S0-ASL-631

Architectural Drafting and Construction

Fourth Edition

Architectural Drafting and Construction

Ernest R. Weidhaas

Professor Emeritus of Engineering Graphics
The Pennsylvania State University

Allyn and Bacon
Boston, London, Sydney, Toronto

Cover administrator: Linda Dickinson
Manufacturing buyer: Tamara McCracken
Editorial-production service: Bywater Production Services

Copyright © 1989, 1985, 1981, 1974, by Allyn and
Bacon, a Division of Simon & Schuster, 160 Gould Street,
Needham Heights, Massachusetts, 02194. All rights reserved. No part of the material protected by this copyright
notice may be reproduced or utilized in any form or by any
means, electronic or mechanical, including photocopy-
ing, recording, or by any information storage and retrieval
system, without written permission from the copyright
owner.

Portions of this material also appear in *Architectural Drafting and Design, Sixth Edition,* by Ernest R. Weidhaas,
Copyright © 1989 by Allyn and Bacon, Inc.

Printed in the United States of America

Library of Congress Cataloging in Publication Data

Weidhaas, Ernest R
   Architectural drafting and construction.

   Includes index.
    1. Architectural drawing. 2. Architecture —
Designs and plans. 3. Building. I. Title
NA2700.W39   1989   720′.28′4   88-34269
ISBN 0-205-11861-5

10 9 8 7 6 5 4 3 2 1 94 93 92 91 90 89

To Julia, Richard, Paul, Patricia, and Mark

Contents

Preface xi

I / Introduction to Architectural Drafting 1

1 Architectural Drafting Tools   3
2 Sketching   12
3 Drafting   17
4 Architectural Technique   28

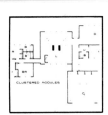

II / Drawing Conventions 35

5 Projections   37
6 Multiview Projections   40
7 Auxiliary Views   47
8 Pictorial Projections   50
9 Architectural Lettering   54
10 Architectural Dimensioning in English Units   60
11 Architectural Dimensioning in Metric Units   67

III / Introduction to Architectural Design 81

12 Architectural History   83
13 Primary Considerations   105
14 Financing   113
15 The Program   117

IV / Components 119

16 Windows   121
17 Doors   130
18 Schedules   138

V/Plans   141

19   Room Design   143
20   Preliminary Layout   159
21   Floor Plans   172
22   The Plot Plan   179

VI/Elevations   185

23   Roofs   187
24   Elevations and Sections   195
25   Stairways   211
26   Fireplaces and Chimneys   220
27   Architectural Models   229

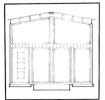

VII/Light Construction   237

28   Light Framing   239
29   Structural Calculations   264
30   Durability   273

VIII/Electrical-Mechanical Systems   281

31   Electrical Conventions   283
32   Plumbing   294
33   Heating and Air Conditioning   302
34   Energy Conservation   321
35   Energy Sources   328

IX/Presentation Drawing   333

36   Perspective   335
37   Shadows   342
38   Architectural Rendering   350
39   Entourage   363

X/Commercial Design and Drafting   369

40   Commercial Drafting   371
41   Design for Accessibility   408
42   Design for Acoustics   417
43   Fire Protection   425
44   The Construction Documents   435

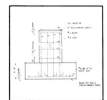

XI/Building Materials   449

45 Wood Products   451
46 Timber Construction   459
47 Concrete Masonry   469
48 Clay Masonry   479
49 Stone Masonry   492
50 Glass Masonry   498
51 Reinforced Concrete   502
52 Structural Steel   518

XII/Building Fabrication   525

53 Steel Fabrication   526
54 Rigid Frames   537
55 Trusses   541
56 Space Frames   551
57 Vaults and Domes   556
58 Cable Roof Structures   563

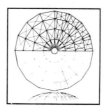

/Appendices   575

A Plans of a Two-Story Residence and a Solar A-Frame   A-1
B Windows   A-17
C Doors   A-23
D Abbreviations   A-27
E Architectural Spelling   A-33
F Glossary of Architectural Terms   A-35
G Microcomputer References and Programs   A-43

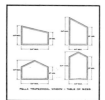

/Index   I-1

Preface

It is projected that more buildings will be erected in the United States during the next thirty years than have been erected to date since colonial times. This building will be in both field-erected and factory-fabricated forms. Buildings will continue to be built up on the site, but using exciting new designs, materials, and methods. Buildings will also be manufactured off the site to provide a substantial portion of the residential and commercial construction market. In both cases, there will be revolutionary advances which will provide challenging opportunities for a new breed of architectural drafter—a person who is equally skilled in drafting techniques, building construction methods, and architectural design. New tools such as computer consoles and data processors will expand his capabilities, but new problems of environmental control and public security will have to be solved.

This book, then, is designed for that creative and energetic individual who seriously intends to prepare for a rewarding career such as this. It is a book on the architectural *drafting* and *construction* of residential and commercial structures. However, whenever architectural drafters draw a line not previously specified by the architect, they are also engaged in *design*. Therefore this book also includes elements of architectural design. To provide continuity, a contemporary home for Mr. and Mrs. A is designed from preliminary program to finished rendering. The plans for this house are included in the relevant chapters. The plans for a split-level modular home for Mr. and Mrs. M (dimensioned in metric) are given in Chapter 11, and a two-story, traditional home for Mr. and Mrs. Z and an A-framed solar home for Mr. and Mrs. S are given in Appendix A. Also included are the plans for a five-story commercial building of bolted and welded steel construction. Photographs of this building being erected are in Chapter 40. A chapter on accessibility follows, for public buildings must be accessible to *all* people.

Each chapter is self-sufficient to the extent possible, so the chapters may be rearranged or omitted according to the available class time. The introduction to each chapter shows the relative importance of that chapter and how it fits into the overall process of drafting and design. A conscious attempt has been made to arrange the descriptive material into an interesting, easy-to-read format. Illustrations have been drawn for maximum clarity and accuracy. For greater realism, pictorials have been drawn in perspective. A variety of photographs taken through the country are included to illustrate practical applications of building principles.

Lumber sizes conform to the new American Softwood Lumber Standard PS 20-70, and structural steel designations conform to the latest revisions recommended by the American Institute of Steel Construction. Specifications follow the CSI Format. The new R-values are used to designate insulation.

This fourth edition includes revised sections on computer-aided drafting stations, interactive graphic programs, microcomputer references, construction documents, and earthquake protection. New sections have been added including postmodern architecture, radon control, low-E glass, and fiber glass roofing. Several topics have been included that are often omitted from other drafting texts. Topics such as architectural acoustics, durability of building materials, and cable roof structures should be of interest to students, even though they may be excluded from the formal course outline.

Although the primary aim of this book is to present information vital to the profession of architectural drafting, it may also lead readers into one of the many allied fields of work. But neither this book nor any other can provide all the extensive information needed to become a registered architect or architectural engineer. Most states require graduation from an approved university (usually a five-year program), plus three years of practical experience under the direction of a professional, plus the successful completion of a comprehensive written examination, as the minimum requirements for professional registration as an architect or engineer.

The author would be most grateful to receive suggestions and correspond with readers interested in this book.

Ernest R. Weidhaas

Illustration Acknowledgments

Chapter 1: Figures 1–4, 6, 8, 9, 18, Frederick Post Company; 5, 11, 12, Gramercy Instruments; 7, Eagle Pencil Company; 10, 13–16, Rapidesign; 17, 19, 20, Keuffel & Esser Company; 21, 22, Hamilton Industries; 23, The Rand Corporation; 24–26, Professor Raymon J. Masters, The Pennsylvania State University; 27, Professor Richard W. Quadrel, Rensselaer Polytechnic Institute. **Chapter 9:** Figures 1–3, Paratone, Inc.; 10, William B. Meister, Jack W. Risheberger, William L. Cunningham, James E. Black, and Richard I. Whidet; 13, 14, Letraset, Ltd. **Chapter 11:** Figure 5, The Construction Specifications Institute; 6–13, Professor M. Isenberg, The Pennsylvania State University. **Chapter 12:** Figures 2, 22, G. E. Kidder Smith; 14, 18, 20, 21, 23, 25, Photo Alinari, Florence, Italy; 24, The British Travel and Holidays Association; 26, 27, Ewing Galloway; 45, Rolscreen Company; 46, American Iron and Steel Institute (E. S. Preston & Associates, consulting engineers; General American Transportation Corporation, fabricators); 47, American Iron and Steel Institute (Edward Durell Stone and Associates, architects; Chicago Bridge and Iron Company, fabricators); 48, Gruen Associates, Architects-Engineers-Planners; 49, 53, 56, photos by Bill Hedrich, Hedrich-Blessing; 50, Bill Engdahl, Hedrich-Blessing; 51, 52, Bethlehem Steel Corporation; 57, Baltazar Korab, photographer. **Chapter 16:** Figure 1, Bill Hedrich, Hedrich-Blessing; Andersen Corporation; 2–5, 7, 13–16, Andersen Corporation; 6, Rolscreen Company (Irving Robinson, architect; Avery Construction Company, builder); 10, 12, Rolscreen Company. **Chapter 17:** Figures 6, 12, 16–17, Morgan Company; 7, Rolscreen Company; 8, Rolscreen Company (Starlite Village Restaurant and Lounge, Fort Dodge, Iowa; Eugene Haire, designer, Ackerman Company, builder); 9, Rolscreen Company (Peninsula Golf Club, San Mateo, Calif.); 14, 15, Educational Facilities Laboratories (photo Rondal Partridge); 19, Frantz Manufacturing Company. **Chapter 19:** Figures 2–9, Chambers Corporation; 10, Mr. and Mrs. M. C. Mateer (Philip F. Hallock, architect); 11, Rolscreen Company; 15, 20, Mr. and Mrs. Donald W. Hamer; 17, National Forest Products Association; 18, 26, California Redwood Association; 24, Hardwood Plywood Manufacturers Association; 32, American Institute of Steel Construction. **Chapter 20:** Figure 3, Weyerhaeuser Company; 10, Mr. and Mrs. Donald W. Hamer; 13, Computervision Corporation. **Chapter 21:** Figures 1–3, Mr. and Mrs. Donald W. Hamer. **Chapter 22:** Figure 3, Figures 4–7, Bethlehem Steel Corporation; 6, 7, Forest Products Promotion Council; 8, Callaway Gardens, Pine Mountain, Ga.; 9, California Redwood Association (Thomas Babbitt, architect); 10, Eliot Noyes & Associates, architects; 11, Perkins & Will, architects (photo by Bill Hedrich, Hedrich-Blessing); 12, American Iron and Steel Institute (Walker O. Cain & Associates, architects; R. L. Stinard and Associates and Severud-Perrone-Sturn-Conlin-Bandel, consulting engineers); 13, Synergetics, Inc.; 15, Rolscreen Company (Good Shepherd Methodist Church, Park Ridge, Ill.: Stade-Dolan & Associates, architects; Vern Benston, builder; Hedrich-Blessing, photo). **Chapter 24:** Figure 1, Rolscreen Company (G. C. Hann residence, Minneapolis, Minn.: Newt Griffith, Peterson, Clark & Griffin, Inc., architects; Johnson & Jasper, builder); 6, Bethlehem Steel Corporation; 30–40, Mr. and Mrs. Donald W. Hamer. **Chapter 25:** Figures 6, 7, Armstrong Cork Company; 12, Bilco Stairguide; 14, 15, 19, 21, Julius Blum & Co., Inc. (The Colorail® System in Figure 14 covered by U. S. patents and pending patent applications; patterns in Figure 21 are covered by U. S. patents); 13, 16, 20, Blumcraft of Pittsburg (Copyrights for Figures 13, 16 are registered, the stock treillage designs in Figure 20 are covered by U. S. patents and pending patent applications). **Chapter 26:** Figure 2, Mr. and Mrs. M. C. Mateer (Phillip F. Hallock, architect): 9, 10, Vega Industries, Inc.; 12, 14, 15, Condon-King Division of the Majestic Company; 13, Acorn Fireplaces, Inc. **Chapter 27:** Figure 1, The Cairo Museum (photograph by the Egyptian Expedition, The Metropolitan Museum of Art); 15, 16, Department of Architecture, The Pennsylvania State University; 17, Bethlehem Steel Corporation; 18, Artesano, Inc., San Francisco; 19, Perkins & Will, architects (photo by Bill Hedrich of Hedrich-Blessing); 20, Balthazar Korab, photographer. **Chapter 28:** Figure 25, Timber Engineering Company; 32, 33, California Redwood Association; 40, Rolscreen Company; 42–44 American Iron and Steel Institute (Ziegelman & Ziegelman, architects;

Samuel V. Tavernit, structural engineers). **Chapter 30:** pp. 272–75, B. E. Beneyfield; Figure 4, Mr. and Mrs. M. C. Mateer (Philip F. Hallock, architect); 9, Bethlehem Steel Corporation; 10, 11, United States Steel Corporation. **Chapter 31:** Figure 1, Armstrong Cork Company. **Chapter 33:** Figures 22–27, Richard E. Kummer, Associate Professor of Architectural Engineering, The Pennsylvania State University and Mary J. Kummer, Assistant Professor of Engineering Graphics, The Pennsylvania State University. Figures 36–39, Mr. Peter Hollander. **Chapter 34:** Figures 7–9, American Iron and Steel Institute (Vincent G. Kling, architect; Oliver & Smith, associated architects; Fraioli-Blum-Yesselman, structural engineers; Kling-Leopold, Inc., mechanical-electrical engineers): 10, Clivus Multrum. **Chapter 35:** Figures 2, 3, Thermograte; 5, Automatic Power Division of Penwalt Corporation; 6, Delta Enfield Cables Limited; 8, DAF-Indal Limited. **Chapter 38:** Figures 5, 7, 17, Dr. Milton S. Osborne, Professor Emeritus of Architecture, The Pennsylvania State University; 8, 10, Rolscreen Company; 15, 20, 25, 27, Gruen Associates, Architects-Engineers-Planners; 16, 23, Department of Architecture, The Pennsylvania State University; 18, 19, Masonite Corporation (George A. Parenti, designer); 26, Balthazar Korab, photographer. **Chapter 40:** All illustrations and drawings of South Hills Office Building courtesy of Jack W. Risheberger & Associates, Registered Architects and Engineers; Figures 43–46, First Church of Christ, Scientist, State College, Pa., designed by Roy D. Murphy & Associates, architects, Urbana, Ill. **Chapter 41:** Professor John N. Grode, The Behrend College of The Pennsylvania State University. **Chapter 42:** Figure 20, Department of the Air Force; 21, United States Steel Corporation. **Chapter 43:** Figure 14, United States Steel Corporation. **Chapter 44:** Figures 1–8, The Construction Specifications Institute. **Chapter 45:** Figures 1, 2, St. Regis Paper Company; 7, 10, Hardwood Plywood Manufacturers Association; 11, 12, Masonite Corporation. **Chapter 46:** Figures 1, 15, American Institute of Timber Construction; 8, Vetter Stone Company; 11–14, Weyerhaeuser Company; 25, 27–30, 32–34, American Plywood Association. **Chapter 47:** Figures 3, 4, 6–17, 19, 20, 26–29, Portland Cement Company; 30, American Institute of Steel Construction. **Chapter 48:** Figures 3, 4, 6, 7, 9–13, 15, 18, 19, 21, 22, Structural Clay Products Institute; 16, Glen-Gery Company. **Chapter 49:** Figure 2, Cold Spring Granite Company; 3, The Brier Hill Stone Company; 4, 5, 11, (Alabama Limestone Division of) The Georgia Marble Company; 6, 8, Vermont Marble Company; 7, Buckingham-Virginia Slate Company; 9, Indiana Limestone Company; 10, Pittsburgh Corning Corporation. **Chapter 50:** Figures 2–5, 7, 8, Pittsburgh Corning Corporation. **Chapter 51:** Figures 2, 3, United States Steel Corporation; 4, Western Wood Products Association; 8–11, 18–21, Gateway Building: Products; 14, 33, Nelson Stud Welding Division of Gregory Industries; 34, American Institute of Steel Construction. **Chapter 52:** Figures 6, 7, Jones & Laughlin Steel Corporation. **Chapter 53:** Figures 1, 2, United States Steel Corporation; 4, 5, Republic Steel Corporation; 8, Bethlehem Steel Corporation; 11–13, Nelson Stud Welding Division of Gregory Industries; 14–22, 25–27, The James F. Lincoln Arc Welding Foundation; 23, 24, American Institute of Steel Construction. **Chapter 54:** Figures 8, 10, 11, American Institute of Steel Construction; 9, Weyerhaeuser Company. **Chapter 55:** Figures 3–5, Teco; 6, 9–11, 16–19, 21, 22, 24, 25, Bethlehem Steel Corporation; 7, Department of the Air Force; 12–15, 20, 23, 26, Vetter Stone Company. **Chapter 56:** Figures 9, 10, American Institute of Steel Construction; 11–18, Department of the Air Force. **Chapter 57:** Figures 7, 8, American Institute of Steel Construction; 9–12, Department of the Air Force; 18–20, Synergetics, Inc. **Chapter 58:** Figures 1, 6–12, 14, 24–28, Bethlehem Steel Corporation; 2–5, The James F. Lincoln Welding Foundation. **Appendix A:** Figure 12, Dr. Milton S. Osborne, Professor Emeritus of Architecture, The Pennsylvania State University; Figures 13–17, Richard E. Kummer, Associate Professor of Architectural Engineering, The Pennsylvania State University and Mary J. Kummer, Assistant Professor of Engineering Graphics, The Pennsylvania State University. **Appendix B:** Figures 1–7, Andersen Corporation; 8, Rolscreen Company. **Appendix C:** Figures 1–3, Morgan Products, Ltd.; 4, Frantz Manufacturing Company.

I / Introduction to Architectural Drafting

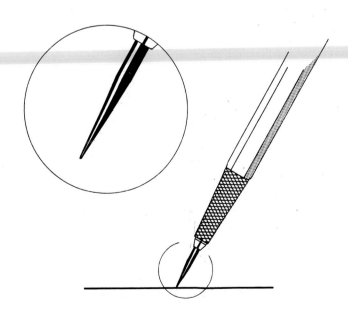

1 / Architectural Drafting Tools

To do any job properly and efficiently, you must have the proper tools. This is true of all trades and professions—whether carpentry or drafting, surgery or architecture. Keep this in mind when you select your basic drawing tools or add more advanced and special equipment. Purchase tools of good quality, since they represent an investment that you can carry with you into your career as an architectural drafter.

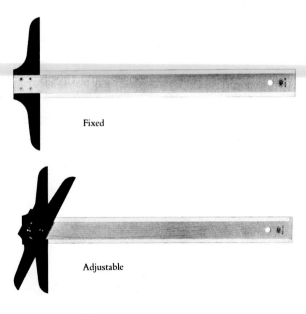

Figure 1   *Drawing board.*

BASIC EQUIPMENT

You should be thoroughly familiar with the following basic tools of the drafter.

Drawing board. Although the majority of architectural drafting work is mounted with tape directly to the drafting table, the drawing board (Figure 1) does have the advantage of portability. Select a smooth-surfaced board without any warpage. The ends should be true and square. Either solid basswood, hollow basswood, or metal-edged basswood is satisfactory.

T square. Make certain that the blade of the T square (Figure 2) is perfectly straight (except for a desirable bow away from the drawing surface) and free of nicks. For accurate work, the blade must be fastened securely to the head (fixed T square) or capable of being fastened securely (adjustable T square).

Fixed

Adjustable

Figure 2   *T squares.*

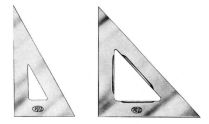

Figure 3   *Triangles.*

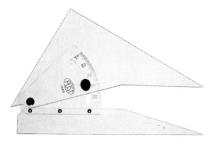

Figure 4   *Adjustable triangle.*

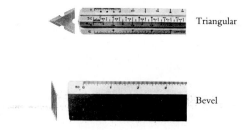

Triangular

Bevel

Figure 5   *Scales.*

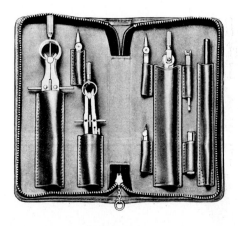

Figure 6   *Drawing instrument set.*

Figure 7   *Mechanical drafting pencil.*

Triangles. Clear-plastic triangles (Figure 3) are used in sets of two: 30°–60° triangle and 45° triangle. As with the T-square blade, the outer edges should be flat and nick-free. Some drafters prefer an adjustable triangle (Figure 4), which permits lines to be drawn at any angle.

Scales. The architectural drafter normally uses an architect's scale, although on occasion he may need an engineer's or mechanical engineer's scale. Either triangular or bevel scales are used according to preference (Figure 5). The architectural scales are:

$12'' = 1'$ (full scale)

$6'' = 1'$

$3'' = 1'$

$1\frac{1}{2}'' = 1'$

$\frac{3}{4}'' = 1'$

$\frac{3}{8}'' = 1'$

$\frac{3}{16}'' = 1'$

$\frac{3}{32}'' = 1'$

$1'' = 1'$

$\frac{1}{2}'' = 1'$

$\frac{1}{4}'' = 1'$

$\frac{1}{8}'' = 1'$

$\frac{1}{16}'' = 1'$

Notice that there are really *two* architectural scale systems. One is based on the full scale and proceeds to smaller scales; the other is based on a $\frac{1}{16}'' = 1'$ scale and proceeds to larger scales. Combined, these two architectural scale systems offer a wide range of scale choice.

Drawing sets. A satisfactory drawing set (Figure 6) should contain as a minimum: dividers, pencil compass, pen compass, and drafting pen or technical fountain pen. Many sets also contain mechanical drafting pencils. The instruments in the better sets are constructed of stainless steel or nickel silver; cheaper sets are of chrome-plated brass.

Drafting pencils. One refillable drafting pencil (Figure 7) with an assortment of different grade leads is sufficient for the classroom. A professional drafter, however, has a number of refillable pencils—each color-coded to one lead grade so that no time will be lost in switching leads. Drafting pencil leads are graded from 9H (hard) to F (firm) to 6B (black), as shown in Table I. Some drafting pencils are designed to hold leads that require sharpening, but thin-lead drafting pencils hold leads of such small diameter that no sharpening is needed. Thin leads are available in diameters of 0.3 mm, 0.5 mm (recommended for architectural drafting), 0.7 mm, and 0.9 mm.

Lead pointers. A mechanical lead pointer (Figure 8) provides an easy method to obtain perfectly formed conical points. The abrasive liners can be replaced quickly and easily.

Erasers. A wide variety of pencil erasers (Figure 9) are available. A satisfactory eraser should be capable of completely removing pencil and ink lines without roughing the surface of the paper or leaving colored marks. The artgum eraser is designed to remove smudges rather than lines. Electric erasing machines are helpful when a great amount of erasing is needed.

Lettering guides. A number of devices to assist in drawing guidelines for lettering are available. The Rapidesign guide illustrated in Figure 10 is operated by placing the pencil point through the proper hole and moving the guide and pencil along the T square. Some drafters prefer the Ames lettering instrument or Braddock-Rowe lettering triangle.

Technical fountain pen. Some drafters prefer the technical fountain pen (Figure 11) to the standard ruling pen since they can obtain a variation in line weight by changing the speed of the stroke. This is most useful in preparing presentation drawings.

ADVANCED AND SPECIAL EQUIPMENT

The following equipment, although not normally found in a school drafting room, is often used in a professional drafting office.

Table I *Grades of Pencil Leads*

9H	
8H	
7H	
6H	
5H	
4H	
3H	
2H	
H	Used for most architectural work
F	
HB	
B	
2B	
3B	
4B	
5B	
6B	

Figure 8   *Pencil pointer.*

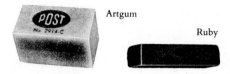

Figure 9   *Erasers.*

Artgum

Ruby

Figure 10   *Lettering guide.*

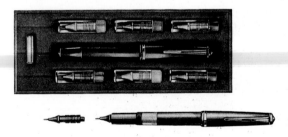

Figure 11   *Technical fountain pen and set. Available line widths are shown at the right.*

Figure 12   *Proportional dividers.*

Figure 13   *Circle template.*

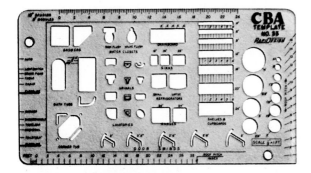

Figure 14   *Architectural template.*

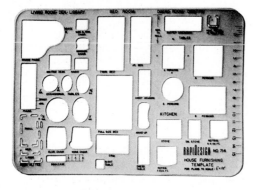

Figure 15   *Furniture template.*

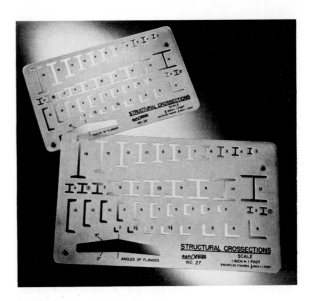

Figure 16   *Structural templates.*

Figure 17   *Lettering set.*

Proportional dividers. The instrument in Figure 12 is very useful for enlarging or reducing a drawing. Proportional dividers are usually calibrated to obtain ratios from 1:1 up to 10:1.

Templates. The architectural drafter uses a large variety of templates to speed the work. A circle template (Figure 13) may be used to supplement the compass. The architectural template (Figure 14) simplifies the drawing of kitchen and bathroom fixtures, and the furniture template

(Figure 15) helps in the preliminary design stage to draw furniture the proper size. Many other specialized templates are available, such as the structural template (Figure 16), which gives the cross-sectional shapes of beams, channels, and angles.

Lettering sets. Although pencil lettering is best drawn freehand, ink lettering may be improved by the use of lettering stencils (Figure 17). These stencils can provide a variety of sizes and styles of letters. Figure 12 of Chapter 9 shows an architectural alphabet formed with the aid of a lettering stencil.

Parallel-rule drawing board. A parallel-rule drawing board (Figure 18) may be used in place of the standard drawing board and T square. The straightedge can be moved up and down, and it is designed to remain perfectly horizontal—thus allowing accurate work.

Drafting machines. Drafting machines may be used in place of the standard drawing board, T square, triangles, scales, and protractor. As with the parallel-rule drawing board, a straightedge remains horizontal. In addition, though, there is a vertical edge. Both edges are graduated to act as scales and may be rotated to any position by pressing a release button. The X-Y plotter (Figure 19) and arm type (Figure 20) perform similar functions.

Drafting tables. Automatic drafting tables (Figure 21) are used for large scale commercial drafting. Drafting table surfaces can be adjusted for height and tilted up to 90° by means of electrical, mechanical, hydraulic, or pneumatic actuators. A drafting table with an endless belt drafting surface is useful for very large drawings. A drawing taped to the belt can be moved horizontally or vertically to a convenient position for the drafter with the unused portion of the drawing rolled to the back side of the drafting surface.

Figure 20 *Drafting machine, arm type.*

Computer-aided drafting stations. Modular drafting and computer stations (Figure 22) are designed to be easily expanded as new technical systems become available. Components of the station are interchangeable so that drafting machines, computer terminals, keyboards, printers, and plotters can be added, removed, or repositioned.

FUTURE TRENDS*

Remarkably, the present-day drafting tools described have been used for many hundreds of years. For example, the use of paper can be traced to 105 A.D., vellum to 1400 B.C., and papyrus to 2500 B.C. Tools for drawing lines and circles on these materials have not changed greatly during this time; in fact, many of our "newer" tools also have a long history. Stencils were used by Greek builders in 400 B.C.; a compass for drawing ovals and spirals was invented in 1565; a parallel ruler, in 1713; and a technical fountain pen, in 1864. It is likely that these same tools will be used for many more years.

Today, there are new types of drafting devices being designed and produced. Future drafting rooms may include *cathode-ray tubes* (often abbreviated as *CRTs*) to display plans and pictorials, and *line plotters* to produce exact drawings on paper or film using technical pens. Because the CRT display does not produce a permanent record, it is called a *soft-copy* device, and the line plotter, which does produce a permanent record, is called a *hard-copy* device. These devices, when coupled with the computational and storage facilities of a computer, present a wide range of possibilities for architectural drafting and design.

Graphic devices. CRTs can be divided into two classes: *Direct-view Storage Tubes,* also known as *DVSTs,* and *Refresh CRTs.* The DVST is widely used because of its high resolution and relatively

Figure 18 *Parallel-rule drawing board.*

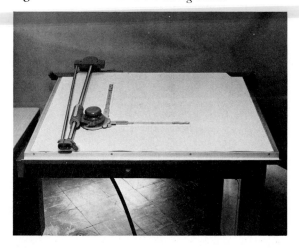

Figure 19 *Drafting machine, X-Y plotter type.*

* Courtesy of Professor Richard W. Quadrel, Rensselaer Polytechnic Institute, and Professor Raymon J. Masters, The Pennsylvania State University.

Figure 21   *Automatic drafting table.*

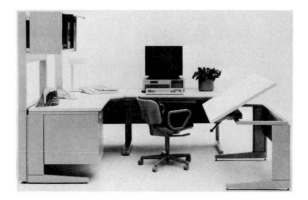

Figure 22   *Computer-aided drafting table.*

Figure 23   *A digitizer and CRT display.*

low cost. With this device, the picture image is drawn once on the screen, and is maintained by *high-persistence phosphors* which coat the back of the display tube. The DVST can display an unlimited number of lines on the screen, but in order to erase or add images to the current picture, the entire screen must be erased and the updated image redrawn. Refresh CRTs, on the other hand, use *low-persistence phosphors,* implying that the image will fade after it has been drawn on the screen. A somewhat more sophisticated processor must then be employed to redraw, or "refresh" the screen, usually at a rate of 30 times per second. This refreshing process, however, allows the drafter to create animation, and permits immediate interaction such as adding to or erasing the picture image. The Refresh CRT is somewhat more expensive and is limited by the number of lines that can be displayed.

The architectural drafter typically gives commands to the computer by using an alphanumeric keyboard and a digitizer. The *alphanumeric keyboard* is similar to a typewriter and is used to transmit and receive alphabetical and numerical commands. The *digitizer* is a special device for giving graphic information (in the form of coordinates) to the computer. The digitizer can also be used to select options from *menus,* each of which may perform a different function. Options such as draw, zoom-in, and erase are commonly seen on graphics menus.

The ARK-2 system. Researchers have studied the application of computer graphics to architectural drafting and design for over thirty years. However, it was not until the early 1970s that reduced costs and modern computational techniques made feasible the common use of such devices by architectural firms. *ARK-2,* a popular computer graphics system used by architectural offices, incorporates a minicomputer, CRT terminal, line plotter, and facilities for storing graphics-library data bases on either magnetic tapes or disks. The system contains a full repertoire of programs for graphics data analysis and design. The following description of a typical application will illustrate how the system is used.

The designer sits at a design console consisting of a CRT display, an alphanumeric keyboard, and a digitizer (Figure 23). The digitizer is composed of a transparent sheet of glass coated with invisible electrical conductors in both horizontal and vertical directions. When a special pen contacts the surface of this tablet, the computer electrically senses the exact location of the pen and records the X and Y coordinates of its position. Lines can be described to the computer simply by registering the coordinates of the endpoints. Circles, arcs, and other geometric shapes can be described by locating centers and extreme points.

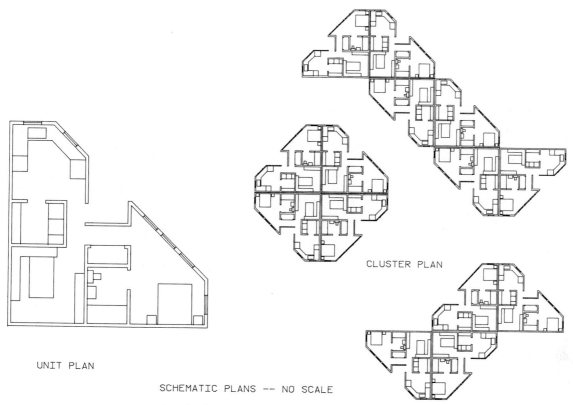

CLUSTER PLAN

UNIT PLAN

SCHEMATIC PLANS -- NO SCALE

Figure 24   *A computer-produced study plan.*

For example, to design a facility composed of repeated elements such as motel rooms, the designer would first sketch a typical room and then place the transparent digitizer tablet over the sketch and digitize each corner of the room. The computer, as it receives this information, automatically corrects the sketch, making all lines straight and true and all arcs circular. The work is continually displayed and updated on the CRT display, and if a mistake occurs, the designer can place the digitizer in front of the CRT screen and indicate to the computer what lines need to be added, deleted, or revised.

After the room has been completely described to the computer, the drafter can use a combination of computer commands to store and retrieve the image, to have it scaled up or down in size, moved, repeated at different positions, or combined with previously described elements to create a complete plan. This plan then can be stored for possible revision later. Hard copies can be obtained by using a line plotter. An example of such a drawing is shown in Figure 24.

When the project progresses into the working-drawing stage, the designer can call up libraries of standard building details previously stored on magnetic tape or disk. These details are displayed on the CRT so that the designer can edit portions

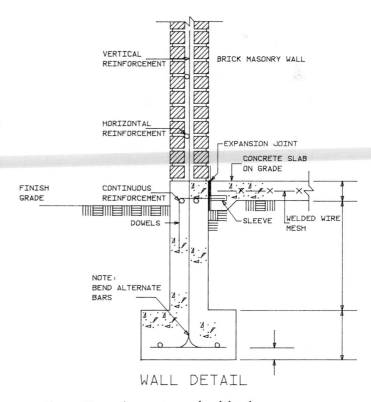

WALL DETAIL

Figure 25   *A computer-produced detail.*

and change dimensions to tailor the detail to the specific needs of the project. The final detail can then be plotted directly on the working drawings. A typical computer-produced detail is shown in Figure 25.

Computer-assisted pictorials. Computer-assisted drafting is not limited to plans, elevations, and details. It is a simple task for a computer to generate accurate perspectives of a building as viewed from any vantage point. The computer first requires information on the three-dimensional nature of the building to calculate and plot a perspective image. Normally, this information is in the form of X, Y, and Z coordinates that describe the corners, lines, and other elements of the building. These coordinates can be described in several ways. One of the more commonly used techniques incorporates a system of geometric descriptions that defines the building as a combination of planes, rectangular prisms, cylinders, and so on. Such systems save considerable time by eliminating the tedious task of describing every coordinate point. Another technique cross-references digitized plans and elevations to determine X, Y, and Z coordinates. There are also three-dimensional digitizing devices that may be used if a scale model is available.

These X, Y, and Z coordinates can be stored in a permanent file and then retrieved by programs that can calculate and plot the appropriate perspective view. Figure 26 is an example of a perspective plot from such a program. Because every line in the building is visible, this type of drawing is often called *wire-frame.* Some more advanced programs can calculate and plot only those portions of a building that are visible to the observer.

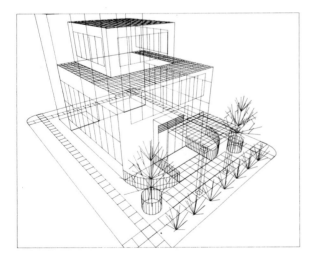

Figure 26 *A computer-produced wire-frame perspective.*

Such programs are described as having *hidden-line removal* capabilities and produce *solid models.* An example of a solid-model perspective, as plotted with the hidden lines removed, is shown in Figure 27.

Solid modeling. Computers produce solid-model perspectives in a variety of ways. Complex images may be built from a number of *primitives,* much like a child's castle constructed from small building blocks. Primitives consist of basic geometric shapes such as cubes, planes, cylinders, and spheres. The primitives may undergo a number of logical operations: the joining of two shapes is called a *union,* the volume that is shared by two overlapping shapes is called the *intersection.* Primitives can also be *subtracted* from each other to produce a resultant object. This process of creating complex forms by performing logical operations on primitives is called *Constructive Solid Geometry.*

Other solid-modeling methods do not deal with three-dimensional primitives but with the synthesis of two-dimensional shapes. *Sweep Geometry* allows the designer to "sweep" a two-dimensional shape (such as a floor plan) into the third dimension (the building's height) to produce a three-dimensional solid. *Boundary Geometry* produces a solid image by describing the locations of two-dimensional shapes (walls, floors, roof) that make up its surface. Ideally, a designer would prefer a variety of techniques to produce a computer representation of the building.

Interactive systems. Some computer graphics systems, called *interactive systems,* allow the user to communicate instantaneously with programs and permit the use of dynamic input devices such as lightpens or joysticks. A *lightpen* is a penlike device containing a photoelectric sensor that indicates positions on the CRT display without the need for a digitizer. A *joystick* is a computer input device that a user can move in any direction. A program can sense changes in the position of a joystick and interpret them to change viewing parameters. For example, movement of the joystick could alter the observer's position for a perspective drawing; as the user moves the joystick, the computer-drawn perspective image on the CRT changes to reflect the observer approaching or circling the building. If the displayed perspective image changes fast enough to simulate true animation, the display is called *real-time.* Because such systems are quite sophisticated and require extensive computer support, they are rarely used for general work.

Although the drafter's older tools will continue to be used, computer technology will play an important role in the architecture office of the future. The computational power and high stor-

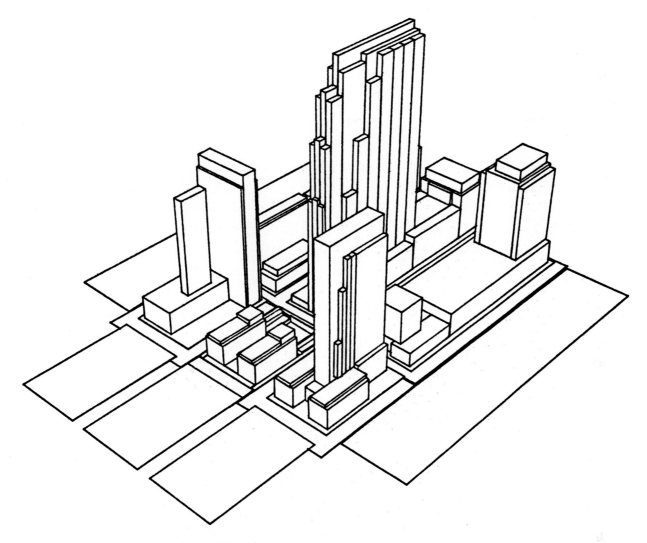

Figure 27 *A computer-produced solid-model perspective.*

age capacities of these systems will influence not only the production of architectural drawings but also the entire architectural process itself.

STUDY QUESTIONS

1. Distinguish between:
   a. Lettering guide and lettering stencil
   b. Dividers and proportional dividers
   c. Adjustable T square and fixed T square
   d. Adjustable triangle and 45° triangle
   e. Triangular scales and bevel scales
   f. Ruling pen and technical fountain pen
   g. Plans produced on CRTs and line plotters

2. Prepare a list of:
   a. Architectural scales from $\frac{1}{16}'' = 1'$ to full size
   b. Pencil grades from 6H to 2B

3. (For the advanced student) After a thorough study of drafting tools used in the past few decades, give your prediction of the kind of "drafting room" that will be used:
   a. Twenty-five years hence
   b. One hundred years hence

2 / Sketching

Each profession has a symbol that has been generally accepted as the hallmark of the field. Often the symbol is an instrument or device commonly used by the members of that profession: a palette for art, a baton for music, a transit for surveying, a stethoscope for medicine. For architects, the pencil has been the symbol, and for draftsmen, the T square. A pencil represents freehand sketching at the initial design stage, and the T square represents the accurate drafting of the final plans. A successful architectural drafter certainly must be proficient in using the tools of the trade: the pencil and the T square. Chapter 2 and 3, then, share with you the sketching and drafting methods that other architectural drafters are now using to do their jobs quickly and accurately.

SKETCHING

Freehand sketching is *not* difficult! An extremely steady hand or other special skill is not necessary. All that is needed is an understanding of what *is* required and what is *not* required to produce an excellent sketch. Just remember that you control your hand; your hand does not control you.

Lines. A freehand sketch should not look like an instrumental drawing with perfectly straight and accurate lines. In fact, the unevenness of a properly sketched line is more attractive and interesting than a mechanically perfect line. The weight, direction, and proportions of sketched lines *are* important, however, and the following rules should help. But please remember to concentrate on the desired *results* rather than on the rules.

1. A soft pencil (such as an F grade) is best for sketching. The point should be long and tapered as shown in Figure 1. The point is slightly rounded rather than needle-sharp. After sketching each line, twist your pencil slightly to avoid developing a flat portion. This will reduce the number of necessary sharpenings.
2. As you might expect, a right-handed person sketches short horizontal lines from left to right* and short vertical and inclined lines from

* A left-handed person sketches from right to left.

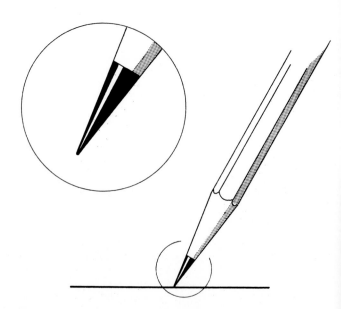

Figure 1   *Lead point for sketching.*

12

top to bottom as shown in Figure 2. If the angle of a line seems awkward for you, turn your paper to a more comfortable position. This is the reason that drafters don't tape sketches to a drawing board as they do when drafting with instruments.

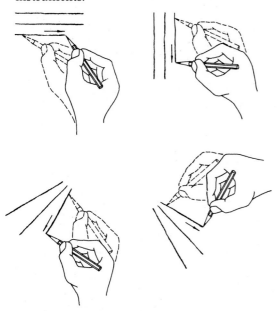

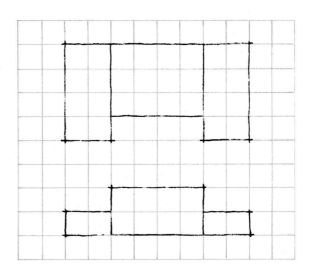

Figure 2   *Sketching short lines.*

3. To sketch a line, rest your hand on the drawing surface and pivot only your fingers. Most persons cannot sketch a line longer than 1″ without sliding their hand. Therefore, sketch lines longer than 1″ in short intervals, with a small gap left between each interval, as shown in Figure 3. Do not omit these gaps, for they add a professional touch to a sketch.

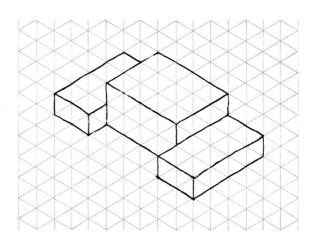

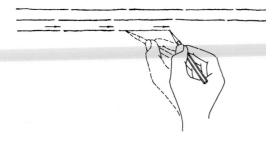

Figure 3   *Sketching long lines.*

4. The correct *direction* of a sketched line is most important. Horizontal lines should be horizontal and not inclined. Vertical lines should be vertical and not leaning. The easiest way to accomplish this is to sketch on graph paper or on tracing paper placed over graph paper. Graph paper with ¼″ grids is commonly used (Figure 4, top). Special tracing vellum with grid lines that disappear when reproduced is also avail-

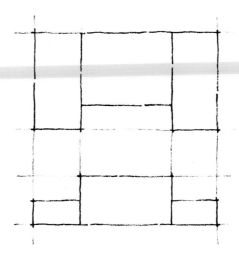

Figure 4   *Top: Sketching on 1/4″ graph paper. Center: Sketching on isometric graph paper. Bottom: blocking lines to aid direction and proportion.*

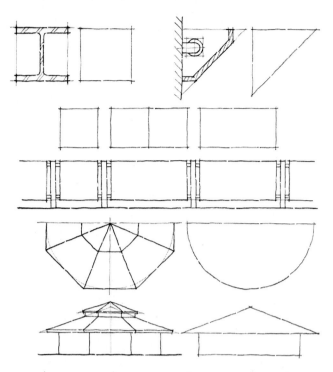

Figure 5 *Proportioning by comparision with geometric forms.*

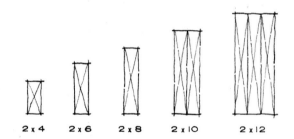

Figure 6 *Lumber proportions.*

2 x 4   2 x 6   2 x 8   2 x 10   2 x 12

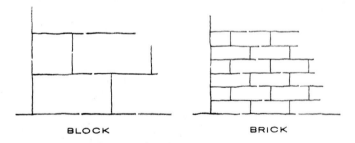

BLOCK   BRICK

Figure 7 *Masonry proportions.*

able. Isometric paper may be used for pictorial sketching (Figure 4, center).

Another advantage of tracing paper is that alternate schemes can be sketched and studied. Details that are to remain unchanged can be

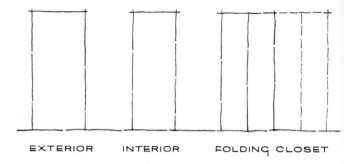

EXTERIOR   INTERIOR   FOLDING CLOSET

Figure 8 *Door proportions.*

traced easily from the initial scheme. Often an architectural drafter will find it easier to correct mistakes by retracing than by erasing.

5. When graph paper is not used, the sketch is blocked in using very light construction lines (Figure 4, bottom). These construction lines give you a chance to study your sketch for the proper line direction and proportion before you darken it with the final outlines.

6. Good *proportion* is important to all design and immediately distinguishes an excellent sketch from a mediocre one. Proportion is simply a matter of relating one length or area to another —for example, the relation of the width of an object to its height (is the width twice the height or two and one-half times the height?), or the relation of one portion of an object to another portion. The overall proportions of an object are especially important, for they will determine the proportions of all smaller elements.

Often areas can be compared with a simple geometric form such as a square, triangle, or circle. Rectangles can be divided easily by eye into several squares. Examples are shown in Figure 5.

Many building components occur so often that it is worthwhile to study and sketch them to become familiar with their proportions: 2″ lumber, 8″ × 16″ concrete block modules, $2\frac{2}{3}″ × 4″ × 8″$ brick modules as shown in Figures 6 and 7. In Figure 8, notice how only a slight change in the proportion of an object—a door—will change the type of door. With such basic materials properly proportioned, other elements will fall into place more easily.

Circles and arcs. Large circles are best sketched by inscribing them inside a square of light construction lines as shown in Figure 9. The center lines determine the tangent points. Small circles can be sketched using only the center lines.

Ellipses. When a circle is inclined to the picture plane, it will appear as an ellipse. Consequently, ellipses often must be drawn in pictorial sketches. As with circles, the best method is to sketch first the center lines with light lines and then the enclosing rectangle with very light construction lines. Then draw tangent arcs at the ends of the major and minor axes, and complete the ellipse by connecting these tangent arcs. See Figure 10.

These sketching techniques are shown in Figure 11.

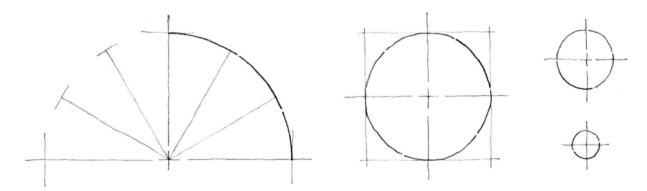

Figure 9   *Sketching circles.*

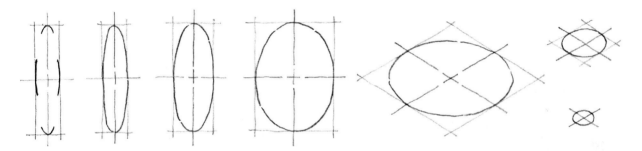

Figure 10   *Sketching ellipses.*

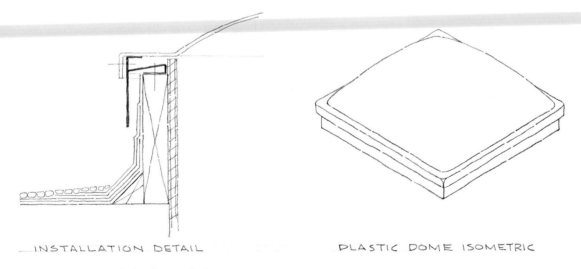

INSTALLATION DETAIL   PLASTIC DOME ISOMETRIC

Figure 11   *Pencil sketching technique.*

STUDY QUESTIONS

1. Give the reason for:
   a. Leaving gaps in sketched lines
   b. Twisting the pencil between each sketched line
2. Give the direction of stroking for the following lines sketched by a right-handed person:
   a. Horizontal lines
   b. Vertical lines
   c. Lines inclined down to the right
   d. Lines inclined down to the left
3. Give a technique for:
   a. Obtaining proper line direction when graph paper is not used
   b. Obtaining proper proportions when graph paper is not used
   c. Sketching circles and arcs
   d. Sketching ellipses

LABORATORY PROBLEMS

1. On $8\frac{1}{2}'' \times 11''$ graph paper, lay out twelve $2\frac{1}{4}''$ square areas. Using correct sketching technique, draw the patterns shown in Figure 12.
2. Draw a random, broken-course-and-range stone wall as illustrated in Figure 13. Include an area 18″ high by 3′-0 wide to a scale of $1\frac{1}{2}'' = 1'\text{-}0$.
   a. Sketch on $\frac{1}{4}''$ graph paper.
   b. Sketch on unruled paper.
3. Draw a low wall (2″ high × 6′ long) constructed of 12″-square concrete screen blocks patterned as shown in Figure 14. Use $\frac{1}{2}''$ mortar joints. Scale: $1'' = 1'\text{-}0$.
   a. Sketch on $\frac{1}{2}''$ graph paper.
   b. Sketch on unruled paper.
4. Refer to a standard structural steel reference and sketch cross sections of the following structural steel members:
   a. W 12 × 40
   b. W 8 × 31
   c. W 8 × 20
   d. S 8 × 18.4
   e. C 8 × 11.5
   f. L 4 × 4 × $\frac{1}{4}$
   g. HP 8 × 36
5. Draw the installation detail of the plastic dome shown in Figure 11.
   a. Sketch on $\frac{1}{4}''$ graph paper.
   b. Sketch on unruled paper.
6. Draw the isometric pictorial of the plastic dome shown in Figure 11.
   a. Sketch on isometric graph paper.
   b. Sketch on unruled paper.
7. Prepare sketches as assigned by your instructor.
   a. Use $\frac{1}{4}''$ graph paper.
   b. Use unruled paper.

Figure 12

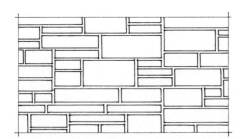

Figure 13

Figure 14

3 / Drafting

Drafting usually refers to drawing with the aid of drafting instruments such as the T square and triangles, discussed in Chapter 1. With the help of these drafting instruments, drawings can be produced quickly and accurately. In some instances, they are even used as patterns for finished products.

Straight lines are drawn with the aid of a straightedge; and circular lines, with the aid of a compass. Here are some techniques used by experienced drafters.

Drafting pencil (Figure 1). The point of your drafting pencil should be long and tapered, as shown in Figure 1, and slightly sharper than the

pencil point used for sketching. There is another difference between sketching and drafting. In drafting, the pencil is rotated slightly *during* the drawing of each line (rather than *after* the line is drawn). This keeps the point uniform so that you can produce lines of constant weight.

Horizontal lines (Figure 2). A right-handed person draws horizontal lines from left to right* using the top edge of the T square, parallel rule, or drafting machine as a guide. When using a T square, first press its head firmly against the working edge of the drawing board or table with your left hand (Figure 2). Then you move your left hand to the middle of the blade of the T square to hold it down (Figure 3). Your left hand is now in a position to also hold a triangle pressed against the top of the blade, if you wish to draw vertical lines.

Vertical lines (Figure 3). A right-handed person draws vertical lines upward using the left edge of a triangle.*

You should realize that these recommendations for the direction of drawing lines are not arbitrary rules. Rather, they are determined by the direction of light that illuminates the drawing surface. Right-handed drafters prefer light from their left rather than their right because this reduces objectionable shadows from their right hands. Consequently, they draw horizontal lines from left to right, and vertical lines using the left edge of a triangle. Also, all drafters prefer light from the front rather than the rear since this reduces objectionable shadows from the body. Consequently,

* Left-handers: In general, reverse these rules. Draw horizontal lines from right to left holding your T square with your right hand with the head of the T square at the right. Draw vertical lines upward by using the right edge of the triangle. Draw most inclined lines from right to left.

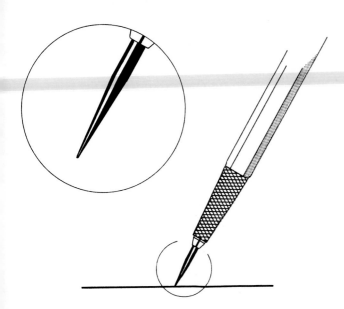

Figure 1   *Lead point for drafting.*

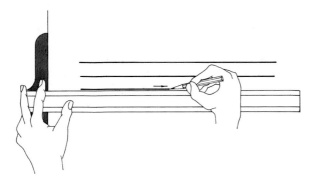

Figure 2   *Drafting horizontal lines.*

Figure 4   *Drafting inclined lines.*

draw horizontal lines using the top edge of the T square. You must, however, draw vertical lines upward to prevent your hand from blocking your vision.

Inclined lines (Figure 4). Most inclined lines are drawn from left to right using the top edge of a triangle.*

Circles and arcs (Figure 5). Drafters use wedge points rather than conical points for compass leads. A wedge point is needed to keep the compass sharp, for it is not possible to rotate the compass lead (with respect to the direction of the line being drawn) as with drafting pencils. A wedge point is formed by sanding just one flat surface. That flat surface may face inward or outward depending on the design of the compass and the radius to be drawn. As shown in Figure 5, the lead should be perpendicular rather than inclined to the surface of the paper. Also, the needle point should extend slightly farther than the lead point.

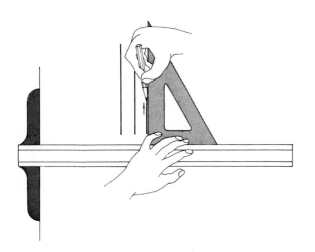

Figure 3   *Drafting vertical lines.*

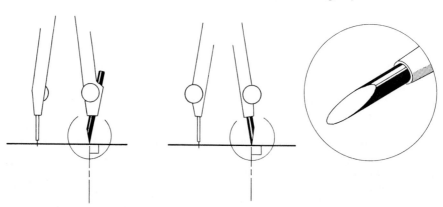

Figure 5   *Lead point for compasses.*

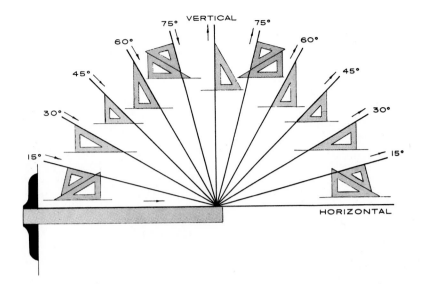

Figure 6

GEOMETRIC CONSTRUCTIONS

Inclined lines (Figure 6). Lines inclined 30°, 45°, and 60° to the horizontal can be drawn using the 30°–60° and 45° triangles. Lines inclined 15° and 75° can be drawn using both triangles in combination. Any angle can be measured or drawn using the adjustable triangle or protractor.
Applications: Pictorial drawings, auxiliary views, section symbols.

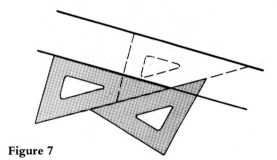

Figure 7

Parallel lines (Figure 7). A line parallel to a given line can be drawn by aligning any one edge of a triangle with the given line, and then sliding another edge of the triangle along a second triangle (or along the T square) to the desired position. Or an adjustable triangle can be used.
Application: A basic construction used in all forms of projection.

Perpendicular lines (Figure 8). A line perpendicular to a given line can be drawn by aligning one leg of a triangle with the given line, and then sliding the hypotenuse of the triangle along a second triangle (or along the T square) to the desired position. Or an adjustable triangle can be used.
Application: A basic construction used in all forms of projection.

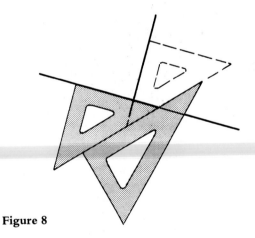

Figure 8

Line tangent to arc (Figure 9). A line can be drawn through a point tangent to an arc by aligning one leg of a triangle to the arc and through the point. Slide the hypotenuse of the triangle along a second triangle (or along the T square) so that the second leg is aligned with the center of the arc. The intersection of the second leg and the arc locates the point of tangency. Slide the triangle back to its original position, and draw the required tangent line. Or use an adjustable triangle.
Application: Accurate location of tangent points.

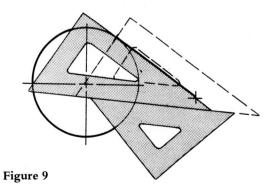

Figure 9

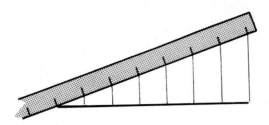

Figure 10

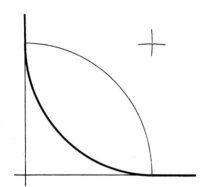

Figure 11

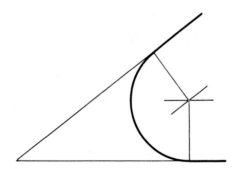

Figure 12

Figure 13

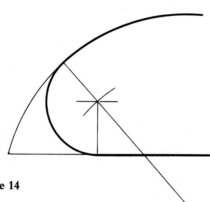

Figure 14

Dividing a line (Figure 10). A line can be divided into any number of equal or proportional parts by the principle of proportional triangles. Construct a triangle with the given line as one leg and an easily divisible construction line as a second leg. Project the divisions, parallel to the third leg, back to the given line.
Application: Layout of repetitive elements such as stairs.

Arc tangent to perpendicular lines (Figure 11). An arc of desired radius can be drawn tangent to two perpendicular lines by striking an arc of the desired radius from the intersection of the perpendicular lines to locate the points of tangency. Strike arcs from the points of tangency to locate the center of the desired arc.
Application: Rounded corners.

Arc tangent to two lines (Figure 12). An arc of desired radius can be drawn tangent to any two lines by drawing construction lines parallel to the given lines, and at a distance equal to the radius, to locate the center of the arc. Drop perpendiculars from the center to the given lines to locate the points of tangency.
Application: Straight forms having fillets or rounds.

Arc tangent to arcs (Figure 13). An arc of desired radius can be drawn tangent to any two arcs by striking construction arcs from the centers of the given arcs using a radius equal to the given arc radii plus (or minus, if desired) the desired radius. This locates the center of the desired arc. Draw construction lines from the center of the desired arc to the center of each given arc to locate the points of tangency.
Application: Curved forms having fillets or rounds.

Arc tangent to line and arc (Figure 14). An arc of desired radius can be drawn tangent to any line and any arc by combining the principles of the two previous geometric constructions.
Application: Combined straight and curved forms.

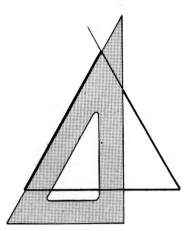

Figure 15

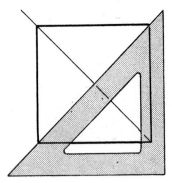

Figure 16

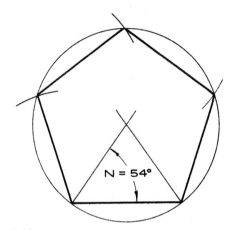

Figure 17

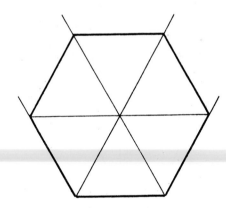

Figure 18

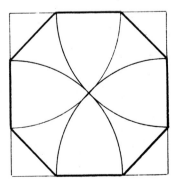

Figure 19

Equilateral triangle (Figure 15). Given a side, an equilateral triangle can be constructed by drawing 60° lines inward through the ends of the side.
Application: A basic proportional element.

Square (Figure 16). Given a side, a square can be constructed by drawing 45° construction lines inward through the ends of the side. Draw adjacent sides at 90° to the given side.
Application: A basic proportional element.

Pentagon (Figure 17). Given a side, a pentagon can be constructed by drawing 54° construction lines inward to the ends of the side to locate the center of the circumscribing circle. Draw this circle and step off the remaining sides.*
Applications: Plan shapes, polyhedra.

Hexagon (Figure 18). Given a side, a hexagon can be constructed by drawing 60° construction lines in both directions through the ends of the side to locate the center of the hexagon. Draw a construction line through the center of the hexagon and parallel to the given side to locate adjacent corners. Draw 60° lines inward through these corners to locate the remaining corners.
Applications: Plan shapes, polyhedra.

Octagon (Figure 19). Given a side, an octagon can be constructed by drawing 45° sides outwardly. Construct a square through the given side and the far ends of the 45° sides. Swing arcs with centers at the corners of the square, and radii equal to half the length of the diagonal of the square. Add the remaining sides to complete the octagon.
Applications: Plan shapes, polyhedra.

* This construction can be used for *any* regular polygon by using an angle of

$$90° - \frac{180°}{N}$$

when N equals the required number of sides.

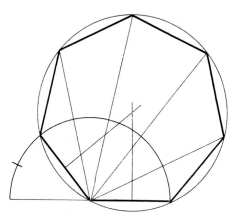

Figure 20

Ellipse (trammel method) (Figure 22). Given the major and minor axes, an ellipse can be constructed by using a trammel (a paper straight-edge). On the trammel, mark off half of the major axis (M) and half of the minor axis (N) from a common origin (O). Then place the trammel in any convenient direction so that the major axis mark falls on the minor axis and the minor axis mark falls on the major axis. The origin mark locates one point on the ellipse. Rotate the trammel to obtain as many points as desired. Using an irregular curve, complete the ellipse by drawing a smooth curve through the origin marks. Two methods are illustrated.

Regular polygon (Figure 20). Given a side, a regular polygon of any number of sides (N) can be constructed by drawing a semicircle on the given side as illustrated. Divide the semicircle into N equal parts, and draw an adjacent side through the second outermost division. Draw perpendicular bisectors of these sides to locate the circumscribing circle. Draw radial construction lines through the divisions of the semicircle to locate the remaining corners of the polygon.
Applications: Plan shapes, polyhedra.

Conic sections (Figure 21). When a right circular cone is cut by a plane surface, the intersection is called an *ellipse* when the plane is inclined at an angle smaller than the base angle of the cone; a *parabola* when inclined at the same angle; and a *hyperbola* when inclined at a greater angle.

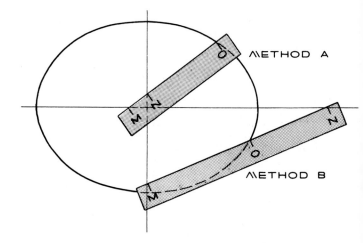

Figure 22

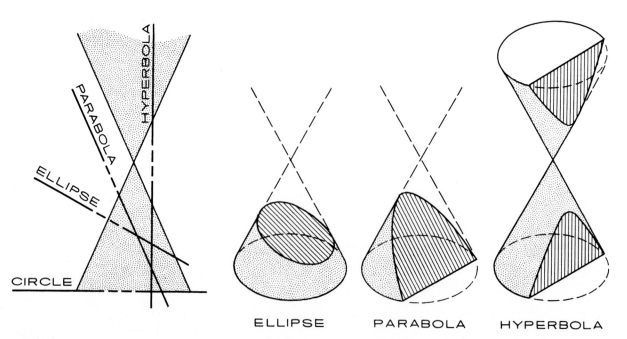

Figure 21

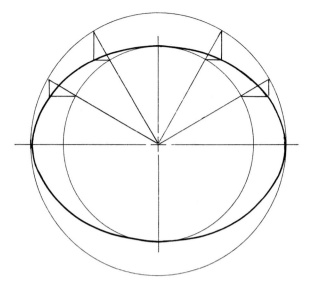

Figure 23

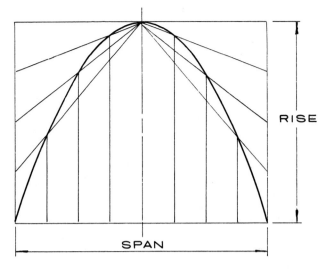

Figure 24

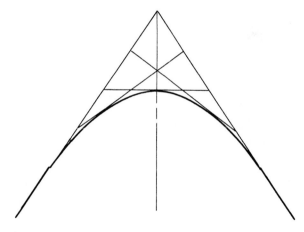

Figure 25

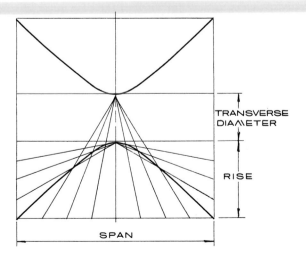

Figure 26

Often only one quadrant of the ellipse need be plotted, for you can mark your irregular curve and use it for the remaining three quadrants.
Application: Circles which project as ellipses.

Ellipse (concentric circle method) (Figure 23).
Given the major and minor axes, an ellipse can be constructed by drawing two concentric circles having diameters equal to the major and minor axes. Draw any convenient number of radial construction lines. Draw construction lines parallel to the major axis through the intersection of the radial lines and the inner circle. Draw construction lines parallel to the minor axis through the intersection of the radial lines and the outer circle. Using an irregular curve, complete the ellipse by drawing a smooth curve through the intersections of the construction lines.

Often only one quadrant of the ellipse need be plotted, for you can mark your irregular curve and use it for the remaining three quadrants.
Application: Circles which project as ellipses.

Parabola of given rise and span (Figure 24).
Given the rise and span, a parabola can be constructed by drawing a rectangle having the span as a base and an altitude equal to the rise. Divide the altitude and half the base into the same number of equal parts. The intersections of the construction lines locate points on the parabola as illustrated.
Applications: Approximate catenary curve, sound- and light-reflecting surfaces, bending moment at any point of a uniformly loaded beam.

Parabola tangent to two lines (Figure 25).
Given two lines, a tangent parabola can be constructed by extending the lines to their intersec-

tion. Divide the line extensions into the same number of equal parts. Draw construction lines as illustrated. The parabola will be tangent to these construction lines.

Applications: Arch forms, warped roof surfaces.

Hyperbola of given diameter, rise, and span (Figure 26). Given the transverse diameter, rise, and span, the hyperbola can be constructed by drawing a rectangle having the span as a base and an altitude equal to the rise. Divide the altitude and half the base into the same number of equal parts. Intersections of the construction lines locate points on the hyperbola as illustrated.

Application: Warped roof surfaces.

Catenary (Figure 27). Given any three points, a catenary curve can be drawn by hanging a fine chain through the three points marked on a vertical drawing board. Prick the desired number of guide points through the links of the chain. A catenary is not a conic section but can be approximated by a parabola as illustrated. For accurate results, use formulas or tables found in standard references such as *Marks' Handbook*.

Application: Cable-supported roofs, uniform cross-sectional arches.

Cylindrical helix (Figure 28). Given the cylindrical diameter and lead, a helix can be generated by dividing the circumference of the cylinder and the lead into the same number of equal parts. Project the circumference marks to the adjacent view until they intersect the lead lines. Draw the helix through these intersections as illustrated.

Applications: Spiral stairways and ramps.

Conical helix (Figure 29). Given the conic diameter, conic altitude, and lead, a helix can be generated by dividing the base of the cone and the lead into the same number of equal parts. Project the base marks to the edge view of the base in the adjacent view, and then to the vertex of the cone until they intersect the lead lines. Draw the helix through these intersections as illustrated. The plan view of the conical helix is called the *spiral of Archimedes*.

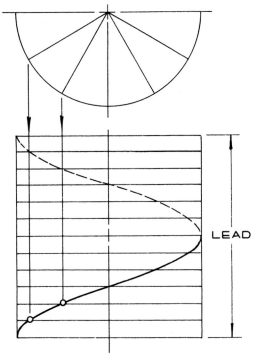

Figure 28

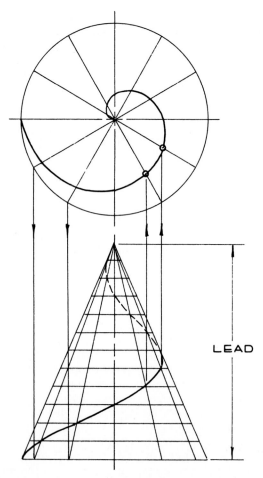

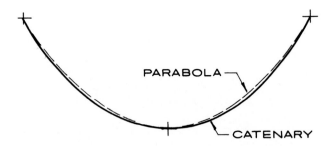

Figure 27

Figure 29

Conical helix of uniform slope (Figure 30).
Given the conic diameter, conic altitude, rise, and run, a helix can be generated by dividing the cone vertically into sections equal to the desired rise, and by projecting these sections to the plan view as concentric circles. Strike arcs equal to the desired run. Draw the helix as illustrated.
Applications: Conical stairways and ramps.

Spherical helix (Figure 31). Given the spherical diameter and lead, a helix can be generated by dividing the circumference of the sphere and the lead into the same number of equal parts. Project the circumference marks to the adjacent view until they intersect the lead lines. Draw the helix through these intersections as illustrated.
Application: Ornamental space curve.

Spherical helix of uniform slope (Figure 32).
Given the spherical diameter, rise, and run, a helix can be generated by dividing the sphere vertically into sections equal to the desired rise, and by projecting these sections to the plan view as concentric circles. Strike arcs equal to the desired run and draw the helix as illustrated. Notice that the desired slope cannot be maintained beyond the tangent point of the slope line on the spherical surface.
Applications: Spherical stairways and ramps.

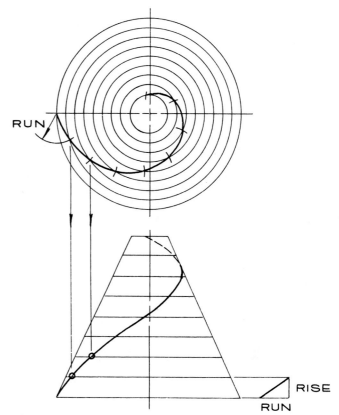

Figure 30

STUDY QUESTIONS

1. Give the direction of stroking for the following instrumental lines drawn by a right-handed drafter:
   a. Horizontal lines
   b. Vertical lines
   c. Lines inclined down to the right
   d. Lines inclined down to the left
2. Give the reason for:
   a. Rotating your pencil while drafting
   b. Drafting horizontal lines from left to right
   c. Drafting horizontal lines using the top edge of your T square
   d. Drafting vertical lines upward
   e. Drafting vertical lines using the left edge of your triangle
3. Give the reason for:
   a. Sharpening a compass lead to a wedge point
   b. Adjusting the needle point of a compass beyond the lead point
   c. Changing the direction of a compass lead's flat surface

LABORATORY PROBLEMS

1. On $8\frac{1}{2}'' \times 11''$ drawing paper, lay out twelve $2\frac{1}{4}''$ square areas. Using drafting instruments, draw the

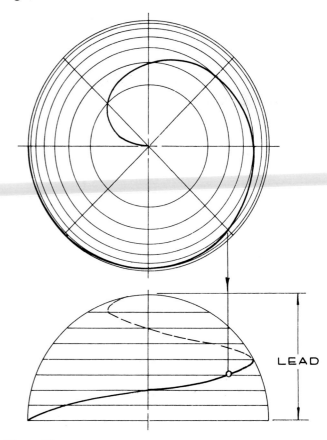

Figure 31

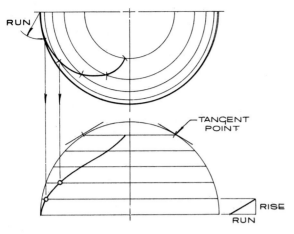

Figure 32

patterns shown in Figure 33. Estimate all dimensions to obtain similar proportions.

2. Using the table placement and dimensions in Figure 34, lay out a 21' × 23' dining room to contain the maximum number of tables. Scale: $\frac{1}{2}$" = 1'-0.
   a. Sketch on graph paper.
   b. Draw with drafting instruments.

3. Draw a random, broken-course-and-range stone wall as illustrated in Figure 35. Include an area 18" high × 3'-0 wide to a scale of $1\frac{1}{2}$" = 1'-0.

4. Draw a low wall (2' high × 6' long) constructed of 12"-square concrete screen blocks patterned as shown in Figure 36. Use $\frac{1}{2}$" mortar joints. Scale: 1" = 1'-0.

5. Draw the plan of a 33'-long serpentine wall using the dimensions given in Figure 37. Scale: $\frac{1}{4}$" = 1'-0.

6. Prepare instrumental drawings as assigned by your instructor.

7. Using drafting instruments, prepare a display sheet

Figure 33

illustrating how these geometric constructions may be obtained:

a. Lines inclined 0°, 15°, 30°, 45°, 60°, 75°, and 90° with the horizontal
b. Arcs tangent to two lines, two circles, and a line and a circle.
c. Parabola tangent to two lines
d. Any polygon
e. Equilateral triangle, square, pentagon, hexagon, octagon
f. Ellipse, parabola, and hyperbola
g. Cylindrical, conical, and spherical helices
h. Cylindrical, conical, and spherical helices of uniform slope

8. Prepare geometric constructions as assigned by your instructor.

Figure 34

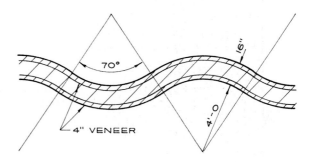

Figure 35

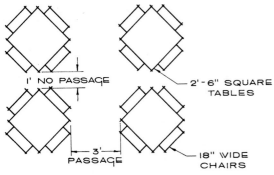

Figure 36

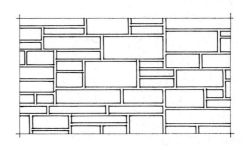

Figure 37

4 / Architectural Technique

The technique of linework on architectural drawings is of a nature completely different from that used on other forms of mechanical drawing. In fact, the difference is so great that it is diffiult for a drafter trained in another field—engineering drafting, for example—to make the switch to architectural drafting, since doing so means "unlearning" many accepted rules and practices. The reason for this dissimilarity is the difference in the goals of the two fields. Whereas engineers must turn out a perfectly exact and cold-blooded indication of their needs to be used by persons trained in their own fields, architects want to produce an artistically complete picture to be read by trained workers and laymen alike. Basically, architects must sell their product. And to do this, their plans must be infinitely more appealing and warm.

LINE CHARACTER

The first point to be remembered is that you are not only a drafter, but an artist as well. Don't be afraid to let your lines run past each other at their intersections (Figure 1). A better end result will be obtained if the mind and hand are not cramped by trying to stop at a given point.

Use a soft pencil. Many architects will never touch a pencil harder than 2H grade. It is impossible to obtain line quality in a drawing done with a hard pencil. The two skills to be mastered with a soft pencil are the slight twisting to keep the point sharp and the extra care required to keep the paper clean. Recommended grades are shown in Figure 2.

Lines (other than dimension lines and a few others) are often *not* drawn uniform in weight. Indeed, they may nearly fade out in the middle. The

POOR   GOOD   BEST

Figure 1   *Line technique at corners.*

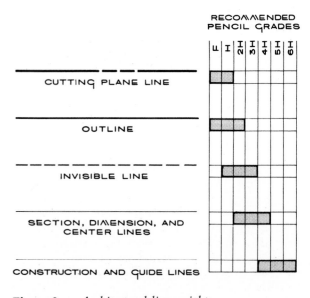

Figure 2   *Architectural line weights.*

28

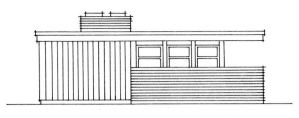

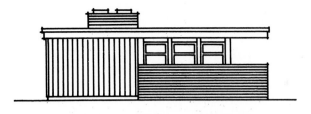

LINES TOO LIGHT FOR PROPER REPRODUCTION

LINES HEAVY, BUT NO CONTRAST

Figure 3   *Poor techniques.*

ends of the lines are accentuated and should come to a distinct stop rather than just fade away.

All instruments and materials should be kept in perfect condition. A violinist might as well try to play with boxing gloves on as a drafter try to draw with a blunt pencil point. If a good drafter is forced to use poor materials and produces an acceptable drawing, he does so in spite of them, not because of them. No good artistic work is sloppy.

Keep your drawings clean and smudge-free. These suggestions will help:

1. All your drafting equipment should be cleaned frequently. Soap and water, if thoroughly dried off, will not injure triangles and T squares. Use a clean cloth or paper towel to clean your desk top before beginning work.
2. Wash your hands. Try to keep your hands off the face of your drawing. Never allow anyone else to touch your drawing. When lettering, place a clean paper shield under your hand.
3. Do not sharpen your pencil over the desk top. Be certain that all graphite particles fall only on the floor. Blow or wipe off your pencil point immediately after sharpening. Wipe off each drafting instrument regularly.
4. Cover the un-worked-on portion of your drawing with a clear paper shield so that it is not smudged and dirty before you start to draw. Cover any completed portion of your drawing with a clean paper shield also.
5. Do not slide your triangles and T square across your drawing; lift them slightly.
6. Keep all lines (especially construction lines) sharp and accurate to reduce the amount of erasing to a minimum.
7. Either blow or brush off any excess graphite from your drawing after drawing each line.
8. Some drafters find that a special cleaning powder (known under various trade names such as Dry-Clean Pad, Draft-Clean Powder, Dust-it, Scumex) will aid in keeping their drawings smudge-free.
9. As a last resort, change pencil grades. A harder

pencil grade will not smudge as readily as a soft pencil grade.

LINE TECHNIQUE

Architectural drafters develop their own styles of linework just as they develop their own styles of lettering. Linework consists of a combination of light and dark lines. As shown in Figure 3, avoid lines of all one, monotonous weight. Some of the most successfully used styles of line techniques are illustrated in Figure 4.

Cutting-plane technique. This technique is used for section views. The lines formed by the cutting plane are darkened.

Distance technique. It is possible to show depth in an architectural drawing by emphasizing the lines closest to the observer. Even if the plan in Figure 4 had been omitted, you would be able to visualize the shape of the building by this technique.

Silhouette technique. The silhouette is emphasized by darkening the outline. One of the oldest techniques, it is still used today.

Shadow technique. Recessions and extensions can be shown by darkening the edges away from the light source. The light is usually assumed to be coming from the upper left.

Major-feature technique. This is a commonly used technique. The major elements are outlined, and the elements of lesser importance are drawn in with finer lines. The diagrams in this text are drawn using this technique.

Obviously, all of the above techniques cannot be used simultaneously. You will develop your own favored style, but remember to remain flexible enough to be able to adapt your personal technique to the standards set up by a particular office.

ARCHITECTURAL SYMBOLS

A system of architectural symbols to indicate certain materials and features has developed through the years. Properly used, these symbols complement the architectural linework and form an attractive and useful language.

Figure 5 shows the symbols most often used on architectural sections, and Figure 6 shows those used on architectural elevations. Notice that most materials have different symbols for section and elevation views. Also remember that all section and elevation symbols should be drawn lighter than the outlines.

Figure 7 shows some common structural shapes used in architectural design. Either the W-shape or S-shape beam may be specified for house girders. The W shape is often used as a column in industrial buildings, but pipe columns are used in residences. The angle sections may be used to support masonry over wall openings; they may be obtained with equal or unequal legs. Both angle and channel sections are generally used as elements of built-up sections for commercial structures.

Steel is also obtainable in round bar shapes, square bar shapes, and rectangular plates.

Wall symbols are shown in Figure 8, together with the accepted dimensioning practices: to the outside face of the studs for frame walls, and to the outside of the masonry for masonry walls. Notice that no section symbol is specified for the frame wall. A wood symbol or poché (darkening of wall by shading or light lines) may be used.

All fixed equipment supplied by the builder should be included in the plans, whereas equipment furnished by the owner is omitted. Figure 9 shows an assortment of symbols that may be used. An invisible line may represent an invisible object (like the dishwasher shown built in under the counter) or a high object (like the wall cabinets that are *above* the plane of the section).

The conventions used to indicate windows and doors in a frame wall are shown in Figure 10. Although the doors are shown opened a full 90°, an angle of 30° may also be used. These same window and door conventions may be adapted to other kinds of walls, as shown in Figure 11. Notice the definite contrast in line weight between the walls and conventions.

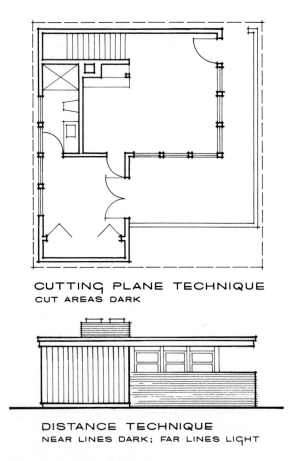

CUTTING PLANE TECHNIQUE
CUT AREAS DARK

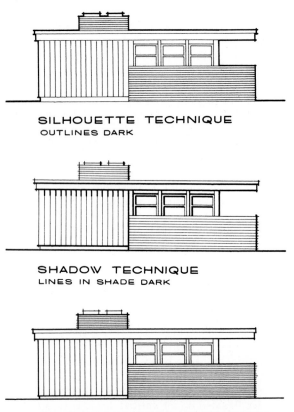

SILHOUETTE TECHNIQUE
OUTLINES DARK

SHADOW TECHNIQUE
LINES IN SHADE DARK

DISTANCE TECHNIQUE
NEAR LINES DARK; FAR LINES LIGHT

MAJOR-FEATURE TECHNIQUE
MAJOR ELEMENTS DARK

Figure 4 *Good techniques.*

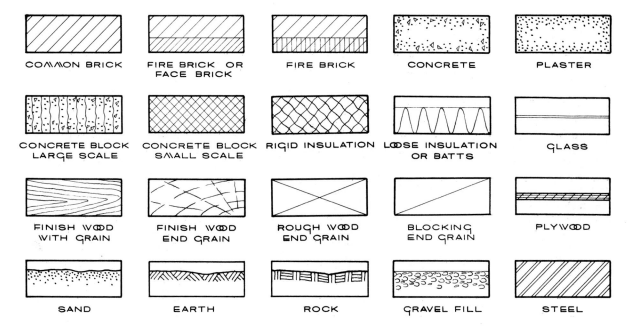

Figure 5 *Architectural symbols in section.*

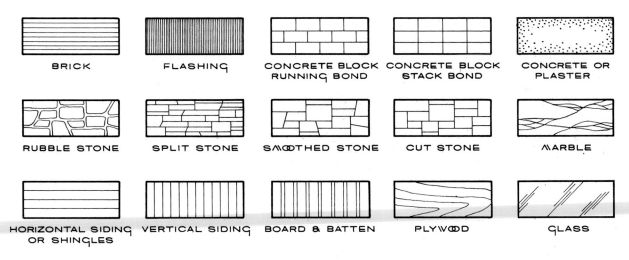

Figure 6 *Architectural symbols in elevation.*

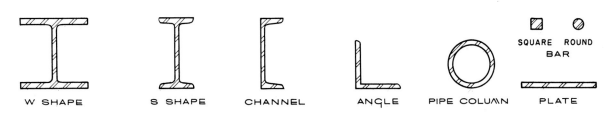

Figure 7 *Structural steel shapes.*

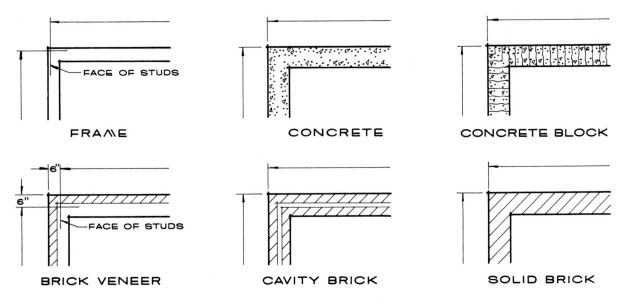

Figure 8 *Wall symbols.*

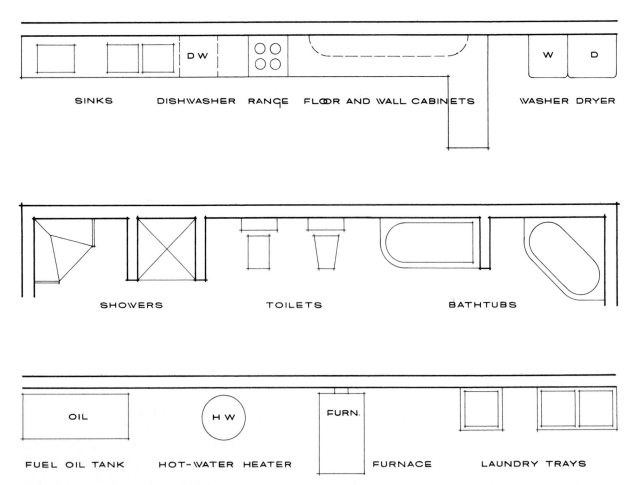

Figure 9 *Fixed equipment symbols.*

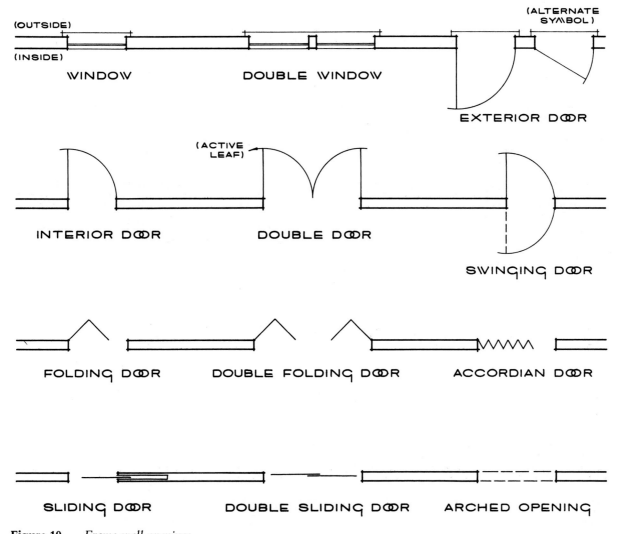

Figure 10 *Frame wall openings.*

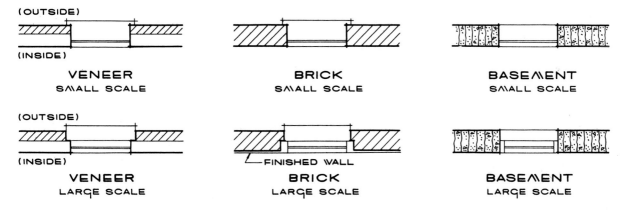

Figure 11 *Masonry wall openings.*

STUDY QUESTIONS

1. What is the difference between linework used on engineering drawings and architectural drawings?
2. Suggest several methods to keep architectural drawings free of smudges.
3. What is the advantage of using:
   a. Hard pencil grades
   b. Soft pencil grades
4. List five different types of line techniques used by architectural drafters.

LABORATORY PROBLEMS

1. Prepare a legend that lists and illustrates:
   a. Architectural section symbols
   b. Architectural elevation symbols
   c. Structural steel shapes
   d. Wall symbols
   e. Window and door symbols
   f. Fixed equipment symbols
2. Prepare classroom illustrations showing the five types of architectural line techniques.
3. Lay out the 10'-6" × 8'-0 awning window wall shown in Figure 12. Use appropriate pencil technique. Scale: $\frac{1}{4}$" = 1'-0.
4. Draw the elevation of a stacked bond wall containing a 2'-8" × 8'-0 door and transom as indicated in Figure 13. Masonry units are 8" × 8" × 16". Use appropriate pencil technique. Scale: $\frac{1}{4}$" = 1'-0.
5. Draw an elevation of the helicoidal concrete stairway shown in Figure 14. Use appropriate pencil technique. Scale: $\frac{1}{4}$" = 1'-0.
6. Draw the cross section of a small theater using the dimensions indicated in Figure 15. Use appropriate pencil technique. Scale: $\frac{1}{8}$" = 1'-0.

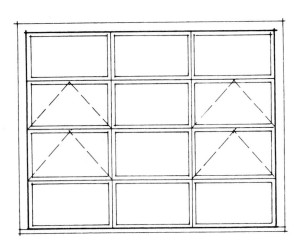

Figure 12

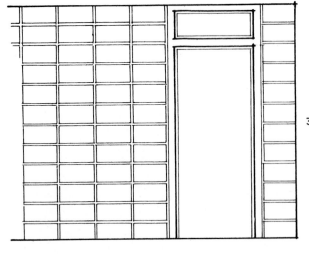

Figure 13

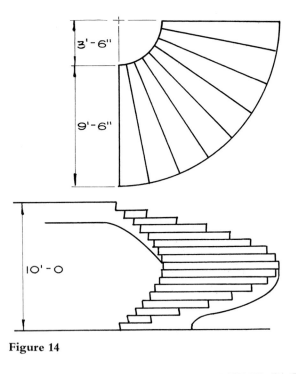

Figure 14

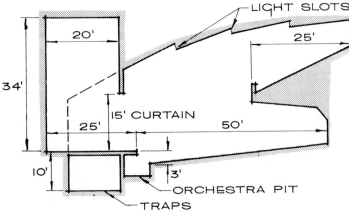

Figure 15

II / Drawing Conventions

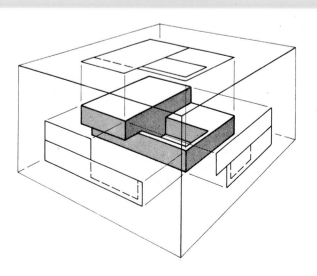

5 / Projections

Since early days, the ability to communicate complex ideas was one of the talents that distinguished humans from other forms of life. The first methods of communication were spoken languages and picture languages. The picture languages have developed through the years into a great number of written languages and one universally accepted graphic language. This universal graphic language is based upon a theory of *projections*. That is, it is assumed that imaginary sight lines, called *projectors,* extend from the eye of the observer to the object being described. The projectors transmit an image of the object onto an intervening transparent surface called the *picture plane*. This image is called a *projection* of the object.

Perspective projection. When the projectors all converge at a point (the observer's eye) as shown in Figure 1, the resulting projection of the object on the picture plane is called a *perspective projection*. Perspective projections are often used by archi-

tects to present a realistic picture of a proposed building. As shown in Figure 4 and Table I, there are three types of perspective projection: *one-point, two-point,* and *three-point* perspective. Detailed information can be found in Chapter 36.

Parallel projection. When the projectors are all parallel to each other (as if the observer had moved to infinity), the resulting projection is called a *parallel projection.* Parallel projectors angled (oblique) to the picture plane result in an *oblique projection* as detailed in Chapter 8, but for most architectural drafting, the projectors are assumed to be perpendicular to the picture plane, resulting in an *orthographic projection.** There are two kinds of orthographic projection depending upon the relation of the object to the picture plane. These are called *multiview projection* (Figure 2) and *axonometric projection* (Figure 3).

* *Ortho* is a Greek prefix meaning "at a right angle."

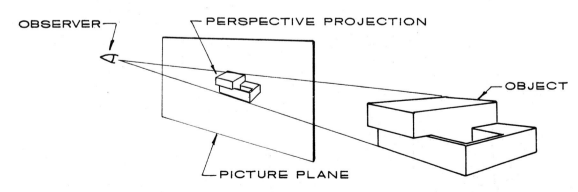

Figure 1   *Perspective projection.*

Table I *Types of Projections*

			Type	Relation of Projectors to: Each Other	Relation of Projectors to: Picture Plane	Relation of Object Faces to Picture Plane
Perspective			One-point	Converging	Many angles	One face parallel
			Two-point	"	" "	Vertical faces oblique
			Three-point	"	" "	All faces oblique
Parallel	Orthographic	Multiview	First-angle	Parallel	Perpendicular	Parallel
			Third-angle	"	"	"
		Axonometric	Isometric	Parallel	"	Three equally oblique
			Dimetric	"	"	Two equally oblique
			Trimetric	"	"	Three unequally oblique
	Oblique		Cavalier	Parallel	Oblique	45°
			Cabinet	"	"	Arc tan 2

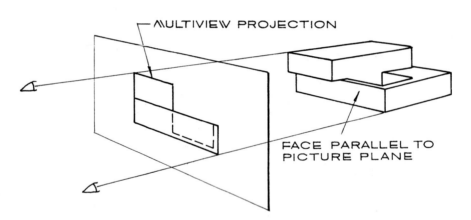

Figure 2   *Multiview projection.*

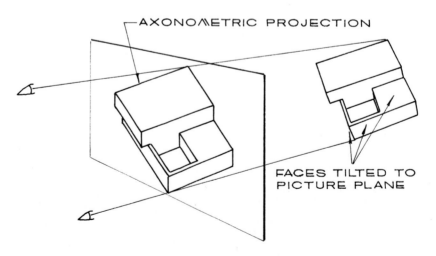

Figure 3   *Axonometric projection.*

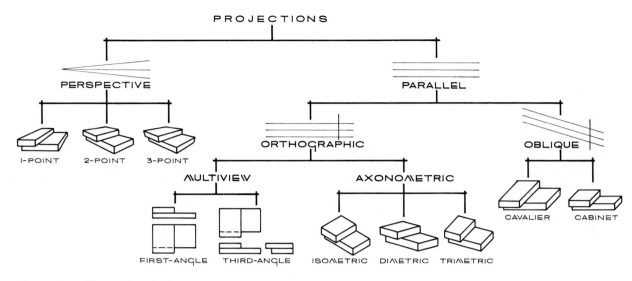

Figure 4 *Types of projections.*

Multiview projection.* In multiview projection, the object is positioned so that its principal faces are parallel to the picture planes. This is the type of projection most useful to architects because principal lines and faces appear true size and shape on the picture plane. The term *multiview* is used because more than one view is required to show all three principal faces. See Chapter 6 on multiview projections for more detail.

Axonometric projection.** In axonometric projection, the object is tilted with respect to the picture plane so that all faces and axes are visible but not in true shape. Axonometric projections are easier to draw than perspectives and, consequently, are used often. See Chapter 8 on pictorial projections for more detail.

* *Multi* is a Latin prefix meaning "many."

** *Axono* is a Greek prefix meaning "axis."

The different features of each type of projection are illustrated in Figure 4 and Table I. Study them carefully and refer back to them often as you read related Chapter 6 on multiview projections, Chapter 8 on pictorial projections, and Chapter 36 on perspective projections.

STUDY QUESTIONS

1. Distinguish between:
   a. Perspective projection and parallel projection
   b. Orthographic projection and oblique projection
   c. Multiview projection and axonometric projection
2. Give the relationship of the projectors to each other and to the picture plane in the following types of projection:
   a. Multiview
   b. Axonometric
   c. Oblique
   d. Perspective

6 / Multiview Projections

All buildings and nearly all elements of a building are three-dimensional, but they are designed and specified by means of two-dimensional plans. A three-dimensional object can be described on a flat, two-dimensional plan by any of the types of projection discussed in the previous chapter, but the type of projection most useful, and therefore most commonly used, is *multiview projection*. Multiview projection is so popular because the exact shape of each face of a building and the elements of a building can be shown without distortion. Also, the length of every line can be shown true size or to a convenient scale.

The "glass box." The easiest way to understand multiview projection is to imagine the object placed inside a "glass box" so that all six faces (front, rear, plan, bottom, and both ends) are parallel to the faces of the glass box. This is illustrated in Figure 1, where an object (a clay model of a building) has been surrounded by imaginary, transparent planes. Now, if projectors were dropped perpendicularly from the object to each face of the glass box (Figure 2), a number of projection points would be obtained which could then be connected to give a true-size and -shape projection of the six principal faces of the object. If the glass box is then unfolded, as shown in Figure 3, all six faces can be illustrated upon a single sheet of paper as shown in Figure 4. Note the terms *height, width,* and *depth. Height* is a vertical distance, *width* is an end-to-end distance, and *depth* is a front-to-rear distance.

Study Figure 4 and notice that all adjacent views must be in projection. For example:

1. The front view must be in projection with the rear and end views. These four views all have the same *height* and are often called *elevations* (such as front elevation, rear elevation, right-end elevation, and left-end elevation). In drafting, the projection between elevations is accomplished by aligning these views horizontally using a T square.
2. The front view must be in projection with the plan and bottom views, since these views all have the same *width*. In drafting, this projection is accomplished by aligning these views vertically by using a drafting triangle.*
3. Also notice that four views (plan, bottom, and both ends) have a common element of *depth*. In

* Width dimensions can be projected to the rear view using dividers.

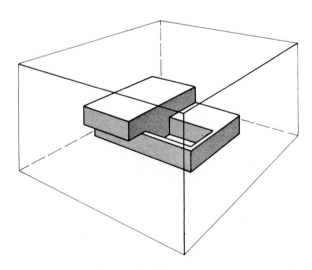

Figure 1   *The "glass box."*

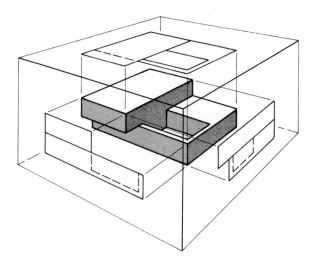

Figure 2 *Projecting to the "glass box."*

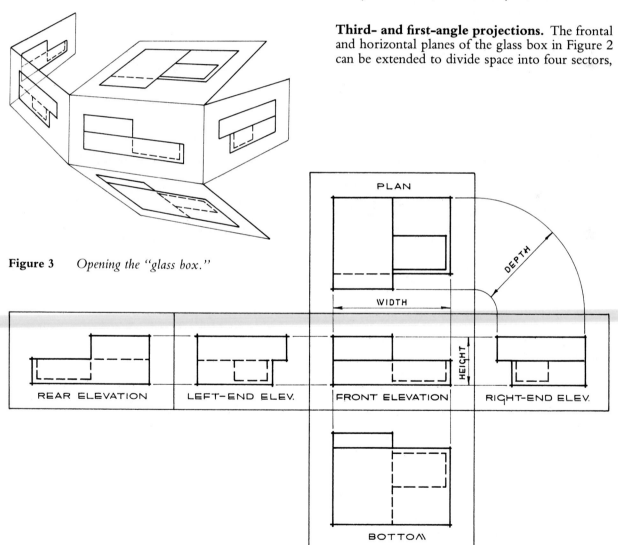

Figure 3 *Opening the "glass box."*

Figure 4 *Standard arrangement of the principal views.*

drafting, depth measurements may be transferred by dividers, by scale, by using a 45° miter line, or by drawing 90° circular arcs (Figure 5).

In architectural drafting, views of an entire building are often so large that each view requires an entire sheet of paper. In such cases, titles or other identifications are used to clarify the relationships between views.

Number of views. Six views are seldom drawn. A simple architectural detail usually requires only two or three views, but a complex building might require a great number of views in addition to sections and details. Partial views may also be drawn. The governing rule is to draw as many views as necessary to describe the object clearly and accurately—no more, and certainly no fewer.

Third- and first-angle projections. The frontal and horizontal planes of the glass box in Figure 2 can be extended to divide space into four sectors,

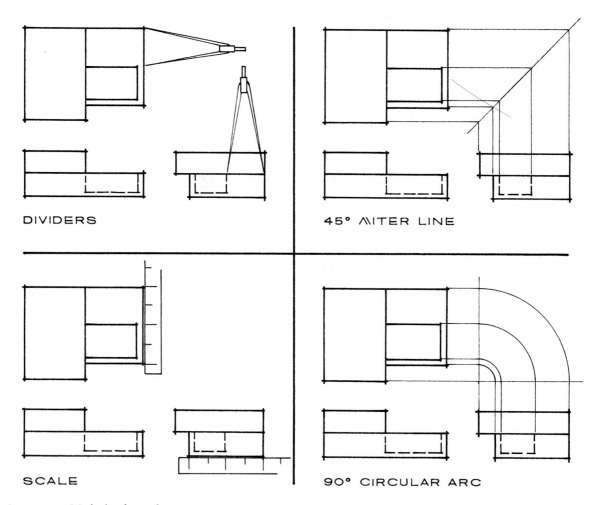

DIVIDERS

45° MITER LINE

SCALE

90° CIRCULAR ARC

Figure 5   *Methods of transferring measurements.*

known in geometry as *quadrants* (Figure 6). The object can be placed in any quadrant and projected to the projection planes. The horizontal plane is folded clockwise into the frontal plane as shown by the arrows in Figure 6. This results in four alternate arrangements of views, called first-, second-, third-, and fourth-angle projections.

Third-angle projection produces the relationship between views previously described in the "glass-box" paragraph in which the plan view is *above* the front elevation. First-angle projection produces a slightly different relationship between views, in that the plan is *below* the front elevation. In first-angle projection, the picture plane is *beyond* the object rather than *between* the object and observer. Second- and fourth-angle projections produce overlapping views and are not used.

Third-angle projection is used for most architectural and technical drafting in this country. Occasionally, however, first-angle projection is used in architectural drafting when it is more convenient to place a plan below an elevation. In Figure 5 of Chapter 26, notice that the plan and front ele-

vation of each fireplace is in first-angle projection, whereas the front and end elevations are in third-angle projection.

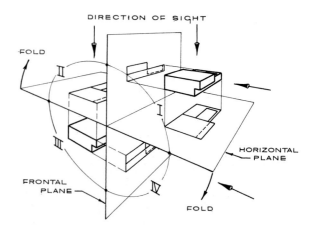

Figure 6   *The four quadrants.*

Language of lines. Nine types of lines constitute the basic "alphabet" of drafting. They are all illustrated in Figure 7. Notice that these lines are drawn using five different line weights. *Line weight* refers to the blackness and thickness of a line and ranges from an extremely heavy cutting-plane line to barely visible construction lines and guidelines. A heavy line is obtained by using a soft pencil (such as an F grade), a slightly rounded point, and some hand pressure. A light line is obtained by using a hard pencil (such as a 6H grade), a sharp point, and less pressure.

Outline. Outlines (also called *visible* lines) are heavy lines used to describe the visible shape of an object including edges, edge views of planes, and contours of curved surfaces.

Invisible line. Invisible lines (also called hidden lines) are outlines that cannot be seen by the observer because they are covered by portions of the object closer to the observer. The locations of such invisible edges are indicated when necessary to accurately describe the object. The dashes of invisible lines are about $\frac{1}{8}''$ in length and $\frac{1}{32}''$ apart. Invisible lines are medium-weight lines.

Cutting-plane line. The cutting-plane line represents the edge view of a cutting plane sliced through the object to reveal inner features. It is drawn as the heaviest-weight line so that the location of a section can be identified easily.

Section line. Section lines are used to crosshatch any cut portion of an object. A number of sectioning symbols are shown in Figure 5 of Chapter 4. Section, center, dimension, and extension lines are all drawn the same light weight.

Center line. Center lines indicate axes of symmetry. Most center lines consist of alternating $\frac{1}{8}''$ short dashes and $1''$ long dashes spaced about $\frac{1}{32}''$ apart. In small-scale drawings, spaces may be omitted.

Dimension line. Dimension lines are used to indicate the direction and limits of a linear dimension. Some types of arrowheads used with dimension lines are illustrated in Figure 1 of Chapter 10.

Extension line. Extension lines serve as an extension of a feature on the object so that dimensions can be placed *next* to a projection rather than crowded *on* the projection.

Construction line. Construction lines are extremely light lines barely visible to the eye. They are used to lay out a view or to project between views.

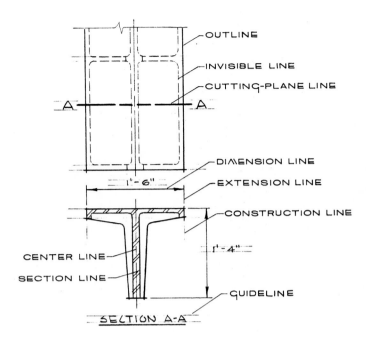

Figure 7 *The language of lines.*

Guideline. Horizontal and vertical guidelines are construction lines used to guide hand lettering. See Figure 5 in Chapter 9.

"Reading" a drawing. In addition to drawing the projections of an object from a mental picture, an architectural drafter must be able to "read" drawings. That is, given a projection of an object, the drafter must be able to visualize its shape and features. The following rules may help:

1. The same features must always be in projection in adjacent views. Consequently, a point or line in one view may be projected to and read in an adjacent view to help understand what it represents.
2. Read views simultaneously rather than one at a time. Staring at a single view usually will not be particularly helpful. Your eyes should project a feature back and forth between views until you are able to visualize the feature and eventually the entire object.
3. There is a rule called the *rule of configuration* which states that the configuration (shape) of a plane remains about the same in all views, unless the plane appears in its edge view. For example, a five-sided surface will always have five sides—not four or six—unless it appears on edge.

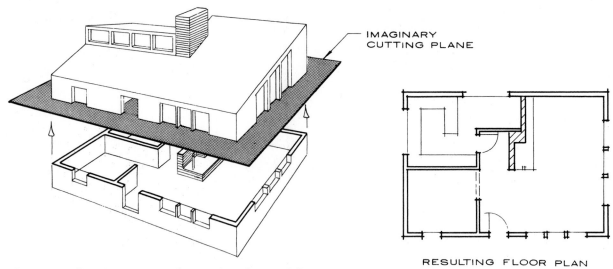

IMAGINARY
CUTTING PLANE

RESULTING FLOOR PLAN

Figure 8 *Imaginary cutting plane used to obtain a full section.*

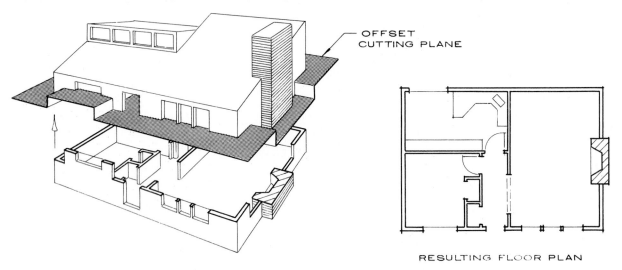

OFFSET
CUTTING PLANE

RESULTING FLOOR PLAN

Figure 9 *Cutting-plane offset to show all desired features.*

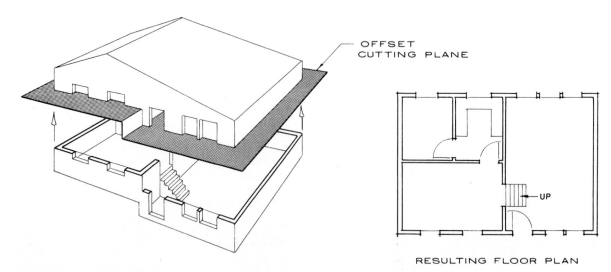

OFFSET
CUTTING PLANE

RESULTING FLOOR PLAN

UP

Figure 10 *Cutting-plane offset to obtain a floor plan of a split-level house.*

Sectioning. Architectural components are seldom solid objects as discussed in the preceding sections. Rather, they consist of complex assemblies that require sectional views to adequately describe them. A section is an imaginary cut through a component (part) or an assembly of components. All the material on one side of the cut is removed so that the interior can be studied. Often, sections are drawn through entire structures, walls, floors, roofs, foundations, structural assemblies, stairs, and fireplaces. The scale of sectional views is often increased to further clarify the details. Cutting-plane lines are used only when needed to show where the cut was taken. Sight direction arrows are added to the ends of cutting-plane lines only when needed to show the direction of sight.

Full section. A full section is a cut through the entire building or component. As shown in Figure 8, when a horizontal cutting plane is passed through an entire building, a floor plan results. The horizontal cutting plane is assumed to be located 4' above the floor (midway between floor and ceiling).

Cutting planes can be vertical as well as horizontal. A vertical cut through the long dimension of a building is called a *longitudinal section,* and through the short dimension of a building, a *transverse section.* Both cuts are helpful in analyzing the building's structure and detailing.

Offset section. The cutting plane can be *offset* (bent) to permit it to cut through all necessary features. For example, although a horizontal cutting plane through an entire building is usually assumed to be about 4' above floor level, it would be offset *upward* to cut through a high strip window as shown in Figure 9, and offset *downward* to cut through a lower level of a split-level house as shown in Figure 10. Usually such offsets need not be indicated by a cutting-plane line.

Half-section. A half-section is a cut to remove only *one-quarter* of a symmetrical component. Thus

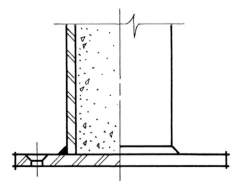

Figure 11 *A half-section of a welded steel column.*

both the exterior and interior can be shown in one view as indicated in Figure 11.

Broken-out section. A broken-out section has the advantage of permitting the drafter to select the most critical area for sectioning and still present the exterior appearance of the component—all in one view. See Figure 12.

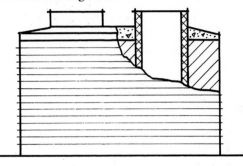

Figure 12 *A broken-out section of a chimney cap.*

Revolved section. A revolved section is a section that has been revolved 90° and drawn on the exterior view of a component. Like a broken-out section, this permits the showing of a greater amount of information in a small space. See Figure 13.

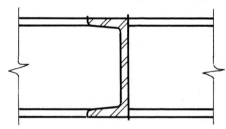

Figure 13 *A revolved section of a steel channel.*

Revolved partial sections are used to indicate the sectional profile of a special column, jamb, or molding. See Figure 14.

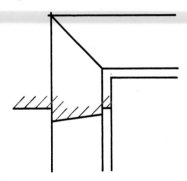

Figure 14 *A revolved partial section of door trim.*

Removed section. A removed section is simply a revolved section that has been removed to another location and often drawn to a larger scale. A cutting plane should be used to indicate where this sectional cut was taken.

STUDY QUESTIONS

1. Distinguish between first-angle projection and third-angle projection.
2. Distinguish between height, width, and depth.
3. Describe four methods of transferring depth measurements between the plan and end elevations.
4. Using a line-weight scale of 5 (very heavy) to 1 (very light), give the weight of each type of line:
   a. Outline
   b. Invisible line
   c. Center line
   d. Cutting-plane line
   e. Section line
   f. Dimension and extension lines
   g. Guidelines and construction lines
5. What is the advantage of:
   a. Half-sections
   b. Offset sections
   c. Broken-out sections
   d. Revolved sections
   e. Partial sections
   f. Removed sections
6. Distinguish between:
   a. Full section and half-section
   b. Longitudinal section and transverse section

LABORATORY PROBLEMS

1. Draw multiview projections of the mass models shown in Figure 15 as assigned:
   a. Sufficient views to describe model
   b. Front elevation, end elevation, and plan
   c. Plan and all elevations
2. Draw the multiview projections as assigned by your instructor.
3. Draw a full section of an 8″ × 16″ reinforced concrete footing for an 8″ concrete block foundation wall.
4. Draw half-sections of a 3½″ concrete-filled steel pipe column at its base and cap.
5. Draw an elevation and a revolved section of the following:
   a. W 8 × 31 steel beam
   b. C 8 × 13.75 steel channel
   c. L 6 × 4 × ½ steel angle

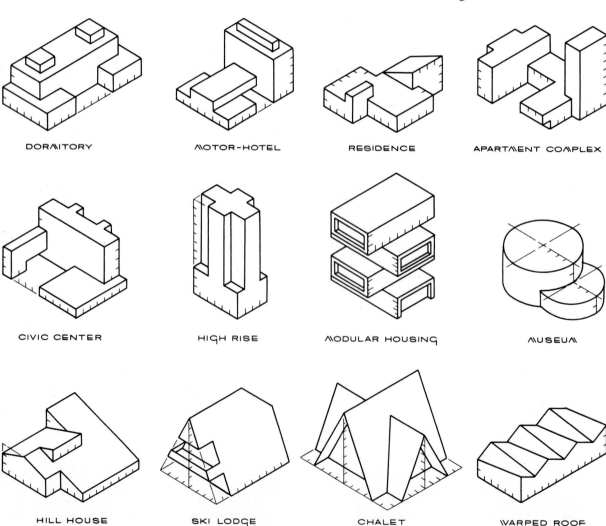

DORMITORY   MOTOR-HOTEL   RESIDENCE   APARTMENT COMPLEX

CIVIC CENTER   HIGH RISE   MODULAR HOUSING   MUSEUM

HILL HOUSE   SKI LODGE   CHALET   WARPED ROOF

Figure 15

7 / Auxiliary Views

Occasionally in architectural drafting, a view which is not a principal view is required. Such views are called *auxiliary views* and may show the true size and shape of an inclined or oblique surface or the true length of an inclined or oblique edge. Auxiliary views are classified as primary auxiliary views and secondary auxiliary views. A *primary auxiliary view* is a view that is perpendicular to only one of the three principal planes of projection and is inclined to the other two. A *secondary auxiliary view* is an auxiliary view that is obtained by projection from a primary auxiliary view.

Primary auxiliary view. A primary auxiliary view is obtained by projection from a principal view. Common examples in architectural drafting are the auxiliary views needed to show the true size and shape of each face of a building that has walls or wings that are not at a 90° angle to each other. An example is shown in Figure 1. The procedure used to draw a true-size and -shape elevation of the inclined wall 1-2-3-4 is as follows:

Step 1. Draw the edge view of a projection plane parallel to the edge view of plane 1-2-3-4. This is usually called a *reference line*. Since the auxiliary view is to be projected from the plan, label the reference line *P/A* (P for *plan* and A for *auxiliary elevation*).

Step 2. All points on the inclined face are projected from the adjacent view (the plan view in this example) to the auxiliary elevation view. Projection lines are *always* drawn perpendicular to their reference line. In this example, points 1 and 4 project along the same projector. Also, points 2 and 3 project along the same projector.

Step 3. Locate points 1, 2, 3, and 4 in the auxiliary elevation view by transferring distances from a related view (the front elevation in this example). *Related views* are two views that are adjacent to the same view. Dividers are often helpful in transferring these measurements. Connect the points in the auxiliary view in the proper order.

Secondary auxiliary view. Secondary auxiliary views are auxiliary views projected from a primary auxiliary view. Although not commonly used in architectural drafting, they are occasionally required for accurate shape description or to solve structural problems. An example is shown in Figure 2, which illustrates the procedure to find the true size and shape of face 1-2-3 of the geodesic dome so that a pattern can be made. Two auxiliary views are required, because an edge view of face 1-2-3 must be drawn before the true-size and -shape view can be found.

Step 1. Analyze the problem. Before the true size and shape of face 1-2-3 can be found, the edge view must be drawn. To find the edge view of any plane, the point view of a line in that plane is found. The point view of any line can be found by projecting parallel to the true-length view of that line. Since line 2-3 is true length in the plan view, project parallel to it by drawing a perpendicular *P/A* reference line.

Step 2. Project face 1-2-3 to the primary auxiliary view so that it appears as an edge view.

Step 3. Draw an *A/B* reference line parallel to the edge view of face 1-2-3. Project face 1-2-3 to the secondary auxiliary view so that it appears true size and shape.

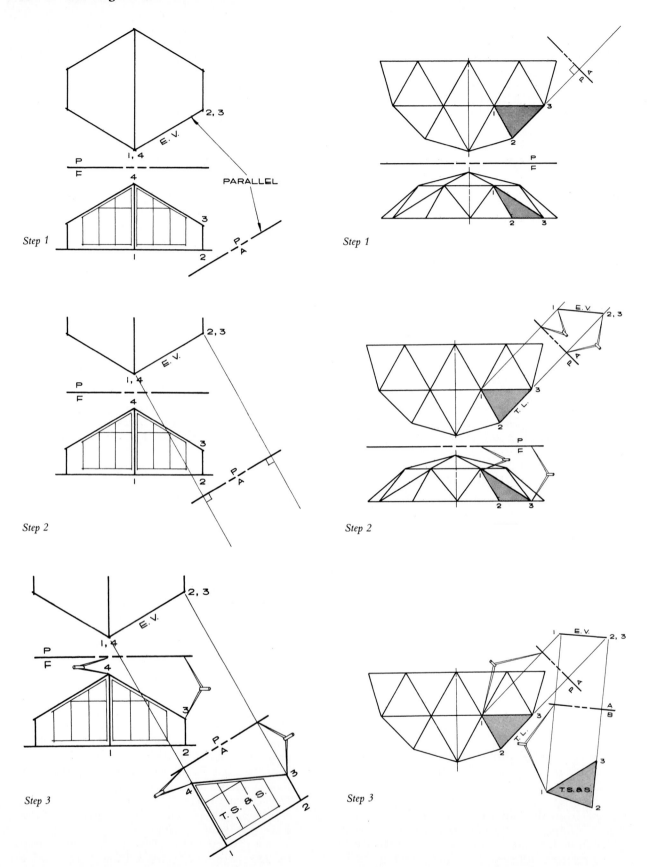

Figure 1   *Drawing a primary auxiliary view.*

Figure 2   *Drawing a secondary auxiliary view.*

STUDY QUESTIONS

1. Distinguish between a primary auxiliary view and a secondary auxiliary view.
2. Are projection lines parallel or perpendicular to:
   a. Each other
   b. Their reference lines

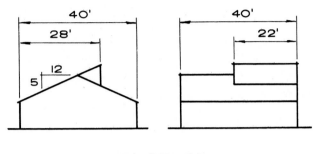

RESIDENCE

Figure 3

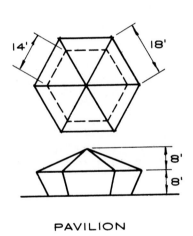

PAVILION

Figure 4

LABORATORY EXERCISES

1. Using primary auxiliary views, find the true size and shape of each roof section of the residence shown in Figure 3. Compute the number of squares of roofing required (1 square = 100 sq. ft.).
2. Using a secondary auxiliary view, find the true size and shape of a typical roof section of the pavilion shown in Figure 4. Compute the number of squares of roofing required for the entire roof.
3. Using a secondary auxiliary view, find the true size and shape of a typical wall of the pavilion shown in Figure 4. Compute the square feet of insulation required for one wall section.
4. (For the advanced student) Using the required auxiliary views, find the following data for the cable-supported roof shown in Figure 5 so that proper angle brackets can be specified:
   a. The angle between each cable and the mast
   b. The angle between each cable and the roof

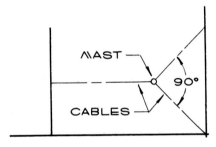

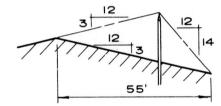

CABLE-SUPPORTED ROOF

Figure 5

8 / Pictorial Projections

In addition to multiview projections, pictorials are often used by architects because they better describe the actual appearance of an object. In pictorials, all three principal faces of an object can be shown in one view, and such pictures are easily understood by persons not trained in reading multiview projections.

Pictorial projections can be classified as *perspective* and *parallel*. Perspective projections are more realistic, but parallel projections are easier to draw. Perspective drawings are described in Chapter 36. Parallel pictorial projections are classified as *axonometric* and *oblique* as follows.

Axonometric projection. As in multiview projection, the projectors in axonometric projection are parallel to each other and perpendicular to the picture plane. But the object has been tilted with respect to the picture plane so that all three principal faces are seen in one view, but not in true size or true shape. When the object is tilted so that all three principal faces are equally inclined to the picture plane, the axonometric projection is called an *isometric projection*. When only two faces are equally inclined to the picture plane, a *dimetric projection* results. When *no* two faces are equally inclined, a *trimetric projection* results. A form of isometric projection, called *isometric drawing,* is by far the most popular pictorial method.

Isometric projection. An isometric projection can be obtained by revolving an object 45° about a vertical axis as shown in Figure 1. Then the object is tilted forward so that all principal edges form equal angles with the picture plane. This angle is approximately 35°-16'. Dimetric and trimetric projections can be obtained by similar methods, but this is a cumbersome procedure and, consequently, is seldom used.

STEP I   A MULTIVIEW PROJECTION OF AN OBJECT

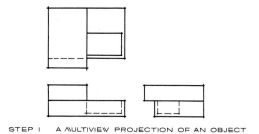

STEP 2   THE OBJECT REVOLVED

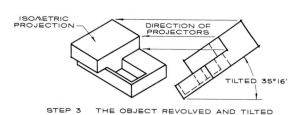

STEP 3   THE OBJECT REVOLVED AND TILTED

Figure 1   *The theory of isometric projection.*

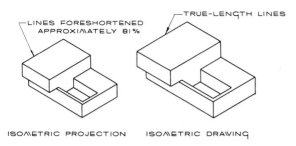

Figure 2 *Comparison of isometric projection and isometric drawing.*

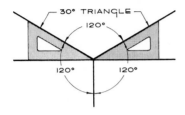

Figure 3 *The isometric axes.*

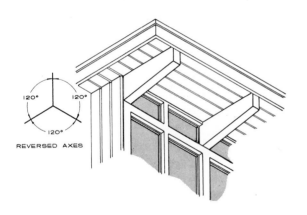

Figure 4 *A reversed isometric drawing.*

Isometric drawing. Isometric drawing differs from isometric projection in that the principal edges are drawn true length rather than foreshortened (Figure 2). Therefore, isometric drawings can be drawn directly and quite quickly. The principal edges appear as vertical lines or as lines making an angle of 30° to the horizontal (Figures 3 and 4).

It is important to realize that in isometric drawing, only isometric lines (principal edges) are drawn true length. Consequently, nonisometric lines cannot be obtained by direct measurement but by offset measurement. *Offset measurement* is simply the procedure of boxing in a shape so that the position of any point can be measured along isometric lines as shown in Figures 5 and 6.

Circles in isometric drawing appear as ellipses. But rather than plotting these ellipses by offset measurement, an elliptical template can be used. For large ellipses, a four-center approximation can also be used (Figure 7). An example of an approxi-

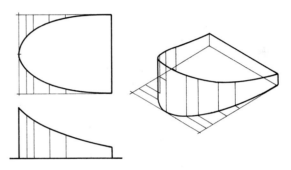

Figure 6 *Plotting irregular curves using offset measurements.*

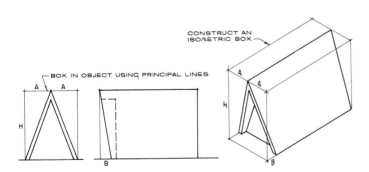

Figure 5 *Drawing nonisometric lines by offset measurement.*

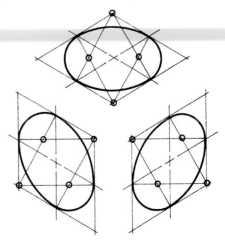

Figure 7 *A four-center ellipse can be drawn in all principal planes.*

mation for a semicircle is shown in Figure 8. The procedure is as follows:

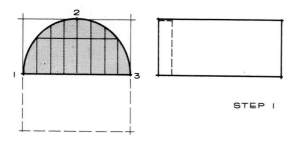

STEP 1

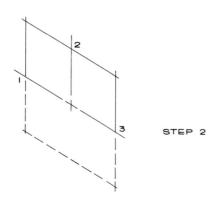

STEP 2

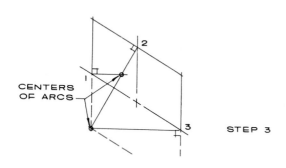

CENTERS OF ARCS

STEP 3

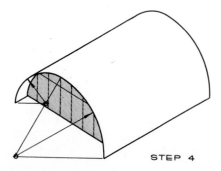

STEP 4

Figure 8 *Plotting a semicircle in isometric drawing by the approximation method.*

Step 1. A square is assumed to be placed tangent to the semicircle at the three intersections with its center lines (points 1, 2, 3).

Step 2. The tangent square and center lines of the circle are drawn in the isometric drawing.

Step 3. Perpendiculars are erected to the sides of the isometric square at points 1, 2, and 3. The intersections of these perpendiculars are the centers of two arcs tangent to the isometric square at 1, 2, and 3.

Step 4. Using a compass, draw two arcs tangent to the isometric square.

Oblique projection. An oblique projection (Figure 9) is obtained by parallel projectors that are oblique rather than perpendicular to the picture plane. The projectors can be assumed to be at any angle to the picture plane, but it is most common to project them to produce receding lines that will appear at an angle of 45° to the horizontal. Usually these 45° lines are drawn to the right.

The angle of the projectors also determines the amount of foreshortening of the receding lines. For example, the receding lines can be reduced to half size (a *cabinet* drawing) or drawn to full scale (a *cavalier* drawing, Figure 10). The proportions $\frac{2}{3}$ and $\frac{3}{4}$ are also used.

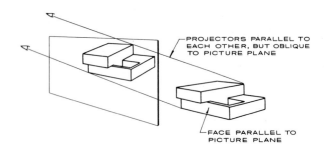

PROJECTORS PARALLEL TO EACH OTHER, BUT OBLIQUE TO PICTURE PLANE

FACE PARALLEL TO PICTURE PLANE

Figure 9 *Oblique projection.*

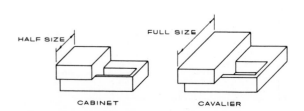

HALF SIZE

FULL SIZE

CABINET

CAVALIER

Figure 10 *Comparison of cabinet and cavalier drawings.*

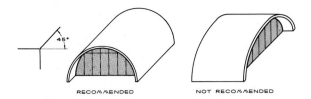

RECOMMENDED   NOT RECOMMENDED

Figure 11 *Positioning curved faces parallel to the picture plane.*

A major advantage of oblique drawing is that one face of the object is parallel to the picture plane and therefore remains in its true size and shape. Consequently, it is common sense to position the object so that the most irregular outline is the face parallel to the picture plane. The faces not parallel to the picture plane are distorted and must be constructed using offset measurements. For example, circles in the parallel face can be drawn as circles (Figure 11), but circles in the receding faces must be plotted by offsets or by the four-center ellipse method.

A disadvantage of oblique drawing is that receding lines do not converge and, consequently, appear to the eye to be distorted. The distortion can be minimized by positioning the object, when possible, so that the largest dimensions are parallel to the picture plane rather than receding.

STUDY QUESTIONS

1. Distinguish between:
   a. Perspective projection and parallel projection
   b. Orthographic projection and oblique projection
   c. Multiview projection and axonometric projection
   d. Isometric drawing and isometric projection
   e. Dimetric projection and trimetric projection
   f. Cavalier drawing and cabinet drawing
2. Why are offset measurements used to draw nonisometric lines?
3. Why is the most irregular face of an object positioned parallel to the picture plane in oblique drawings?
4. Hidden lines are usually omitted from pictorial drawings. Why?

LABORATORY EXERCISES

1. Draw pictorials of the 2″ × 4″ wood joints shown in Figure 12 as assigned:
   a. Assembled isometric drawings
   b. Exploded isometric drawings
   c. Exploded cavalier drawings
2. Draw pictorials of the buildings shown in Figure 15 of Chapter 36 as assigned:
   a. Isometric drawing
   b. Dimetric drawing
   c. Trimetric drawing
   d. Calvalier drawing
   e. Cabinet drawing
3. Draw the pictorial projections as assigned by your instructor.

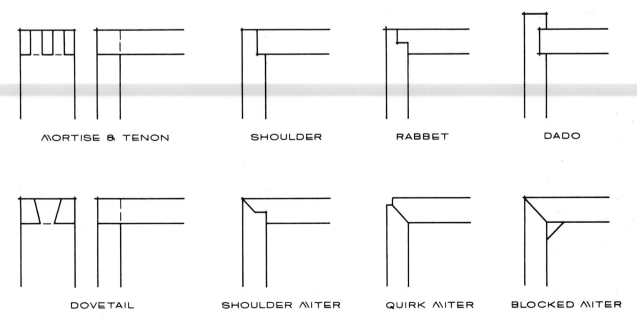

MORTISE & TENON   SHOULDER   RABBET   DADO

DOVETAIL   SHOULDER MITER   QUIRK MITER   BLOCKED MITER

Figure 12

9 / Architectural Lettering

The ability to letter is as important to a drafter as the ability to paint is to an artist. An artist who has an idea for a painting must be able to put that idea on canvas in a neat, orderly fashion using a definite technique. Similarly, an architectural drafter who has ideas for a building must be able to put those ideas on vellum in a clear, orderly manner using a definite system of notation. The ability to do a professional job of lettering is considered so important by most employers that they require a lettering sample to be submitted at the time of application for employment.

LETTERING STYLES

Of the many styles of lettering, *Old English, Roman,* and *Gothic* are best known.

Old English lettering (or **Text**) is shown in Figure 1. Although it is attractive, it is not widely used today because it is difficult to letter and read. Most high school and university diplomas use Old English lettering because of its elegant appearance.

Roman letters have strokes of different widths. Notice in Figure 2 that the horizontal lines are thin and the verticals thick. This is because the early pen points (quills) were flat and made lines that varied in width depending upon the direction of stroke. Also notice the small lines at the ends of every stroke. These are called *serifs.* Roman lettering is used extensively by book and magazine publishers, but not by engineers or architects. You may find Roman lettering on monumental structures cut into stone or metal plaques.

Gothic lettering (Figure 3) differs from Roman lettering in two important aspects: (1) All strokes are exactly the same width, and (2) no serifs are used. Of the many types of Gothic lettering, only *one* type has been approved by ANSI* for use on engineering and architectural drawings. This one approved type of Gothic lettering, called *Commercial Gothic,* is used on all engineering drawings.

Figure 1   *Old English lettering.*

Figure 2   *Roman lettering.*

Figure 3   *Gothic lettering.*

* American National Standards Institute (formerly American Standards Association), American National Standard Drafting Manual: Y14.2–1979.

ABCDEFGHIJKLMNOPQRSTUVWXYZ

(14) FLOOR PLAN

1/4" LETTERING FOR TITLES AND DRAWING NUMBERS

ABCDEFGHIJKLMNOPQRSTUVWXYZ 0123456789

JAMB DETAIL

1/8" LETTERING FOR HEADINGS

ABCDEFGHIJKLMNOPQRSTUVWXYZ 0123456789

2" × 8" JOIST

3/32" LETTERING FOR DIMENSIONS AND NOTES

Figure 4 *USASI Commercial Gothic lettering.*

On architectural drawings, it is often altered slightly to suit the taste of the draftsman or the style of a particular office. Let us first study the standard Commercial Gothic lettering and then look at the usual methods by which it can be altered to better suit architectural needs.

Commercial Gothic. Figure 4 shows the American Standard Commercial Gothic lettering in the three sizes used on architectural drawings: $\frac{1}{4}''$ for important titles and drawing numbers, $\frac{1}{8}''$ for lesser headings, and $\frac{3}{32}''$ for dimensioning and notes. The form and proportion of each letter should be studied carefully since this alphabet is used universally.

LETTERING SECRETS

There are six lettering "secrets" which have been collected by professional drafters who use Commercial Gothic lettering. Practice your lettering with these secrets in mind.

Guidelines. *A professional drafter always uses guidelines* when lettering. Guidelines are very light lines (usually drawn with a 4H pencil) that aid in

forming uniformly sized letters. Guidelines are *not* erased, since they are drawn so lightly that they are not objectionable. They should be visible to you when lettering, but invisible when you hold the drawing at arm's length.

The horizontal guidelines used for capital letters (like *ABC*) are a base line and a cap line. The horizontal guidelines used for lowercase letters (like *abc*) include also a waist line and a drop line (Figure 5). Lowercase lettering, however, is seldom used in architectural work. If you wish to simplify the task of measuring and drawing guidelines, the Rapidesign guide, Ames lettering device, or Braddock-Rowe lettering triangle may be used.

Either vertical or inclined guidelines are also used. These are spaced at random and are used to keep all letters vertical, or slanting at a uniform slope of $67\frac{1}{2}°$.

CAP LINE
WAIST LINE
BASE LINE
DROP LINE
VERTICAL GUIDE LINES

Figure 5 *Guidelines.*

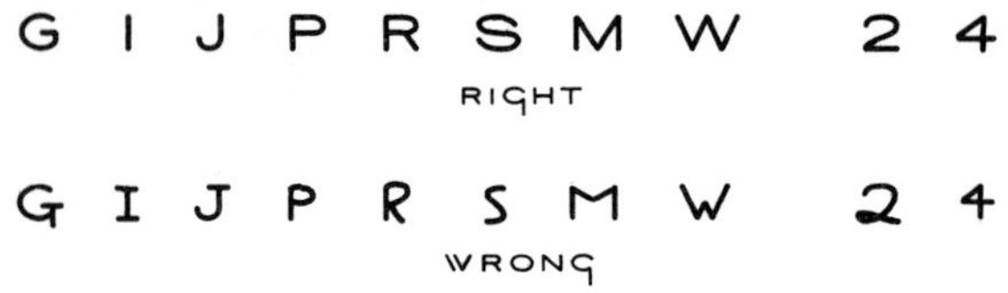

G I J P R S M W   2 4

RIGHT

G I J P R S M W   2 4

WRONG

Figure 6   *Common lettering errors.*

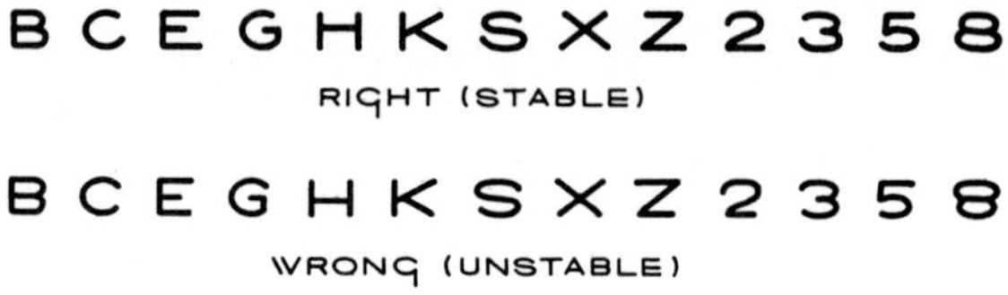

B C E G H K S X Z 2 3 5 8

RIGHT (STABLE)

B C E G H K S X Z 2 3 5 8

WRONG (UNSTABLE)

Figure 7   *Stability of letters.*

Form. The exact form of every Commercial Gothic letter should be memorized and used. This task is much simplified if you notice that all capital letters (except S) are based upon *straight* and *circular* lines. The numerals (and the letter S) are based upon *straight* and *elliptical* lines. Some of the common mistakes made in forming letters are shown in Figure 6.

Stability. You must also remember that *letters and numerals should appear stable* whenever possible. Stability means that the letters and numerals should be able to "stand on their own two feet." To prevent any possibility of appearing *unstable* or top-heavy, the letters B, C, E, G, H, K, S, X, and Z and the numerals 2, 3, 5, and 8 are drawn with their lower portions slightly larger in area than their upper portions. Examples of stability in lettering are shown in Figure 7.

Proportion. Of all the lettering secrets, this is the most important one to the beginner: *Make your letters much wider than you think they should be.* Notice in Figure 4 that nearly all letters are as wide as they are high. Thus the O and Q are perfect circles. The M and W are even wider than they are high. Also notice that the letters are somewhat wider than the numerals.

Letters that are narrower than standard are called *condensed,* and letters wider than standard are called *extended.* Condensed lettering is used only when it is absolutely necessary to fit many letters into a small space. Slightly extended lettering, on the other hand, is often used, since it is more readable and better looking than standard lettering. All of the notes on the illustrations in this book are lettered in extended lettering.

Density. *Black lines should be used for lettering.* This is necessary for two reasons: to improve the appearance of the lettering and to improve its readability so that it will show up well when reproduced. If your lettering is not black enough, simply use a softer pencil (such as H or F) and *bear down* harder on the paper. Of course you must still remember to keep a sharp point. Professional drafters sharpen their pencils after every two or three words.

Spacing. Proper spacing of letters to form words, and words to form sentences, is a "must." The best lettering has the *letters close together* to form words but the *words far apart* to form sentences. The spacing of letters is not measured directly, but is done by the eye so that the areas between letters are visually equal. Notice at the left of Figure 8 that the spaces between the letters in the words BLDG FELT were carefully measured, with the result that the space between the L and T appears too large. The second part of the figure shows proper optical spacing, all letters having the same *area* between them.

Figure 9 shows a simple method of spacing words: Imagine the letter *O* (a circle) between each word.

Remember when you practice your lettering, use the six lettering secrets:

1. Guidelines
2. Straight lines and circular lines
3. Stable lettering
4. Fat lettering
5. Black lettering
6. Close spacing

ARCHITECTURAL LETTERING

Unless beginning architectural drafters have training in letter design, they should use the Commercial Gothic letter forms without change. In-

Figure 8   *Spacing of letters.*

Figure 9   *Spacing of words.*

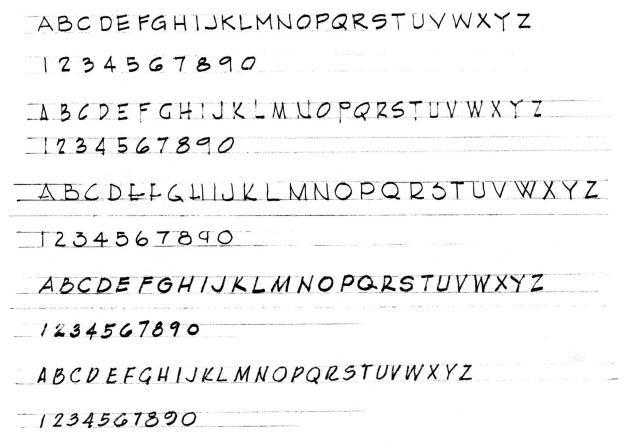

Figure 10   *Examples of architectural lettering by practicing architects.*

Figure 11   *Architectural lettering.*

deed, even some drafters with many years' experience feel that these forms cannot be improved. However, most architectural drafters are not content to use Commercial Gothic lettering because it is, after all, the standard for *engineering* rather than for *architectural* drawing. Since there exists no standard architectural alphabet, most architects take great pride in developing their own style (see Figure 10). It has been said that there are as many styles of lettering as there are architects! An architect will, of course, stick to his own style, and that style will appear uniformly on all of his drawings. If one keeps in mind that a prime function of the architect is to *sell* his work, then it seems natural that the lettering used be as attractive as possible. However, no matter how fanciful his style in lettering titles and headings, he will always use straightforward Commercial Gothic numerals when it comes to dimensioning.

Figure 11 shows a legible and attractive alphabet. You may wish to practice these letters first and then revise some letters until you find a type of lettering that feels right to you. During this test period, keep these rules in mind:

1. Rapidity of execution is an important factor. Time is money; do not get in the habit of drawing excessively time-consuming letters. This

ABCDEFGHIJKLMNOPQRSTUVWXYZ

DINING ROOM

Figure 12 *The architectural alphabet, obtained from a standard lettering stencil.*

means that the letters should be single-stroke, and that stylized portions of individual letters should be drawn in a free and natural fashion. (For example, you should not use the elliptical form of C and D in Figure 11 if it does not seem natural to you.)

2. Accentuate the ends of the strokes. This detail comes naturally to some, and very hard to others. If you find that you cannot easily produce attractive results with these accents after a fair trial, then do not attempt them further.

3. In most cases, only vertical capitals are used. Lower and upper drop lines are useful in uniformly ending those lines that drop below or above the normal guides. Each drop line is one-third the capital height. The capital letters G, Q, R, T, and Y may drop down, and the capital letter L may extend upward.

4. Lettering should be legible. It can be safely stated that architectural lettering can be as fanciful as you please—as long as it is easily read.

PRESENTATION DRAWING

The large majority of architectural working drawings are drawn in pencil, and therefore freehand pencil lettering is used. Occasionally, though, ink drawings are used for special requirements. A presentation drawing (a display drawing to show the prospective client) may be done in ink or even a combination of pencil and ink. Also, drawings to be printed in newspapers, magazines, or books are best reproduced when drawn in ink.

Lettering stencils. Although the ink lettering on presentation drawings may be drawn freehand, a lettering stencil is usually used. Some of the popular trade names are LeRoy, Wrico, and Varigraph. These stencils may be obtained in a variety of stock sizes and styles, or they may be ordered in custom-made styles. Often the stock Commercial Gothic stencil is adjusted slightly to obtain lettering with an architectural flavor. Figure 12 shows an architectural alphabet obtained by using a standard LeRoy extended lettering stencil. A similar alphabet was used for the illustrations in this book.

Appliqué (pressure-sensitive transfer). Prepared lettering sheets may be obtained from which drafters can transfer individual letters to their drawings merely by rubbing the letter as shown in Figure 13. Figure 14 shows only a few of the hundreds of lettering styles available. Some popular trade names are ACS Instant Lettering, Paratone Alphabets, and Mico/Type.

1. Transfer of letters is effected by registering guide lines on type sheet with guide on artwork. With a very soft pencil or ballpoint pen rub down letter with light pressure.

2. Carefully lift away type sheet — letter is now transferred — repeat procedure until setting is complete. Finally place backing sheet over setting and burnish for maximum adhesion.

Figure 13 *How to use appliqué.*

ABC89   ABCD89
ABCD9   ABCD34
ABCD12   ABCst6!
ABCDEF89! ABCD23
ABCDEFG34 ABCDEF.
ABCD78; ABG9

Figure 14 *Styles of appliqué lettering.*

ABCDEFGHIJKLMNOPQRSTUVWXYZ

Figure 15 *Single-line instrumental lettering.*

ABCDEFGHIJKLMNOPRS

Figure 16 *Double-line instrumental lettering.*

Instrumental lettering. Drafting instruments are seldom used for lettering because they are too slow. Occasionally, however, a large presentation drawing may require a special title. Figure 15 shows one of the many possible styles of single-line lettering, and Figure 16 one style of double-line (boxed) lettering. The boxed letters may be filled in if desired.

Title box. Professional offices use vellum with printed border lines and title boxes to save drafting time. As shown in Figure 17, title boxes are usually of a horizontal, vertical, or corner format. A sample 2″ × 4″ title box is shown in Figure 18. There are many other sizes and types of title boxes, but all should contain the following information as a minimum:

1. Name and location of structure
2. Name and address of owner
3. Name and address of architect
4. Name of sheet (such as "First-Floor Plan")
5. Number of sheet
6. Date
7. Scale
8. Draftsman's initials

STUDY QUESTIONS

1. Name and show an example of three styles of lettering.
2. What sizes of Commercial Gothic lettering are used on architectural drawings?
3. List the six "secrets" of good lettering.
4. Are guidelines erased? Why?
5. Show the difference between a drop line, base line, waist line, and cap line.
6. What is meant by *stability* in lettering? Give examples.
7. What is the difference between:
   a. Vertical and inclined guidelines
   b. Condensed and extended lettering
8. Why is it important for architecural lettering to be dense black?

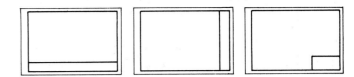

Figure 17 *Common forms of title boxes.*

ROBERT A. FALLIS	
REGISTERED ARCHITECT	TUCSON, AZ
SCALE	DRAWN	DATE	SHEET

Figure 18 *Appliqué title box used by professional architects.*

9. What is the proper method for spacing letters and words?
10. When is ink lettering used in architectural work?
11. List the minimum information contained in every title box.

LABORATORY PROBLEMS

1. Four sample alphabets incorporating common architectural lettering practices are shown in Figure 10. Repeat the alphabets on drawing paper. This lettering should be ¼″ high—a common title height. Remember to use guide lines. If you are not satisfied with your results, try again on a second line.
2. Figure 11 shows an architectural alphabet. Repeat this alphabet on drawing paper using letters ⅛″ high. Repeat until you are satisfied with the results.
3. On drawing paper, design a style of lettering that feels right to you. Take great care that each letter is just what you want, since you will be required to adhere to this style on all drawings. Your instructor will indicate his approval of each letter type. Use the sizes assigned:
   a. ¼″
   b. ⅛″
   c. $\frac{3}{32}$″
   d. 5 mm
   e. 3 mm
   f. 2 mm

10 / Architectural Dimensioning in English Units

To read architectural plans, you must become familiar with the graphic language used in two different professions: architecture and surveying. The architect uses architectural drawing to provide the instructions for constructing a building, and the surveyor uses topographical drawing to describe the plot of land occupied by the building. The dimensioning practice in each of these fields differs slightly. Let us look at both.

ARCHITECTURAL PLAN DIMENSIONS

Architectural dimensioning practices depend entirely upon the method used to construct the building. The masonry portion of a building, therefore, is dimensioned quite differently from the frame or veneered portion. For example, in masonry construction, the widths of window and door openings are shown since these dimensions are needed to lay up the wall. Openings in a frame

wall, however, are often dimensioned to their center lines to simplify locating the window and door frames. In masonry construction, dimensions are given to the faces of the walls. In frame construction, overall dimensions are given to the outside faces of studs because these dimensions are needed first. Masonry partitions are dimensioned to their faces, whereas frame partitions are usually dimensioned to their center lines. The thicknesses of masonry walls and partitions are indicated on the plan, but frame wall thicknesses are indicated on the detail drawings where construction details may be shown to a larger scale.

Masonry veneer on a wood-frame wall is dimensioned as a frame wall would be (to the outside faces of the studs) since the wood frame is constructed before the veneer is laid up. Figures 2–4 illustrate these differences.

Some additional rules of architectural dimensioning follow.

1. Dots, small circles, triangles, perpendicular lines, or diagonal lines (as shown in Figure 1) may be used in place of arrowheads. Dots should always be used when dimensioning small distances in tight spaces.
2. Dimension lines are spaced about $\frac{3}{8}''$ apart. Often three lines of dimensions are needed on each wall: a line of dimensions close to the wall locating windows and doors, a second line locating wall offsets, and finally an overall dimension.
3. Extension lines may or may not touch the plan, but be consistent. To avoid crossing extension and dimension lines, place the longer dimensions farther away from the plan, as in Figures 2–4.

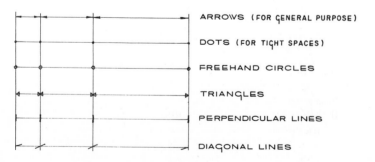

ARROWS (FOR GENERAL PURPOSE)

DOTS (FOR TIGHT SPACES)

FREEHAND CIRCLES

TRIANGLES

PERPENDICULAR LINES

DIAGONAL LINES

Figure 1 *Arrowhead types.*

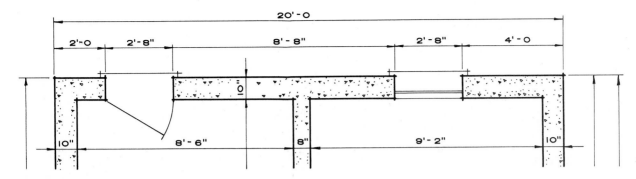

Figure 2 *Dimensioning masonry construction (concrete, concrete block, solid brick, and cavity brick).*

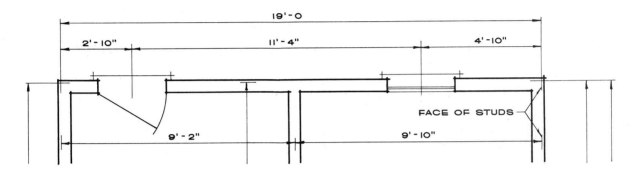

Figure 3 *Dimensioning frame construction.*

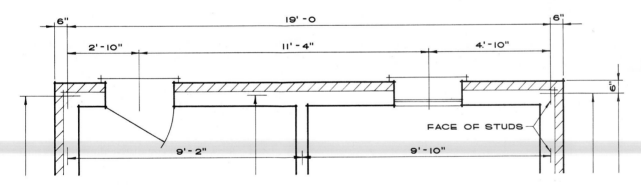

Figure 4 *Dimensioning veneer construction.*

4. Dimension lines are continuous with the numerals lettered above them. Numerals are placed to read from the bottom and right-hand side of the drawing.
5. Dimensions may be placed on the views, but avoid dimensioning over other features. Several complete lines of dimensions in both directions are ordinarily needed to locate interior features.
6. Dimension numerals and notes are lettered $\frac{3}{32}''$ high.
7. Give all dimensions over 12″ in feet and inches (to the nearest $\frac{1}{16}''$). The symbols for feet (′) and inches (″) are used except for zero inches. For example:

$$6'' \quad \text{not} \quad 0'\text{-}6''$$
$$1'\text{-}0 \quad \text{not} \quad 1'\text{-}0''$$
$$1'\text{-}6'' \quad \text{not} \quad 1'\text{-}6$$

8. Do not try to "fancy up" dimensions with artistic numerals. *Legibility* is the only concern.
9. Never crowd dimensions.
10. No *usable* dimension is omitted even though the dimension could be obtained by addition or subtraction of other dimensions. Be sure to include overall dimensions, any change in shape of outside walls, all rooms, halls, win-

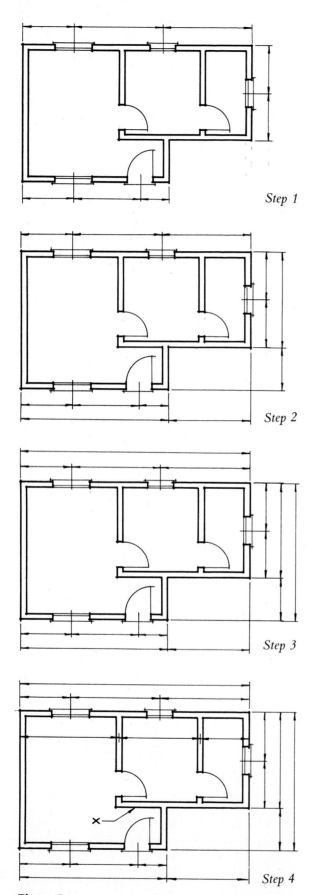

Step 1

Step 2

Step 3

Step 4

Figure 5

dow locations, and exterior door locations. A common mistake is failing to check cumulative dimensions with overall dimensions. Incorrect dimensions can cause the builder much delay and added expense.

11. All obvious dimensions *are* omitted. For example:
    a. Interior doors at the corner of a room need not be located.
    b. Interior doors centered at the end of a hall need not be located.
    c. The widths of identical side-by-side closets need not be dimensioned.

12. Columns and beams are located by dimensions to their center lines.

13. To free the plan from excessive dimensions, the sizes of windows and doors are given in window and door schedules.

14. House drawings are usually made to a scale of $\frac{1}{4}'' = 1'$-0. Larger buildings are usually drawn to a scale of $\frac{1}{8}'' = 1'$-0. Details are drawn to larger architectural scales. *Always* indicate the scale used near the drawing or in the title block.

EXAMPLE

Show the dimensions needed on the plan of the simple frame cottage shown in Figure 5.

Step 1: Window and door locations. A line of dimensions is placed on every outside wall containing a window or door to locate them for the builder. This dimension line is positioned about $\frac{3}{8}''$ beyond the farthest projection (such as a chimney, window, or doorsill). Dimension lines are spaced by eye rather than actually measured.

Step 2: Wall locations. A second line of dimensions is placed on every wall containing offsets to provide the builder with the subtotal of dimensions for each wall.

Step 3: Overall dimensions. Both overall dimensions are placed. Check that all cumulative dimensions equal the subtotal dimensions and that the subtotal dimensions equal the overall dimensions.

Step 4: Partition locations. Lines of interior dimensions are placed to locate partitions and interior features. In this example, only one line of dimensions is required since partition X is located by alignment with the exterior wall. Note that location dimensions for interior doors are not necessary since their positions are obvious. Additional required notes and schedules will complete the dimensioning. See the drawings of the A residence in Chapter 21 for the dimensioning required on a larger plan.

ELEVATION DIMENSIONS

Of the many different methods of indicating elevation dimensions, the two following are most often used.

Finish dimensions. This method indicates the actual dimension of the inside of the room when completely finished. Thus the distance between the *finished floor* and the *finished ceiling* is specified. This method is often used by the designer since he can quickly specify a desired room height. The height 8'-0 is often used for the first floor, and 7'-6" for the second floor.

Construction dimensions. This method indicates the dimensions actually needed by the contractor when framing a building. Thus, in platform framing, the distance between the *top of subflooring* and the *top of plate* indicates the exact height to construct the sections of walls and partitions. This method is preferred by builders. The National Lumber Manufacturers Association recommends a first-floor height of 8'-1½" and a second-floor height of 7'-7½". These dimensions will result in 8'-0 and 7'-6" room heights after the finished floor and ceiling have been added.

When in doubt as to the correct method of dimensioning an architectural drawing, there is one simple rule to follow: put yourself in the place of the builder and give the dimensions that will help him build with a minimum amount of calculation. Refer to the elevation dimensions of the A residence in Chapter 24 for a complete example.

SECTIONAL DIMENSIONS

The sectional view provides an opportunity to specify the materials and sizes not shown on the plans and elevations. Since sectional views are drawn to a larger scale, more detailed dimensions may be shown. The dimensions, material, and location of all members are specified, leaving nothing to the imagination of the builder. Nominal ("name") sizes are used for rough material, but actual sizes are used for finish material, as in:

1" × 8" subflooring (Use nominal dimensions)
¾" × 7" fascia (Use actual dimensions)

Some offices attempt to show rough material by omitting the inch marks from nominal dimensions. Thus the dimension 2" × 4" would indicate finished lumber measuring 2" × 4", whereas the dimension 2 × 4 would indicate rough lumber measuring 1½" × 3½". See the A residence sections in Chapter 24 for examples of the dimensions required on sectional views.

TOPOGRAPHICAL DIMENSIONS

A complete study of topographical drawing would be quite lengthy. Fortunately, the architec-

tural drafter is usually interested only in the areas of topography related to the plot plan.

The boundaries of a plot are described by dimensions given in hundredths of a foot (two places beyond the decimal point), such as 151.67'. However, the surveyor will, whenever possible, lay out plots using even lengths (such as 100'). When this is done, the dimension is given simply as 100' rather than 100.00'. Bearings (such as N 5° 10' 15" E) are also given to show the compass direction of the boundaries. The bearings are given starting at one corner of the plot and proceeding around the perimeter until the starting point is again reached. Thus two opposite and parallel sides of a plot have opposite bearings (such as N 30° E and S 30° W).

Contour lines are dimensioned by indicating their elevation above sea level or some other datum plane like a street or the floor of a nearby house. The elevations of the land at the corners of the plot and the house are also shown. An engineer's scale is used rather than an architect's scale, 1" = 20' being quite common. The plot plan of the A residence in Chapter 22 shows these required dimensions.

MODULAR COORDINATION

Module (from the Greek "measure") means a standard unit of measurement. A modular system, then, is a system of design in which most materials are equal in size to an established module or a multiple of that module. Such a system is called *modular coordination* because the materials will fit together—or *coordinate*—without cutting. For example, let us plan an open barbecue pit to be built of 8" × 8" × 16"* concrete blocks with inside dimensions approximately 3' square. If we designed this pit without giving thought to the size of the blocks, we would find that the four corner blocks in each course must be cut from 16" down to 12" (Figure 6).

If, however, we planned on an 8" module as shown in Figure 7, there would be no cutting required, and we would obtain a larger barbecue pit without using additional blocks.

Advantages. From this simple example, it is evident that modular coordination has some definite advantages:

1. It reduces cutting and fitting.
2. It reduces building costs.
3. It standardizes sizes of building materials.
4. It reduces drafting errors by reducing fractional dimensions.

* The actual size of an 8" × 8" × 16" block is 7⅝" × 7⅝" × 15⅝". When laid up with a ⅜" mortar joint, however, the blocks fit in an 8" module.

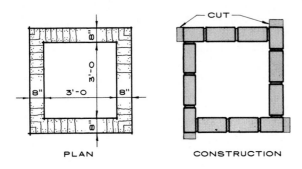

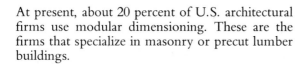

PLAN   CONSTRUCTION

Figure 6   *Nonmodular barbecue pit design.*

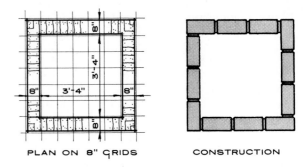

PLAN ON 8" GRIDS   CONSTRUCTION

Figure 7   *Modular barbecue pit design.*

At present, about 20 percent of U.S. architectural firms use modular dimensioning. These are the firms that specialize in masonry or precut lumber buildings.

Size of module. Any convenient size module may be used. An 8″ module was used in the preceding example. A 4′ planning module is useful in layout work. A 20′ structural module is often used in steel factory construction. The most useful module, however, is 4″, since brick, block, structural tile, window frames, and door bucks are all available in multiples of 4″. Countries with metric rather than English measurements use a 100-mm module (4″ = 101.6 mm).

Rules of modular dimensioning

1. Show light 4″ grids on all plans, elevations, and sections drawn to a scale of $\frac{3}{4}$″ = 1′ or larger. For smaller scales, only a 4′ planning grid is shown since it is impractical to show 4″ grids.
2. Whenever possible, fit the building parts *between* grid lines or *centered on* grid lines. Occasionally an edge arrangement is necessary (Figure 8). Typical walls in plan are shown in Figure 9.

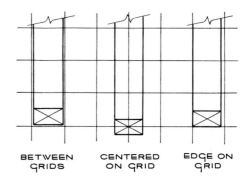

BETWEEN   CENTERED   EDGE ON
GRIDS   ON GRID   GRID

Figure 8   *Relation of a stud wall to a grid line.*

3. To indicate location of building parts, use grid dimensions (dimensions from grid line to grid line). Use *arrows* for grid dimensions as shown in Figure 10. These arrows are used to indicate grid dimensions even when the grid lines do not appear on the drawing (as on the 4′ planning module).
4. To indicate any position *not* on a grid line, use a dot.
5. The plans and elevations will contain mostly grid dimensions. But since many materials are

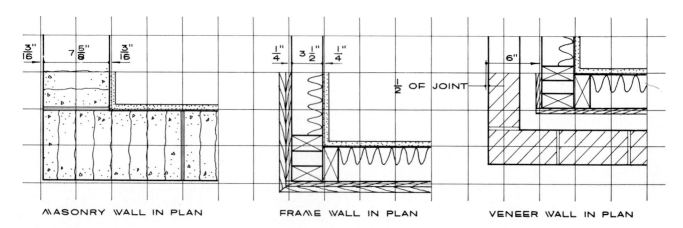

MASONRY WALL IN PLAN   FRAME WALL IN PLAN   VENEER WALL IN PLAN

Figure 9   *Dimensioning typical walls using modular coordination.*

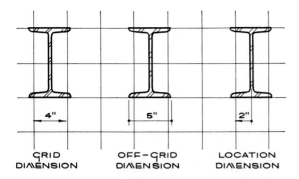

Figure 10 *Modular grid dimensions, off-grid dimensions, and location dimensions.*

not sized in 4″ modules (3½″ studs, for example), these materials are related to the nearest grid line by means of location dimensions in the section views. Location dimensions will have an arrow on the grid end and a dot on the off-grid end.

6. The 4″ module is three-dimensional, applying to both horizontal and vertical dimensions. Elevation grids are established as follows (Figure 11):

   a. The top of the subfloor in wood-frame construction coincides with a grid line.

   b. The top of a slab-on-ground coincides with a grid line.

   c. The actual finished floor in all other types of construction is located ⅛″ below a grid line.

For plans containing some elements of modular dimensioning, see the split-level house in Chapter 11 and the South Hills Office Building in Chapter 40.

Unicom system. The National Lumber Manufacturers Association recommends a modular system of house construction called *unicom* (for "uni-

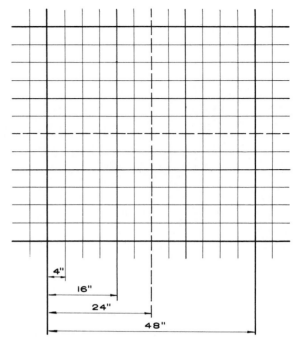

Figure 12 *Four related modules included in the unicom grid system.*

form components"). In the unicom system, components such as wall, window, and door sections are all based upon a 16″ or 24″ module, thus requiring suppliers to stock a smaller number of different sized components. Houses may be erected using only these prefabricated components, or framed in the conventional manner.

Unicom grid. The unicom grid is based upon the 4″ modular grid but with several variations. Figure 12 shows a unicom grid containing three weights of grid lines and a hidden line. The lightweight grids indicate 4″ modules, the medium-weight 16″

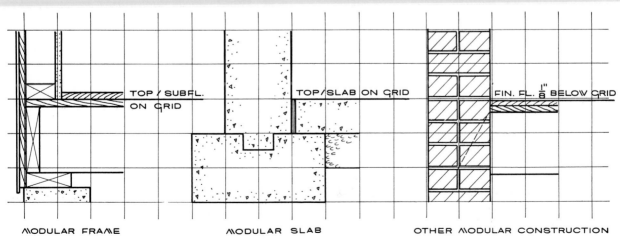

Figure 11 *Vertical positioning in modular coordination.*

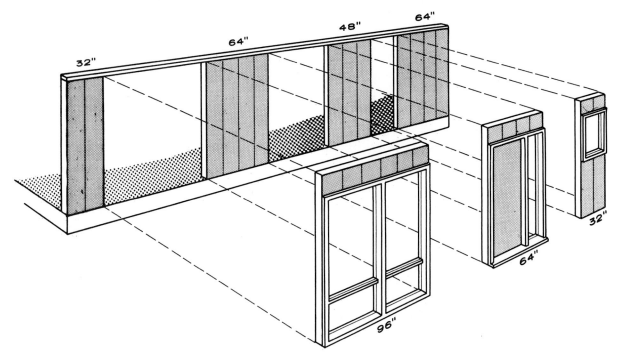

Figure 13   *Unicom wall, window, and door components.*

modules, and the heavyweight 48″ modules. The hidden line indicates 24″ modules.

Unicom panels. Some typical wall, window, and door panels are shown in Figure 13. These panels are multiples of the 16″ module and can be combined without cutting into the desired modular design. Floor panels, roof panels, partitions, roof truss components, and stairs are also available to unicom specifications.

STUDY QUESTIONS

1. Compare the methods of dimensioning a window in a masonry wall and a window in a wood-frame wall.
2. Give the proper method of indicating the following dimensions on an architectural drawing:
   a. Four inches
   b. Fourteen inches
   c. Four feet
   d. Four feet, four inches
3. Give the recommended:
   a. Distance between dimension lines
   b. Height of dimension numerals
   c. Height of architectural notes
4. Give examples of some dimensions that may be omitted from an architectural drawing.
5. What is the purpose of window and door schedules?
6. What would be the probable English scale of the architectural drawings of:
   a. A residence
   b. A 20′ × 40′ store
   c. A church (capacity = 200)

7. Give two methods of indicating elevation dimensions. When is each method used?
8. When are nominal sizes and actual sizes used to dimension materials?
9. On a plot plan of a rectangular lot, why do parallel lot lines have different bearings?
10. What is meant by:
    a. Modular coordination
    b. The unicom system
11. List four advantages of the unicom system.
12. What module size is most commonly used?
13. In modular dimensioning:
    a. When are 4″ and 4′ grids shown?
    b. When are an arrow and a dot used?
14. In modular elevation dimensioning, what is the position of the floor with respect to a grid line in:
    a. Wood-frame construction
    b. Slab-on-ground construction
    c. Other types of construction

LABORATORY PROBLEMS

1. Using $\frac{1}{4}$″ cross-section paper, sketch a typical exterior corner of a residence constructed of the following. Indicate the method of dimensioning and completely note all materials.
   a. Frame
   b. Brick veneer
   c. 10″ cavity brick
   d. 8″ concrete block
2. Complete the dimensioning on your plans of the A residence.
3. Complete the dimensioning of the building assigned by your instructor.
4. Complete the dimensioning of your original house design.

11 / Architectural Dimensioning in Metric Units

The metric system was conceived over three hundred years ago by Gabriel Mouton, a Frenchman, who designed a decimal system based upon the circumference of the earth. The unit of length was called the meter, from the Greek "metron" ("measure"). In 1960 the meter was redefined internationally in terms of the wavelength of a specific color of light. Most industrialized countries have adopted this system, known as the SI (Système International) metric system. France officially adopted metric units in 1795. The United Kingdom finished its conversion in 1975, and Canada in 1978. The United States is following on a voluntary—but steady—basis. Due to this voluntary approach, *hard* conversion of building products from English to metric will vary considerably depending upon the publication of technical standards and the speed of manufacturing conversion.

Soft and hard conversion. The terms *soft conversion* to metric and *hard conversion* to metric are often used. *Soft conversion* refers to changing the English dimensions of a product to metric dimensions without changing the size of the product. *Hard conversion* refers to changing both the dimensions and the size of a product to a rational metric size. For example, in soft conversion terms, the size of a 4′ × 8′ plywood sheet would be unchanged but called a 1220 × 2440 mm sheet. In hard conversion terms, it would be changed to a modular size and manufactured as a 1200 × 2400 mm sheet.

* Portions of this chapter courtesy *The Construction Specifications Institute.*

THE SI METRIC SYSTEM

Use of SI units. The SI sytem is based upon the following seven units which are of interest to the architect and builder. Multiples and submultiples are expressed as decimals.

1. Length: meter (m)
2. Time: second (s)
3. Mass: kilogram (kg)
4. Temperature: kelvin (K)
5. Electric current: ampere (A)
6. Luminous intensity: candela (cd)
7. Amount of substance: mole (mol)

Prefixes are used to eliminate insignificant digits and decimals. For example, 3 mm (3 millimeters) is preferred to 0.003 m (0.003 meter). Metric prefixes are shown in Table I.

Table I *Metric Prefixes*

Prefix	SI Symbol	Multiplication Factor	
tera	T	10^{12}	(1 000 000 000 000)
giga	G	10^{9}	(1 000 000 000)
mega	M	10^{6}	(1 000 000)
kilo	k	10^{3}	(1 000)
hecto	h	10^{2}	(100)
deka	da	10^{1}	(10)
deci	d	10^{-1}	(0.1)
centi	c	10^{-2}	(0.01)
milli	m	10^{-3}	(0.001)
micro	μ	10^{-6}	(0.000 001)
nano	n	10^{-9}	(0.000 000 001)
pico	p	10^{-12}	(0.000 000 000 001)
femto	f	10^{-15}	(0.000 000 000 000 001)
atto	a	10^{-18}	(0.000 000 000 000 000 001)

Wherever possible, use multiple and submultiple prefixes representing steps of 1000. For example, express length in millimeters, meters, and kilometers. Avoid using the centimeter and the decimeter. Do not use a period after an SI symbol except when it occurs at the end of a sentence (e.g., 2 mm not 2 mm.). To assist in reading numbers with four or more digits, and to eliminate confusion by the European use of commas to express decimal points, place digits in groups of three separated by a space, without commas, starting both to the left and right of the decimal point (e.g., 12 625 not 12,625). The space is optional with a four-digit number however (e.g., either 1500 or 1 500). Figure 1 is an architectural plan dimensioned in metric units.

Use of non-SI units. Some non-SI units are so commonly used that they will continue to be accepted. For example, we will continue to indicate time in the English units of minutes, hours, and days in addition to the SI unit of seconds. Angles will continue to be measured in the English units of degrees, minutes, and seconds in addition to the SI unit of radians.

Also some new non-SI terms will be introduced. For example, the term *metric ton* is not an approved SI unit, but it is now being used to indicate 1000 kg.

Some non-SI symbols will also be used. The SI symbol for liter, for example, is the lowercase *l*. Because this symbol is so easily confused with the numeral 1, the capital *L* is commonly used.

USE OF SI UNITS ON ARCHITECTURAL DRAWINGS

Working drawings. The preferred SI measurement unit on working drawings scaled between 1:1 and 1:100 is the millimeter. The symbol (mm) is deleted, but the note "All dimensions in millimeters except as noted" should be added. On drawings of large structures scaled between 1:200 and 1:2000, the preferred measurement unit is the meter, taken to three decimal places (e.g., 8.500). Again, the symbol (m) is deleted, but a note, "All dimensions in meters except as noted," added.

Plot plans. Surveyors indicate land distances on plot plans in meters (and on maps in kilometers). Surveyors normally measure to an accuracy of about 1 cm, and therefore such distances on plot plans are shown as meters taken to two decimal places (e.g., 8.50). Contour lines are usually established at 0.5-m intervals, 1-m intervals, 2-m intervals, and 5-m intervals. The 0.5-m interval is shown in Figure 6.

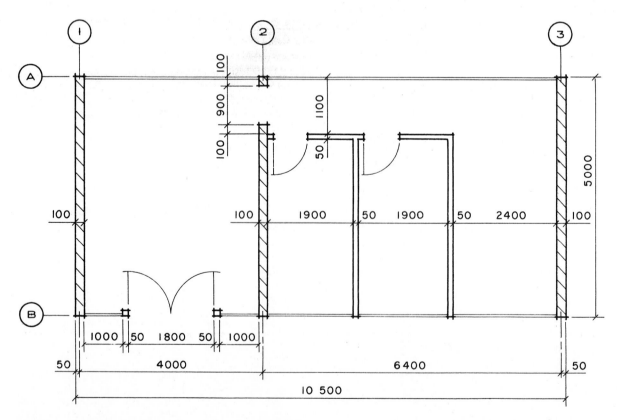

Figure 1   *A plan dimensioned in metric units (millimeters).*

Angles. According to the National Bureau of Standards,* plane angles will be specified in three ways: (1) The SI unit (the radian) will be used in calculations. (2) Engineers will specify angles in degrees with decimal submultiples (e.g., 11.25°) on engineering and construction drawings. (3) Surveyors will continue to specify angles in degrees, minutes, and seconds (e.g., N 10° 12′ 30″ E) on plot plans.

Metric modules. It is anticipated that 100 mm (about $\frac{1}{16}$″ less than 4″) will be accepted as a basic metric module. Figure 2 shows a unicom grid based upon the 100-mm module with multiples of 400 mm (approximately 16″), 600 mm (approximately 24″), and 1200 mm (approximately 48″). Compare this grid with the related grid in the previous chapter. It is expected, then, that hard conversion of building materials will result in metric sizes as discussed in the following sections.**

LUMBER

Rough lumber. U.S. standards for softwood lumber have not yet been established, but the American National Metric Council (ANMC) has recommended that English lumber sizes be soft-converted to the nearest mm and specified in actual rather than nominal sizes. Thus a 2″ × 4″ having actual dimensions of $1\frac{1}{2}$″ (38.1 mm) × $3\frac{1}{2}$″ (88.9 mm) would be specified as 38 × 39. Other similar metric conversions are shown in Table II.

The International Organization for Standardization (ISO), however, has established nominal size standards as shown in Table III. The ISO consists of standards organizations in each country such as the American National Standards Institute (ANSI), the British Standards Institution, and the Canadian Standards Association. The lumber sizes commonly available in European countries are shown in Table IV. Notice that lumber in rough widths of 100 mm (4″), 150 mm (6″), 200 mm (8″), 250 mm (10″), and 300 mm (12″) are all available in a rough thickness of 50 mm (2″). Only the smaller sizes of 100 mm and 150 mm are also available in a thickness of 38 mm ($1\frac{1}{2}$″). Notice that strapping is commonly available in 19 mm ($\frac{3}{4}$″) by 75 mm (3″) and 100 mm (4″) as well as in 25 mm (1″) by 100 mm (4″) and 150 mm (6″).

---

* *Recommended Practice for the Use of Metric (SI) Units in Building Design and Construction*, U.S. Department of Commerce/National Bureau of Standards, reprinted with corrections June 1977.

** These examples of the modular sizes of building materials should be considered tentative until standards are established and manufacturing changeovers are announced.

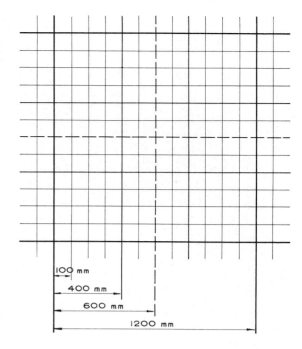

Figure 2 *The unicom grid system using metric modules.*

Table II *Some Metric Sizes Recommended by ANMC for Rough Softwood*

Nominal English Size	Actual English Size	Actual Metric Size
1″	$\frac{3}{4}$″	19 mm
2″	$1\frac{1}{2}$″	38 mm
3″	$2\frac{1}{2}$″	64 mm
4″	$3\frac{1}{2}$″	89 mm
6″	$5\frac{1}{2}$″	140 mm
8″	$7\frac{1}{4}$″	184 mm
10″	$9\frac{1}{4}$″	235 mm
12″	$11\frac{1}{4}$″	286 mm

Table III *Some Nominal Metric Sizes Recommended by ISO for Rough Softwood*

Thickness		Width	
Nominal Metric Size	Approx. Equivalent English Size	Nominal Metric Size	Approx. Equivalent English Size
19 mm	$\frac{3}{4}$″	75 mm	3″
25 mm	1″	100 mm	4″
38 mm	$1\frac{1}{2}$″	150 mm	6″
50 mm	2″	200 mm	8″
		250 mm	10″
		300 mm	12″

Table IV   *Some Nominal ISO Sizes Available in Metric Countries for Rough Softwood (with approximate equivalent English sizes)*

	75 mm (3″)	100 mm (4″)	150 mm (6″)	200 mm (8″)	250 mm (10″)	300 mm (12″)
19 mm ($\frac{3}{4}$″)	⊠	⊠				
25 mm (1″)		⊠	⊠			
38 mm (1$\frac{1}{2}$″)		⊠	⊠			
50 mm (2″)		⊠	⊠	⊠	⊠	⊠

Table V   *Lumber Lengths Recommended by ISO*

Metric Size	Approx. Equivalent English Size
2.4 m	8′
3.0 m	10′
3.6 m	12′
4.2 m	14′
4.8 m	16′
5.4 m	18′
6.0 m	20′

Regarding nomenclature, the familiar 2 × 4 may be called a 50 × 100. However, you should realize that the nominal size is a value assigned for the purpose of convenient designation and may exist in name only. Consequently, terms such as *2 × 4* and *2 × 6* may continue to be used for some time. For example, the term *8-penny nail* is still used even though such nails can no longer be purchased for 8 cents per hundred.

Table V shows the ISO standard lengths of joists and rafters. These lengths are commonly available in metric countries. A 2.4-m length is approximately 1$\frac{1}{2}$″ (1$\frac{1}{2}$ percent) shorter than an 8′ length.

Current joist and rafter spacings of 16″ oc (on center) and 24″ oc convert to spacings of 400 mm and 600 mm.

Finish lumber. Finish (dressed) lumber is commonly available in metric countries in 12-mm (approximately $\frac{1}{2}$″) and 19-mm (approximately $\frac{3}{4}$″) thicknesses. As shown in Table VI, the dressed widths are 5 mm smaller than the rough widths shown in Table IV.

Panels. Sheets of plywood, fiberboard, and hardboard will be available in a 1200 × 2400-mm size. The 4′ × 8′ size will also be stocked for some time since the 1$\frac{1}{2}$″ difference between English and metric sizes can cause serious problems. For example, the smaller metric panel would not fit in a modular building designed to English dimensions, nor would it serve as a suitable replacement panel in the renovation of an old building. Similarly, each of the larger English panels would have to be trimmed to fit in a metric modular building. Some thicknesses of plywood available in metric countries are listed in Table VII.

Table VII   *Some Thicknesses of Plywood Available in Metric Countries*

Metric Thickness	Approx. Equivalent English Thickness
12 mm	$\frac{1}{2}$″
16 mm	$\frac{5}{8}$″
19 mm	$\frac{3}{4}$″
25 mm	1″

Table VI   *Some Sizes Available in Metric Countries for Finished Softwood (with approximate equivalent English sizes)*

	45 mm (1$\frac{3}{4}$″)	70 mm (2$\frac{3}{4}$″)	95 mm (3$\frac{3}{4}$″)	145 mm (5$\frac{3}{4}$″)	195 mm (7$\frac{3}{4}$″)	245 mm (9$\frac{3}{4}$″)	295 mm (11$\frac{3}{4}$″)
12 mm ($\frac{1}{2}$″)	⊠	⊠	⊠	⊠			
19 mm ($\frac{3}{4}$″)	⊠	⊠	⊠	⊠	⊠	⊠	⊠

MASONRY

Concrete masonry. Concrete masonry units, usually called *concrete blocks,* are manufactured in modular sizes based upon the 4″ module. The 8″ × 8″ × 16″ stretcher unit is most often used. The actual size of such a block is $7\frac{5}{8}″ \times 7\frac{5}{8}″ \times 15\frac{5}{8}″$ to allow for $\frac{3}{8}″$ mortar joints. Converted to metric, such units are 200 × 200 × 400 mm nominally. Actual size is 190 × 190 × 390 mm to allow for 10-mm mortar joints. Larger block and smaller partition block convert to metric sizes as shown in Table VIII.

Brick masonry. Four common types of modular brick are shown in Figure 3 and Table IX. Actual sizes are 10 mm smaller than nominal sizes to allow for mortar joints.

Reinforced concrete. Rebars (reinforcing bars) are available in English sizes from #2 ($\frac{1}{4}″$ diameter) to #18 ($2\frac{1}{4}″$ diameter) in $\frac{1}{8}″$ increments. Hard conversion in most metric countries resulted in rebars sized as shown in Table X.

Table VIII   *Concrete Block Modular Widths*

Metric Size	Approx. Equivalent English Size
50 mm	2″
75 mm	3″
100 mm	4″
150 mm	6″
200 mm	8″
250 mm	10″
300 mm	12″

Table X   *Rebar Sizes (diameter)*

Metric Size	Approx. Equivalent English Size
6 mm	$\frac{1}{4}″$
8 mm	$\frac{5}{16}″$
10 mm	$\frac{3}{8}″$
12 mm	$\frac{1}{2}″$
16 mm	$\frac{5}{8}″$
20 mm	$\frac{3}{4}″$
25 mm	1″
32 mm	$1\frac{1}{4}″$
40 mm	$1\frac{1}{2}″$
50 mm	2″

Table IX   *Brick Sizes*

	Nominal Metric Dimensions			Nominal English Dimensions		
	Width	(3-course) Height	Length	Width	(3-course) Height	Length
Modular brick	100 mm	200 mm	200 mm	4″	8″	8″
Roman brick	100 mm	150 mm	300 mm	4″	6″	12″
Norman brick	100 mm	200 mm	300 mm	4″	8″	12″
SCR brick	150 mm	200 mm	300 mm	6″	8″	12″

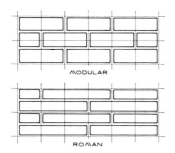
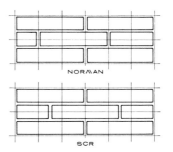

Figure 3   *Modular coordination of brick types.*

STEEL

Steel plate. Availability of steel plate varies depending upon the plate mill, but most mills supply plate in the following English thicknesses:

$\frac{1}{32}''$ increments up to $\frac{1}{2}''$
$\frac{1}{16}''$ increments over $\frac{1}{2}''$ to $2''$
$\frac{1}{8}''$ increments over $2''$ to $6''$

Although the availability of steel plate in metric sizes also varies depending upon the mill, the following thicknesses are supplied as a minimum:

1-mm increments up to 12 mm
2-mm increments over 12 mm to 20 mm
5-mm increments over 20 mm to 60 mm
10-mm increments over 60 mm to 160 mm

Steel beams. Hard conversion of steel beams to metric sizes occurs only during the last stages of conversion. Soft conversion tables, however, are now available. These tables give the properties of customary beams in metric terms. For example, a W 6 × 15.7 (a W-shape beam sized 6″ × 6″ weighing 15.7 lb./ft.) is converted to 152 mm × 152 mm having a mass (weight)* of 23 kg/m.

* *Weight* is a commonly used term, but in technical work it is correct to use the term *mass* to indicate quantity of matter.

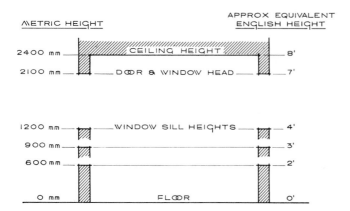

Figure 4 *Metric ceiling, head, and sill heights.*

Table XI *Door Openings*

Metric Width	Approx. Equivalent English Width
600 mm	2′-0
700 mm	2′-4″
800 mm	2′-8″
900 mm	3′-0
1000 mm	3′-4″
1500 mm	5′-0
1800 mm	6′-0

METRIC DESIGN

Ceiling, head, and sill heights. The minimum comfortable ceiling height for a habitable room is 8′ (in English units) and 2400 mm (in metric units), as shown in Figure 4. Also shown are commonly specified head heights of doors and windows (measured from finished floor to the bottom of rough opening at the head) and windowsill heights (measured from finished floor to the top of rough opening at the sill).

Width of door openings. In most metric countries, the rough opening widths are 600, 700, 800, and 900 mm for interior doors and 900, 1000, 1500, and 1800 mm for exterior doors. These widths are shown in Table XI.

Width of window openings. In metric countries, the rough opening width for most windows varies from 600 mm to 1800 mm as shown in Table XII.

Metric scales. Common metric scales used in architectural drawing are listed in Table XIII together with their equivalent English scales.

For an example of plans dimensioned in metric units, see the M residence, Figures 6–13.

Table XII *Window Openings*

Metric Width	Approx. Equivalent English Width
600 mm	2′-0
700 mm	2′-4″
800 mm	2′-8″
900 mm	3′-0
1000 mm	3′-4″
1100 mm	3′-8″
1200 mm	4′-0
1500 mm	5′-0
1800 mm	6′-0

Table XIII *Common Architectural Scales*

Metric Scale	Approx. Equivalent English Scale	Used for:
1:1	12″ = 1′-0 (1:1)	Full-scale patterns
1:5	3″ = 1′-0 (1:4)	Detail sections
1:10	1½″ = 1′-0 (1:8)	Wall sections
1:20	¾″ = 1′-0 (1:24)	Structural sections
1:50	¼″ = 1′-0 (1:48)	Large-scale plans and elevations
1:100	⅛″ = 1′-0 (1:96)	Small-scale plans and elevations
1:200	1″ = 20′ (1:240)	Large-scale plot plans
1:500	1″ = 50′ (1:600)	Small-scale site plans

DUAL DIMENSIONING

Occasionally architectural drawings must be dimensioned in dual units. For example, dual dimensioning is used when a building component has been manufactured to English sizes but must be mated with a component manufactured to metric sizes. Dual dimensioning is simply the placing of the metric counterpart after the English dimension, e.g., 1″ (25.4 mm). Dual dimensioning may be shown by any of the methods illustrated in Figure 5.

A number of countries are now using a metric system that varies slightly from the SI metric system. For projects in such countries, determine what metric system is used, and then give dual dimensioning using that country's metric units followed by SI units.

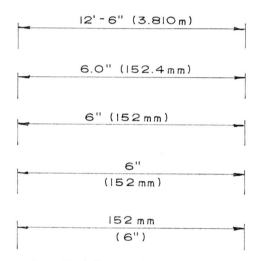

Figure 5   *Dual dimensioning systems.*

Table XIV   *English-Metric Conversions*
(accurate to parts per million)

1 inch = 25.4 millimeters
1 foot = 0.304 8 meter
1 yard = 0.914 4 meter
1 mile = 1.609 34 kilometers
1 quart (liquid) = 0.946 353 liter
1 gallon = 0.003 785 41 cubic meter
1 ounce (avdp) = 28.349 5 grams
1 pound (avdp) = 0.453 592 kilogram
1 horsepower = 0.745 700 kilowatt

1 millimeter = 0.039 370 1 inch
1 meter = 3.280 84 feet
1 meter = 1.093 61 yards
1 kilometer = 0.621 371 mile
1 liter = 1.056 69 quarts (liquid)
1 cubic meter = 264.172 gallons
1 gram = 0.035 274 0 ounce (avdp)
1 kilogram = 2.204 62 pounds (avdp)
1 kilowatt = 1.341 02 horsepower

English-metric conversions. Conversions from English to SI units can be made with the help of Table XIV. Retain in all conversions the number of significant digits so that accuracy is neither sacrificed nor exaggerated. Conversion is quite easy using a pocket calculator: $1\frac{1}{16}″ = 1.0625 \times 25.4 = 27$ mm. Building site or plot plans are generally dimensioned in decimals, such as 101.24′. Conversion of these dimensions is simple: e.g., $101.24′ = 101.24 \times 0.3048 = 30.86$ m.

STUDY QUESTIONS

1. What is the difference between soft and hard conversion?
2. Give the SI units for:
   a. Length
   b. Mass
   c. Temperature
   d. Electric current
3. Give the meaning of the following abbreviations:
   a. ANSI
   b. ISO
   c. kg
   d. m
   e. mm
4. Give the probable hard conversion size of:
   a. 2″ × 4″ wood studs
   b. 1″ × 10″ finished wood shelving
   c. $\frac{1}{2}″$ × 4′ × 8′ plywood
   d. 4″ × 8″ × 16″ concrete block
   e. $\frac{1}{4}″$ rebar
   f. 3′-wide × 4′-high window opening
5. Which quantity is greater?
   a. A 100-mm or a 4″ module
   b. 1200 × 2400-mm or 4′ × 8′ plywood
   c. A meter or a yard
   d. A kilometer or a mile
   e. A metric ton or an English ton
   f. A kilogram or a pound.
6. What would be the probable metric scale of:
   a. A floor plan of a residence
   b. A plot plan of a residence
   c. A floor plan of a shopping mall
   d. A site plan of a shopping mall and its parking area

LABORATORY EXERCISES

1. Complete the SI dimensioning on your plans of the A residence.
2. Complete the SI dimensioning of the building assigned by your instructor.
3. Complete the SI dimensioning of your original house design.
4. Dimension your building using:
   a. English system
   b. SI metric system
   c. Dual dimensioning
5. Draw the following M residence wall sections:
   a. Kitchen
   b. Dining room

NOTE : ALL DIMENSIONS IN METERS

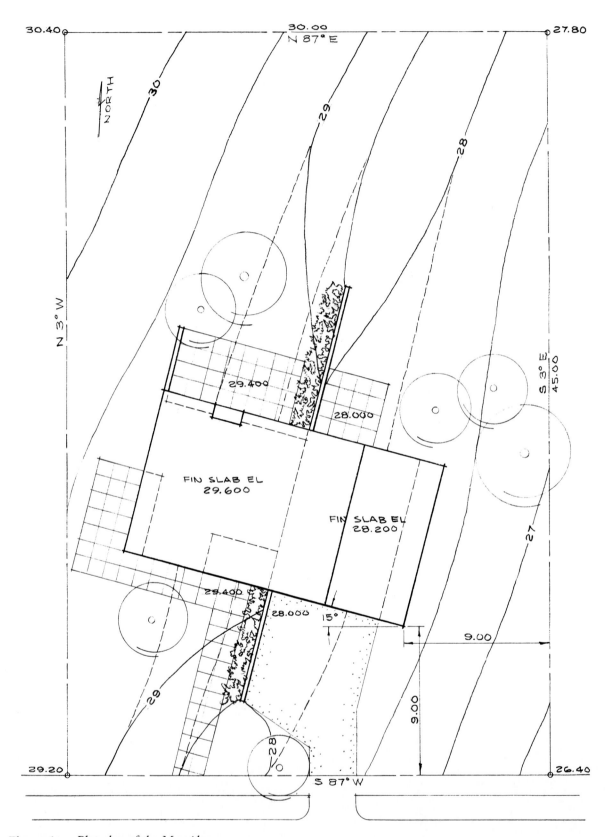

Figure 6 *Plot plan of the M residence.*

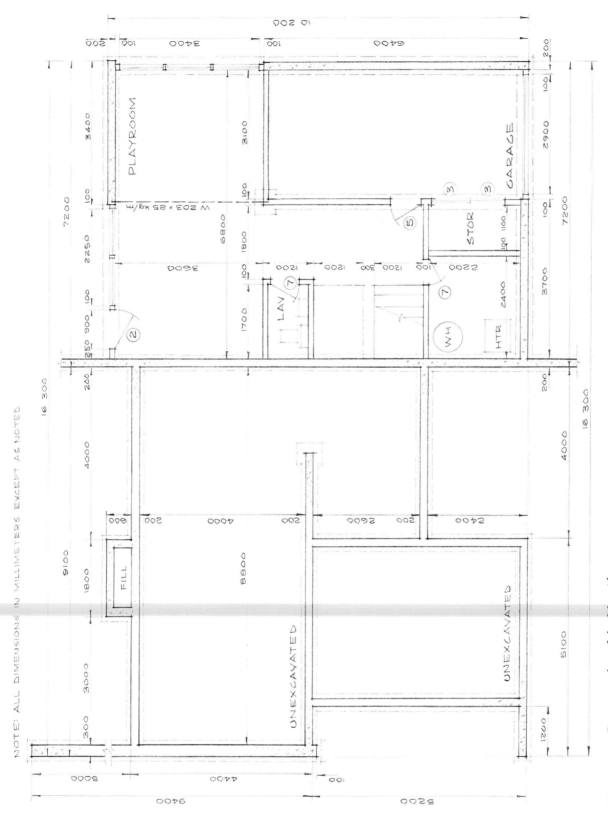

Figure 7 Basement plan of the M residence.

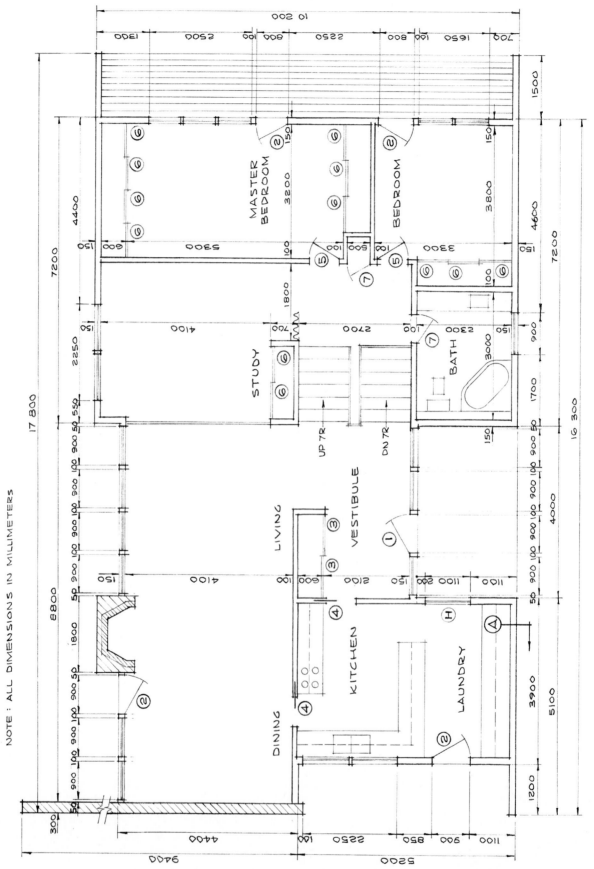

Figure 8 *Floor plan of the M residence.*

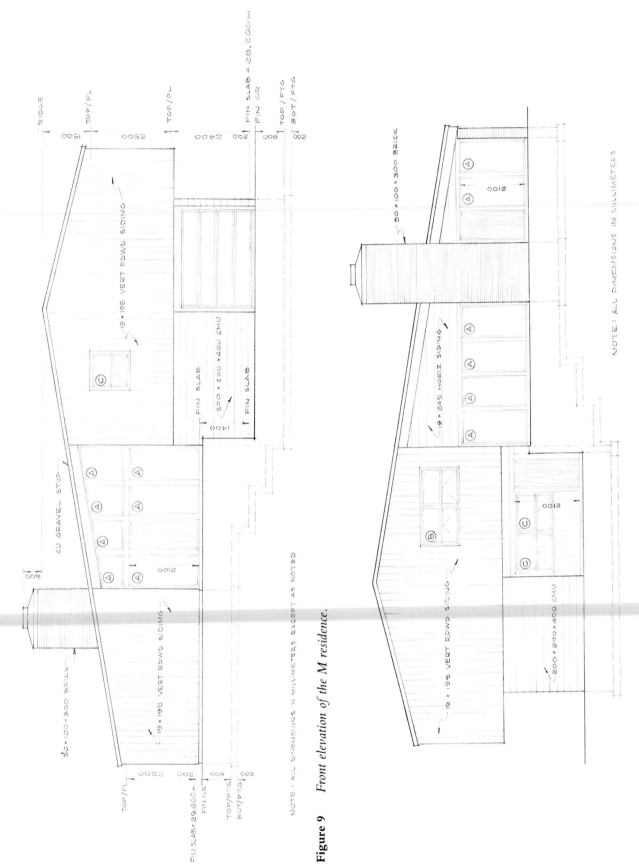

Figure 9 *Front elevation of the M residence.*

Figure 10 *Rear elevation of the M residence.*

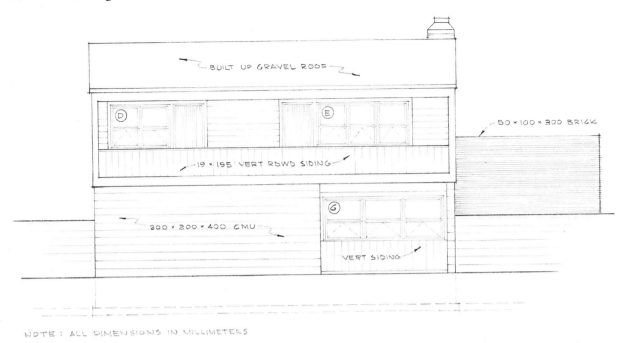

Figure 11 *Right-end elevation of the M elevation.*

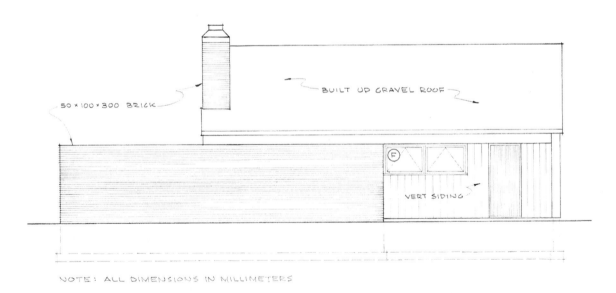

Figure 12 *Left-end elevation of the M elevation.*

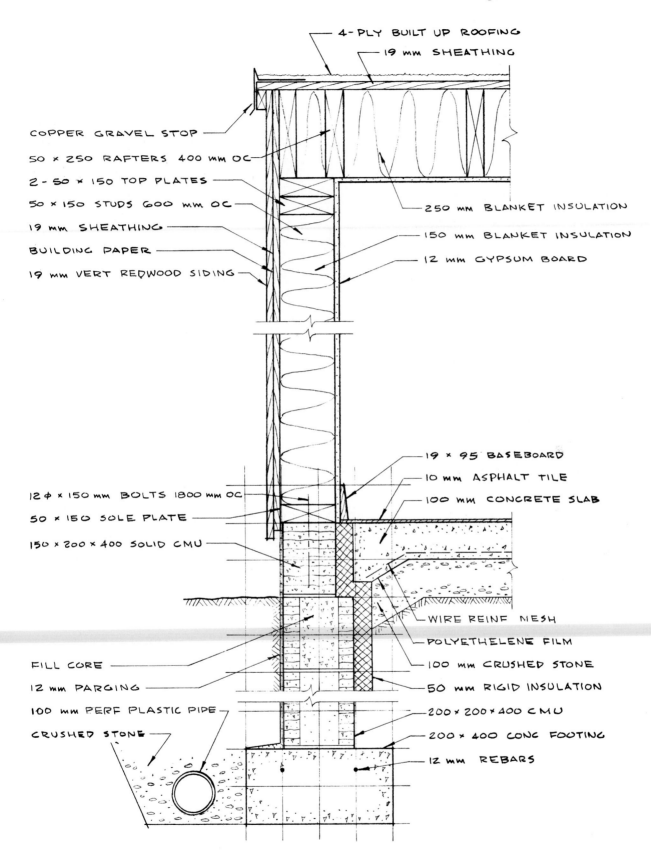

4-PLY BUILT UP ROOFING
19 mm SHEATHING

COPPER GRAVEL STOP
50 × 250 RAFTERS 400 mm OC
2 - 50 × 150 TOP PLATES
50 × 150 STUDS 600 mm OC
19 mm SHEATHING
BUILDING PAPER
19 mm VERT REDWOOD SIDING

250 mm BLANKET INSULATION
150 mm BLANKET INSULATION
12 mm GYPSUM BOARD

19 × 95 BASEBOARD
10 mm ASPHALT TILE
100 mm CONCRETE SLAB

12 φ × 150 mm BOLTS 1800 mm OC
50 × 150 SOLE PLATE
150 × 200 × 400 SOLID CMU

WIRE REINF MESH
POLYETHELENE FILM
100 mm CRUSHED STONE
50 mm RIGID INSULATION

FILL CORE
12 mm PARGING
100 mm PERF PLASTIC PIPE
CRUSHED STONE

200 × 200 × 400 C M U
200 × 400 CONC FOOTING
12 mm REBARS

Figure 13   *Section A through laundry of the M residence.*

III / Introduction to Architectural Design

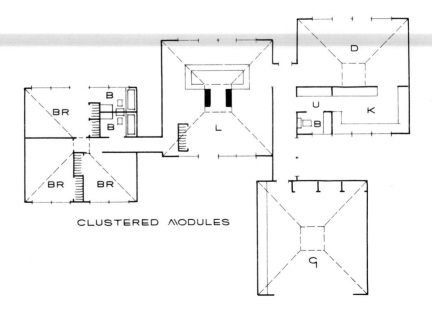

CLUSTERED MODULES

12 / Architectural History

In this age of new styles, new materials, and new building methods, we are apt to think of the contemporary house as having no ancestry—no history. Actually, the house we live in today is not a completely original design, but the outgrowth of many centuries of architectural development. No significant architectural style stands alone; rather it is the result of evolution. Every building that has ever been built is a composite idea of all the centuries of ideas that have preceded. It is thus with our present "modern" house, and the trends today will dictate the architecture of the future. We study the history of architecture, therefore, not only to enable us to appreciate the many public buildings previously built in classic styles, but also to aid in the design of present-day buildings.

In the following discussion, architectural history has been divided into separate chronological groups. But it should be remembered that architectural development is a steady and continuous process. Each age has made its contribution. Then we will see this century in true perspective and realize that no age is an ultimate—but merely one step in this continuing process.

The principal historical styles of architecture are as follows. Each is an evolution of, or has been influenced by, earlier styles.

Egyptian, Assyrian, Persian
Greek
Roman
Byzantine, Romanesque
Gothic
Renaissance
Classic Revival, Eclecticism
International, Contemporary

PREVIEW

If a beginning must be found, the architecture of the Egyptians will serve well. The Greeks drew on Egyptian, Assyrian, Persian, and Phoenician ideas. The Romans borrowed the ideas of the Greeks and added to them. History has approved the architecture of the Greeks and Romans to such an extent that many modern public buildings have been built in imitation of it. Later, the acceptance of domed and arched construction permitted the new styles of Byzantine and Romanesque. The Gothic style further developed vaulting, keeping many of the forms of its predecessors. During the Renaissance, the classic civilizations were studied and revived. But this return to ancient styles led eventually into a period called Eclecticism, which virtually stopped any real architectural development. In reaction to Eclecticism, architects searched for a new and true form of shelter. This was found in the Contemporary.

STRUCTURAL SYSTEMS

The history of architecture is closely tied to the development of methods of spanning the open space between two columns. To accomplish this spanning, five fundamental structural systems have been used (Figure 1):

1. Lintel
2. Corbel
3. Arch
4. Cohesive construction
5. Truss

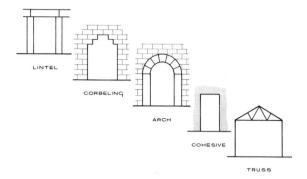

Figure 1 *Fundamental structural systems.*

The *lintel* is simply a horizontal member spanning an opening to carry the weight above. The weight of the lintel and any weight above it cause a vertical downward thrust to the columns. The Egyptians and Assyrians used the lintel almost exclusively. The Greeks developed the column and lintel, in an aesthetic sense, to perfection.

A *corbel* is a block projecting from a wall and supporting a weight. The cantilever is based upon the same principle. The Persians used corbeling extensively.

The *arch* is composed of wedge-shaped blocks, each supporting a share of the load by wedging the adjoining blocks. The weight of the blocks and any weight above cause not only a downward thrust but also outward thrusts. The Assyrians built a few arched structures, but the Romans are credited with much further development. The application of the principle of the arch

to the dome is credited to the Roman and Byzantine periods, and the vault reached its height in the Gothic period.

Cohesive construction employs materials that are shaped while plastic and allowed to harden into a homogeneous structure. The Romans used a kind of cohesive construction in their domes. Reinforced concrete is a modern application of this system.

A *truss* is a rigid arrangement of comparatively short members spanning a wide space.

EGYPTIAN ARCHITECTURE

It is a tribute to Egypt that her works dating back to 3500 B.C. are still standing. The surviving architecture, however, does not represent homes or even palaces, but rather tombs and monuments to the dead. In earliest history, graves were marked by piles of stones called *cairns*. The most noted outgrowth of these cairns are the pyramids built of stone or brick. There are over a hundred pyramids, varying in size and design, each containing intricate passageways designed to confuse anyone entering. Actually, no entrance can be found easily, since the tunnel was blocked once the mummy was in place. It is known that some pyramids were completed on a smaller scale, and successive outer layers were then added on. The pyramid was thus complete in case of the king's early death, and was enlarged as time permitted.

The actual construction method of the Egyptians is one of the mysteries of the past. It is true that hundreds of thousands of workers were employed in these huge monuments, but even so it is not clear how stones weighing up to thirty tons were raised. It has been suggested that a temporary sand ramp was erected, and the stone blocks were rolled up this ramp into position. The Egyptian temples of later periods could have been constructed in the same manner, the interior of the temple being filled with sand as the walls and columns were erected, and then dug out at completion. Another theory is that the stones were rocked in place using wooden rockers, which have been unearthed. It has been suggested that the stone was rocked enough for a shim to be inserted under one side, and then rocked again to insert a shim on the other side. This process could continue until the stone reached any required height.

The three largest pyramids are at Ghizeh (Figure 2), the most famous being the Great Pyramid of Cheops (Figure 3). This is the only remaining one of the original seven Wonders of the World. The dimensions of the Great Pyramid were originally 764′ square × 482′ high. Its present dimensions are 746′ square × 450′ high. It was built of limestone blocks upon a leveled rock plateau and

Figure 2 *The Sphinx and the Great Pyramid at Ghizeh.*

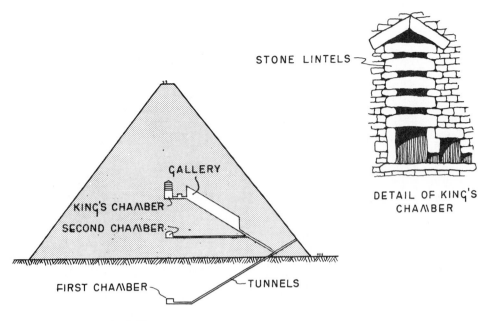

Figure 3   *The Great Pyramid of Cheops.*

was coated with smooth bands of colored granites. The king's marble sarcophagus is located in the upper chamber, reached by low tunnels and bridged by stone lintels topped by a sort of lintel-arch. A large gallery, 5' wide × 28' high, is connected to this chamber. Two additional burial chambers were prepared earlier. The first was cut into solid rock 102' below ground level. The second was built below the king's chamber and was once thought to be the queen's chamber.

A small temple for the worship of the king was connected to each pyramid. These have been mostly destroyed, but a few ground plans have been discovered, and one called the Temple of the Sphinx (Figure 4) is nearly complete. It contains square columns supporting massive square lintels which in turn support the roof slabs—a very simple forefather of the elaborate columns of later periods.

While only kings built pyramids, lesser rulers built *mastabas* (Figure 5). These were long, rectangular tombs of stone or brick with only a slightly sloping exterior wall and a flat roof of stone slabs. They always faced east, as did one of the four sides of the pyramids. The interior was divided into three chambers, the first being the chapel where offerings were made to sustain the *Ka*, or the double of the deceased. Secondly, there was a sealed and secret inner chamber containing statues and colored reliefs of the Ka. These were meant to entertain the Ka until the soul, or *Ba*, could arrive before the tribunal of Osiris. The last chamber, the *well*, was deep underground and led to the mummy chamber.

As time passed, these mastabas evolved into tremendous temples (ca. 1500 B.C.) for the deifica-

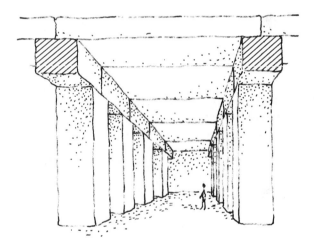

Figure 4   *The Temple of the Sphinx.*

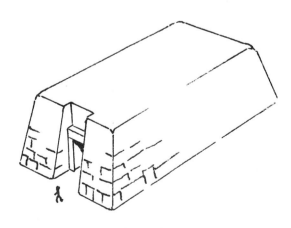

Figure 5   *A typical mastaba.*

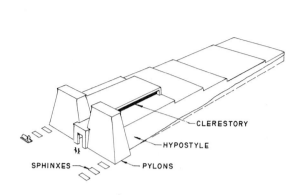

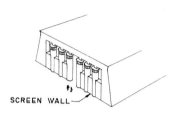

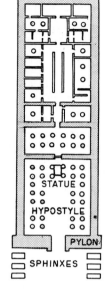

Figure 6   *Typical Egyptian temple.*

Figure 7   *A facade of a later period.*

Figure 8   *An Egyptian temple plan.*

tion of the kings. These temples were built on a diminishing plan (see Figure 6); that is, the chambers were smaller, darker, and more mysterious the farther they were penetrated. Also, the floors became higher and the roofs lower as the chambers receded. The exteriors of the temples were windowless oblong boxes fronted by two pylons, somewhat reminiscent of the pyramids, flanking the entrance. Two rows of facing sphinxes might border the approach.

The most noteworthy of these structures is the Karnak Temple, which was built and added to for seven hundred years, finally reaching dimensions of 376' wide × 1,215' long. The first chambers entered, called *hypostyle halls,* were entered at times by the Egyptian upper class for solemn worship. A clerestory allowed light to enter this chamber. In later periods a screen wall (Figure 7) was built between the front columns. The wall extended only half the column height to allow light to penetrate to the hieroglyphics on the inner walls and columns. Behind the hypostyle were countless darkened inner chambers accessible only to the priests (Figure 8).

With few exceptions, Egyptian construction was based on the column and lintel. The columns were richly carved and painted; lintels were square, plain, and massive. The entire structure was heavy—much heavier than was actually required for strength. The earliest example of an Egyptian arch dates back to 500 B.C. The principle of the 3-4-5 triangle was also known to the Egyptians and used in laying out floor plans. A cord tied in a circle with twelve equally spaced knots was

pegged in the earth to produce walls perpendicular to each other. This was a priestly ritual called the *cording of the temple.*

ASSYRIAN ARCHITECTURE

Though we have no Assyrian architectural remains as old as the pyramids of Egypt, these civilizations were nearly chronologically parallel. The surviving structures are not too similar, for the Egyptians have given us their tombs to study, and the Assyrians have given us palaces and fortifications. Moreover, although the Egyptian stone monuments have withstood the years, the Assyrian clay brick structures have crumbled.

Looking at the plan of an Assyrian palace shown in Figure 9, you will first notice the lack of symmetry, which is so different from the Egyptian temple plan. The palace was laid out with open courtyards surrounded by many small rooms and hallways, all arranged in a haphazard fashion. Probably one group of rooms and courtyards housed the ruler, another his harem, and others the soldiers and servants. Large rooms are not found. Since the Assyrians did not use columns, the room width was limited to the length of its ceiling beam. The arch was known to them: arched drainage systems have been found. An inclined vaulting system (Figure 10) was used to hold the blocks in place as they were laid. (The vertical keystone system requires supports until the top block is in place.) Long, narrow, horizon-

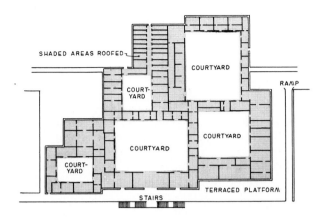

Figure 9 *An Assyrian palace.*

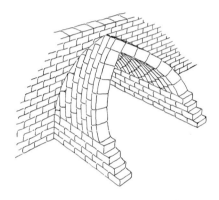

Figure 10 *The Assyrian vaulting system.*

tal openings directly beneath the roof served as the only kind of window.

Throughout history, fortifications have been built on elevated land. In the case of the Assyrians, this was impossible, since the land was perfectly flat. They solved this problem by constructing an artificial mountain, or platform, to raise the palace above the plains. This terraced platform was ascended by stairs and ramps.

Although the structures themselves were simple, there was much *applied* ornament—that is, ornament added after the structure was built. Bold colors were used—often the seven planetary colors: gold, silver, white, black, red, yellow, and blue.

PERSIAN ARCHITECTURE

The architecture of any country is influenced by the architecture of countries it knows or conquers. For example, the raised platform of the Assyrians also appears in Persian architecture. The Assyrians built entirely of brick, but the Persians built solid stone gateways and pilasters with brick filling between. The centuries have destroyed the brick, but the stone remains.

Extensive use was made of a kind of corbeled arch (Figure 11). The Persians used columns, but of more slender proportions and spaced farther apart than the Egyptians'. The Great Hall of Xerxes is a memorable work. It was twice the size of the Great Hypostyle Hall at Karnak, but the columns were spaced so much farther apart that the same roof area was supported by only one-fourth the number of columns. The capitals were composed of the heads of two monsters, the space between the heads supporting the beam (Figure 12).

GREEK ARCHITECTURE

The Grecian period (500 B.C.–100 B.C.) produced some of the most remarkable works of art and architecture known. The Greeks were a highly civilized and intelligent race, and they built temples of the finest proportion and detail. Their work was influenced by Egyptian, Assyrian, Persian, Phoenician, and Lycian architecture. The Greeks developed an architecture of columned monuments and temples, but the column was used in a manner different from that used in the Egyptian temples. The Egyptians used columns for internal support, the exteriors being for the most part completely blank walls, whereas the Greeks surrounded their tem-

Figure 11 *The Persian corbeled arch.*

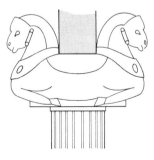

Figure 12 *A Persian column.*

Figure 13 *The Greek orders.*

ples with columns, making them the primary elements of exterior design. The number and arrangement of these columns varied greatly, but the plan was the same. The enclosed building itself, called the *cella,* was long, narrow, and windowless. The cella housed the statue of a deity and was open to the public. A small temple might have a single chamber in the cella which would be entered from one end. Columns might be only at that end, or on both ends. A larger temple, such as the Parthenon, might be divided into two chambers and completely surrounded by one or more rows of columns. Interior columns might also be used. Walls and columns were of marble, and the low-pitched roof was wood, covered with marble or terra-cotta tiles. Color was used on the interior and exterior reliefs, blue and gold being most popular. Moldings like the *egg-and-dart* carvings were simple but refined.

There are three styles of Greek columns, each with its own base, shaft, capital, and entablature constituting what is called an *order* (Figure 13). These three orders have been called the *Doric, Ionic,* and *Corinthian.* The tribes of Dorians and Ionians have given the name to the two styles traditionally Greek, whereas the Romans must be credited with fully developing the Corinthian order.

The Doric column was four and one-third to seven diameters high with sixteen to twenty elliptical flutes. It had a simple capital, but no base, resting directly on a stepped platform. The finest example of Doric architecture is the Parthenon (Figures 14 and 15) on the Acropolis of Athens.

Figure 14 *The Parthenon as it appears today.*

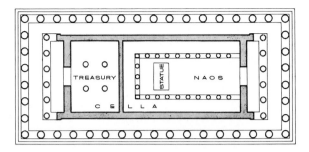

Figure 15   *A plan view of the Parthenon at Athens.*

Figure 16

It was built in 440 B.C. to enshrine the goddess Athena Parthenos and to commemorate the victory of the Athenians over the Persians. The marble blocks were cut to fit together with amazing accuracy and laid without mortar. The details were executed with exquisite refinement, giving rise to the comment that the Greeks "built like Titans and finished like jewelers." Many lines on the Parthenon that look perfectly straight were actually slightly curved to counteract the optical illusion of curvature. Columns have a slight convex curve (only 1″ in their 32′ height) so that they do not appear concave. Also, the axes of the columns lean a bit inward to prevent a top-heavy look. The steps and eaves curve gently down at the ends—also for visual effect. This can be explained by referring to Figure 16. Notice that the horizontal line, which is drawn straight, appears to sag because of the effect of the inclined lines above it. The Greeks took even such details into consideration.

The Ionic column was slender in comparison, being eight to ten diameters in height with twenty-four flutes cut deeper than in the Doric. It stood on a molded base and was finished by a capital with volutes. The only defect with this capital was that it did not readily lend itself to use as a corner column. To correct this problem, the corner volute was set at 45° so that it could be faced on both sides. The gables on Ionic buildings were frequently sculptured in relief, as were the Doric. Two examples of Ionic buildings are outstanding. One is the Erechtheion, also on the Acropolis, which is noted for its unsymmetrical plan. It enshrined many deities and heroes. Perhaps the most well known feature of this temple is the Caryatid Porch, which has robed female figures (caryatids) for columns. An Ionic tomb, the Mausoleum at Halicarnassus, was built by the widow of King Mausolus in 354 B.C. It had a pyramidal roof reminiscent of Egyptian architecture.

The Corinthian order was similar to the Ionic except that the capitals had smaller volutes entwined with rows of acanthus leaves. The most celebrated example of Greek Corinthian is the circular Monument of Lysicrates in Athens.

ROMAN ARCHITECTURE

Roman architecture was influenced by the Dorians, Phoenicians, Etruscans, and, most of all, the Greeks. The Romans never reached the Greek perfection of design, but they extended the services of architecture to theaters, baths, basilicas, bridges, aqueducts, and monuments—all well-engineered structures.

The three Greek orders were adopted as a direct consequence of the Roman conquest of Greece. Not only did the Romans bring home artistic wealth as part of the spoils of war, but they also brought home the desire to make Rome as magnificent as the Greek cities they had destroyed. The Greek orders were modified into what are called the five Roman orders: Tuscan, Doric, Ionic, Corinthian, and Composite. The Tuscan was a simplified Etruscan Doric, with a column seven diameters high. The Doric was similar to the Greek Doric, with a column eight diameters high and often devoid of any fluting. The Ionic was almost identical to the Greek Ionic, with a column nine diameters high. The Corinthian had a column ten diameters high. As previously stated, this order was perfected by the Romans and became the most characteristic order, probably because its ornateness appealed to the Romans. The Composite can be described as a Corinthian column with the volutes enlarged, giving it an Ionic look.

The Romans established sets of rules to simplify the orders which, many feel, were to their detriment. For example, fine elliptical moldings and flutes were cut circular to simplify the construction. However, their tremendous output of architecture probably could not have been accomplished if this kind of standardization had not been introduced. The columns, incidentally, were often cut in one piece (called *monolith*), instead of being built up from smaller sections, as were the Greek columns.

The Romans are credited with the development of the vault and arch. The Etruscans first used vaults; the vaulted great sewer of Rome (500 B.C.) still remains. Roman vaults are basically of three types: barrel, groined, and dome. The barrel vault is a semicylinder, the groined is formed from two intersecting barrel vaults, and the dome is a hemisphere supported on a wall of circular plan. The hemisphere supported on a wall of square

Figure 17   *The arch order.*

plan was later developed as the typical Byzantine dome. The vaults were cast over a wooden form, unlike the inclined vault, which required no forms. When hardened, the vault formed a cohesive curved lintel which did not extend the outward thrust of the stone block construction.

The Romans outdid themselves in the use of the arch, combining it with the column and lintel. This combination has been called the *arch order* (Figure 17) and is a characteristic feature of Roman architecture. It is also the poorest feature, because of its inherent inconsistency; either the arch or the lintel has to be redundant. The Romans considered ornateness above function, however, and this sham did not bother them. Lintels were even scored with false joints to make them look like smaller blocks. Much Roman work, especially

theaters, used the arch order. False columns were applied to the exterior, a different order for each level.

Many Roman public buildings were built around the basilica located in the Forum. The Forum was to Rome what the Acropolis was to Athens, the basilica being a meeting place and courthouse. The buildings were large and partially or completely roofed, the higher center portion affording a clerestory. Constantine built the first vaulted basilica; previous ones had wooden roofs.

Among the most remarkable Roman structures is the Colosseum in Rome (Figure 18), which seated eighty thousand. Erected to house the bloody battles between men and beasts, it could even be flooded to create sea fights. Titus finished the Colosseum in A.D. 80. The plan was a 600′ × 500′ ellipse; the walls were 153′ high arranged in four levels. The three lower levels were based on the arch orders, using Doric half-columns at the lower level, then Ionic, and then Corinthian. The upper level was composed of Corinthian columns with windows between them. A huge silk awning was stretched from this height over the galleries. The arena itself was uncovered. Ramps led to subterranean vaults which were used to house beasts and machinery.

The Circus Maximus outdid the Colosseum in that it measured 400′ × 2,100′ and seated two hundred sixty thousand. It was used for chariot races.

The Pantheon of Rome (Figure 19), built in A.D. 138, has been described as the noblest of all circular temples. It is roofed with a dome that admits light through a round opening at the top

Figure 18   *The Colosseum as it appears today.*

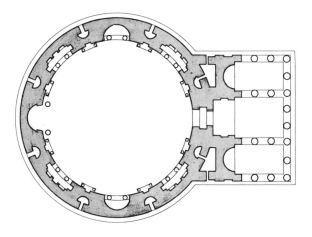

Figure 19   *A plan view of the Pantheon at Rome.*

Figure 20   *The interior of the Pantheon at Rome.*

called the "eye." Rich paneling and statues cover the interior walls (Figure 20).

The Roman Thermae, or baths, constructed about A.D. 300, illustrate the luxury in which the Romans loved to indulge. These tremendous structures contained rooms for gymnastic exercises and games, gardens, and usually three pools: the hot baths (Caldarium), warm baths (Tepidarium), and cold baths (Frigidarium).

Less ornamentation was lavished on the Roman aqueducts and bridges; instead the arch was used in its pure form. As a consequence, these are perhaps the Romans' best works. They were built in layers of arches, the greater arches at the bottom. The smaller, topmost arches were adjusted to the exact height required.

Due to Vesuvius's eruption in A.D. 79, we have a very good picture of the Roman house—at least the house in the provinces. A small vestibule led to the atrium, open to the sky and containing a pool to catch rainwater. A second vestibule led from the atrium to the inner court, the peristyle. The peristyle (Figure 21) was also open, but was a bit larger, with a garden and statues. Both courts, the front "living" room and the rear "family" room, were surrounded by smaller chambers, in a manner similar to the Assyrian plan.

BYZANTINE ARCHITECTURE

Byzantine architecture is characterized by a dome rising from a square base using transitional curved surfaces called *pendentives*. Initially, windows were pierced into the dome, allowing a crown of light to enter. Later, the dome was set upon a cylindrical tower, the windows cut in the tower instead of in the dome. Brick and stone were used for domes instead of the Roman concrete. The extra support

needed was supplied by buttresses. The Hagia Sophia at Constantinople (A.D. 538) is the most renowned example of the architecture of this period (Figure 22).

Figure 21   *The peristyle of a house at Pompeii.*

Figure 22   *The Hagia Sophia at Istanbul (Constantinople).*

Figure 23   *Notre Dame.*

Figure 24   *Westminster Abbey, London.*

ROMANESQUE ARCHITECTURE

The transitional period from Roman and Byzantine to Gothic (ninth to twelfth centuries) has been termed *Romanesque*. The foremost examples of Romanesque architecture are churches which appear with variations in many different countries. The square Byzantine plan was replaced by a rectangular plan, quite long and narrow, the interior divided by rows of arches called *arcades*. The round arch and stone vault (usually a kind of groined vault) were still used, but no longer singly. The column was moved inside again and, in fact, was built in a compound form called a *pier*.

GOTHIC ARCHITECTURE

The Gothic style developed in Western Europe between 1150 and 1450 as an outgrowth of the Romanesque. The Gothic was still an architecture of cathedrals, but it attacked some of the structural problems of vaulting in a different way. First, the groined vaults were supported entirely by comparatively few piers. The wall between the piers was filled in with marvelous pointed arch windows of stained glass and tracery. Second, the outward thrust of the vaults was countered by an exterior combination of arches and buttresses called

flying buttresses. These flying buttresses were capped with gables or small steeplelike pinnacles. The third distinguishing Gothic feature is the pointed arch, which was first developed to facilitate the construction of groined vaults on a rectangular plan. The stone vaulted roofs of the cathedrals were covered with a wooden gable roof to protect them from the elements. There are innumerable fine examples of Gothic architecture in use. Outstanding are the Cathedral of Notre Dame at Paris (Figure 23), Cologne Cathedral, the Cathedral of Seville, and Westminster Abbey (Figure 24).

RENAISSANCE ARCHITECTURE

The decline of feudalism and a new freedom of expression in art, literature, and architecture characterized the period known as the Renaissance (1420–1700). The classic civilizations were rediscovered, studied, and imitated. The objection to the architecture of the Renaissance is that the structural framework was hidden beneath a false classical facade. Also, the classical orders were applied in many instances where they did not fit. Knowledge of the Roman orders was the chief stock-in-trade of the architect of this period.

The first example of this new style was the Cathedral of Florence (1420). The Pantheon in

Paris is noted for its strict adherence to classical detail. The largest church in existence today is a Renaissance church: St. Peter's in Rome is 600' long and 405' high. Other notable examples are the Louvre in Paris (Figure 25), St. Paul's Cathedral in London, and the Doge's Palace in Venice.

MECHANICAL SYSTEMS

Although the history of architecture is closely allied with that of structural systems, the "mechanical" systems (heating, lighting, and sanitation) are interesting studies each in their own right.

Heating. The earliest heating systems were, of course, open wood fires. Holes in the rooves of caves and tents, used to remove smoke, were later replaced by chimneys in buildings. Early buildings in cold climates had a single fireplace or stove for heating and cooking; fireplaces were built of stone or brick with wood chimneys. The first stoves were of brick or tile and later cast iron, and fuel was wood or dried peat. Houses of several rooms had a fireplace or stove located in the kitchen, and hot coals in warming pans were used for sleeping on cold nights. The first built-in house stoves had a stove door on the outside of the building with the remaining three sides within the house, sometimes heating two stories. In 1744 Benjamin Franklin invented an improved iron stove (the Franklin stove) that wasted less heat because the hearth was extended into the room and the stove was connected to the chimney by a funnel-shaped transition duct.

Central heating systems became common during the nineteenth century, but local heating was still used in many locations. Fuel was coal, oil, or gas with heat distributed by warm air, hot water, or steam. Electric heating and active solar heating developed during the twentieth century.

Lighting. Ancient Egyptians, Greeks, and Romans obtained light by using pottery or bronze dish lamps: wicks were set inside dishes filled with grease or olive oil. Candles made from fats or cooking greases were used for light for many centuries, but in the eighteenth century it was discovered that a flame burns more brightly and with less smoke when it is in a glass chimney. This discovery, combined with increased activity in whaling and the availability of whale oil, created the popular oil lamp. A distilling process to refine oil from coal was discovered by a Canadian geologist, Abraham Gesner, in 1854. This new substance was called coal oil or kerosene and was used both as a lamp fuel and a heating fuel. At about the same time, both natural gas and manufactured gas started to be used for lighting, heating, and cooking.

Figure 25 *The Louvre.*

Natural gas was discovered several thousand years ago and used in temples in China, Japan, India, Russia, and Greece. Ancient Greeks built the temple of Apollo at Delphi over a natural gas crevice. An oracle breathed the fumes (thought to be the breath of Apollo) and predicted future happenings. "Eternal" flames in temples were often fueled by natural gas. In the early seventeenth century it was discovered that gas could be manufactured from coal, but manufactured gas was not used for lighting until the early nineteenth century. The first gas lamp posts were installed along the Pall Mall in London in 1807. The first U.S. city to use manufactured gas street lamps was Baltimore in 1816. The first city to use natural gas street lamps was Fredonia, N.Y., eight years later. Gas ranges for cooking began being manufactured in the late 1800s. At the same time electricity began to replace gas for lighting, and the electrical convenience outlet made available a wide range of appliances for work and leisure.

Sanitation. Early methods of sanitation usually consisted of the disposal of waste in fields and street gutters, but improved sanitary systems were also designed and built. The Romans built aquaducts of stone, brick, tile, or lead to carry fresh water to buildings and to flush the underground sewers that ran from the buildings to the Tiber River. Ancient cities in India contained paved bathrooms and drains of terracotta pipes, and other waste was discarded through wall chutes to waste bins in the street, but there was little progress in sanitation during the dark ages. The first modern valve toilet (still called a "water closet") was invented in 1596 by the Englishman John Harington (thought to be the origin of the slang term "the john"), but indoor plumbing was only slowly accepted. Piping began to be installed inside walls only in the early 1900s. Hand-cranked wells and separate outhouses are still in use today.

DOMESTIC ARCHITECTURE

Throughout the previous discussion, private dwellings have not often been used as examples. The reason is that only monumental buildings were of sufficiently durable construction to survive time and the elements. However, we do have examples of comparatively recent private dwellings in all countries. For simplicity, let us look only at North American architecture.

The first shelters of the English colonists in the New World (Plymouth and Jamestown) were lean-tos called *English wigwams*. They were not like Indian tents, however, but were framed with poles and covered with woven twigs called *wattle*, brush, and mud or clay. Sod huts partially buried in the ground with staked walls were also built.

The log cabin was introduced by the Swedes in Delaware. This was the type of dwelling the poorer classes had used in the mother country and was unknown to the Indians. Log construction was adopted by other colonists for use in stockades and prisons. In fact, *log house* meant, at first, a jail. Later, the log house and overhanging blockhouse moved west with the frontier.

It should be noted here that traditional North American architecture has its roots in the architecture of the mother countries, particularly England. There was no Indian influence, nor was it the intention of the colonists to found a new architectural style. All they desired was to build a civilization similar to the one they had left. However, available materials and the North American climate soon dictated certain modifications of the European methods.

Around 1600, the typical English middleclass house was of half-timbered construction. That is, a heavy wooden frame was pegged together and filled in with clay-covered wattle or rolls of clay and straw called *cat and clay*. In the severe New England climate, however, this construction had to be covered with a horizontal sheathing called *weatherboards* (also known in England). Due to the abundance of timber, the clay or brick filling was gradually omitted, being replaced by the hollow frame construction known today. Of course in areas where there was a supply of good building stone (Pennsylvania), or clay for brick making (Maryland), these materials were used.

For the roof covering, thatch was replaced by shingles split from the forests of cedar. In fact, the North Americans abandoned thatched roofs almost two hundred years before the English.

Classic revival. During the first half of the nineteenth century, the *Classical Revival* held sway. Even the United States turned from its wooden version of the English Georgian (called *Colonial*) to Classic Revival in stone and concrete. Examples of Classic Revival in the United States are the White House (Figure 26), the national Capitol (Figure 27), several state capitols, and many churches. This artificial return to the past slowed down any real architectural progress.

Eclecticism. The Classic Revival was shortly replaced by *Eclecticism,* a conglomeration of various historical styles, any number of which might be used in a single structure. This searching for ancient methods of enclosing modern structures brought architectural progress to a halt. At first, even the advent of structural steel framing did not change the Egyptian, Classical, Byzantine, and Renaissance coverings. Only when the simple structural lines of the American skyscraper were left undisguised did architecture move on. Today, Eclecticism is synonymous with all that is false in architecture.

International style. Although the United States led the way in nontraditional design for commercial building, Europe quickly applied this new *functionalism* (the doctrine that a feature should have a *function* and should not be applied for deco-

Figure 26 *A view of the south side of the White House (executive mansion).*

Figure 27 *The Senate wing of the Capitol Building.*

ration only) to private dwellings. Led by Gropius of Germany and Le Corbusier of France, a type of architecture called the *International Style* developed which was characterized by simple, blocklike exteriors, concrete walls with no roof overhang, and windows located at the corners rather than the sides of walls. Unfortunately, the skillful block proportions used to advantage on North American commercial structures, culminating in buildings like the Empire State Building (1931) and Rockefeller Center (1930–1950), gave these smaller buildings a boxy, factorylike appearance. When the International Style of domestic architecture spread to England and then to the United States, it was not readily accepted. The lack of eaves, the corner windows, and other features of the style were rejected as not being truly functional, but rather false, applied styling. However, the major premise of the International Style, that of planning the exterior around the interior, even though revolutionary, was quickly adopted. This idea of "form follows function" is the guiding spirit of architecture today—made possible, in reality, by the free use of a combination of old and new building methods.

With this general background of the development of domestic architecture in North America, let us look in more detail at some common examples of residential architecture. The characteristics of these buildings make up what is called *architectural styling*.

ARCHITECTURAL STYLING

A working knowledge of architectural styling is important for two reasons:

1. The first decision to be made when planning to build a house is its styling. Will it be traditional or modern? Ranch house or split-level? The choice will be affected by the fact that the style, or exterior appearance, influences the interior layout. Some styles, for example, require a one-floor house, others one and a half or two floors. Certain styles call for a symmetrical design with a central hall.
2. Even if you have definitely decided upon the styling for a particular house, you should be able to understand and appreciate the advantages of other types.

We shall first discuss the styles and types in more common use, and then show how to pick the style that will best suit a set of requirements. There are two general classifications of popular architectural styles: traditional and contemporary. Let us take each in turn.

TRADITIONAL

A house built in the traditional style today is a copy, with certain modifications, of a kind of house built previously. There are many dwellings built in the traditional style, but the trend has been toward contemporary. Many people feel that some traditional styles overly limit freedom of layout. Also, many traditional styles are of European, not truly North American, origin. However, the traditional house has stood the test of years and will always have a place in the hearts of those who put tradition before expediency.

English. English houses (Figure 28) are fashioned after the type built in England before the eighteenth century. Historical subdivisions of English architecture are Old English, Tudor, and Elizabethan. Each has its own particular characteristics, but all have common features as well. For example, the interior layout is informal and unsymmetrical due to the lack of exterior symmetry. Walls are of stone, brick, or stucco, and are sometimes half-timbered. The gable ends may be of darkstained, hand-hewn beams. If the second floor overhangs the first, carved drops may be used at the corners. Fenestration (the arrangement of windows in a wall) is completely random; occasionally a window may appear to be built right through a chimney. The windows are casements (side hinged) and are made of small diamond panes after the prototype, a style that developed because large sheets of glass were not manufactured at the time. Roofs are steeply pitched, the eaves and ridges being at various levels.

The fireplace used to have a more important function in the home than it does today, since it furnished all cooking and heating facilities. Massive chimneys were usually topped off with chimney pots (vertical extensions of tile or brick). Although some features of the English house may be used in constructing small homes, the style is at its best in larger houses.

Although you will find many examples of English homes in the United States today, most of

Figure 28   *English styling.*

Figure 29 *Georgian styling.*

Figure 30 *Regency styling.*

them were built more than fifty years ago. The English style is not popular for new homes (although occasionally individual features are copied) because builders today cannot build in stone, brick, or stucco at a reasonable price. Moreover, the trend in this country is away from continental ideas and toward American Colonial and modern styles.

Georgian. As we have seen in the section on architectural history, the Renaissance was characterized by the rebirth of the architecture of the classical civilizations. Georgian architecture (1714–1760) was also developed from classical principles of formality and symmetry (Figure 29). Many classical details were used, such as pedimented doorways (triangular areas above the doorways), elaborate cornices, and pilasters (bas-relief columns).

The Georgian house (so called for the kings under whom it flourished) is a large one, two or more floors high, with a gently sloping hip roof. The front of the house must be religiously symmetrical. The front entrance is at dead center with windows equally spaced on either side, the second-floor windows directly above the first-floor windows. Symmetry is carried through even to the chimneys—one at either end. If only one chimney is required, a false one is included so that symmetry will be preserved. We often find pilasters, sidelights, and columned porches two stories high. The interior plan is, of course, a center-hall one, with bedrooms on the second floor. These restrictions of symmetry do not affect the design of the rear of the house, however.

We shall soon see how the Georgian house served as the inspiration for the various American Colonial styles—becoming adapted to wood instead of stucco and stone.

Regency. The king of England at the time of the American Revolution was George III. His son was appointed regent by the English Parliament to reign in his father's place when George III became too old to rule. This period in English history, known as the *Regency,* gave birth to a particular architectural style.

The Regency-style house (Figure 30) is similar to the Georgian but has cleaner lines and finer

Courtesy of Scholz Homes, Inc.

Figure 31 *A contemporary home with a classic heritage.*

Figure 32 *New England Colonial styling.*

details. Exterior walls are usually brick, often painted white. The Georgian formality and hip roof still prevail. Other typical Regency details are long shutters at the first-floor level, curved copper bay or porch roofs, curved side wall extensions, and fancy iron-work tracery around porches. Contemporary homes may show their classic heritage (Figure 31), even though not designed to a specific style.

Colonial. The term *colonial* is loosely applied to any style developed by colonizers. Colonial architecture, or—to be more specific—English Colonial architecture, consists of Early American (before 1720) and American Colonial (after 1720). American Colonial is a modification of Georgian and consists of various regional types, such as New England, Southern, and Dutch.

Even though there were no trained architects in North America before the Revolution, many well-designed houses were built. The reason is that a workable knowledge of architecture was part of every gentleman's training. Each landowner designed his own house (Jefferson designed his own and several others) with the aid of English architectural handbooks which simplified the use of the Renaissance orders. If these handbooks were followed, the landowner could not go wrong. For materials, wood was plentiful in all the colonies, although brick was often used in the south and stone in the middle colonies.

New England Colonial. The New England house (Figure 32) was simple and unpretentious, but of such good design and proportion that it has been copied through the years. Since this style is modeled after the Georgian, the front elevation is symmetrical. Wood was plentiful in the North and was used even for classical columns and pilasters. Exterior finish was a narrow clapboard with vertical boards covering the corners so that the clapboards did not have to be mitered. The roof pitch was steep to shed the heavy snows, and sometimes the eaves at the rear dropped a floor lower than the eaves at the front of the house. In early houses, one chimney was located at the center to serve as many rooms as possible, and in later work there were two chimneys, one at either end. The first win-

dows were glassless and closed by wooden shutters. These were replaced by diamond-paned casements imported from England, and eventually by the double-hung (nicknamed *guillotine*), rectangular-paned window. This house was called a *salt box* because it looked like the salt boxes sold in early general stores.

Garrison. Like all colonists, the new arrivals in North America tried to duplicate the type of house they had known at home. One of the first breaks with this tradition was the garrison house (Figure 33), modeled after the blockhouses the colonists used to fight off Indian raids. These blockhouses had overhanging second stories, which made them difficult to scale and easier to defend. In imitation of these forts, some houses were built with an overhanging second floor, although they were otherwise similar to the New England Colonial. The ends of the heavy timbers projecting down below the overhang were frequently carved in some fashion.

Cape Cod. The Cape Cod section of Massachusetts has become known for its charming small homes. Although a true Cape Cod house (Figure 34) has very definite characteristics, nearly any small house having a steeply pitched gable roof with the eave line at the top of the first story may be called Cape Cod. Actually, a true reproduction will have the following details: double-hung, small-paned windows with shutters, shingle or clapboard walls, a wood-shingled roof (or an imitation), a main entrance in the center of the front elevation, and a massive center chimney. Small dormers at the front or a shed dormer (jokingly called a *dustpan*) at the rear adds greatly to the us-

Figure 33 *Garrison styling.*

Figure 34 *Cape Cod styling.*

Figure 35   *Southern Colonial styling.*

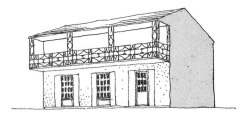

Figure 36   *Dutch Colonial styling.*

Figure 37   *French Colonial styling.*

ability of the second floor. An American architect associated with the Cape Cod house is Royal Barry Wills.

Southern Colonial. It is true that better examples of architecture can be found in the larger, more expensive houses than in the small ones. This is natural, since only the wealthy could afford the expense of the details of styling. This distinction was particularly true in the South where some very lovely plantation houses were built (Figure 35). They differed from the New England Colonial mainly in that a flat porch, two stories high and supported by columns, was used to shade the front windows. Brick was the usual material. Today the Southern Colonial style is not as popular as the colonial styles of the North because the high porch looks ungainly on any but a very large house.

Dutch Colonial. Dutch and German settlers in New Amsterdam (New York), New Jersey, and Pennsylvania built houses with steeply pitched roofs, called *gambrel* roofs (Figure 36). This type of roof was invented by a French architect named Mansard, who designed a double-pitched roof, permitting the attic to be used as another floor. The tale goes that this was done originally to evade the heavier tax on two-story houses. When this roof runs on four sides, it is called *mansard* after the originator; when it is on only two sides, *gambrel* or *Dutch Colonial.* The more authentic example of Dutch Colonial has a slightly curved projecting eave with a continuous shed dormer window. Stone construction should be used.

Courtesy of Scholz Homes, Inc.

Figure 38   *A contemporary home in the style of a French chateau.*

Figure 39   *Spanish styling.*

Figure 41   *Split-level styling.*

Figure 40   *Ranch styling.*

Figure 42   *Modern styling.*

French Colonial. The best examples of authentic French Colonial architecture (Figure 37) can be found in the old French Quarter of New Orleans. Here, buildings are crowded together, all with common characteristics, but each different. The hallmark of this style is a flat facade relieved only by wrought-iron balconies. The balconies contain fancy scroll work and may be supported by delicate iron columns or trellises. The plastered fronts are tinted pink, yellow, or green. A contemporary home in the style of a French chateau is shown in Figure 38.

Spanish. A Spanish house (Figure 39) should appear to have adobe walls, in keeping with the material originally available. Roofs are tiled and low-pitched. A close reproduction should be built around a patio and have open-timbered ceilings of rough-hewn logs.

CONTEMPORARY ARCHITECTURE

Many terms such as *modernistic, futuristic,* and *functional* have been used to distinguish nontraditional architecture from traditional. The two terms most widely accepted are *contemporary* and *modern.* To be perfectly correct, *contemporary* indicates any building erected at the present time regardless of style. However, since present-day construction consists mainly of ranch, split-level, and modern, we will restrict this term to these three types. Occasionally *contemporary* is used synonymously with *modern.*

Ranch. The popularity of the ranch house (Figure 40) today is partly due to its blend of past and

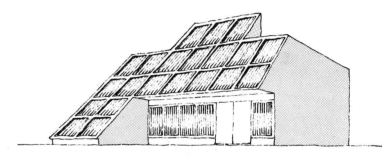

Figure 43   *Solar house.*

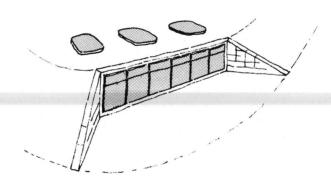

Figure 44   *Underground house.*

present. Most contemporary conveniences can be incorporated into a ranch house design without appearing too extreme. Also, the demand for light construction and low, land-hugging designs has increased, as has the desire for one-floor plans with no stairs to climb.

Nearly any one-story house is called a ranch house today, although it should be rambling, have

Figure 45   *A modern house combining form and function.*

an informal plan and a low-pitched roof, preferably hipped. The ranch is well suited to large, flat lots and may be built in the high, medium, and even low price ranges.

Split-level. A split-level house (Figure 41) is arranged so that floor climbing is limited to half-flights of stairs. It is a kind of combination of ranch and two-story construction. It might be laid out with bedrooms and bath on the highest level; living, dining, and kitchen half a floor lower; and garage and "free room" half a floor lower still (under the bedroom level). A free room is usually a recreation or family room built in "found" or "free" basement areas. The levels may be split between ends or between front and back depending on the terrain. Although the majority of split-levels are built on a more or less stock plan, infinite variations are possible. These should offer a real challenge to the designer.

Modern. A truly modern building (Figure 42) should be "honest." That is, it should have a fresh approach to requirements such as shelter, light, and circulation. The modern architect feels that drawing on the styles of the past to any great extent is "dishonest." He designs each house to suit

Figure 47   *A water tank on the campus of the State University of New York at Albany. Edward Durell Stone and Associates, architects.*

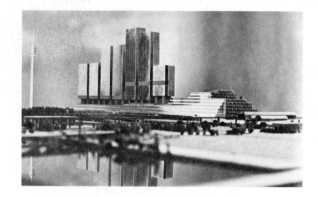

Figure 48   *Model of the proposed United Nations Organizations Headquarters for Vienna, Austria. Gruen Associates, architects.*

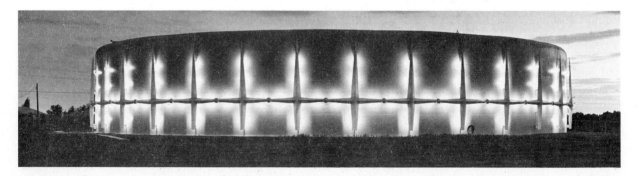

Figure 46   *A water tank in Columbus, Ohio.*

Figure 49   *Farnsworth House at Plano, Illinois. Mies van der Rohe, architect.*

Figure 50   *Architecture Hall at the Illinois Institute of Technology. Mies van der Rohe, architect.*

the requirements of those living in it without being fettered by historical styling, symmetry, or useless decoration. Some fine examples are homes that apply new technological advances without attempting to hide them behind decorative facades. The requirement for large areas of solar collectors affects the design of solar homes (Figure 43), and the requirement for earth covering affects the design of underground homes (Figure 44).

A key word used in modern architecture is *functional*. This means that every element of the house should have a function—a reason for existing. The expression "form follows function" is a simplification of the idea that exterior appearance, or form, should be subordinated to the functional and structural aspects (Figure 45).

But the modern house should not be merely a "machine for living," since it also has the function of meeting the family's aesthetic needs. This one factor—a sensitivity to aesthetic need—distinguishes the truly great modern design from the mediocre. Even a mundane structure such as a water tank, when designed by an inspired architect-engineer, can be a community asset rather than a visual pollutant. The 10-million-gallon tank in Figure 46 is braced by star-shaped steel members and illuminated indirectly at night. The slender steel tower shown in Figure 47 encloses a 320,000-gallon water tank which is set in a reflecting pool. A sixteen-bell carillon is installed in the cage at the top of the spire.

Since sensitivity and originality are objectives of the modern architect, there can be no typical example of modern. However, the style is often marked by a simple (but interesting) design; both native and machine-produced materials; low structures with flat, shed, or clerestory roofs; provision for indoor-outdoor living; and great expanses of glass. Some architects who stand out in modern architecture are Alvar Aalto, Le Corbusier, Walter Gropius, Victor Gruen (Figure 48), Philip Johnson, Louis Kahn, Ludwig Mies van der Rohe (Figures 49 and 50), Pier Luigi Nervi, Rich-

Figure 51   *Yale University hockey rink, New Haven, Connecticut. Eero Saarinen & Associates, architects.*

Figure 52   *Dulles International Airport terminal near Washington, D.C. Eero Saarinen & Associates, architects.*

Figure 53   *Fallingwater, a private residence at Bear Run, Pennsylvania. Frank Lloyd Wright, architect.*

ard Neutra, Oscar Niemeyer, Ioh Ming Pei, Eero Saarinen (Figures 51 and 52), Edward Durell Stone (Figure 47), Louis Sullivan, Frank Lloyd Wright (Figures 53–55) and Minoru Yamasaki (Figures 56 and 57).

Postmodern. Postmodern architecture applies the ornamentation of past classical designs to the clean lines of contemporary buildings, often in a tongue-in-cheek fashion. For example, classical columns might be used for decoration without supporting any lintels. One of the earliest examples of post-

modern architecture is the AT&T Headquarters in New York City, designed by Philip Johnson and John Burgee. Constructed in the 1980s, this 645-foot tower is finished with a Chippendale roof (Figure 58).

STUDY QUESTIONS

1. Sketch and name the five fundamental structural systems. Give the civilization responsible for introducing each system.
2. Prepare an outline naming the major civilizations responsible for architectural development.
   a. Include the approximate dates of each.
   b. Indicate the structural systems used.
   c. Give examples of well-known buildings in each period.
3. Discuss the contribution to archtectural development made by the following civilizations. Give the methods of construction of each and examples.
   a. Egyptian
   b. Assyrian
   c. Greek
   d. Roman
   e. Gothic
4. Trace the development of architecture in North America from simple huts to contemporary buildings.
5. (For the advanced student) After a thorough study of building trends over the past one hundred years, give your estimate of architectural styles:
   a. twenty-five years hence
   b. one hundred years hence
6. (For the advanced student) Prepare a report on the life and accomplishments of one or more of the following. Include examples of structures built and proposed by each. Show how his work was influenced by his predecessors.

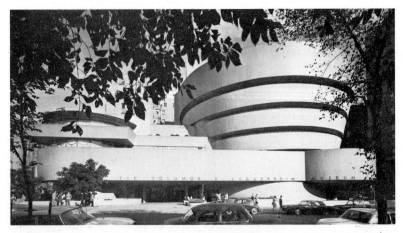

The Solomon R. Guggenheim Museum, New York.

Figure 54   *The exterior of the Solomon R. Guggenheim Museum, New York City. Frank Lloyd Wright, architect.*

The Solomon R. Guggenheim Museum, New York.

Figure 55   *The interior of the Guggenheim Museum. Frank Lloyd Wright, architect.*

a. Frank Lloyd Wright
b. Walter Gropius
c. Le Corbusier
d. Mies van der Rohe
e. Eero Saarinen
7. Classify the residences built today into major categories.
   a. Give a brief description of each.
   b. Include a sketch of a typical example of each.
   c. Give your estimation of the future popularity of each.

LABORATORY PROBLEMS

1. Prepare a chart showing the five fundamental structural systems.
2. Build a model of each of the five fundamental structural systems.
3. Prepare a chart of the major civilizations responsible for architectural development.
4. Build a model of one or more of the following (*for advanced students only):
   a. Pyramid of Cheops (cutaway to show interior passages)
   b. Assyrian palace
   c. Parthenon
   *d. Acropolis
   *e. Pantheon
   *f. Cathedral of Notre Dame
   *g. St. Peter's
   h. White House
   i. U.S. Capitol building
   *j. Fallingwater
   k. Farnsworth House

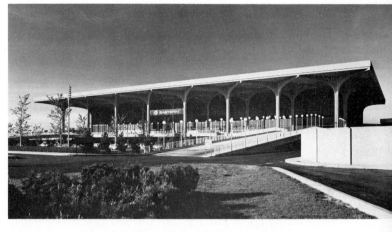

Figure 57 *Eastern Airlines terminal, Boston, Massachusetts. Minoru Yamasaki and Associates, architects.*

Figure 56 *Manufacturers and Traders Trust Building, Buffalo, New York. Minoru Yamasaki and Associates, architects.*

Figure 58 *AT&T Headquarters, New York City, Philip Johnson and John Burgee, architects.*

5. Build a model of a typical residence of one or more of the following types:
   a. Egyptian
   b. Greek
   c. Roman
   d. English
   e. Colonial
   f. Ranch
   g. Split-level
   h. Modern
   i. Solar
   j. Underground
   k. Postmodern
6. Arrange for a practicing architect to visit the class and discuss contemporary architectural design.

13 / Primary Considerations

Talk to persons who have recently designed a home. Ask them if they would do it again, and you'll get a variety of replies. Some will tell you that this was a most satisfying and rewarding experience; others will say it was entirely frustrating. After further questioning, you'll find that those who were most successful have an important characteristic: *sensitivity*. The successful designer has the ability to be sensitive to many factors. Some of these factors are aesthetic (such as feeling the potentials of the site), some are empathic (such as understanding the desires of his client), and some are practical (such as keeping within the budget). The designer must be sensitive to many such factors throughout the entire design process. But some factors should be considered before starting to sketch a preliminary layout (Chapter 20) or even listing program requirements (Chapter 15). These are called *primary considerations* and are discussed in this chapter:

1. The site
2. Architectural styling
3. Basic structure
   Energy system
   Size
   Number of floors
   Shape of plan
   Foundation
   Roof
   Expansion
4. Building codes and zoning
5. Cost

THE SITE

To the sensitive designer, each site has an individ-ual character which suggests the most appropriate structure and style of home. The contour of the land, shape of the plot, kind of trees, surrounding views, and type of community all give broad hints toward a satisfactory solution. For example, a *sloping* contour suggests a split-level or modern house. A *narrow* plot restricts the choice of styles and requires special planning to prevent a cramped appearance. A *wide* plot offers more freedom of planning, permitting a low, rambling design or several connected modules. Try to keep excavation to a minimum, for the less the natural contour of the site is disturbed, the less Nature will try to disturb the occupants of that site (Figure 1).

Take advantage of existing trees, especially if they are large; it will take many years for newly planted trees to mature. Evergreen trees to the windward are excellent natural windbreaks, and deciduous trees located on the southern side of the site are natural "automatic" solar screens. They shade a building from the undesirable summer sun (thereby reducing the interior temperature by about 10°) and, when they shed their leaves in the winter, permit the desirable winter sunlight to filter through.

It has always been an architectural goal to provide a building that shields the occupant from a sometimes hostile environment. In so doing, however, the occupant does not wish to lose contact with the friendly parts of the environment. Thus exterior living space adjacent to interior living space should be provided. Also glass window walls can face the best views and unpleasant views or noisy streets can be shielded. Be sensitive to the nature of the surrounding community and avoid building in a style that is incompatible with nearby architectural styles.

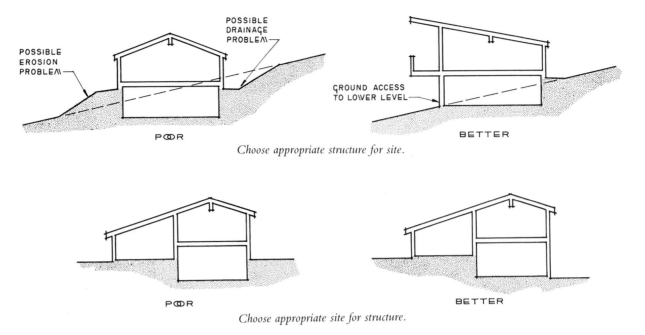

Choose appropriate structure for site.

Choose appropriate site for structure.

Figure 1

EXAMPLE

The plot belonging to Mr. and Mrs. A* is narrow and relatively flat with an excellent view to the rear. The views to the front and left are undesirable.
Decision: Clerestory windows or atrium.

ARCHITECTURAL STYLING

As indicated in Chapter 12, the architectural styling should be considered before preliminary sketches are drawn. Although many factors influence the choice of style, the owner's personal preference will be the outstanding consideration.

EXAMPLE

The need to eliminate all front windows prevents traditional styling.
Decision: Contemporary.

BASIC STRUCTURE

The nature of the site and the architectural styling desired provide important clues to the type of basic structure required. Now is the time to make tentative decisions on the size and type of struc-

* In this book, a house will be designed for Mr. and Mrs. A from beginning to end. They are not necessarily an average family, and their home is not to be considered a model for your future designs.

ture, number of floors, and general plan shape. However, if an "alternate" energy system (such as solar heating) is to be specified, the requirements of the system may affect any of these decisions.

Energy system. A "conventional" heating system, such as one provided by an oil furnace or electric panels, will have little effect on the design of a building, but an alternate energy system often determines many of the design elements. For example, a passive solar heating system requires southern orientation to gain solar exposure. An active solar heating system having flat-plate roof panels will need a roof that is sized in multiples of the dimensions of the panels; this then determines the dimensions of the floor plan as well.

EXAMPLE

The plot belonging to Mr. and Mrs. A has an adjacent plot to the south which contains a commercial structure.
Decision: Insufficient southern exposure is available for a passive solar heating system of wall panels, but an active solar heating system would be possible if the commercial structure were not too high to block southern exposure to solar collector roof panels. Or separate solar collectors could be installed in the rear yard beyond the shading of the commercial structure.

Size. The number of rooms and their special requirements are primary considerations since they determine the size of the structure. Usually a balance must be reached between the number of rooms desired and the number that can be afforded.

Careful thought should be given to the number of bedrooms. A common error on the part of young couples with no children or a single child is building a one- or two-bedroom house with the thought that they can sell or add on if another bedroom is needed. A house with fewer than three bedrooms is difficult to sell, and actually adding a room (not finishing an existing one) is more costly than including it in the original plans, not to mention the sacrifice in exterior appearance.

Even minor rooms like bathrooms should be carefully planned to answer questions of: how many? what size? simple or with contemporary sectioned areas? a powder room near the front entrance? These questions, and many others, must be answered before the plans are begun.

EXAMPLES

Mr. and Mrs. A have two children, ages three and nine.
Decision: Three bedrooms: a master bedroom with shower and two additional bedrooms served by one main bathroom.

The A family does much entertaining (parties of four to fifty).
Decision: Provision for living area overflow to family area, basement recreation room, and patio.

Mr. A has built a 12′ power boat which he stores on the property.
Decision: Oversize or double garage, provision for future shop.

Mrs. A desires more storage space than she has had in previous kitchens.
Decision: Utility room with shelves adjacent to kitchen.

Number of floors. The number of floors is a basic decision (Figure 2). Should there be two floors, one and a half floors, one floor, or one of the combinations afforded by split-level designs?

The two-floor home, with sleeping areas on one floor, and living-dining-cooking areas on another, usually provides more "gracious living." Areas are definitely separated, making it easier to clean (or not to clean), to entertain, and to get all the privacy desired. A special effort is needed to relieve the vertical appearance (Figure 3).

The one-and-a-half-story house is an attempt to capture the advantages of the two-story house and to reduce the cost by reducing the outside wall area. (Of course, portions of the bedrooms must have sloping ceilings.) Remember that the use of too many dormers will reduce any cost advantage.

For those who dislike stair climbing and want a low-cost home (two bedrooms, no dining room), the one-floor house is the answer. Remember, however, that a moderately large number of rooms (six or seven) will cost more in a one-floor plan since larger roof and foundation areas are re-

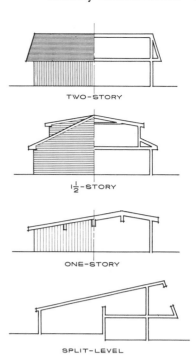

TWO-STORY

1½-STORY

ONE-STORY

SPLIT-LEVEL

Figure 2 *Number of floors.*

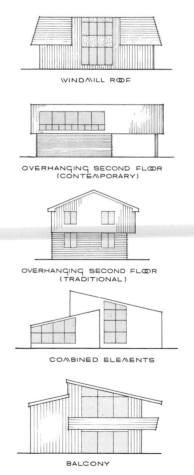

WINDMILL ROOF

OVERHANGING SECOND FLOOR (CONTEMPORARY)

OVERHANGING SECOND FLOOR (TRADITIONAL)

COMBINED ELEMENTS

BALCONY

Figure 3 *Methods of relieving vertical appearance.*

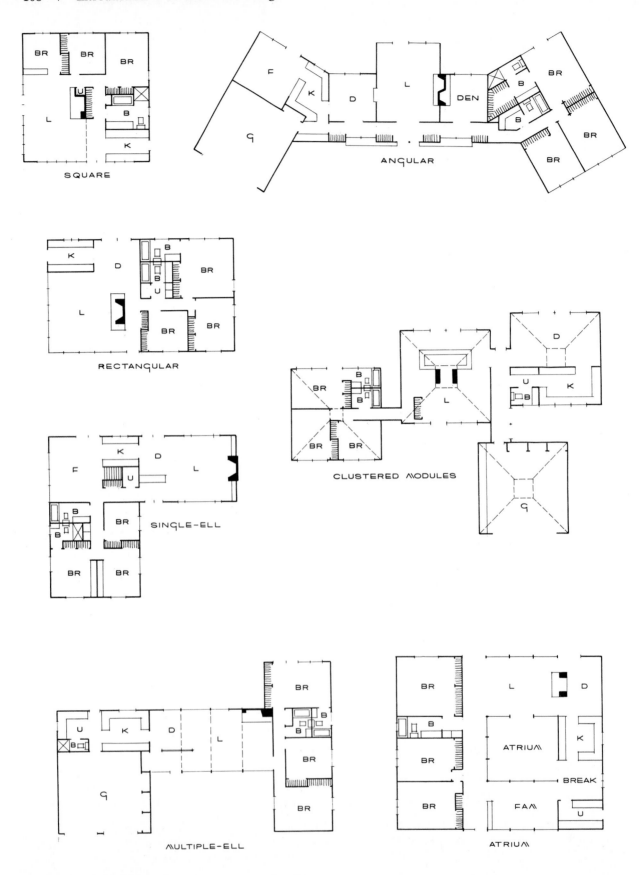

Figure 4 *Plan shapes.*

quired. In general—one floor for four or five rooms, two floors for six or more.*

EXAMPLE

The A residence will require five and one-half rooms; an atrium is desired.
Decision: Group rooms to create atrium; all rooms on one floor for more light into atrium.

Shape of plan. Since the shape of the floor plan affects house styling and cost, it should be given special consideration (Figure 4). In general, it is best to create a plan that is irregular enough to be interesting and to supply the needed wall area for lighting all rooms. But keep in mind that each extraneous corner adds to the total cost. If low cost is a primary objective, a square plan is the best choice since a square encloses a given volume with a minimum of wall area. In practice, a rectangular plan is more often used because of its appearance and planning advantages. The addition of ells (L-shaped, T-shaped, or C-shaped) is costly and should be weighed against the advantages.

EXAMPLE

To illustrate the effect of the number of floors and plan shape on the total house cost, compare the two houses in Figure 5. Each has identical floor area, the differences being the plan shape and the number of floors.
    House A is a two-floor house with 30′ × 30′ = 900 sq. ft. of floor area on each floor, giving a total of 1,800 sq. ft. Its plan is square. House B is a one-floor house with 60′ × 30′ = 1,800 sq. ft. of floor area. Its plan is rectangular. The total area of walls, roof, and slab floor needed to enclose house A is 3,871 sq. ft. The total area needed to enclose house B is 5,583 sq. ft. Although there are some discrepancies in any comparison such as this (house A must have an additional interior floor and heavier foundation), the increase in outside area needed to enclose this one-floor rectangular house over the two-floor square house is:

$$\frac{5,583 - 3,871}{3,871} \times 100 = 44\%$$

	House A	House B
Front and rear elevations	1,080 sq. ft.	1,440 sq. ft.
End elevations	960 sq. ft.	480 sq. ft.
Roof	931 sq. ft.	1,863 sq. ft.
Slab	900 sq. ft.	1,800 sq. ft.
Total	3,871 sq. ft.	5,583 sq. ft.

* Living room, dining room, kitchen, bedroom, den, playroom, and enclosed heated porch are each considered one room. Attached rooms such as dining ell or kitchenette are considered as half-rooms. Bath, porch, breezeway, basement, and attic are not considered rooms.

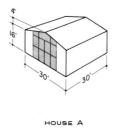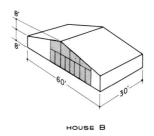

Figure 5

Foundation. There is continuing controversy over whether or not to provide a basement in new house construction. The advantages of a basementless house are:

1. Room for the furnace, water heater, laundry, workshop, storage area, and playroom is more convenient if located on the first floor.
2. A slight saving may be realized due to the omission of floor joists and basement stairway.
3. The house can be kept just as warm and dry as if a basement were built.
4. This is the ideal construction if a ledge is encountered on the land.
5. This may be preferred in areas having a high water table (water level in the ground).

    The advantages of a basement are:

1. The total cubage enclosed by a basement cannot be provided above ground at comparable cost.
2. Due to drainage problems, a basement should be provided when building on a steeply sloping plot.
3. There is little or no saving in omitting the basement from a house built in a cold climate since footings must go 4′-6″ or more in depth.
4. There is little or no saving in omitting a basement from a house of two or more floors.
5. In some localities, zoning laws prohibit basementless construction.
6. Prevailing public opinion is in favor of basements. For this reason, banks and loan agencies will favor a house with a basement.

    As you can see, there is no one simple answer for all conditions, because plot contour, climate, house size, zoning, and cost must be considered. The major advantage of a basementless house is elimination of stair climbing. Rooms above ground level are warmer and lighter, but unfortunately houses without basements are seldom designed with suitable space for all the functions a basement provides.

Studies have been conducted to determine actual savings in eliminating the basement. It has been found that slab construction reduces the cost of the foundation by 25 percent. But if space is added at the first-floor level for the functions of a basement, no saving is realized since additional foundation walls and roof must be provided. A large, rambling, one-floor house will produce the greatest saving if the basement is omitted. This is not true of a house with two or more floors since it requires a more substantial foundation and because in such a house, the basement takes up a smaller proportion of the total house cubage.

In your decision, various combinations should also be considered. Today many houses are built with a basement under one portion and slab construction or a crawl space under another. The split-level house is a good example of this solution. It may have the garage under the sleeping area and the basement under the living-eating area.

EXAMPLE

The A residence will include an emergency shelter and provision for a future recreation room. Also, Mr. A wants a shop for his hobby of woodworking.
Decision: Full or partial basement.

Roof. The choice of a pitched or flat roof is somewhat dependent upon house styling (Figure 6). Although the final choice will probably depend upon personal taste, both possibilities have advantages.

The advantages of a flat roof are:

1. Storage space such as is provided by an attic is more convenient if located on the ground floor.
2. A saving can be realized due to the reduction of framing and omission of the stairway.
3. A complicated floor plan is more easily covered with a flat roof.
4. A properly installed flat roof gives satisfactory service. Snow can accumulate on the roof, serving as insulation in the winter, and a *water-film roof* serves as insulation (reflector) against summer heat.

The advantages of a pitched roof are:

1. A pitched roof with attic provides cheap storage, play, and expansion area. A pitched roof with sloping ceilings provides a major design feature.
2. Certain architectural styles demand the use of a pitched roof.
3. In some localities, zoning laws prohibit flat roof construction.
4. Prevailing public opinion is in favor of a pitched roof.

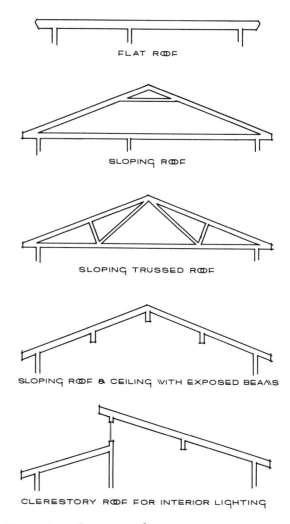

Figure 6   *Common roof types.*

Again, there is no one answer, and many factors must influence the decision. However, if low cost is a primary objective, the flat roof will offer a saving. A flat roof will, of course, restrict the style of the house. As far as function is concerned, flat roofs have been used satisfactorily on urban buildings for centuries.

EXAMPLE

A cathedral ceiling is desired in the living room. Undesirable views suggest windows above eye level to permit light without view.
Decision: Gable or clerestory roof.

Expansion. If low original cost is an object, a house can be very carefully designed so that a room or garage can be added later without a loss

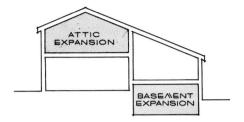

Figure 7   *Plan for future expansion.*

to the exterior appearance either before or after the addition (Figure 7). The simplest forms of expansion are the expansion attic and unfinished basement. The expansion attic will cost the owner only as much as a shed dormer, an unfinished stairway, and some electrical and heating extensions, certainly an economical provision for several additional rooms.

EXAMPLE

Mr. and Mrs. A would like to provide for the possibility of a third child, increased recreational area, and a woodworking shop.
Decision: (1) One child's bedroom to be oversized for possible future use by two children. (2) A full (or partial) basement to be finished into a recreation room and shop at a later date.

BUILDING CODES AND ZONING

Building codes govern building construction while zoning ordinances govern land use. Combined, they serve to protect the health, safety, and welfare of the public.

Building codes. Building codes are regulations which give minimum standards for building design, materials, construction, and maintenance. They are usually administered by the government of local communities. Often a local government adopts one of the model national building codes rather than writing its own unique code. The most popular model national codes are:

1. National Building Code of the American Insurance Association
2. Basic Building Code of the Building Officials and Code Administrators International
3. Uniform Building Code of the International Conference of Building Officials
4. Southern Standard Building Code of the Southern Building Code Congress International

The Basic Building Code predominates in the eastern states of the U.S.—the Uniform Building Code

in the western states and the Southern Standard Building Code in the southern states. In addition there are a number of specialized codes such as the National Electric Code and the National Plumbing Code.

To assure building code compliance, a building inspector must review architectural plans before issuing a building permit to start construction. During and after construction, the inspector visits the site to certify that plans are accurately followed before issuing an occupancy permit.

Zoning ordinances. Zoning ordinances are established by local communities to coordinate land development and promote the health, safety, and welfare of the public. A zoning ordinance includes an official zoning map which establishes four basic types of land development zones:

1. Residential
2. Commercial
3. Industrial
4. Agricultural

These four categories are then further subdivided. For example, residential zones could be established as:

R1   One-family dwelling, church, school, park, or playground
R2   Any R1 use plus two-family dwelling or professional office
R3   Any R2 use plus multiple dwelling, fraternity, or sorority house
R4   Any R3 use plus rooming house or tourist home

Exceptions to zoning ordinances are permitted in special circumstances:

1. *Nonconforming use.* A structure is permitted to be used in a manner not conforming to its zone when the structure was in existence before the zoning district was established. Normal maintenance of a nonconforming structure is permitted, but it cannot be expanded.
2. *Conditional use.* After a public hearing and when found to be in the best interest of the community, facilities such as hospitals, airports, and public utilities may be permitted to be constructed in a zone normally excluding them.
3. *Variance.* Each community has a Zoning Appeals Board which may grant variances from the ordinance when there are requests for minor variations from the zoning laws or unusual circumstances (such as steeply sloping land that prevents the normal setback from a property boundary).

Local zoning ordinances may be quite restrictive as to the position of a house, its cubage in relation to surrounding dwellings, and even its style. A copy of the ordinances can be obtained from any town hall. These should be studied carefully before planning is begun.

EXAMPLE

The most important zoning limitations that apply to the location of the A residence were found to be:

30′ minimum front yard setback
8′ minimum side yard setback
25′ maximum building height

COST

Although we list cost last, it should certainly be a major consideration, influencing nearly every other factor. To be enjoyed, a home must be within the owner's means. No one wants a house that will be impossible to keep up, and might finally be lost. The following chapter on financing relates the house cost to income.

STUDY QUESTIONS

1. Indicate the most suitable style of house to build on the following type of land:
   a. A wide, flat plot
   b. A narrow, flat plot
   c. A steeply sloping plot
2. A friend tells you he has purchased a small, five-and-a-half-room house. What kinds of rooms does that house probably contain?
3. Most families live in three-bedroom houses. If no more than two children are to occupy a single bedroom, show how the three bedrooms should be utilized by the following families:
   a. One son
   b. One son and one daughter
   c. One son and two daughters
   d. Three daughters
   e. Two sons and two daughters
4. List the advantages of:
   a. The two-floor house
   b. The one-and-a-half-floor house
   c. The one-floor house
5. Low-cost housing containing 1,500 sq. ft. of floor area is to be built with a flat roof and full basement. Which of the following alternatives would cost the least to construct? Which would cost the most? Why?
   a. A rectangular one-floor plan
   b. A rectangular two-floor plan
   c. An L-shaped one-floor plan
   d. An L-shaped two-floor plan
6. Should a basement or slab be specified under each of the following conditions?
   a. Low-cost housing on flat land, southern states
   b. Moderate-priced housing, New England states
   c. Known ledge, 2′-6″ below surface
   d. Steeply sloping land
7. Should a flat roof or pitched roof with attic be specified for:
   a. A Cape Cod house
   b. A modern house with a floor plan containing several ells
   c. A retirement cottage for a couple unwilling to climb stairs

LABORATORY PROBLEMS

1. Complete the skeleton outline of primary considerations for your original house design:

Type of plot: _____
House style desired: _____
Number of rooms needed: _____
Number of floors desired: _____
Plan shape desired: _____
Basement or no basement: _____
Flat or sloping roof: _____
Expansion requirements: _____
Zoning limitations: _____
Tentative cost: _____

14 / Financing

The planning and building of a home is an important step in the life of every family. A house is usually the largest single purchase a family will make. There are a number of rules of thumb that will aid in deciding if this purchase—and how large a purchase—can be afforded. However, none of these rules can take into consideration the "sacrifice factor"—that is, that some persons with moderate incomes want their own homes so much that they are willing to make many sacrifices. Others will never be able to make ends meet no matter how high a salary level they reach. The following rules and information should help with these financial decisions. In the final analysis, though, only each individual knows all the details of his present financial status and earning potential.

MORTGAGE CALCULATIONS

Yearly income. The total amount invested in a house and lot should not exceed two and one-half times the yearly income.

EXAMPLE

Mr. and Mrs. A earn $40,000 a year. This would justify their spending $100,000 on a house and lot.

Down payment. A down payment of 25 percent of the total house cost is advisable, although some lending agencies accept 20 percent or less. Of course, the larger the down payment, the smaller the mortgage interest charges.

EXAMPLE

Mr. and Mrs. A decide to make a down payment of 30 percent of the $100,000 total cost. This requires a down payment of $30,000, leaving $70,000 to be borrowed.

Points. In addition to the down payment, there are a number of additional expenses in obtaining a mortgage; often these fees will total about 5 percent of the total mortgage. The largest fee is the bank's service charge: a percentage of the mortgage called "points."

EXAMPLE

Mr. and Mrs. A are charged 4 points for their $70,000 mortgage. Therefore they must pay an additional fee of $2,800 (4% × $70,000 = $2,800).

Weekly income. The monthly shelter expenses (mortgage payments, taxes, insurance) should not exceed the weekly income.

EXAMPLE

Mr. and Mrs. A earn $40,000 a year, or $769 a week. This would justify their spending $769 a month on a house. Table II shows that a 15-year mortgage at 10 percent on $70,000 ($100,000 total cost minus the $30,000 down payment) would be about $752 a month ($537.31 for $50,000 + $214.93 for $20,000 = $752.24). This allows only $17 leeway for taxes and insurance. A 20-year mortgage at 10 percent would be about $636 a month, allowing $133 toward taxes and insurance.

Construction loan. A mortgage can be obtained only on a finished house. During building, a construction loan is obtained, usually at the same interest rate as the mortgage.

Table I   *Monthly Payments on Mortgages at 8 Percent**

Amount of Mortgage	Length of Mortgage			
	10 yr.	*15 yr.*	*20 yr.*	*25 yr.*
$10,000	$121.33	$ 95.57	$ 83.65	$ 77.19
$20,000	$242.66	$191.14	$167.29	$154.37
$30,000	$363.99	$286.70	$250.94	$231.55
$40,000	$485.32	$382.27	$334.58	$308.73
$50,000	$606.64	$477.83	$418.23	$385.91

* Taxes and insurance are normally added to above payments.

Table II   *Monthly Payments on Mortgages at 10 Percent**

Amount of Mortgage	Length of Mortgage			
	10 yr.	*15 yr.*	*20 yr.*	*25 yr.*
$10,000	$132.16	$107.47	$ 96.51	$ 90.88
$20,000	$264.31	$214.93	$193.01	$181.75
$30,000	$396.46	$322.39	$289.51	$272.62
$40,000	$528.61	$429.85	$386.01	$363.49
$50,000	$660.76	$537.31	$482.52	$454.36

* Taxes and insurance are normally added to above payments.

Table III   *Monthly Payments on Mortgages at 12 Percent**

Amount of Mortgage	Length of Mortgage			
	10 yr.	*15 yr.*	*20 yr.*	*25 yr.*
$10,000	$143.48	$120.02	$110.11	$105.33
$20,000	$286.95	$240.04	$220.22	$210.65
$30,000	$430.42	$360.06	$330.33	$315.97
$40,000	$573.89	$480.07	$440.44	$421.29
$50,000	$717.36	$600.09	$550.55	$526.62

* Taxes and insurance are normally added to above payments.

Table IV   *Monthly Payments on Mortgages at 14 Percent**

Amount of Mortgage	Length of Mortgage			
	10 yr.	*15 yr.*	*20 yr.*	*25 yr.*
$10,000	$155.27	$133.18	$124.36	$120.38
$20,000	$310.54	$266.35	$248.71	$240.76
$30,000	$465.80	$399.53	$373.06	$361.13
$40,000	$621.07	$532.70	$497.41	$481.51
$50,000	$776.34	$665.88	$621.77	$601.89

* Taxes and insurance are normally added to above payments.

Mortgage. Nearly every home bought today is financed by means of a mortgage. Most of these mortgages provide for uniform monthly payments consisting of interest, amortization, and taxes. As time passes, the proportion of the monthly payments going toward amortization (that is, payment of the principal) increases, and the amount going toward interest decreases. Thus the early payments are nearly all interest payments, and the last payments are nearly all amortization payments. If the property tax increases, the amount of the monthly payment increases proportionately.

A good mortgage should include the following features:

1. Monthly payments, which include taxes and sometimes insurance.
2. Prepayment of part or all of the mortgage before the end of the period if the borrower wishes.
3. An open-ended clause allowing the borrower to reborrow a sum equal to the amount amortized for the purpose of expanding or finishing.

Mortgage interest rate. A home mortgage interest rate varies from place to place and year to year. Bank interest rates have ranged from 8 to 18 percent, an FHA-insured (Federal Housing Administration) mortgage is lower, but added charges raise the total to approximately the same cost. For example, *mortgage insurance* (to protect the *bank* against loss on the mortgage) may add a 1 percent insurance premium.

Length of mortgage. In normal times, mortgage payments should be made over as short a term as possible. But in times of expected continuing inflation, long-term mortgages have the advantage of repayment with money of lessened value.

EXAMPLE

Mr. and Mrs. A calculated they would have to pay a total of $191,000 on a 25-year mortgage ($70,000 amortization and $121,000 interest) at 10 percent. They decided on the fifteen-year mortgage since they would pay only $135,000 total ($70,000 amortization and $65,000 interest).

Satisfaction piece. When the last payment is made, the bank will send a document stating that the mortgage has been paid in full. This is called a *satisfaction piece.* Also, the mortgage will be returned. The satisfaction piece should be recorded; the mortgage can be burned.

Other types of mortgages. In addition to the conventional mortgage described above, a number of nonconventional types of mortgages are available each having some advantages and disadvantages. The most popular types are graduated payment, adjustable rate, and renegotiated rate mortgages.

Graduated payments. Mortgage interest rates have become so high that many people cannot afford the payments. Graduated payment mortgages, however, have lower payments in early years when the homeowner's income is modest, but higher payments in later years when income is expected to be greater. For example, the monthly payments for a $50,000, 30-year, graduated payment mortgage at 10 percent would be $346.47 during the first year, but would increase to $497.41 after the fifth year (*see* Table VII). In comparison, monthly payments for a conventional 10 percent mortgage would be $454.36. Because amortization begins slowly, the graduated payment mortgage has a greater total cost.

Adjustable rates. The interest rate on an adjustable rate mortgage depends on some economic index (such as a Treasury bill index) and may change each year. Usually the interest rate increase is limited to 2 percent per year with a maximum increase of 5 percent over the life of the mortgage. The interest rate may also decrease but only if a previous increase has occurred. Adjustable rate mortgages do have the advantage of an initial interest rate that is about 1 percent lower than that of a conventional mortgage.

Renegotiated rates. The interest rate on a renegotiated rate mortgage remains constant over a given period—usually five years—at which time the rate is renegotiated. An interest rate increase is usually limited to 3 percent every five years. Renegotiated rate mortgages also have interest rates that are lower than conventional mortgages.

COST ESTIMATION

To avoid building an unaffordable house, an accurate estimate of cost is needed. There are two commonly used methods of estimating house cost. One method is based on the volume, or cubage, of the building, the other on the floor area.

Cubage: $2.00–$10.00/cu. ft.
Floor area: $20.00–$30.00/sq. ft. inexpensive, unfinished
$30.00–$50.00/sq. ft. moderate
$50.00–$100.00/sq. ft. good materials and workmanship

The unit cost of a house (by cubage or floor area) will vary considerably from one location to another and even from one year to another. Also, a small house will have a greater unit cost than a large one, since some expenses (such as the heating plant) remain almost the same regardless of the size of the house.

Calculation by cubage. Calculations for volume include all enclosed areas, such as the garage, basement, attic, dormers, chimneys, and enclosed porches. Outside dimensions are used (from the

Table V *Monthly Payments on Mortgages at 16 Percent**

Amount of Mortgage	Length of Mortgage			
	10 yr.	15 yr.	20 yr.	25 yr.
$10,000	$167.52	$144.72	$139.13	$135.89
$20,000	$335.03	$289.43	$278.26	$271.78
$30,000	$502.54	$434.14	$417.38	$407.67
$40,000	$670.06	$578.85	$556.51	$543.56
$50,000	$837.57	$723.56	$695.63	$679.45

* Taxes and insurance are normally added to above payments.

Table VI *Monthly Payments on Mortgages at 18 Percent**

Amount of Mortgage	Length of Mortgage			
	10 yr.	15 yr.	20 yr.	25 yr.
$10,000	$180.19	$161.05	$154.34	$151.75
$20,000	$360.38	$322.09	$308.67	$303.49
$30,000	$540.56	$483.13	$463.00	$455.23
$40,000	$720.75	$644.17	$617.33	$606.98
$50,000	$900.93	805.22	$771.66	$758.72

* Taxes and insurance are normally added to above payments.

Table VII *Monthly Payments on a Graduated Payment Mortgage ($50,000 for 25 years at 10%)*

First year	$346.47
Second year	$372.46
Third year	$400.39
Fourth year	$430.42
Fifth year	$462.70
Remaining years	$497.41

outside of walls, roof, and floor slab). Open porches and areaways are included at half volume.

Calculation by area. All enclosed areas are included in the area calculations, but some are reduced in the following proportions:

Garage: $\frac{2}{3}$
Enclosed porch: $\frac{2}{3}$
Open porch: $\frac{1}{2}$
Unfinished basement: $\frac{1}{2}$
    (finished basement: full area)
Carport: $\frac{1}{2}$

Land cost. The total developed land cost includes the cost of the lot, street, sidewalk, water pipeline, and sanitary sewer. The total developed land cost typically ranges from 15 percent to 25 percent of the cost of a residence.

REDUCING COST

Many persons cut building costs by doing some of the construction themselves. Figure 1 shows the areas which will produce the greatest savings. The percentages on this pie chart represent percentages of total cost of a wood-framed house. Each category can be further split fifty-fifty, half of each category representing labor, half material. Several thousand dollars should be added to cover miscellaneous building equipment, landscaping, and other expenses.

Warning. Anyone who has recently built a home will tell you that they have spent 10 to 25 percent more than they originally intended. Indeed, ex-apartment-dwellers will sometimes spend over 50 percent more than their estimated cost when they are furnishing and buying tools and equipment.

STUDY QUESTIONS

1. The *total cost* of a house should not exceed
_____.
2. The *monthly cost* of a house should not exceed
_____.
3. When obtaining a house mortgage, an advisable down payment is _____.
4. Distinguish between:
  a. The construction loan and the house mortgage
  b. Mortgage interest and mortgage amortization

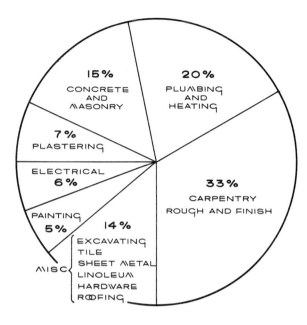

Figure 1 *Where your building dollar goes.*

  c. Area cost estimation and volume cost estimation
  d. Graduated payment, adjustable rate, and renegotiated rate mortgages

LABORATORY PROBLEMS

1. Obtain the mortgage interest rate and an interest table from your local bank. Prepare a table of monthly mortgage payments similar to that shown in Table I.
2. Mr. and Mrs. B have a yearly salary of $50,000. Prepare a list of financial considerations for them as follows:
  a. Yearly income:_____
  b. Weekly income:_____
  c. House cost:_____
  d. House area:_____
  (Use average construction cost)
3. Prepare a list of financial considerations as indicated in problem 2 to meet the requirements of a client as assigned by your instructor.
4. Prepare a list of financial considerations for your original house design as follows:
  a. Estimated yearly income:_____
  b. Weekly income:_____
  c. House cost:_____
  d. Amount of mortgage:_____
  e. Length of mortgage:_____
  f. Interest rate of mortgage:_____
  g. Amount of down payment:_____
  h. Amount of monthly payments:_____
  i. House area:_____

15 / The Program

The first problem confronting an architect engaged to design a home is to find the type of house that will best suit the family's requirements and budget. To prevent items from being forgotten, a list of requirements is drawn up at the first meeting between the owner and architect. This list is called the *program*.

In studying architectural drafting, you are probably planning your own home, and thus you are taking the parts of both owner and architect. However, you will find that you should still prepare a program to help you keep your goals clearly in mind.

Your program should look somewhat like the program for the A residence.

GENERAL REQUIREMENTS

Size: 2,500–3,000 sq. ft.
Cost: Lot: $20,000. House: $80,000
Style: Contemporary.
Exterior finish: Vertical board and batten siding, brick or stone.
Roof: No preference.
Second floor: No.
Basement: Full or partial basement to be finished into recreation room later.

ORIENTATION

Living: West (to view).
Dining: No preference.
Kitchen: No preference.
Master bedroom: West (to view).
Other bedrooms: Not west.

ROOM REQUIREMENTS

Living area: Conversational area (fireplace with raised hearth), bridge area, and music area. Cathedral ceiling desired.
Dining area: Informal (combine with kitchen or family room).
Kitchen: U-type kitchen with baking island, built-in-wall ovens, burners, dishwasher, and garbage disposer. Allow for refrigerator-freezer and breakfast bar. Connect to garage.
Utility room: For storage of canned foods and miscellaneous items.
Family area: Include if possible without exceeding cost limitations. Provide fireplace if possible.
Bedrooms: Master bedroom with double bed, separate closets for Mr. and Mrs. A, large picture window view of Mount Nittany, and attached bathroom with shower. Separate bedrooms for two children· Mark, age nine; and Beth, age three. Beth's bedroom adjacent to master bedroom, if possible.
Hobby room: Use family room or basement.
Entertainment: Much entertaining (parties of 4 to 50).
Bathrooms: Main bathroom with toilet, lavatory, bathtub, and shower; master bathroom with toilet, lavatory, and stall shower; and powder room with toilet and lavatory (or use main bathroom).
Laundry: Locate on first floor. Provide for electric washer and dryer.
Storage: Two closets in master bedroom, one in other bedrooms, linen closets, large front entrance guest coat closet, broom closet, garden tools.
Basement: Unfinished. Future use will be general recreation, table tennis, snack bar and workshop. Provide outside entrance to future workshop.
Garage: One-car, attached, 12′ power boat.
Porch: None.
Emergency shelter: For four persons.
Terrace: To rear of plot next to living area.
Garden: Flowers, not vegetables.
Fireplaces: Living area, family area, and recreation room.
Miscellaneous: Front entrance vestibule preferred. Atrium or clerestory required due to narrow lot and unpleasant views.

ROOM SIZES*

Living area: 15′ × 25′
Dining and family area: 15′ × 20′
Kitchen: 12′ × 15′
Master bedroom: 12′ × 15′
Other bedrooms: 10′ × 12′, 12′ × 15′
Bathrooms: Average size.
Hall width: 3′ to 3½′
Stair width: 3′ to 3½′
Closets: Large.
Garage: 14′ × 21′

MECHANICAL REQUIREMENTS

Plumbing: Copper tubing, several outside bibbs.
Heating: No exposed radiators.
Air conditioning: Omit, but plan for future addition.
Electrical: Outside convenience outlets, silent switches.
Special equipment: Telephone wiring to each room. Television conduits to living room, family room, and master bedroom.

SITE

Location: West side of Outer Drive.
Size: 75′ × 140′ deep.
Zoning limitations: 30′ minimum front yard setback. 8′ minimum side yard setback, 25′ maximum height.
Best view: West to Mount Nittany.
Trees: Eight birch, five sumac, one cherry (remove as few as possible).
Garden wanted: As extensive as possible.

After studying this program, it might be well to turn to the final plans (Chapter 21) and elevations (Chapter 24) to discover how the final product compares with the program. You will notice that nearly every requirement has been satisfied.

LABORATORY PROBLEMS

1. Complete the program for your original house design using the following skeleton outline:

General requirements

Size:_____
Cost:_____
Style:_____
Exterior finish:_____

Roof:_____
Second floor:_____
Basement:_____

Orientation

Living:_____
Dining:_____
Kitchen:_____
Master bedroom:_____
Other bedrooms:_____

Room requirements

Living room or living area:_____
Dining room or dining area:_____
Kitchen:_____
Utility room:_____
Family room:_____
Master bedroom:_____
Other bedrooms:_____
Den or study:_____
Bathrooms:_____
Laundry:_____
Storage:_____
Basement:_____
Garage:_____
Porch:_____
Terrace:_____
Fireplace:_____
Miscellaneous (special preferences or provisions for pets, hobbies, etc.): _____

Room sizes

Living room:_____
Dining room:_____
Kitchen:_____
Master bedroom:_____
Other bedrooms:_____
Bathrooms:_____
Hall width:_____
Stair width:_____
Closets:_____
Garage:_____

Mechanical requirements

Plumbing:_____
Heating:_____
Air conditioning:_____
Electrical:_____
Special equipment:_____

Site

Location:_____
Size:_____
Zoning limitations:_____
Best views:_____
Trees:_____
Garden:_____

* Note: Room sizes should be determined only after careful comparison with familiar rooms of known size.

IV / Components

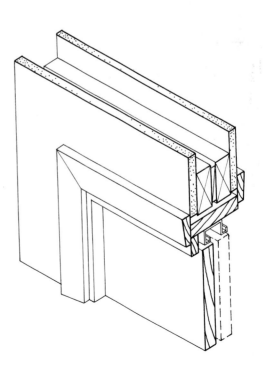

16 / Windows

The architectural drafter should be thoroughly familiar with *all* the building components to be specified and detailed. However, the window is probably the most important single component in the design of a successful building. The proper selection and placement of windows is necessary for aesthetic as well as functional reasons. In addition to providing light and air, windows can change the interior of a room by providing framed views or window walls, and can change the exterior of a building by the fenestration (Figure 1). The energy costs of a building may be dramatically affected by the size and orientation of windows. For example, heating costs in cold climates are increased by the heat lost through windows on north-facing walls, and cooling costs in warm climates are increased by the heat gained through windows on south-facing walls.

Figure 1   *A successful design created by attractive fenestration.*

TYPES

There are many different types of windows now on the market. Some of the most commonly used are:

Casement
Awning
Hopper
Projected
Sliding
Double-hung
Pivoted
Jalousie
Fixed

CASEMENT
SASH LOCK

CASEMENT
HINGES

These windows can be obtained in many metals, wood, and clad wood (wood with plastic or metal sheathing) in nearly any size ranging from small lavatory windows to entire window walls. Let us look at each in turn.

Casement. A casement window (Figure 2) is hinged at the side and usually swings outward so that the inside drapes are not disturbed. Screens, then, are hung on the inside. When more than two casement windows are installed side by side, it is often the practice to specify fixed-sash for the middle windows, and a hinged-sash at each end.

When the sash is hinged at the top, it is called an *awning* window; when the sash is hinged at the bottom, it is called a *hopper* window. To prevent rain from entering the open windows, awning windows swing outward and hopper windows swing inward.

Projected. A projected window (Figure 3) is somewhat different from a casement window in that some form of linkage other than the hinge is used. A projected window will swing open and slide at the same time. Projected windows may

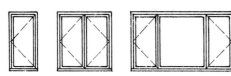

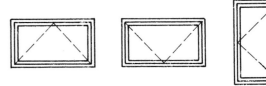

Figure 2 *Casement windows.*

Figure 3 *Projected windows.*

also be classified as casement, awning, or hopper according to the direction of swing. Metal projected windows are commonly used on commercial buildings, whereas wooden casement (non-projected) windows are commonly used on residences.

Sliding. Sliding or gliding windows (Figure 4) are designed to run on horizontal tracks in pairs.

The tracks are curved so that the sash are in line when closed but will move past each other when opened. Most sliding windows contain sash that can be removed from the frame for easy cleaning. The screen is installed on the outside of the window.

Double-hung. The double-hung window (Figure 5) is usually specified for Colonial-type

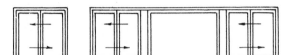

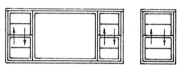

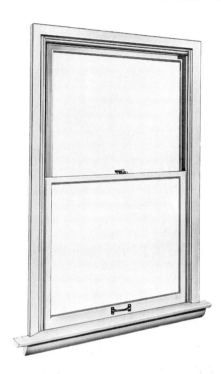

Figure 4   *Sliding windows.*

Figure 5   *Double-hung windows.*

Figure 6 *Trapezoidal fixed window units.*

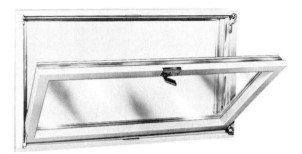

Figure 7 *Basement windows.*

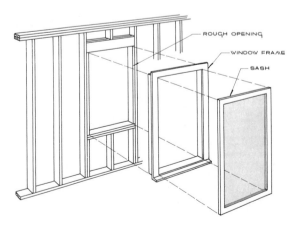

Figure 8 *Window installation.*

houses. This window contains two sash which slide in vertical tracks. A spring-balance arrangement is used to counterbalance the weight of the sash and hold them in any desired position. The sash are easily removed for window cleaning. Double-hung windows may be obtained with self-storing screens and storm windows.

Pivoted. The pivoted window revolves on two pivots—one at the center of the top of the sash, and the other at the center of the bottom of the sash. Not often specified for houses, the pivoted widow is common in taller buildings because of the ease of cleaning.

Jalousie. The jalousie window is a series of small awning panes, all operated together. It has not become very popular because the view through it is interrupted by the many intersections.

Fixed. When views and light are desired without ventilation (as is often true of air-conditioned buildings), fixed windows are specified. Large fixed windows are sometimes called *picture windows*. Some fixed windows are designed so that they can be opened only by window washers for cleaning. Fixed windows are stocked in both rectangular and trapezoidal shapes (Figure 6 and Appendix B).

Basement windows. The most often specified basement window is a reversible awning-hopper window (Figure 7). The sash is designed so that it can be easily removed from the frame and installed to swing up (awning) or down (hopper). In both cases the swing is toward the inside. Since a basement window is installed at the inner side of the foundation wall, there is no danger of rain entering. The screen is installed on the outside of the frame.

INSTALLATION

Before studying specifications and the detailing of windows, it is necessary to understand how a window is installed in a building wall (Figure 8). The glass and its immediate framing members are called the *sash*. Except in fixed windows, the sash is designed to be opened for ventilation or entirely removed for easy cleaning. The sash is surrounded by the *window frame,* which is permanently fastened to the rough wall (studs). The window frame has an L-shaped cross section, the outer portion of which is called the *blind stop.* The blind stop helps to properly position the frame in the rough opening. Stock windows are obtained with the sash already installed in the frame so that the entire window unit can be set into the rough opening. The rough opening is constructed several inches larger than the window frame to allow for leveling the window. After the window is in place, exterior and interior trim is used to close the cracks between the frame and the rough opening.

TERMINOLOGY

Many special terms are used to describe the various parts of a window. Figure 9 shows a cutaway

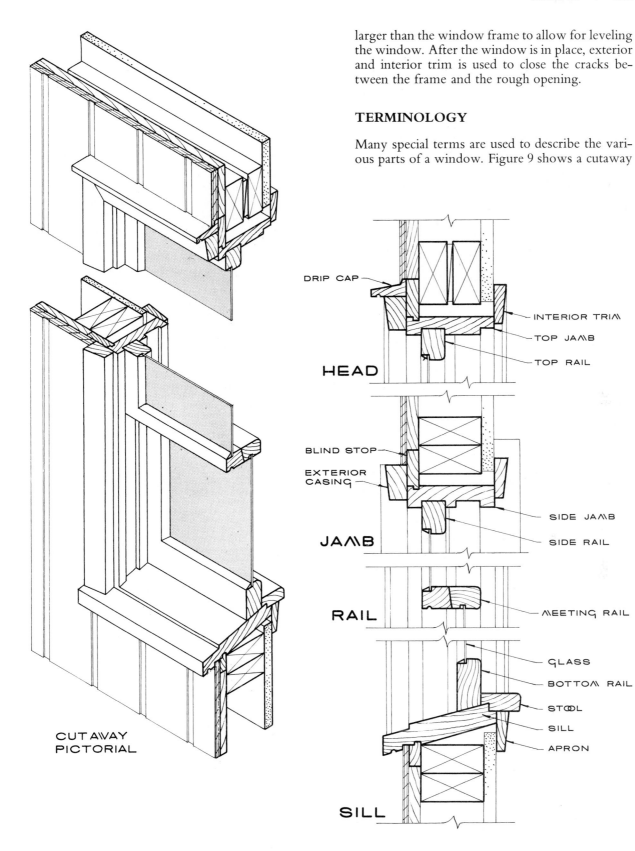

CUTAWAY PICTORIAL

HEAD

DRIP CAP

INTERIOR TRIM

TOP JAMB

TOP RAIL

JAMB

BLIND STOP

EXTERIOR CASING

SIDE JAMB

SIDE RAIL

RAIL

MEETING RAIL

GLASS

BOTTOM RAIL

STOOL

SILL

APRON

SILL

SECTION

Figure 9 *Double-hung window in a wood-frame wall.*

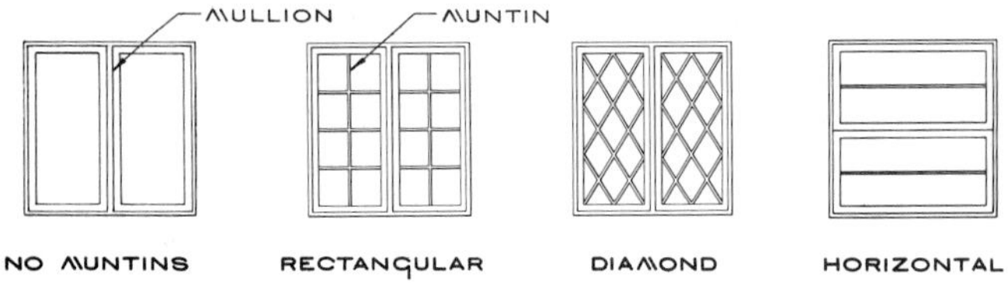

Figure 10 *Removable muntins.*

pictorial of a double-hung window and the corresponding sectional details. The terms *head, jamb, rail,* and *sill* indicate that the sectional cuts were taken through the head (the upper horizontal members), jamb (side vertical members), meeting rail (middle horizontal members), and sill (lower horizontal members).

Sash. The members of the upper sash are called *top rail, meeting rail,* and *side rails.* The lower sash members are called *meeting rail, bottom rail,* and *side rails.*

Window frame. The members of the window frame are called *top jamb, side jamb, sill,* and *blind stop* (or *windbreaker*).

Interior trim. The interior trim and *apron* cover the crack between the window frame and the interior finished wall.

Exterior casing. The exterior casing (which may be called *trim*) also covers wall cracks. In addition, it serves as the frame around the *storm sash* or *screens.*

Drip cap. The drip cap prevents water from seeping into the window head. Note the *drip groove* on the underside which prevents water from seeping inward underneath the drip cap. *Flashing* can be used in place of the wooden drip cap.

Double glazing. A second glass pane may be installed on the sash, creating a dead-air space to provide insulation and prevent condensation on the inside pane. Also, the outside pane can be manufactured with a micro-thin transparent coating, called *low-E glass,* which reflects outside heat in summer and inside heat in winter.

Mullions and muntins are shown in Figure 10. Mullions are members (usually vertical) that separate adjacent windows. Muntins are smaller members used to subdivide large glass areas. Many manufacturers offer removable muntins so that the windows may be subdivided to any taste. Also, these muntins may be removed for easy cleaning.

SPECIFYING WINDOWS

The type of window to be specified for a building will be determined by the building style and the client's desire. Once the style is decided, the size must be determined from the many sizes available in each style. As an example, let us study the Andersen casement windows. Six window heights are obtainable, each height recommended for a different condition. Figure 11 shows how these different window sizes will fit into different types of rooms.

Manufacturers do not offer a wide variety of window widths since wide windows are obtained by specifying a number of individual units side by side. Andersen casements may be obtained in four widths, CR (reduced casement), CN, C, and CW (wide casement).

Each manufacturer has its own set of window sizes and catalog numbers. To simplify window specifications, tables showing the size and numbers may be obtained from the manufacturers. Tables for Andersen casement, sliding, double-hung, and basement windows and a table for Pella fixed trapezoidal windows (much used in contemporary design) are shown in Appendix B.

DETAILING

In addition to supplying size tables for the convenience of architectural drafters, manufacturers also supply *tracing details.* These tracing details

Andersen Catalog Number	Rough Opening Height	Recommended for:
2	2′-0⅝″	Extreme privacy
3	3′-0½″	Lavatory, Bedroom
35	3′-5⅜″	Kitchen
4	4′-0½″	Dining area
5	5′-0⅜″	Living area
6	6′-0⅜″	Solar wall
Andersen Catalog Number	**Rough Opening Width**	**Preferred for:**
CR	1′-5½″	Emphasis on vertical lines
CN	1′-9″	General applications
C	2′-0⅝″	General applications
CW	2′-4⅞″	Wider uninterrupted view

may be slipped under tracing vellum and all applicable details copied. Although the manufacturer attempts to supply tracing details for nearly all possible types of construction, some modification is often necessary to fit the window into a particular type of wall. Tracing details for Andersen casement, sliding, double-hung, and basement windows are shown in Appendix B.

WINDOW ARRANGEMENTS

Stock windows may be stacked horizontally or vertically to obtain countless distinctive arrangements. Figure 12 shows various combinations of Pella casement and fixed windows. Figures 13–16 show some arrangements of Andersen windows.

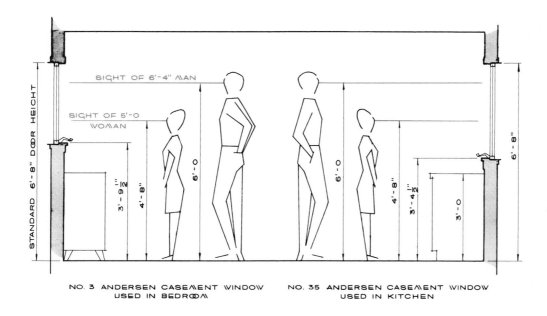

NO. 3 ANDERSEN CASEMENT WINDOW
USED IN BEDROOM

NO. 35 ANDERSEN CASEMENT WINDOW
USED IN KITCHEN

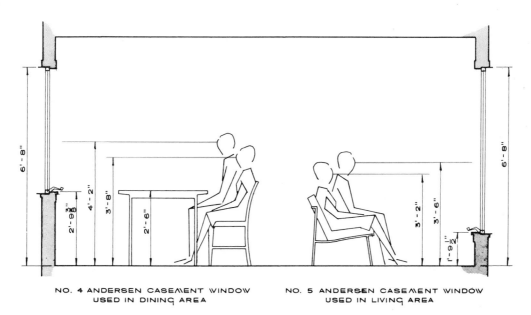

NO. 4 ANDERSEN CASEMENT WINDOW
USED IN DINING AREA

NO. 5 ANDERSEN CASEMENT WINDOW
USED IN LIVING AREA

Figure 11   *Selection of window height.*

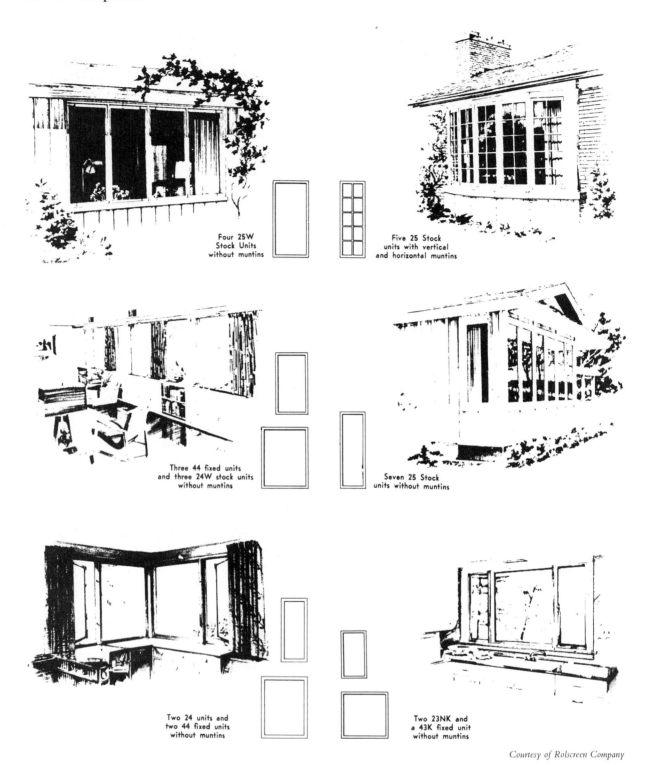

Four 25W
Stock Units
without muntins

Five 25 Stock
units with vertical
and horizontal muntins

Three 44 fixed units
and three 24W stock units
without muntins

Seven 25 Stock
units without muntins

Two 24 units and
two 44 fixed units
without muntins

Two 23NK and
a 43K fixed unit
without muntins

Courtesy of Rolscreen Company

Figure 12   *Arrangements of casement and fixed window combinations.*

Figure 14   *A window wall for a select view.*

Figure 13   *Gliding units combined to form a patio window wall.*

STUDY QUESTIONS

1. List the types of windows and indicate how each is opened.
2. Define these window terms:
   a. Sash
   b. Window frame
   c. Rough opening
   d. Blind stop
   e. Apron
   f. Casing
   g. Stool
   h. Removable muntin
   i. Clad window
   j. Low-E glass
3. What is the difference between these window terms?
   a. Head, jamb, and sill
   b. Top rail, bottom rail, and meeting rail
   c. Storm sash and double glazing
   d. Drip cap and drip groove
   e. Mullion and muntin
   f. Blind stop and windbreaker
   g. Awning window and hopper window
   h. Awning window and jalousie window
   i. Fixed window and picture window
   j. Pivoted window and projected window

Figure 15   *Fixed and projected units combined.*

LABORATORY PROBLEMS

1. Prepare a classroom illustration showing:
   a. Types of windows
   b. Window terminology
2. (For the advanced student) Design a type of window entirely different from those commonly used.
3. Complete the design of the windows for the building assigned by your instructor.
4. Complete the design of the windows for your original building design.

Figure 16   *A dramatic window arrangement of fixed and awning units.*

17 / Doors

Doors, like windows, are important components in the design of a successful building. The main entrance door is particularly important, since it will be the first detail experienced by visitors. The other doors should also be carefully chosen; a building can be no better than its details.

TYPES

Doors are available in a wide range of types and materials. Residential doors most commonly used are:

Hinged
Sliding
Folding
Accordion

These doors may be obtained in single and double units. Wood is usually used, but metal and glass doors are also popular.

Hinged. Hinged doors (Figure 1) may be flush, paneled, or louvered. The flush door (Figure 6) is most popular due to its perfectly clean lines and low cost. It may be either solid-core or hollow-core. The solid-core flush door is constructed of solid wood covered with wood veneer and is preferred for exterior doors. The hollow-core flush door has an interior of honeycombed wood strips also covered by veneer. The most popular veneers are mahogany and birch.

Paneled doors consist of Ponderosa pine members framing wood or glass panels. The framing members are called *top rail, bottom rail,* and *side rails.* The midheight rail is called a *lock rail.*

Figure 1   *Hinged doors.*

Figure 2   *Sliding doors.*

Louvered doors are constructed like paneled doors, but with louvers replacing the panels. They are often used as closet doors to permit circulation of air.

Hinged doors may be installed as a *double* unit (two doors, one hung on the right jamb, the other on the left) to allow a larger and more dramatic passageway. Hinged double doors with glass panels are called *French doors*. A *Dutch door*, on the other hand, is a single door that has been cut in halves so that the top half can be opened for light and air without opening the bottom half. Simulated Dutch doors which open like ordinary doors are specified to give the appearance of a Dutch door without the function. A door hung on special hinges which permit it to swing in both directions is called a *swinging door* and is often used between the kitchen and dining area to permit operation by a simple push.

Sliding. Sliding doors (Figure 2) are used to save the floor space that is required for hinged doors. They are especially useful in small rooms. Sliding doors are hung from a metal track screwed into the door frame head. A single sliding door slides into a pocket built into the wall. Double sliding doors are usually installed so that one door slides in front of the other. This has the disadvantage of opening up only one half of the doorway space at a time. Exterior sliding doors of glass (Figure 7) serve the double purpose of a doorway and window wall.

Folding. A folding door (Figure 3) is partially a hinged and partially a sliding door. Two leaves are hinged together, one being also hinged to the door jamb. The other leaf has a single hanger sliding in a track. Although some floor space is required for the folding door, it has the advantage of completely opening up the doorway space. Single (total of two leaves) and double (total of four leaves) units are available.

Accordion. A door that operates on the principle of the folding door, but contains many narrow leaves, is called an *accordion door* (Figure 4). These leaves may be made of hinged wood or a flexible plastic material. Accordion or folding partitions are used to provide an entire movable wall between rooms. The folds of the retracted partition may be left exposed or hidden by a wall pocket (Figures 8 and 9).

MATERIALS

In addition to wood doors, metal-clad wood doors (called *kalamein doors*) or hollow metal doors are

Figure 3   *Folding doors.*

Figure 4   *Accordion doors.*

used for fireproofing and strength. Metal door frames (called *door bucks*) are also available. Even all-glass doors are used. Bronze, aluminum, and glass doors are commonly used for public buildings, but wood remains the popular choice for residential construction. Figure 5 shows how a door frame fits into the rough opening in the same way as a window. The door, in turn, fits into the door frame.

TERMINOLOGY

Figure 10 shows a cutaway pictorial of a hinged exterior door, and the corresponding sectional details. Figure 11 shows the pictorial and details of a

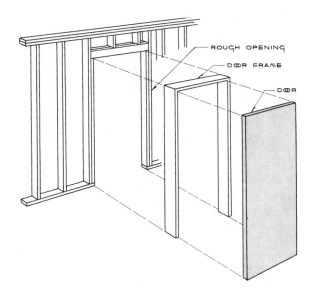

Figure 5 *Door installation.*

Figure 6 *Typical light and louver openings in flush doors.*

Figure 7 *A window wall of sliding glass doors.*

Figure 8 *Folding doors offer maximum flexibility and efficiency (Pella 558 series for $5\frac{5}{8}''$ panels).*

Figure 9 *Heavier folding partitions can fill openings of any width (Pella 1058 series for $10\frac{5}{8}''$ panels).*

sliding interior door. Notice that a saddle is used to weatherproof the exterior door, but such protection is not necessary for the interior door.

SPECIFYING DOORS

The type of door to be specified for each location will be determined by functional and aesthetic

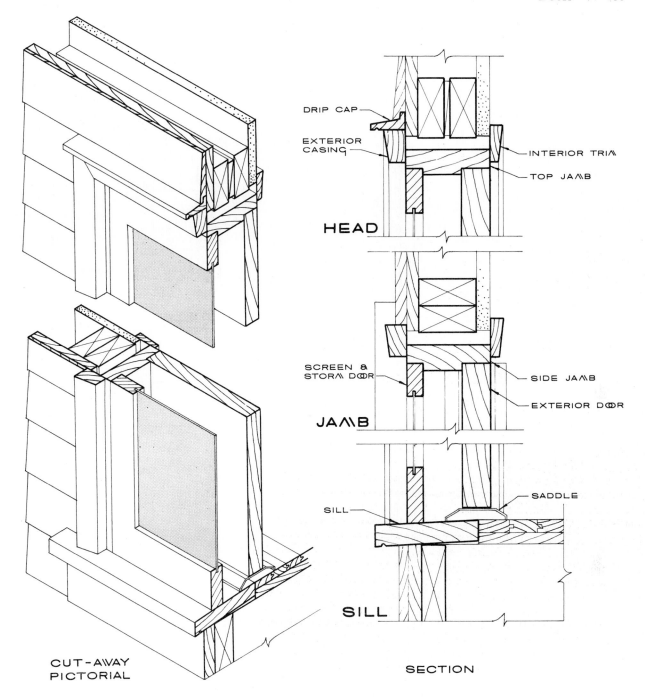

Figure 10 *An exterior door in a wood-frame wall.*

considerations. Manufacturers' catalogs should be consulted for available styles and sizes. In general, exterior doors are $1\frac{3}{4}''$ thick and interior doors are $1\frac{3}{8}''$ thick. Widths from 2'-0 to 3'-0 in even inches are available, although some manufacturers offer doors as narrow as 1'-6'' and as wide as 4'-0. Residential doors are obtainable in 6'-6'' to 7'-0 heights in even inches. The most popular height is 6'-8''. See Appendix C.

Interior doors: $2'-6'' \times 6'-8'' \times 1\frac{3}{8}''$
Front entrance door: $3'-0 \ \times 6'-8'' \times 1\frac{3}{4}''$
Other entrance doors: $2'-8'' \times 6'-8'' \times 1\frac{3}{4}''$

The rough opening must be considerably larger than the door sizes. The frame for a 3'-0 × 6'-8'' door, for instance, would require a $3'-2\frac{3}{4}'' \times 6'-11''$ (top of subfloor to bottom of header) rough opening.

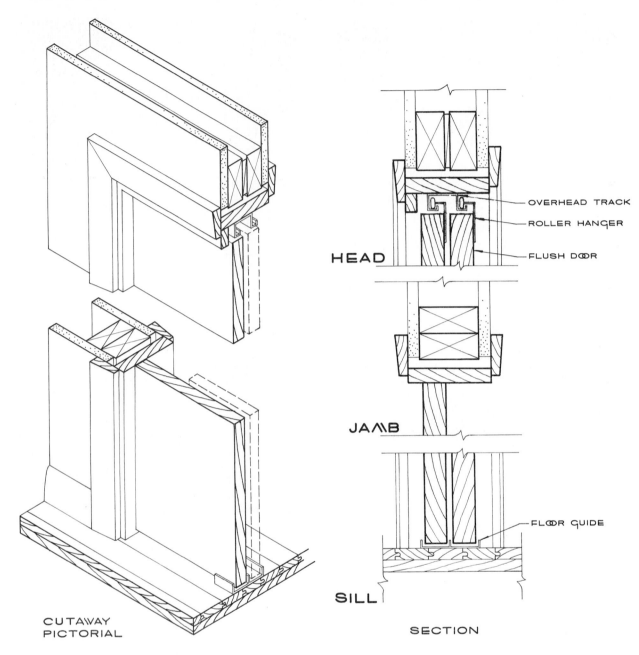

HEAD

OVERHEAD TRACK

ROLLER HANGER

FLUSH DOOR

JAMB

FLOOR GUIDE

SILL

CUTAWAY
PICTORIAL

SECTION

Figure 11   *A double sliding door in an interior wall.*

ENTRANCES

The entrance provides the first close introduction to a building and therefore should be attractive and representative as well as functional (Figures 12–15). A completely designed entrance may be obtained from stock. Details and sizes are shown in Appendix C. Sidelights are obtainable as separate units in a variety of sizes, colors, and patterns (Figure 16). A selection of contemporary and traditional entranceways is shown in Figure 17.

HARDWARE

The hardware for doors is specified by indicating the desired manufacturer and catalog number in a hardware schedule. Some of the many hardware items are:

Door butts (hinges)
Lock sets
Doorstops
Door checks (for public buildings)
Cabinet hinges, handles, and catches

Figure 12   *A simple double-door entranceway.*

Courtesy of Scholz Homes, Inc.

Figure 13   *An ornamental double-door entrance-way.*

Figure 14   *An office building entranceway with glass doors.*

Figure 15   *Interior view of Figure 14.*

GARAGE DOORS

Most residential garage doors are of the overhead type (Figure 18). An overhead door is composed of several hinged sections that roll up to the ceiling on tracks. Adjustable springs are used to counterbalance the weight of the door. Between 3″ and 13½″ of headroom (depending on the hardware type and door size) is required above the bottom of the header. Garage doors may be operated by means of remote-controlled motors.

Residential garage doors are usually stocked in 6′-6″ and 7′-0 heights × 1⅜″ thick. Common widths for single doors are 8′-0 and 9′-0; double doors are 16′-0 wide. See Figure 19 and Appendix C for more detail.

In addition to wood, garage doors may be obtained in aluminum and fiberglass in the same range of sizes. Fiber-glass doors are also available in 18′-0 widths.

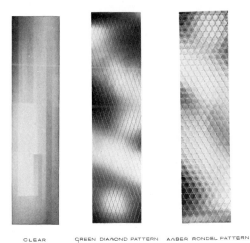

CLEAR   GREEN DIAMOND PATTERN   AMBER RONDEL PATTERN

Figure 16   *Sidelights.*

CABINETS

A wide range of cabinets for the kitchen, laundry, and bathroom are available from stock. They include storage, china, corner, all-purpose, and ironing board cabinets.

STUDY QUESTIONS

1. List the types of doors and indicate how each is opened.
2. Define these door terms:
   a. Door saddle
   b. Sidelight
   c. Kalamein door
   d. Sectional overhead door
   e. Tilt-up overhead door
3. What is the difference between the following door terms:
   a. Solid-core and hollow-core door
   b. Flush, paneled, and louvered door
   c. Top rail, bottom rail, side rail, and lock rail
   d. French door and Dutch door
   e. Door butt and door buck
   f. Doorstop and door check
4. Give the common sizes of the following doors:
   a. Interior door
   b. Front entrance door
   c. Rear entrance door

Figure 17 *Suggestions for contemporary and traditional entranceways.*

Figure 18 *Double-width garage door.*

LABORATORY PROBLEMS

1. Prepare a classroom illustration showing:
    a. Types of doors
    b. Door terminology
2. (For the advanced student) Design a type of door entirely different from those now commonly used.
3. Complete the design of the doors for the building assigned by your instructor.
4. Complete the design of the doors for your original house design.

INDUSTRIAL GARAGE DOOR
AVAILABLE TO 24' x 20'

RESIDENTIAL GARAGE DOOR
AVAILABLE FROM 8'-0" x 6'-6" TO 18' x 7'

COMMERCIAL GARAGE DOOR
AVAILABLE TO 20' x 16'

Figure 19 *Garage door sizes.*

18 / Schedules

A building is composed of a tremendous number of parts. In fact, if all of these parts were indicated on the plans, the plans would become so crowded that they would not be readable. Therefore the designer includes much of this information in *schedules* on the working drawings or in the written *specifications* (see Chapter 44 for a discussion of specifications writing).

DOOR AND WINDOW SCHEDULES

Figures 1 and 2 show minimum layouts for door and window schedules. Although this information may be included on the drawings in the form of notes, it is usually considered better practice to use

DOOR SCHEDULE

MK	NO.	SIZE	ROUGH OPENING	DESCRIPTION	REMARKS
1	1	3'-0 x 6'-8" x $1\frac{3}{4}$"	3'-2$\frac{3}{4}$" x 6'-11"	14 PANEL WP, 4 LTS	
2	1	2'-8"x6'-8" x $1\frac{3}{4}$"	2'-10$\frac{3}{4}$" x 6'-11"	FLUSH WP, 1 LT	
3	2	2'-8"x6'-8"x $1\frac{3}{4}$"	2'-10$\frac{3}{4}$" x 6'-11"	2 PANEL WP, 3 LTS	
4	10	2'-6" x 6'-8"x $1\frac{3}{8}$"	2'-8$\frac{3}{4}$" x 6'-11"	FLUSH BIRCH	
5					
6					

Figure 1

WINDOW SCHEDULE

MK	NO.	SIZE	ROUGH OPENING	DESCRIPTION	REMARKS
A	1	G65	6'-0$\frac{1}{2}$" x 5'-0$\frac{1}{2}$"	ANDERSEN GLIDING	DOUBLE GLAZED
B	1	C24-2	8'-0$\frac{5}{8}$" x 4'-0$\frac{1}{2}$"	" CASEMENT	" "
C	3	C23	4'-0$\frac{1}{2}$" x 3'-0$\frac{1}{2}$"	" "	" "
D					
E					

Figure 2

schedules and keep the actual plans and elevations uncluttered. Of course, a reference mark or symbol must be placed upon each door in the plan and each window in the elevations. These marks are repeated in the door and window schedules, the schedules then giving all the necessary sizes and information. A numeral is used for doors and most other scheduled items, but a letter is used for windows. The usual place for the door schedule is near the plan, and the window schedule should be placed near the elevations. Use a different mark for different sizes or types of doors and windows, but use the same mark for similar doors and windows. Such marks should be enclosed in circles, which are drawn about $\frac{1}{4}''$ in diameter.

ADDITIONAL SCHEDULES

In addition to doors and windows, other materials may be specified by the use of schedules. Figures 3–7 show the outlines of some other commonly used schedules. The plans for a large, well-detailed building might contain many other types of schedules in addition to those illustrated.

Some of the customs and rules of writing schedules follow.

1. Rather than take the time to letter the same words many times over, use the ditto mark (as in Figure 2) or the note "DO" (short for *ditto,* as in Figures 6 and 7).
2. Abbreviations are often used to reduce the size of the schedule. Standard abbreviations should be used and listed in a table of abbreviations on the drawings. The abbreviations used on Figures 1–7 are:*

CL	Closet
ELEV	Elevation
FIN	Finish
S	American Standard I beam
LAV	Lavatory
LT	Light (window glass)
MK	Mark
NO.	Number
REINF	Reinforce
T & G	Tongue-and-groove
WP	White pine
W/	With
L	Angle
#	Pounds or number

3. When spaces on the schedule do not apply to a material, they may be left blank (as in the Fig-

---

* For a more extensive list of commonly used abbreviations see Appendix D.

COLUMN AND BEAM SCHEDULE

MK	NO.	DESCRIPTION	LENGTH	REMARKS
1	4	$3\frac{1}{2}''$ STEEL PIPE COLUMN W/PLATES	7'-0	
2	1	S 7 x 15.3 FLOOR GIRDER	42'-0	
3				
4				

Figure 3

LINTEL SCHEDULE

MK	NO.	DESCRIPTION	LENGTH	REMARKS
1	6	L 5 x $3\frac{1}{2}$ x $\frac{3}{8}$	4'-8"	
2				
3				

Figure 4

FOOTING SCHEDULE

MK	A	B	C	ELEV	REINF	REMARKS
1	8"	1'-4"	8"	93.4'	2 #4	
2	10"	1'-6"	8"	93.4'	2 #4	
3	8"	1'-4"	8"	97.4'	NONE	
4						

Figure 5

FINISH SCHEDULE

MK	ROOM	FLOOR	FIN	WALL	FIN	CEILING	FIN	TRIM	FIN
1	LIVING ROOM	T&G OAK	VARN-ISH	SHEET ROCK	PAINT	ACOUST. TILE	—	PINE	PAINT
2	LAV	ASPHALT TILE	—	CERAMIC TILE	—	SAND PLASTER		DO	DO
2A	LAV CL	DO	—	SAND PLASTER	—	DO	—	DO	DO
3									
4									

Figure 6

ELECTRICAL SCHEDULE

LOCATION	SYMBOL	NO.	WATT	DESIGNATION	EXAMPLE
GARAGE	⊖	2	100	DUPLEX OUTLET	
	O_A	2	100	CEILING MOUNT	PASS & SEYMOUR #41
LIVING ROOM	⊖	6	100	DUPLEX OUTLET	
	O_B	1	100	WALL MOUNT	GENERAL #1606
	O_C	12	60	WALL VALANCE	PASS & SEYMOUR #41
KITCHEN	⊖	4	100	DUPLEX OUTLET	
	O_D	1	100	FLUSH CEILING	HOLOPHANE #RL-732
	O_E	1	100	DO	DO #RL-796
BEDROOM					

Figure 7

ure 1 remarks column) or filled with a strike line (as in the Figure 6 ceiling finish column).

4. The desired manufacturer of a product may be specified (as in Figure 2, Andersen windows) or merely given as an example of an acceptable product (as in Figure 7, Pass & Seymour electric fixtures).

STUDY QUESTIONS

1. Why are schedules used in preference to notes or dimensions?

2. List several building components that may be specified by means of schedules.
3. When using schedules, a _____ mark is used to indicate windows, and a _____ mark is used to indicate doors.
4. In a schedule, what is the meaning of "DO"?

LABORATORY PROBLEMS

1. Prepare the schedules of the building assigned by your instructor.
2. Prepare the schedules for your original house design.

V / Plans

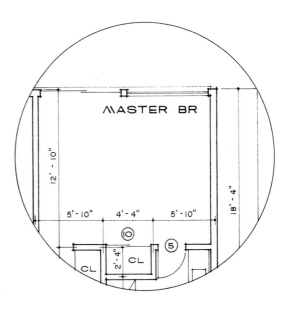

19 / Room Design

There are two major considerations in the design of the floor plan of a house. First, each room must be designed so that it is pleasant, functional, and economical; and second, the rooms must be placed in the correct relationship to one another. This second consideration may be likened to working out a jigsaw puzzle in which the pieces may change in shape and size, giving various solutions. Some of these solutions will be better than others, but in the design of a house, the overall plan can be no better than the design of the individual rooms.

To give some starting point, minimum and average room sizes are given in the accompanying table. Notice that the rooms are not long and narrow (which makes them too hall-like) nor square (which makes furniture placement difficult). Actually, there is no such thing as an average, or standard, or even ideal, size or shape for a room. De-

sign a size and shape that will best meet the requirements of function, aesthetics, and economy.

The desired furniture arrangement will have a considerable effect on the design of each room. Professional designers find that furniture templates or underlays greatly simplify the design process. The furniture underlay (Figure 1) may be used when drawing floor plans to a $\frac{1}{4}'' = 1'\text{-}0$ scale. Simply slip it into position under your paper and trace off the desired elements.

KITCHEN DESIGN

When a builder puts up a low-priced house, there are a number of ways to cut corners and reduce cost. However, you have probably noticed that even the smallest house has a carefully designed and well-equipped kitchen. The reason is that builders realize prospective buyers demand an efficient and cheerful kitchen. As a matter of fact, this is the first room many will want to see. The average homemaker walks two hundred miles a year in the performance of household tasks—half of this in the kitchen. Consequently, in designing any house for yourself or others, you cannot spend too much time in perfecting the kitchen design.

A kitchen should be thought of as a group of three activity centers:

1. Storage
2. Preparation and cleaning
3. Cooking and serving

Room	Minimum (inside size)	Average
Living room	12′ × 16′	14′ × 20′
Dining room	10′ × 12′	12′ × 13′
Dining area	7′ × 9′	9′ × 9′
Bedroom (master)	11½′ × 12½′	12′ × 14′
Bedroom (other)	9′ × 11′	10′ × 12′
Kitchen	7′ × 10′	8′ × 12′
Bathroom	5′ × 7′	5½′ × 8′
Utility (no basement)	7′ × 8′	8′ × 11′
Hall width	3′	3½′
Closet	2′ × 2′	2′ × 4′
Garage (single)	9½′ × 19′	12′ × 20′
Garage (double)	18′ × 19′	20′ × 20′
Garage door (single)	8′ × 6½′	9′ × 7′
Garage door (double)	15′ × 6½′	16′ × 7′

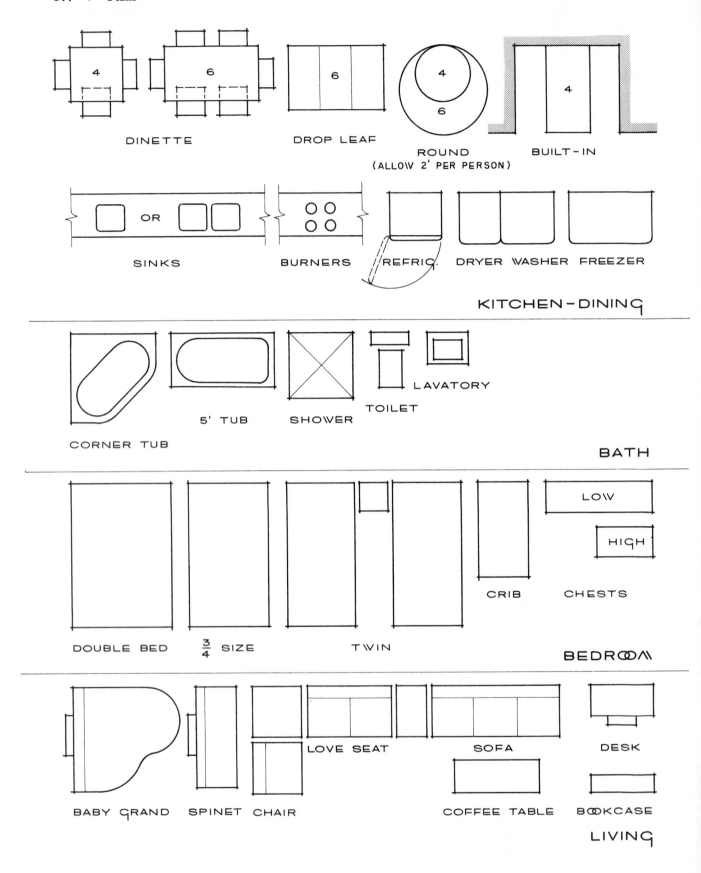

Figure 1 *Furniture underlay for ¼″ = 1″-0 scale.*

Figure 2   *Over-and-under refrigerator-freezer (left).*

Figure 3   *Side-by-side refrigerator-freezer (right).*

Storage. The focal point of the storage center is the refrigerator, although many cabinets for nonrefrigerated food, dishes, and utensils must be provided. To save steps, the refrigerator may be located near the delivery door, or nearest the door to the living-dining area. Also consider a freezer or refrigerator-freezer (Figures 2 and 3), although a freezer is often removed from the kitchen itself to another area.

Preparation and cleaning. This center is built around the sink and its adjoining counter space. Do you want to include an automatic dishwasher (Figure 4) or garbage disposal unit? Most people want their sink by a window.

Cooking and serving. The cooking center is grouped around the range (Figures 5 and 6). In addition to electric coils and gas burners, range cooktops are available in solid ceramic disks, magnetic induc-

Courtesy of Chambers Corporation.

Figure 4   *Electric dishwasher.*

Kitchen Equipment

	Width	Depth	Height
Base cabinets		2'-0	3'-0
Wall cabinets		1'-0	2'-6"
Range, oven below	1'-8"	2'-1"	3'-0
Range, oven at side	3'-6"	2'-1"	3'-0
Range, built-in	2'-8"	1'-8"	
Oven	2'-0	2'-0	2'-4"
Microwave	2'-0	1'-6"	1'-4"
Sink	2'-0	2'-0	3'-0
Sink and drainboard	3'-6"	2'-0	3'-0
Refrigerator, 7 cu. ft	2'-1"	2'-3"	4'-6"
Refrigerator, 14 cu. ft.	2'-8"	2'-3"	5'-4"
Washer	2'-0	2'-3"	3'-1"
Dryer	2'-6"	2'-3"	3'-1"

tion surfaces, and tungsten halogen surfaces. A built-in oven, being less used, may be located at a more isolated position than the range. Range-oven combinations are standardized at 36" high, so counters should be designed at the same height. If a house is designed for especially tall or short persons,

Figure 5   *Electric surface range.*

Figure 6   *Gas surface range.*

Figure 7   *Built-in self-cleaning electric oven (left).*

Figure 8   *Built-in electric self-cleaning double oven (right).*

Figure 9 *Electric barbecue.*

these major appliances may be built in at a convenient height. Choose a microwave oven if you wish to decrease cooking time. Consider an exhaust fan or hood and fan above the range cooktop.

A planning center consisting of a desk or table and a telephone is included in many modern kitchens. Allow space for cookbooks, recipe index, and so forth.

As a rule, the laundry (automatic clothes washer, dryer, and ironing board) is best placed in its own utility room. If it must be placed in the kitchen, it should have its own separate area.

These activity centers may be combined in a number of ways in various-shaped rooms designed so that work progresses from right (storage) to left (serving). The often-used combinations shown in Figure 14 are:

1. Pullman (or corridor or two-wall)
2. U-shaped
3. L-shaped
4. Peninsula (or island)
5. One-wall

Figure 10 *Kitchen-dining area separated by a folding door.*

Figure 11   *An exposed kitchen in a dramatic design.*

Pullman. The pullman kitchen, consisting of a long corridor with utilities on either side, is often used where space is at a premium. Doors may be at either end or at one end only. Although this design is somewhat factorylike, it is efficient in saving space and steps.

U-shaped. The U-shaped kitchen has cabinets on three walls, the sink usually in the middle, and the refrigerator and stove on opposite sides. Space for dining may be allowed near the fourth wall. This plan is adaptable to large and small rooms.

L-shaped. This is probably the most commonly used arrangement since it is efficient, allows for two doors without any interruption of countertop area, and may be nicely used with a breakfast table.

Peninsula. This kind of layout may be used only with large rooms. It is called *peninsula* when the counter or *breakfast bar* runs pependicular to a wall, and *island* when it is freestanding.

One-wall. This layout is used when a kitchen must be fitted into a long, narrow space. It is not an ideal arrangement.

Although it may seem from the previous discussion that the kitchen is greatly standardized, this is not the case. The kitchen should be original and pleasant. Avoid the monotony of the "factory" look. Consider built-in ranges, ovens, and refrigerators. Materials like brick and copper; color in appliances; and careful floor, window, and lighting design will all add to a kitchen's attrac-

Figure 12   *A peninsula kitchen.*

Courtesy of Scholz Homes, Inc.

Figure 13   *An exciting kitchen design.*

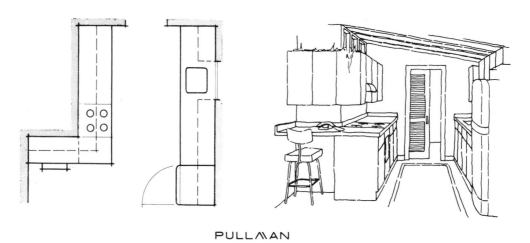

PULLMAN

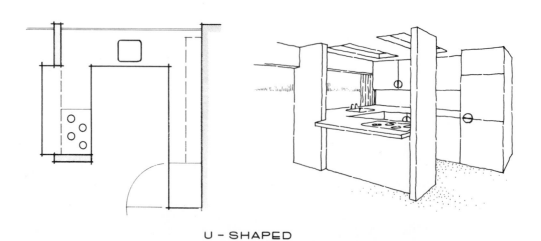

U - SHAPED

Figure 14   *Kitchen design.*

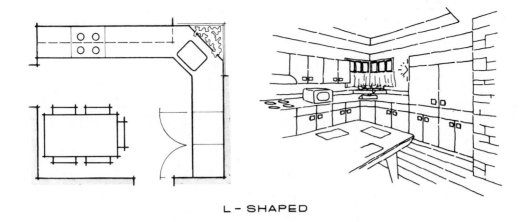

L - SHAPED

PENINSULA

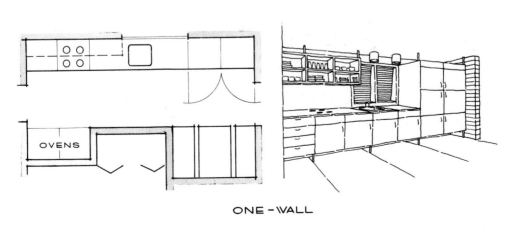

ONE - WALL

Figure 14 *continued.*

Figure 15   *Living room of the A residence, looking toward the atrium.*

Figure 16   *A window wall is the major feature of this living area.*

tiveness. Working areas should be continuous; they may turn corners but should not be interrupted by doors. Remember that the cabinet space in an inside corner cannot be *fully* utilized.

The minimum area recommended by the Public Housing Authority for a kitchen and eating space is 100 sq. ft.

Figure 17   *Pool integrates atrium with living area.*

Figure 18   *A sunken conversational area.*

LIVING AREA DESIGN

Many people feel that since guests are entertained in the living room, it should be as large and gracious a room as can be afforded. The minimum area recommended by the Public Housing Authority is 160 sq. ft. The shape of the living area is often rectangular, the length one-third longer than the width.

Two factors should be given careful consideration in the design of the living area: circulation and furniture grouping.

Circulation. Movement within a room and from one room to another is called *circulation*. Most persons feel the *center-hall* house arrangement is ideal because circulation to all rooms is easily accomplished without using the living room as a hallway or vestibule. When a room is not used as a throughway, it is called a *dead-end room*. There is much merit in dead-end rooms, but remember that they are not as interesting as a room that "goes somewhere." At any rate, a living room should never have to be used for trips between bedroom and bath.

Furniture grouping. The major furniture grouping should be arranged so that the circle of chairs falls within a 12′ diameter. A living room that has a fireplace as the focal point of this major furniture grouping is at a disadvantage when the fireplace is not in use. Rather than place furniture facing a black hole, a picture window or television set might be better choices. Consider also any special living room areas for music, reading, study, or cards.

Figure 19 shows a living room designed for a contemporary executive mansion. The client required an area that could be used for large, formal receptions as well as small, intimate parties. The design requirements included provision for indoor and outdoor gatherings in the day or evening. Notice that this design met these various requirements by the creation of areas that could be used individually or combined. The room itself, for ex-

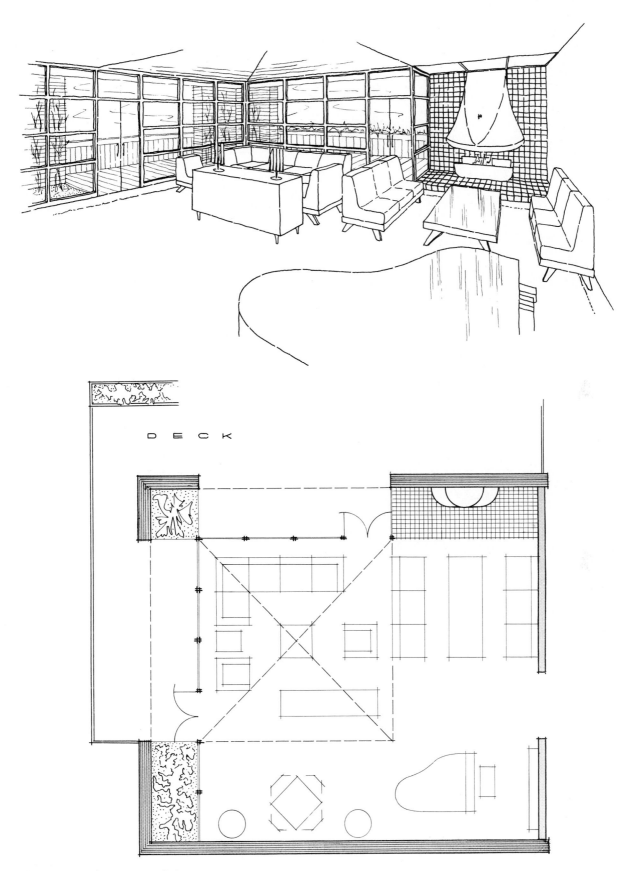

Figure 19 *Living room design.*

Figure 20   *Dining area of the A residence showing the breakfast bar and kitchen.*

Courtesy of Scholz Homes, Inc.

Figure 21   *A combined dining-family room.*

Courtesy of Scholz Homes, Inc.

Figure 22   *A kitchen area reserved for dining.*

ample, is separated into four major furniture groupings: (1) the major formal conversational grouping, emphasized by the ceiling design; (2) a secondary conversational grouping in front of the fireplace; (3) a music area; (4) an area for card playing. For large gatherings, the outside deck could be added by opening the French doors at the two locations. To provide contrast with the long distance view through the window walls, plantings were specified immediately outside these windows. These plantings, backed by brick piers, could be illuminated in various ways depending upon the mood desired.

Undoubtedly you will want to design a much smaller living room than this example. Please notice, though, that the plan by itself does not tell the entire story. An interior perspective of the room was needed to verify that the design requirements were met satisfactorily.

DINING AREA DESIGN

Periodically, the dining room loses and gains popularity. It can be dropped from new house plans to reduce costs, but a separate dining room is sometimes wanted.

The size of a dining room depends entirely on the size of the table and amount of accessory furniture. A good compromise between the dining room and breakfast nook is the living-dining area or kitchen-dining area. The living-dining combination is economical and tends to increase the apparent size of the living room. Kitchen eating space may also be provided if desired.

The dining room shown in Figure 23 was planned for a small city lot that allowed no pleasant views. The windows were arranged high on the walls to block the view without preventing natural lighting. On the rear wall, the window was combined with an enclosed courtyard designed to be landscaped. The double-entry doors, centered on the wall opposite the courtyard, provide a dramatic entrance.

BEDROOM DESIGN

The minimum area recommended by the Public Housing Authority is 80 sq. ft. for a single bed-

Figure 23 *Dining room design.*

room, and 120 sq. ft. for a master bedroom. As a general rule of thumb, bedrooms are often designed with the length 2′ longer than the width. The rooms should be large enough that the beds can be freestanding (that is, with only the head of the bed touching the wall), to make them easier to make. In a small bedroom, combine areas used for dressing, circulation, and closet access into one larger area rather than three small ones.

Small, high windows allow greater freedom of furniture arrangement and provide privacy. However, windows should not be so small and high that escape in case of fire is impossible.

The master bedroom shown in Figure 27 has been planned to include an element of symmetry in an oriental motif. The designer has located all the major items of furniture so that there will be enough room for each. This is particularly impor-

Figure 24 *Dining with an oriental flair.*

Courtesy of Scholz Homes, Inc.

Figure 25 *An open bedroom.*

Figure 26   *Dining area under balcony, bedrooms overhead.*

Closets

	Width	Depth	Height
Clothes closet	4'-0	2'-0	
Walk-in clothes closet	6'-0	4'-0	
Linen closet	2'-0	1'-6"	1'-0 between shelves
Suits, trousers, jackets, shirts, skirts		2'-0	3'-9"
Dresses, overcoats		2'-0	5'-3"
Evening gowns		2'-0	6'-0
Children, 6–12 years		1'-8"	3'-9"
Children, 3–5 years		1'-4"	2'-6"

tant when unusually large or irregularly shaped furniture is to be used.

Closets that are carefully designed to provide room efficiently for all sorts of clothing are becoming popular. These *storage walls* may have drawers, replacing bureaus and chests. The table gives sizes which might be of help in closet design.

BATHROOM DESIGN

A bathroom may be designed to be as small and compact or as large and compartmented as you wish. The trend is toward a compartmented room —keeping the toilet and tub or shower in separate, enclosed areas.

For economy in plumbing, keep the bathrooms near the kitchen. If possible, avoid specifying a window behind a bathroom fixture. A window behind a tub or toilet is awkward, and one behind a lavatory interferes with the mirror.

The economy bathroom shown in Figure 28 has been provided with a wall-hung toilet and lavatory. These will give the effect, visually, of enlarging the room. In addition, the floor will be easier to clean. A one-piece plastic tub and shower unit eliminates the need for wall tile.

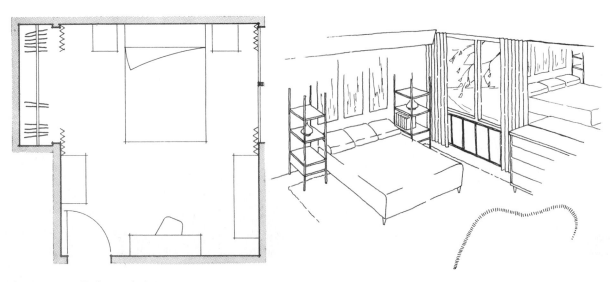

Figure 27   *Bedroom design.*

Bathroom Equipment

	Width	Depth	Height
Lavatory (washstand)	1′-10″	1′-7″	2′-9″
Built-in lavatory	2′-0 min.	1′-10″	2′-9″
Bathtub	5′, 5′-6″, 6′	2′-6″	1′-4″
Shower	3′-0	3′-0	7′-0
Toilet	1′-8″	2′-4″	2′-4″
Medicine cabinet	1′-2″	4″	1′-6″

Minimum clearance between:

Front of toilet and wall	1′-6″
Side of toilet and wall	6″
Front of lavatory and wall	2′-0
Front of lavatory and lower fixture	1′-6″
Edge of tub and wall	2′-0
Edge of tub and other fixture	1′-6″

The compartmented bathroom shown in Figure 28 has been provided with two lavatories (for a larger family), a built-in tiled vanity, a corner whirlpool bath, and a stall toilet with swinging doors for privacy.

LAUNDRY DESIGN

The homemakers of today spend less time in the laundry than did their predecessors. However, more time is spent on laundry chores than on any other work with the exception of food prepa-

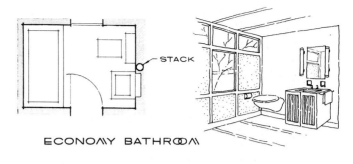
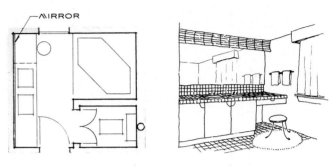

ECONOMY BATHROOM

COMPARTMENTED BATHROOM

Figure 28   *Bathroom design.*

Courtesy of Scholz Homes, Inc.

Figure 29   *A dressing room with private solarium.*

Courtesy of Scholz Homes, Inc.

Figure 30   *A lavish bathroom design.*

ration. The laundry, then, should be carefully planned. There is a sequence of laundry work just as there is a sequence of kitchen work. Proper planning should provide for each of the following steps:

1. Collection of laundry (hampers, laundry chute)
2. Treating of spots (a sink for pretreating spots and stains)
3. Washing and drying (the core of the laundry)
4. Finishing (a table or counter for folding and ironing; may be away from the area where the washing is done)

A storage area for soap and supplies must be specified also.

There are a number of possible locations for a laundry (Figure 31).

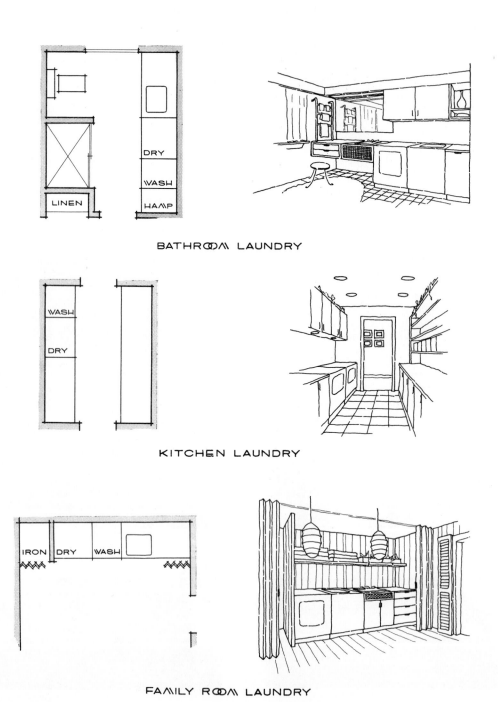

BATHROOM LAUNDRY

KITCHEN LAUNDRY

FAMILY ROOM LAUNDRY

Figure 31 *Laundry design.*

Bathroom. The most efficient location for a laundry is near the bedrooms and bath, where most soiled clothes originate. Additional advantages of a bathroom location are economy of plumbing and suitable interior finish. A disadvantage to be considered is the sacrifice of privacy. A combination bathroom and laundry should be a good-sized room that is well vented to remove excess moisture. Figure 31 shows a possible arrangement. The hamper is filled from the hall and emptied from the laundry. The shower doubles for drip-drying clothes.

Kitchen. The kitchen is the most obvious laundry location since placement here simplifies plumbing connections. However, a well-planned kitchen-laundry combination provides for separate areas or rooms so that clothes and cooking are not competing for the same space. Notice that the M residence has a small utility room containing the laundry adjacent to the kitchen.

Family room. The family room is an ideal laundry location for the large family; the homemaker can watch the children while doing the laundry chores. Although some might object to the appearance of laundry equipment here, this can be overcome by the use of folding, sliding, or accordion partitions.

Entry. A rear hall or area may be the perfect solution in some cases, especially if a rear mud room, which already requires plumbing connections, is specified.

Basement. Basement locations are often desired, since the "free" basement area is used instead of prime first-floor area. Also, a washer that accidentally overflows will cause less damage in the basement. The major disadvantage of the basement location is the additional stair climbing required.

STORAGE DESIGN

Anyone will tell you that no house can have too much storage room. As a minimum, a well-designed house will have one closet per bedroom, two closets in the master bedroom, a linen closet, a utility closet, coat closets, and provision for exterior storage. The most economical way to build storage space into a residence is by use of a *closet wall:* a double wall containing closets that serve rooms on opposite sides. Closets should be designed 2′ deep and wide enough to serve their function.

A small house should have approximately the sizes of closets shown in the accompanying table.

Closet Sizes

Each bedroom closet	2′ × 4′
Master bedroom closets	two 2′ × 4′
Linen closet	1′-6″ to 2′ × 2′
Utility closet	2′ × 4′
Guest closet	2′ × 2′
Family coat closet	2′ × 4′
Exterior storage	2′ × 10′

In addition, it is advisable to plan for storage walls for special activities: a home computer and printer, a bridge table, photographic equipment, hobbies, toys, musical instruments, records, shop tools, and seldom-used equipment.

PORCH DESIGN

If a porch is desired, it is usually located at the rear of the house for maximum privacy. Also, it should be conveniently near the kitchen if outdoor meals are to be served. Consider screening the porch for comfort in the summer and glazing it for winter use.

GARAGE DESIGN

A garage is usually attached to the house in some manner to provide a sheltered entry. This may be done by an attached first-floor garage, a breezeway, or a garage built into the basement. A basement garage will fit well in a split-level house; it is economical and offers heat as well as shelter. An attached garage or breezeway fits well in a small house design since it lengthens the house exterior. The breezeway may double as an open or closed porch. When completely enclosed, this space may be more efficiently used for living.

Consider a carport if you do not wish an enclosed garage. The carport is economical, but it does not offer the same protection from snow and rain. The deciding factor between garage and carport is usually climate. Whatever method is used to house the automobile, remember to include a sizable storage wall for automotive equipment, gardening tools, and toys.

FUTURE TRENDS

In this chapter, we have concentrated upon the design of the types of rooms found in the average house today. To get a picture of the house interior

Figure 32 *This concourse between two old buildings uses the "air rights" for maximum land use, San Francisco.*

of the future, we need only look at the more advanced designs of contemporary architects. Using these contemporary designs as a guide, it is possible to predict the features likely to be found in future houses:

1. Rooms will be of all shapes—from circular or free-form to completely plastic surfaces, blending floor, wall, and ceiling into one uninterrupted flowing surface.
2. The trend will be away from the individual room concept toward multipurpose rooms and flexible areas that may be quickly rearranged by folding doors or retractable walls.
3. Multilevel floors and varying ceiling heights will become more common.
4. Furniture will often be an integral part of the architecture. (One example is the sunken living area surrounded by a carpeted lounge.)
5. The outdoors will be brought indoors through the greater use of glass walls and interior planting.
6. New materials will make an appearance. Wood, stone, brick, and plaster will be gradually replaced by materials manufactured by yet-to-be-discovered methods.
7. Assemblyline housing will become popular—packaged rooms that can be assembled in various combinations, and completely packaged houses. Conversely, there will also be a greater demand for custom-designed homes.
8. Revolutionary appliances will appear. Many will be built in—dust-repellent surfaces; completely concealed heating, cooling, and lighting elements; home computers and communication systems; and improved systems of food storage and preparation. Cleaning facilities as we know them may become unnecessary because of the use of disposable utensils and clothing.
9. New systems of building will be developed so that less desirable land (and water) can be used. Refer to Figure 32 for one example.

STUDY QUESTIONS

1. Name the three activity centers included in a kitchen. What appliances are associated with each?
2. Name five kinds of kitchen layouts. Include the advantages and disadvantages of each.
3. What is meant by *room circulation?*
4. Give the advantages and disadvantages of a dining-living combination as opposed to a separate dining room and living room.
5. How many bathrooms should be specified for the following houses? List the fixtures required in each.
   a. Economy one-bedroom summer house
   b. Moderate-priced three-bedroom ranch house
   c. Higher-priced four-bedroom, two-story colonial house
6. Name the four activity centers included in a laundry. What appliances are associated with each?
7. (For the advanced student) After a thorough library search, prepare an illustrated paper on the history of the development of house interiors to date. Include changes in the number of rooms, room sizes, and the number and types of windows and doors.
8. (For the advanced student) After a thorough search of contemporary architectural periodicals, give your prediction of the type of house interior:
   a. Twenty-five years hence
   b. One hundred years hence

LABORATORY PROBLEMS

1. Sketch to scale or draw (as assigned) individual room layouts for the following rooms. Show the placement of major furniture.
   a. 15′ × 22′ living room with fireplace
   b. 12′ × 14′ dining room with alcove for a serving table
   c. 14′ × 18′ family room with fireplace and pass-through counter from kitchen
   d. 10′ × 12′ U-shaped kitchen
   e. 12′ × 14′ master bedroom with "his" and "hers" closets
2. In preparation for the layout of the rooms for your original house design, list the rooms familiar to you (your own home, neighbors' homes, and relatives' homes), their exact sizes (do not guess but actually measure or pace off), and your impression of their size (too small, satisfactory, or too large).
3. Using the information obtained from problem 2, prepare a list of the rooms of your original house design showing the sizes you wish.
4. Using the sizes drawn up for problem 3, sketch to scale or draw (as assigned) individual room layouts for your original house design.

20 / Preliminary Layout

The preparation of a satisfactory preliminary layout is undoubtedly the most difficult but yet most satisfying phase of architectural design. As mentioned in Chapter 19, the placing of all the rooms in the correct relationship to each other may be likened to completing an unusual jigsaw puzzle composed of flexible pieces which must fit together in a workable pattern. This puzzle is further complicated by some considerations in addition to those of the individual room designs and their relationships:

1. The program requirements
2. Orientation
3. Circulation
4. Efficiency
5. Elevations

Each of these will be considered in turn.

THE PROGRAM REQUIREMENTS

The designer must meet *all* the requirements set up in the program. The program, you recall, reflects the decisions previously made on the primary considerations of type of plot and energy system, styling, number of rooms and floors, shape of plan, inclusion of basement or attic, expansion, zoning, and cost.

ORIENTATION

The term *orientation* refers to the compass location of the various rooms of the house to make best use of sun, topography, breezes, and views.

Solar orientation. Major living areas should face south for winter solar heat, and the minor areas should face north. The breakfast room should face east to get the morning sun. Children's bedrooms should *not* face west if the occupants are expected to go to bed early.

Topographical orientation. This refers to orientation designed to take full advantage of the land contour. For example, a house on a sharply sloping plot might be designed so that lower-level rooms would open directly to the low portion of the plot, and the upper-level rooms would open to the high portion of the plot. In general, it is well to keep excavation to a minimum, for the less the natural contour of the site is disturbed, the less Nature will try to disturb the occupants of that site.

View orientation. Major rooms such as the living room and master bedroom should be oriented to obtain the best possible view of the interesting features of the surrounding countryside. Minor rooms such as the utility room, laundry, and garage can face the less desirable views. In fact, some city dwellings have been built with no windows at all in the outside walls; all windows open upon landscaped interior courts.

Wind orientation. Major living areas should be located to take advantage of prevailing summer breezes, and the minor areas may serve to block off the winter winds.

Designing for orientation. The best method to design for optimum orientation is to sketch the plot showing the direction of the sun, slope of land, wind, and best views. Figure 1 shows an orienta-

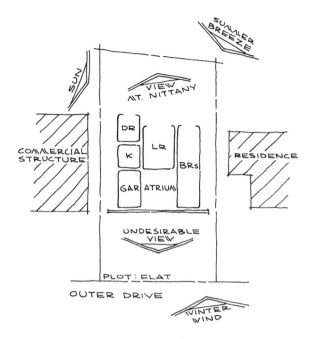

Figure 1 *Orientation sketch for the A residence.*

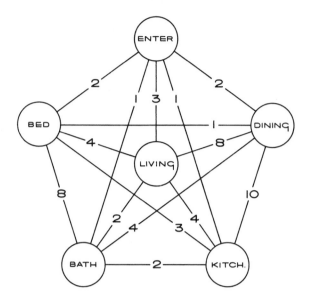

Figure 2 *House circulation guide. The numbers indicate the average number of daily trips between rooms.*

CIRCULATION

The designer must carefully consider the patterns of traffic among rooms to ensure convenient and, at the same time, efficient circulation. Circulation areas are halls, stairs, and the lanes of travel through rooms. Successful circulation means that there are convenient pathways between the rooms or areas that have the most connecting traffic. Usually this is accomplished by planning these rooms adjacent to each other with a common doorway. When halls are used, they should be kept as short as possible; when rooms are used for circulation, they should be planned so that the most direct route is across a corner or along one side of the room. With this arrangement, traffic will be less likely to disturb those using the room.

Probably the best way to ensure satisfactory circulation is to group all the individual rooms into three main zones:

1. Living (living room, front entrance foyer, powder room)
2. Sleeping (bedrooms and bathrooms)
3. Dining (dining areas, kitchen, service door)

Rooms of the same zone must be planned to have

tion sketch for the plot of the A residence. A study of this sketch and the program requirements will indicate the best location of many of the rooms.

excellent circulation. For example: (1) The living room should be adjacent to the entrance foyer. (2) It should be easy to reach a bathroom from any bedroom. (3) The kitchen and dining room should not be separated by a hall.

In addition, the most often used rooms of different zones should be planned to have good circulation. The dining areas should be easily reached from the living area, for instance. Figure 2 shows the relative circulation between the areas of an average home. The numbers in the lines connecting the rooms are the number of trips made each day between those rooms by the average occupant. Compare circulation between *entrance* and *living* (three trips) and *entrance* and *kitchen* (one trip). This shows that it is more important to have the living room near the front entrance.

EFFICIENCY

Halls serve a very definite purpose, but should be kept at a minimum. They should not occupy more than 10 percent of the total area. The *efficiency*, or *tare*, of a house shows the percentage of area actually occupied by rooms. As you know, the first-floor area may be taken up by stairs, heating unit, halls, walls, closets, and vestibules. Although these are all necessary items, they must be kept to a minimum in the efficient—or low-cost—house. Seventy-five percent is considered excellent efficiency. Under 70 percent is considered poor efficiency.

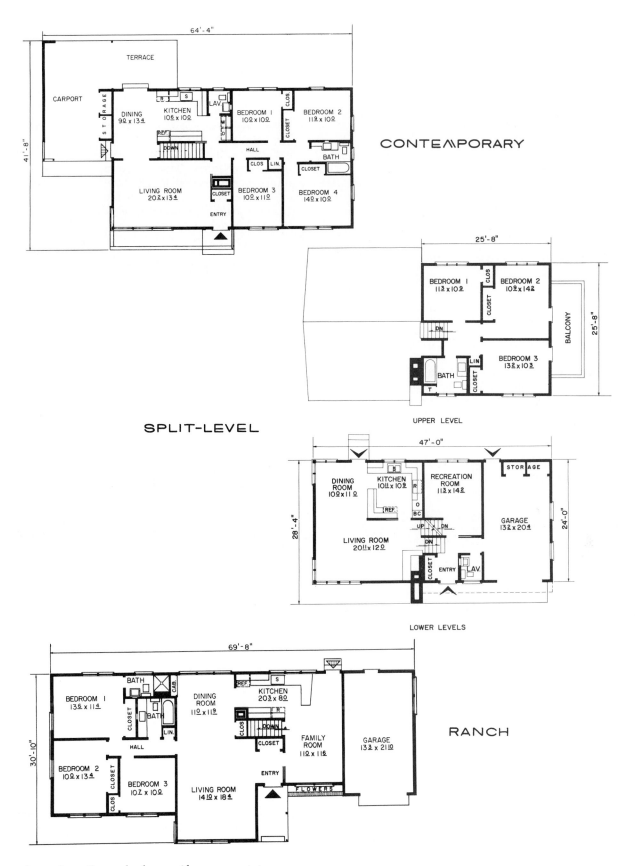

Figure 3 *Source books provide many prototypes.*

ELEVATIONS

The plans of the house should not be developed too far before elevations and framing are considered. Actually, the good architect will not completely finish one drawing at a time, but will jump from one to another until all the major plans are finished simultaneously.

PLANNING PROCEDURE

Designers do not all have the same approach to obtaining a satisfactory preliminary layout. There are, however, four methods which are widely used:

1. Prototype
2. Templates
3. Interior planning
4. Overall planning

Let us look at each of these methods from the simple to the sophisticated. Then you can decide on the method you will want to use.

Prototype. The method of planning recommended for inexperienced persons is that of the prototype. A prototype is an example that you wish to copy fully or partially. The prototype may be an actual house you have seen and admired or a set of plans that appears to meet your requirements. Plans may be found in a variety of sources: popular home magazines, books on residential design, and newspapers. These sources publish houses that have been designed by architects, and they are able to furnish a complete set of drawings and specifications at comparatively low cost. Figure 3 shows three typical layouts from booklets published by Weyerhaeuser. Some other sources are listed at the end of this chapter. Building material suppliers also have sets of "stock" plans that may be borrowed or purchased.

Probably you will not be fortunate enough to find a good plan that meets all the requirements of your program, but you may find a plan that will be satisfactory after some modifications and alterations are made. If major alterations are necessary (such as moving the location of a stairway), you will find that you will need to redesign the entire plan.

Excellent results have been obtained using the prototype method, but remember that this is not original designing; it is merely copying someone else's design!

Templates. A second method of planning is by use of templates: first a set of furniture templates to obtain the individual room design, and then a set of individual room templates to obtain the preliminary layout.

A furniture template should be made for each existing or proposed piece of furniture. The templates may be cut from graph paper or cardboard using a reasonable scale. The furniture underlay in the previous chapter was drawn to a scale of $\frac{1}{4}'' = 1'$, which has proved to be a satisfactory working scale. Obviously much measuring will be saved if $\frac{1}{4}''$ grid paper is used.

The furniture templates can be moved to various positions until a satisfactory grouping is obtained. Then draw the outline of the furniture templates together with lines showing the size and shape of the entire room. Remember to allow for circulation areas, doors, windows, and closets.

EXAMPLE

To design one of the bedrooms for the A residence, templates (Figure 4) are made for the principal pieces of furniture: the bed, night table, chest, vanity and its chair, and boudoir chair. These templates are shown in Figure 5 arranged in two groupings. When you study Figure 5, you will notice an inherent disadvantage in the template method of design: The furniture will have to be rearranged if the doors and windows must be placed at another location. And any change in furniture arrangement usually means a change in room dimensions also.

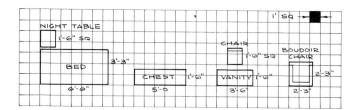

Figure 4 *Furniture templates.*

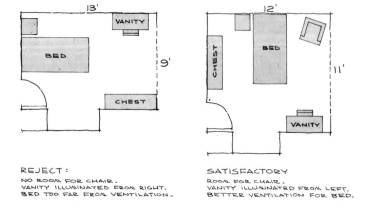

Figure 5 *Room layout using method of templates.*

After the dimensions of each room are determined by use of furniture templates, room templates may be made and used in a similar manner to determine alternate floor plan layouts. However, you must remember to leave spaces between the room templates—small 6″ spaces for the wall thickness and large 3′ or 4′ spaces for closets, stairs, and halls.

EXAMPLE

To design the first-floor layout for the A residence, templates are made for the living area, dining area, kitchen, garage, and bedrooms as shown in figure 6. Since the sizes of the atrium and lavatories are not considered to be critical, no templates are made for them. These areas are kept in mind, however, just as are halls, closets, walls, and a stairway. The first trial proved unsatisfactory for the reasons noted in Figure 7. A later scheme shows improvement, but the last scheme shown in Figure 7 meets all established requirements. It is important that a record be made of all acceptable schemes so that they may be compared to arrive at the very best solution.

Interior planning. A widely used system of architectural planning is called interior planning. Neither prototype drawings nor templates are used, but rather a series of sketches is made to develop the house plan. The architect first shows only basic concepts by use of *thumbnail* sketches, and then works up through a series of larger and more detailed sketches until a satisfactory finished sketch is obtained. The order of procedure is shown by an example from the A residence.

Thumbnail sketches. Figure 8 shows several thumbnail sketches made to show the general location of various areas. These are purposely drawn very small, or *thumbnail,* so that there is no possibility of getting bogged down with detail at this early stage. Thus the designer is forced to consider only the essential elements.

Preliminary sketches. Using the thumbnail sketch as a guide, a preliminary sketch as shown in Figure 9 is prepared. This will normally be done to $\frac{1}{8}″ = 1′$ scale on graph paper, as many beautiful ideas are seen to be obviously impossible when sketched to scale. Main attention is directed to room layout, circulation, and orientation, with no attention yet given to details such as door swings and exact window locations. The dwelling front will face the bottom of the sheet regardless of compass direction. Compass direction is indicated, however. Notice that the walls have been *pochéd* or darkened so that the plan will be easier to read. This is standard practice in preliminary and finished sketching.

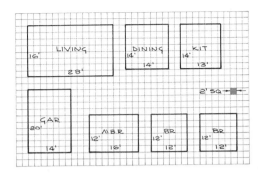

Figure 6   *Room templates.*

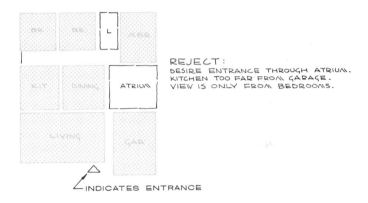

REJECT:
DESIRE ENTRANCE THROUGH ATRIUM.
KITCHEN TOO FAR FROM GARAGE.
VIEW IS ONLY FROM BEDROOMS.

∠ INDICATES ENTRANCE

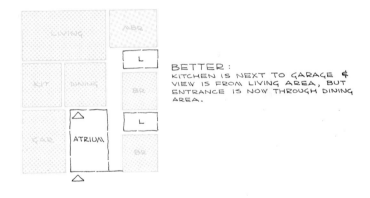

BETTER:
KITCHEN IS NEXT TO GARAGE &
VIEW IS FROM LIVING AREA, BUT
ENTRANCE IS NOW THROUGH DINING
AREA.

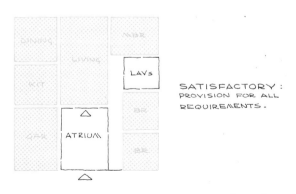

SATISFACTORY:
PROVISION FOR ALL
REQUIREMENTS.

Figure 7   *House layout using method of templates.*

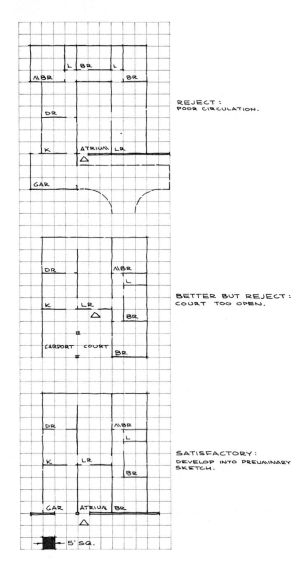

Figure 8   *Thumbnail sketches for the A residence.*

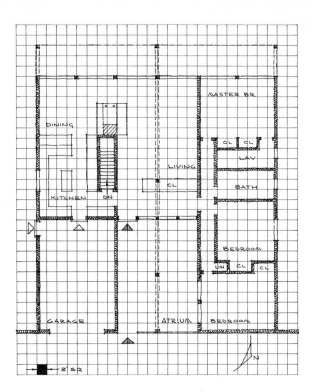

Figure 9   *Preliminary sketch of the A residence.*

Finished sketches. The finished sketch may be a carefully drawn freehand sketch or a drawing done with drafting instruments. The scale is usually ¼″ = 1′ for a small residence and ⅛″ = 1′ for larger buildings. Rough outside dimensions and approximate inside room dimensions are indicated.

Figure 10 shows a finished sketch of the A residence made using the preliminary sketch as a model. Notice that all the requirements of the program have now been met and that considerably more detail has been added. Some additional minor changes will be made and details added when the finished sketch is eventually redrawn as the final plan.

Overall planning. Experienced designers and architects use the concept of overall planning since it

is likely to produce the best results. The actual procedure for overall planning is identical to the procedure for interior planning except that other elements in addition to the floor plan are considered. Thus preliminary elevations are sketched along with preliminary floor plan, plot plan, and details.

The choice of house styling may affect the type of planning. A ranch house or modern house might be planned from the inside out (interior planning), but a symmetrical, traditional structure would be planned somewhat from outside in (overall planning). For example, Figure 11 shows two alternate front elevations of the A residence which were sketched when the plan was developed. Notice that the side elevations were not sketched, allowing the windows and doors to fall at random. The front elevation, then, represents overall planning; the side elevations represent interior planning only.

PLAN ANALYSIS

The ability to critically analyze a plan—whether designed by you or by someone else—is a talent you must develop. The entire design process is really a series of these analyses, but the most comprehensive analysis should be made of the finished

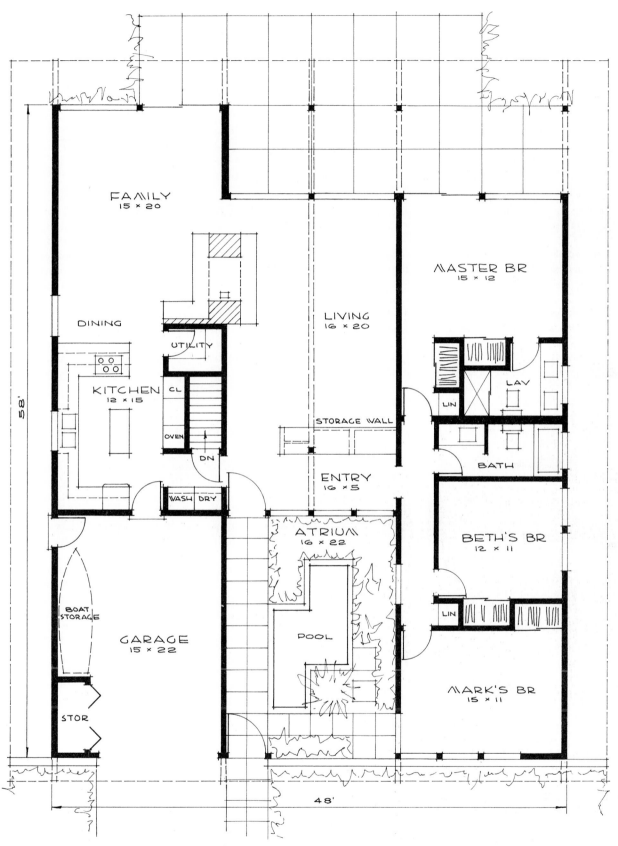

Figure 10 *Finished floor plan sketch of the A residence. Compare with the thumbnail sketches and preliminary sketches, and with the finished drawings.*

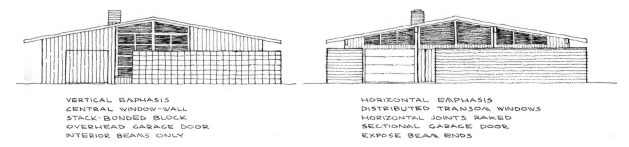

VERTICAL EMPHASIS
CENTRAL WINDOW-WALL
STACK-BONDED BLOCK
OVERHEAD GARAGE DOOR
INTERIOR BEAMS ONLY

HORIZONTAL EMPHASIS
DISTRIBUTED TRANSOM WINDOWS
HORIZONTAL JOINTS RAKED
SECTIONAL GARAGE DOOR
EXPOSE BEAM ENDS

Figure 11 *Preliminary front elevation sketches of the A residence.*

sketch, since it will serve as the basis for the working drawings.

Procedure. Each planning item that has been discussed should be studied for possible flaws or omissions:

1. *Program.* Each program requirement must be satisfied. Do not trust to memory; go through the program item by item.
2. *Orientation.* Check each room for the orientation of sun, wind, and views desired. Has best use been made of topography?
3. *Circulation.* Do not trust a visual check. Rather, take a pencil and actually trace the path of common circulation patterns. They should be simple and uncomplicated.

EXAMPLE

A typical early-morning pattern would be:

bedroom → bathroom → bedroom → kitchen → dining area → kitchen → coat closet → garage

4. *Efficiency.* Calculate hall area percentage (should be less than 10 percent) and house efficiency (should be greater than 70 percent).

EXAMPLE

Check hall area percentage and house efficiency of the A residence (see Figure 10).

Approximate total area: 2,200 sq. ft.
Approximate hall area: 150 sq. ft.
Approximate room area: 1,600 sq. ft.

Hall area percentage $= \dfrac{150}{2,200} \times 100 = 7\%$ O.K.

House efficiency (tare) $= \dfrac{1,600}{2,200} \times 100 = 73\%$ O.K.

5. *Elevations.* Carefully consider how the floor plan will coordinate with the exterior elevations. Also consider details and construction. The framing method may affect the maximum room size.
6. *Utilities.* Has space been allowed for utilities such as plumbing walls, heating, and chimney? Are the kitchen and bathroom plumbing adjacent for economy? Are bearing partitions on different floors directly over one another?
7. *Individual room design.* Study each room separately to see if it meets its requirements of function, aesthetics, and economy. Compare the proposed room sizes with your list of familiar rooms and their sizes. Are the rooms too commonplace and ordinary? Or have you planned extreme features which will be costly and eventually embarrassing? Figure 12 shows some common planning errors.

COMPUTER-AIDED DESIGN*

The computer as an architectural design tool has been more than a theoretical possibility for many years. Advancements in electronic technology during the 1970s and 1980s have greatly reduced the cost of computing, and a majority of larger architectural/engineering firms now find this technology an efficient and cost-effective tool. A number of design-oriented computer graphics systems have been developed and are available for purchase or rental. Each system contains a repertoire of standard programs and graphic symbols as well as special programs and data as desired by individual firms. The ARK−2 system, described in Chapter 1, is one such system. Another system, marketed by the Computervision Corporation, Figure 13, is more general in application and is widely used by architectural and engineering firms for many of the traditional office drafting and design tasks. A typical setup for an architectural office would appear as follows.

The Computervision system. A drafter, working on what appears to be a standard drafting table, can now use a special parallel ruling device that is actually a digitizer. A small microcomputer can

---

* Courtesy of Professor W. Quadrel, Rensselaer Polytechnic Institute and Professor Raymon J. Masters, The Pennsylvania State University.

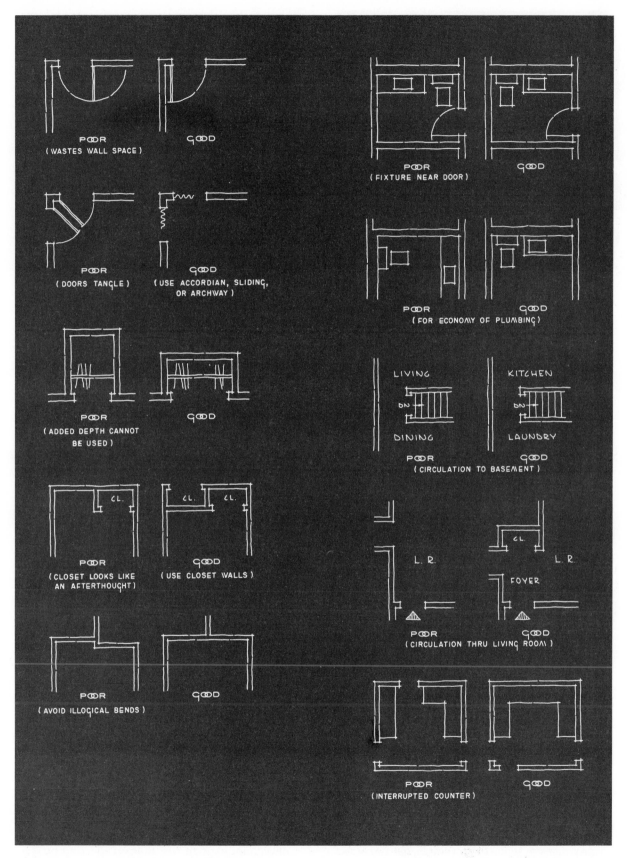

Figure 12 *Correction of common planning errors.*

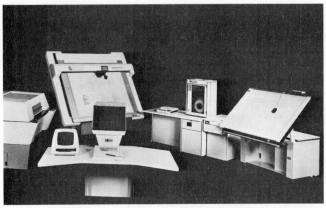

Courtesy of Computervision Corporation.

Figure 13   *The Computervision's Designer System.*

detect and locate any point on the drafting table to within .005 inches by sensing the position of the digitizer arm. For instance, the drafter may be tracing a preliminary sketch of a floor plan with the device, and when standard items such as bathtubs, plumbing and electrical fixtures, or door frames are required, he or she can have them located at an indicated position by pressing a coded button on a keypad. There are many such buttons on this keypad, and each one represents a standard graphical element. The buttons can be redefined to represent new elements by indicating the desired change to the microcomputer. As the drafter works, a CRT (cathode ray tube) continually displays what he is describing (digitizing), and mistakes are quickly noticed and easily corrected. After the plan is described in this manner, it can be stored, rescaled, or changed as desired.

The digitizer used by this system is special in that it can reverse its function and, under the control of the microcomputer, become a line-plotting device. A special holder accommodates a technical pen, and the entire sketch can be redrafted quickly in a form more precise and complete than the original sketch. All the lines are precisely horizontal, vertical, or at the specified angle, and all desired symbols are present.

If more accurate drawings are required, the computer can store the drawing on a small magnetic cassette tape that can be read by other microcomputers with larger plotting devices. One such device is produced by the Xynetics Corporation. It is a flatbed plotter incorporating a unique linear drive motor that is capable of producing drawings at high speeds; lines can be drawn at speeds up to sixty inches per second.

Architectural databases. Computervision is one among many systems that produce multiview and pictorial drawings of buildings. Other systems em-ploy analytical programs to solve structural, mechanical, and energy problems in buildings. Both types of systems require geometric information about the building in order to perform their tasks, although in many cases graphic functions and analytical (numerical) functions are kept entirely separate. By forming a *database* containing the building representation, both analytical and graphic data can be stored in a common location. The building representation contains geometric information (such as the location of walls and roofs) and attribute information (such as insulation, fire-hour ratings, and acoustic absorption). The efficiency of the computer system is greatly increased because both analytical programs and graphic programs can draw information from a common database. As updates are made to the building design, the database is also updated, which in turn produces different analytical results as well as new drawings reflecting the designer's changes. To create such a system, a considerable amount of research has been devoted to developing an adequate scheme for the building representation. All of the building elements must be linked geometrically for the computer to understand how the building's pieces fit together. Once the building geometry is described, the computer can integrate various programs for solving some of the nongraphical problems, which might include some of the following topics.

Architectural management. Problems associated with the management of multiple design projects may be solved through computer techniques. To increase the efficiency of the office, the computer can store information on these projects, and, by analyzing their requirements, help allocate the necessary manpower and resources to each project at the most appropriate time. Other computational techniques such as the *critical path method* are useful for scheduling and controlling the progress of a building project from its inception through construction. A particularly useful feature of this type of management is the ability to control the cash flow of a project in order to reduce cost.

Estimating. Architectural drafters are often required to prepare quantity takeoffs, schedules for items such as doors and finishes, cost estimates, and specifications for the building construction contracts. Computers can simplify the task of those processes that may involve careful measuring of material quantities as shown on architectural drawings. If the drawings have been developed through a computer program and the information stored in a database, then it is possible for quantities to be automatically calculated, schedules produced, and current cost indexes added to produce a cost estimate.

Specifications. Computerized specification writing was one of the first applications of computers to the building design field. The computer maintains a master file of current product specifications and produces basic specifications by request from the architect. The documents are then assembled and printed within minutes. Word processing allows fast additions to and deletions from the text and automatically formats the specifications to produce a final copy.

Architectural engineering. Another common area of computer application is the engineering of structural, mechanical, and electrical systems. It is possible for an engineer to describe, graphically or numerically, a design concept for computer analysis. After the appropriate loading conditions have been keyed into the computer, it can analyze the structure and produce stress diagrams. A structural engineer can quickly determine the most efficient solution for the building framing to minimize the weight, difficulty of construction, and cost of the project. After the final design changes have been completed, the computer will produce the shop fabrication drawings. Heating, ventilating, and air conditioning systems can be analyzed in a similar fashion. Plumbing and electrical systems can be sized and optimized and pictorials produced.

Code checking. The process of checking a building design against state building codes is one of the most time-consuming, yet most important, tasks in the design process. The computer can be used to determine if a given building design meets the code requirements for accessibility and fire safety. For example, the computer can check the distance between each room and the nearest exit for safe evacuation. It can also check widths and clearances for maneuvering wheelchairs. Many violations of the codes can be brought to the attention of the architect for redesign.

Site analysis. Site features, prevailing winds, and solar orientation can be studied by the computer to determine the placement of the building to minimize energy losses and conflicts with natural systems. Cut-and-fill studies can be performed to reduce the cost of site development. Roadway alignment, parking, and storm runoff can be checked to ensure feasible, economical, and safe solutions.

Creative design. One of the most controversial areas of architectural research is the use of computers in creative design. Despite considerable investigation in this area, researchers have yet to produce a comprehensive computer program to model the creative design process. There are prob-

ably two major reasons for this. First, the human design process is not clearly understood, sometimes not even by the designers themselves. Much of the process depends on intuition, pattern recognition, and cognitive synthesis: traits that are not readily programmable into a computer. Secondly, current computer systems only process information serially, which does not necessarily pattern the human thought process. Researchers are currently trying to develop special types of computers capable of *artificial intelligence* (also called *cybernetics*). The construction of this computer will allow it to learn through experience, recognize patterns, draw inferences, and perform other "creative" tasks. Computer systems displaying this "intelligence" will have a major impact on the creative design process.

The Computer as a consultant. Computers and computer programs in use today are basically to assist the designer in making better design decisions. Computers help in structuring problems by organizing the criteria and variables of the design problem so that they can be efficiently solved. These programs are most effective when they can answer "What if . . . ?" questions. The architect may typically ask, "What if I change the building form? How will that affect the structural systems, energy systems, building cost?" By organizing the criteria and variables of the problem, the computer can be used to answer these questions quickly and ultimately aid the architect in creating a better environment.

Computer access: Time sharing vs. workstations. The extent of the usefulness and acceptance of a computer graphics system will depend to a large degree on its cost effectiveness. While it may be feasible for larger firms to own or lease advanced systems, smaller firms may have difficulty in generating enough use to justify obtaining their own system. An alternate solution is to connect to a large central computer through remote terminals. These terminals use ordinary telephone lines to communicate with a host computer that may be many miles away. The host computer can support hundreds of such remote terminals through *time sharing*. As the term implies, the remote terminals share the resources of the central computer. At any given instant, a large number of these remote terminals may be idle—perhaps while the drafters view displays and make decisions. When this happens, the central computer processes problems submitted by other active terminals instead of simply idling. In this way, the efficiency of the total system can be increased, and the costs to individual subscribers lowered.

There is an increasing trend towards the decentralization of time sharing systems in the 1980s;

and lower hardware prices are encouraging architects to purchase *workstations* instead. A workstation consists of a graphics CRT, a digitizer, and a hardcopy device attached to a powerful microcomputer. Occasionally, a small number of other CRTs may be networked to the main workstation. Workstations have enough computational power to solve most graphic and analytic problems and have the advantage of maintaining the architect's independence from a central computer system.

Speech processing. Looking again to the future, we can expect to see more "user friendly" computer systems that will recognize human voice and respond by synthetic voice rather than requiring manual operation of keyboards. Some systems now available commercially permit voice-actuated telephone dialing, stock market quotations, and machine control.

REFERENCE PLAN SOURCES

Better Homes and Gardens, 1716 Locust Street, Des Moines, IA 50336

Brick Institute of America, 11490 Commercial Park Drive, Suite 300, Reston, VA 22091

Good Housekeeping, 959 Eighth Avenue, New York, NY 10019

Homes for Living, Inc., 107-40 Queens Boulevard, Forest Hills, NY 11375

Home Planners, Inc., 23761 Research Drive, Farmington Hills, MI 48024

National Forest Products Association, 1250 Connecticut Avenue NW, Washington, DC 20036

National Home Planning Service, 37 Mountain Avenue, Springfield, NJ 07801

Portland Cement Association, Old Orchard Road, Skokie, IL 60077-4321

Sunset, The Magazine of Western Living, Lane Publishing Co., 80 Willow Road, Menlo Park, CA 94025-3691

STUDY QUESTIONS

1. In architecture, what is meant by the term *orientation?* Name four different kinds of architectural orientation.
2. In architecture, what is meant by the terms:
   a. Circulation
   b. Prototype
   c. Poché
3. Indicate which sets of rooms should be planned adjacent to each other in residential design:
   a. Kitchen and dining room
   b. Kitchen and bedrooms
   c. Bath and bedrooms
   d. Bath and dining room
   e. Living and dining room
4. What is the main advantage in planning the kitchen, laundry, and bathrooms close to one another?
5. A house of 1,500 sq. ft. total floor area contains 1,150 sq. ft. of area actually occupied by rooms and 100 sq. ft. of hall area. Is this an efficient house?
6. What is the difference between:
   a. Furniture templates and room templates
   b. Interior planning and overall planning
   c. Thumbnail sketches and preliminary sketches

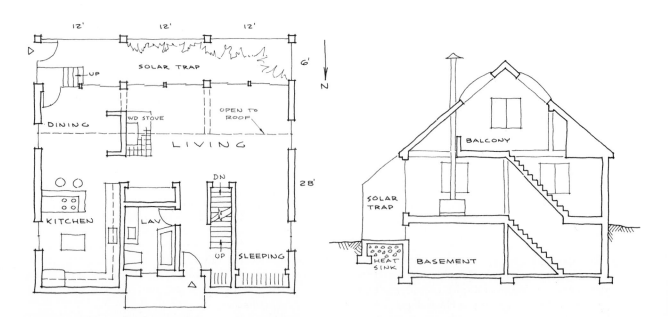

Figure 14   *Thumbnail sketches of a passive solar home*

LABORATORY PROBLEMS

1. Using a scale of $\frac{1}{8}'' = 1'$, prepare a preliminary layout of the A residence making any improvements you feel are desirable.
2. A one-floor summer cottage is to be planned to have a living area, kitchen, bedroom, bathroom, and garage. Make a thumbnail sketch showing the location of each room if the plot has the following features: level, best view to the west, winter wind from the north, summer breezes from the southwest.
3. Using the method of templates, design a master bedroom to contain 3'-3" × 6'-6" twin beds, 2'-0 × 4'-0 chest of drawers, 1'-6" × 3'-0 cedar chest, 1'-6" × 3'-0 kidneyshaped dressing table, 2'-2" × 2'-2" chair, and 1'-6" × 1'-6" night table.
4. Using the method of templates, lay out a residence having the following rooms: 13' × 19' living area, 9' × 9' dining area, 9' × 12' kitchen, 11' × 13' master bedroom, 9' × 11' bedroom, small bathroom, and full basement.

5. Using the thumbnail sketches shown in Figure 14 as a guide, prepare the following preliminary or finished sketches (as assigned by your instructor) for a low-cost, passive solar home:
   a. First floor plan
   b. Balcony floor plan
   c. Structural section (see Chapter 24)
   d. Elevations (see Chapter 24)
6. Make a preliminary layout for a house meeting the requirements assigned by your instructor.
7. Make the preliminary layout for your original house design using the planning procedure assigned by your instructor:
   a. Prototype
   b. Templates
   c. Interior planning
   d. Overall planning
8. Make a critical plan analysis for your original house design by listing its strong and weak features.

21 / Floor Plans

WORKING DRAWINGS

The finished drawings made by the architect and used by the contractor are called working drawings. The working drawings, together with the specifications and the general conditions, form the legal contract between the owner and contractor. Since the working drawings are a major portion of the contract documents, they should be very carefully drawn.

A complete set of working drawings includes the following sheets in this order:

1. Title page and index (a perspective is often included)
2. Plot plan
3. Foundation plan
4. First-floor plan
5. Second-floor plan
6. Elevations
7. Sections
8. Typical details
9. Schedules
E1. Electrical requirements
H1. Heating and air conditioning
P1. Plumbing
V1. Ventilation
S1. Floor framing plan
S2. Roof framing plan
S3. Column schedule
S4. Structural details

Usually all of the working drawings are drawn to the same scale ($\frac{1}{8}'' = 1'$ or $\frac{1}{4}'' = 1'$), with the exception of details, which are drawn to a larger scale, and the plot plan, which is drawn to an engineer's scale.

Before starting finished drawings, most draftsmen prefer to prepare *mock-ups* of each sheet. This organizes the set of working drawings so that related information fits on the same or adjacent sheets, and ensures that no drawing will have to be redrawn due to its poor placement on a sheet.

Mock-ups are merely sketched forms (usually rectangles) in proportion to the finished drawings. They should allow room for all expected dimensions and notes. Mock-ups are also called *layouts, dummies,* or *cartoons.*

FLOOR PLANS

Of all the different kinds of working drawings, the floor plan is the most important since it includes the greatest amount of information. The floor plan is the first drawing started by the designer, but it may be the last finished because the designer will transfer attention to the sections, elevations, and details required to complete the floor plan design.

A floor plan is actually a sectional drawing obtained by passing an imaginary cutting plane through the walls about 4' above the floor (midway between floor and ceiling). The cutting plane may be offset to a higher or lower level so that it cuts through all desired features (such as a high strip window). In the case of a split-level house, the cutting plane must be considerably offset.

If the finished sketch has been carefully made, the floor plan can be drawn without much trouble. Notice in the accompanying floor plan of the A residence (Figure 1), the similarity with the finished sketch of Figure 10 in Chapter 20. Of course, if the designer feels a sketch can be improved upon, it is done.

The steps used in drawing a floor plan are illustrated in Figure 2. A portion of the first-floor plan of the A residence is used as an example.

FIRST-FLOOR PLAN

Step 1: Wall layout. Lay out the exterior and interior walls very lightly on tracing vellum using a hard, sharp pencil. A scale of $\frac{1}{4}'' = 1'$ should be used for a residence, $\frac{1}{8}'' = 1'$ for a larger structure. Always indicate the scale in the title block or on

DOOR SCHEDULE

MK	NO	SIZE	DESCRIPTION
1	1	4'-0 x 7'-0 x 1"	CEDAR GATE
2	1	3'-8" x 6'-8" x 1 3/4"	3 PANEL WP
3	3	2'-8" x 6'-8" x 1 3/4"	FLUSH-SOLID WP
4	5	2'-6" x 6'-8" x 1 3/8"	FLUSH-HOLLOW BIRCH
5	2	2'-4" x 6'-8" x 1 3/8"	" " "
6	2	3'-6" x 6'-8" x 1 3/8"	LOUVER BI-SWING WP

MK	NO	SIZE	DESCRIPTION
7	1	2'-4" x 3'-4" x 1 3/8"	LOUVER BI-SWING WP
8	2	2'-0 x 3'-4" x 1 3/8"	" " "
9	4	7'-6" x 7'-0 x 1"	BI-SLIDE ALUMINUM
10	4	4'-0 x 6'-8" x 1 3/8"	FLUSH BI-SLIDE BIRCH
11	2	3'-0 x 6'-8" x 1 3/8"	FLUSH SLIDE WP
12	1	6'-0 x 6'-8" x 1 3/8"	FLUSH BI-FOLD WP
13	1	11'-6" x 7'-0 x 1 3/8"	4 PANEL OVERHD GAR WP

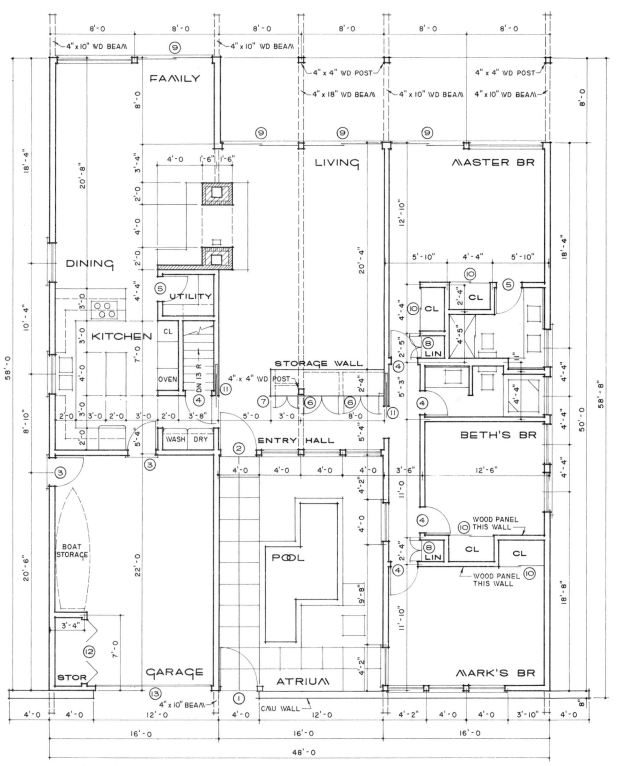

Figure 1   *Floor plan of the A residence.*

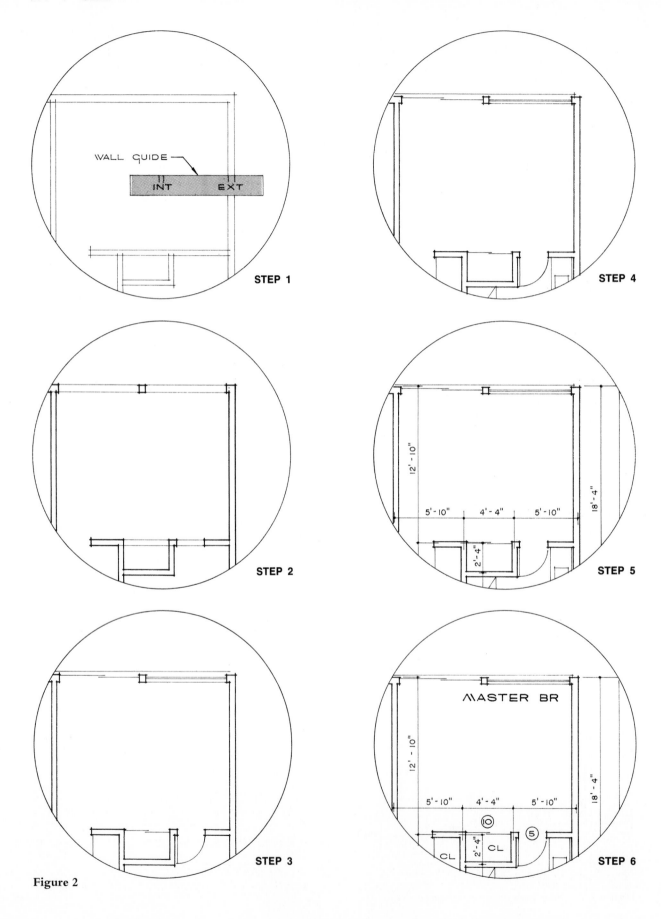

Figure 2

the drawing. To save time measuring the thicknesses of exterior and interior walls, a wall guide may be made by marking the wall thicknesses on a strip of paper. The wall sizes shown in the accompanying table may be used.

Wall Sizes

	Thickness
Wood-frame walls	
Exterior walls	6"
Interior partitions	5"
Brick-veneered walls	10"
Brick walls	
With two courses of brick	8"
With two courses of brick and air space	10"
With three courses of brick	12"
Concrete block walls	
Light	8"
Medium	10"
Heavy	12"

Step 2: Wall completion. Still using a hard, sharp pencil, locate the windows and doors on the wall layout.

Windows. The final placement of windows is determined, keeping fenestration, compass direction, pleasantness of view, and amount of light and air required in mind. Window selection depends on the style, design, and appearance of the building. See Chapter 16 for more detail.

The width of the windows given on the plan is that of the sash opening. Remember to allow room for the surrounding framing in close conditions.

Doors. The final door placement should take into consideration the door swing and furniture placement. Plan for unbroken wall spaces where they are needed, making sure no unnecessary doors are specified. Remember that every swinging door takes up valuable floor space (the area through which it swings) and two wall areas (the area containing the door and the area the door swings against). Do not discount sliding and accordion doors for closets, and especially for little-used openings.

Interior doors:	2'-6" × 6'-8" × 1⅜"
Allow for approximately 2'-9" rough opening	
Front door:	3'-0 × 6'-8" × 1¾"
Allow for approximately 3'-3" rough opening	
Rear door:	2'-8" × 6'-8" × 1¾"
Allow for approximately 2'-11" rough opening	

Doors opening into rooms from a hall should swing into the room against the wall. Use sliding, folding, or accordion doors if space is at a premium, but remember that these should not be specified for often-used bedroom and bath doors since they require more time and energy to operate. As a rule, swinging doors should be used on all but closets.

Occasionally it is better to use archways in place of doors for the sake of economy, appearance, and spaciousness. They should be shown on the plan by two dashed lines.

After all windows and doors have been located, the wall lines are darkened using a soft pencil. The wood frame wall convention is shown in the illustration of step 2.

Step 3: Details. Using a sharp, but black, line weight, add the floor plan details.

Windows. Show the sill and glass as indicated in Chapter 16.

Doors. Show the doors and their swings. Show the sill on exterior doors.

Stairs. A preliminary cross-sectional layout must be first drawn to determine the total run and the number and size of treads and risers. This layout is saved and used later as the basis for the finished stair details. Draw about half of the full stair run and letter a small "UP" at the stair foot, and "DN" (down) at the stair head. Indicate the number of risers. (For example: UP-14R.) See Chapter 25 for more detail.

Fireplace. Show the overall width and depth of brickwork, location of basement flue, ash drop, and the outline of the fireplace opening and hearth. Cross sectioning is used to indicate the brickwork. See Chapter 26 for more detail.

Step 4: Equipment. Show all built-in equipment, such as bathroom fixtures (bathtub, toilet, lavatory, and medicine cabinet), kitchen fixtures (cabinets, sink, built-in wall ovens, countertop burners, and built-in refrigerator or freezer), and closet fixtures (shelves and clothesrod). The location of a movable stove or refrigerator is shown even if it is not included in the contract. Notice that the wall cabinets are shown as hidden lines. A hidden line on an architectural plan may refer to a feature (cabinet, archway, or beam) *above* the level of the imaginary cutting plane. The locations of lighting and heating devices are included only when they will not make the floor plan crowded. Occasionally all furniture placement is shown.

Step 5: Dimensioning. Dimension all walls and partitions using dimension lines spaced approximately $\frac{3}{8}''$ apart. The dimension lines are continuous with the $\frac{3}{32}''$-high figures lettered above them. The dimension figures should be in feet and inches (to the nearest $\frac{1}{16}''$), and should read from the bottom or right-hand side of the drawing. In frame construction, the dimensions are given from the outside faces of the studs in exterior walls and to the center lines of interior partitions. Cumulative dimensions should lie in one line if possible, but try to avoid dimensioning over other features. Also remember to allow some open spaces for lettering the room names later on. Dots or small circles may be used in place of arrowheads. Check carefully that no *necessary* dimension is omitted, but some *minor* dimensions can be omitted for the sake of clarity. For example, the width of some closets may have to be scaled from the drawing. This is accepted practice since the exact location of these partitions is not critical. See Chapter 10.

Step 6: Lettering. Letter room names in the center or lower left-hand corner of each room without lettering over other features. Room lettering should be approximately $\frac{3}{16}''$ high. Special explanatory notes on materials and construction are added using $\frac{3}{32}''$-high lettering. See Appendix E for the proper spelling of words often misspelled on architectural drawings.

A $\frac{1}{8}''$-high schedule mark (a number for doors and a letter for windows) is assigned to each door or window of the same size and type. The door numbers are placed within $\frac{1}{4}''$-diameter circles in a convenient location near the doors. The door schedule is added as shown in Chapter 18. Window marks and the window schedule may be included also, although they usually appear on the elevations.

Any additional information necessary for proper construction should be added at this point. Include such details as concrete porches, window areaways, hose bibbs, and electrical fixtures if they do not appear elsewhere.

Step 7: Checking. In a professional drafting room, checkers have a most responsible position. They must certify that they have checked and approved every line and dimension on the drawings. If done correctly, this procedure should guarantee that nothing has been omitted and that nothing is in error.

In a classroom, however, there is no professional checker, and you must check your own work. This is very difficult to do properly since you will, in all likelihood, repeat any drawing errors in your checking. If possible, it is a good idea to trade the responsibility of checking with another student. If this is not possible, you should check the drawing only after it has been put aside for several days to assure a fresh outlook.

SECOND-FLOOR PLAN

After the first-floor plan is completed, related plans such as those for the basement and second floor are started by tracing common features from the first-floor plan. The exterior walls may usually be traced, together with bearing partitions, plumbing walls, stairways, and chimney location. Principal walls should be over one another from foundation to roof insofar as possible, to ensure a stiffer frame and facilitate plumbing and heating installations. Also, the fenestration may require that first- and second-floor windows be directly over one another.

BASEMENT PLAN

The basement plan or foundation plan (Figure 3) is begun by tracing common features from the first-floor plan: the outside lines of exterior walls, the stairway, and the chimney location. The foundation wall sizes shown in the accompanying table may be used.

A hidden line is used to indicate the size of foundation footings and column footings.

Dimensioning practice is somewhat different from that used for the floor plans, in that dimensions will run from the faces of all masonry walls or partitions rather than from their center lines. Also the openings for windows and doors in masonry walls are dimensioned to faces rather than to center lines.

Some special considerations in designing basements must be remembered:

1. The size and location of columns and girders.
2. The size, spacing, and direction of joists (double-headed arrow indicates joist direction).

Foundation Wall Sizes

	Thickness
Under wood-frame house	
Concrete block	8", with pilasters 16' oc
Poured concrete	10"
Under veneered construction	
Concrete block	10"
Poured concrete	10"
Under solid masonry construction	
Concrete block	12"
Poured concrete	12"

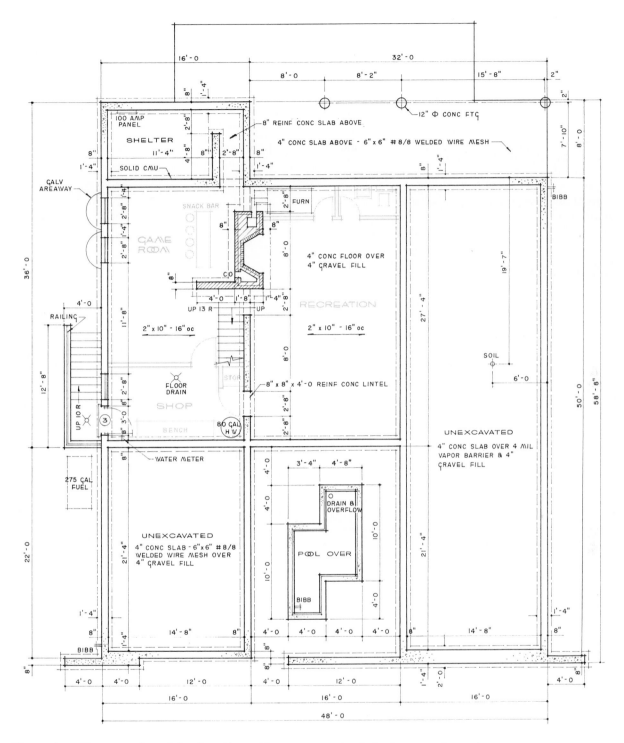

Figure 3 *Basement plan of the A residence (future construction is in the screened area.)*

3. Stiffening pilasters, needed on long, straight runs of wall.
4. The furnace, located near chimney flue (within 10′).
5. Provision for fuel storage, near the driveway but removed from the furnace (beyond 10′).
6. The hot-water heater.
7. The water meter, located near water line entrance.
8. Floor drains.
9. Electrical entrance panel, located near entrance pole.

10. Labeling of unexcavated areas, crawl spaces, and concrete floors, together with any additional helpful information. For example, the thickness of a basement floor is usually noted on the basement plan. Specify 3″ minimum concrete for a basement floor and 4″ minimum concrete for a garage floor or finished slab floor.

Notice that the basement of the A residence has been designed for the future construction of a recreation room, game room, shop, and lavatory. This allows better planning in locating necessary utilities.

STUDY QUESTIONS

1. List the drawings normally included in a set of residential working drawings.
2. Sketch a section of each of the following walls, showing the actual size of materials to illustrate the total wall thickness normally used on a plan:
   a. Exterior wood-frame wall
   b. Interior wood-frame partition
   c. Exterior brick-veneered wall
3. List the most commonly used size (width, height, and thickness) of the following doors:
   a. Front entrance door
   b. Rear entrance door
   c. Interior doors
4. What other drawings must be considered before the floor plan is completed?
5. What does a hidden line on an architectural plan represent? Give three examples.
6. When drawing a second-floor plan, what features may be traced from the first-floor plan?
7. When drawing a basement plan, what features may be traced from the first-floor plan?
8. In the layout of a basement plan, what special considerations must be made in the location of:
   a. Furnace
   b. Fuel storage
   c. Water meter
   d. Electrical entrance panel
9. Should bedroom doors swing into the bedroom or hall? Why?

LABORATORY PROBLEMS

1. Prepare a title page and index for your set of working drawings to include:
   a. Title information (name of project, location, name of designer, date)
   b. Index listing number and title of each sheet
   c. Legend of symbols used
   d. List of abbreviations used
   e. Modular dimensioning note
   f. Interior perspective
   g. Exterior perspective
2. Using a scale of $\frac{1}{4}″ = 1′$, draw the following plans of the A residence:
   a. First-floor plan
   b. Basement plan
3. Draw the plans of the building assigned by your instructor:
   a. First-floor plan
   b. Second-floor plan
   c. Basement plan
4. Draw the plans of a residence for the family assigned:
   a. Bank president and spouse; no children; income, $300,000; wide musical interests; large art collection; two cars
   b. Physics professor and spouse, a lawyer; two children; combined income, $160,000; large library and research laboratory in home; two cars
   c. Architectural drafter and spouse; three children; income, $60,000; office for additional work done at home; two cars
   d. Managing editor of magazine; one child; income, $50,000; computer terminal in home office for work at home; one car
   e. Bachelor airplane navigator; income, $45,000; hobby: large model railroad layout; one car
   f. High school physical education director and spouse; four children; combined income, $40,000; spouse conducts dancing studio and piano lessons at home; one car
   g. Assistant manager of chain store; one child; income, $25,000; hobbies, cooking and ceramics; one car
5. Draw a plan showing your concept of a dwelling to be built under one of the following conditions:
   a. Flexible plan required (must be used equally well by families with one to four children)
   b. Low-cost, mass-produced
   c. Unpleasant view in all directions
   d. Physically handicapped couple
6. (For the advanced student) Draw a plan showing your concept of a dwelling of the future to be built:
   a. In a desert area
   b. On extremely mountainous terrain
   c. Entirely over water
   d. Completely underground
   e. Occupying a minimum amount of land
7. Complete the plans of your original house design:
   a. First-floor plan
   b. Second-floor plan
   c. Basement plan

22 / The Plot Plan

The plot plan shows the location of the house on the plot together with information on terraces, walks, driveways, contours, elevations, and utilities. A roof plan or landscaping plan may be included.

The steps used in drawing a plot plan are illustrated in Figure 1. We will use the plot plan of the A residence (Figure 2) as an example.

STEP 1: PROPERTY LINES

Lay out and dimension the property lines using a medium-weight center line. The information is obtained from the site survey (Figure 1 of Chapter 28). The plot plan is usually drawn to an engineer's scale (such as 1″ = 20′) rather than to an architect's scale (such as $\frac{1}{16}$″ = 1′). Show the "north" arrow.

Bearings are given to show the compass direction of the property lines. Notice in Figure 2 that the opposite and parallel property lines have opposite bearings (such as S 65°10′W and its opposite N 65°10′E), because the surveyor started at one corner and surveyed clockwise around the perimeter until reaching the starting corner again.

STEP 2: CONTOUR LINES

A contour line is an imaginary line representing a constant elevation on the lot. The vertical distance between adjacent contour lines is called the *contour interval* and is usually 1′ for a residential lot.

The easiest way to learn to read contour lines is to imagine that you are constructing a model of the plot. For example, a model of the small section of sloping land shown in Step 2 of Figure 1 could be built by cutting out cardboard sections shaped to the contour lines.

Contour lines are drawn freehand and dimensioned by indicating their elevation above sea level or some other datum plane such as a nearby street or house. This information is also obtained from the site survey. On the plot plan of the A residence (Figure 2) notice that the contour lines indicate gently sloping ground, with the lowest point being the south-west corner. The elevations of any permanent markers at the plot corners should also be transferred from the site survey.

STEP 3: ZONING

The first-known zoning law was passed in ancient Rome to prevent industries from locating too near the central forum of the city. This established the principal that private property can be restricted in favor of the general welfare. The first comprehensive zoning ordinance in the United States was passed in New York City in 1916 as a consequence of a tragic fire at the Triangle Shirtwaist factory. Over one hundred dressmakers, mostly young girls, died in that building, which was higher than the reach of firefighting equipment, had no sprinklers, and had an uncompleted fire escape.

Most communities now have zoning ordinances that restrict the size and location of buildings to prevent crowding and encourage the most appropriate use of the land. It is imperative that the designer be familiar with, and adhere to, all zoning regulations and building codes. Several regulations of one community's zoning ordinance are given in Table I. Using these regulations, the following calculations are made for the A residence:

179

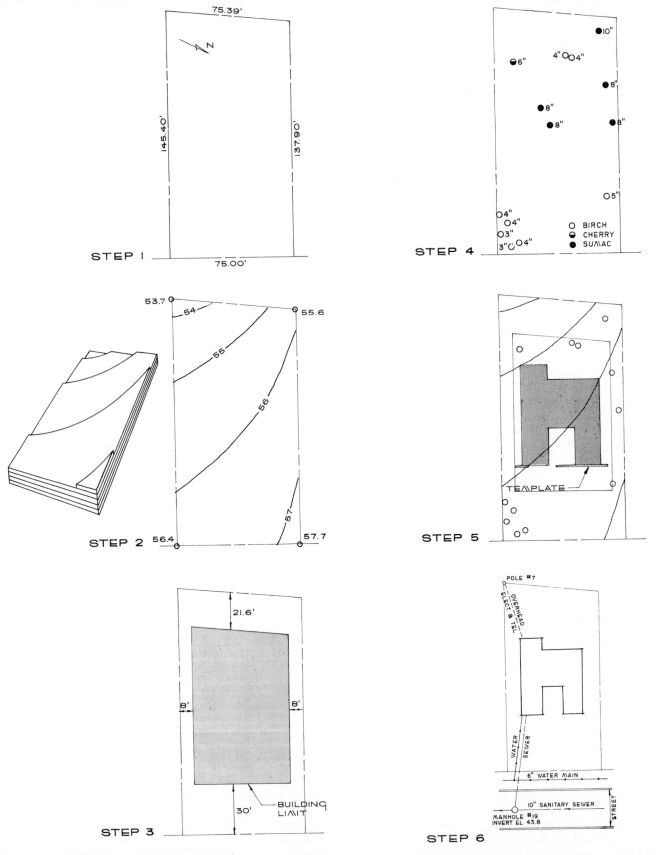

Figure 1   *Preparing a plot plan.*

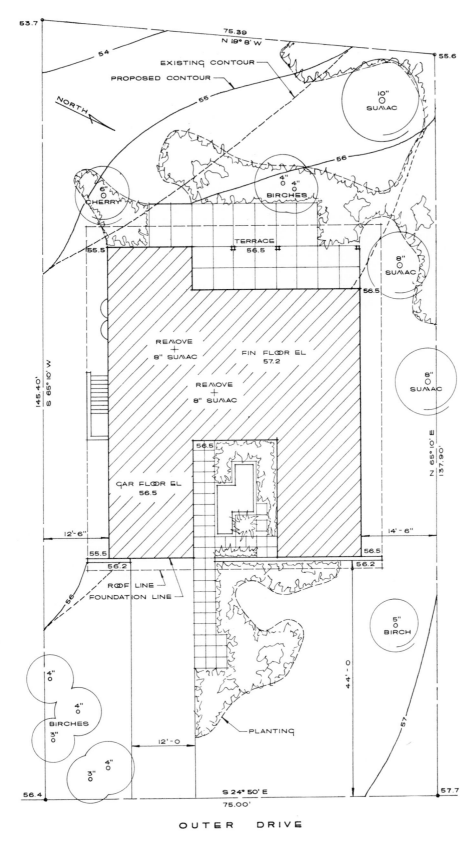

Figure 2 *Plot plan of the A residence.*

Table I   *Sample of Zoning Regulations*

Article V—Residence District

Section 501. Each lot in this district shall comply with the following minimum requirements:

501-1) Lot area:
   One-family dwelling   10,000 sq. ft.
   Two-family dwelling   12,000 sq. ft.

501-2) Lot width:
   One-family dwelling   75′
   Two-family dwelling   100′

501-3) Front yard depth:
   Dwelling 30′
   Nondwelling 40′

501-4) Side yard width:
   Dwelling and accessory building 8′
   Nondwelling 20′

501-5) Rear yard depth:
   The rear yard depth shall be at least 20 per-cent of the depth of the lot measured from the front building line to the nearest point of rear lot line but in no case shall this be less than 15′.

Section 502. The maximum height of structures in this district shall be:

502-1) Dwellings 26′ (not exceeding two stories)

502-2) Accessory building 16′ (not exceeding one story)

502-3) Nondwelling 40′

Check on lot area: $75 \times 141.6 = 10{,}620$ sq. ft. O.K. (greater than required 10,000 sq. ft.)
Check on lot width: 75′ O.K. (equal to required minimum of 75′)
Minimum front yard depth: 30′
Minimum side yard width: 8′
Minimum rear yard depth: $0.20(137.9 - 30) = 21.6′$ O.K. (greater than required 15′)
Check on dwelling height: 14′ O.K. (less than 26′ maximum)

Using light construction lines, show the front, side, and rear yard limits calculated on page 179 and above so that you know exactly where you are permitted to place your house.

STEP 4: TREES

The lot of the A residence contains birch, sumac, and cherry trees. These are plotted so that the house and driveway may be located without removing many of them. The type and diameter of each tree should be noted on the plot plan to aid in identification. No tree should remain within 5′ of the foundation because the excavation will disturb the roots so much that it will eventually die.

Figure 3 *Plan landscaping to provide both planting groups and uninterrupted lawn.*

Courtesy of Scholz Homes, Inc.

Figure 4   *A terrace well integrated with the interior plan.*

STEP 5: LOCATION OF HOUSE

The house may now be located in the position that will satisfy all requirements of solar orientation, wind orientation, topography, landscaping, zoning, and utilities. A paper template in the shape of the basement plan is useful since it can be shifted to various locations. When the final position is determined, draw in the plan with heavy lines using the outside basement dimensions. The plan may be sectioned if desired. Hidden lines are used to indicate roof overhang. On structures with fairly involved roof intersections, a roof plan is shown in place of a section to indicate ridges, valleys, and hips.

Show the elevation of the finished first floor and complete all details such as walks, drives, street names, notes, and scale.

STEP 6: UTILITIES

Existing utilities—such as electric, telephone, sewer, water, and gas lines—are often noted or ac-

tually located since they may affect the house location. For example, some of the factors to be considered in the location of the branch drain from the house to the street manhole connection are:

1. A minimum downward grade of $\frac{1}{4}''$/ft. must be maintained to the invert elevation (the bottom inside) of the sewer line.
2. The branch line must remain below the frost line to prevent damage from freezing.
3. The line must be straight, since changes in direction or grade, which collect sediment, should occur only at manholes.
4. If there are trees, cast-iron drains with poured-lead joints must be used instead of vitreous tile to prevent the roots growing into and blocking the drain.

STEP 7: ADJUSTMENT OF CONTOUR LINES

When the existing land contour is not satisfactory, it must be adjusted by cutting away or filling in. This is indicated on the plot plan by showing the proposed position of the contour lines with a solid line; the existing contours are still indicated, but as broken lines. Figure 2 shows how all of these steps are finished into the plot plan. It was decided to show the utilities on later mechanical plans to prevent overcrowding of the plot plan.

The ultimate goal of a plot plan is to show how the building will integrate with its environment. Two successful results are shown in Figures 3 and 4.

STUDY QUESTIONS

1. Distinguish between a contour line and a contour interval.
2. List the utilities to be considered when drawing a plot plan.

3. Why is it necessary to be familiar with the local zoning ordinance when drawing a plot plan?
4. List the bearings of the remaining property lines of a rectangular lot that has a front bearing of N 72°E and a right side bearing of N 18°W.

LABORATORY PROBLEMS

1. Draw the plot plan of the A residence.
2. Draw the plot plan of the building assigned by your instructor.
3. Complete the plot plan for your original house design.

VI / Elevations

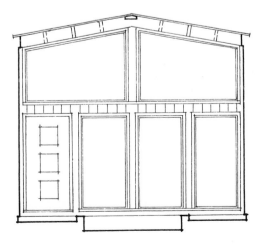

VI Elections

23 / Roofs

The type of roof specified for a house is a very important factor in exterior design. It also affects the interior. In a traditional house, the type of roof is pretty well determined by the house style. When the building is in a contemporary style, however, a wide variety of roof types may be used. The shape of the plan may also affect the roof choice. Whereas a rectangular plan could be roofed in nearly any manner, a rambling plan would be most economically covered by a flat roof. A hip roof, in such a case, would require much additional cutting and fitting.

The various types of roofs may be classified very broadly into two categories: roofs used mostly on traditional houses and roofs used mostly on contemporary houses. Let us look at each in turn.

TRADITIONAL ROOF TYPES
(Figure 1)

Gable. To be perfectly correct, the gable is the triangular portion of the end of the house, and this type of roof is a gabled roof. The gable roof is the most common form of roof since it is easy to construct, is pitched for drainage, and is universally accepted. This roof should be pitched high enough that louvers can be installed to allow warm air and moisture to escape. This roof may also be used in contemporary design.

Hip. A hip roof is more difficult to construct than a gable, but is still used with a low pitch on ranch houses. However, every hip or valley increases chances for leakage.

Gambrel. The gambrel roof is used on Dutch Colonial designs to increase headroom on the second floor. Since the framing is complicated, it is not widely used today.

Mansard. This type was named after the French architect who originated it. The Mansard roof is not built today but it was extensively used on French-styled houses at one time.

DORMER TYPES (Figure 2)

Gable. A dormer is used to let light into an otherwise dark area. The designer must weigh the expense of dormers against the expense of an additional story.

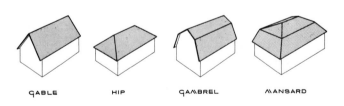

GABLE   HIP   GAMBREL   MANSARD

Figure 1   *Traditional roofs.*

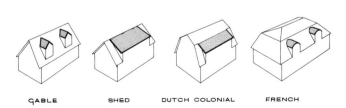

GABLE   SHED   DUTCH COLONIAL   FRENCH

Figure 2   *Dormers.*

187

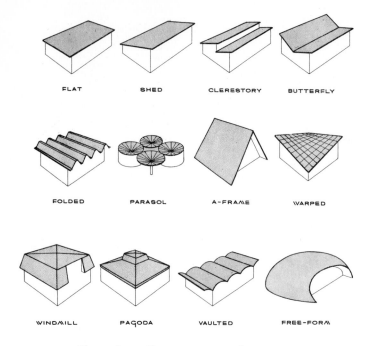

FLAT   SHED   CLERESTORY   BUTTERFLY

FOLDED   PARASOL   A-FRAME   WARPED

WINDMILL   PAGODA   VAULTED   FREE-FORM

Figure 3   *Contemporary roofs.*

Shed. A shed dormer will give nearly all the advantages of a full story, without disturbing the one-floor look of the house. This dormer type is sometimes called a *dustpan.*

Dutch Colonial. A Dutch Colonial dormer might be termed a shed dormer on a gambrel roof. The second-floor wall may be set back from the first-floor wall.

French. Rounded dormer tops indicate French influence.

CONTEMPORARY ROOF TYPES
(Figure 3)

Flat (Figures 4 and 5). The flat roof is the most common type of commercial roof. Most roofs that appear flat actually have a slight slope of $\frac{1}{4}''$/ft. to $\frac{1}{2}''$/ft. for drainage. Roofing is laid in layers (called *plies*) of tar and gravel or with membranes of plastic or other flexible material.

Some roofs are designed as perfectly flat thus allowing water to remain on them. This is called a *water-film roof* and the water serves as insulation from cold in winter and insulation from heat (by reflection and evaporation) in summer. Other roofs are designed to slope, but may become deflected so that *ponding* (puddles) occur. In either case, there is a great possibility of roof leaks. Standing water encourages growth of vegetation, producing roots that force their way through the roof seams, and fungi growth that deteriorates organic roofing materials. Also water that penetrates the roofing plies will freeze and further delaminate the roof.

Shed. The shed roof is ideally suited to the solar house if the high wall faces south. It will also give interesting interior effects if the beams are left exposed. Beams measuring $4'' \times 10''$ spaced 4' oc might be used. This roof takes standard roofing material. Contemporary roofs are often unique and do not fit into standard categories. The roof shown in Figures 6 and 7 is an example.

Clerestory. This roof solves the problem of introducing light into the center of a house. The clerestory may be used with a sawtooth roof as shown in Figure 3 or with other roof types.

Butterfly. The pitch and length of each side of the butterfly roof need not be equal. This roof

Figure 5   *A flat roof on a commercial design.*

Figure 4   *A flat roof on a residential design.*

"opens up" the house, providing plenty of light and air. Drains may be at the end of the valley or in the middle—running down through the center of the house.

Folded. Some roofs are so new that some imagination must be used to find descriptive names. As the name implies, the folded or pleated roof looks as though it were folded from a sheet of paper, and is quite popular in office and motel design. Roofing material may be exterior-grade plywood or metal.

Parasol (Figure 8). The parasol roof has become popular since the success of Wright's Johnson's Wax Building. Round and square variations are possible. Often the material used is reinforced concrete.

Free-form. The shape of free-form roofs may depend upon the method of construction. Urethane foam can be sprayed on a *knit jersey* material stretched over a pipe frame. It has proved to be strong, weather-resistant, and self-insulating, but some foamed plastics are dangerously flammable and toxic. See Figure 10 for a sprayed concrete house. A unique petal-shaped roof is shown in Figure 11.

A-frame. Originally specified for low-cost summer or winter cabins, the A-frame roof has been adapted to larger structures such as churches. The classic A-frame roof is a gable roof that reaches the ground on two sides. A variation is shown in Figure 9.

Warped. Beginnings have been made in the development of warped surfaces for roofs. In most cases, this warped surface is a hyperbolic parabo-

Figure 7   *Another view of the residence shown in Figure 6.*

Figure 8   *A beach pavilion with parasol roofs.*

Figure 6   *A wood-shingled roof of unique design for a hillside plot.*

Figure 9   *A metal roof on an A-frame.*

Figure 10 *Hobe Sound Bubble House, constructed by spraying concrete on an inflated plastic balloon.*

Figure 11 *A contemporary library with a petal-shaped roof.*

loid, that is, a surface generated by a line moving so that its ends are in contact with two skew lines. This produces a superior roof due to the high resistance to bending. Warped roofs have been constructed of molded plywood, reinforced concrete, and sprayed plastic.

Windmill. The windmill roof is often used on two-story town houses to lend interest to an otherwise simple design. This roof looks best when wood-shingled.

Pagoda. The pagoda roof provides an interesting interior, as well as exterior, design. The Oriental flavor should be extended to other elements of the building. Connected clusters of pagoda-roofed rooms have been successfully designed.

Vaults and domes. Vaults and domes have staged a comeback from the Byzantine days. More often used on commercial than residential buildings, they limit considerably the possible shapes of the floor plan.

A *geodesic dome* is framed of members nearly equal in length which are joined to form triangular patterns. The triangles are then joined to form pyramids, giving a double-faced structure of great strength. The framing members are usually straight rather than curved. Consequently, the roof shape is a polyhedron rather than a true spherical dome. See Figure 12. The steel geodesic dome shown in Figure 13 was specified for a tank car rebuilding plant. It is 384′ in diameter and 116′ high, one of the largest clear-span enclosures in the world.

Figure 12 *Close-up of the geodesic shaping of the Princeton gymnasium.*

Figure 13 *Union Tank Car Shop, Baton Rouge, Louisiana.*

ROOFING MATERIALS

Although several new roofing materials and methods have been mentioned, the large majority of residential roofs are constructed of built-up tar and gravel or membrane roofing when the roof is flat and of shingle when the roof slopes more than 3″/ft.

Built-up roofing. Built-up tar and gravel roofing is used on flat and slightly sloping roofs. It is constructed of alternate layers of roofing felt and mopped-on hot tar or asphalt. Three to five layers (called *plies*) are used and topped by crushed gravel or marble chips imbedded in the tar. Roofing contractors will bond a three-ply economy roof for ten years, and a five-ply roof for twenty years.

Membrane roofing. Membrane roofing is rapidly replacing built-up roofing for use on flat and slightly sloping roofs. Easy to apply and repair, membrane roofing is lighter in weight and a better heat reflector than built-up roofing. Most membranes are also available in various colors. The membrane is a thin layer (about $\frac{1}{8}″$ thick) of plastic, rubber, bitumen, or aluminum. Available in rolls or large sheets, the membrane is applied over mopped-on adhesive or may be loose-laid and covered with ballast of crushed gravel or marble chips. Joints are heat-sealed or spliced using a contact adhesive pressure-sealed by roller. Membranes also can be applied in fluid form by spray, brush, or squeegee. The membrane then hardens through chemical curing or evaporation of a solvent in the mixture. The manufacturer's bond for defective material is usually for fifteen years, but the roofer's guarantee for proper installation is usually only for two to five years.

Shingles. Fiber glass shingles, consisting of a fiber glass mat saturated with asphalt, are now commonly used in house construction because they are durable and their cost is moderate. Asphalt shingles, consisting of a cellulose mat saturated with asphalt, are still available. Wood shingles and shakes (Figures 14 and 15) are often of cedar or redwood and present a handsome appearance. Unfortunately the fire hazard is great. Roofing shingles are sold by *squares*. A square is the amount of shingling needed to roof 100 sq. ft.

Slate and tile (Figure 16) are occasionally used for roofing materials. Both are relatively heavy and expensive, however. Metal roofs of tin, copper, zinc, aluminum, and lead are often used on commercial buildings.

Plastic foam. Sprayed urethane foam roofs offer exciting possibilities for new architectural concepts. All free-form shapes are possible, construc-

Courtesy of Scholz Homes, Inc.

Figure 14   *A wood-shingled hip roof.*

Courtesy of Scholz Homes, Inc.

Figure 15   *A wood-shingled conical roof.*

Courtesy of Scholz Homes, Inc.

Figure 16   *A tile roof used with a contemporary design.*

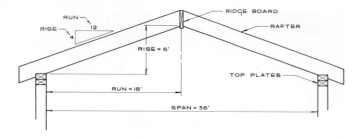

Figure 17   *Roof pitch terms.*

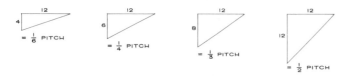

Figure 18   *Alternate method of specifying pitch.*

tion is economical, and it has three times the insulating value of common insulating materials. These roofs are formed by spraying on large balloons, inflatable forms, or fabric stretched over lightweight tubing. Spraying is continued until a thickness of 5″ is obtained.

Urethane foam is an organic polymer formed by chemical reaction between two liquids (isocyanate and polyol). These liquids are pumped from separate tanks to a mixing spray gun where the mixture begins to foam immediately, expanding to thirty times its original volume. Within a few minutes, the foam has hardened. It will adhere to most surfaces. Final density is about 3 lb./cu. ft. A serious disadvantage is that some forms of urethane foam are very flammable. Consequently, the foam should be covered by a fireproof material rather than installed exposed. Sprayed urethane

Table I   *Recommended Roof Pitch*

Type of Roofing	Recommended Roof Pitch
Built-up	Under 3-12
Fiber glass shingles	
Interlocking*	2-12 or more
Self-sealing*	2-12 or more
Cemented*	2-12 or more
Heavyweight*	2-12 or more
Heavyweight	3-12 or more
Regular	4-12 or more
Wood shingles	4-12 or more
Slate shingles	6-12 or more

* Double layer of roofing for underlay must be used.

foam should always be protected against any possible source of combustion.

ROOF PITCH

Some roof pitch terms are shown in Figure 17. The terms *rise* and *run* are used in two ways:

1. To describe the rise per unit of run. For example, the roof shown in Figure 17 has a rise of 4″ in a run of 1′.
2. To describe the *actual* dimensions of a roof. For example, the roof in Figure 17 has a rise of 6′, run of 18′, and span of 36′.

The roof pitch is also described in two ways:

1. By a pitch triangle on the elevations showing the rise in whole inches per 12″ of run. For example, the 4-12 pitch triangle shown in Figure 17 indicates a rise of 4″ for a run of 12″.
2. By a fraction whose numerator is the rise and denominator is the span. For example, a roof with a rise of 6′ and a span of 36′ has a $\frac{6}{36}$ pitch, which would be reduced and called a $\frac{1}{6}$ pitch. See Figure 18.

In general, the steeper roofs are found in areas where there are heavy snowfalls, since snow is naturally shed from a steep roof.

Special steps must be taken with low-pitched, shingled roofs to prevent wind from lifting the tabs and allowing water to seep under them. Several solutions are possible, as indicated in Table I:

1. Use interlocking tab shingles.
2. Use self-sealing shingles that have factory-applied adhesive on the underside.
3. Cement each tab with a spot of quick-setting adhesive during installation.
4. Use heavyweight shingles (300#, 15″ × 36″), which are stiffer than regular shingles (210#, 12″ × 36″) and are sized for triple overlap.

FLASHING

Thin sheets of soft metal are used to prevent leakage at critical points on roofs and walls. These sheets are called *flashing* and are usually of lead, zinc, copper, or aluminum. Areas that must be flashed are:

Intersections of roof with chimney, soil pipe, and dormer (see Figure 7, Chapter 26)
Roof valleys

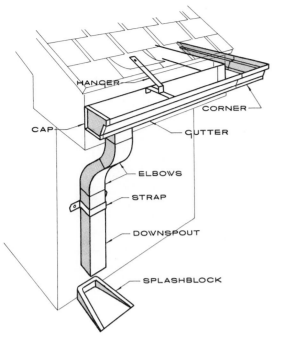

Figure 19 *Guttering terms.*

GUTTERING

Gutters are used when the soil is likely to be eroded by rain dripping from the roof, or when roof overhangs are less than 12″ (in a one-story structure) or 24″ (in a two-story structure). Downspouts conduct the water down the wall to a storm sewer (*not* a sanitary sewer), dry well, or splashblock (a concrete pad placed to prevent soil erosion) as shown in Figure 19. When gutters are omitted, a diverter is used to protect the entrances to the house from rainwater. Guttering is made of galvanized iron, copper, aluminum, zinc alloy, or wood, or it may be built into the roof as shown in Figure 28 of Chapter 28. Seamless guttering is formed from 200′-long rolls of aluminum.

SKYLIGHTS

Plastic domes are often used to light the interior of industrial buildings. Recently, skylights have been

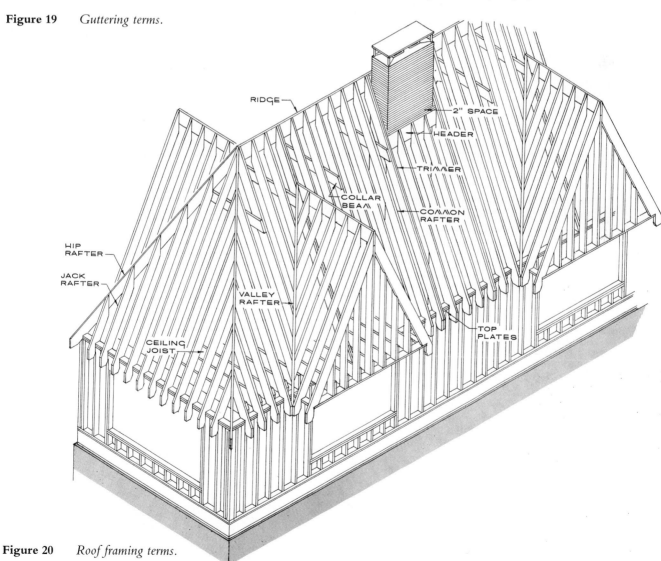

Figure 20 *Roof framing terms.*

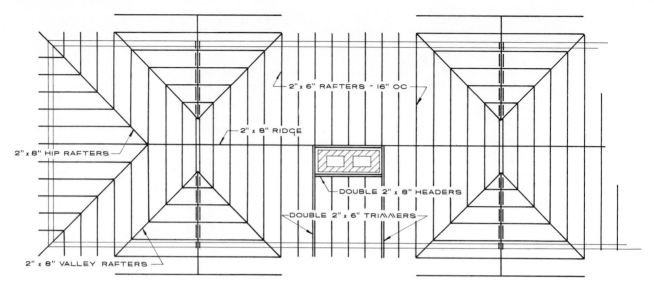

Figure 21   *Roof framing plan.*

used in residences to obtain specific effects. Both fixed and ventilation types are available in sizes ranging from 24″ square to 48″ square.

CONSTRUCTION

Roof framing is described in Chapter 28. Tables for the selection of rafters are given in Chapter 29. Figure 20 shows some common terms used in roof construction.

Framing plan. When unusual or difficult roof construction is necessary, a roof framing plan is included in the working drawings. Figure 21 shows the roof framing plan for the roof shown in Figure 20. Notice that a single heavy line is used to indicate each rafter. Floor framing plans and ceiling joist framing plans are also included when necessary.

STUDY QUESTIONS

1. List four types of traditional roofs.
2. Sketch four types of traditional roofs.
3. List twelve types of contemporary roofs.
4. Sketch twelve types of contemporary roofs.
5. List four types of dormer windows.
6. Sketch four types of dormer windows.
7. Should a roof sloping 3″/ft. be covered by ordinary fiber glass shingles? Why?
8. Name three types of roof shingles and give the advantages of each.
9. Sketch and label the pitch triangle for a $\frac{1}{4}$ pitch roof.
10. Give two methods of indicating the pitch of a roof having an 8′ rise in a 32′ span.

11. What is the purpose of flashing? Give several examples.
12. Describe in words or by sketches the following terms:
    a. Common rafter
    b. Jack rafter
    c. Hip rafter
    d. Valley rafter
    e. Ridge board
    f. Collar beam
    g. Header
    h. Trimmer
    i. Span
    j. Run
    k. Rise
    l. Roofing square
    m. Roofing ply
13. List four methods to prevent wind from lifting roof shingles.
14. Distinguish between built-up roofing and membrane roofing.

LABORATORY PROBLEMS

1. Prepare a classroom illustration showing:
    a. Traditional roofs
    b. Contemporary roofs
    c. Dormer windows
    d. Roof construction terminology
2. Construct a series of study models to illustrate various types of contemporary roofs.
3. (For the advanced student) Design a type of roof that is entirely different from those now commonly used.
4. Complete the roof framing plan for the A residence.
5. Complete the roof framing plan for the building assigned by your instructor.
6. Complete the roof design for your original house design.
7. Complete the roof framing plan for your original house design.

24 / Elevations and Sections

An architectural elevation is a view of a building containing a height dimension. When elevations show the inside of a building, they are called *interior elevations;* when they show the outside, they are called simply *elevations.*

INTERIOR ELEVATIONS

Interior elevations are included in a set of working drawings only when there is some special interior construction to be illustrated. This is quite often the case in kitchen design. Figure 2 shows the interior elevations of the kitchen of the A residence. Notice that the arrangement of the elevations is in relation to the floor plan—as though the four walls had fallen backward. To prevent this awkward appearance, the interior elevations may be removed to an upright position and even placed on a separate drawing sheet. The relation of each elevation to the plan is then shown by sight arrows as indicated in Figure 3. A right arrow shows the drawing number on which the detail appears. Sight arrows $\frac{1}{4}$, $\frac{2}{4}$, etc., are interpreted as detail #1 on drawing #4, detail #2 on drawing #4, and so on.

ELEVATIONS

The exterior elevations are as necessary to the satisfactory appearance of a building as the floor plan is to its satisfactory functioning. Normally the elevations of the four sides of a building are sufficient to describe it. In some cases, however, more than the four elevations are needed. For example, a structure built around an open court would require additional exterior elevations to illustrate the building as seen from the court.

ELEVATION DESIGN

The procedure used in the design of elevations is similar to the procedure used in the design of floor plans.

Thumbnail sketches. Thumbnail sketches of elevations are somewhat simpler to draw than the thumbnail sketches of a floor plan since overall di-

Figure 1   *A front elevation provides the first indication of the character of a building.*

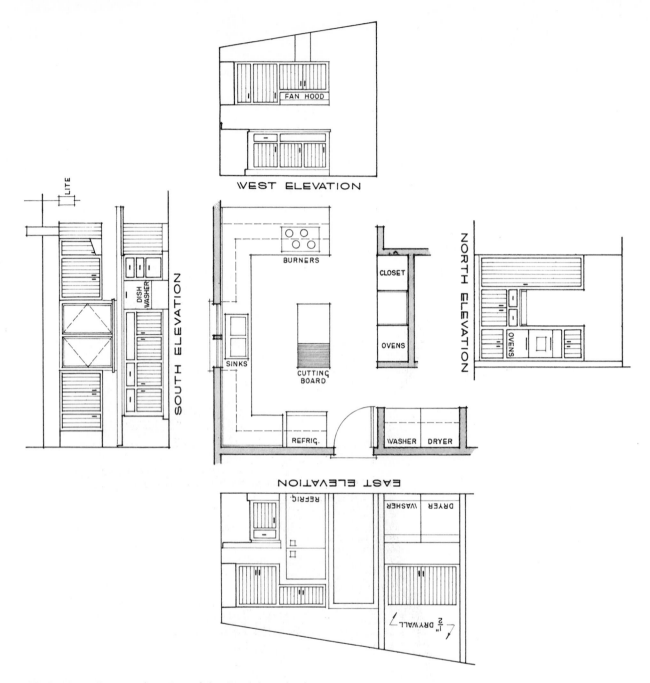

Figure 2 *Interior elevations of the A residence kitchen.*

mensions, window locations, and door locations may be transferred from the plan. The prime purpose of the elevation thumbnail is to help decide the general exterior styling. In Figure 4, compare the thumbnail sketches for the A residence. Although they appear to be different buildings, actually they are different ways of styling the same building.

The final choice may be influenced by the character of the neighborhood. Although it is not necessary or desirable to have a neighborhood composed entirely of the same style and size houses, the surroundings will influence the appropriateness of a particular design to some extent. For example, it would not be appropriate to place a charming Cape Cod house in the midst of a section of highly experimental modern houses.

Preliminary sketches. Using the thumbnail sketch as a guide to the general styling, prepare a preliminary sketch. This will normally be done to $\frac{1}{8}'' = 1'$ scale on graph paper because the location

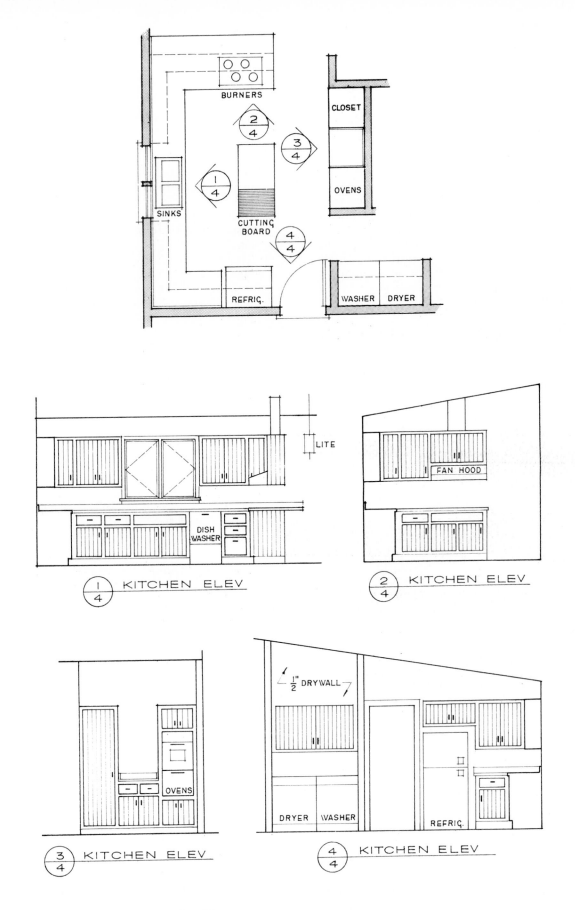

Figure 3   *Interior elevations, preferred layout.*

197

and proportion of features are very important at this stage. Main attention is given to the proportions of walls and openings and the fenestration of the window and door openings. Also consider the harmony of materials and features and the effects of orientation and shadows.

Proportion. Most people can look at a finished building and decide if it is well proportioned (Figure 5). However, designing a building so that it will have good proportion requires talent and training (Figure 6). In general, the term *proportion* deals with the size and shape of areas and their relation to one another. Some of the most important rules of good proportion are:

1. Avoid square areas or multiples of squares since a rectangular area that cannot be visually divided into squares is more interesting and pleasing (Figure 7).

2. Balance areas so that they do not appear unstable. Thus the lightest-appearing material or area should be above the heaviest or darkest (Figure 8).

3. Areas should be either completely symmetrical or obviously unsymmetrical (Figure 9). These principles are further illustrated in Figures 18 and 19.

4. One leading area should dominate the entire design, with the other areas subordinate (Figure 10).

5. Repetition of elements may be used to advantage or disadvantage depending upon the circumstances. The repeated window arrangement shown in Figure 11 is superior, but the repeated drawer arrangement in Figure 12 is not.

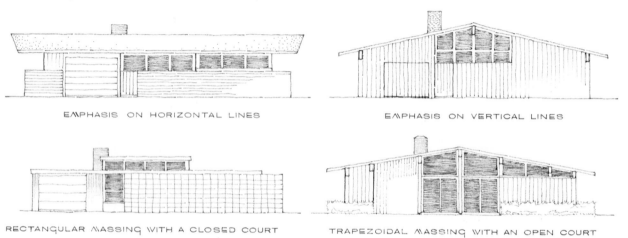

EMPHASIS ON HORIZONTAL LINES

EMPHASIS ON VERTICAL LINES

RECTANGULAR MASSING WITH A CLOSED COURT

TRAPEZOIDAL MASSING WITH AN OPEN COURT

Figure 4 *Thumbnail sketches of the A residence.*

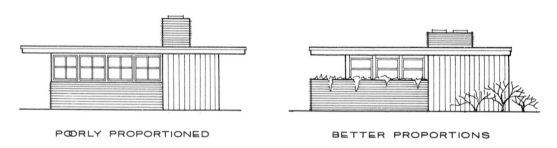

POORLY PROPORTIONED

BETTER PROPORTIONS

Figure 5 *Effect of proper proportions.*

Figure 6 *Proportional massing lends interest to this factory warehouse.*

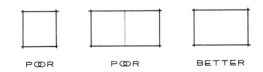

POOR   POOR   BETTER

Figure 7   *Shape*

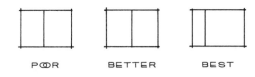

POOR   BETTER

Figure 8   *Stability.*

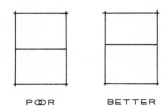

POOR   BETTER   BEST

Figure 9   *Symmetry.*

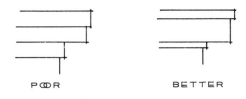

POOR   BETTER

Figure 10   *Domination.*

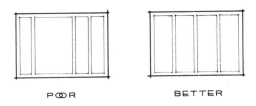

POOR   BETTER

Figure 11   *Horizontal repetition.*

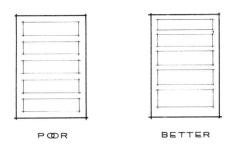

POOR   BETTER

Figure 12   *Vertical repetition.*

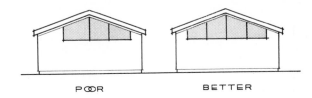

POOR   BETTER

Figure 13   *Symmetrical fenestration.*

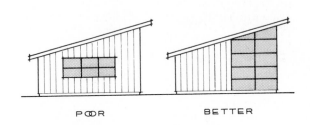

POOR   BETTER

Figure 14   *Unsymmetrical fenestration.*

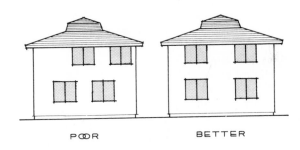

POOR   BETTER

Figure 15   *Vertical alignment of windows.*

VERY POOR

Figure 16   *Disorderly fenestration.*

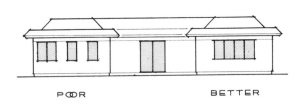

POOR   BETTER

Figure 17   *Orderly fenestration.*

Courtesy of Scholz Homes, Inc.

Figure 18   *A symmetrical entranceway.*

Courtesy of Scholz Homes, Inc.

Figure 19   *An unsymmetrical entrance design.*

Fenestration. The term *fenestration* deals with the arrangements of windows (and doors) in a wall. Some of the rules for satisfactory fenestration are:

1. Arrange windows symmetrically in a symmetrical elevation (Figure 13), but off center in an unsymmetrical elevation (Figure 14).
2. Line up windows on different floors. This is important for both aesthetic and structural reasons (Figure 15).
3. Do not use a variety of types and sizes of windows (Figure 16).
4. Arrange windows in groupings when possible (Figure 17).

Harmony. All features should harmonize to present a uniform elevation. Materials also should be selected to harmonize with one another. In general, it is wise to use no more than two different types of materials on one building (Figure 20).

Shadows. Consider the effect of solar orientation upon each elevation. A very simple elevation may become more interesting when designed to take full advantage of shadows. Figure 21 shows a house designed with a second floor slightly overhanging the first floor. The simple shadow lines are made more interesting by a variation in the surface casting the shadow (Figure 22), or by varying the surface receiving the shadow (Figure 23).

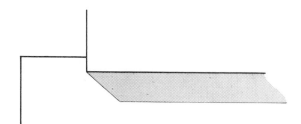

Figure 21   *Shadow too simple.*

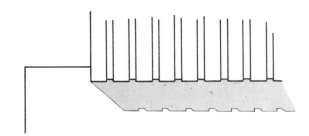

Figure 22   *Shadow made more interesting by use of boards and battens.*

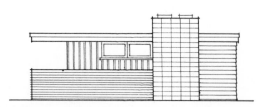

Figure 20   *Lack of harmony—too many materials used.*

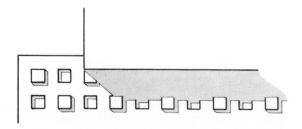

Figure 23   *Shadow made more interesting by use of extended and recessed concrete blocks.*

Finished sketches. The finished sketch may be a carefully drawn freehand sketch or a drawing done with drafting instruments. If the preliminary sketch was very carefully drawn, the designer may omit the finished sketch and proceed directly to the finished elevation drawing. The scale of both is usually $\frac{1}{4}'' = 1'$ for a small residence and $\frac{1}{8}'' = 1'$ for larger buildings. Occasionally one or two major elevations are drawn to the large $\frac{1}{4}'' = 1'$ scale, and the less important elevations are drawn to the smaller $\frac{1}{8}'' = 1'$ scale. Since these are fairly large-scale drawings, the exact size of all features must be considered together with their correct representation.

Window and door sizes. As a general rule, it is a good idea to align the tops of all exterior doors and windows. This simplifies construction by allowing the builder to use one size of header for all normal wall openings and, incidentally, simplifies the drawing of the elevations. A front door will usually be $3'\text{-}0 \times 6'\text{-}8''$ (actual size of the door), and a rear door will be $2'\text{-}8'' \times 6'\text{-}8''$. A single garage door averages $9'\text{-}0 \times 7'\text{-}0$ high, and a double garage door $16'\text{-}0 \times 7'\text{-}0$ high. Window sizes must be chosen from manufacturers' catalogs, which offer a great variety of sizes and types. Windows fall into the following general types:

Fixed
Double-hung (slides vertically)
Sliding (slides horizontally)
Awning (hinged at top and swings outward)
Hopper (hinged at bottom and swings inward)
Casement (hinged at side and usually swings outward)
Pivoted (hinged at center, half swings outward and half inward)
Jalousie (many individually hinged panes)

Only one or two types of windows should be specified for a house, although their sizes can be varied to suit the need.

Window and door representation. Since most architectural features are too complicated to draw in detail, certain simplifications and conventions have been established to lessen the work of the drafter. For example, windows and doors are shown considerably simplified. Figure 24 shows how a door and window would appear if drawn completely. Fortunately this type of representation is never used. Figure 25 shows standard representations—with lines only for the opening, the trim, and panels. Notice that even the doorknob should be omitted.

A further simplification is often used: one window on an elevation is detailed as in Figure 25 and all other similar windows are merely outlined

Figure 24   *Actual representation (not used).*

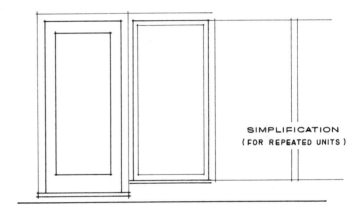

Figure 25   *Standard representation.*

Figure 26   *Representation of hinged windows.*

by a rectangle. The hidden lines in Figure 26 indicate a hinged window. The hinge is located where the hidden lines meet.

Material representation. Like windows and doors, materials are also represented by drawing only a few lines. Brick, for example, is indicated by several horizontal lines spaced about 3″ apart (to the proper scale) rather than showing each brick and mortar joint. When bricks are laid on edge for windowsills or window and door heads, they

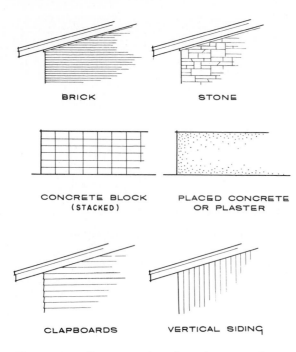

Figure 27 *Representation of exterior materials.*

should be shown also. Figure 27 shows the usual representation of brick, stone, concrete block, placed (poured) concrete, clapboards, and vertical siding. Roofs may be left blank.

Footings and areawalls. Hidden lines are used to indicate the location of footings, below-grade windows, and their areawalls. An areawall is a retaining wall that holds the earth back from a below-grade opening. Common materials used for areawalls are concrete, masonry, and corrugated sheets of galvanized iron. Take particular note of the hidden foundation and footing lines. Notice that the footing and the outside wall of the foundation *are* shown, but the basement floor and inside wall of the foundation are *not* shown. It is easy to remember which lines to include in an elevation view: just imagine that the ground has been removed and show only those lines that you would then see.

Labeling views. Two methods are used to label elevation views:

1. Front elevation   2. North elevation
   Rear elevation   East elevation
   Right-end elevation   South elevation
   Left-end elevation   West elevation

In the second method, the north elevation is the elevation that faces generally northward, but it

does not have to face exactly north. When an interior elevation is designated as a north elevation, this means the *outside* of the wall faces north, and the *inside* of the wall faces south.

Dimensioning. Elevation dimensions are limited to vertical dimensions since horizontal dimensions have already been shown on the plan. Show the depth of the footing below grade, the finished-floor-to-finished-floor heights (or finished-floor-to-finished-ceiling height for the topmost story), the roof height, and the height of the chimney above the roof. The following inside room heights (finished floor to finished ceiling) are the minimum allowable:

Basement: 6'-2" (clear of all low beams, ducts, or pipes)
First floor: 7'-10"
Second floor: 7'-4"
Garage: 8'-0

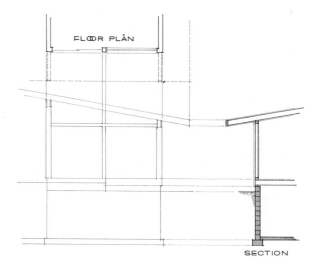

Figure 28 *Step 1: Layout.*

Figure 29 *Step 2: Details.*

Of course, when you give finished-floor-to-finished-floor heights, you must allow for the thickness of the floor (finished flooring, subflooring, joists, and ceiling). This will amount to about 1 ft.; the exact amount can be calculated by adding the actual sizes of these members as indicated on the typical section. Chimneys should extend at least 2′ above a nearby ridge line. The window schedule may be placed in any convenient location.

Changes. Remember that it is quite probable that some changes and additions in the elevations will be necessary after all the other drawings are completed.

Elevation drawing. After the elevations have been designed by use of thumbnail, preliminary, and finished sketches, the final drawing may be started. The steps used in drawing elevations are illustrated as follows. We will use the rear elevation of the A residence as an example.

Step 1: Layout. Lay out the elevation very lightly on tracing vellum using a hard, sharp pencil (Figure 28). Using dividers or a scale, transfer horizontal dimensions from the floor plan and vertical dimensions from the sectional drawing. A scale of $\frac{1}{4}'' = 1'$ or $\frac{1}{8}'' = 1'$ is used and indicated in the title block or near the drawing. If the plan and section are drawn to the same scale as the required elevation, they may be taped in position and dimensions projected directly using a triangle and T square. (If the plan and section have not been drawn yet, they should be drawn in rough form at this point. Save these rough drawings since they will help finish the final plan and section.)

Windows and doors are located horizontally by projecting from the plan; they are located vertically by projecting from the window and door details or simply by aligning the tops of the windows with the tops of the doors.

Step 2: Details. The elevation details to be included will vary depending upon the style of the house. In the case of the A residence, the following details are added (Figure 29):

1. Roof fascia
2. Roof beams
3. Chimney, saddle, and flashing
4. Window representation (if you wish, only one window is detailed)
5. Grade lines
6. Footings
7. Material representation
8. Darkened building outline

Figure 30   *Front elevation of the A residence.*

Figure 31   *Rear elevation of the A residence.*

Figure 32   *Atrium of the A residence.*

Step 3: Dimensioning. Elevation dimensions and notes are added (Figures 33–37):

1. Height of roof (in this example, the roof beam height determines the roof height)
2. Depth of footings
3. Height of other features such as masonry wall and chimney
4. Height of windows (in this example, the windows fit directly under the roof and roof beams)
5. Roof slope indication
6. Window schedules
7. Titles and notes indicating materials and special details

Compare the elevations as drawn with the photographs of the finished A residence, Figures 30 to 32.

203

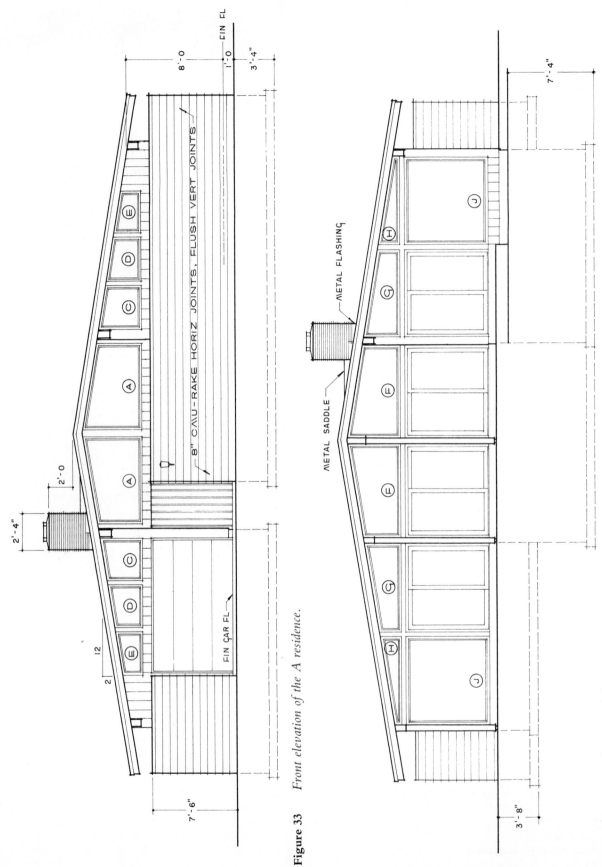

Figure 33 *Front elevation of the A residence.*

Figure 34 *Rear elevation of the A residence.*

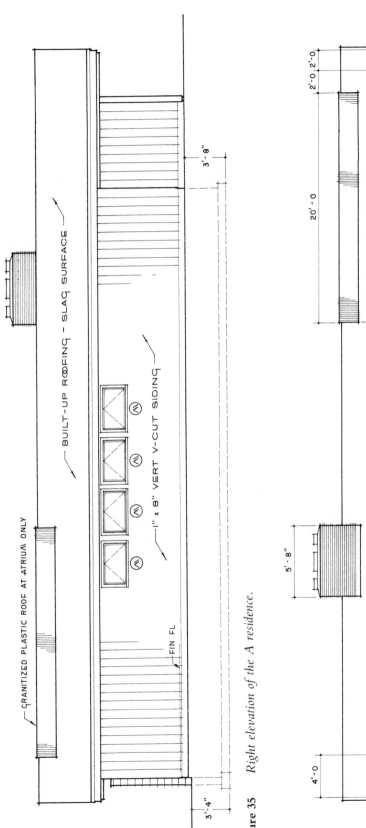

Figure 35 *Right elevation of the A residence.*

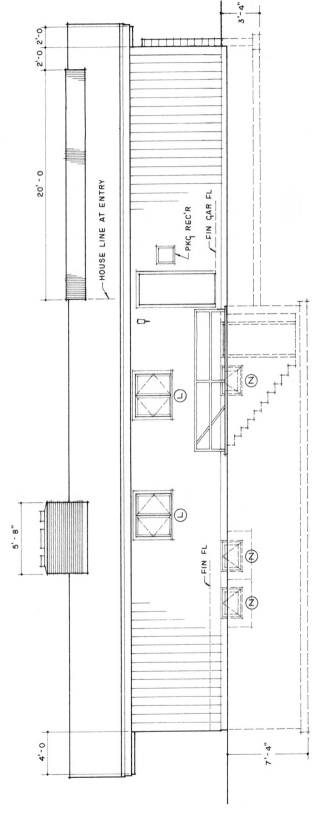

Figure 36 *Left elevation of the A residence.*

WINDOW SCHEDULE

MK	NO	SIZE	DESCRIPTION
A	2	90" x 42" x 57"	1/4" FIXED PLATE GLASS
B	3	44" x 80"	" " " "
C	2	44" x 34" x 41"	" " " "
D	2	44" x 26" x 33"	" " " "
E	2	44" x 18" x 25"	" " " "
F	2	90" x 38" x 53"	" " " "
G	2	90" x 22" x 37"	" " " "
H	2	90" x 6" x 21"	" " " "
J	2	90" x 84"	" " " "
K	2	AP421	ANDERSEN AWNING-FIXED
L	2	C235	CASEMENT
W	4	A41	AWNING
N	3	2820	BASEMENT

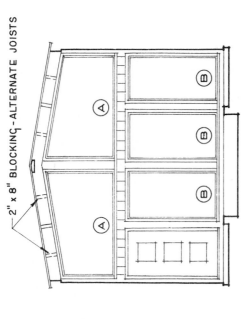

FRONT ATRIUM ELEVATION

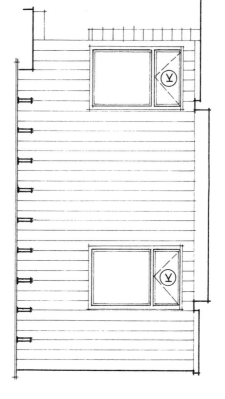

RIGHT ATRIUM ELEVATION

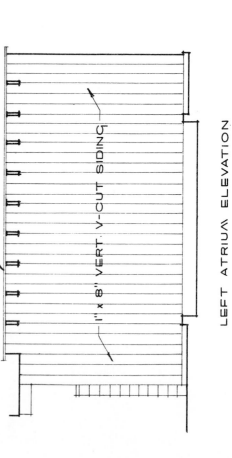

LEFT ATRIUM ELEVATION

Figure 37 *Atrium elevations of the A residence.*

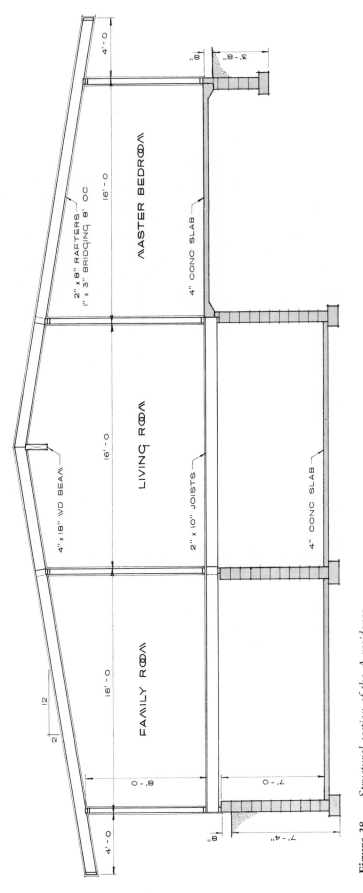

Figure 38 *Structural section of the A residence.*

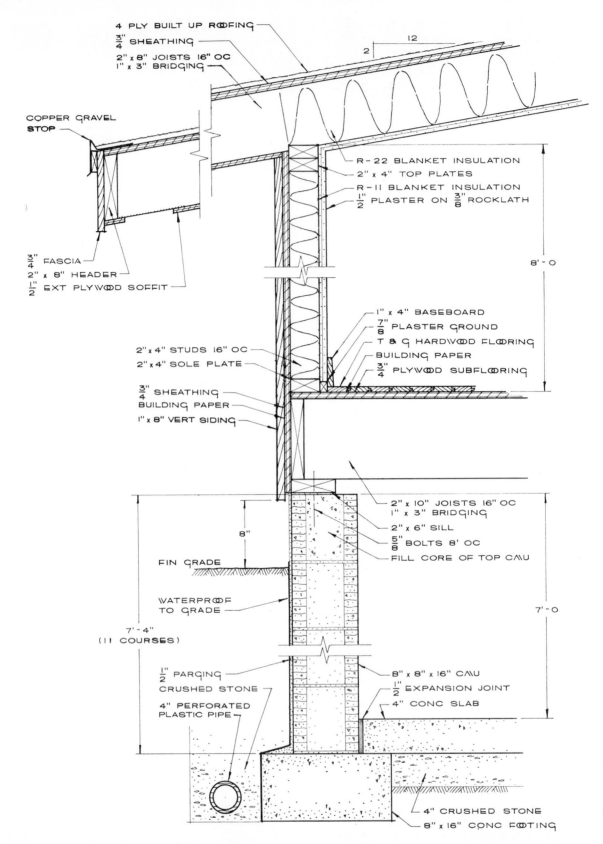

Figure 39 *Typical section of the A residence.*

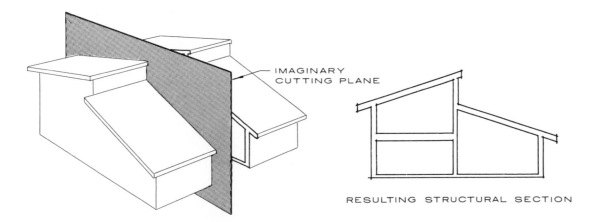

Figure 40 *Imaginary cutting plane used to obtain a structural section.*

SECTIONS

The designer shows the entire building construction by means of a few drawings called *sections*. He lays out the sections in much the same order that the workmen will use in actual construction. A complete set of construction drawings would contain one or more of each of the following types of sections:

Structural section. A structural section shows the entire building construction, as shown in Figure 40. A $\frac{1}{4}'' = 1'$ scale is often used. Figure 38 shows a structural section for the A residence. This would be useful in planning for structural strength and rigidity, determining the length of members, and specifying sizes.

Wall section. A wall section shows the construction of a typical wall to a larger scale than the structural section ($1\frac{1}{2}'' = 1'$ is often used). Figure 39 shows a wall section for the A residence. Notice that floor-to-ceiling heights are shown, together with sizes and material specifications for all rough and finished members.

Detail section. Any deviations from the typical wall sections may be shown in detail sections. Also any special or unusual construction must be detailed, as shown in Figure 41. These sections may be drawn to a large scale (up to full size).

STUDY QUESTIONS

1. How many exterior elevations are needed to describe a building having:
   a. A rectangular floor plan
   b. An L-shaped floor plan

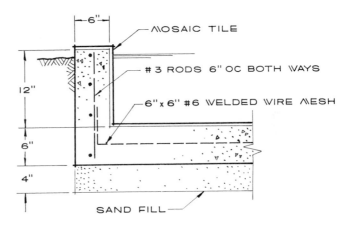

Figure 41 *Atrium pool detail for the A residence.*

   c. A U-shaped floor plan
   d. An S-shaped floor plan
2. What is the purpose of each of the following? Give the probable scale of each.
   a. Thumbnail elevation sketches
   b. Preliminary elevation sketches
   c. Finished elevation sketches
   d. Finished elevation drawings
3. Explain how each of the following words is associated with the rules of good proportion:
   a. Squares
   b. Stability
   c. Symmetry
   d. Domination
   e. Repetition
4. Explain how each of the following words is associated with the rules of fenestration:
   a. Symmetry
   b. Alignment
   c. Variety
   d. Grouping

5. Give the most commonly used size for the following:
   a. Front door
   b. Rear door
   c. Single garage door
   d. Double garage door
6. State two methods of simplifying the representation of doors and windows.
7. How is the location of window hinges indicated on elevation drawings?
8. What is the rule for determining the below-grade lines to be shown by hidden lines, and the below-grade lines to be entirely omitted?
9. If an interior elevation of a room is called a *south elevation*, in what direction does the inside wall face?
10. Sketch and name three types of sectional drawings. What scale might be used for each?
11. Indicate information on wall sections:
    a. Not found on other kinds of architectural plans
    b. Repeated on other kinds of architectural plans

LABORATORY PROBLEMS

1. Using a scale of $\frac{1}{4}'' = 1'$, draw the following elevations of the A residence:
   a. Front elevation
   b. Rear elevation
   c. Right-end elevation
   d. Left-end elevation
   e. Atrium elevations
2. Draw the elevations of the building assigned by your instructor.
3. Complete the elevations for your original house design.
4. Draw the typical wall section of the A residence.
5. Complete the structural section for your original house design.
6. Complete the typical wall section for your original house design.
7. Complete the detail sections for your original house design.

25 / Stairways

An important consideration in a house having more than one level is the stairway design. Often the stairway is specifically planned for its architectural effect and it can be a major design element in both traditional and contemporary house styles. In addition, the stairway must be carefully planned to conveniently perform its function of vertical circulation. Since the stairway is usually associated with the halls, it may be the key to circulation throughout the entire house.

TYPES

See Figure 1. Straight-run stairs take up the least amount of floor area and are the simplest to construct. However, some designs require a stair that turns or is shorter in length. In these cases, the designer specifies a U-type or L-type stair with a platform at the turn. The platform does have the safety feature of breaking up a long run of stairs and providing a place to pause and rest. When space is restricted, diagonal steps called *winders* are used in place of the platform. Winders are designed so that the same tread depth is maintained at the normal path of travel: 18″ from the inside corner. Since the tread depth is reduced inside the normal path of travel, it is obvious that winders are dangerous and should be used only as a last resort. Also avoid single steps to sunken rooms. There is less likelihood of a person tripping on two or more steps. Spiral stairs may be obtained in packaged units and will satisfy unique design requirements.

TERMS

The terms generally used in stairway design are illustrated in Figure 2.

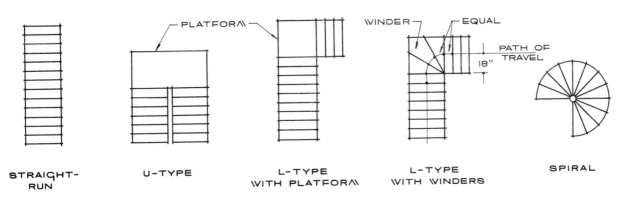

Figure 1 *Stair types.*

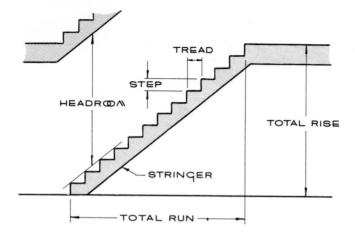

Figure 2 *Stairway terminology.*

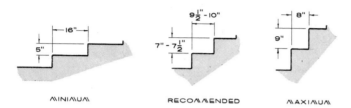

Figure 3 *Stair pitch.*

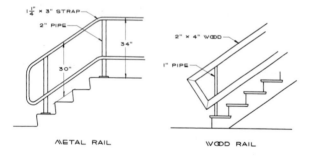

Figure 4 *Contemporary handrails.*

Step, or *riser:* The vertical distance from one tread top to another.

Tread, or *run:* The horizontal distance from the face of one riser to the next. Notice that there will always be one fewer tread than risers.

Total rise: The vertical distance from one finished floor to the next. This is a basic measurement in stair planning.

Total run: The horizontal distance of the entire stairway.

Headroom: The vertical distance from the outside edge of the step to the ceiling above.

Nosing: The projection of the tread beyond the riser. It should be about 1⅛", as shown in Fig-

ure 6, and is not considered as part of the stair tread when laying out the stairway.

DESIGN

All stairways do not have the same slope, or pitch. They may vary from a 5-16 pitch (that is, a 5" rise with a 16" run) to a 9-8 pitch (a 9" rise with an 8" run). A pitch less than the 5-16 limit will require a ramp; a pitch greater than 9-8 will require a step-ladder or rung ladder. Figure 3 shows the minimum pitch of 5-16, which may be used for outside or monumental stairs; the recommended pitches for most stairways of 7-10–7½-9½; and the maximum possible pitch of 9-8. The 9-8 pitch is not recommended in a house but may be used on board ship almost like a ladder. It is assumed that no one would use such steep stairs without holding the handrails. An 8-9 pitch (not to be confused with a 9-8 pitch) is very satisfactory for basement stairs.

In Figure 3 notice that as the run dimension decreases, the rise dimension increases so that the overall distance from step to step remains about the same. This fact has given us this general rule:

Rule 1   rise + run = 17

For example, if you decide upon a 7" rise, the tread should be 10". Two slightly more sophisticated rules may be used for additional checks:

Rule 2   2 × rise + run = 24 to 25

Notice that the 9" rise and 8" run would not be satisfactory according to this rule since 2 × 9 + 8 equals 26. The 7-10 pitch, however, equals 24, which is acceptable.

Rule 3   rise × run = 70 to 75

The 7-10 pitch used in the two preceding examples equals 7 × 10 = 70, which is acceptable. None of the preceding rules should be used to check for monumental stairs.

Allow 7'-0 minimum headroom on a stairway, but 7'-6" is preferred. A 6'-6" headroom may be used for basement stairs. The most comfortable handrail height is 30" on a stair and 34" on a landing, as shown in Figure 4. The minimum comfortable stair width is 3'-0, but 3'-6" or 4'-0 is better for moving furniture.

LAYOUT

Tables like Table I have been devised to simplify some of the stair calculations. A stairway is best laid out using the following method:

Table I *Stair Dimensions*

Total Rise	Number of Risers	Riser	Tread	Total Run
8'-0	13	7.38"	9½"	9'-6"
8'-6"	14	7.29"	9¾"	10'-6¾"
9'-0	15	7.20"	9¾"	11'-4½"
9'-6"	16	7.13"	10"	12'-6"
10'-0	17	7.06"	10"	13'-4"

Step 1. Draw two horizontal lines representing the finished floors to a scale of $\frac{1}{2}" = 1'-0$. In Figure 5, the distance between finished floors (total rise) is 9'-0.

Step 2. Using Table I, we shall have 15 risers of 7.20" each and 14 treads (treads = risers − 1) of 9¾" each, with a total run of 11'-4½". Lay out the total run to scale.

Step 3. Since there are 15 risers, divide the total rise into 15 equal parts using your scale at an angle so that the zero mark is on the other finished floor.

Step 4. Since there are 14 treads, divide the total run into 14 equal parts in the same manner using the zero mark and the 7" mark.

Step 5. Darken in the outline of the stairway, adding details like those shown in Figure 18.

A similar procedure is used for U-type, L-type, and circular stairs.

CONSTRUCTION

Figures 6–10 show different types of stairs. A 2" × 12" member would be used for the open stringer in Figure 11. Incidentally, the triangular pieces cut from this 2" × 12" are often nailed to a 2" × 4"—serving as a middle stringer for extra support. Closed stringers are slightly different from open stringers in that no triangular pieces are cut from the stringer (Figure 11). Rather, ½" grooves are routed to receive the treads and risers, which are wedged and glued in place. This completely conceals their ends. The tongue-and-groove construction between riser and tread is often omitted for economy. Prefabricated stairways are becoming increasingly popular. Figure 12 shows one method of simplifying stair construction by the use of preformed metal stair guides.

Stock components are often used for stairs and railings in commercial buildings. In addition to the metal systems shown in Figures 13–15, a ½" tempered-glass railing is available (Figure 16).

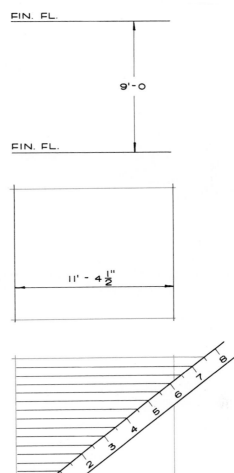

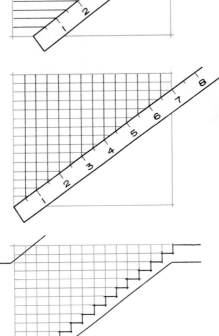

Figure 5 *Stair layout (new steps shown in dark blue).*

Figure 6 *A large-radius spiral stairway.*

Figure 7 *Stair treads cantilevered from a central support.*

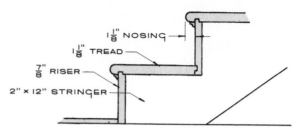

Figure 8 *Closed-riser stair.*

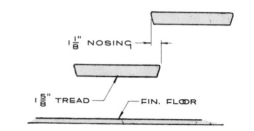

Figure 9 *Open-riser stair.*

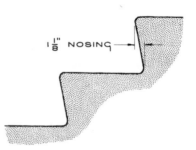

Figure 10 *Concrete stair.*

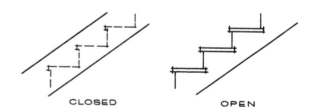

Figure 11 *Stringer types.*

STAIR DETAILS

A complete set of stair details includes a section or elevation together with a plan view of each stairway. Details of tread construction and handrail construction may be included. Some of these drawings may be incorporated with other plans. The stair plan, for example, may be satisfactorily shown on the floor plan. Notice in Figure 18 that arrows with the notation "UP" and "DN" are used to show stair direction. The number of risers is also included. Always use capital letters for "UP" and "DN" notations since, when viewed

Figure 12 *Installing metal stair guides.*

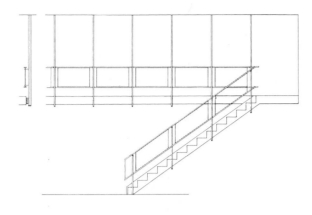

BRACKET ASSEMBLY

The **Colorail** bracket assembly has two interlocking parts which, engaged with the bracket arm, clamp the tee-shaped handrail support bar for convenient field assembly without drilling and tapping.

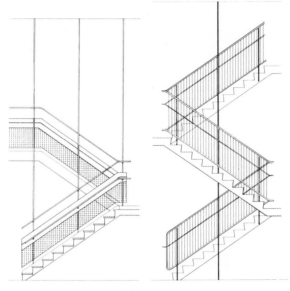

Figure 13   *Some stock metal railing designs.*

BRACKET AND SUPPORT SECTION

The handrail bracket can be tilted to conform to stair angle. Bracket extensions allow variation in length to conform to varying conditions. Tee-shaped support sections give **Colorail** the required stiffness.

POST CONSTRUCTION

Post assemblies include plastic-clad aluminum post whose hollow core houses concealed fastening devices. Sleeves provide color variation in one of five colors.

Figure 14   *Details of a metal railing system.*

FLOOR MOUNTING

Floor mounting is provided for three post sizes. An aluminum floor cover flange is used for finished appearance. Posts may be embedded in concrete or mechanically fastened under flooring.

from the opposite direction, a lowercase "up" looks like "dn" and a lower case "dn" looks like "up." When there are both "up" and "down" stairs over one another, they are separated by a break line.

Figures 17 and 18 show details of the stairs for the A residence and the Z residence.

RAILINGS

Balcony railings and retaining walls require special attention to safety considerations. The national standard requires a minimum height of 3'–6" because that height is above the center of gravity of even a tall person. Railing bars should be less than 5" apart to prevent children from squeezing through.

Most standards presently require that railings be strong enough to withstand at least 200 pounds of impact pressure, but much greater strength than that is advisable.

TREILLAGE*

Treillage is used for building facing, partitions, room dividers, privacy fences, or concealment of unsightly elements. Stock components are available in many patterns (Figures 19–21).

* Pronounced *trail-lige* in French, with the accent on the first syllable. The last syllable is pronounced like the last syllable in the word *pillage*.

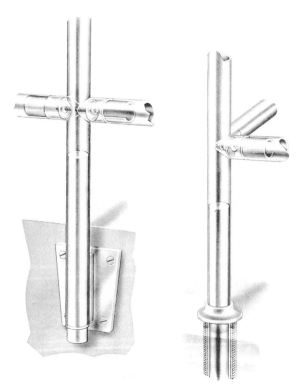

OPTIONS FOR MOUNTING
Connectorail® posts may be embedded in floor slab or side mounted on facia or stringer by means of facia flanges. A solid aluminum rod insert is used at the base of the post for added strength and stiffness.

MECHANICAL CONNECTIONS
Non-welded connections eliminate welding discoloration and expensive grinding. Strong structural adhesive, stainless steel machine screws with lock washers, and threaded tubular rivets assure positive connections at joints.

ADJUSTABLE BRACKETS
An adjustable bracket may be fitted to the post by means of a simple adapter. The handrail bracket tilts to conform to stair angle. Recommended for ramps or unusual stair angles.

Figure 15   *Details of a pipe railing system.*

STUDY QUESTIONS

1. Give the main advantage and disadvantage of:
   a. Introducing a platform into a straight run of stairs
   b. Using winders in place of a platform in an L-type stairway
2. What is the difference between:
   a. Rise and total rise
   b. Run and total run
   c. 8-9 pitch and 9-8 pitch
   d. Open stringer and closed stringer
   e. Open riser and closed riser
3. Using each of the three rules of rise and run proportions, figure the tread dimensions for:
   a. A 7″ rise
   b. A 7½″ rise
   c. An 8″ rise
4. How many risers and treads should be specified for a total rise of:

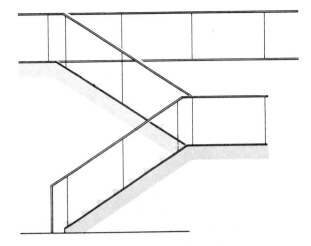

Figure 16 *Structural glass railing.*

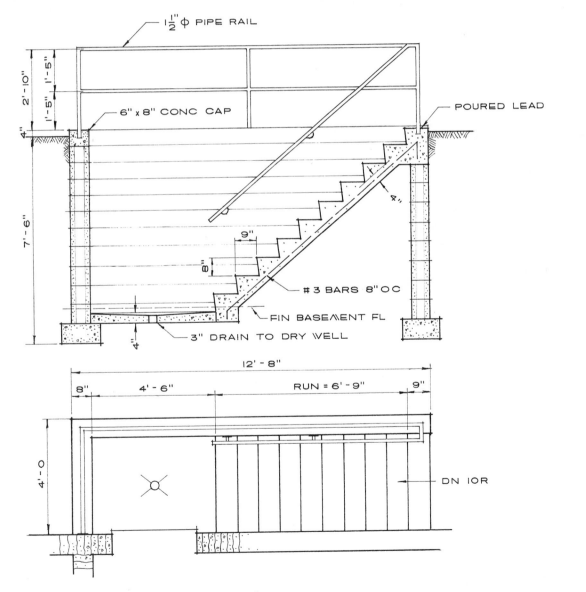

Figure 17 *Exterior stairway detail of the A residence.*

a. 8'-9"
b. 4'-9" (split-level house)
c. 1'-9" (sunken room)

5. Show how to divide any line into three equal parts using the following. Do not use trial-and-error solutions.
   a. Your scale
   b. Your dividers
6. (For the advanced student) After a thorough library search, prepare an illustrated paper on the history of the development of the various methods of vertical circulation in buildings.
7. (For the advanced student) After a thorough library search, give your estimate of the status of the various methods of vertical circulation fifty years hence.

LABORATORY PROBLEMS

1. Draw the plan and sectional elevation of:
   a. Interior stairway of the A residence
   b. Exterior stairway of the A residence
   c. Main stairway of the Z residence
2. Draw the plan and sectional elevation of the following stairways and fill the requirements that are listed:
   a. Straight-run, 13 risers to the basement of a ranch house, total rise = 8'-6"
   b. Straight-run, 7 risers between two levels of a split-level house, total rise = 4'-3"
   c. U-type, 7 risers each between three levels of a split-level house, total rise = 8'-8"

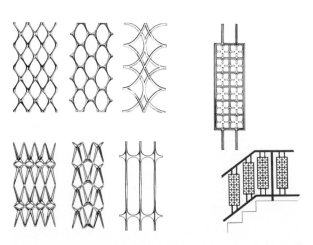

Figure 19   *Use of treillage for architectural effect.*

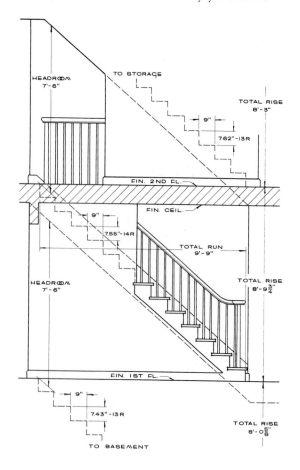

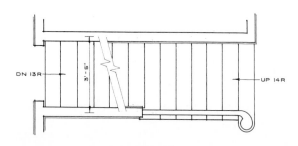

Figure 18   *Stair detail of the Z residence.*

Figure 20   *Some treillage patterns.*

d. L–type, 3 risers and 11 risers (14 risers total) to the second floor of a two-story apartment, total rise = 8′-9″
3. Prepare a classroom illustration showing:
   a. Stairway terminology
   b. Stairway construction
   c. Recommended stairway dimensions for tread, rise, width, headroom, and handrail heights

4. (For the advanced student) Design a means of vertical circulation that is entirely different from those now commonly used.
5. Draw the stairway details for the building assigned by your instructor.
6. Complete the stairway details for your original house design.

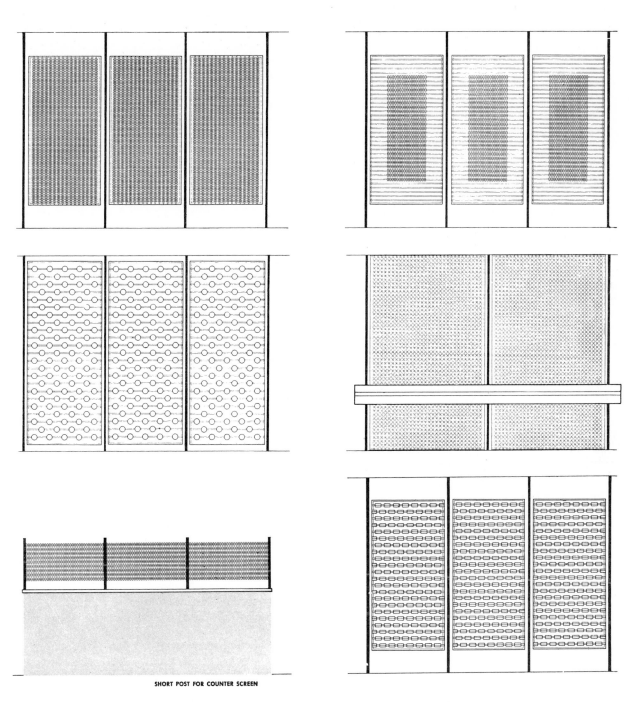

SHORT POST FOR COUNTER SCREEN

PANELS WITH SPANS OVER 4′-0″ WIDTH AND 4′-6″ HEIGHT MUST USE A CENTER SUPPORT

Figure 21   *Some stock treillage designs.*

26 / Fireplaces and Chimneys

The fireplace, although no longer a necessity as the major heat source, is considered by many to be a "must" luxury. A blazing fire or glowing embers on a cold winter day create a mood of cheerfulness and comfort that cannot be achieved by a concealed heating system. The fireplace is usually the major element of interior design in a living room or family room. In addition, it is occasionally specified for the family-type kitchen or master bedroom. Careful planning and thoughtful design are always required to obtain proper styling, the best location in a room, and coordination with the heating plant and the other fireplaces in the house.

STYLING

Several types of fireplaces are illustrated in Figure 1. Notice that the designer may work with a great variety of sizes and styles of fireplace openings, hearths, mantels, and materials. Fireplace openings may be single-faced (the basic type), double-faced (with faces on adjacent or opposite sides), three-faced (serving as a peninsula partition between two areas), or even freestanding (in the center of an area). Multifaced fireplaces are associated with contemporary design, but corner fireplaces have been in use for many years. The double-faced (opposite sides) and three-faced fireplaces are often used as room dividers but they are not particularly useful for heating since the open design reduces the reflection of heat. Also, large flues must be used to obtain an adequate chimney draft. Cross-drafts may cause smoke to enter the room unless glass fire screens are added.

Hearths may be flush with the floor or raised to any desired height. The back hearth serves as the base for the fire; the front hearth protects a combustible floor from sparks. The front hearth and edges of the fireplace opening may be surfaced with an ornamental material such as a ceramic tile, which is highly heat resistant. Mantels may be of various designs or omitted entirely. Brick, block, stone, tile, and metal are used for fireplace construction. When the fireplace is used as the primary element in the decorative scheme, log bins, shelves, or cabinets are often included.

FUEL

The usual fuel is wood: softwood for kindling and logs of hickory, birch, beech, ash, oak, or maple. Andirons or some form of grating may be an integral part of the fireplace design. A suspended grill might be considered for indoor charcoal grilling.

LOCATION

A fireplace may be located on a wall, in a corner, on a projecting corner, or freestanding. When the fireplace is to be located on a wall, the designer must choose between interior and exterior walls. Most chimneys in older houses were located in the center of the house; here they drew better and the heat could not escape directly outdoors. Newer houses tend to have exterior-wall chimneys to save floor space. The exterior chimney can be a distinct feature of the exterior design; however, more flashing and finish brick is required. Re-

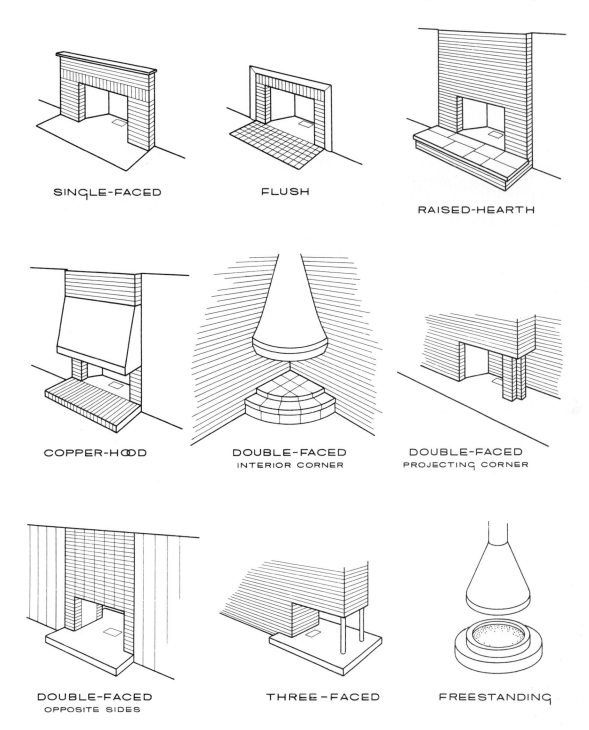

SINGLE-FACED

FLUSH

RAISED-HEARTH

COPPER-HOOD

DOUBLE-FACED
INTERIOR CORNER

DOUBLE-FACED
PROJECTING CORNER

DOUBLE-FACED
OPPOSITE SIDES

THREE-FACED

FREESTANDING

Figure 1 *Fireplace types.*

member that a frame structure is weakened by having a masonry fireplace and chimney on an exterior wall; a masonry structure is stiffened.

Split-level houses pose a special problem because the chimney should not emerge at a location close to higher-elevation roofs. The chimney will not draw properly unless it is extended at least 2′ higher than any portion of the roof located within 10′ (see Figure 3).

SIZE

Figures 4 and 5 give minimum and recommended dimensions for single- and multifaced fireplace designs; some of these dimensions will vary according to the size category as shown in Table I. The size category will depend upon the room size and the emphasis to be placed upon the fireplace. For

Figure 2   *A single-faced fireplace with raised hearth.*

Figure 3   *Minimum chimney height.*

example, the *medium* fireplace might be specified for a living room of 300 sq. ft.; the *medium-large* for a living room of 350 sq. ft. Notice that the dimensions in Figure 4 are nearly all multiples of 4″. To reduce the amount of brick trimming and waste, it is important to establish a modular system such as that shown in Figure 6. Here a $2\frac{1}{6}″ \times 3\frac{1}{2}″ \times 7\frac{1}{2}″$ modular brick is laid up with $\frac{1}{2}″$ joints, resulting in a 4″ module. Table III may be consulted for a quick reference of modular sizes of brick, tile, and block. If you are using common brick, Norman brick, Roman brick, or some other tile or block size, it is a good idea to make up a similar table. The actual sizes of these bricks are given in Table II.

CONSTRUCTION

A chimney is a complete structure in its own right —unsupported by any wooden member of the house framing. Recall how often you have seen a

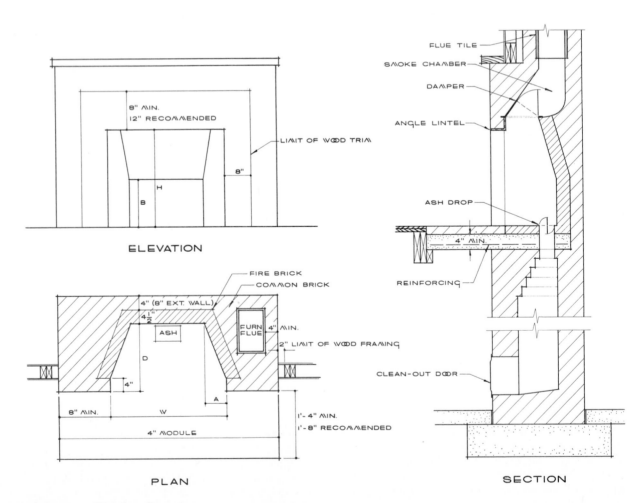

Figure 4   *Fireplace dimensions.*

Table I *Sizes for Fireplace Design*

Size Category	Width of Opening (W)	Height of Opening (H)	Depth of Opening (D)	A*	B*	Nominal Flue Size
Single-faced						
Very small	2'-0	2'-0	1'-5"	6"	1'-0	8" × 12"
Small	2'-8"	2'-3"	1'-8"	$6\frac{1}{2}$"	1'-2"	12" × 12"
Medium (most common)	3'-0	2'-5"	1'-8"	$6\frac{1}{2}$"	1'-2"	12" × 12"
Medium large	3'-4"	2'-5"	1'-8"	$6\frac{1}{2}$"	1'-2"	12" × 16"
Large	4'-0	2'-8"	2'-0	9"	1'-4"	16" × 16"
Very large	5'-0	3'-1"	2'-0	9"	1'-4"	16" × 20"
Double-faced, corner						
Small	2'-8"	2'-3"	1'-8"		1'-2"	12" × 16"
Medium	3'-0	2'-5"	1'-8"		1'-2"	16" × 16"
Medium large	3'-4"	2'-5"	1'-8"		1'-2"	16" × 16"
Large	4'-0	2'-5"	2'-0		1'-2"	16" × 16"
Double-faced, opposite sides						
Small	2'-8"	2'-5"	3'-0			16" × 16"
Medium	3'-0	2'-5"	3'-0			16" × 20"
Medium large	3'-4"	2'-5"	3'-0			16" × 20"
Large	4'-0	2'-8"	3'-0			20" × 20"
Three-faced						
Small	3'-4"	2'-3"	3'-0			20" × 20"
Medium	3'-8"	2'-3"	3'-0			20" × 20"
Medium large	4'-0	2'-3"	3'-0			20" × 20"
Large	4'-8"	2'-3"	3'-0			20" × 24"

* See Figure 4 or 5.

house that has burned to the ground, while the chimney remained standing. It is equally improper to use the chimney as a support for girders, joists, or rafters since a wooden member framing into a chimney may eventually settle and crack it. Actually, no framing lumber should come closer than 2" from the chimney due to the fire hazard. The 2" space should be filled with noncombustible material to act as a fire stop. Subflooring, flooring, and roof sheathing may come within $\frac{3}{4}$" of the chimney.

Figure 7 shows the type of overlapping flashing used at the roof. This allows movement between the chimney and roof due to settling without damage to the flashing.

The construction of a fireplace and chimney should be entrusted only to experienced workmen since improper construction can cause a fire hazard or a smoking fireplace. Due to its great weight, the chimney should have a sizable footing. Each fireplace is fitted with an ash dump (5" × 8" is a common stock size) to the ash pit which is fitted in turn with a clean-out door (12" × 12" is often used). The hearth is supported by a 4"-thick concrete slab reinforced with $\frac{3}{8}$"-diameter bars spaced 6" oc both ways. The opening to the fireplace is spanned by a steel angle lintel using 4" × $3\frac{1}{2}$" × $\frac{5}{16}$" stock. The back and sides of the fireplace are fire brick laid up in fire-clay mortar which is more heat-resistant than ordinary brick and mortar. The sides are sloped to direct the heat toward the room and the smoke to the smoke chamber. A metal damper set below the smoke chamber is used to control the draft. The damper and the base of the smoke chamber form a smoke shelf which is im-

Table II *Masonry Sizes*

Modular brick	$2\frac{1}{8}$" × $3\frac{1}{2}$" × $7\frac{1}{2}$"
Common brick	$2\frac{1}{4}$" × $3\frac{3}{4}$" × 8"
Norman brick	$2\frac{1}{8}$" × $3\frac{1}{2}$" × $11\frac{1}{2}$"
Roman brick	$1\frac{1}{2}$" × $3\frac{1}{2}$" × $11\frac{1}{2}$"
Fire brick	$2\frac{1}{2}$" × $4\frac{1}{2}$" × 9"
Tile	$4\frac{8}{8}$" × $7\frac{1}{2}$" × $11\frac{1}{2}$"
Block	$7\frac{5}{8}$" × $7\frac{5}{8}$" × $15\frac{5}{8}$"

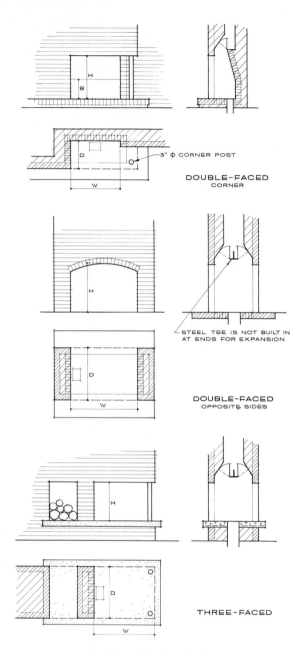

H
B
D
W

3" ⌀ CORNER POST

DOUBLE-FACED
CORNER

H

STEEL TEE IS NOT BUILT IN
AT ENDS FOR EXPANSION

D
W

DOUBLE-FACED
OPPOSITE SIDES

H
D
W

THREE-FACED

Figure 5   Multifaced fireplace designs.

portant in preventing backdraft. The smoke chamber is corbeled into the flue itself, which conducts the smoke and waste gas safely outside.

Tile flue. The flue is often constructed of rectangular terra-cotta tiles surrounded by 4″ or 8″ masonry. For proper draft, the area of the flue should not be less than $\frac{1}{10}$ the area of the fireplace opening. When computing the flue size of multifaced fireplaces, the areas of *all* faces must be included. The flue tile sizes given in Table I meet this requirement. A sharp chimney capping, usually obtained by extending the flue tile 4″ above the masonry, also improves draft. Remember to extend the chimney 2′ higher than any portion of a roof located within 10′. A tall chimney has a naturally better draft than a short chimney.

Each fireplace or furnace must have a separate flue to prevent the interference of drafts, although these flues may all be combined within a common chimney. This is usually stated, "a flue for every fire." For example, an average home may have two flues: one for the oil furnace and another for the living room fireplace. Both the flues should be set side by side in one chimney separated by 4″ of brick (called a *wythe*). Even a house with no fireplace must have a chimney if it is heated by an oil, coal, or gas-fired furnace. For the flue size, see the manufacturer's specifications; 12″ × 12″ is often used.

Prefabricated flue. The prefabricated, nonmasonry flue and chimney shown in Figure 8 consist of insulated and fireproof flue sections and a metal housing placed above the roof to simulate a masonry chimney. This costs considerably less than a masonry chimney and is often used for oil and gas furnace flues. Some installation details are shown in Figures 9 and 10.

Fireplace liner. Since a skilled mason is needed for the proper construction of a masonry fireplace, metal fireplace liners are often used (Figure 11). These liners consist of the fireplace sides and back, damper, smoke shelf, and smoke chamber all in one prefabricated unit and provide a form for the

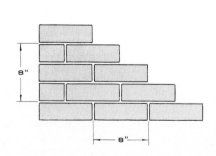

8"
8"

Figure 6   Common brick modular dimensions.

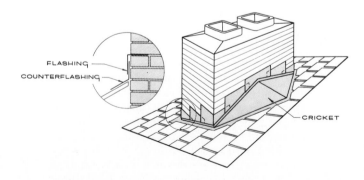

FLASHING
COUNTERFLASHING
CRICKET

Figure 7   Chimney flashing.

Table III *Masonry Sizes (3 brick + 3 joints = 8")*

Modular Brick	Tile	Block	Size	Modular Brick	Tile	Block	Size
1			2⅔"	51		17	11'-4"
2	1		5⅓"	52	26		11'-6⅔"
3		1	8"	53			11'-9⅓"
4	2		10⅔"	54	27	18	12'-0
5			1'-1⅓"	55			12'-2⅔"
6	3	2	1'-4"	56	28		12'-5⅓"
7			1'-6⅔"	57		19	12'-8"
8	4		1'-9⅓"	58	29		12'-10⅔"
9		3	2'-0	59			13'-1⅓"
10	5		2'-2⅔"	60	30	20	13'-4"
11			2'-5⅓"	61			13'-6⅔"
12	6	4	2'-8"	62	31		13'-9⅓"
13			2'-10⅔"	63		21	14'-0
14	7		3'-1⅓"	64	32		14'-2⅔"
15		5	3'-4"	65			14'-5⅓"
16	8		3'-6⅔"	66	33	22	14'-8"
17			3'-9⅓"	67			14'-10⅔"
18	9	6	4'-0	68	34		15'-1⅓"
19			4'-2⅔"	69		23	15'-4"
20	10		4'-5⅓"	70	35		15'-6⅔"
21		7	4'-8"	71			15'-9⅓"
22	11		4'-10⅔"	72	36	24	16'-0
23			5'-1⅓"	73			16'-2⅔"
24	12	8	5'-4"	74	37		16'-5⅓"
25			5'-6⅔"	75		25	16'-8"
26	13		5'-9⅓"	76	38		16'-10⅔"
27		9	6'-0	77			17'-1⅓"
28	14		6'-2⅔"	78	39	26	17'-4"
29			6'-5⅓"	79			17'-6⅔"
30	15	10	6'-8"	80	40		17'-9⅓"
31			6'-10⅔"	81		27	18'-0
32	16		7'-1⅓"	82	41		18'-2⅔"
33		11	7'-4"	83			18'-5⅓"
34	17		7'-6⅔"	84	42	28	18'-8"
35			7'-9⅓"	85			18'-10⅔"
36	18	12	8'-0	86	43		19'-1⅓"
37			8'-2⅔"	87		29	19'-4"
38	19		8'-5⅓"	88	44		19'-6⅔"
39		13	8'-8"	89			19'-9⅓"
40	20		8'-10⅔"	90	45	30	20'-0
41			9'-1⅓"	91			20'-2⅔"
42	21	14	9'-4"	92	46		20'-5⅓"
43			9'-6⅔"	93		31	20'-8"
44	22		9'-9⅓"	94	47		20'-10⅔"
45		15	10'-0	95			21'-1⅓"
46	23		0'-2⅔"	96	48	32	21'-4"
47			10'-5⅓"	97			21'-6⅔"
48	24	16	10'-8"	98	49		21'-9⅓"
49			10'-10⅔"	99		33	22'-0
50	25		11'-1⅓"	100	50		22'-2⅔"

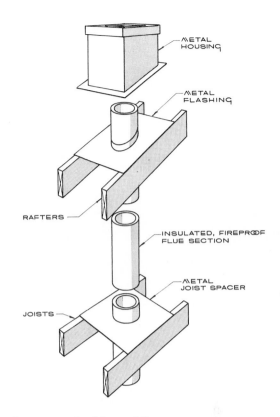

Figure 8 *Prefabricated flue.*

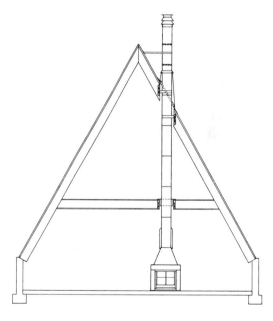

Figure 9 *Installation of a metal fireplace prefabricated flue.*

mason to work to. They also contain a duct system that draws in the room air through inlet registers, warms it, and then discharges it back to the room through outlet registers. This increases the heating capacity of the fireplace.

Metal fireplaces. Fireplaces constructed entirely of metal have been used for many years, and faithful simulations of these early models are still manufactured. Some contemporary types made of sheet steel are shown in Figures 12–15.

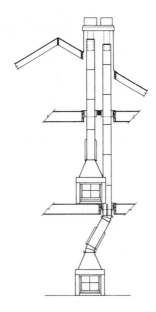

Figure 10   *Installation of metal fireplaces on two levels.*

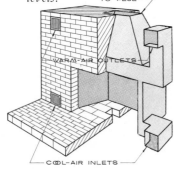

Figure 11   *Metal fireplace liner.*

Since a metal fireplace is usually used with a metal chimney, the cost is quite low. In addition, a metal fireplace heats up faster and gives more heat than a masonry fireplace.

Metal fireplaces are sold in a variety of sizes, colors, and coatings. Some are made of porcelain enamel steel in a choice of colors. Others use black-painted sheet steel. Others come with a factory prime coat over heavy-gauge sheet steel—leaving the final choice of color to the user. Steel fireplaces can be hung from a wall or ceiling, stand on a platform on their own legs, or be recessed into the floor.

FIREPLACE AND CHIMNEY DETAILS

The architect shows the fireplace and chimney design by means of detail drawings and specifications. The detail drawings usually consist of a front elevation showing the design of the fireplace opening and trim, and sectional plans showing dimensions of the fireplace and chimney together with flue placement. A side vertical section may be included. A scale of $\frac{1}{2}'' = 1'$-0 is often used. Some dimensions, such as the height of the chimney above the roof, are shown in the house elevation views.

Figure 16 shows the detail drawings of the fireplaces for the A residence. Notice that dimensions are based upon the 4″ module to reduce the amount of brick cutting.

Figure 12   *Wood-burning metal fireplace.*

Figure 13 *Wall-hung steel fireplace.*

Figure 14 *Ceramic fireplace available in several colors.*

STUDY QUESTIONS

1. Compare the advantages and disadvantages of a chimney located on an interior wall with a chimney located on an exterior wall.
2. Why should a chimney be extended higher than any nearby construction?
3. What is the actual size of:
   a. Common brick
   b. Modular brick
   c. Fire brick
   d. Roman brick
   e. Norman brick
4. Why is it considered poor practice to frame a girder into a chimney?
5. What is the purpose of the:
   a. Ash dump
   b. Clean-out door
   c. Front hearth
   d. Damper
   e. Smoke shelf
   f. Fire brick
   g. Flue
   h. Steel lintel over fireplace opening
6. How many flues are required for an oil-heated house with two fireplaces?
7. What are the advantages of a fireplace liner?
8. What are the disadvantages of multifaced fireplaces?

LABORATORY PROBLEMS

1. Draw the fireplace details for the A residence.
   a. First-floor fireplace
   b. Basement fireplace
2. Draw the fireplace and chimney details as assigned by your instructor:

Location:	a. Interior wall
	b. Exterior wall
	c. Corner
Size:	a. Small
	b. Average
	c. Medium large
Styling:	a. Traditional
	b. Contemporary
Fireplace openings:	a. Single-faced
	b. Double-faced with adjacent faces
	c. Double-faced with opposite faces
	d. Three-faced
	e. Four-faced

Figure 15 *Metal fireplace in an office setting.*

Materials: a. Modular brick
b. Norman brick
c. Roman brick
d. Common brick with ceramic tile
e. Block
f. Stone

Hearth: a. Flush with floor
b. Raised 12″ from floor

Accessories: a. Log bin
b. Built-in book shelves
c. Built-in record cabinet
d. Fireplace liner with air registers
e. Tempered glass doors
f. Outside air intake

3. Complete the fireplace and chimney details for your original house design.

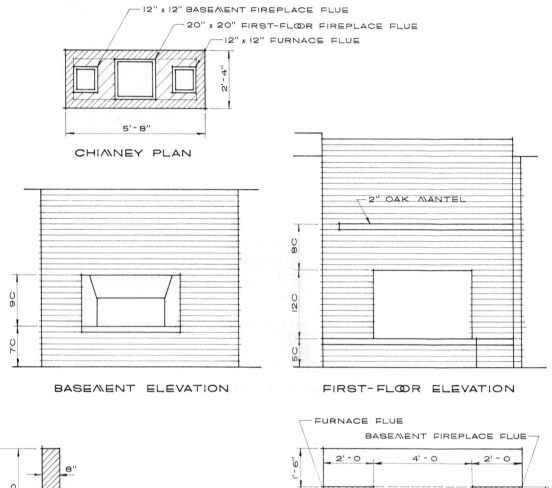

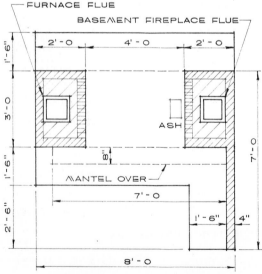

Figure 16 *Fireplace details of the A residence.*

27 / Architectural Models

Models have always been an important tool of the architect. Before the discovery of the blueprinting process, architects used models to describe their projects to craftsmen. It was common practice to scale measurements directly from working models. Architects also used presentation models to attract new patrons, carrying models of their best works from town to town.

Figure 1 *Model of an Egyptian residence. Cairo Museum. Photograph by the Egyptian Expedition. The Metropolitan Museum of Art.*

The model of an Egyptian residence shown in Figure 1 was taken from the XI Dynasty tomb of Meket-Re. It is one of the oldest known models, dating to 2500 B.C. It was built of carved, painted wood. Walls were mitered together and mortised to the base. Tree branches, leaves, and fruit were made of doweled wood, and the atrium pool was lined with copper sheet to hold water.

Nearly everything we use in today's living was first constructed in model form. The ground, water, and air vehicles we ride in, the commercial, industrial, and educational structures we work in, and the residences we live in were all modeled before they were actually built. The construction of architectural models, therefore, is a definite part of the services performed by the architect and is a useful skill for the architectural drafter.

TYPES OF MODELS

Various kinds of architectural models are used for different purposes. In general, though, architectural models fall into two categories: study models and presentation models.

Study model. The study model, as the name implies, is constructed by designers to help them *study* the function or appearance of a building. A study model is built during the planning stage and may be modified many times before a satisfactory solution is found. Obviously, then, a study model is not a carefully constructed finished model. In fact, very crude materials may be used. A *mass model,* for example, is used to study the general effect of the position (or *massing*) of architectural ele-

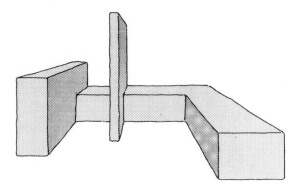

Figure 2 *Mass model.*

ments (see Figure 2). Modeling clay is an excellent medium for this, although balsa wood, styrofoam, soap, and even raw potatoes are used. Other types of *thumbnail* models may be used to study plot contours, roof intersections, landscaping, interiors, and the like.

Presentation model. A presentation model is a finished scale model showing *exactly* how a proposed building will appear and function. It may be built after the preliminary planning stage to help the architect explain the concept to the clients, or it may be built after the finished plans are drawn to help the clients raise money for the actual construction. In larger offices, the presentation models are built by a special model-making department; smaller offices often contract with professional architectural model-building concerns.

In the following pages we will discuss some materials and methods used in building presentation models. First, however, two important rules in architectural model building—neatness and scale—should be discussed.

Neatness. Take great care to be accurate and neat in all phases of the building. A sloppy modeling job is completely useless because it will not serve its main function—that of selling the design to the client.

Scale. Every feature of the structure, down to the smallest detail, must be built to the same scale. When this is carefully done, the model will have the professional look of a scale model; when it is not, it will look like a toy. The most commonly used scales are $\frac{1}{8}'' = 1'$ and $\frac{1}{4}'' = 1'$.

MATERIALS

The most often used and versatile material for architectural modeling is heavy cardboard. Properly selected, cardboard can serve as finished walls and roofs, or as the base for the application of other finished materials. It is known as *mat board, mount board,* or *display cardboard.* Fourteen-ply cardboard ($\frac{1}{8}''-\frac{3}{16}''$ thick) of the best quality should be used. These boards may be obtained permanently embossed with scaled surface detail of several types (see Table I).

Another popular architectural modeling material is two- or three-ply *Strathmore drawing paper,* plate surface. It is often used for trims and overlays since it has a hard, tough surface, cuts cleanly, can be bent sharply without tearing, and will take paint without wrinkling.

These cardboards are cut with a new razor or razor knife, using a steel straightedge as a guide. The first cut should be fairly light, the cuts being repeated until the edge cuts through. The outside corners of walls must be carefully mitered. Good work can be done only with *sharp* instruments.

Some professional model makers prefer wood to cardboard. Basswood and ponderosa pine are used for their fine, even grain, and balsa wood is used for its extreme softness. Table II shows the available sizes of these woods in sheets, strips, and structural shapes. Thin wood may also be cut by razor, but heavier stock is best cut by a razor saw.

Table I *Available Mat Boards*

	Surfaces	Sheet Size	Sca
	Smooth surface	30″ × 40″	
	Pebbled surface	30″ × 40″	
	Embossed surfaces		
	9″ weatherboard or shiplap	3″ × 22″	$\frac{1}{8}''$
	12″ weatherboard or shiplap	3″ × 22″	$\frac{1}{8}''$
	12″ board and batten	3″ × 22″	$\frac{1}{8}''$
	brick siding	3″ × 22″	$\frac{1}{8}''$ an
	concrete block siding	3″ × 22″	$\frac{1}{8}''$ an
	stucco siding	3″ × 22″	$\frac{1}{8}''$ an
	shake roofing	3″ × 22″	$\frac{1}{8}''$ an

Household cement (such as Dupont Duco) may be used for cementing cardboard, paper, and wood. After setting one hour it will make a glue joint that is stronger than the materials joined. Rubber bands, drafting tape, straight pins, and small *lills* are used as clamps to hold the materials until set. To prevent model parts from adhering to a template, waxed paper may be used over the template.

BASE

Since a structure is designed in relation to its surroundings, the model is constructed showing some of its surrounding topography. The usual procedure is to select a base that is scaled to the plot size and shape. Plywood $\frac{1}{2}$″ thick is quite satisfactory for this purpose.

Flat plot. The plywood base may be finished directly with paint, flocking, or a loose material sprinkled over glue (such as dyed sawdust or sand). Sandpaper or black garnet paper may be glued face up with rubber cement to give the effect of concrete or asphalt driveways.

Contoured plot. To obtain an accurate reproduction of a contoured plot, the usual procedure is to build up successive layers of chipboard which have been cut to conform to the contour lines on the plot plan. Chipboard is an inexpensive cardboard available in thicknesses of $\frac{1}{16}$″, $\frac{3}{32}$″, $\frac{1}{8}$″, and $\frac{5}{64}$″. The thickness is selected to equal the scaled contour interval (vertical distance between contour lines). For example, the contour interval in Figure 3 is 2′. If the contour model is to be built to a $\frac{1}{8}$″ = 1′ scale, each layer of chipboard must be $\frac{1}{4}$″ thick. Therefore, two $\frac{1}{8}$″ chipboards should be used. Usually this kind of contour model is left in terraced steps for easy comparison with the plot plan rather than being smoothed to shape. It is finished in the same manner as the flat plot.

Hillside plot. When the plot has a very steep slope, the contour plot method described requires too many layers of cardboard. The professional modeler then uses an alternate technique, building up the land model using bandsawed wood forms and covering them with wire screening as

The materials in the table at left are obtainable from model suppliers such as Walthers, 1245 N. Water St., Milwaukee, Wisconsin 53202 (ask for their ARCHITECTURAL INDUSTRIAL CATALOG OF MODEL SUPPLIES) and America's Hobby Center, 146 W. Twenty-Second St., New York, New York. 10011 (ask for their model train catalog; this includes architectural modeling materials).

Table II   *Available Wood Sizes*

Sheet balsa (36″ × 2″, 3″, 4″, and 6″) $\frac{1}{32}$″, $\frac{1}{16}$″, $\frac{3}{32}$″, $\frac{1}{8}$″, $\frac{3}{16}$″, $\frac{1}{4}$″

Strip balsa (36″ long)

	$\frac{1}{16}$″	$\frac{3}{32}$″	$\frac{1}{8}$″	$\frac{3}{16}$″	$\frac{1}{4}$″
$\frac{1}{16}$″	√		√	√	√
$\frac{3}{32}$″		√	√		
$\frac{1}{8}$″	√	√	√		√
$\frac{3}{16}$″	√			√	
$\frac{1}{4}$″	√		√		√

Sheet pine (22″ × 1″, 2″, and 3″) $\frac{1}{32}$″, $\frac{1}{16}$″, $\frac{3}{32}$″, $\frac{1}{8}$″, $\frac{3}{16}$″, $\frac{1}{4}$″

Strip basswood (24″ long)

	$\frac{1}{32}$″	$\frac{1}{16}$″	$\frac{3}{32}$″	$\frac{1}{8}$″	$\frac{5}{32}$″	$\frac{3}{16}$″	$\frac{1}{4}$″
$\frac{1}{32}$″	√	√	√	√	√	√	√
$\frac{1}{16}$″	√	√	√	√	√	√	√
$\frac{3}{32}$″	√	√	√	√	√	√	√
$\frac{1}{8}$″	√	√	√	√	√	√	√
$\frac{5}{32}$″	√	√	√	√	√	√	√
$\frac{3}{16}$″	√	√	√	√	√	√	√
$\frac{1}{4}$″	√	√	√	√	√	√	√

Milled basswood ($3\frac{1}{2}$″ × 24″ sheets)

	$\frac{1}{32}$″	$\frac{1}{16}$″	$\frac{1}{8}$″
6″ and 9″ clapboard ($\frac{1}{8}$″ scale)			√
6″ clapboard ($\frac{1}{4}$″ scale)	√		
12″ board and batten ($\frac{1}{8}$″ scale)		√	
9″ board and batten ($\frac{1}{4}$″ scale)		√	
3″, 4″, 6″, 9″, and 12″ scribed planking ($\frac{1}{8}$″ scale)		√	
3″, 4″, 6″, and 9″ scribed planking ($\frac{1}{4}$″ scale)	√		
shingled siding ($\frac{1}{4}$″ scale)			√
brick siding ($\frac{1}{8}$″ and $\frac{1}{4}$″ scale)		√	
concrete block siding ($\frac{1}{4}$″ scale)			√
flagstone ($\frac{1}{8}$″ and $\frac{1}{4}$″ scale)		√	√

Structural shapes (24″ long)

	$\frac{3}{64}$″	$\frac{1}{16}$″	$\frac{5}{64}$″	$\frac{3}{32}$″	$\frac{1}{8}$″	$\frac{3}{16}$″	$\frac{1}{4}$″
angles	√	√		√	√	√	
tees	√	√		√	√	√	√
channels			√	√	√	√	√
WF beams					√	√	√
I beams					√	√	√
quarter round	√			√	√		

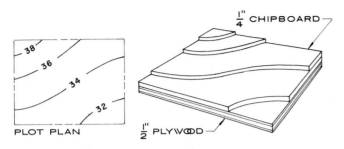

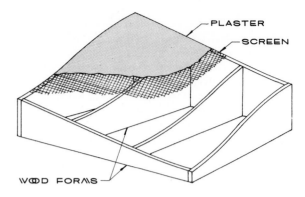

Figure 3   *Modeling a contoured plot.*

Figure 4   *Modeling a hillside plot.*

shown in Figure 4. The screening is plastered with a ¼″-thick mix of 50 percent (by volume) plaster, 50 percent mineral fibers, dry color, and water. Mineral fibers of the type used for insulation greatly increase the strength of the mix (like the aggregate in concrete). The dry colors are obtained from an art store and are sometimes called *earth colors*. A brown color is used so that the plaster will look like earth if it is chipped. This mix is troweled on roughly to indicate rock outcrops, and smoothed or stippled with a brush to indicate grass areas. Thin washes or oil stains are used

for the final painting. The following colors are common:

> Grass: Color varies from pale yellow to olive green
> Brown soil: Burnt umber stain
> Reddish soil: Burnt and raw sienna stain
> Brown rock: Van Dyke brown stain
> Reddish rock: Van Dyke brown and burnt sienna stain
> Gray rock: Thin wash of black

Table III   *Available Plastic Material*

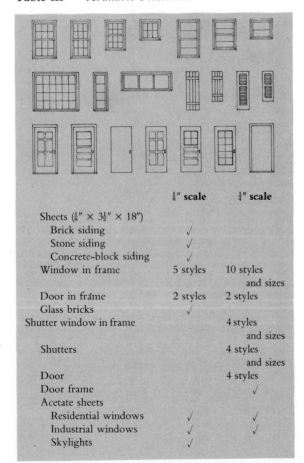

	⅛″ scale	¼″ scale
Sheets (⅛″ × 3½″ × 18″)		
Brick siding	√	
Stone siding	√	
Concrete-block siding	√	
Window in frame	5 styles	10 styles and sizes
Door in frame	2 styles	2 styles
Glass bricks	√	
Shutter window in frame		4 styles and sizes
Shutters		4 styles and sizes
Door		4 styles
Door frame		√
Acetate sheets		
Residential windows	√	√
Industrial windows	√	√
Skylights	√	

WALLS

The selection of the method and materials used for wall construction depends upon the scale of the model. When models are built to a scale smaller than ⅛″ = 1′, the walls are usually built of painted mat board. The recommended order of procedure is:

1. Accurately lay out all wall sizes in pencil on the mat board using T square and triangles. Cut out with a *sharp* razor knife (Figure 5).
2. Paint the walls using poster paint (tempera) carefully mixed to the desired colors. When they are dry, rule on white or black lines (depending upon the color of the desired mortar mix) representing brick or stone joints and wood siding. These lines need not be completely ruled—only enough to give the impression of the surface (Figure 6).
3. Since stock windows are not available—or desirable—for such small scales, windows are painted on or outlined by scaled strip wood (Figure 7). The professional model builder uses a flat black or dark gray for glass areas, since this is the actual appearance of windows. Muntins and mullions are ruled on in white ink (such as Pelikan white drawing ink) with a ruling pen or technical fountain pen.

4. Miter corners and assemble, being careful not to smudge the prepainted surfaces. All corners must be square (Figure 8).

Models built to a scale of $\frac{1}{8}''$ or $\frac{1}{4}'' = 1'$ are somewhat simpler to construct since a great variety of stock material is available in these scales. These are common scales for residential models and probably the best ones for the beginner. Some plastic materials available in these scales are shown in Table III, and some paper materials are shown in Table IV. The procedure for building these larger scaled models is as follows:

1. Select the desired material from Tables I–IV. Milled basswood, embossed mat board, and balsa wood are all satisfactory materials. If the model is to have a removable roof so that rooms inside can be viewed, the thickness of the material should scale to the actual wall thickness. Although it requires much more work, custom siding can be constructed by cementing thin strips of Strathmore paper to sheet stock (Figure 9).
2. Accurately lay off all walls, windows, and doors in pencil on the siding (Figure 10). If stock windows and doors are to be used, some adjustment may have to be made to fit the available material to your plan. Cut out walls, windows, and doors using a *sharp* razor knife.
3. Windows and doors may also be custom-built (Figure 11). The construction of a sliding window is illustrated.
4. Carefully miter all corners and assemble the sides directly upon a floor plan cut from sheet stock. If this sheet stock is sufficiently thick, it can serve as the exposed portion of the foundation. Use pins or tape to hold the model until dry (Figure 12).

ROOFS

Flat built-up roofs of all scales can be made very simply of sandpaper glued face up to mat board and finished with the desired color latex paint.

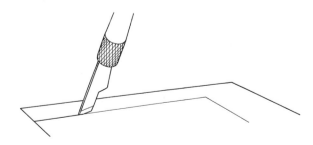

Figure 5 *Use of the razor knife.*

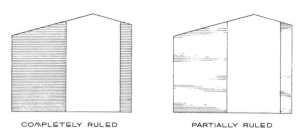

COMPLETELY RULED   PARTIALLY RULED

Figure 6 *A model wall.*

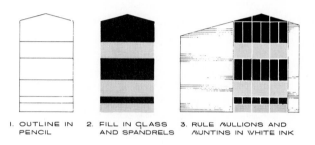

1. OUTLINE IN PENCIL   2. FILL IN GLASS AND SPANDRELS   3. RULE MULLIONS AND MUNTINS IN WHITE INK

Figure 7 *A model window.*

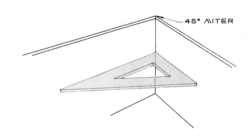

45° MITER

Figure 8 *Miter and square corners.*

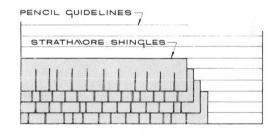

PENCIL GUIDELINES
STRATHMORE SHINGLES

Figure 9 *Modeling a shingle roof.*

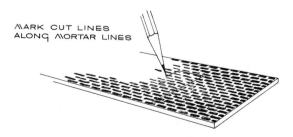

MARK CUT LINES ALONG MORTAR LINES

Figure 10 *Lay out on mortar lines.*

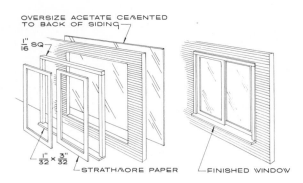

Figure 11   *Custom-built window construction.*

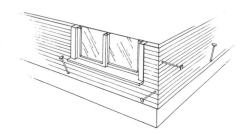

Figure 12   *Pin corners until cement dries.*

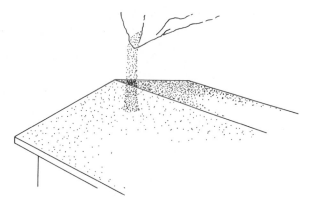

Figure 13   *Built-up roofing simulation.*

Marble chip roofs are simulated by sprinkling fine sand or salt on the wet white paint to add sparkle to the surface (see Figure 13). Preformed shingle roof material is available, but roofs may be custom-built by gluing strips of notched Strathmore paper to a mat board roof base.

Sheet metal roofs and flashing are modeled with strips of drafting tape cut to shape and painted copper or silver. A properly scaled fascia of strip basswood provides a finished look to any roof. Gutters and downspouts are built of properly scaled wire or strip basswood.

Chimneys should be cut from a balsa wood block with the horizontal brick joints scribed in (Figure 14). Bricks are painted on over a white undercoat to represent mortar. Of course, any of the stock brick sheet material may be used.

Figure 14   *Modeling a chimney.*

ACCESSORIES

Accessories added to the structure (such as front door lamps), those added to the topography (such as shrubs and trees), and entourage (such as cars and people) may be custom built or purchased from stock. Some architectural modelers find it more convenient to obtain supplies from a model railroad supplier. For this purpose, it is necessary to know that O gauge is $\frac{1}{4}''$ scale, HO gauge is approximately $\frac{1}{8}''$ scale, and N gauge is approximately $\frac{1}{16}''$ scale. See Table V for the exact conversion size.

Nearly any architectural modeling element may be purchased, but often custom-built accessories are less toylike and more professional looking. Realistic trees may be modeled from dried yarrow or culex weeds dipped in shellac to prevent deterioration, shrubs and ground cover formed from lichen obtainable in many colors, hedges from sponge rubber or styrofoam, people carved from erasers or soap, and stylized cars from balsa blocks. Care must be taken that all accessories are properly scaled.

Table IV   *Available Building Paper*

		$\frac{1}{8}''$ scale, 6″ × 9″ sheets	$\frac{1}{4}''$ scale, 9″ × 12″ she
Red brick		✓	✓
Yellow brick		✓	✓
Brown fieldstone		✓	✓
Gray fieldstone		✓	✓
Gray flagstone		✓	✓
Brown ashlar stone		✓	✓
Gray ashlar stone		✓	✓
Yellow ashlar stone		✓	✓
Concrete block		✓	✓
Brown wood shingles		✓	✓
Gray wood shingles		✓	✓
Green wood shingles		✓	✓
Gray slate		✓	✓

Figure 15 *Model contemporary house, student design by William Travis, Jr. (Scale: 1/8 = 1'-0.)*

Figure 16 *Another view of the model house shown in Figure 15.*

Some architectual models by students and professionals are shown in Figures 15–20.

CUTAWAY MODELS

A cutaway model of a structure is used to show actual construction methods and materials. Such models are very popular classroom projects since they must be built up of studs, sheathing, and finish material in much the same manner as in current building practice. For example, a wall is constructed by pinning each stud and plate over a framing drawing. The framing is glued together rather than nailed, with wax paper used to prevent it from sticking to the drawing. This is followed by wood sheathing, felt paper, and finish siding—each layer cut back so that the previous layer is left exposed for inspection. Insulation, heating ducts, and piping may also be shown in the walls. Other procedures are similar to those already described in this chapter. Recommended scales are $\frac{3}{8}'' = 1'$ and $\frac{3}{4}'' = 1'$.

Figure 17 *Scale model of museum helped designers to plan aircraft placement, Air Force Museum, Dayton, Ohio.*

Table V *Scale Conversions*

Model Railroad Gauge	Equivalent Architectural Scale
O gauge	$1'' = 1'-0$
S gauge	$\frac{3}{16}'' = 1'-0$
HO gauge*	$\frac{1}{8}'' = 1'-0$
TT gauge	$\frac{1}{10}'' = 1'-0$
N gauge*	$\frac{1}{16}'' = 1'-0$
Z gauge*	$\frac{1}{20}'' = 1'-0$

* Actually HO gauge is 3.5 mm = 1', which is approximately 1/7.3'' = 1'-0, N gauge is 1:160, which is approximately 1/13.3'' = 1'-0, and Z gauge is 1:220, which is approximately 1/18.3'' = 1'-0.

Figure 18 *Professional architectural model of a housing complex.*

Figure 19   *Model of Madison Square Garden Sports and Entertainment Center.*

Figure 20   *Architectural model of the Lecture Center, University of Illinois, Chicago.*

STUDY QUESTIONS

1. How does a study model differ from a presentation model?
2. Why are neatness and scale important in building presentation models?
3. Match these modeling requirements with the materials to be used:
   a. Temporary fastener   Lills
   b. Permanent fastener   Acetate sheet
   c. Window and door trim   Mat board
   d. Window glass   Household cement
   e. Walls and roof   Strathmore drawing paper
4. How is the size of the base of a model determined?
5. Describe the modeling technique used to build the following bases:
   a. Flat plot
   b. Contoured plot
   c. Hillside plot
6. Describe the technique used to build model walls to a scale of:
   a. $\frac{1}{16}'' = 1'$
   b. $\frac{1}{4}'' = 1'$
7. What materials are used to model:
   a. Built-up roofs
   b. Shingle roofs
   c. Flashing
   d. Guttering
8. Give the equivalent architectural scale for:
   a. O gauge
   b. S gauge
   c. HO gauge
   d. TT gauge
   e. Z gauge
9. What materials are used to model these accessories:
   a. Trees
   b. Shrubs
   c. Hedges
   d. People
   e. Automobiles

LABORATORY PROBLEMS

1. Construct a study model of:
   a. The building assigned by your instructor
   b. Your original house design
2. Construct a presentation model of:
   a. The A residence
   b. The building assigned by your instructor
   c. Your original house design
3. Construct a cutaway model of a building using the specifications given by your instructor.

VII / Light Construction

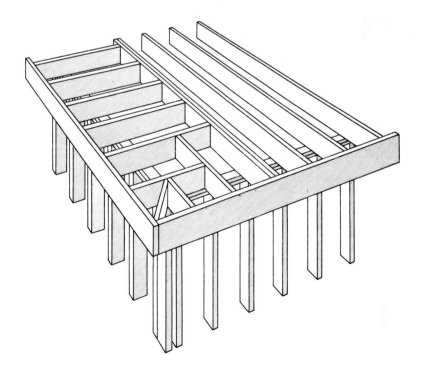

28 / Light Framing

It is extremely important that you, as a student of architectural drafting, be thoroughly familiar with standard construction practices. An architectural drafter attempting to design a building without knowledge of its construction would be like a contractor trying to build without being able to read blueprints. In either case, chaos would result.

Although there are many different types of acceptable construction in use today, we shall proceed by studying in detail the most commonly used type: the *platform frame*. This will be done step by step, starting with the site survey and excavation, and working up to the roof and finish materials—as though we were actually building. Later we will look at other kinds of construction to see how they differ from the platform frame.

SURVEY

Before starting construction, the house lot should be surveyed by a registered surveyor who will accurately locate the property lines. The property corners are marked with 30″-long galvanized iron pipes driven almost completely into the ground. The surveyor may also stake out the corners of the house, checking the local building ordinance for requirements on minimum setback from the road, and minimum side and rear yards. The ordinance may state that the front of the building must align with adjacent buildings.

As previously mentioned, if there are trees on the site, the house should be placed to save a maximum number. As a rule, all trees within 5′ of the proposed building are cut down, since the excavation will disturb their roots so much that they will die.

The surveyor will also establish correct elevations, usually using the adjoining road or house as references. All of this information is placed on a survey map which will be the basis of the plot plan. Figure 1 shows a survey map for the A residence.

STAKING

Although the surveyor may stake out the house foundation, this is usually done by the building

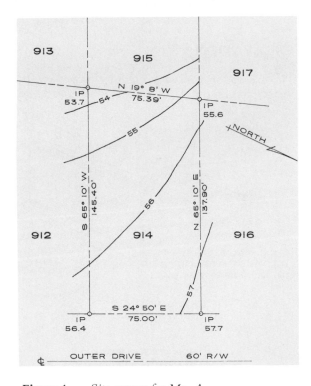

Figure 1   *Site survey for Mr. A.*

239

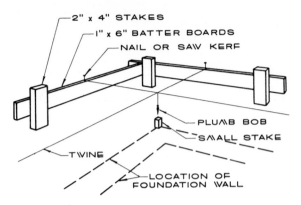

Figure 2 *Staking.*

contractor who locates the future outside corners of the foundation and marks these points with tacks in small stakes. Then, since these stakes will be disturbed by the excavation, larger 2″ × 4″ stakes are driven 4′ beyond the foundation lines, three at each corner. Figure 2 shows 1″ × 6″ batter boards nailed to these stakes so that their tops are of the same elevation. Using a plumb bob, the contractor stretches stout twine across the batter boards directly above the corner tacks. Saw kerfs (cuts) or nails are located on the batter boards where the twine touches to establish a more permanent record of the foundation lines (Figure 3). Of course, it is particularly important to check for squared corners. This may be done with surveying instruments, by measuring diagonals, or by using the principle of the 3-4-5 triangle (Figure 4).

EXCAVATION

The excavation is usually done by power equipment. First, about 1′ of topsoil is removed and

stored at the side of the lot to be used later in the finish grading. Then the excavation itself is made, the depth depending upon these factors:

1. On sloping land, the foundation must extend above the highest perimeter point of finished grade by:
   a. 8″ in wood-frame construction to protect the wood from rotting due to moisture
   b. 2″ in brick construction to protect the first brick course from constant exposure to moisture which may eventually work into the joints
2. The footing must extend below the lowest perimeter point of finished grade by the prevailing frost-line depth. This is necessary to prevent upheaval when the ground freezes. Figure 5 may be consulted for a general indication of frost-line depth, but a more accurate depth for a particular area may be obtained from local architects and builders.
3. When a full foundation is to be built, allow a minimum of 6′-9″ from the top of the basement floor to the bottom of the floor joist as shown in Figure 6. Remember that a girder under the joist will reduce the headroom. The minimum comfortable ceiling height for a habitable room is considered to be 7′-6″; 8′-0″ more often is used for the main living areas.
4. When a crawl space (for inspection and repair) is to be built, allow a minimum of 18″ to the bottom of the joists. Specify 2′-6″ for a more comfortable working height. Prevent water from accumulating in the crawl space by:
   a. Locating the crawl space 1½″ above the outside finish grade
   b. Providing a special drain to a lower elevation or storm sewer
   c. Relying on local soil conditions which may

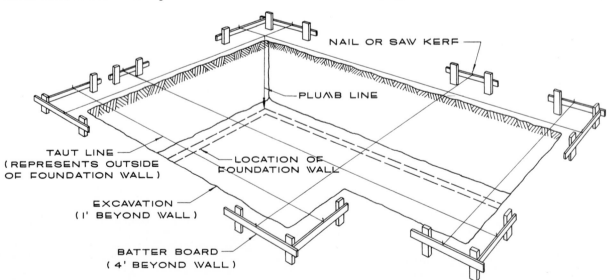

Figure 3 *Excavation.*

be such that water will naturally drain from the crawl space

5. The excavation should extend down to *unfilled* ground. Because it is so important that a good bearing surface be provided, the trench for the footings should be dug shortly before pouring the concrete to prevent a possible softening of the bearing ground by exposure to rain and air.

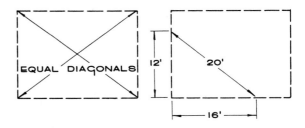

Figure 4   *Methods of squaring corners.*

FOOTING

Footings increase the bearing surface of the house upon the ground so that there will be less settling. The footings should be of concrete poured on undisturbed land. Average residential construction on firm land calls for footings twice as wide as the foundation wall, from 16″ to 24″. The depth of the footing should equal the wall thickness, ranging from 8″ to 12″. Side forms may be omitted if the ground permits sharply cut trenches. Reinforcing steel is used when the footing spans pipe trenches. As mentioned previously, the frost line determines the minimum depth of footing excavation, this varying from 1′-6″ in Florida to 4′-6″ in Maine.

The bottom of footings should always be horizontal, never inclined. Thus on sloping land, *stepped footings* such as shown in Figure 10 are used. The horizontal portion of a step footing should not be less than 32″; the vertical portion should not exceed 24″. To reduce cutting when building the foundation wall, these dimensions should be in modular block units. The horizontal and vertical portions of the stepped footing should be of equal thickness, and both portions should be poured at the same time.

Footings are also required for chimneys and columns. Since column footings must support as much as one-quarter of the total weight of the house, they are stepped out even farther (usually to 24″ square or 30″ square). By the use of the tables in Chapter 29, it is possible to calculate the required sizes of foundation, chimney, and column footings.

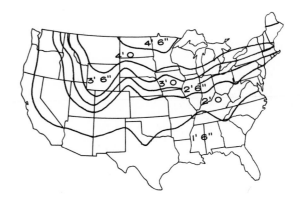

Figure 5   *Footing depth.*

DRAINAGE

To provide drainage around the foundation and ensure a dry basement, 4″ perforated pipes are laid in the foundation excavation or footing excavation. Two types of drain pipe are available:

1. A rigid, perforated plastic pipe, 4″ diameter in 10′ lengths joined by plastic fittings.
2. A flexible, perforated plastic pipe, 4″ diameter in 250′ rolls.

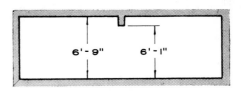

MINIMUM BASEMENT HEIGHTS

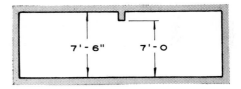

MINIMUM HABITABLE ROOM HEIGHTS

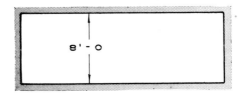

RECOMMENDED ROOM HEIGHT

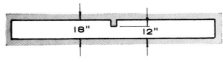

MINIMUM CRAWL SPACE

Figure 6   *Minimum design heights.*

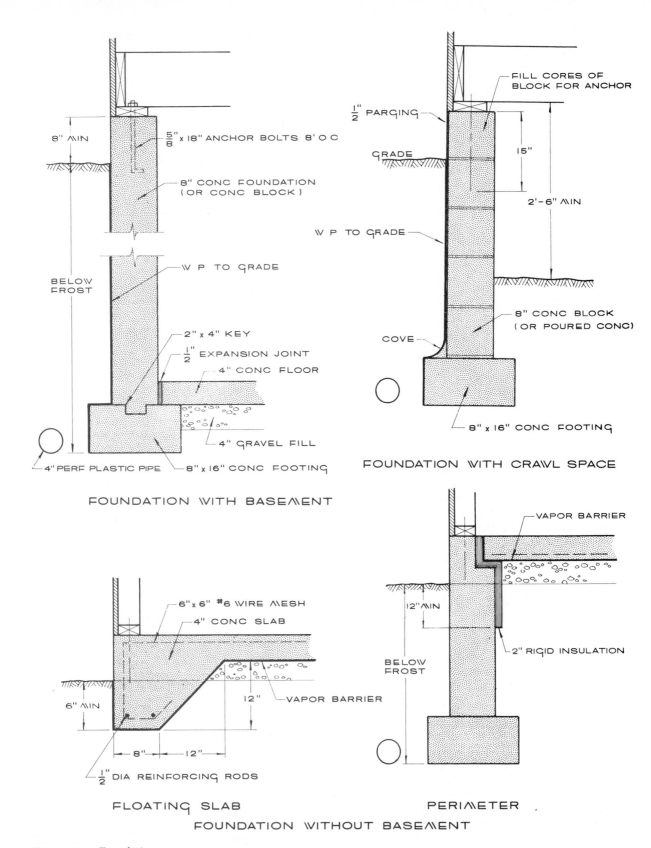

8" MIN

5/8" x 18" ANCHOR BOLTS 8' O C

8" CONC FOUNDATION
(OR CONC BLOCK)

W P TO GRADE

BELOW
FROST

2" x 4" KEY

1/2" EXPANSION JOINT

4" CONC FLOOR

4" GRAVEL FILL

4" PERF PLASTIC PIPE   8" x 16" CONC FOOTING

FOUNDATION WITH BASEMENT

FILL CORES OF
BLOCK FOR ANCHOR

1/2" PARGING

GRADE

15"

2'-6" MIN

W P TO GRADE

8" CONC BLOCK
(OR POURED CONC)

COVE

8" x 16" CONC FOOTING

FOUNDATION WITH CRAWL SPACE

6" x 6" #6 WIRE MESH

4" CONC SLAB

6" MIN

12"

VAPOR BARRIER

8"   12"

1/2" DIA REINFORCING RODS

FLOATING SLAB

VAPOR BARRIER

12" MIN

BELOW
FROST

2" RIGID INSULATION

PERIMETER

FOUNDATION WITHOUT BASEMENT

Figure 7   *Foundations.*

Ground fill above either type encourages drainage to the drain pipes. The drain line should slope slightly ($\frac{1}{16}''$/ft. minimum) to a catch basin, dry well, or sewer.

FOUNDATION

Foundations (Figure 7) may be constructed to provide a basement or crawl space. When a concrete floor is poured at ground level, it is called *slab* construction. It may be floating or perimeter. The floating slab requires reinforcing since it is meant to "float" as an integral unit on the ground. Although this construction has been used in cold climates, it is best suited to areas where frost penetration is no problem. The perimeter foundation, on the other hand, provides a complete foundation wall for the protection of the slab from frost. The rigid insulation reduces heat loss from the house.

Materials. The two most common foundation materials are poured concrete ($8''$–$12''$) and concrete blocks ($8''$, $10''$, or $12''$).

Poured concrete. The poured concrete foundation is usually considered superior because it is more likely to be waterproof and termite-proof. A 1-$2\frac{1}{2}$-5 concrete mix is often used. This means 1 part cement, $2\frac{1}{2}$ parts fine aggregate (sand), and 5 parts coarse aggregate (gravel or crushed stone). Poured concrete walls are sometimes battered (sloped) from $12''$ thickness at the bottom to $8''$ thickness at the top. This is to prevent any adhesion between the walls and clay ground due to freezing and to guard the wall from being lifted by frost action. The outside faces of the foundation and footing are mopped with hot tar or asphalt for additional protection against water. For this purpose, emulsified or hot tar (pitch) is superior to asphalt, since asphalt in continual contact with moisture may eventually disintegrate.

Concrete block. A $\frac{1}{2}''$ layer of cement plaster (called *parging*) is applied to the outside block wall and covered with hot tar or asphalt waterproofing. It is good practice to fill the cores of the top course of concrete blocks with concrete to prevent passage of water or termites. Long stretches of wall are often stiffened with $8'' \times 16''$ pilasters every $16'$ as shown in Figure 11. This is particularly important when using walls of only $8''$ block.

Foundation height. Remember that the foundation must extend above the highest perimeter point of finished grade by $8''$ in wood-frame con-

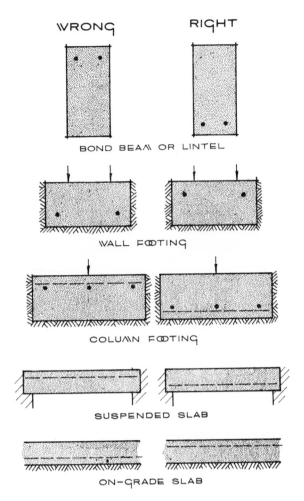

Figure 8 *Placement of reinforcing steel in light construction.*

struction to protect lumber from ground moisture. When a brick-veneer construction is used, the foundation should extend at least $2''$ above the finished grade.

Reinforcing. Concrete has excellent strength in *compression*, but is weak in *tension*. Therefore when any portion of a concrete member is expected to be subjected to tension, steel rods or steel wire mesh is cast in that portion to resist the tension. This is called *reinforcing steel*. In light construction, reinforcing is used in concrete bond beams, concrete lintels, and occasionally in concrete slabs and footings. This reinforcing should be placed near the *bottom* of bond beams, lintels, column footings, and suspended slabs to best resist the tension there. It is common building practice to also place reinforcing near the bottom of wall footings and on-grade slabs upon the assumption that these mem-

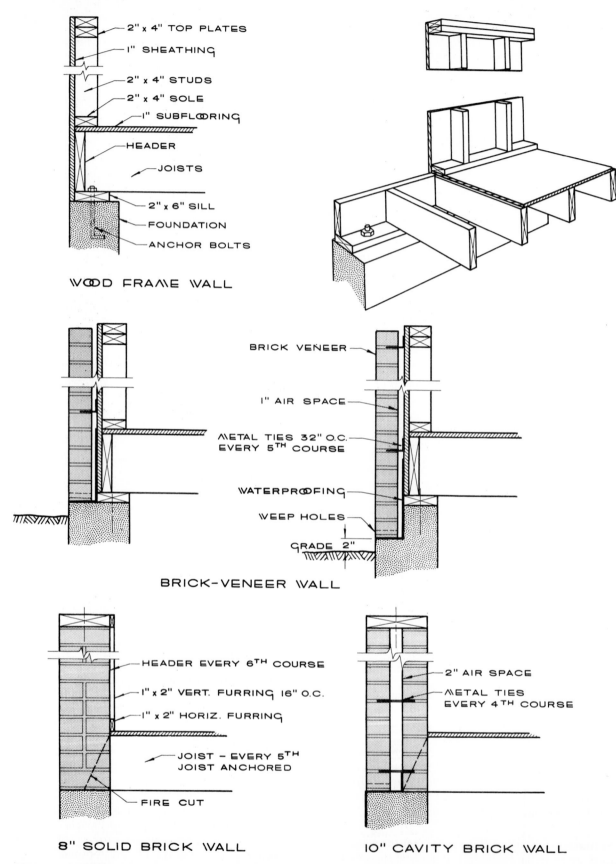

2" x 4" TOP PLATES
1" SHEATHING
2" x 4" STUDS
2" x 4" SOLE
1" SUBFLOORING
HEADER
JOISTS
2" x 6" SILL
FOUNDATION
ANCHOR BOLTS

WOOD FRAME WALL

BRICK VENEER
1" AIR SPACE
METAL TIES 32" O.C.
EVERY 5TH COURSE
WATERPROOFING
WEEP HOLES
GRADE 2"

BRICK-VENEER WALL

HEADER EVERY 6TH COURSE
1" x 2" VERT. FURRING 16" O.C.
1" x 2" HORIZ. FURRING
JOIST – EVERY 5TH JOIST ANCHORED
FIRE CUT

8" SOLID BRICK WALL

2" AIR SPACE
METAL TIES EVERY 4TH COURSE

10" CAVITY BRICK WALL

Figure 9 *Walls.*

bers are similar to bond beams. However, many engineers now specify that reinforcing rods in wall footings be near the *top* to better prevent cracking which could then extend up into the wall above. Reinforcing wire mesh in slabs poured on grade is also specified near the *top* of the slab to better control cracking which would affect the exposed floor surface. See Figure 8.

SILL

The sill is a 2″ × 6″ plank resting directly on top of the foundation wall. Notice in Figure 9 that the sill is set back about 1″ from the outside wall so that the sheathing, which is nailed to the sill, will be flush with the outside foundation wall. Some builders allow for irregularities in the face of the foundation wall by setting the sill flush so that the sheathing projects beyond the outside of the foundation wall. This is illustrated in Figure 13 of Chapter 11. The sill should be fastened by $\frac{1}{2}$″, $\frac{5}{8}$″, or $\frac{3}{4}$″ bolts spaced 8′ apart. These extend 6″ into a poured concrete foundation and 15″ into a concrete block foundation. Holes are drilled into the sill, a bed of mortar (called *grout*) is spread on the foundation, and the sill is tapped into a level position. The nuts and washers are tightened by hand. Several days later they may be wrench-tightened. The grout provides a level bed for the sill and makes an airtight joint.

HEADER

Headers and joists are the same size. The header is spiked upright to the top outside edge of the sill. Where a basement window or door breaks the foundation wall, it is good practice to let the header, rather than the sill, act as the spanning member. This is best accomplished by a ledger strip spiked to the header and extending at least 6″ beyond the opening, as shown in Figure 12. The joists are cut to rest on the ledger and are also spiked to the header. A steel angle lintel may also be used.

GIRDER

The dimensions of most houses are so great that joists cannot span the foundation walls. In that case, a wood girder (that is, several 2″-thick members spiked together) or steel beam is used, as shown in Figure 13. Notice that the girder is also too long to span the foundation walls and must be

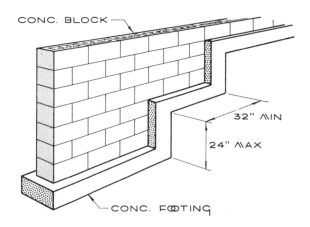

Figure 10   *Stepped footing.*

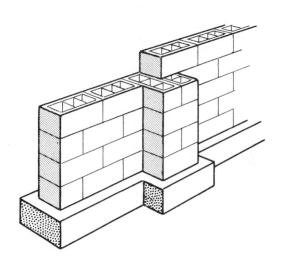

Figure 11   *Pilaster construction.*

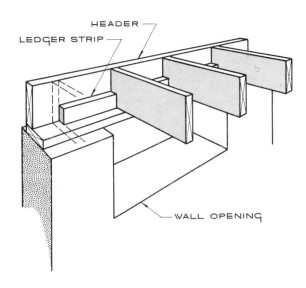

Figure 12   *Use of a ledger strip.*

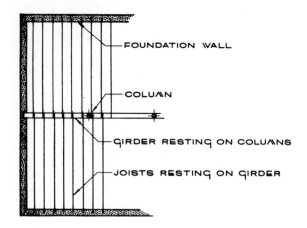

Figure 13 *Use of a girder.*

supported by wood or steel columns as in Figure 14. Steel pipe columns (usually referred to by the trade name *Lally columns*) are capped with a steel plate to increase the bearing surface with the wood girder. A 3½″-diameter column is large enough for ordinary requirements.

The girder is framed into the foundation wall as shown in Figure 16 so that it bears a minimum of 4″. Incidentally, this is a good rule to remember: *always provide the greatest possible bearing surface between two members.* In case of wood, the length of bearing surface should not be less than 4″ (see Figure 15) for safest construction. However, to save headroom, joists are occasionally framed level with the girder using iron stirrups, ledger strips, or framing anchors. Joists may also be set "level" with a steel beam. (Actually, such joists are installed with their upper edges 1″ above the steel

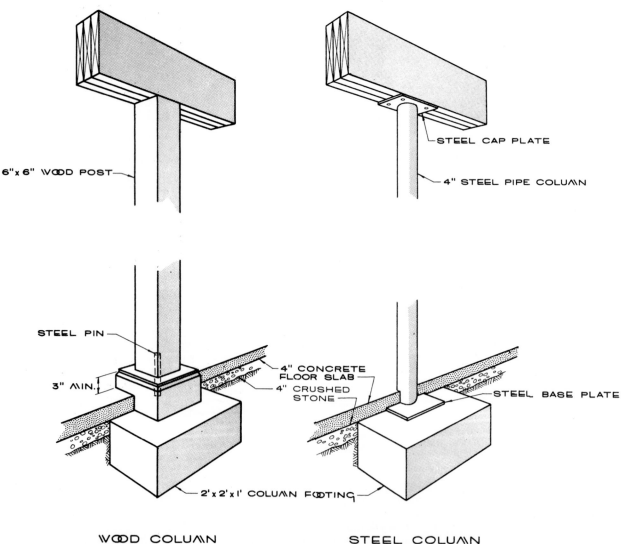

WOOD COLUMN   STEEL COLUMN

Figure 14 *Use of columns.*

beam to allow for wood shrinkage and to prevent a bulge in the floor above.)

The wall pocket for a wood girder should be large enough to allow a minimum of $\frac{1}{2}''$ air space at the sides and ends of the girder. This allows moisture to escape and reduces the possibility of decay.

Sizes of wood girders and steel beams may be calculated as shown in Chapter 29.

FLOOR JOISTS

Because so much material is made in 4′ lengths (4′ × 8′ plywood, plasterboard, rigid insulation, 4′ rocklath lengths, and so forth), it is desirable that floor joists, wall and partition studs, and rafters be spaced either 12″, 16″, or 24″ oc (all even divisions of 4′) to avoid cutting. Since 24″ oc is usually too weak and 12″ oc is wasteful, 16″ oc is normally used. The joist sizes are determined by the tables in Chapter 29. Joist spans are often 14′–16′.

Joists and headers are doubled around all openings (such as stairwells and chimneys) as shown in Figure 17. When a partition runs parallel to a joist, its entire weight must be supported by one (or two) joists. Since this weight might cause excessive bending, such a joist is also stiffened by doubling. When partitions run at right angles to

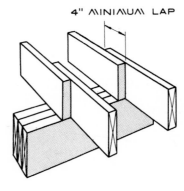

**JOISTS
OVER WOOD GIRDER**

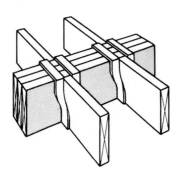
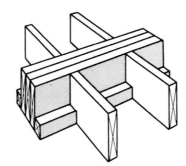
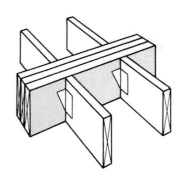

USING IRON STIRRUPS | USING LEDGER STRIPS | USING FRAMING ANCHORS

JOISTS LEVEL WITH WOOD GIRDER

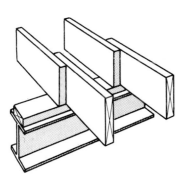
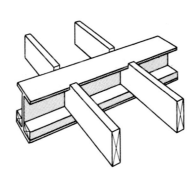
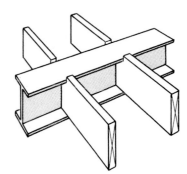

**JOISTS
OVER STEEL BEAM**

RESTING ON WOOD NAILERS | RESTING ON BEAM

JOISTS LEVEL WITH STEEL BEAM

Figure 15   *Methods of framing joists.*

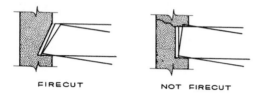

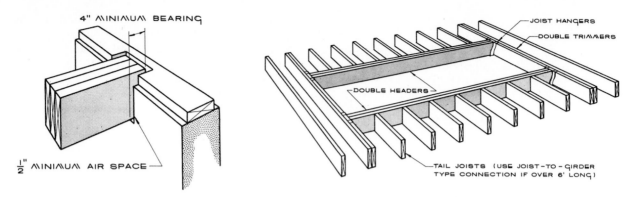

Figure 16 *Girder pocket.*

Figure 17 *Stairwell framing.*

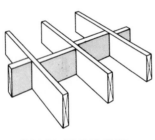

Figure 18 *Use of firecutting.*

joists, no extra support is necessary. Joists may be spaced 12″ oc instead of the usual 16″ oc under bathrooms and occasionally under kitchens to allow for weakening caused by pipes being set into the floor.

When joists frame into masonry walls as in Figure 9, their ends should be firecut to prevent the walls being pushed outward if the joists should sag. Firecutting also helps prevent cracks in the masonry wall due to the joists settling (see Figure 18).

BRIDGING

Bridging (Figure 19) is used to keep the joists vertical and in alignment, and to distribute a concentrated load on more than one joist. Solid wood blocking, 1″ × 3″ wood bridging, or metal straps may be used. Rows of bridging should be spaced a maximum of 7′ apart. Since the subflooring has a tendency to align the joist tops, the lower end of the wood and strap bridging is not nailed until the subflooring is laid.

SUBFLOORING AND FLOORING

Subflooring is a wood floor of $\frac{5}{8}$″ plywood or 1″ boards laid over joists to serve as a base for the finished floor. The finished floor is usually of tongue-and-grooved hardwood; oak, maple, and birch are used. When plywood or boards laid diagonally are used for subflooring, the finished flooring is laid parallel to the long dimension of the room; when boards laid perpendicular to the joists are used for subflooring, the finished flooring must be laid perpendicular to the subflooring regardless of the room proportions. Building paper is laid between subflooring and flooring as a protection against air and moisture.

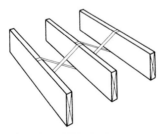

SOLID BLOCKING

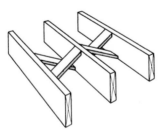

1″ × 3″ WOOD BRIDGING

METAL STRAP BRIDGING

Figure 19 *Bridging.*

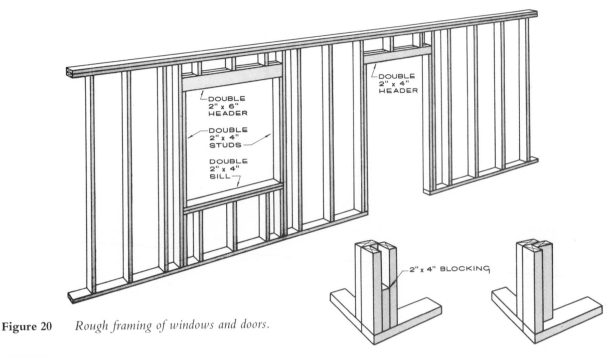

Figure 20   *Rough framing of windows and doors.*

STUDS

A *wall* means an exterior wall; a *partition* means an interior wall. Partitions may be either bearing or curtain (nonbearing). A wall or partition consists of vertical members spaced 16″ oc called *studs,* a lower horizontal sole plate, and doubled top plates, as shown in Figure 9. All of these members may be 2″ × 4″ lumber. When a 4″ cast-iron soil stack is used, however, the wall is made of 2″ × 6″ lumber to conceal it. In cold climates, studs of 2″ × 6″ lumber spaced 24″ oc are used to increase the wall thickness so that more insulation can be installed in the walls. Often an entire wall, including sole and top plates, is assembled horizontally on the subflooring and then raised and braced in position while the sole is spiked to the subfloor-ing. This method avoids toenailing the stud to the sole. Sheathing serves as an additional tie between wall, header, and sill.

WINDOW AND DOOR OPENINGS

The horizontal framing member above a window or door opening is called a *header,* and the horizontal framing member below the window is called the *rough sill* (Figure 20). All members framing an opening should be doubled for greater strength and to provide a nailing surface for trim. The headers are laid with the long edge vertical to provide greater strength. They must be shimmed, however, to increase their 3″ (2 × 1½″) thickness to 3½″. The size of the headers ranges from doubled 2″ × 4″ members up to doubled 2″ × 12″ mem-

Figure 21   *Methods of framing corner post.*

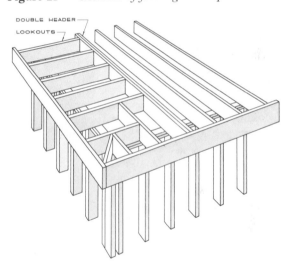

Figure 22   *Cantilever framing.*

bers, depending upon the span and superimposed load. Table XIII in Chapter 29 may be used to determine the required size of headers.

CORNER POSTS

Corner posts must provide surfaces for nailing the sheathing at the corner and the lath at both interior walls. Two methods of accomplishing this are illustrated in Figure 21.

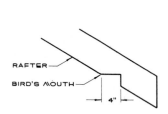

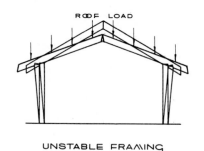

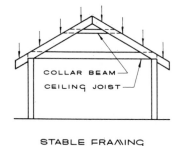

Figure 23   *Bird's mouth.*

Figure 24   *Framing for outward thrust.*

CANTILEVER FRAMING

Figure 22 shows the method of framing for canti-levered construction such as the second-floor overhang of a garrison house. The length of the lookouts should be at least three times the length of the overhang.

SHEATHING

Sheathing is nailed to the exterior of the studs in a manner similar to that used for the subflooring. Common sheathing materials are:

1. $\frac{5}{16}$" minimum × 4' × 8' plywood
2. $\frac{1}{2}$" minimum × 4' × 8' composition board. Composition board has the advantage of providing some additional insulation but does not make a good base for exterior finish nailing, nor does it provide the diagonal bracing strength of plywood. When composition board is used as outside sheathing, it should be as-

Figure 25   *Erecting trussed rafters.*

phalt-coated to prevent disintegration and serve as a moisture barrier.
3. 1" × 6" boards applied diagonally. If the boards are applied horizontally, corner braces must be let into the studs to stiffen the wall.
4. 1" rigid insulation. When rigid insulation is used for sheathing, plywood is substituted at corners to stiffen the wall.

Plywood or 1" boards should be used for roof sheathing.

BUILDING PAPER

Building paper is asphalt-saturated felt or paper used between subflooring and finished flooring, sheathing and finished wall covering, and roofers and roof covering. It prevents wind and water from entering the building between cracks, while still allowing water vapor to escape.

RAFTERS

Rafter size and spacing may be determined by Table XI in Chapter 29. A 16" or 24" spacing is often used. The upper end of the rafter is spiked to a 1"- or 2"-thick ridge board, the depth of which is not less than the end cut of the rafter. The lower end of the rafter is cut to obtain a full bearing on the top plate. This cut is called a *bird's mouth* (see Figure 23).

ROOF THRUST

A sloping roof exerts not only a *downward* thrust on the exterior walls, but also an *outward* thrust which tends to push the exterior walls apart as shown in Figure 24. The result of this outward thrust may be prevented by the following measures:

1. Run the ceiling joists parallel to the rafters together with 1" × 6" or 2" × 4" collar beams spaced 4' oc.

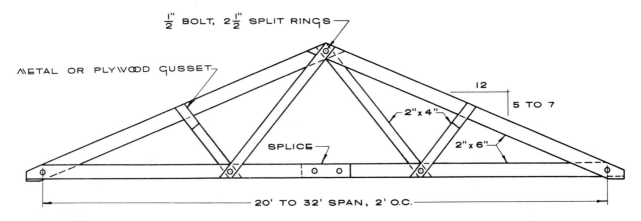

Figure 26   *Typical trussed rafter.*

2. Support the rafters at the ridge by a bearing partition or beam.
3. Roof trusses or trussed rafters* (Figure 25) may be used for large spans without bearing partitions, allowing great freedom in room planning. Notice, though, that a truss greatly reduces the usefulness of the attic space. Because a truss is composed of a number of small spans, the members need not be heavy. A typical trussed rafter is shown in Figure 26. The Timber Engineering Company of Washington, D.C., publishes a reference book that is very helpful to designers planning to specify trusses or trussed rafters.

FLAT ROOFS

Flat roofs may be laid level to hold water on the roof (called a *water-film roof*) or, more commonly,

* A trussed rafter is a truss spaced close enough to adjacent trusses that purlins are unnecessary.

sloped slightly to prevent water from collecting. The roof joists rest directly on the top plates and serve a double purpose, as roof rafters and ceiling joists. When a wide overhang is desired, the roof joists are framed for cantilever framing, as shown in Figure 22. Although wood roof joists are used to frame flat roofs in residential construction, steel *open-web joists* (also called *bar joists,* Figure 27) are normally used in commercial construction since they can span up to 48'. Because shingles cannot be used for a flat roof covering, a *built-up* roof finish is used. A built-up roof is constructed by laying down successive layers of roofing felt and tar or asphalt topped with roll roofing, gravel, or marble chips.

CORNICES

Figure 28 shows cornice construction over a frame wall, brick wall, and brick-veneer wall. Also the methods of framing various overhangs are shown, ranging from wide overhangs to a flush cornice.

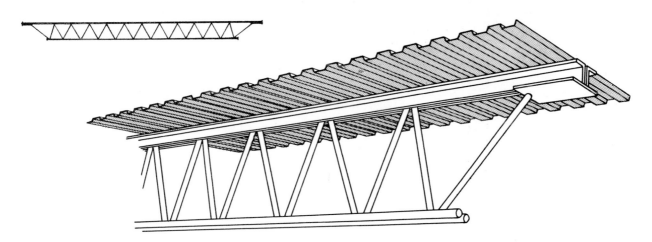

Figure 27   *Open-web joist.*

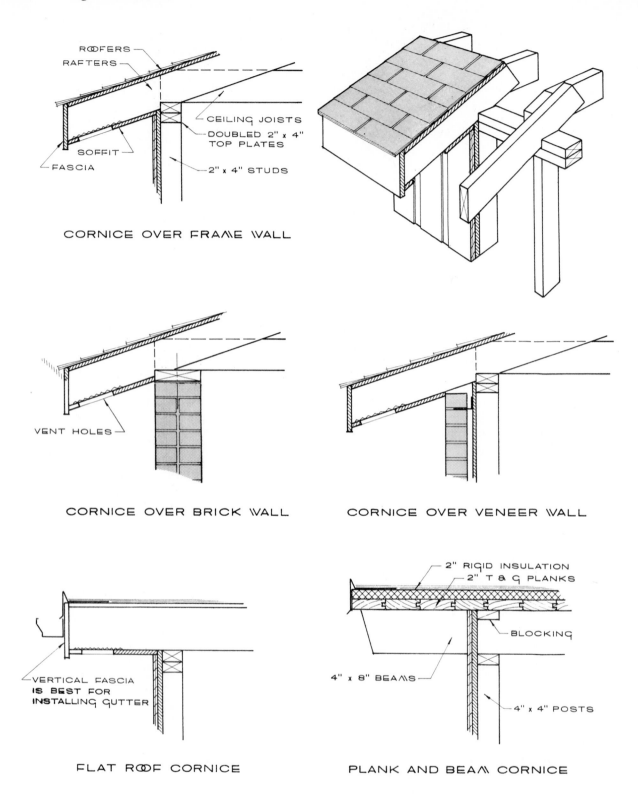

ROOFERS
RAFTERS
CEILING JOISTS
DOUBLED 2" x 4"
TOP PLATES
SOFFIT
FASCIA
2" x 4" STUDS

CORNICE OVER FRAME WALL

VENT HOLES

CORNICE OVER BRICK WALL

CORNICE OVER VENEER WALL

VERTICAL FASCIA
IS BEST FOR
INSTALLING GUTTER

FLAT ROOF CORNICE

2" RIGID INSULATION
2" T & G PLANKS
BLOCKING
4" x 8" BEAMS
4" x 4" POSTS

PLANK AND BEAM CORNICE

Figure 28   *Cornices.*

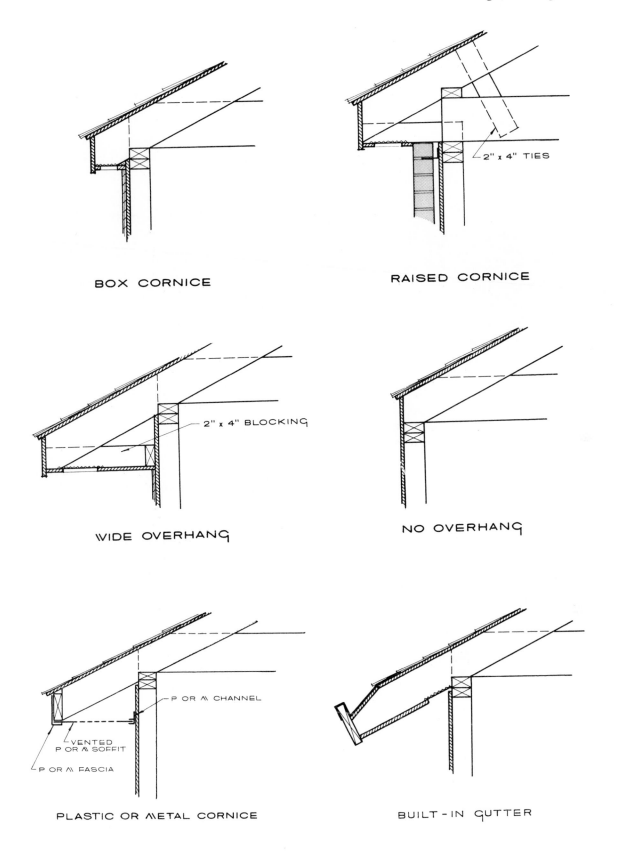

BOX CORNICE

RAISED CORNICE

2" x 4" TIES

WIDE OVERHANG

2" x 4" BLOCKING

NO OVERHANG

PLASTIC OR METAL CORNICE

P OR M CHANNEL

VENTED
P OR M SOFFIT

P OR M FASCIA

BUILT-IN GUTTER

Figure 28 *continued.*

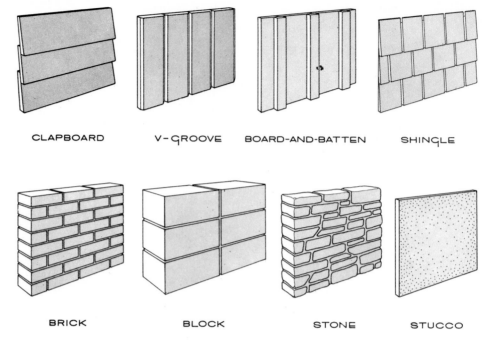

Figure 29   *Types of exterior finish.*

EXTERIOR FINISH

The raised cornice is used to provide an additional foot of headroom in the attic space or, in the case of wide overhangs, to provide more clearance above the windows beneath the cornice. Since roof gutters are often unsightly, they may be built into the roof as shown. Obviously, built-in gutters must be very carefully flashed.

Exterior wall finish (Figure 29) covers the sheathing and building paper. Since the choice of finish will greatly influence the final appearance and upkeep of a house, the materials should be carefully selected.

Plastic and metal siding, installed over sheathing, is available in horizontal clapboard and vertical V-groove styles. Plastic siding, usually vinyl, and metal siding, usually aluminum, is manufactured in a variety of colors and textures. Advantages include durability and low maintenance.

Wood siding is usually of red cedar, cypress, or California redwood because these materials have superior weather resistance. Corners may be mitered for a neat appearance, but wood or metal corners are more durable (see Figure 30). The style of the house will also influence the corner treatment.

Board-and-batten wood siding is relatively inexpensive and presents an attractive finish.

Wood shingles are also of red cedar, cypress, or redwood. Hand-split shakes may be used for a special effect. Shingles are often left unpainted and unstained to obtain a delightfully weathered finish. Red cedar and California redwood weather to a dark gray color; cypress weathers to a light gray with a silver sheen. Various types of composition siding—hardboard, fiberboard, asbestos, asphalt, and so forth, in imitation of wood, brick, or stone

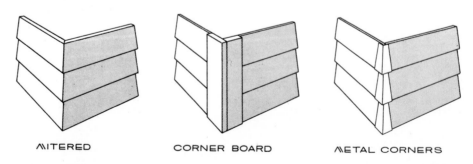

Figure 30   *Siding corner construction.*

—have certain advantages. But they must be carefully specified so that they do not cheapen the appearance of the building.

Brick and stone finishes are durable, require very little upkeep, and present a fine appearance. Types of brick bonds are shown in Figure 31. The word *bond* used in reference to masonry has several meanings. *Mortar bond* is the adhesion of the mortar to the brick or block units. *Structural bond* is the method of overlapping the masonry units so that the entire wall is a single structural member. *Pattern bond* is the decorative pattern formed by the use of various units in different combinations. The pattern may result from the type of structural bond specified (as an 8″ solid brick Flemish bond wall using full brick laid as stretchers and headers), or it may be purely decorative (as a 4″ brick-veneer Flemish bond wall using full brick and half-brick).

The *stretcher* or *running bond* is the most popular bond. Since no headers are used, this is often used in single-width walls (veneer and cavity) with metal ties. The *common bond* is a variation of the running bond with a course of headers every fifth, sixth, or seventh course to tie the face wall to the backing masonry. The *English bond* is laid with alternate courses of headers and stretchers, and the *Flemish bond* is laid with stretchers and headers alternating in each course. The *stack bond* is a popular contemporary pattern. Because of the alignment

of all vertical joints, reinforcing is needed in the horizontal joints. A masonry wall may be varied by diamond, basket weave, herringbone, and other patterns. Also, brick can be recessed or projected for special shadow effects. Decorative variations are endless.

Concrete block lends itself well to contemporary designs. Special effects may be obtained by the bond or by the block itself, which can be specified in many textured and sculptured surfaces.

Stucco is a cement plaster which may be used on exterior walls for special effects.

Combinations of exterior finishes. As mentioned in Chapter 24, it is not wise to mix many different kinds of exterior finishes on one house, as this will result in a confusing appearance. Normally no more than two finishes should be used, and the lighter finish should be above the heavier finish. (Notice that the M and the Z residences have wood siding stories over masonry stories.)

INTERIOR FINISH

Interior walls are often of plaster or dry-wall finish. Ceilings may be of the same finish or of ceiling tile. Figures 32 and 33 illustrate contemporary

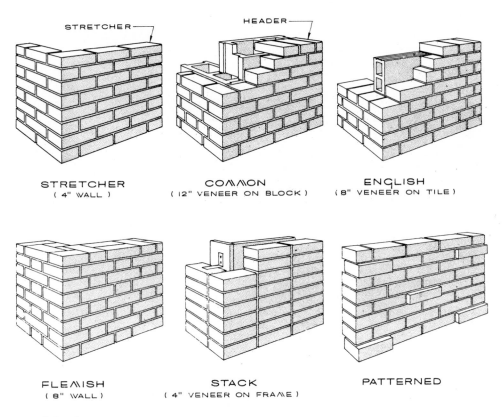

Figure 31 *Brick bonds.*

Figure 32   *Interior finished with horizontal planking.*

Figure 33   *Interior finished with vertical planking.*

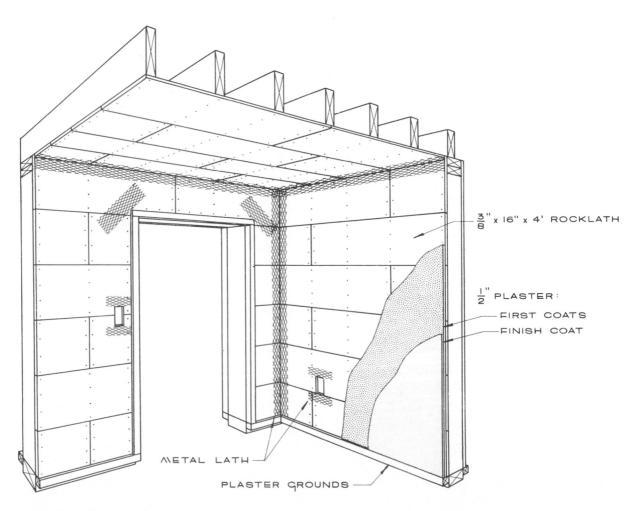

$\frac{3}{8}$" x 16" x 4' ROCKLATH

$\frac{1}{2}$" PLASTER:

FIRST COATS

FINISH COAT

METAL LATH

PLASTER GROUNDS

Figure 34   *Plastered finish.*

interiors finished in horizontal and vertical red-wood planking.

Plaster. Plaster finishing is considered superior to dry-wall finish, but it has the following disadvantages:

1. It is more likely to crack.
2. Wet plaster requires many days to dry, during which all construction must be halted.
3. Wood framing is completely soaked with moisture during the drying period and may warp.

Gypsum lath measuring $\frac{3}{8}'' \times 16'' \times 4'$ (usually referred to as *rocklath*) or $27'' \times 8'$ metal lath is nailed to the studs and joists as a base for the plaster. Notice in Figure 34 that a gypsum lath base requires strips of metal lath to reinforce the areas most susceptible to cracking: wall and ceiling intersections, the upper corners of door and window openings, and other openings such as electric outlets. Wood grounds, equal in thickness to the lath and plaster, are installed around openings and near the floor.

They serve as a leveling guide for the plaster, and act as a nailing base for the finished trim and the baseboard. Steel edges must be used on outside corners to protect the edges from chipping.

Three coats of plaster—a scratch coat (so called because it is scratched to provide a rough bond with the next coat), a brown coat (which is leveled), and a finish coat—are used over metal lath. Two-coat, *double-up* plaster (the scratch coat and brown coat combined or *doubled up*) is used over rocklath. The finished coat may be a smooth, white coat that is painted or wallpapered, or it may be a textured coat (called *sand finish*), which usually has the color mixed into the plaster so that no finishing is necessary. A moisture-resistant plaster (called *Keene's cement*) is used in the kitchen and bathrooms. It is also possible to plaster with only a single $\frac{1}{4}''$ coat of finish plaster when applied over a special $\frac{1}{2}'' \times 4' \times 8'$ gypsum lath.

Dry wall. The most common type of dry-wall material is $\frac{3}{8}''$ or $\frac{1}{2}''$ gypsum board, as shown in Figure 35. When finished, this wall will look just like a plastered wall. Other kinds of dry-wall finishes,

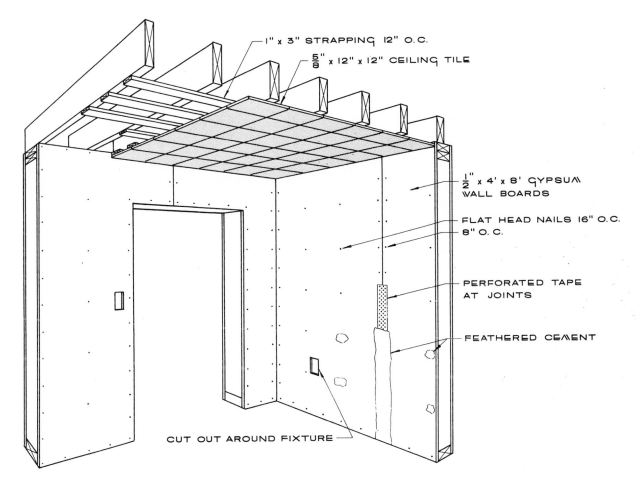

Figure 35 *Dry-wall finish.*

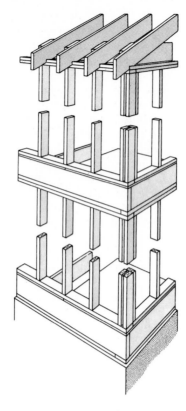

Figure 36 *Platform construction.*

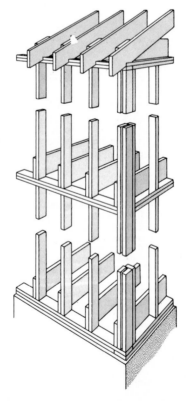

Figure 37 *Modern braced construction.*

such as ¼″ plywood panels (with a hardwood veneer) are used for special effects such as a single bedroom wall or fireplace wall. A den may be completely paneled, but take care that paneling is not overdone. For all dry-wall finishes, it is important that the studs or joists be carefully aligned.

Gypsum board. Gypsum board consists of a cardboard sandwich with a gypsum filler. It is installed by nailing 4′ × 8′ sheets directly to the studs or joists, and slightly setting the nailheads. Joint cement then covers the nailheads; joint cement over perforated paper tape is used at the joints. When the joint cement has been sanded, a smooth wall results.

OTHER CONSTRUCTION TYPES

Platform framing (Figure 36), in which framing studs only one story high rest on a complete platform, has been discussed in detail. Other construction types are *braced* framing, *balloon* framing, and *plank-and-beam* framing.

Braced framing. Braced framed construction was used in colonial times and is still used today in modified forms (Figure 37). Braced framing utilized heavy (4″-thick) sills and corner posts. In two-story construction, the corner posts ran the full height of the building, with heavy girts let into them to support the second floor. In early braced framing, the studs served only as a curtain wall, carrying no load. Recently, a type of modular construction using corner and wall posts in a manner similar to braced framing has been gaining popularity.

Balloon framing. The balloon-framed house is characterized by studs resting directly on the sill and extending the full height of the stories, as shown in Figure 38. Second-floor joists rest on a ledger, which is spiked to the studs. The joists are also lapped and spiked to the studs. This type of framing has been largely replaced by platform framing, but balloon framing does have the advantage of lessening vertical shrinkage, and therefore is best for two-story brick-veneer or stucco construction. However, additional fire stopping of 2″ blocking must be provided to prevent air passage from one floor to another. Recently, balloon framing has been used in cold climates to minimize air infiltration, because balloon framing permits the vapor barrier to be installed without gaps at the tops and bottoms of walls.

Plank-and-beam framing. A building method called *mill* construction has been used for years in factories and warehouses where the loads are heavy and the fire danger high. In mill construction, a few heavy posts and beams support a solid wood floor 3″ to 6″ thick—since a few large members will resist fire longer than many small members. Although mill construction has been largely replaced by steel and concrete construction methods, an adaption has been widely used in residential construction. This is called plank-and-beam construction.

In plank-and-beam construction, 2″-thick tongued-and-grooved planks replace the 1″ subflooring of conventional framing, 4″ × 8″ beams 4′ to 7′ oc replace conventional 2″ joists 16″ oc, and 4″ × 4″ posts under the beams replace the conventional 2″ × 4″ studs.

Plank-and-beam framing in residential construction developed from the trend toward picture windows and window walls, which made it necessary to frame a number of large openings in the exterior walls. Consequently, it is usually used in the construction of modern houses. Other advantages are:

1. A few large structural members replace many small members.
2. Planks and beams are left exposed, eliminating the need for additional interior finish such as plastering and cornices.
3. A saving is made on the total height of the building.
4. Fire hazard is reduced.

Some disadvantages of this type of construction are:

1. Special furring must be used to conceal pipes and electrical conduits installed on the ceiling.
2. Additional roof insulation must be used due to the elimination of dead air spaces between the roof and ceiling.
3. It is more difficult to control condensation. Exhaust fans are used to reduce moisture in the house to a minimum.

Figure 39 shows a typical plank-and-beam construction. Notice that the large open areas between posts may be used for window walls as shown in Figure 40 or may be enclosed with curtain walls. It should be mentioned that combinations of plank-and-beam and conventional construction are possible, using the advantageous features of each type.

Theory of plank-and-beam construction. Compare the deflection of single-span planks and continuous-span planks as shown in Figure 41 and notice that the continuous-span will deflect less. In fact the

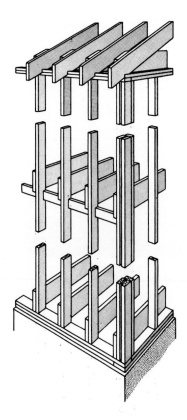

Figure 38   *Balloon construction.*

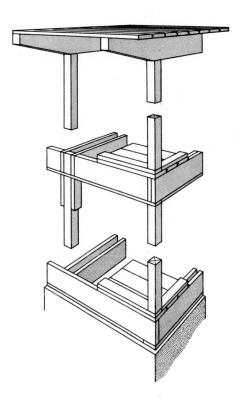

Figure 39   *Plank-and-beam construction.*

Figure 40   *A cathedral ceiling and window walls provided by plank-and-beam framing.*

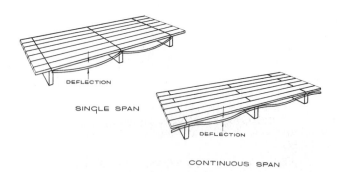

Figure 41   *Plank-and-beam construction theory.*

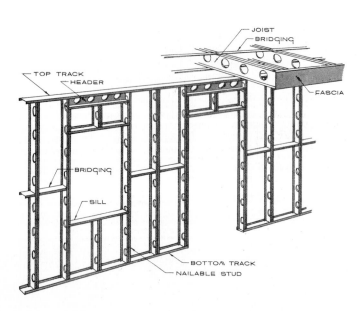

Figure 42   *Metal framing components.*

continuous-span will have about twice the stiffness of the single-span. Of course it is important that the floor be constructed so that it acts as one homogeneous unit. This is done by using tongue-and-groove planks with staggered end joints.

Metal framing. Metal framing is commonly used for constructing commercial and industrial buildings; and wood framing, for residences. Wood members are widely available, easily fabricated, and economical, but they are combustible and may be weakened by decay or termites. Wood can be pressure-treated with fire-retardant chemicals or decay- and termite-resistant preservatives. Metal framing, however, is superior in many aspects of safety and durability.

Galvanized steel and aluminum components are manufactured for use as studs, sills, headers, joists, bridging, fascia, window framing, door framing, and doors. See Figure 42. Components are cut to length using a power saw with a metal cutting blade. Then they are assembled by snap-in clips, bolting, or welding. Stud depths are usually $2\frac{1}{2}''$, $4''$, and $6''$. Joist depths are $6''$, $8''$, $9''$, $10''$, and $12''$. Standard lengths of most sections are available up to $32'$ long, or they can be ordered cut to special lengths at the mill. Wall and ceiling surfaces can be attached to nailable studs and joists by means of nailing grooves which hold spiral-shank nails tightly in place (Figure 43), or they can be

Figure 43   *Nailable metal stud.*

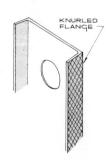

Figure 44   *Screw stud with knurled flanges.*

attached to screw studs through knurled flanges using power driven self-drilling, self-tapping, sheet metal screws (Figure 44).

In addition to the obvious advantage of incombustibility, metal framed structures have the advantage of easier piping and electrical installation through prepunched holes. However, grommets must be used to prevent pipe rattling and wire fraying.

FUTURE CONSTRUCTION METHODS AND MATERIALS

Today's methods of building construction are based mostly on lumber and nails put together in a specific way. It certainly does not take much foresight to realize that there will be revolutionary changes in building construction in the next few decades. It is quite possible that some of these changes will be evident by the time you actually begin to practice architectural drafting. Already many companies are manufacturing precut buildings (with lumber cut to the correct size), prefabricated ones (with entire wall sections already factory assembled), and even entirely mass-produced buildings. Assembly-line methods are not the only answer, however, since most people want custombuilt homes. Some companies have made complete breaks from traditional construction, and still more have launched full-scale research and development programs in the housing field.

Most mobile home manufacturers have departed from the traditional design to build *expandable* mobiles (having sections that can be telescoped or folded during transit), *double-wide* mobiles (two mobile units joined at the site), *sectional* mobiles (double-wide mobiles placed on a permanent foundation), and *modular* units (transportable units that can be connected side by side, end to end, or stacked several stories high in various combinations). Figure 45 illustrates a bank that was factory-built in three sections weighing $7\frac{1}{2}$ tons each, transported to the site (Figure 46), and bolted together. The structural system is a welded three-dimensional truss made of steel tubular beams and columns. Four lift rings are provided on the roof for a crane (Figure 47) to move each unit to a flatbed train or truck. All panels, glass, and interior finishes are installed at the factory. Final erection can be completed in three days.

Although we can easily predict changes, it is impossible to predict their exact form and direction, since they will depend upon future engineering research and development. Be alert to these changes and accept them readily. For the present, though, learn all you can about current construction methods and materials.

STUDY QUESTIONS

1. In proper order, list the steps necessary for staking the excavation of a 26' × 44' house.
2. Indicate the factors that determine the depth of excavation under the following conditions:
   a. Wood-frame construction with a full foundation in Augusta, Maine
   b. Brick-veneer construction with a crawl space in San Diego, California

Figure 45 *Interim Branch Bank, Bank of the Commonwealth, Detroit, Michigan.*

Figure 46 *Trucking modular units to the site.*

Figure 47 *Crane lifting modular unit from flatbed truck.*

c. Brick and slab construction on low land (to be filled 4' higher) in Baltimore, Maryland
3. A heavy downpour occurs immediately after the footing trenches have been dug and before the concrete is poured. What must be done? Why?
4. A one-story, flat-roofed house with full basement has the dimensions of 30' × 40' with three columns spaced 10' oc. Estimate:
   a. The total load to be carried by the foundation walls
   b. The load on each column
5. A residence built on firm ground has 10"-thick concrete block foundation walls. What would be the probable width and depth of its wall and column footings?
6. Under what conditions would you specify:
   a. Poured concrete foundation walls
   b. Concrete block foundation walls
   c. Concrete blocks filled solid with concrete
   d. Pilasters
   e. Reinforcing rods in footings
   f. Reinforcing rods in slabs
   g. Stepped footings
7. What is the difference between:
   a. Sill and sole
   b. Ledger and girt
   c. Girder and joist
   d. Wall and partition
   e. Flooring and subflooring

f. Rafter and truss
g. Precut and prefabricated
8. Describe briefly each term:
   a. Grout
   b. Lath
   c. Expansion joint
   d. Bridging
   e. Bird's mouth
   f. Built-up roof
9. Give the normal oc spacing of:
   a. Anchor bolts
   b. Joists
   c. Studs
   d. Roof trusses
10. For an average-sized, one-story, platform-framed house, give the probable nominal size of:
    a. Poured concrete foundation wall
    b. Concrete block foundation wall
    c. Anchor bolts
    d. Sill
    e. Header
    f. Joists
    g. Cross-bridging
    h. Subflooring
    i. Sole
    j. Studs
    k. Top plate
    l. Sheathing
11. What lumber size is required to span 13 ft. if Ponderosa Pine is to be used spaced 16" oc?
    a. Floor joists
    b. Ceiling joists
    c. 1 in 12 slope roof joists
    d. 6 in 12 slope rafters
12. When would floor joists be:
    a. Spaced 12" oc
    b. Doubled
13. a. List the advantages of a built-up wood girder over a solid wood girder.
    b. What is the principal advantage of a solid wood girder (used exposed under a living area ceiling) over a built-up wood girder?
14. Sketch three methods of framing joists level with a wood girder.
15. What is the reason for using:
    a. Cross-bridging
    b. Building paper
    c. The *key* between footing and foundation wall
16. What length lookouts should be specified for a 1'-8" second-story overhang?
17. Show three methods of counteracting the outward thrust of a gable roof upon its supporting walls.
18. When would the following types of cornice be used?
    a. Raised cornice
    b. Cornice with built-in gutter
    c. Cornice with wide overhang
    d. Flush cornice
    e. Plastic or metal cornice
19. What materials are normally used for siding? Why?
20. Compare plaster and dry-wall finishes by listing the advantages of each.
21. What type plaster should be used:
    a. Over metal lath
    b. Over gypsum lath
    c. In a laundry room

22. List the advantages and disadvantages of:
    a. Plank-and-beam construction
    b. Metal framing
23. Distinguish between:
    a. Expandable mobile homes
    b. Double-wide mobiles
    c. Sectional mobiles
    d. Modular mobiles

LABORATORY PROBLEMS

1. Draw a typical wall section of a one-story house with requirements as assigned by your instructor:

Foundation:

a. With basement
b. With crawl space
c. Without basement, floating slab
d. Without basement, perimeter foundation

Wall:

a. Wood frame
b. Brick veneer
c. Solid brick
d. Cavity brick

Roof:

a. Pitched 6 in 12
b. Pitched 4 in 12
c. Pitched 2 in 12
d. Flat

Cornice:

a. No overhang
b. 8″ overhang
c. 4′ overhang
d. Raised
e. Built-in gutter
f. Vinyl or aluminum

2. (For the advanced student) Draw a typical wall section of a building showing your conception of a framing system that is entirely different from those now in use.
    a. Using standard materials readily obtainable
    b. Using revolutionary materials
3. Construct a cutaway model showing the method of building:
    a. Platform-framed house
    b. Balloon-framed house
    c. Plank-and-beam framed house
4. (For the advanced student) Construct a cutaway model showing your conception of a framing system that is entirely different from those now in use.
5. (For the advanced student) After a thorough library search, prepare a set of pictorial drawings or panoramas illustrating the history of the development of building methods to date.

29 / Structural Calculations

In professional offices, architectural design is the responsibility of registered architects, and structural design is the responsibility of registered architectural engineers. However, most architects and engineers appreciate the drafter who has the ability to make simple design and structural decisions independently. When the principal architect or engineer is busy or away from the office, many hours can be wasted if the drafter is not willing to make such decisions and continue working. Of course it is very important that the principal be informed of such tentative decisions at a more appropriate time for approval or revision.

STRUCTURAL MEMBERS

The tables* in this chapter will enable the architectural drafter to size the structural members in the average house or small building. However, for unusual framing methods or loading conditions, these tables will be inadequate. Each of the following structural members will be considered in turn:

1. Footings:
   Wall footings
   Column footings
2. Columns:
   Wood posts
   Steel columns
3. Beams:
   Wood girders
   Steel beams

* For more complete tables than are given in this book, see the *AISC* (American Institute of Steel Construction) *Handbook,* *FHA* (Federal Housing Administration) *Bulletins,* or *Architectural Graphic Standards.*

4. Joists:
   Floor joists
   Ceiling joists
   Roof joists
   Rafters
5. Headers and lintels

Loads. The size and spacing required for any structural member depends upon a combination of elements—the distance spanned, the material used, and the load applied. The total applied load supported by the structural members of a house consists of a live load and a dead load. The live load is the weight supported by the house (furniture, people, wind and snow loads), and the dead load is the weight of the house itself. Although these loads may be fairly accurately calculated using the typical weights of materials given in *Architectural Graphic Standards,* a quicker method is to assume each floor has a live load of 40 lb./sq. ft. and a dead load of 20 lb./sq. ft. Attic live load may be assumed as 20 lb./sq. ft. if used for storage only, and a dead load of 10 lb./sq. ft. if not floored. When interior partitions exist, add an extra 20 lb./sq. ft. to the dead load of the whole floor upon which the partitions rest, remembering that these partitions also transmit any additional weight resting on them. Since roofs usually rest on exterior walls only, they should not normally add to the total girder or column load. However, if they are included, add 30 lb./sq. ft. (snow and wind) live load and a dead load of 10 lb./sq. ft. (for asphalt shingle) or 20 lb./sq. ft. (for built-up tar and gravel, slate, or tile).

For convenient reference, these loads are listed in Table I.

Tributary area. Each structural member supports a certain proportion of the total house weight or area, called the *tributary area*. The word *tributary* refers to the weight *contributed* to each member. Figure 1 illustrates the tributary area of a column and a beam of the Z residence. One beam running the length of the house will normally have a tributary area equal to half the total floor plan area. When columns are used, the tributary area is reduced in proportion to the reduction of the beam span. If joists run uncut across the beam, the beam supports five-eighths of the weight above instead of one-half. Notice in Table I that values are given in pounds per square foot. Therefore, the live and dead loads must be multiplied by the tributary square foot area to determine the total load supported by a member.

Table I   *Residential Live and Dead Loads*

	Live	Dead
Each floor	40 lb./sq. ft.	20 lb./sq. ft.
Attic (storage only)	20 lb./sq. ft.	20 lb./sq. ft.
Attic (not floored)	0	10 lb./sq. ft.
Roof (built-up)	30 lb./sq. ft. (snow and wind load)	20 lb./sq. ft.
Roof (asphalt-shingled)	30 lb./sq. ft. (snow and wind load)	10 lb./sq. ft.
Partitions	0	20 lb./sq. ft.

Table II   *Weights of Materials*

Type of Material	Pounds per Cu. Ft.
Poured concrete	150
Concrete block (including mortar)	80
Brick (including mortar)	120

Table III   *Safe Ground Loadings*

Type of Ground	Pounds per Sq. Ft.
Ledge rock	30,000
Hardpan	20,000
Compact gravel	12,000
Loose gravel	8,000
Coarse sand	6,000
Fine sand	4,000
Stiff clay	8,000
Medium clay	4,000
Soft clay	2,000

Table IV   *Safe Loads for Wood Posts (in kips)*

Lumber	Size	Unbraced Length			
		6'	7'	8'	9'
Spruce and pine*	6" × 6" (5½" × 5½")	16.7	16.4	15.9	15.3
	8" × 8" (7½" × 7½")	31.5	31.3	31.0	30.6
Douglas Fir**	6" × 6" (5½" × 5½")	29.5	29.0	28.1	26.8
	8" × 8" (7½" × 7½")	56.2	55.6	55.0	54.3

Adapted from *Light Frame House Construction*, U.S. Department of Health, Education, and Welfare.
* Red, White, and Sitka Spruce; the White Pines, No. 1 Common.
** Douglas Fir, Southern Pine, and North Carolina Pine, No. 1 Common.

FOOTINGS

Using Tables I, II, and III, it is possible to calculate the required sizes of footings for foundation walls, columns, and chimneys. The procedure is to calculate the total weight to be contributed to the footing using the Live and Dead Load table (I) and the Weights of Materials table (II). When calculating tributary areas, remember it is the usual practice to support the roof by exterior walls, not interior partitions. The pressure of the footing on the ground may not be greater than the safe ground loadings given in Table III.

Calculations for the footings of the Z residence will be used as an example.

FOUNDATION FOOTING CALCULATIONS

Find the load per running foot on the foundation footing. In Figure 2 notice that the live and dead loads have been multipled by half the joist spans to obtain the total load.

COLUMN FOOTING CALCULATIONS

Find the total load carried by a column footing. In Figure 3 notice that the average load per square foot has been multiplied by the tributary area to obtain the total load.

WOOD POSTS

Structural framing of a small house might consist of wood posts (usually 6" × 6" or 8" × 8") supporting the center girder (usually 8" × 8" or three 2" × 10"s spiked together), which in turn supports the floor joists. Table IV is used to determine the post size required.

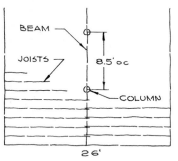
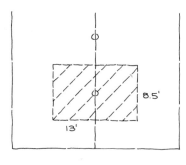
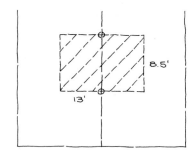

PLAN OF THE Z RESIDENCE   TRIBUTARY AREA OF COLUMN   TRIBUTARY AREA OF BEAM

Figure 1   *Calculation of tributary areas.*

EXAMPLE

The load on each post of the Z residence was calculated in Figure 3 to be 22.1 kips.* If 7′-long Douglas Fir posts are to be used, a 6″ × 6″ size will be satisfactory, since they will safely support 29.0 kips.

STEEL PIPE COLUMNS

Wood post and girder framing is not practical for larger houses since the posts might have to be spaced so close together that use of the basement is restricted. Furthermore, deeper timbers for girders

* 1 kip = 1,000 lb.

are too costly and either add to the house cubage or reduce headroom.

The solution, then, is to use steel columns and steel girders—as are specified in many building codes. Because steel is so much stronger than wood, steel columns can be spaced farther apart, giving more free basement area, and steel girders can be shallower than wood girders, saving on the cubic content or giving more basement headroom. W shapes, S shapes, and even channels are used for industrial building columns; round, hollow piping called *pipe columns* are used for houses. The hollow center of the pipe column may be filled with concrete to further increase its strength. Notice that a cap and base plate must be used (see Figure 14, Chapter 28).

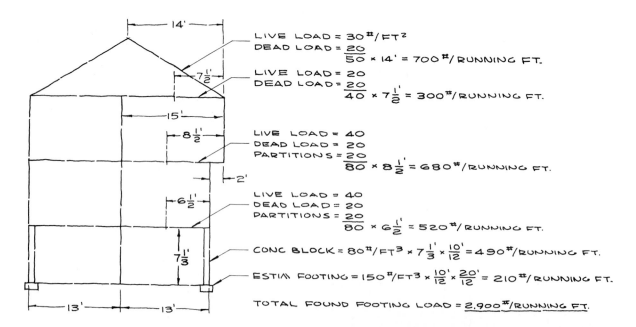

Figure 2   *Foundation footing calculations.*

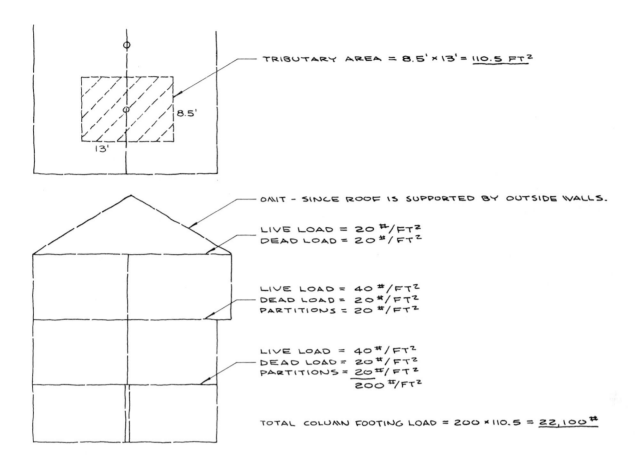

TRIBUTARY AREA = 8.5' × 13' = 110.5 FT²

OMIT - SINCE ROOF IS SUPPORTED BY OUTSIDE WALLS.

LIVE LOAD = 20 #/FT²
DEAD LOAD = 20 #/FT²

LIVE LOAD = 40 #/FT²
DEAD LOAD = 20 #/FT²
PARTITIONS = 20 #/FT²

LIVE LOAD = 40 #/FT²
DEAD LOAD = 20 #/FT²
PARTITIONS = 20 #/FT²
200 #/FT²

TOTAL COLUMN FOOTING LOAD = 200 × 110.5 = 22,100 #

IF GROUND IS MEDIUM-STIFF CLAY, COLUMN FOOTING AREA MUST BE $\frac{22,100 \#}{6,000 \#/FT²}$ = 3.7 FT²
∴ 20" SQ (2.8 FT²) IS TOO SMALL, BUT 24" SQ (4 FT²) IS O.K.

Figure 3   *Column footing calculations.*

The column diameter can be obtained by referring to a table published by the Lally Company, a popular manufacturer of pipe columns. A portion of this table is shown as Table V.

EXAMPLE

In the Z residence, the previously calculated load of 22.1 kips on a 7'-long column will be amply supported by a $3\frac{1}{2}''$ Lally column, since it will safely support 35.1 kips.

Table V   *Safe Loads for Heavyweight Columns (in kips)*

Column Diameter	Unbraced Length			
	6'	*7'*	*8'*	*9'*
$3\frac{1}{2}''$	37.9	35.1	32.3	29.4
4"	49.2	46.1	43.1	40.1
$4\frac{1}{2}''$	61.8	58.5	55.3	52.0

WOOD GIRDERS

Wood girders built up of 2" lumber spiked together or solid wood beams are often used in combination with steel columns. Table VI may be used to determine the safe span of various sizes of wood girders.

EXAMPLE

For the Z residence, the structure width is approximately 26', and the building is two-story supporting a bearing partition. If we wish to space columns 8'-6" oc, we must use a wood girder greater than 6" × 12", because Table VI shows that a 6" × 12" girder will safely span only 6'-2".

STEEL BEAMS

Steel beams of various sizes are especially useful when spanning distances greater than 10'. Steel

Table VI *Safe Spans* for Wood Girders*

Structure Type	Girder Size (solid or built-up)	Structure Width		
		22'–24'	*26'–28'*	*30'–32'*
One-story supporting	6″ × 8″	8'-1″	7'-5″	6'-6″
Nonbearing partitions	6″ × 10″	10'-4″	9'-6″	8'-4″
	6″ × 12″	12'-7″	11'-7″	10'-2″
Two-story supporting	6″ × 8″	4'-7″	—	—
Bearing partition	6″ × 10″	6'-0	5'-1″	4'-6″
	6″ × 12″	7'-2″	6'-2″	5'-5″

Adapted from *Manual of Acceptable Practices*, U.S. Department of Housing and Urban Development.
* Based upon allowable fiber stress of 1,500 psi (such as Douglas Fir or Southern Pine).

beams are obtained cut to length (up to 60') and in various weights (an 8″ W-shape beam weighing 20 lb./ft. will support more than an 8″ W-shape beam weighing 17 lb./ft.). Only the more popular sizes stocked by suppliers are shown in Table VII.

EXAMPLE

For the Z residence, the desired span is 8'-6″, and the load to be supported is found as shown in Figure 4 to be 22.1 kips. Reading between the 8' and 9' columns in Table VII, it will be seen that the W 8 × 17 beam will just support this weight. To be on the safe side, specify W 8 × 20, which will support approximately 26 kips.

JOISTS

The sizes of floor joists, ceiling joists, roof joists, and rafters are determined by Tables VIII–XI. Notice that you must know the span, spacing, and material.

EXAMPLE

For the Z residence, No. 2 Southern Pine floor joists 16″ oc are to span 13'. From Table VIII, we see that 2″ × 8″ joists will span only 12'-10″, and 2″ × 10″ joists

Table VII *Safe Loads for Steel Beams (in kips)*

Size*	Span					
	8'	*9'*	*10'*	*11'*	*12'*	*13'*
S 7 × 15.3	17.3	15.4	13.9	12.6		
W 8 × 17	24	21	18.8	17.1	15.7	
W 8 × 20	28	25	22.6	20.6	18.9	17.4
W 10 × 21	36	32	29	26	24	22
W 10 × 25	44	39	35	32	29	27

Adapted from FHA standards. For more complete information, see *Minimum Property Standards for One and Two Living Units*, Federal Housing Administration.
* Note: S 7 × 15.3 refers to an S-shape I beam 7″ high weighing 15.3 pounds per foot of length; W 8 × 17 refers to a W-shape beam 8″ high weighing pounds per foot of length.

will span 16'-5″. Therefore 2″ × 10″ should be used for first-floor joists, but 2″ × 8″ will be satisfactory for second-floor joists because of the slightly smaller second-floor load.

Ceiling joists over the master bedroom must span 15'. From Table IX, we see that 2″ × 6″ joists will span only 12'-3″, and 2″ × 8″ joists will span 16'-2″. Therefore use 2″ × 8″ ceiling joists 16″ oc.

Rafters must span 14'. From Table XI, we see that 2″ × 8″ rafters will span 15'-8″. Therefore, use 2″ × 8″ rafters 16″ oc or 2″ × 6″ rafters of a higher grade than shown in the table.

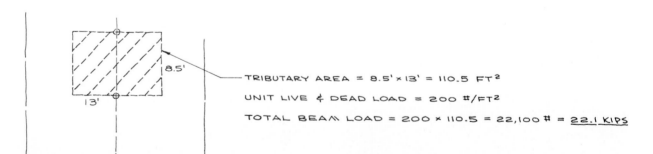

Figure 4 *Steel beam calculations.*

Table VIII   *Floor Joist Sizes (40 lb. live load)*

Size	Spacing (oc)	No. 1 Southern Pine	No. 2 Southern Pine	No. 3 Southern Pine
		Maximum Span		
2″ × 6″	16″	9′-11″	9′-9″	7′-10″
	12″	10′-11″	10′-9″	9′-0
2″ × 8″	16″	13′-1″	12′-10″	10′-3″
	12″	14′-5″	14′-2″	11′-11″
2″ × 10″	16″	16′-9″	16′-5″	13′-1″
	12″	18′-5″	18′-0	15′-2″
2″ × 12″	16″	20′-4″	19′-11″	16′-0
	12″	22′-5″	21′-11″	18′-5″

Table IX   *Ceiling Joist Sizes (plaster ceiling, limited attic storage)*

Size	Spacing (oc)	No. 1 Southern Pine	No. 2 Southern Pine	No. 3 Southern Pine
		Maximum Span		
2″ × 4″	24″	7′-0	6′-10″	5′-6″
	16″	8′-0	7′-10″	6′-9″
2″ × 6″	24″	10′-11″	10′-9″	8′-3″
	16″	12′-6″	12′-3″	10′-1″
2″ × 8″	24″	14′-5″	14′-2″	10′-10″
	16″	16′-6″	16′-2″	13′-3″
2″ × 10″	24″	18′-5″	18′-0	13′-10″
	16″	21′-1″	20′-8″	16′-11″

Table X   *Roof Joist Sizes (30 lb. live load, any slope, plaster ceiling)*

Size	Spacing (oc)	No. 1 Southern Pine	No. 2 Southern Pine	No. 3 Southern Pine
		Maximum Span		
2″ × 6″	24″	9′-7″	8′-10″	6′-9″
	16″	10′-11″	10′-9″	8′-3″
2″ × 8″	24″	12′-7″	11′-7″	8′-10″
	16″	14′-5″	14′-2″	10′-10″
2″ × 10″	24″	16′-1″	14′-9″	11′-4″
	16″	18′-5″	18′-0	13′-10″
2″ × 12″	24″	19′-7″	18′-0	13′-9″
	16″	22′-5″	21′-11″	16′-10″

Table XI   *Rafter Sizes (30 lb. live load, light roofing, slope over 3 in 12, no ceiling)*

Size	Spacing (oc)	No. 1 Southern Pine	No. 2 Southern Pine	No. 3 Southern Pine
		Maximum Span		
2″ × 4″	24″	7′-4″	6′-8″	5′-0
	16″	8′-9″	8′-2″	6′-1″
2″ × 6″	24″	10′-8″	9′-8″	7′-5″
	16″	13′-1″	11′-11″	9′-1″
2″ × 8″	24″	14′-1″	12′-9″	9′-9″
	16″	17′-2″	15′-8″	11′-11″
2″ × 10″	24″	17′-11″	16′-4″	12′-5″
	16″	21′-11″	20′-0	15′-3″

Tables VIII–XI adapted from *Southern Pine Maximum Spans for Joists and Rafters* of the Southern Forest Products Association.

LAMINATED DECKING

Laminated wood decking from $2\frac{1}{4}''-3\frac{3}{4}''$ thick is often used for floors and roofs. Table XII gives the maximum allowable uniformly distributed load for floors or roofs up to 3-12 pitch.

EXAMPLE

A plank-and-beam building is designed on a 12' module. If the total live and dead roof load is determined to be 50 lb./sq. ft., a 3"-thick laminated Ponderosa Pine roof deck is required, since a $2\frac{1}{4}''$ deck will support only 30 lb./sq. ft.

ROOFS

It is good practice to use the exterior walls, and not interior partitions, for roof support. If the span between exterior walls is so great that ordinary rafters cannot be used, either wood trusses or steel beams are employed. Probably, a sloping roof would call for wood trusses, and a flat roof would call for steel open-web joists.

HEADERS

Large openings for windows and doors are spanned by wood or steel structural members. Wood members are called *headers*, and steel members are called *lintels*. Table XIII gives the maximum safe span for wood headers in light frame construction. For unusual loading conditions, special design is necessary.

EXAMPLE

Several 8'-wide window openings in the Z residence will require two 2" × 12" headers, since two 2" × 10" headers will span only 7'-6" safely.

LINTELS

To span openings in masonry walls, wood headers are not satisfactory because wood shrinkage will cause cracks in the masonry above. Instead, steel angle lintels are used as shown in Figure 5. The $3\frac{1}{2}''$ horizontal leg provides support for a $3\frac{3}{4}''$-wide brick, and the vertical leg provides the resistance to bending. Table XIV may be used to find the lintel size required in a simple masonry wall. If joists or other members frame into the wall above the lintel, their contributing weight must also be supported, and a larger size of lintel will be necessary.

EXAMPLE

In the Z residence, the angles needed to span the 3'-4" and 4'-0 fireplace openings are found to be $4'' \times 3\frac{1}{2}'' \times \frac{5}{16}''$.

Table XII *Allowable Loads for Laminated Decking*

Finished Thickness*	Span	Allowable Uniformly Distributed Total Roof Load** (lb./sq. ft.)	
		Ponderosa Pine	Hem-fir
$2\frac{1}{4}''$	8'	101	142
	10'	52	72
	12'	30	42
3"	12'	71	100
	14'	45	63
	16'	30	42
$3\frac{3}{4}''$	16'	61	82
	18'	43	57
	20'	31	42

Adapted from *Koppers Company Design Manual.*
* Laminated decking sizes and load-carrying capacities may vary between manufacturers.
** Based upon controlled random layup continuous over at least three spans. Deflection limited to 1/240.

Table XIII *Safe Spans for Headers*

Size	Span
Two 2" × 4"	3'-6"
Two 2" × 6"	4'-6"
Two 2" × 8"	6'-0
Two 2" × 10"	7'-6"
Two 2" × 12"	9'-0

Table XIV *Safe Spans for Lintels in 4" Masonry ($3\frac{1}{2}''$ leg horizontal)*

Size	Span
$3\frac{1}{2}'' \times 3\frac{1}{2}'' \times \frac{1}{4}''$	3'
$4'' \times 3\frac{1}{2}'' \times \frac{5}{16}''$	5'
$5'' \times 3\frac{1}{2}'' \times \frac{5}{16}''$	6'

VENEER   10" CAVITY   8" SOLID   12" SOLID

Figure 5   *Use of angle lintels in brick wall openings.*

GENERAL EXAMPLE

Mr. and Mrs. X decide that they want a full basement under their 24′ × 48′ flat-roofed house. Design one girder running the length of the basement down its center, giving 12′ floor joist spans. Find the size of the girder and the number and size of the columns.

Loads. First calculate the total live and dead load acting on the girder, remembering that in this plan the roof must be supported by interior partitions.

First-floor live load	40 lb./sq. ft.
First-floor dead load	20 lb./sq. ft.
First-floor partitions	20 lb./sq. ft.
Roof live load	30 lb./sq. ft.
Roof dead load	20 lb./sq. ft.
Unit live and dead load	130 lb./sq. ft.

The tributary area is 12′ × 48′ = 576 sq. ft. Therefore the total live and dead load acting on the beam is 130 lb./sq. ft. × 576 sq. ft. = 74,880 lb. = 75 kips.

Beam. Now determine the number of columns and size of the beam by trial and error, as shown in Figure 6 and the accompanying table.

The first three trials are no good, but the last three are possible. The final selection might be influenced by the future location of basement partitions or the difference in cost. (Since steel is sold by the pound, the lighter-weight beams should be compared with the cost of extra columns.)

Column. If the four-column solution is selected, the load on each column will be the tributary weight plus the weight of the girder:

Column load = 15 kips + (10 × 17 lb.)
             = 15.2 kips

Using Table V, the $3\frac{1}{2}''$-diameter pipe column will be more than sufficient, and any length may be chosen ($6\frac{1}{2}'$–7′ is common).

The footing, joist, and header sizes are calculated in the manner previously shown.

STUDY QUESTIONS

1. Name three factors that affect the size and spacing of structural members.
2. Distinguish between:
   a. Live load and dead load
   b. Wood beam, wood girder, and wood post
   c. Header and lintel
   d. Kip and ton
3. Give two methods used to determine dead loads.
4. What is meant by *tributary area*?
5. How much does a 20′-long, W 10 × 25.4 beam weigh?
6. Why are lintels used in place of headers to support masonry construction?
7. What size of (a) steel column and (b) Southern Pine post would be specified to support a 40-kip tributary load if the unbraced length of column is 7′-6″?
8. What size steel beam would be specified to support a 25-kip tributary load over a 10′ span?
9. What size No. 2 Southern Pine floor joists would be specified to span 13′-6″ in a residence if the joist spacing is to be 16″ oc?

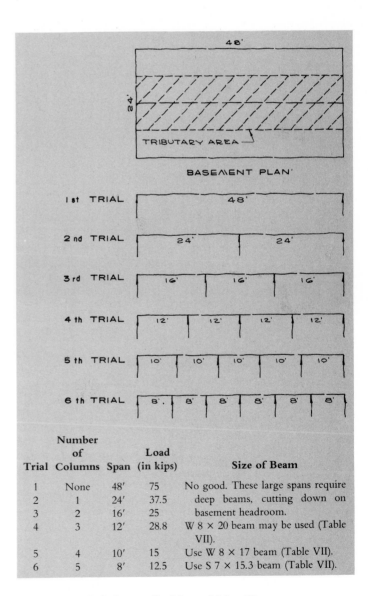

Trial	Number of Columns	Span	Load (in kips)	Size of Beam
1	None	48′	75	No good. These large spans require
2	1	24′	37.5	deep beams, cutting down on
3	2	16′	25	basement headroom.
4	3	12′	28.8	W 8 × 20 beam may be used (Table VII).
5	4	10′	15	Use W 8 × 17 beam (Table VII).
6	5	8′	12.5	Use S 7 × 15.3 beam (Table VII).

Figure 6 *Calculations for Mr. and Mrs. X.*

10. What size header should be used for a 4′ opening in a frame wall?
11. What size lintel should be used for a 4′ opening in an 8″ masonry wall?

LABORATORY PROBLEMS

1. Calculate the minimum safe sizes of the structural members of the Z residence assuming the following specifications:
   a. Wall footing: medium clay ground
   b. Column footing: medium clay ground
   c. Steel column: 6′-8″ unbraced length
   d. Wood girder: Douglas Fir
   e. Joists: Douglas Fir
   f. Headers: 7′-6″ maximum span
   g. Lintels: 4′-4″ maximum span
   Use the examples given in this chapter as a guide, but note that some of the specifications have been changed.
2. Calculate the sizes of the structural members of the building assigned by your instructor.
3. Calculate the sizes of the structural members of your original building design.

30 / Durability

MOISTURE CONTROL*

Two unseen elements play an important part in the life and livability of houses — temperature and moisture. Temperature is relatively easy to control through the use of adequate insulation and a properly designed and functioning heating system. Moisture also can be easily controlled through proper building design and construction. However, since the control of moisture is so little understood, moisture damage is undoubtedly the most prevalent of all problems connected with the home.

Water vapor. Water vapor, moisture, humidity, and steam are all the same. They are just different

* Courtesy B. E. Beneyfield, Moisture Control Consultant.

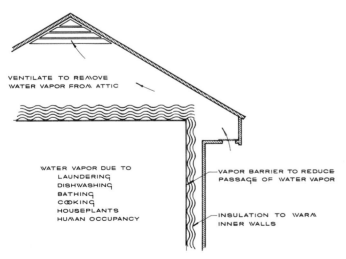

Figure 1   *Water vapor protection.*

names given to water when it has evaporated to a gas state. Water vapor is invisible, but it is present to some degree in nearly all air. Two factors associated with water vapor should be clearly understood: vapor pressure and condensation.

Vapor pressure. The water vapor in wet air always tries to flow toward drier air to mix with it. This *vapor pressure* causes the water vapor in a house to seek escape to the drier air outside, traveling through walls and roof (Figure 1). Water vapor is a gas, like air, and can move wherever air can move. It is not generally understood that water vapor can travel through materials that air cannot readily penetrate, such as wood, brick, stone, concrete, and plaster. Under the vapor pressure of warm, moist air, the vapor constantly tries to escape through most building materials to the cooler outside where the pressure is lower.

The extent of this problem may be realized when you consider the numerous sources of water vapor in a home: laundering, dishwashing, bathing, cooking, house plants, and human occupancy. All this may amount to 20 gal. of water per week which enter the air and must escape from the home.

Condensation. When warm, moist air is cooled, as happens when it comes in contact with a cold surface, the water returns to a liquid state, or *condenses*. Figure 2 shows water vapor condensing into droplets of liquid water upon contact with the cold surface of a glass of iced tea. The same condensation will occur when water vapor, under pressure to escape from a warm house, comes in contact with cooler surfaces in attics, crawl spaces, and wall interiors. This trapped condensation may cause mildewing and decay of structural members;

273

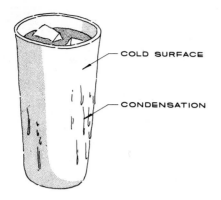

COLD SURFACE

CONDENSATION

Figure 2 *Condensation.*

MINIMUM NET VENTILATION AREA
(RATIO TO CEILING AREA)

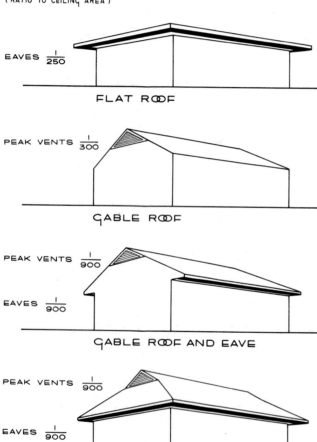

EAVES $\frac{1}{250}$

FLAT ROOF

PEAK VENTS $\frac{1}{300}$

GABLE ROOF

PEAK VENTS $\frac{1}{900}$

EAVES $\frac{1}{900}$

GABLE ROOF AND EAVE

PEAK VENTS $\frac{1}{900}$

EAVES $\frac{1}{900}$

HIP ROOF

Figure 3 *Roof ventilation.*

damage to plaster, insulation, and roofing; blistering and peeling of paint; window sweating; musty odors; and many other problems.

Comfort. Although some people believe that high humidity is beneficial to health, this question is unsettled and probably academic. Florida is a health resort and has a high humidity; Arizona, too, is a health resort and has low humidity. Neither state shows superior advantages for all people. Moisture can cause more damage than its slight comfort benefits can offset. It is best to get rid of excess moisture in order to protect clothing, tools, and leather goods as well as the building itself.

Control. There are two principal ways of controlling water vapor and preventing moisture damage. One is to stop the passage of vapor through the structure so that it cannot reach a surface cold enough to cause condensation. This can be done by the use of *vapor barriers* on the inside (warm side) of walls. The second is to *ventilate* the outer walls and ceilings so that any water vapor reaching the outer surfaces of the structure can continue flowing to the colder outside air.

Vapor barriers. A vapor barrier is any material that resists the passage of water vapor. Among the commonly used vapor barriers are:

1. Membrane vapor barriers which cover the entire wall and ceiling with openings only at the windows, doors, and electric boxes
2. Blanket insulation containing a barrier on one side
3. Aluminum-foil reflective insulation
4. Aluminum primer under wall paint
5. Asphalt coating on the back of interior wall surfaces

In every case, the vapor barrier must be kept warm by installation on the warm side of the wall. If it is installed on the cold side, condensation will form immediately. Storm windows and double-glazed windows operate on the same principle—condensation on the window is reduced in proportion to the temperature of the inside glass. Also, since no vapor barrier will completely prevent the passage of all water vapor, it is important that any penetrating vapor be permitted to continue flowing through the cold side of the wall to the outside air. This is the reason that building paper is made water-resistant but not vapor-resistant.

Ventilation. Although little can be done to reduce the amount of water vapor poured into a house, much of this vapor can be removed by ventilation in one or more of the following areas:

1. Openings at the eave and ridge of the roof. The ratios given in Figure 3 can be used to calculate the minimum net ventilation area required.

Figure 4   *Roof ventilation disguised in gable design.*

Often unsightly roof vents can be disguised by careful design as shown in Figure 4.

2. Crawl space ventilation together with a ground covering of waterproofed concrete or vapor barrier to reduce moisture entering from the ground (Figure 5)
3. Exhaust fans in kitchen, bathrooms, laundry, and basement
4. Venting of gas appliances, since water vapor is a product of gas combustion
5. Outside cold-air intake on hot-air furnace, damper controlled

EXAMPLE

Find the size of ventilators for a 25′ × 36′ gable-roofed home with flush cornice.

Solution

1. Calculate the ceiling area: 25′ × 36′ = 900 sq. ft.
2. Using Figure 3, a gable house with a flush cornice, calculate the minimum net ventilation area:

$$\frac{1}{300} \times 900 = 3 \text{ sq. ft.}$$

3. Double this area due to louvers, reducing the actual opening area: 3 sq. ft. × 2 = 6 sq. ft.
4. Since two ventilators are used, each must be 3 sq. ft. minimum.

TERMITE CONTROL

Nature has provided insects whose primary function is to accelerate the reduction to dust of dead wood on the forest floor (or on a house). These insects are of two kinds: subterranean termites located in the southern part of the United States as shown in Figure 6, and dry-wood termites located only in southern California and southern Florida.

Dry-wood termites can live in wood without having contact with moisture or the ground. Fortunately though, they are fewer in number and less of a threat than the subterranean termites. Subterranean termites breed underground and then tunnel through the earth for the wood they need for food. They will even construct tunnels *above* ground, as shown in Figure 7, to reach wood within 18″ of the ground. In areas of termite hazard, the following precautions must be taken in building:

1. Keep wood members 18″ above ground. Since this is not always possible, termite shields of 16-oz. copper (Figure 8) can be installed over the foundation walls and under the sill.
2. Solid concrete walls with reinforcing to prevent cracks are necessary, since termites are soft-bodied and able to squeeze through a paper-thin fissure. They may even tunnel through low-grade concrete.

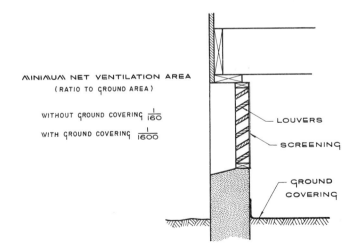

Figure 5   *Crawl space ventilation.*

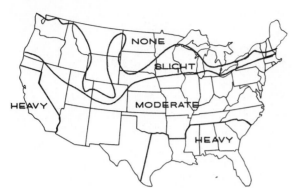

Figure 6   *Areas of termite danger.*

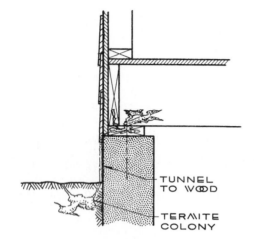

Figure 7   *Termite damage.*

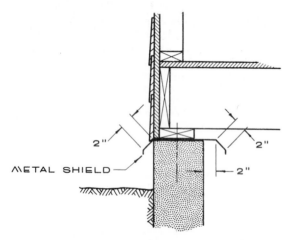

Figure 8   *Termite shield.*

3. If wood must be in contact with the ground (as in the case of wooden steps), use a concrete base under the wooden member, use the heartwood of redwood or cypress, and pressure-treat the lumber with coal tar creosote or zinc chloride.

4. Properly drain the area surrounding the house since subterranean termites need moisture to live.
5. Remove all dead wood from the building vicinity and treat the ground with antitermite chemicals.
6. Make sure that all areas such as crawl spaces are accessible for periodic inspections.
7. Screen all openings (such as attic ventilation) with 20-mesh bronze screening.

CARPENTER ANT CONTROL

In addition to termites, carpenter ants also live in wood. Unlike termites, carpenter ants do not eat wood but merely chew enough room for nests. They may colonize and expand termite nests after the termites have been exterminated, or they may nest in existing cracks in beams or hollow-core exterior doors. Carpenter ants usually seek out moist wood that has begun to decay. Since they fly, they will chew nests at any height, giving an indication of a serious moisture problem in a building. Therefore carpenter ants are best controlled by proper roofing and flashing to prevent water leaks. Other precautions are similar to those described above.

DECAY PREVENTION

Nature has also provided a low form of plant life, called fungus, which, like termites, serves to disintegrate wood. Fungus may be of a type that merely produces mold or stains (unsightly but not structurally dangerous), or of a type that produces actual decay.

Major conditions necessary for decay are:

1. Moisture in a moderate amount. Dry wood (less than 20 percent moisture content) and wood kept under water will not decay. Even so-called dry rot requires moisture.
2. Moderately high temperature (70°F.–85°F.). High temperature such as used in kiln drying will kill fungus, but low temperature merely retards it.

Since the conditions necessary for the survival of fungus are similar to those needed by termites, the preventive measures are fortunately the same.

1. Protect lumber from wetting by using wide cornice overhangs, proper construction and flashing, painting, and keeping all wooden members at least 8″ above ground.
2. Use the heartwood of redwood, cedar, and cy-

press, pressure-treated with creosote or zinc chloride. The heartwood of all lumber is more resistant to decay than the sapwood. Heartwood of redwood, cedar, and cypress is especially resistant to decay.

3. Make sure there is proper drainage of the ground surrounding the building. A vapor barrier, waterproofed concrete, or sand spread over crawl areas reduces the ground moisture evaporation.
4. Remove all dead wood from the area of the building since fungi spores float through the air from decayed wood.
5. Ventilate enclosed spaces.

CORROSION PREVENTION

Whereas wood is distintegrated by termites and decay, metal is disintegrated by rusting (corrosion). Rather than attempting to remove the conditions that cause corrosion, such as moisture, the best prevention is simply to use metals that are more corrosion-resistant.

Nonferrous metals such as bronze, copper, brass, and aluminum are corrosion resistant and therefore should be used for piping, flashing, guttering, and screening.

Ferrous metals such as steel, wrought iron, and cast iron are susceptible to corrosion but may be used for interior structural members without fear of their weakening. When they are exposed to moisture, however (as in exterior work), they must be constantly protected by painting or galvanizing (coating with zinc). Stainless steel can also be used.

Weathering steel is steel with a unique means of corrosion protection. Rather than painting or galvanizing, the steel's own corrosion serves as its protective coating. This coating forms in several years into a dense, hard oxide which effectively protects the steel from further corrosion. If the coating should be scratched, it is "self-healing." When first installed, weathering steel construction has a disappointingly rusty look. However when exposed to the weather for a year or two, it darkens in color to a rich, dark brown patina. For uniform results, though, care must be taken during installation that the material is handled as a finished product. Rainwater running over weathering steel will stain other porous or light-colored building components. This can be prevented by proper design of overhangs as shown in Figure 9. The entire exterior of Pittsburgh's U.S. Steel Building (Figure 10) is clad in a curtain wall system of weathering steel.

The first commercial office building of weathering steel was designed by Eero Saarinen and built in 1961 (Figure 11).

Figure 9   *Design of overhang to prevent staining.*

Figure 10   *A curtain wall of weathering steel.*

Figure 11   *Deere & Company Building, Moline, Illinois, Eero Saarinen, architect.*

Table I *Metals Subject to Galvanic Corrosion*

1. Aluminum
2. Zinc
3. Steel
4. Iron
5. Nickel
6. Tin
7. Lead
8. Stainless steel
9. Copper
10. Monel metal

Galvanic corrosion. Galvanic corrosion occurs when different metals come in contact in the presence of an electrolyte, as in an electric battery. This process will cause one of the metals to corrode. Therefore certain combinations of metals should not be used in exterior construction, since water may act as a weak electrolyte. The lower-numbered metals in Table I will be corroded by contact with a higher-numbered metal; in addition, the corrosion will increase in proportion to the difference between their numbers.

EXAMPLE

1. If aluminum storm windows are installed over stainless steel casement windows, the aluminum will corrode.
2. If galvanized nails (iron and zinc) are used to fasten copper gutters, the nails will corrode.

LIGHTNING PROTECTION

In locations of frequent thunderstorms, a lightning conductor system should be installed to protect the occupants of a building and the building itself. Lightning protection consists of paths that permit lightning to enter or leave the earth without passing through a nonconducting part of the building such as wood, masonry, or concrete. These paths can be metal air terminals (often called *lightning rods*) with ground conductors or grounded structures of metal. There are many advantages to including lightning protection in the initial design of a building instead of adding it later. To ensure that the system will be effective, it should be designed by an architectural engineer. See the *National Fire Codes* for recommended practices.

EARTHQUAKE PROTECTION

Earthquakes are caused by the breaking and sudden shifting of rock plates under the earth's surface. When the edges of the plates are smooth, the plates will slide slowly. But when the edges are rough, they lock together allowing stress to build for years until they finally break apart and produce an earthquake. Often such earthquakes occur in cycles of 20 to 200 years, the longer cycles generating the largest quakes. Consequently some of the most serious earthquakes have occurred in areas thought to be dormant and safe.

Moderate earthquakes have occurred in nearly every state in the United States, and major (killer) earthquakes have occurred in Alaska, California, Hawaii, Idaho, Missouri, Montana, South Carolina, Utah, and Washington. Obviously then, both residential and commercial buildings must be designed to protect occupants from the hazards of earthquakes.

Most building codes include seismic requirements. Many cities adopt model codes such as the Uniform Building Code published by the International Conference of Building Officials. The earthquake design rules in nearly all codes are similar and easy to follow. For nonengineered buildings such as single residences, the codes specify the construction details such as foundation reinforcing, quantity and size of anchor bolts, size and nailing of wood members, bracing of the frame, and chimney reinforcing. For commercial buildings, codes written before 1980 specify that buildings must be able to withstand a horizontal* force equal to 8 percent of the building's total weight. More recent codes, however, specify that each building be specially designed to consider the amount of seismic hazard, ground conditions, the building's natural period of vibration, ductility of the building's members, and other factors.

RADON CONTROL

Radon is a harmful, radioactive gas produced in the ground by the decay of radium. It enters into buildings by leaks in basements and slabs such as cracks, joints, hollows in concrete blocks, floor drains, and plumbing penetrations. Consequently radon can be controlled by careful building design and construction such as:

1. Reducing or sealing all basement and slab joints and cracks with flexible, urethane caulking.
2. Specifying concrete fill in the cores of the top course of concrete masonry basement walls.
3. Reversing air movement from inward to outward through a ventilation system that replaces and dilutes indoor air with outdoor air.

* During an earthquake, the ground vibrates in both vertical and horizontal directions. Because the horizontal vibration is usually greater than the vertical, and because buildings are stiffer vertically, collapse during an earthquake is caused by the horizontal vibration.

4. Reversing air movement from inward to outward through an air to air heat exchanger which replaces and dilutes indoor air with outdoor air. A heat exchanger is more efficient than a ventilation system because some heat is recovered from exhaust air and transferred to the incoming air.
5. Avoiding using backfill or building materials that contain excessive radium.

Radon control becomes particularly urgent when:

1. A sleeping area will be located in the lowest level of a building.
2. Children will occupy a building.
3. Occupants of a building have the habit of smoking.

Radon concentrations in buildings can be measured by charcoal detectors (for one-week testing) or track-etch detectors (for one- to twelve-month testing). Readings below 4 picocuries/liter of air are considered acceptable, but readings above 20 picocuries/liter of air require correction.

More detailed information can be obtained from the U.S. Environmental Protection Agency, Research Triangle Park, NC 27711.

STUDY QUESTIONS

1. Give two methods to control:
   a. Temperature
   b. Moisture
2. Give three additional names for water vapor.
3. Why does water vapor in a building tend to escape to the outside?
4. List the sources of water vapor in the home.
5. What causes water vapor to condense?
6. List five commonly used vapor barriers.
7. List five commonly used methods of ventilation.
8. Why is building paper made *water* resistant but not *vapor* resistant?
9. List the precautions to be taken:
   a. When building in high termite hazard areas
   b. For protection from decay
   c. To protect ferrous metal from rusting
   d. For lightning protection
   e. For earthquake protection
   f. For radon control
10. Why would it be poor practice to use lead flashing in direct contact with aluminum fittings?

LABORATORY PROBLEMS

1. Find the size of ventilators for:
   a. A 24' × 40' flat-roofed building
   b. A 30' × 40' gable-roofed home with eaves
   c. A 30' × 50' hip-roofed house
2. Calculate the ventilator sizes for each of the following:
   a. The Z residence
   b. The building assigned by your instructor
   c. Your original house design
   Also indicate the type of vapor barrier to be used.

VIII / Electrical-Mechanical Systems

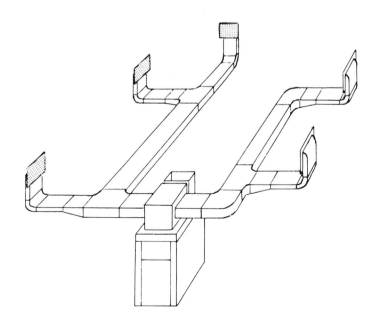

31 / Electrical Conventions

An electrical lighting system is an important part of a building, contributing both to its aesthetic effect and usefulness. The lighting system provides the major design feature during nighttime hours and, as shown in Figure 1, may affect the mood in some rooms during daytime as well. Nearly all the mechanical servants in the home—necessities and luxuries—are operated by electricity.

To design an electrical system properly, the architectural drafter must be thoroughly familiar with the available fixtures, switches, and outlets; the symbols used for them; and how to combine these symbols properly.

FIXTURES

The symbol used for an electric fixture is either a $\frac{3}{16}$"-diameter circle for an incandescent lamp or a $\frac{1}{8}$"-wide rectangle for a fluorescent lamp on a $\frac{1}{4}' = 1'$-0 scale plan (Figure 3). These simple symbols may, however, represent a wide variety of fixture types and mountings, the exact design being further detailed to a larger scale and outlined in the specifications.

Fixture types may be either (1) direct lighting, as provided by the more commonly used fixtures, recessed lights, and spotlights, or (2) indirect lighting, as provided by valance and cove lighting. Some fixtures provide a combination of direct and indirect lighting.

A detailed classification of fixture types and mountings is given in Figure 2.

All of the fixture types shown in Figure 2 (except spotlighting) may be obtained with either incandescent or fluorescent lamps. Fluorescent lamps are more efficient than incandescent lamps;

that is, a fluorescent lamp emits many times more light than an incandescent lamp having the same wattage. Also, the average life of the fluorescent lamp is many times longer. Fluorescent lamps may be obtained in lengths between 6" and 24" at 3" intervals, and also in 3', 4', 5', and 8' lengths.

Figure 1 *This library's lighting system is an important part of the building design—in both night and day.*

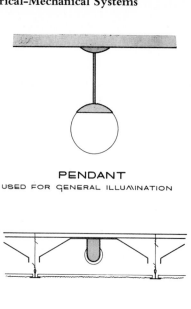

PENDANT
USED FOR GENERAL ILLUMINATION

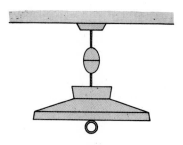

REEL
PERMITS FIXTURE TO BE ADJUSTED
TO DESIRED HEIGHT

LUMINOUS CEILING
USED WITH A SUSPENDED CEILING

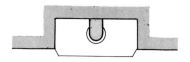

RECESSED
PERMITS BUILT-IN LIGHTING AT
SELECTED POSITIONS

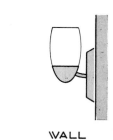

WALL
USED FOR GENERAL OR DECORATIVE
ILLUMINATION

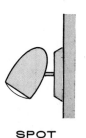

SPOT
USED FOR ACCENT ILLUMINATION

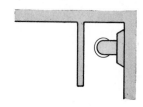

VALANCE
USED AT EDGE OF CEILING AND UNDER
KITCHEN CABINETS

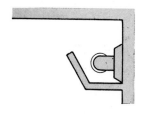

COVE
REFLECTS UP AT CEILING FOR SOFT,
INDIRECT LIGHTING

Figure 2   *Fixture types.*

SWITCHES

Wall switches are often used to control the fixtures in rooms and halls. In living rooms and bedrooms, the switch may also control one or two convenience outlets. As in the case of fixtures, the symbol for a switch (the letter *S*, Figure 3) may represent a wide variety of switch types. The most inexpensive switch is a simple on-off *toggle switch,* although most persons prefer a *quiet switch* (very faint click) or a *mercury switch* (completely silent).

Push-button types come in a wide range of button sizes ranging up to the *push plate* (in which the entire plate acts as the button). For special requirements, you may specify a *dimmer switch* (enabling a full range of light intensity to be dialed) or a *delayed-action switch* (which gives light for one minute after the switch has been turned off).

Switches are usually located 4′ above the floor and a few inches from the doorknob side of each entrance door to a room. They are placed inside most rooms. Occasionally it may be convenient to place the switch outside the room entrance (as in a walk-in closet). Three-way switches are used when a room contains two entrances over 10' apart. Two sets of three-way switches are used at the head and foot of stairs: one set for the upstairs hall, and the other for the downstairs hall. When it is desirable to control a fixture from three or more locations, three-way switches are used at two locations, and four-way switches must be used for each additional location. (Figure 4 shows the wiring of these switches.) Automatic door switches for each clothes closet are useful. Closet ceiling lights, when installed above shelves, should be recessed fixtures, thus preventing accidental contact of combustible material against a hot light bulb.

OUTLETS

Room outlets should be duplex and specified no farther than 10' apart. They should be provided wherever they might be needed so that no extension cord longer than 6' need be used. Include short wall spaces, fireplace mantels, bathroom shaving, kitchen clock, and other special requirements. Consider how the outlets will serve furniture groupings; also consider possible future changes in the use of the room. Hall outlets should be specified for every 15' of hall length. Outlets are located 18" above the floor except for higher positions in the kitchen and dining areas to accommodate counter appliances. Symbols for convenience outlets are given in Figure 3. The circles are $\frac{1}{8}$" in diameter on a $\frac{1}{4}$" = 1'-0 scale plan. The two-line symbol indicates a 120-V outlet, and the three-line symbol indicates a 240-volt, heavy-duty outlet such as would be required for a range, oven, or dryer. Outdoor outlets for Christmas decorations or patio should be marked "WP" (weatherproof) on the plan.

In addition to individual outlets, *plug-in strips* are available containing outlets spaced 6", 18", 30", or 60" apart. These plug-in strips are often used behind kitchen counters when many outlets are required. They are also available as replacements for room baseboards as shown in Figure 5. Both individual outlets and plug-in strips may be wired to obtain constant electrical service on one of a set of dual outlets, and switch-controlled service on the

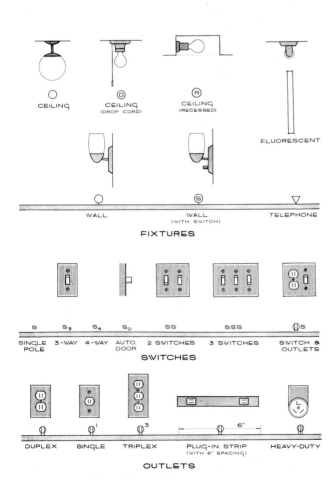

Figure 3   *Electrical symbols.*

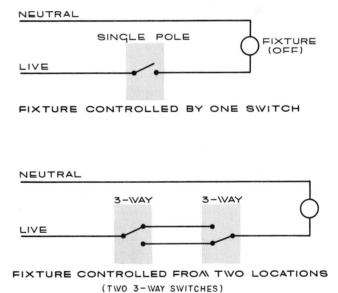

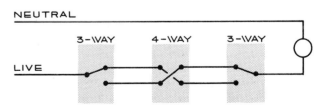

Figure 4   *Theory of electric switches.*

other. A tabulation of the minimum electrical requirements (fixtures and outlets) for a residence is given in Table I.

TELEPHONES

Even though only one telephone is planned in a new home, it is well to run concealed wires to all possible future telephone locations. As a minimum, one telephone should be specified on each active floor level. Also consider the kitchen planning center, master bedroom, den or study, living room, teen-ager's bedroom, guest room, recreation room, patio, and workshop. Consider as well dual telephone lines to a home computer center to permit linking the home computer with the office computer simultaneously with telephone conversation. Some occasionally used rooms may be equipped for portable plug-in telephones. Most telephone companies will prewire residential and commercial structures while under construction upon request of the owner, unless concealed wiring can be provided after completion of construction. At added expense, telephone lines can be run underground from the street to the house.

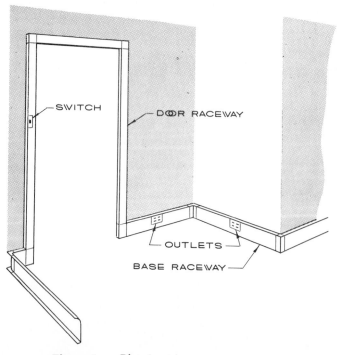

Figure 5 *Plug-in strip.*

USE OF CONVENTIONS

After you have decided upon the number of fixtures, switches, and outlets desired, together with their locations, the completion of the electrical plan is a simple matter. A freehand hidden line is shown connecting each fixture with its controlling switch(es). Remember this line does not represent an actual electric wire but merely indicates that a particular switch controls a particular fixture or outlet. Examples of some typical plans are shown in Figure 6. Study them carefully. Figure 8 shows the electrical plan for the A residence.

SERVICE

Electricity is normally supplied to the home by means of an overhead three-wire service with a capacity for 150 amperes (A). The minimum wire size for this service is #2-gauge wire (see Figure 7). A large home (over 3,000 sq. ft.) or a home with electric heat would require a larger service of 200 A. At extra cost, unsightly overhead wire can be eliminated by underground conductors.

CIRCUITS

To distribute electricity throughout the house, branch circuits of various capacities are installed. Several outlets or fixtures may be placed on one branch circuit for protection by a common circuit breaker in the entrance panel. Normally house circuits are of three types:

1. *Light-duty* circuits (outlets, 2,400 watts [W] maximum*)

   Amperage: 20
   Voltage: 120**
   Wire size: #12-gauge wire
   Description: Ordinary lights

2. *Appliance* circuits (one circuit for kitchen, one circuit for laundry, and so forth)

   Amperage: 20
   Voltage: 120**
   Wire size: #12-gauge wire
   Description: Refrigerator, freezer, toaster, ironer, washer, TV

* 20 A × 120 V = 2400 W.

** These voltages may be 120–240 V, 115–230 V, or 110–220 V, depending upon the service supplied by the power company.

Table I *Minimum Electrical Requirements*

Room	Minimum Fixtures	Minimum Outlets
Living area	Valance, cove, or accent fixtures	Outlets 10' apart plus smaller usable spaces One or several outlets controlled by switches Fireplace mantel outlet
Dining area	One ceiling fixture Possible valance or cove fixtures	Outlets 10' apart plus smaller usable spaces Table-height appliance outlets near buffet and table
Kitchen	Ceiling fixture for general illumination Fixture over sink, controlled by switch near sink Possible under-cabinet valance fixtures	Appliance outlets 4' apart Refrigerator-freezer outlet Dishwasher outlet Kitchen clock outlet Heavy-duty range outlet Heavy-duty oven outlet
Laundry	Ceiling fixture at each work center	Outlets for iron Heavy-duty outlets for washer and dryer
Bedroom	One ceiling fixture per 150 sq. ft. or major fraction, possibly controlled from bed location in addition to entrance door	Outlets 10' apart plus smaller usable spaces Possibly one or several outlets controlled by switch
Bathroom	One ceiling fixture if area greater than 60 sq. ft. Two wall fixtures on either side of mirror One vaporproof ceiling fixture in enclosed shower stall, sauna, or jacuzzi	One outlet for electric shaver
Hall	Ceiling fixtures 15' apart controlled from both directions	Outlets 15' apart
Stairways	One ceiling fixture on each floor or landing, controlled from both directions	None
Closets	One recessed ceiling fixture in each clothes closet controlled by wall switch or automatic door switch	None
Front and trades entrances	One or several weatherproof fixtures per entrance Bell or chime button	Weatherproof outlet for decorative lighting and electrical lawn care equipment
Recreation room	One flush ceiling fixture per 150 sq. ft. or major fraction Possible valance, cove, or wall fixtures	Outlets 10' apart plus smaller usable spaces
Porch, patio	One ceiling fixture per 150 sq. ft. or major fraction	Weatherproof outlets 15' apart
Utility room, basement	One ceiling fixture per 150 sq. ft. or major fraction Fixtures over workbenches	Workshop outlets as required Special outlets for heating and electric hot water heater
Garage	One ceiling fixture per two cars	One weatherproof outlet per two cars
Attic	One ceiling fixture	One outlet

3. *Heavy-duty* circuits (one individual circuit for each appliance)

Amperage: 30
Voltage: 240**
Wire size: #6-gauge wire
Description: Range top, oven, water heater, clothes dryer, air conditioner

Notice that the lower the wire gauge number, the heavier the wire. Copper wires offer resistance to the flow of electricity; the smaller the wire, the greater the resistance. Since electric energy is necessary to overcome this resistance, and underdesigned wire will heat up, causing inefficient and expensive operation (a 10 percent voltage drop reduces the light from a lamp by 30 percent), and possibly a fire hazard.

Electrical wiring is usually of copper, but aluminum is occasionally used. Although aluminum wire is less costly than copper wire, it tends to shrink and loosen at connections. When this happens, there is danger of an electric arc that is, of course, a fire hazard. For this reason, special clamps should be used at the ends of aluminum wire to assure tight connections.

LOW-VOLTAGE SYSTEM

An electric system requiring a transformer to furnish low voltage (24 V) has been gaining popularity recently. The major advantage of this system (also called the *remote-control system*) is that a fixture may be controlled from a multitude of switch

REQUIRED:

1 CEILING FIXTURE CONTROLLED BY
1 SWITCH,
RECESSED CLOSET LIGHTS
CONTROLLED BY AUTOMATIC DOOR
SWITCHES.

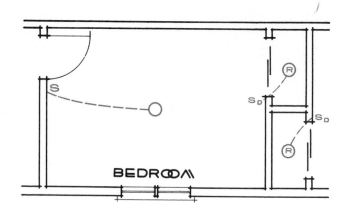

REQUIRED:

2 CEILING FIXTURES CONTROLLED BY
1 SWITCH

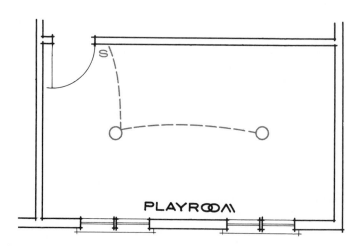

REQUIRED:

2 WALL FIXTURES CONTROLLED BY
1 SWITCH
            OR
2 WALL FIXTURES WITH INTEGRAL
SWITCH

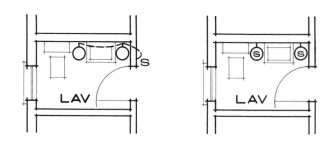

REQUIRED:

1 FLUORESCENT CEILING FIXTURE
CONTROLLED BY 2 SWITCHES

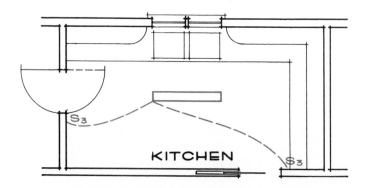

Figure 6   *Typical electrical plans.*

REQUIRED:

I VESTIBULE CEILING FIXTURE,
I FAMILY ROOM CEILING FIXTURE,
2 OUTDOOR WALL FIXTURES,
CONTROLLED BY 3 SWITCHES IN I PLATE

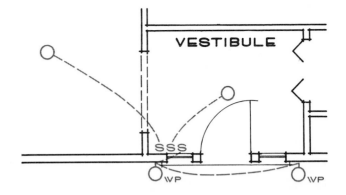

REQUIRED:

FIRST FLOOR HALL FIXTURE AND
SECOND FLOOR HALL FIXTURE
CONTROLLED BY SWITCHES ON
BOTH FLOORS

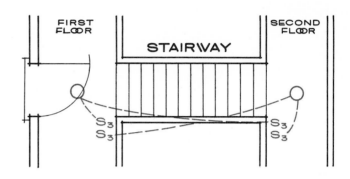

REQUIRED:

CONVENTIONAL NUMBER OF OUTLETS,
2 CONTROLLED BY SWITCH

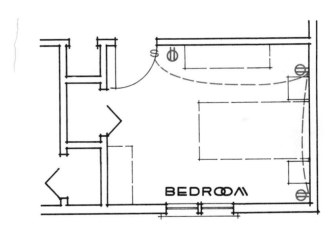

REQUIRED:

PLUG-IN STRIP WITH OUTLETS
SPACED 18" APART

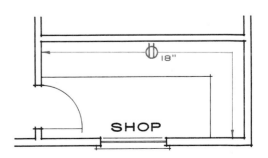

Figure 6 *continued.*

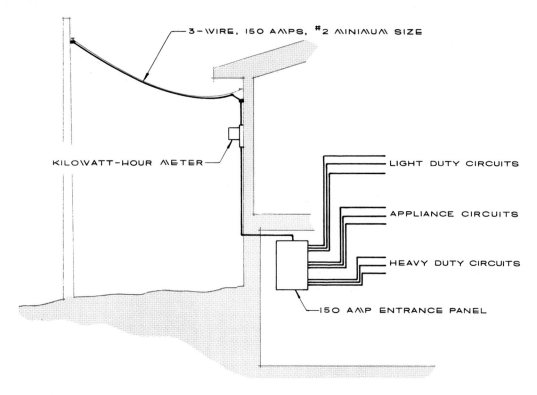

Figure 7 *Typical electrical supply to the home.*

locations, the wiring being simpler than for the conventional system. Master switches may be installed that control all the house circuits. For example, all the house lights can be turned off by one master switch located in the master bedroom. Many other conveniences are possible, such as turning on the front entrance light from a kitchen location, turning off a radio or TV from the telephone locations, or controlling an attic fan from the lower house levels.

CIRCUIT-BREAKERS

Circuit-breakers, installed in the entrance panel, are protective devices that automatically interrupt (break) a circuit in the event of an electric overload or short circuit, thus preventing a fire hazard. Whenever a circuit breaker is tripped, the electrical problem must be located and corrected. Then the circuit-breaker can be closed again by means of its switch.

GROUND FAULT INTERRUPTERS

Ground fault interrupters (GFIs), installed in the entrance panel or in individual outlets, are protec-

tive devices which automatically interrupt a circuit in the event of a line-to-ground fault thus preventing an electrical shock. GFIs provide protection in addition to the protection provided by circuit-breakers. A circuit-breaker opens only when the current exceeds its rating; ratings of 15 and 20 amps are common. A GFI opens when a ground fault causes the frame of an appliance to become "hot." Such an electrical defect may result in only a small current flow, but an electrical shock of even a fraction of an ampere can be fatal.

The National Electrical Code requires that circuit-breakers with GFIs be used for all 120 volt, single-phase, 15 and 20 amp bathroom outlets and outdoor outlets.

SMOKE DETECTORS

Smoke detectors, while not infallible, offer the earliest warning of a potential fire. Photoelectric-type detectors are better at sensing slow smoldering fires than fast flaming fires; ionization-type detectors sense flaming fires better than smoldering fires. The National Fire Protection Association recommends that smoke detectors be installed in the immediate vicinity outside of each separate sleeping area and on each additional story of a living

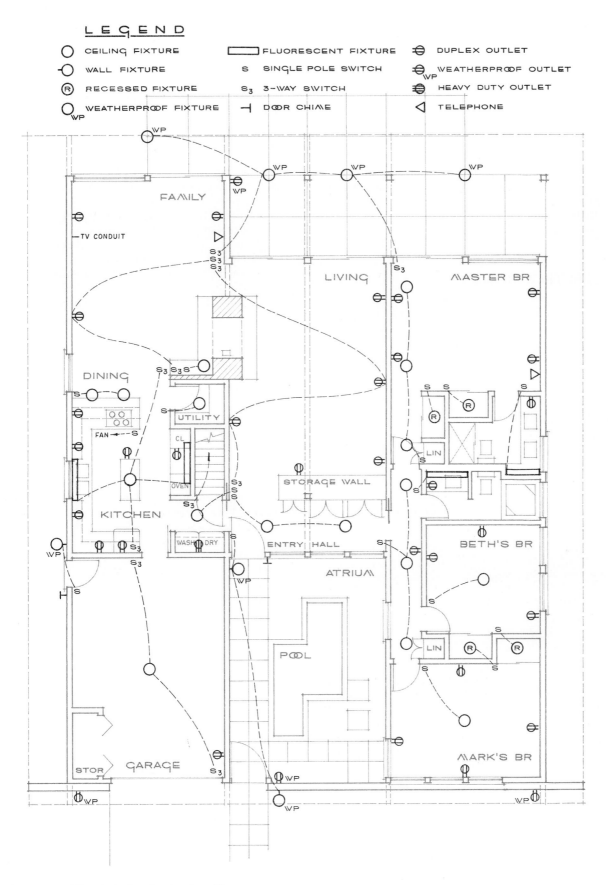

Figure 8 *Electrical plan for the A residence.*

unit including the basement. When a detector is installed in a nonsleeping area such as a furnace room, the alarm should sound in the sleeping area.

CODES

In the design of any electric system, try to meet all the special requirements of your client. Also check that all wiring meets the requirements of the National Electric Code and existing state and municipal codes, as well as the requirements of the local utility company.

ELECTROLUMINESCENCE

It is always interesting to speculate on future developments and improvements. In the area of electric lighting, possibly the electroluminescent lamp will become popular. This lamp can be roughly described as a thin sandwich of three sheets of material:

1. The rear sheet of metal
2. The middle sheet of plastic impregnated with zinc sulphide and purposely introduced *impurities*
3. The front sheet of transparent enamel

Courtesy of U.S. Steel.

Figure 9   *The computerized control center in the U.S. Steel Building, Pittsburgh.*

The front and rear sheets are electrically conductive. When alternating current is passed through them, a stream of electrons passes through the middle sheet, emitting light—thus the term *electroluminescent*.

The major advantages of this type of illumination are:

1. It provides glareless, uniform light distribution.
2. It is shockproof (eliminating periodic bulb replacement).
3. An infinite variety of sizes, shapes, and colors are possible, allowing entire walls or ceilings to be light-emitting surfaces. Experimentally produced lamps have been made in the general form of cloth and paper—suggesting drapes or wallpaper of light which may be changed in color by varying the electric frequency. It has also been suggested that an electroluminescent panel will provide the means of copying a television image—allowing flat TV screens to be hung on the walls of each room, like pictures.

A major disadvantage is that the frequencies and voltages necessary for operation are higher than are presently available in the home.

COMMERCIAL CONTROL

The electrical systems in large commercial buildings are monitored through a centralized control room. Figure 9 shows a computerized control panel in Pittsburgh's U.S. Steel Building. The panel is used to operate everything electrical, from light switching and air conditioning to fire alarm and heliport weather monitoring. Equipped to handle any emergency, the control center has a separate power source.

STUDY QUESTIONS

1. State the two general types of electrical fixtures and give two specific examples of each.
2. Give eight different classifications of electrical fixtures. Indicate where each type would be used.
3. List the fixtures and outlets in each major room of your home. Which of these fixtures and outlets are never used? What additional fixtures, outlets, or switches would be desirable?
4. Compare the advantages and disadvantages of incandescent and fluorescent lamps.
5. List seven types of switches, giving the uses of each.
6. When are the following pieces of electrical equipment used?
    a. Three-way switches
    b. Four-way switches

c. Heavy-duty outlets
d. Weatherproof outlets and fixtures
e. Plug-in strips
7. List nine rooms to be considered when planning telephone installations.
8. List three types of house circuits, giving the amperage, voltage, and wire size of each.
9. Will a #6-gauge wire or a #12-gauge wire have the greatest heat loss? Why?
10. Give two advantages of a low-voltage system.
11. (For the advanced student) After a thorough library search, prepare an illustrated paper on the history of the development of electricity to date.
12. (For the advanced student) After a thorough library search, give your estimate of the status of electricity in the home:
a. Twenty-five years hence
b. One hundred years hence

LABORATORY PROBLEMS

1. Prepare a legend of the commonly used electrical symbols. List each type of electrical requirement and show its conventionally used symbol.
2. (For the advanced student) Include in the legend of problem 1 seldom-used electrical symbols. (Hint: Refer to a reference such as *Architectural Graphic Standards*.)
3. Draw the electrical plan for the A residence.
4. Draw the electrical plan for rooms of your own design with the following requirements:
a. 14′ × 23′ living room with fireplace
b. 14′ × 14′ dining room
c. 15′ × 27′ playroom
e. 3½′ × 14′ hall
f. Front entrance vestibule with an outdoor fixture and outlet
g. Stairways appearing on the first-floor plan (to the second floor and basement)
5. Draw a diagram showing how electrical energy is supplied to a house lamp from the street service wire. Include changes in amperage and wire size.
6. (For the advanced student) Construct a working model of cardboard demonstrating:
a. How a fixture is controlled from two locations
b. How a fixture may be controlled from three locations
7. Draw the electrical plan for the building assigned by your instructor.
8. Complete the electrical plan for your original house design. To prevent cluttering the floor plan, the electrical plan is often a separate drawing—the wall, door, and window indications being *lightly* retraced with *darker* electrical symbols.

32 / Plumbing

An understanding of plumbing systems is important to the architectural designer and drafter. Since the plumbing and heating systems account for one-fifth of the total house cost, the designer is interested in obtaining an economical, as well as functional, design. The drafter often prepares mechanical plans—plumbing, heating, electrical, and structural—in addition to the architectural plans. Although plumbing plans may be omitted from the design of a small residence (leaving all decisions to the contractor), they are always included in the design of a larger building.

A plumbing system performs two major functions:

1. Water distribution
2. Sewage disposal

The *water distribution system* consists of the supply pipes that conduct water from the water main or other source to lavatories, bathtubs, showers, and toilets. A portion of this must be routed through a water heater to provide hot water. Most of the water piped into a building must also be drained out together with water-carried wastes. The *sewage disposal system* is composed of the waste pipes that conduct this water to the public sewer or disposal field.

WATER DISTRIBUTION

Piping. A wide variety of water supply pipes are available.

Copper tubing with soldered joints is often used in residential work. The nominal diameter indicates the approximate inside diameter of the tubing. The designations K, L, and M indicate wall thickness from heavy to light. Compare the following inside diameters (I.D.s) and outside diameters (O.D.s):

1″ Cu. Tubing Type K:	0.995″ I.D.	1.125″ O.D.
1″ Cu. Tubing Type L:	1.025″ I.D.	1.125″ O.D.
1″ Cu. Tubing Type M:	1.055″ I.D.	1.125″ O.D.

The designation DWV (drainage, waste, and vent) indicates a still lighter tubing intended for sewage disposal only.

Plastic pipe has become very popular in residential work, since revised plumbing codes permit it to be used for water supply as well as waste disposal. Plastic pipe and fittings are joined by solvent cement. Available nominal diameters (which approximate the inside diameters) are $\frac{3}{8}$″, $\frac{1}{2}$″, $\frac{3}{4}$″, 1″, $1\frac{1}{2}$″, 2″, 3″, 4″, and 6″.

Brass pipe is more rigid than copper and plastic and is used with screwed fittings in large, expensive buildings.

Iron pipe is used for underground supply outside buildings, but is not used inside.

Steel pipe is inexpensive but not durable due to corrosion. Both iron and steel pipe must be galvanized or coated with hot pitch to reduce this corrosion.

Fittings. Pipe is joined by *couplings* to connect straight runs, or *elbows* to connect 45° or 90° bends (Figure 1). *Tees* are used for 45° and 90° branches. *Gate valves* are used to completely shut off the water supply for repair, *globe valves* to provide a range of water regulation from off to on (like a faucet). *Check valves* permit flow in one direction only and are used when there is a possibility of back-pressure. Valves are also called *cocks, bibbs,* and *faucets.*

Cold-water supply. Let us trace the path of the water from the street main to the house faucets as shown in Figure 2. Upon request, the city water department excavates the street to the public water main and installs a *tap* (pipe) to the property line. A gooseneck is included to allow for future settling of the pipe. Two cocks are installed on the tap—one close to the main, called the *corporation cock,* and the other close to the property line, called the *curb cock.* The curb cock is attached to a long valve stem that reaches up to the ground so that water can be disconnected without another excavation.

The contractor connects $\frac{3}{4}''$ copper tubing to the curb cock and runs it in a trench below the frost line to the building. It enters the building through a caulked pipe sleeve, and immediately the *service cock, water meter, check valve,* and *drain valve* are installed. The service cock is a gate valve which allows the owner to shut off water throughout the building. The water meter registers the quantity of water used. The check valve protects against a back flow of unpotable (undrinkable) water as a result of a break in the street main. It also protects the water meter from drainage as a result of a malfunctioning water heater. The drain valve is used when it is necessary to drain all water from the system. If a water softener is to be included, lines for hard-water hose bibbs are first connected.

A $\frac{3}{4}''$ cold-water feeder line is then installed in the basement ceiling with $\frac{1}{2}''$ risers running directly to each fixture. Each riser is extended 2' higher than the fixture connection to provide an air chamber to reduce knocking (water hammer). Valves are installed at the bottom of each riser so that repairs can be made without shutting off the water for the entire house.

Hot-water supply. A tee is installed on the $\frac{3}{4}''$ cold-water supply line so that some water is routed through the water heater—entering at 70°F and leaving at 130°F. A $\frac{3}{4}''$ feeder and $\frac{1}{2}''$ risers are again installed leading to each fixture (the lavatory, tub, and shower require hot and cold water, but a toilet requires only cold). A gate valve is installed at the entrance to the water heater so that it can be shut off for repair. Water may be heated by the existing house heating system or independently by means of electric, gas, or solar heaters. A 66-gal. water heater is adequate for a family of three. A larger family should have an 80-gal. water heater. Electric water heaters are available as quick-recovery units and low-wattage units. To

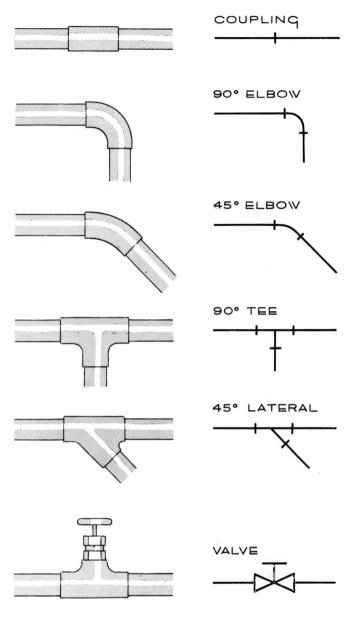

Figure 1   *Pipe fittings.*

conserve energy, the low-wattage units are preferred.

Pipe sizes. Proper pipe sizing depends upon a number of factors, such as the average water consumption, peak loads, available water pressure, and friction loss in long runs of pipe. For the average residence, however, this procedure may be simplified by the use of the minimum sizes recommended by the Federal Housing Administration as shown in Table I. Notice that waste and vent stack sizes are also included to help in sizing the sewage disposal system.

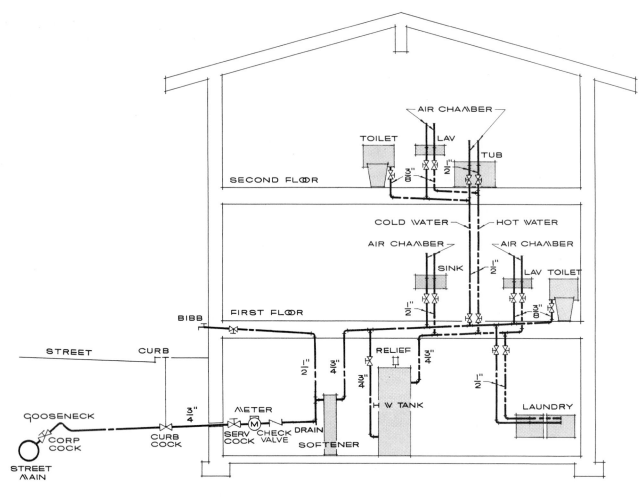

Figure 2   *Water distribution.*

Table I   *Minimum Pipe Sizes*

	Hot Water	Cold Water	Soil or Waste Branches	Vent
Supply lines	$\frac{3}{4}''$	$\frac{3}{4}''$		
Feeder lines				
Bathroom group plus one or more fixtures	$\frac{3}{4}''$	$\frac{3}{4}''$		
3 fixtures (other than bathroom group)	$\frac{3}{4}''$	$\frac{3}{4}''$		
Bathroom group	$\frac{1}{2}''$	$\frac{1}{2}''$		
2 fixtures	$\frac{1}{2}''$	$\frac{1}{2}''$		
Hose bibb plus one or more fixtures		$\frac{3}{4}''$		
Hose bibb		$\frac{1}{2}''$		
Fixture risers				
Toilet		$\frac{3}{8}''$	$3''$	$2''$
Bathtub	$\frac{1}{2}''$	$\frac{1}{2}''$	$1\frac{1}{2}''$	$1\frac{1}{4}''$
Shower	$\frac{1}{2}''$	$\frac{1}{2}''$	$2''$	$1\frac{1}{4}''$
Lavatory	$\frac{3}{8}''$	$\frac{3}{8}''$	$1\frac{1}{4}''$	$1\frac{1}{4}''$
Sink	$\frac{1}{2}''$	$\frac{1}{2}''$	$1\frac{1}{2}''$	$1\frac{1}{4}''$
Laundry tray	$\frac{1}{2}''$	$\frac{1}{2}''$	$1\frac{1}{2}''$	$1\frac{1}{4}''$
Sink and tray combination	$\frac{1}{2}''$	$\frac{1}{2}''$	$1\frac{1}{2}''$	$1\frac{1}{4}''$

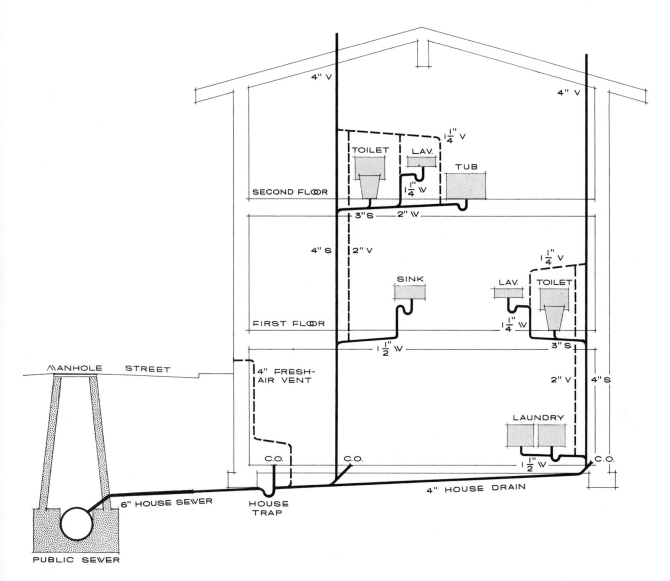

Figure 3 *Sewage disposal.*

SEWAGE DISPOSAL

The water distribution system just described is roughed in a new house before the interior walls are finished. The sewage disposal system which conducts waste water from the home is installed at the same time. The fixtures themselves are added after the interior walls are finished. Let us trace the path of the waste water from the fixtures to the public sewer (shown in Figure 3).

Fixture branches. The fixture branches are nearly horizontal pipes which conduct the waste water from the fixtures to the vertical waste stacks (vertical pipes are called *stacks*). They are pitched $\frac{1}{8}''$–$\frac{1}{2}''$ per foot away from the fixtures, and they

should be as short as possible. Sizes are shown in Table I.

Traps. To prevent sewer gases in the fixture branches from entering the living quarters, a U-shaped fitting called a *trap* is connected close to each fixture. This trap catches and holds waste water at each discharge, thus providing a water seal. Lavatory and bathtub traps like those shown in Figure 4 are installed in the fixture branch lines; toilet traps are cast as part of the fixture.

Vent stacks. A sudden discharge of waste water causes a suction action which may empty the trap. To prevent this, vent pipes are connected beyond the trap and extended through the roof to open air. Vent stacks should be installed not less than 6″ nor more than 5' from the trap. Vent stack sizes may be obtained from Table I. The portion extending through the roof is increased to 4" in diameter to prevent stoppage by snow or frost. The 4" section should begin at least 1' below the roof, extend 1' above the roof, and be no closer than 12' to ventilators or higher windows.

Waste and soil stacks. It would be very costly to carry each fixture branch separately to the sewer; therefore the fixture branches are connected at each floor level to a large vertical pipe. This pipe is called a *waste stack* if it receives discharge from any fixture except a toilet. It is called a *soil stack* if it receives discharge from a toilet, with or without other fixtures. Soil stacks are often 4" in diameter, waste stacks 3" in diameter. As with vent stacks, their upper ends should be 4" in diameter and extend 1' above the roof to open air. This retards the decomposition of organic matter since bacteria do not work in the presence of free oxygen. For maximum economy, fixtures should be grouped so that all fixture branches drain into only one or two stacks.

House drain and house sewer. The soil and waste stacks discharge into the *house drain*—an extra-heavy cast-iron pipe with lead joints under the basement floor. It is a 4"-diameter pipe running under the footing and 5' past the foundation wall. The house drain is then connected to the *house sewer* which may also be of 4" cast iron or of 6" vitrified clay. Both the house drain and house sewer are sloped $\frac{1}{4}$"/ft. to the public sewer.

Clean-outs. Clean-outs are elbows projecting through the basement floor to permit cleaning the house drain and sewer. They are installed in the house drain beyond the last stack, just inside the basement wall, and in between at points not over 50' apart. It is best to include clean-outs at the foot of each waste or soil stack and at each change of direction of the horizontal run. Threaded plugs are used to close the clean-outs.

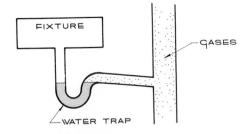

Figure 4 *Fixture trap.*

House trap. The trap installed next to the building in the house drain is called a *house trap*. It furnishes a water seal against the entrance of gas from the public sewer to the building piping. Clean-outs are located at the top of one or both sides of the trap.

Fresh-air inlet. A 4"-diameter air vent installed next to the house trap admits fresh air to the house drain. The fresh-air inlet does not run through the roof, but rather to a place 6" above the ground. It is finished with a gooseneck bend or grille.

Septic tank. In sparsely populated areas without public sewers, private disposal fields are used. Usually the sewage is directed to a 750-gal underground septic tank where solid waste is decomposed by the bacteria contained in the sewage itself. The remaining liquid is distributed to the ground through porous pipes in the disposal field.

PIPING AND PLUMBING PLANS

The water distribution and sewage disposal systems may be shown in an elevation (as in Figures 2 and 3) or in an isometric drawing, but are usually shown in plan (as in Figures 5 and 6). The water distribution system is shown in the *piping plan,* and the sewage disposal system is shown in the *plumbing plan.* Notice that since these plans are schematic drawings, it is not necessary to hold to scale. Some typical instructions appearing on such plans follow.

GENERAL NOTES

1. All underground piping should be type **K** copper (soft temper) with screwed-pressure-type joints.
2. All hot- and cold-water piping inside the building should be type **L** copper (hard-temper) with soldered joints.
3. All soil and waste piping above ground should be type **M** copper with soldered joints.
4. All soil and waste piping under ground should be heavy cast iron with lead and oakum bell and spigot joints.
5. Furnish and install stop valves in all hot- and cold-water lines before fixtures; if visible, valves to have same finish as fixture trim.
6. All fixtures shown on drawings to be furnished and completely connected with approved chrome-plated brass trim, traps, and suitable supports. Furnish and install chrome-plated escutcheon plates where pipes pierce finish walls.

For more detailed information than is given in this chapter, obtain the *ASHRAE Guide* from the American Society of Heating, Refrigerating,

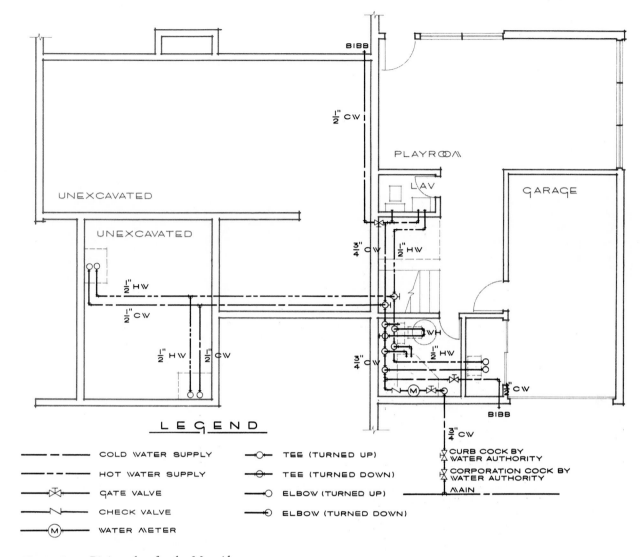

Figure 5 *Piping plan for the M residence.*

and Air Conditioning Engineers; the *National Plumbing Code* from the Government Printing Office in Washington, D.C.; or the *Uniform Plumbing Code* from the International Association of Plumbing and Mechanical Officials.

FUTURE TRENDS

Sovent plumbing. A single-stack, self-venting sewage disposal system was developed recently and holds promise for multistory buildings. The first American installation was in the model apartments (called *Habitat*) at the Expo 67 World's Fair in Montreal, Canada. This system is called *sovent*, indicating a combination of *soil* stacks and *vent* stacks. The key to this system is an aerator fitting located at the connection of each fixture branch to the soil stack. This fitting limits the sewage flow velocity in the stack, thus reducing the suction which would siphon the traps. The solvent stack extends through the roof and acts both as a soil stack and as a vent stack.

Solar water heating. Solar hot water pre-heating has become quite common and is considered to be one of the most cost-effective means of using the sun's energy. This is because hot water is needed year-round, but space heating is needed only during cold weather. The principal elements of most solar hot water systems are a flat plate collector used to directly heat water, a hot water dis-

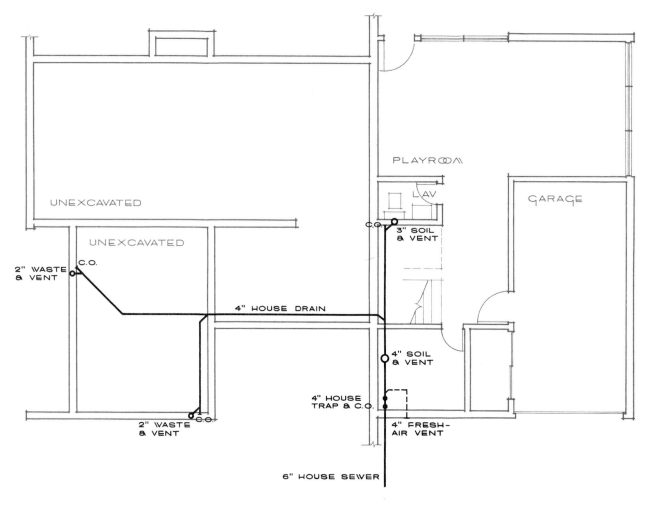

Figure 6 *Plumbing plan for the M residence.*

Figure 7 *A 2-gal./day solar still installed on the roof of a San Diego home.*

tribution system of piping, a hot water storage unit, appropriate automatic controls, and some method of protecting the water from freezing. Several types of solar hot water collectors are described in the heating chapter. A solar hot water heating system, of course, does not require as much collector area as does a space heating system.

Solar heaters for swimming pools are also available in a wide variety of systems.

Solar stills. * In some locations a supply of potable (drinkable) water has become a critical need. The solar still provides an effective solution. The first large solar still used to purify salt or brackish water was built in Chile a century ago (1872). In recent years more than twenty community-size solar stills, ranging from one hundred to several thousand gallons per day, operating on seawater or inland brackish water, have been built in ten different countries. This type of usage predictably will increase.

* Courtesy Horace McCracken, Solar Equipment Consultant.

Small home stills to convert seawater to drinking water are being manufactured by the Sunwater Company of San Diego and have been installed along the coasts of California and Mexico. These stills consist of shallow pans covered by glass panels as shown in Figure 7. Installed on a flat roof, an automatic feed pump provides a constant supply of seawater. The daily output of such an installation is about 1½ gal. of potable water.

Solar farming. The development of solar stills has been expanded to provide the means to farm in areas where only saltwater is available. The process requires air-inflated plastic greenhouses in which the water transpired by vegetable plants is condensed on the plastic roof and then reused for root irrigation.

An integrated plant which supplies potable water and food as well as power was built in the Arabian state of Abu Dhabi by the University of Arizona. Among other benefits, the price of fresh vegetables was lowered enough to provide a new food source for the forty thousand people of the state.

STUDY QUESTIONS

1. Distinguish between:
   a. K, L, M, and DWV copper tubing
   b. Coupling, elbow, and tee
   c. Gate valve, globe valve, and check valve
   d. Corporation cock, curb cock, and service cock
2. Give the minimum pipe sizes for:
   a. Supply lines
   b. Feeder line to a bathroom
   c. Feeder line to a hose bibb
   d. Feeder line to a powder room
   e. Fixture risers to a lavatory
   f. Bathtub
   g. Shower
3. Give the principal reasons for using:
   a. Traps
   b. Vent stacks
   c. Clean-outs
4. Distinguish between:
   a. Soil stack and waste stack
   b. House drain and house sewer
   c. Piping plan and plumbing plan
   d. Solar water heating and solar space heating

LABORATORY PROBLEMS

1. Prepare a legend of the commonly used piping and plumbing symbols. List each requirement and show its conventionally used symbol.
2. (For the advanced student) Include in the legend for problem 1 seldom-used piping and plumbing symbols. (Hint: Refer to a reference such as *Architectural Graphic Standards.*)
3. Draw (a) the piping plan and (b) the plumbing plan for the A residence.
4. Draw a diagram showing:
   a. How water is distributed from street main to fixtures
   b. How waste water is carried from fixtures to the sewer
5. Draw (a) the piping plan and (b) the plumbing plan for the building assigned by your instructor.
6. Draw (a) the piping plan and (b) the plumbing plan for your original building design. To prevent confusing the floor plan, the piping and plumbing plan is often a separate drawing—the wall, door, and window indications being *lightly* retraced with *darker* piping and plumbing symbols.

33 / Heating and Air Conditioning

The earliest known central heating systems were built by the Romans to heat their bathhouses. Tile hot-air ducts were used to heat the buildings, and lead pipes were used to conduct hot water to the baths. Although such systems have been used in palaces for several thousand years, they were not used for small-home heating until about a hundred years ago. Today we can choose from a multitude of systems which include cooling, humidity control, ventilation, and filtering, in addition to heating.

HEATING

The most expensive appliance in a building is the heating system — its initial cost amounts to about 10 percent of the total house cost and the fuel costs amount to several hundred dollars per year. A building's heating system is specified by an architectural engineer (specializing in heating) after consulting with the client. The architectural drafter must be able to prepare heating plans from the heating engineer's calculations and sketches. Therefore the drafter should be familiar with all heating systems, their design and layout, and how they are represented on the heating plan. We will consider heating systems of four general types:

1. Warm-air
2. Hot-water
3. Electric
4. Solar

Let us look at the operation of each, together with its advantages and disadvantages.

Warm-air. In *forced warm-air,* warm air is circulated through sheet-metal supply ducts to the rooms, and cold air is pulled through return ducts to the furnace for reheating (usually to about 150°F). Duct work may consist of a number of small individual ducts leading to each room (*individual duct system,* Figure 1), or a master duct which reduces in size as it branches off to feed the rooms (*trunk duct system,* Figure 2). Circular ducts are 4″-diameter tubes that slip together like stovepipe, with flexible elbows to form any angle up to 90°. Rectangular ducts are custom made to fit in spaces between joists and studs.

A fan, operating either continuously or intermittently, circulates the air. The thermostat* controls the fan in the intermittent system. The fan may be similar to a common electric fan, but more

* A thermostat is an instrument sensitive to changes in temperature. One type contains two metal strips having different temperature coefficients brazed together. One end of the strips is fixed, but the free end will move due to dissimilar expansion of the metals. This closes an electric contact to start a motor which controls the heating and cooling systems.

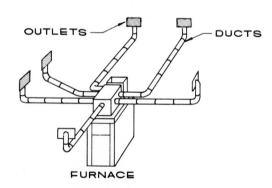

Figure 1   *Individual duct system.*

probably it will be a centrifugal type called a *blower*.

For even temperature throughout the house, the warm air should be delivered to the places that lose heat fastest—the exterior walls. The warm air is supplied through grilles with manually operated louvers located in the exterior walls or floor, preferably under windows. These grilles are called *registers* or *diffusers*. In place of registers, warm-air *baseboard units* (Figure 3) may be used to distribute the heat along a wider portion of the exterior wall.

Since the heating element, air, is actually blown into the room, warm-air heating has the inherent disadvantage of distributing dust throughout the house. This is somewhat checked by *filters*—pads of spun metal or glass coated with oil to catch dust. These must be replaced or cleaned often to be effective. Another method is attracting dust by a high-voltage screen.

Perimeter heating. This forced-warm-air system was developed for a special need—to heat the basementless house. As previously described, warm air is delivered to the exterior walls, or *perimeter,* of a building. Perimeter heating, however, has an additional function—to warm the floor itself, thus replacing the heat lost through the concrete slab floor or wood floor over a crawl space.

The recommended perimeter heating system for a slab floor is the *perimeter loop* (Figure 4). This consists of a 6″-diameter tile duct imbedded in the outer edge of the slab and supplied by warm air fed through radial ducts. The ducts warm the slab, and floor registers in the ducts supply heat to the rooms.

Another perimeter heating method is called the *perimeter radial* system (Figure 5). Radial ducts run directly to the floor registers with no outer loop. This system is often used in crawl spaces.

The *crawl-space plenum* system (Figure 6) utilizes the entire crawl space as a plenum (warm-air reservoir). Short ducts (6′ minimum length) from the furnace heat the crawl-space plenum, which then supplies heat to the rooms through perimeter floor registers. All perimeter heating requires careful insulation of the foundation to prevent excessive heat loss.

Hot-water. In *forced-circulation hot-water,* a hot-water boiler heats the circulating water to 200°F–215°F.* An electric pump controlled by the thermostat circulates the water through narrow ($\frac{1}{2}$″–$\frac{3}{4}$″) flexible tubing to radiators or convectors, giving up heat to the room. The temperature of the return water is about 20°F lower than the boiler

---

* The entire system contains water under slight pressure to prevent the formation of steam at 212°F.

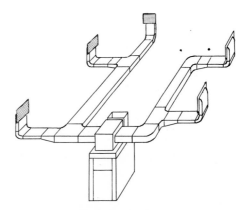

Figure 2   *Trunk duct system.*

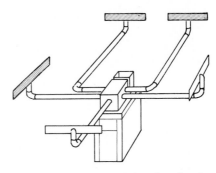

Figure 3   *Warm-air baseboard units.*

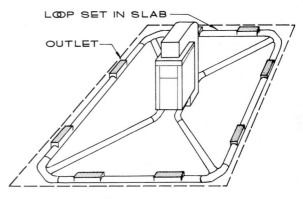

LOOP SET IN SLAB

OUTLET

Figure 4   *Perimeter loop system.*

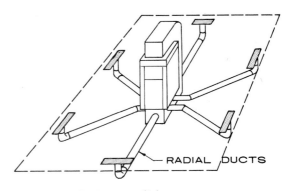

RADIAL DUCTS

Figure 5   *Perimeter radial system.*

delivery. The temperature of the delivery water can be automatically adjusted by a mixing valve which determines the amount of hot water required in the circulating system. Also each radiator can be regulated by automatic or manual

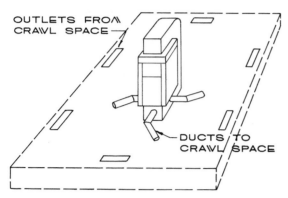

Figure 6   *Crawl-space plenum system.*

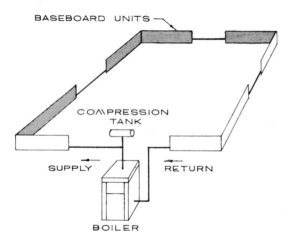

Figure 7   *Series loop.*

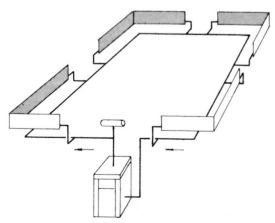

Figure 8   *One-pipe system.*

valves. Usually the boiler is fitted with additional heating coils to supply hot water, winter and summer, to the sinks, tubs, and laundry.

A hot-water system is also called *hydronic* heating. Three hot-water piping systems can be used:

1. Series loop
2. One-pipe system
3. Two-pipe system

Series loop. The series loop system (Figure 7) is, in effect, a single baseboard radiator extending around the entire house and dropping under doorways and window walls. Hot water enters the baseboard near the boiler and travels through each baseboard section and back to the boiler for reheating. It is often used in small homes because it is inexpensive to install, but there can be no individual control of the heating units. Either the entire house is heated, or none of it. A compromise is the installation of *two* series loops in two zones which may be independently controlled.

One-pipe system. The one-pipe system (Figure 8) is often specified for the average-size residence. Hot water is circulated through a main, special tee fittings diverting a portion of the water to each radiator. Radiators can be individually controlled by valves and located either above the main (*upfeed* system) or below it (*downfeed* system). Downfeed is less effective because it is difficult to coax the water into the branches.

Since water expands when heated, a compression tank is connected to the supply main. A cushion of air in the tank adjusts for the varying volume of water in the system as the water temperature changes.

Two-pipe system. The two-pipe system is used for large installations. The hot water is circulated by two main pipes, one for supply and one for return. The water is diverted from the supply main to a radiator, and then flows from the radiator to the return main. In this manner, all radiators receive hot water at maximum temperature. The *reversed return* system of Figure 9 is preferred to the *direct return* system of Figure 10. Piping is saved in the direct return system, but the total length of supply and return piping is the same in the reversed return system, assuring equal flow due to equal friction.

Piping in the one- and two-pipe systems needs no pitch except for drainage. All hot-water systems must be drained or kept operating to prevent their freezing when the house is not occupied.

Heating units. The heating units used in hot-water heating are either radiators, convectors, or combi-

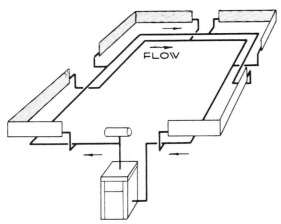

Figure 9   *Two-pipe system, reversed return.*

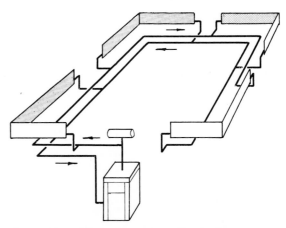

Figure 10   *Two-pipe system, direct return.*

nations of radiator and convector. A radiator has large, exposed surfaces to allow heat to *radiate* to the room. Radiant heat does not depend upon air movement; it passes through the air directly to any object. A convector, however, draws in cool air from the room at the bottom, warms it by contact with closely spaced fins, and forces it out into the room again. Heat is therefore circulated by air movement. The major disadvantage of convection is that the heat rises to the ceiling, leaving the floor cold.

Radiators and convectors (Figure 11) may be recessed into the wall to increase floor space. Baseboard heating may be radiant or convector. The distribution system is identical for conventional and baseboard heating.

Radiant panel heating. In this system the entire floor, the ceiling, or the walls serve as radiators. The heating element may be hot water or steam in tubing, hot air, or even electricity. In the hot-water system, prefabricated loops of tubing are imbedded into a concrete floor (Figure 12) or attached to the ceiling or walls before plastering (Figure 13). In drywall construction, the tubing is installed behind the wall or ceiling panels. In the warm-air system, ducts may be laid in the floor or ceiling, or the entire space above the ceiling may be heated by blowing warm air into it.

Electric heat. Electric heating systems offer many advantages: low installation cost, no exposed heating elements, individual room control, cleanliness, and silent operation. The main disadvantage is the high cost of operation in localities not offering low electric rates. Heavy insulation is required to keep operation costs to a minimum. The most popular electric heating systems for homes are:

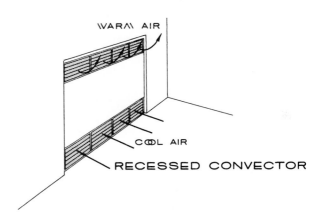

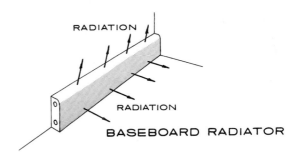

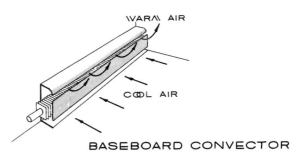

Figure 11   *Types of heating units.*

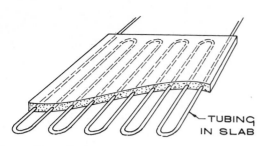

Figure 12   *Radiant floor panel.*

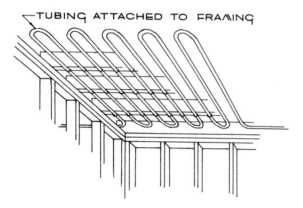

Figure 13   *Radiant ceiling panel.*

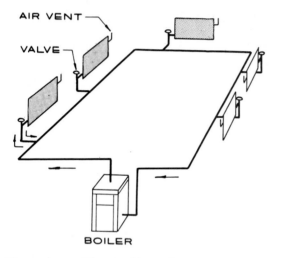

Figure 14   *Electric cable in plaster ceiling.*

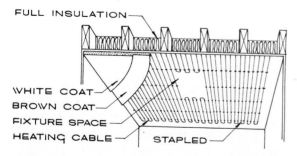

Figure 15   *Electric cable in gypsum-board ceiling.*

1. Electric resistance cable
2. Electric panels
3. Electric baseboards
4. Heat pump

Electric resistance cable. Covered wire cables are heated by electricity and concealed in the ceiling or walls. The wires are manufactured to specific lengths to provide the rated wattage. They are stapled to gypsum lath in a gridlike pattern, only a few inches apart. Then they are covered by a $\frac{1}{2}''$ brown coat and finish coat of plaster (Figure 14) or gypsum board (Figure 15). The temperature of each room can be individually controlled by thermostats.

Electric panels. Prefabricated ceiling panels (Figure 16) are only $\frac{1}{4}''$ thick and constructed of a layer of rubber containing conductive material and backed with insulating material. They cover the entire ceiling and can be painted, plastered, or papered. Smaller glass wall panels are backed with an aluminum grid for the resistance element and are available in radiant, convection, and fan-forced types. These panels are set into the outside walls under the windows and are best suited for supplemental or occasional heating.

Electric baseboard. Most electric baseboards are convection heaters (Figure 17). They consist of a heating element enclosed in a metal baseboard molding. Slots at the bottom and top of the baseboard permit the circulation of warmed air.

Heat pump. The heat pump works on the same principle as the refrigerator, which takes heat out of the inside compartments and discharges it into the room. The heat pump takes heat from the outdoors and brings it into the house. It does this by further "refrigeration" of the outside air. A refrigerant (which acts to absorb heat) circulates between two sets of coils—the evaporator and the condenser. During cold weather the outside air is blown over the evaporator coils. Although this air is cold, the refrigerant is much colder and thus absorbs heat as it changes from liquid to gas. The warmed refrigerant is then pumped to the condenser, where the room air is blown over the coils, and is heated by the refrigerant as it changes back to a liquid. The still-colder outside air is blown back outdoors again. During warm weather the operation is reversed so that heat is removed from the room.

Heated or cooled air from a heat pump can be circulated through supply ducts (Figure 18) in the same manner as it is circulated in a warm air system.

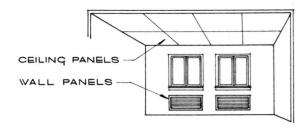

CEILING PANELS
WALL PANELS

Figure 16 *Electric panels.*

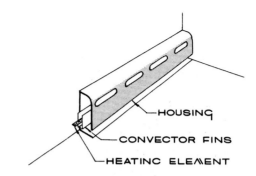

HOUSING
CONVECTOR FINS
HEATING ELEMENT

Figure 17 *Electric baseboard.*

Solar heat. A solar heating system uses the sun's rays as the heating source. Although this is a comparatively new concept, many homes are now being built with solar space heating and cooling or solar hot water heating systems. Because of the diffuse nature of solar energy, most solar heating systems supply only about half of the space heating requirements of a building, the other half being supplied by auxiliary conventional heating systems. Solar heating systems are usually described by the method used to circulate heat through the building. When the heat flows naturally, the system is called *passive;* when the heat flow is forced by some mechanical means, the system is called *active.* Many solar buildings combine passive and active systems. For example, the natural heat flow of a passive system can be accelerated with the addition of a fan.

Passive solar heating systems are usually described by the path of the heat flow, while active systems are usually described by the type of collector used. Some of the most common types are:

I. Passive
  1. Direct gain
  2. Indirect gain
  3. Isolated gain
II. Active
  1. Flat-plate collectors
    A. Air-type collectors
    B. Liquid-type collectors
    C. Trickle collectors
  2. Focusing collectors

PASSIVE SYSTEMS

Direct gain. The direct gain passive system is the simplest and most common of solar heating systems. It consists of a large glass area on the southern wall to permit the sun's rays to *directly* heat the house. As shown in Figure 19, the roof overhang

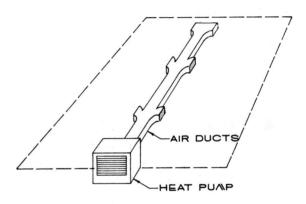

AIR DUCTS
HEAT PUMP

Figure 18 *Heat pump.*

is designed to permit the winter sun swinging low on the horizon to warm the house, but exclude the summer sun which is high in the sky. The exact angle of the sun by hour, date, and latitude is given in standard reference books. Some form of adjustable screen is needed to prevent heat from escaping through the same glass areas during the evening and on cloudy days.

A south-facing window system should be designed to use available solar heat, but without overheating during midday. Some methods used are:

1. Interior designed to permit warm air to rise and heat additional rooms above.
2. Fans to circulate warm air to other parts of the building.
3. Windows facing east of true south to provide quick morning heat and less heat in the afternoon.

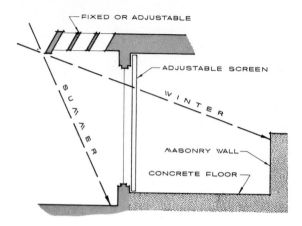

Figure 19 *An adjustable system for direct solar heating.*

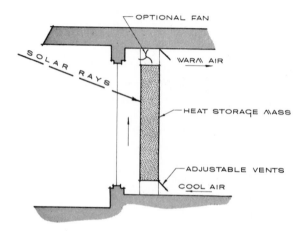

Figure 20 *A thermosyphoning system for indirect solar heat.*

4. A heat storage system such as a masonry wall or concrete floor which absorbs the heat and returns it to the building for a few hours after the sun disappears. Windows facing west of due south are best for this system because they extend the heat return later into the evening.
5. A separately zoned solar heated room such as a greenhouse or sun room, which can be closed off from the other rooms when desired.

Indirect gain. The indirect gain passive system consists of a dark-colored storage mass about 4″ behind the southern glass area. The storage mass absorbs and stores heat, and the heat then flows from the mass to *indirectly* heat the house. This system is also called a *Trombe* system, after the French architect Felix Trombe who pioneered it.

As shown in Figure 20, the heated air can be circulated by natural convection (called *thermosyphoning*) or it can be aided by a fan. Also, the indirect gain system can be designed with adjustable vents at the top and bottom of the storage mass to control heat distribution. As with the direct gain system, adjustable screens can be used to prevent the escape of heat at night.

Isolated gain. The isolated gain passive system consists of a collector and storage unit separated (thermally "isolated") from the area to be heated. The isolated gain system is not as popular as the direct and indirect systems.

EXAMPLE

The S residence, shown in Figures 21–26 and in Appendix A is a solar house with both direct and indirect, passive space-heating systems, and an active, domestic hot-water heating system. The house is a three-level A-frame located on the site so that the front left corner faces south. This permits solar heat to be collected through both the front wall and the left wall. Features of this house are:

1) Solar heat is directly gained through large, glazed areas in the left (southwest) wall that warms the cathedral living level and loft sleeping level. Protection from summer heat is provided by the roof overhang and by tall, deciduous trees.
2) Solar heat is indirectly gained through a greenhouse also on the left wall that takes cooler air from the basement level through operable windows and warms the living level through adjustable wall registers. The greenhouse has a brick floor and water storage containers to extend the time of heat release throughout the evening.
3) Additional early morning solar heat is gained through a sun trap on the front (southeast) wall that warms the basement and living levels, both through operable windows.
4) Two wood-burning stoves are located centrally, one on the living level and another in the basement level.
5) Auxiliary heat is provided as needed through conventional electric baseboard units. Approximately 50 percent of this home's space-heating requirements is provided by solar means, 40 percent through the two wood-burning stoves, and 10 percent by the auxiliary electric heat.
6) To reduce heat loss, the house is insulated by:
   (a) Earthen berms along the rear and right walls.
   (b) Full-thick (R-11) insulation in 4″ walls sheathed with 1″ (R-5) extruded styrofoam giving a total insulating ability of R-16.
   (c) Ten-inch (R-30) insulation in 12″ rafters with 2″ vent space above.
7) Liquid-type flat-plate collectors are on the southeast roof to provide preheating for domestic hot water. Approximately 50 percent of the home's hot water heating requirements is provided by this active solar heating method.

Figure 21   *Kitchen-dining area of the S residence.*

Figure 22   *Wood-burning stove in the S residence.*

Figure 23   *Stairway to the loft sleeping level of the S residence.*

Figure 24   *Cathedral living area of the S residence.*

Figure 25   *Southwest-facing window wall of the S residence.*

Figure 26   *Music area of the S residence.*

ACTIVE SYSTEMS

Flat-plate collectors. A flat-plate collector system consists of exterior solar collectors to heat air or liquids which are then piped to a heat storage container. A second piping loop is used to pipe the heat from the storage container to the building. An auxiliary conventional heating system is included as shown in Figure 27.

For best operation, it is important that flat-plate collectors face the sun. For example, a flat-plate collector in Dallas, Texas (latitude 33°) should face south and be tilted at an angle of 57° (90° − 33° = 57°) with the horizontal.

Air-type collectors (Figures 28 and 29). An air-type collector consists of "flat" panels, each about 4″ thick, 3′ wide, and 7′ long. A solar heat absorber is inside the panel. The absorber surface is made of a good heat conductor such as aluminum, copper, stainless steel, or galvanized steel. The panel is covered with a translucent sheet of tempered glass or plastic. This permits sunlight to enter, but prevents the radiation of longer wavelengths given off by the absorber from leaving. Thus, heat is trapped inside the collector. There is, of course, insulation at the bottom of the panel. The panels can be mounted horizontally, vertically, or inclined. Cool air is drawn through the panel (under the absorber) by an automatic fan which operates only when the absorber temperature is sufficiently high. Usually the air enters at the bottom of an inclined or vertical panel and leaves at the top. The absorber surface is irregular in texture (such as corrugated) to cause the air to tumble. This increases the amount of heat transferred from the absorber to the air underneath. Also, the absorber metal usually has a special surface chemically or electrolytically applied to increase its absorbtion capacity. Viewed closely, it looks like the bluing on a gun barrel, but from a distance the collectors look like dark windows.

Air-type collector systems have lower installation costs than liquid-type collector systems. They have no water freezing problems, and they are, in general, less complicated. However, they are not as efficient for hot-water heating, and they require hot-air ducts which are many times larger than hot-water tubing. Also, rock storage containers (often used with air-type systems) require more space than hot-water storage (used with liquid-type systems).

Liquid-type collectors (Figures 30 and 31). A liquid-type collector is similar in operation to an air-type collector except that the heat transfer medium is water or antifreeze which is pumped through copper tubing soldered to a copper absorber plate. The water system is drained during cold nights to prevent freezing. Some antifreezes are toxic and special precautions must be taken to prevent leakage into the hot-water supply. The water or antifreeze may be pumped either from the eave up to the ridge or from the ridge down to the eave.

Another form of liquid collector, the *evacuated tube,* is shown in Figure 32. This collector consists of three concentric metal or glass tubes. Cool liquid is supplied through the smallest feeder tube to the end of the assembly. The liquid picks up solar heat as it returns through the midsized absorber tube. There is a partial vacuum (an *evacuation*) between the absorber tube and the largest cover tube. The vacuum helps to reduce condensation and heat loss.

Trickle collectors (Figure 33). A trickle collector is a liquid-type collector that has cool liquid flowing from $\frac{1}{32}$″ holes drilled in a header tube and trickling down open absorber channels rather than in closed absorber tubes. After the liquid is warmed, it is collected in an open gutter for distribution to storage. Compared to a closed system, the trickle collector is less costly to install and has fewer freezing problems, but has lower efficiency due to evaporation and condensation on the cover sheet.

Focusing collectors (Figure 34). Focusing collectors concentrate diffuse solar radiation onto a smaller absorber area and at a higher temperature. Figure 34 shows a parabolic reflector that focuses on the absorber pipe. Other reflector shapes have been used. Some systems include automatic tracking control to enable the collector to follow the sun's direction. A focusing collector connected to a heat pump can provide both heating and cooling.

Photovoltaic cells. Photovoltaic cells convert solar radiation directly into electricity rather than into heat. Semiconductor chips are used which develop an electric field in the presence of sunlight. The chips are connected in a grid to produce electric current. This is a costly system, however, and consequently it is not often installed.

Heat storage. In all solar heating systems, heat must be stored for future use in evenings and on cloudy days. Some of the most common types of heat storage are:

1. Rock storage
2. Liquid storage
3. Heat of fusion

Rock storage. Rock is usually used to store heat collected by air-type collectors. The heated air is drawn through an insulated container filled with

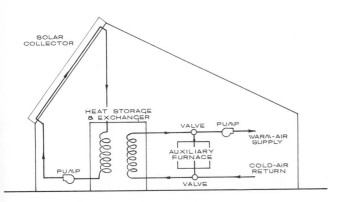

Figure 27   *A flat-plate solar collector system.*

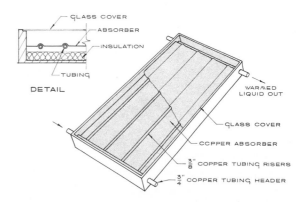

Figure 30   *A water-type solar collector.*

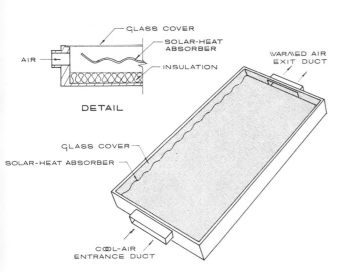

Figure 28   *An air-type solar collector.*

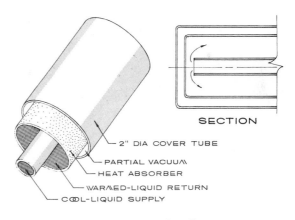

Figure 31   *A water-type assembly.*

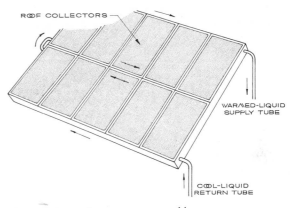

Figure 32   *An evacuated-tube collector.*

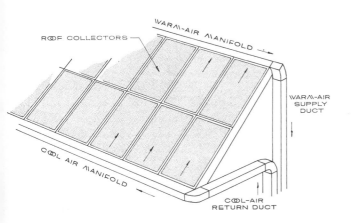

Figure 29   *An air-type assembly.*

pieces of rock or large-sized gravel. As the air flows through the spaces between the rock, the rock is heated and some of that heat will remain for use several days later. The container, however, must be quite large—about 1 cu. ft. for each 2 sq. ft. of collector surface.

Liquid storage. Water is usually used to store heat collected by liquid-type collectors. This can be

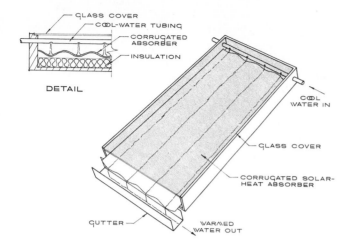

Figure 33 *A trickle-type solar collector.*

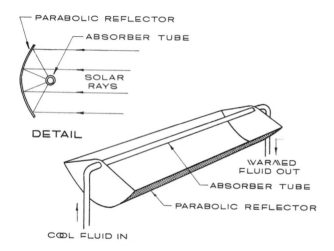

Figure 34 *A parabolic focusing solar collector.*

accomplished by either storing the heated liquid directly in an open-loop system or by circulating the heated liquid through a tank of water in a closed-loop system. The water tank will gain heat from the heated liquid, thus acting as a *heat exchanger.* A liquid storage system requires only about one-third the volume of a rock storage system.

Heat of fusion. The most promising system uses the *heat of fusion* to store heat. A great amount of heat is required to melt a solid into a liquid. When this melting, or *fusion,* occurs, the temperature does not change. For example, 1 Btu of heat is required to raise the temperature of 1 lb. of water 1°F, but 144 Btu are needed to melt 1 lb. of 32°F ice to 32°F water. In the heat of fusion system,

heated air or heated liquid is circulated through tubing surrounded by a chemical compound having a melting point of about 90°F. As the chemical compound is melted from a solid to a liquid, it stores heat until the heat is released later by its changing back to a solid.

Heat distribution. There are two common systems used to distribute stored heat in the building:

1. Forced warm-air
2. Forced-circulation hot-water

They differ from standard distribution systems only in that heat must be delivered in larger volume because it is at a comparatively low temperature. Conventional furnaces deliver warm air at about 150°F and hot water at about 190°F. In comparison, solar storage units deliver heat at about 100°F. Usually an auxiliary conventional heating system is provided which automatically cuts in as needed. If space cooling is desired in addition to space heating, in most cases a liquid system is better adapted than an air system.

Examples of solar-heated buildings. The California residence shown in Figure 35 is a cluster of ten connected rooms. Solar heat enters through automatically adjusted skylights. Heat is stored in interior masonry walls. Auxiliary heat is provided by electric resistance panels.

The Oregon residence in Figure 36 has an air-type solar collector on a roof sloping 60°. The rock storage system contains 60 tons of 2″ stone in a 6′ × 12′ × 18′ insulated bin. Auxiliary heat is electric forced warm air.

The Oklahoma house in Figure 37 has a water-type solar collector on a roof sloping 50°. The open-loop water storage system is a 2,000-gal. concrete basement tank. Auxiliary heat is electric hot water. Earth banked on several sides provides additional insulation.

The Colorado building of Figure 38 has a trickle collector on a 45° roof. The heat storage system is an 1,800-gal. steel water tank sized 4′ × 5′ × 12′. Auxiliary heat is provided by natural gas.

The accompanying table of advantages and disadvantages of different heating systems (Table I) may help in the selection of a heating system for an individual case. You may want to add to it.

Heat-loss calculations. A heating system should be designed by a heating engineer specializing in the field. The drafter will prepare the heating plans, however, and should be familiar with the design process. Let us look, then, at the steps necessary to design a typical system.

Although every heating system must be individually designed, there are certain elements common to all. For example, the total heat loss through the walls, ceiling, and floor of each room

Courtesy of Mr. Peter Hollander.

Figure 35 *Clustered modules with solar skylights.*

Courtesy of Mr. Peter Hollander.

Figure 36 *An air-type solar collector.*

must be balanced by the heat delivered to each room. The first step, therefore, is to calculate the heat losses.

Heat losses. Heat escapes from a room in two ways:

1. Transmission through walls, ceiling, and floor
2. Infiltration through cracks around windows and doors

Transmission losses. Heat loss by transmission will increase in proportion to the area A of the surfaces of the room, the difference between the inside temperature and outside temperature $(t_i - t_o)$, and the coefficient of transmission U:

$$H = AU(t_i - t_o)$$

where: H = Heat loss (Btu/hr.)
      A = Area (sq. ft.)
      U = Coefficient of transmission (see Table II)

t_i = Inside temperature (70°F is often assumed)
t_o = Outside temperature (assume 15°F above lowest recorded temperature; 0°F is used for New York, Boston, and Philadelphia)

The coefficient of transmission is a factor that indicates the amount of heat in British thermal units that will be transmitted through each square foot of surface in one hour for each degree of temperature difference. A poor insulator will have a high U value; a good insulator will have a low U value. Values of U have been computed by tests for a number of surfaces as shown in Table II.

Air-infiltration losses. In addition to the heat that is lost directly through the room surfaces, heat will escape through the cracks between windows and window frames and between doors and door frames according to the following formula:

$$H = 0.018LV(t_i - t_o)$$

Figure 37 *A water-type solar collector.*

Courtesy of Mr. Peter Hollander.

Figure 38 *A trickle-type solar collector.*

Courtesy of Mr. Peter Hollander.

Table I *Comparison of Heating Systems*

	Advantages	Disadvantages
Warm-air	Quick heat	Ducts take up basement headroom
	No radiators or convectors to take up floor space	Ducts convey dust and sound
	Air conditioning and humidification possible	Flue action increases fire danger
	Cannot freeze	Separate hot-water heater required
	Low installation cost	
Hot-water	Low temperature heat possible for mild weather	Retains heat during periods when no longer required
		Slow to heat up
		Radiators require two lines
		Must be drained to avoid freezing when not in use
Radiant	No visible heating device	Slow reponse to heat needs
	Economical operation	Air conditioning must be separate unit
	Good temperature distribution	Repair costly
Electric	No visible heating device	Operation cost high in many locations
	Low installation cost	Heavy insulation required
	Individual room control	
	Clean, silent operation	
Solar	Low operation cost	Supplemental heating system necessary
		High installation cost
		System not fully developed

Table II *Coefficients of Transmission (U) (Btu/hr./sq.ft./degree)*

Walls	
Wood siding, plastered interior, no insulation	0.26
Wood siding, plastered interior, R-11 (3½") insulation	0.07
Wood siding, plastered interior, R-19 (6") insulation	0.05
Brick veneer, plastered interior, no insulation	0.26
Brick veneer, plastered interior, R-11 (3½") insulation	0.07
Brick veneer, plastered interior, R-19 (6") insulation	0.05
8" solid brick, no interior finish	0.50
8" solid brick, furred and plastered interior	0.31
12" solid brick, no interior finish	0.36
12" solid brick, furred and plastered interior	0.24
10" cavity brick, no interior finish	0.34
10" cavity brick, furred and plastered interior	0.24

Partitions	
Wood frame, plastered, no insulation	0.34
4" solid brick, no finish	0.60
4" solid brick, plastered one side	0.51
4" solid brick, plastered both sides	0.44
6" solid brick, no finish	0.53
8" solid brick, no finish	0.48

Ceilings and Floors	
Frame, plastered ceiling, no flooring, no insulation	0.61
Frame, plastered ceiling, no flooring, R-19 (6") insulation	0.05
Frame, plastered ceiling, no flooring, R-30 (9") insulation	0.03
Frame, no ceiling, wood flooring, no insulation	0.34
Frame, no ceiling, wood flooring, R-19 (6") insulation	0.05

Ceilings and Floors, Cont'd.	
Frame, no ceiling, wood flooring, R-30 (9") insulation	0.03
Frame, plastered ceiling, wood flooring, no insulation	0.28
Frame, plastered ceiling, wood flooring, R-19 (6") insulation	0.05
Frame, plastered ceiling, wood flooring, R-30 (9") insulation	0.03
3" bare concrete slab	0.68
3" concrete slab, parquet flooring	0.45
3" concrete slab, wood flooring on sleepers	0.25

Roofs	
Asphalt-shingled pitched roof, no ceiling, no insulation	0.52
Asphalt-shingled pitched roof, plastered ceiling, no insulation	0.31
Asphalt-shingled pitched roof, plastered ceiling, R-19 (6") insulation	0.05
Asphalt-shingled pitched roof, plastered ceiling, R-30 (9") insulation	0.03
Built-up flat roof, no ceiling, no insulation	0.49
Built-up flat roof, no ceiling, 2" board insulation	0.12
Built-up flat roof, plastered ceiling, no insulation	0.31
Built-up flat roof, plastered ceiling, 2" board insulation	0.11

Windows and Doors	
Single-glazed windows	1.13
Double-glazed windows	0.45
Triple-glazed windows	0.28
Glass blocks (8" × 8" × 4")	0.56
1¾" solid wood doors	0.44
1¾" solid wood door with storm door	0.27

Table III *Volume of Infiltration (V) (cubic feet per foot of crack per hour)*

Doors not weatherstripped	111
Doors weatherstripped	55
Windows not weatherstripped	39
Windows weatherstripped	24

Table IV *Radiant (R) and Radiant Convector (RC) Baseboard Outputs (average water temperature = 200°F)*

Type	Height	Rated Output (Btu/hr./ft. of baseboard)
R	Low (7″)	255
R	High (10″)	365
RC	Low (8″)	430
RC	High (10″)	605

where: H = Heat loss (Btu/hr.)

$0.018 = 0.24 \times 0.075$ (0.24 is specific heat of air in Btu/lb.; 0.075 is density of air in lb./cu. ft.)

L = Length of all cracks (ft.)

V = Volume of air infiltration per foot of crack per hour. (see Table III)

t_i = Inside temperature

t_o = Outside temperature

Values for the volume of air infiltration (V) for the average doors and windows are given in Table III.

EXAMPLE

Find the hourly heat loss from the front bedroom of the M residence (Chapter 11) using the following data:

Door: Weatherstripped, $1\frac{3}{4}$″ solid wood with storm door

Windows: Weatherstripped, double-glazed

Walls: Wood siding, plastered interior, $3\frac{1}{2}$″ insulation

Floors: 6″ insulation

Ceiling: 9″ insulation

Solution

	A	U	$(t_i - t_o)$	$H = AU(t_i - t_o)$
Door	20 sq. ft.	0.27	(70 − 0)	378 Btu/hr.
Windows	24 sq. ft.	0.45	(70 − 0)	765 Btu/hr.
Walls	168 sq. ft.	0.09	(70 − 0)	1058 Btu/hr.
Floor	137 sq. ft.	0.05	(70 − 20)	343 Btu/hr.
Ceiling	137 sq. ft.	0.03	(70 − 0)	288 Btu/hr.

Transmission losses = 2823 Btu/hr.

	L	V	$(t_i - t_o)$	$H = 0.018\,LV(t_i - t_o)$
Door	19′	55	(70 − 0)	1317 Btu/hr.
Windows	34′	24	(70 − 0)	1028 Btu/hr.

Infiltration losses = 2345 Btu/hr.

Total heat losses = 2823 + 2345 = 5168 Btu/hr.

System design. After the total heat loss from each room has been calculated, a system must be designed that will replace the loss. For our example, we will assume that a series-loop baseboard, hydronic system is desired for the M residence, and that the baseboard heating units will be selected from the four types shown in Table IV. Two loops

Table V *Baseboard Heating Design*

	Room	Heat Loss (Btu/hr.)	Exterior Wall Available (ft.)	Minimum Output (Btu/hr./ft.)	Baseboard Selected	Baseboard Length (ft.)	Correction Factor	Final Baseboard Length (ft.)
Loop 1	Vestibule	5,950	10	595	RC high 605	9.9	× 1	10
	Kitchen-laundry	6,240	13	480	RC high 605	10.3	× 1.075	11
	Dining-living	10,570	38	280	R high 365	29	× 1.15	33
Loop 2	Bathroom	2,150	4	540	RC high 605	3.6	× 1	4
	Bedroom	5,170	18	290	R high 365	14.2	× 1	14
	Master bedroom	8,000	14	570	RC high 605	13.2	× 1.075	14
	Study	3,670	14	260	R high 365	10	× 1.15	12
Loop 3	Lower level	17,500						

Total heat loss = 59,250 Btu/hr.

will be used on the main levels: one loop through the vestibule, kitchen-laundry, and dining-living areas; and a second loop through the bathroom, bedrooms, and study. The order of design is as follows:

1. Calculate the length of exterior wall available for baseboard heating units in each room and tabulate them in a form like that shown in Table V.
2. Divide the heat loss by the available length of wall to find the minimum output required.
3. Select a baseboard type from Table IV with a slightly greater output than required.
4. Divide the heat loss by the rated output of the baseboard selected to find the revised length of baseboard required.
5. Divide the radiation approximately into thirds. Increase the middle third by $7\frac{1}{2}$ percent and the last third by 15 percent to compensate for the cooling of the water as it proceeds along its run.
6. Select a boiler with a capacity equal to the total heat loss (59,250 Btu/hr.). Boilers for small buildings are usually rated on the basis of the net output rather than the gross output, so a 60,000-Btu/hr. boiler will be large enough to include all heat losses and domestic hot-water demand.
7. Using manufacturers' catalogs, the sizes of the compression tank, pump, and main are determined. In this case, an 8-gal. compression tank and 1″-diameter main are selected. A separate 1″ pump is installed in each of the three loops so that zone control of each loop is possible.
8. Lay out the system as shown in Figure 39.

AIR CONDITIONING

Air conditioning means different things to different people. The average person thinks of air conditioning as the cooling of a building on a hot day. The professional engineer, though, considers air conditioning to have a broader meaning: both heating and cooling in addition to humidity control, ventilation, filtering, and other processing. All of these elements are essential to human comfort and should be considered when planning a building.

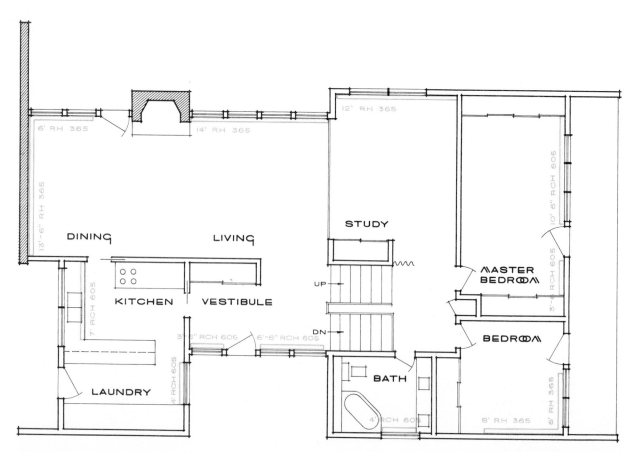

Figure 39 *Heating plan for the M residence.*

Cooling. Heat will transfer from a warm surface to a cooler surface. Air cooling may be accomplished by withdrawing heat from the air by transferring it to the cooler surface of evaporator coils in a refrigerating unit. As described in the section on heat pumps, a *compressor* circulates a *refrigerant* between two sets of coils: *evaporator* coils and *condenser* coils. The refrigerant is a volatile liquid with such a low boiling point that it is a gas (*vapor*) under normal pressure and temperature. Common refrigerants are freon 11 (CCl_3F) and freon 12 (CCl_2F_2). As a vapor the freon is compressed in the compressor, and its temperature increases. At this high pressure and temperature, the vapor passes through the condenser coils to be cooled by the surrounding water and condensed into a liquid as shown in Figure 40. Still under pressure, the liquid refrigerant enters through the expansion valve into the evaporator, where the pressure is lowered by the suction stroke of the compressor. The boiling point of the liquid refrigerant drops, and the refrigerant changes into a gas (*vaporizes*). For this vaporization, a great deal of heat is withdrawn from the air or water surrounding the evaporator coils. The vaporized refrigerant is drawn back into the compressor through the suction valve to be compressed again, in a continuous cycle.

In large air-conditioning systems, water is chilled in the evaporator and piped to the desired portion of the building. In smaller systems, such as unit air conditioners, the air to be cooled is allowed to enter the evaporator cabinet directly.

Humidity control. As far as human comfort is concerned, temperature and humidity are inseparable. In dry air (low humidity), perspiration evaporates readily and cools the skin. Consequently, winter heating should be accompanied by *humidification*. In moist air (high humidity), perspiration will not evaporate, and the skin and clothing become wet and uncomfortable. Summer cooling, then, can be aided by *dehumidification*.

It is generally agreed that a comfortable winter temperature is 74°F with a relative humidity* between 30 and 35 percent. Lower humidity will dry furniture and house members, causing them to crack and warp. A higher humidity causes condensation on windows and possibly on walls. A summer temperature of 76°F at a relative humidity under 60 percent is desirable. Indoor temperatures in the summer are not lowered more than 15° below the outdoor temperatures to prevent an unpleasant chill upon entering or the feeling of intense heat upon leaving the building.

In addition to thermostats for controlling temperature, air conditioners are provided with *hygrostats* (also called *humidistats*) which are sensitive to and control the humidity of the air. Separate humidifiers and dehumidifiers in portable units are also available.

Ventilation. Temperature, humidity, and ventilation are all important to human comfort. A too-warm room having a gentle air motion may be more comfortable than a cooler room containing still, stale air. For air motion, a velocity of about 25 ft./min. is considered satisfactory. Much higher velocities cause uncomfortable drafts. Air-conditioning systems in large buildings continuously introduce some fresh outdoor air and exhaust stale air containing excess carbon dioxide, reduced oxygen, and unpleasant odors. Air from toilets, kitchen, and smoking and meeting rooms is not recirculated but exhausted directly. A complete air

---

* Relative humidity is the ratio of the quantity of water vapor actually present to the greatest amount possible at that temperature.

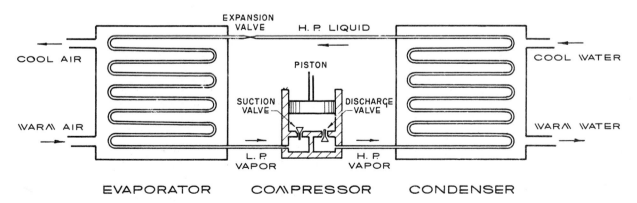

Figure 40 *Mechanical air conditioner.*

change every fifteen minutes is recommended for most activities. In uncrowded homes, natural infiltration provides a satisfactory amount of fresh outdoor air.

Filtering. Air contaminated with dust, smoke, and fumes can be purified by filters and air washers of many designs. The most commonly used air filters are dry filters, viscous filters, and electric precipitators. Dry filters are pads of fibrous material such as spun glass or porous paper or cloth which must be cleaned or replaced to remain effective. Viscous filters are screens coated with viscous oil to trap dust. They may be cleaned by air or water and recharged by dipping in oil. Electric precipitators remove particles by passing the air through a high-voltage field. This charges the particles, which are then attracted to plates of opposite polarity.

Air-conditioning systems. Air-conditioning systems are designated *central* or *unit* systems. A central system may be designed as part of the heating system, using the same blower, filters, ducts or pipes, and registers. Or it may be separate from the heating system, having its own distribution method. In general, a single, combined, all-season system is more economical than two separate systems which must duplicate equipment.

For greater accuracy of control, it is often desirable to divide a building into zones for cooling as well as for heating. Frequently the sections of a house vary in the amount of heating and cooling required due to different exposures to prevailing winds and sun, varying construction materials, and different uses. Thermostats are placed in each zone. The zones may be groups of rooms or individual rooms each with its own thermostat controlling the air conditioning.

Cooling systems may be combined with most heating systems. The warm-air system can supply cooled air as well. Chilled water can be circulated through the same pipes used in hot-water or steam heating systems. In this case the room convectors are equipped with blowers to circulate the warm room air over the chilled coils. The operation of the heat pump can be reversed to either supply or withdraw heat as required.

Self-contained room-sized *unit* systems are particularly effective in buildings with naturally defined zones. The units may be controlled automatically or manually as desired. Room units are built into the exterior walls in new construction and installed in window openings in existing dwellings.

Heat-gain calculations. Summer heat enters a room just as winter heat escapes: by transmission through walls, ceiling, and floor and by air infiltration through cracks around windows and doors. But some additional factors, such as solar radiation, heat produced within the house, and latent heat, must also be considered.

Transmission. Heat gained by transmission is calculated in the manner previously discussed for each area having a temperature difference between the inside of the room and the outside. For example, a wall adjacent to a garage without air conditioning should be included, but a below-grade wall should not.

Solar radiation. In addition to the normal transmission gain through glass, there is also a sun load through unshaded glass. Glass sun load is calculated only for the wall containing the largest area of unshaded glass, because the sun can shine directly on only one wall at a time. For an approximate calculation, assume that solar heat will enter through each square foot of glass on the east, south, and west walls at the rate of 100 Btu/hr. Double this amount for horizontal windows such as skylights. Windows facing north are omitted.

Infiltration. Heat gained by air infiltration is calculated in the same manner as winter infiltration losses. The air-conditioning system can be designed, however, to introduce sufficient outdoor air to maintain an indoor pressure capable of eliminating infiltration.

Occupants. The human body produces heat at an average rate of 300 Btu/hr. Therefore a heat gain for occupants is included by multiplying 300 times the assumed number of occupants.

Lighting. The equivalent heat of each watt of incandescent lighting is 3.4 Btu/hr. Therefore multiply 3.4 times the total wattage generally in use at one time. For fluorescent lights, use 4.0 in place of 3.4.

Table VI   *Heat Emission of Appliances*

Electric oven	10,000 Btu/hr.
Electric range, no hood	4,000 Btu/hr./burner
Electric range, with hood	2,000 Btu/hr./burner
Electric warming compartment	1,000 Btu/hr.
Gas oven	10,000 Btu/hr.
Gas range, no hood	8,000 Btu/hr./burner
Gas range, with hood	4,000 Btu/hr./burner
Gas pilot	250 Btu/hr.
Electric motors	2,544 Btu/hr./horsepower

Appliances. The heat gain due to appliances can be estimated from Table VI. A figure of 1200 Btu/hr. is often used for the average residential kitchen.

Latent heat. Latent heat gains must be included when water vapor has been added to the inside air. If the air conditioner is designed to condense an equal amount of moisture from the room, this factor is omitted.

Sizing the system. The total of all preceding heat gains is termed the *sensible heat gain.* The required size of the unit to be installed is found by multiplying the sensible heat gain by a performance factor of 1.3. A unit having this required heat removal rate in British thermal units per hour can then be selected from the manufacturers' catalogs. Cooling units may also be rated in tons of refrigeration.* A ton is equivalent to 12,000 Btu/hr. The size in tons, therefore, can be found by dividing the required size in British thermal units per hour by 12,000. A small house will usually require a 2- or 3-ton unit, a large house a 5-ton (60,000-Btu/hr.) unit.

A large commercial building might require several thousand tons of refrigeration. A 3,500-ton chiller and its computerized control center (Figure 41) are located on a mechanical floor (the sixty-third floor) of the U.S. Steel building in Pittsburgh. The computer center senses the solar energy being absorbed by the building and makes the required adjustments in the air conditioning.

Solar air conditioning. Research is now under way to perfect an air cooling system powered by some natural process rather than by a costly mechanical process. Recently an experimental solar air-conditioned home was built in Phoenix, Arizona. This building has a flat water-film roof in thermal contact with metal ceilings beneath and covered by horizontal plastic panels. During winter daylight, the panels are retracted to allow the sun to heat the water and the house. The panels are retracted during summer nights also—but for a different reason. This allows the water film to evaporate, which cools the water and the house.

STUDY QUESTIONS

1. Distinguish between these forced warm-air systems:
   a. Individual-duct and trunk-duct
   b. Perimeter-loop and perimeter-radial
2. Distinguish between these forced hot-water systems:

* A ton of refrigeration is the amount of refrigeration produced by melting a ton of ice in twenty-four hours.

Figure 41   *Checking temperature readings at air conditioning control panel. U.S. Steel Building, Pittsburgh.*

   a. Series-loop, one-pipe, and two-pipe
   b. Upfeed and downfeed
   c. Direct-return and reversed-return
   d. Radiator and convector
3. Distinguish between these solar collectors:
   a. Air-type and liquid-type
   b. Evacuated-tube and trickle-type
   c. South-facing window and focusing-type
4. Describe the method of operation of:
   a. The electric baseboard
   b. The heat pump
   c. Solar heat (heat of fusion system)
   d. The mechanical air-conditioning system
5. List the advantages and disadvantages of each of these heating systems:
   a. Warm-air
   b. Hot-water
   c. Radiant
   d. Electric
   e. Solar
6. If a solar collector is sized $14' \times 30'$, estimate the needed volume of:
   a. Rock storage
   b. Liquid storage
7. Name the principle causes of heat gain and heat loss in a building.
8. Give the equations that describe heat loss by transmission and by infiltration.
9. Give the coefficient of transmission for:
   a. Brick-veneer wall, plastered interior, without insulation
   b. Brick-veneer wall, plastered interior, 2" insulation
   c. 10" cavity brick wall, without interior finish
   d. Wood-frame floor, without ceiling below, without insulation
   e. Wood-frame floor, without ceiling below, 4" insulation
10. Distinguish between:
   a. Heat loss and heat gain
   b. Central and unit air conditioning
   c. Compressor, condenser, and evaporator
   d. Thermostat, hygrostat, and humidistat
   e. Infiltration and solar radiation

LABORATORY PROBLEMS

1. Prepare a legend of the commonly used heating and air-conditioning symbols. (Hint: Refer to a reference such as *Architectural Graphic Standards*.)
2. For the A residence:
   a. Make the necessary calculations and draw the heating plan. Use the heating system of your choice
   b. Include central air conditioning
3. Using the following data from the living room of the Z residence:

   Windows: Weatherstripped, double-glazed
   Unshaded area of east windows: 42 sq. ft.
   Unshaded area of south windows: 27 sq. ft.
   Unshaded area of west windows: 27 sq. ft.
   Walls: brick veneer, plastered interior, 2" insulation

   Floor: no insulation
   Outside temperature: 0°F
   First-floor temperature: 70°F
   Second-floor temperature: 70°F
   Basement temperature: 60°F
   Number of occupants: 5
   Wattage generally in use: 1,000

   a. Find the hourly heat loss
   b. Find the hourly summer heat gain
4. For the building assigned by your instructor:
   a. Make the necessary calculations and draw the heating plan.
   b. Include central air conditioning
5. For your original building design:
   a. Make the necessary calculations and draw the heating plan
   b. Include central air conditioning

34 / Energy Conservation

Much of the energy used today is wasted. Obviously if the waste is reduced, the need for additional energy sources is also reduced. Some of the principal areas of residential energy conservation are in the reduction of waste in home heating and cooling, hot-water heating, and electrical use.

HEAT CONSERVATION

Residential and commercial buildings require approximately one-third of the total energy we use. Most of this energy is needed to heat or cool buildings as shown in Figure 1, so the search for improvement has concentrated on improved insulation and other methods to save heat.

Thermal insulation. Houses should be insulated to obtain the maximum efficiency from the heating and cooling systems, and to provide the comfort of a steady temperature. Properly installed insulation can reduce heating and cooling costs by as much as 40 percent while at the same time making the house warm in winter and cool in summer.

Insulation is available in many forms. For new house construction batts or blankets (rolls) are often specified. They are sized to fit snugly between joists or rafters and between studs. Most frame houses in cold climates are now being built with 2″ × 6″ studs spaced 24″ oc (rather than 2″ × 4″ studs at 16″ oc) to permit $5\frac{1}{2}″$ of wall insulation, or with a staggered double row of 2″ × 4″ studs to permit continuous insulation. Ceiling insulation is often 9″ to 12″ thick. However, it is important to understand that the insulating ability of different materials varies considerably. To provide a dependable system of comparison, insulating ability is specified by R-values (resistance values).

R-values. Prior to 1970 the insulating effectiveness of a building section was indicated by its thermal *conductivity* (U-factor). However, U-factors were confusing in that only a small difference in values (such as 0.03 and 0.04) indicated a large difference in insulating effectiveness. Consequently Professor E. C. Shuman of The Pennsylvania State University proposed that insulating effectiveness be indicated by its thermal *resistance,* or R-value. An R-value is the reciprocal of a U-factor, so the above U-factors of 0.03 and 0.04 correspond to R-values of 33 and 25 which are obviously significantly different. Also R-values are additive, while U-factors are not.

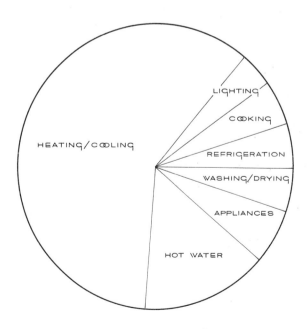

Figure 1   *Home energy consumption.*

321

Table I *Common R-values for Mineral-fiber Batts*

R-value	Thickness
R-11	$3\frac{1}{2}''$
R-19	$6''$
R-30	$9\frac{1}{2}''$
R-38	$12''$

Table II *Recommended Thermal Insulation in Cold Climates*

Building Component	Recommended Insulation
Ceiling	R-30 or R-38
Walls	R-11 or R-19
Basement walls	R-11
Floors (over unheated space)	R-19
Slab on grade	R-7 ($2''$ rigid insulation)

R-values are marked on all types of insulation and are the best indication of insulating effectiveness. A type or brand of insulation with a high R-value has a higher insulating value than insulation with a low R-value. Two different types or brands of insulation with identical R-values will have the same insulating value, even if they have differing thicknesses. Insulation in batts and blankets is commonly produced with R-values of 38, 30, 19, and 11 as shown in Table I. R-values are additive. That is, two R-19 batts equal one R-38 batt. Table II indicates the amount of insulation recommended for houses in cold climates.

Installation. Obviously, insulation will not be very effective if carelessly installed. For example, batts and blankets should fit tightly without "fish-mouth" gaps between the insulation and the studs. Small spaces and cracks should be hand packed with loose wool. As shown in Figure 2, install as much insulation as the available stud and joist depths allow. However, foil-faced insulation must be installed with a $\frac{3}{4}''$ air space as shown in Figure 3 to benefit from the reflective value of the foil.

Most insulation batts and blankets are made with a vapor barrier* on one side, which is installed facing the inside (warm side) of the house to prevent condensation. Condensation occurs only when moisture reaches a cold surface through which it cannot readily pass, and the vapor barrier, when properly installed, does not become cold. If the insulation is improperly installed, with the vapor barrier toward the outside (cold side) of the house, moisture will condense upon contact with the cold vapor barrier, making the insulation ineffective. Also, any breaks in the vapor barrier will decrease its effectiveness. All such breaks should be repaired before the insulation is covered by the wall surface. Proper installation of insulation is important because condensed moisture cannot be dried in the summer. This leads to rotting of wood and rusting of metal.

For fire safety, do not insulate within $3''$ of recessed lighting fixtures or other heat-producing equipment.

Superinsulation. Buildings insulated more heavily than recommended in Table II are termed *superinsulated*. Residences have been built, for example,

---

* The correct technical term is vapor retarder rather than vapor barrier because the flow of vapor is merely retarded and not completely stopped.

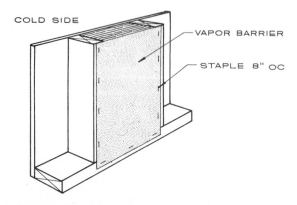

Figure 2 *Nonfoil insulation should completely fill available space.*

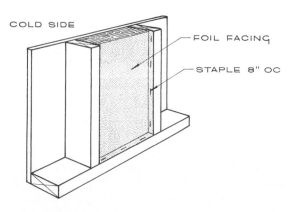

Figure 3 *Foil-faced insulation requires $\frac{3}{4}''$ air gap.*

with R-30 wall insulation by staggering 2" × 4" studs within a 10" wall, thus preventing any heat loss by direct passage through the studs. See Figure 4.

Types of insulation. Two forms of insulation are commonly available: mineral wool (fiber glass and rock wool) and cellulose.

Mineral wool is manufactured in batts, blankets (rolls), and loose-fill. The loose-fill is installed by pouring or blowing under pressure. Mineral wool is preferred over other types of insulation because it is not combustible (since it is made from glass or rock) and does not slump under pressure.

Cellulose, on the other hand, is a paper product and is chemically treated to make it fire-retardant. Unfortunately the chemicals can be driven off by summer heat. Also they leach out when the insulation becomes wet. Cellulose insulation slumps to about half its volume when wet.

Rigid insulation made of asphalt-impregnated fiberboard, and *foamed plastics,* such as Styrofoam® and urethane, are frequently used as insulation under built-up roofs. A common size for these materials is 24" × 48" in thicknesses of $\frac{1}{2}$" to 3" in $\frac{1}{2}$" increments. Foamed plastics are popular as perimeter insulation, installed between the foundation and the floor slab. Perimeter insulation is often 2" thick × 24" wide as shown in Figures 5 and 6. Insulation can also be sprayed on the interior of a building in thicknesses up to 2".

To insulate existing buildings, loose-fill insulation can be poured between studs and joists, or blowing wool can be blow in, filling the walls to the full depth of the studs and to the desired depth between joists.

Additional measures. In addition to insulation, many additional actions can help conserve heat. Some of these activities are:

1. Double glazing (such as thermopanes or storm windows over single panes) reduces heat loss through the windows by about 60 percent. Double glazing of low-E glass (low-emissivity glass manufactured with a microthin, transparent coating that reflects inside heat in the winter and outside heat in the summer) reduces heat loss by about 66 percent. Triple glazing (storm windows over thermopanes) is even more effective and reduces heat loss by about 75 percent. Double and triple glazing also reduce noise and condensation on the windows.

2. Appropriate glazing can also help cool the house in the summer. To reduce solar heat and glare, windows can be glazed with heat-absorbing glass. Such glass, combined with an ingenious design, reduced the solar-heat load by 75 percent in the Norfolk City Hall shown in Figures 7 and 8. An outer window wall is fastened 3' from the inner window wall with tubular steel trusses. This permits a cooling air flow between both layers of glass as illustrated in Figure 9. The upper grid serves as a solar screen and is also used as a walkway for window washers.

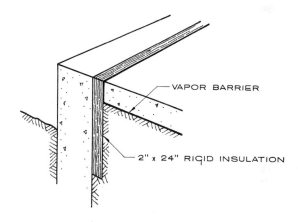

Figure 5   *Perimeter insulation for slab construction.*

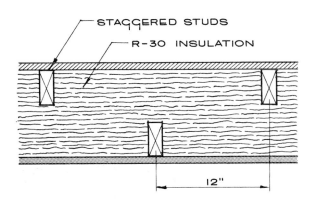

Figure 4   *Plan of a superinsulated wall.*

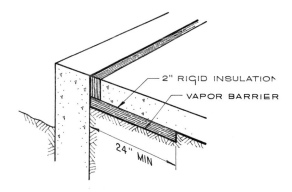

Figure 6   *Alternate method of installing perimeter insulation.*

Figure 7   *Norfolk City Hall.*

Figure 8   *Corner detail of Norfolk City Hall.*

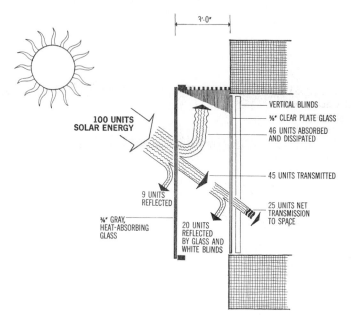

100 UNITS SOLAR ENERGY

3'-0"

VERTICAL BLINDS

¾" CLEAR PLATE GLASS

46 UNITS ABSORBED AND DISSIPATED

45 UNITS TRANSMITTED

9 UNITS REFLECTED

¾" GRAY, HEAT-ABSORBING GLASS

20 UNITS REFLECTED BY GLASS AND WHITE BLINDS

25 UNITS NET TRANSMISSION TO SPACE

Figure 9   *Typical window section of Norfolk City Hall.*

3. Storm doors reduce transmitted heat loss through doors by about 40 percent. Storm doors also reduce the amount of heat lost when the door is opened.
4. Weatherstripping reduces heat lost by infiltration around doors by about 50 percent. Windows also should be weatherstripped if they do not close tightly. Weatherstripping is available in foam rubber, felt strips, flexible vinyl, spring metals, and other materials.
5. For maximum energy conservation, some houses are built partially or completely underground. The earth, with a more uniform temperature than air, protects against both the heat of summer and the cold of winter. At 10' below the surface, the temperature of the earth remains at about the average year-round temperature at that location. This is about 50°F in a temperate zone. *Underground* structures (also called *earth-sheltered* structures) are often built not entirely underground. Designs vary from side-hill exposures to atrium concepts which are open to the sky.

The principal advantages of underground structures are:

1. Energy savings of 50 percent or more due to the temperature moderation of the covering earth
2. Natural air conditioning in hot summer months
3. Insulation from outside noise
4. Protection from fire, storm, and earthquake

The principal disadvantages are:

1. Careful design is needed to reduce an isolated feeling.
2. An earth covering of over 8' is needed for constant temperature. This results in a roof load of 800 lb./ft².

3. Reinforced concrete construction is more costly than standard framing materials.
4. Underground repairs in a concrete wall are difficult.
5. Ground water conditions (such as a high water table) makes many sites unsuitable for efficient underground construction.
6. Some additional energy is needed to heat, dehumidify, and light the building.

Earth-sheltered houses are often designed as passive solar houses. When this is done, the principal window wall should, of course, be facing south. Views from a house which is lower than normal are necessarily limited. Consequently, a site sloping down to the south offers the best opportunity to obtain both passive solar heat and a satisfactory view. When designing underground housing, it is important to remember that all building codes require an operable window or outside door in each bedroom for emergency use as fire exits.

REDUCING ENERGY WASTE

In addition to energy conservation by means of proper insulation and other design and construction features, there are many conservation habits that we should all develop. Most of these suggestions require no capital investment, just common sense.

Reducing heat waste.

1. Keep windows and doors closed.
2. During cold weather, open drapes on south-facing walls to admit warm sunshine, but close drapes at night to keep out cold air. During warm weather, reverse the process. Close out the sun during the day and open drapes during cool nights.
3. Replace broken glass promptly.
4. Close the garage door of a garage attached to a house to reduce heat loss from that side of the house.
5. Keep the heating thermostat set as low as comfort permits. Each degree Fahrenheit lower reduces required heat energy by about 3 percent. Each degree Fahrenheit higher increases required heat energy by about 3 percent.
6. People generate heat. Therefore lower the thermostat about 5°F one hour before guests arrive.
7. Close radiators or heating ducts in unused rooms. Keep the door to these rooms closed.
8. Keep the fireplace damper closed when the fireplace is unused to prevent the natural draft of the chimney from pulling out warm air in the winter and cool, conditioned air in the summer.
9. Use kitchen and bathroom exhaust fans sparingly during the heating season, for they not only waste heat, but also decrease humidity. Low humidity is undesirable in the winter because then a higher temperature is needed for comfort. See the humidity control section in the heating chapter.

Reducing air-conditioning waste.

1. Open windows for moderate cooling rather than operating equipment.
2. Close windows and doors when an air conditioner is operating.
3. Use a window air conditioner to cool the room occupied rather than the entire building. Close doors to other rooms.
4. Place window air conditioners in a north or shaded window. Direct sunlight increases its work load.
5. Do not purchase window air conditioners with energy efficiency ratios (EER) below 8. The EER is the cooling capacity in British thermal units per hour divided by the electrical power input in watts. Try to locate equipment with an EER of 9 or 10.
6. Draw drapes to close out hot sun.
7. Relieve attic heat by ventilation.

Reducing hot-water waste.

1. Reduce standby heat loss by setting the water heater at the lowest acceptable temperature. 130°F is adequate for most purposes.
2. Break the habit of running water needlessly, for instance while shaving.
3. A shower requires only half the water of a bath.
4. Repair all faucet leaks promptly. A slow drip wastes about 100 gal. a month.
5. Insulate long lengths of hot-water pipe.

Reducing electricity waste.

Water heater. Reduce electric water heater waste as just described. For a house that is not heated electrically, about half of the total electric energy is used to heat water.

Lighting.

1. When purchasing incandescent lamps, consider their brightness (measured in lumens) in addition to the electricity used (measured in watts). Remember that large-wattage lamps are more efficient (emit more lumens per watt)

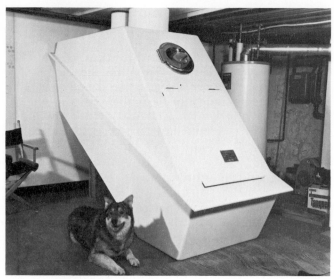

Courtesy of Clivus Multrum.

Figure 10   *A waste processor.*

than small-wattage lamps. For example, one 75-W lamp requires the same wattage as three 25-W lamps, but it will emit about twice as much light. Only wattage is marked on the lamp, but look for the brightness in lumens, which is marked on the carton.

2. Also remember that long-life incandescent lamps emit only about 90 percent as much light as a standard bulb of the same wattage. Consequently they should be installed only when their durability is useful, such as in hard-to-reach places.
3. Choose fluorescent fixtures whenever possible, for fluorescent lamps are many times more efficient than incandescent lamps.
4. Keep lighting fixtures clean to obtain more light for the same wattage.

Refrigeration.

1. To reduce the amount of cold air lost to the room, do not open a refrigerator or freezer door more often or longer than necessary. Plan ahead and remove all items for a meal at the same time.
2. Do not purchase a refrigerator or freezer larger than needed, for the energy used depends upon the size of the refrigerated space regardless of whether it is all or only partially used.
3. Choose a chest-type freezer over an upright, as less cold air is lost when the door is opened.

Cooking.

1. Do not heat more water than needed at any one time.

2. A cooking utensil should completely cover the range-top burner to minimize the heat loss to the room.
3. Choose a microwave oven over a standard oven since only about half as much wattage is needed.

Laundry. A partial load of laundry requires about the same wattage as a full load. Therefore, launder less frequently, but with full loads.

WATER CONSERVATION

The search for ways to better conserve home energy has expanded to conservation of water. One of the reasons that water shortages are predicted is that the same high-quality drinking and cooking water is also used for bathing, washing, and toilet flushing. It is possible to install a water supply system that recycles graywater (from tubs and sinks) for use in flushing. A filtration unit is a necessary part of the system. Another system recycles blackwater (flushing water) over and over again by directing it through a sewage treatment unit. Such a system, designed for use in commercial buildings, is available from Cromaglass Corporation, Box 3215, Williamsport, Pennsylvania 17701.

A third system reduces the amount of water required for each flushing from four gallons to only one gallon by using a high velocity, rather than a high volume, of flushing water. A major manufacturer is Briggs Plumbingware, 4350 W. Cypress St., Tampa, Florida 33607.

A fourth system uses no water for flushing at all. Rather, the toilet and kitchen wastes are collected in a form of compost pile. As shown in Figure 10, the wastes slide down an incline and are converted to humus. Although it takes about two years for the first humus to be produced, the process is then continuous and will produce about 5 gals./person/yr. It is manufactured by Clivus Multrum USA, 14A Eliot Street, Cambridge, Massachusetts 02138.

STUDY QUESTIONS

1. What action would you take to double the insulation value of an R-19 attic floor?
2. What action would you take to reduce to about half:
   a. Transmission loss through single-glazed windows
   b. Transmission loss through exterior doors
   c. Infiltration loss around exterior doors
3. List three methods to conserve:
   a. Heat

b. Hot water
c. Cold water
d. Electricity
e. Refrigeration

4. Given the following data, calculate the probable earth temperature at 10′ below the surface:

Average temperature during December to March: 35°F
Average temperature during April and May: 56°F
Average temperature during June to September: 68°F
Average temperature during October and November: 50°F

5. Distinguish between:
a. Double glazing and triple glazing
b. Graywater and blackwater

LABORATORY PROBLEMS

1. Prepare the insulation specifications for the A residence.
2. Prepare the insulation specifications for the building assigned by your instructor.
3. Prepare the insulation specifications for your original house design.
4. (For the advanced student) Design a building using nontraditional methods to conserve energy.

35 / Energy Sources

The history of the progress of civilization parallels the history of its wise use of the energy available coupled with development of new energy sources. Early energy sources included wood fires for heating and cooking, animal power for farming and land transportation, and wind power for sea transportation. Later, fossil fuels (coal, oil, and gas) were used to power machines such as steam engines and gasoline engines. Reliance on fossil fuels has increased to the extent that they now provide 95 percent of our energy. But it has become evident that these fuels are being rapidly depleted and will have to be conserved and replaced. A worldwide search for new energy sources has concentrated on nuclear reactions, synthetic fuels, ocean energy, geothermal ("earth's heat") energy, solar energy, and others. Some of these sources (such as solar energy) are renewable. Others (such as geothermal energy) are not, but are seldom tapped. The search for new sources of energy for buildings has concentrated on solar energy (see Chapter 33), wood energy, wind energy, and water energy. In most instances, these sources are able to provide only a small portion of our energy needs. Consequently, the designer must carefully investigate all the consequences of using "free" energy. No energy is really "free" since most energy becomes quite costly during its conversion to useful service.

WOOD ENERGY

For centuries wood provided the major source of energy in the United States. Even as late as 1900 almost half of our heat and power was supplied by burning wood. Today, in spite of the increased processing of wood to lumber and paper, there is an abundance of many wood species. This is due partly because of the decline of wood as a fuel and partly because many small Eastern farms have been converted back to forest land. In the search for additional energy, wood provides a partial answer. Also, when wood is intelligently harvested, it can be a renewable energy resource. Approximately five cords* of hardwood are needed to provide heat for an average home in a temperate climate. This could be provided by a woodlot of approximately ten acres. On a larger scale, wood plantations have been used as a "living filter" for disposal of treated sewage effluent. This serves the double purpose of increasing wood growth.

Wood furnaces. Wood-burning furnaces are available that provide hot water as well as hot air. They are fitted with wood storage features that permit wood to feed down as needed during a period of about twelve hours. They often are installed with a supplemental oil burner that automatically ignites when the wood supply burns out. All sources of combustion require safety measures, but the flues of wood furnaces, especially, must be cleaned frequently to avoid flue fires. And emission limits for wood furnaces require them to have catalytic converters to reduce toxic smoke pollution.

Fireplaces. Much of the heat in conventional fireplaces is lost by convection up the flue, but there are several methods of increasing efficiency. The fireplace liner described in Chapter 26 increases heating capacity by drawing in room air, warming it, and discharging it back to the room or to other rooms. A leading manufacturer of heat-circulating fireplace liners is Heatilator Inc. Division, HON

---

* A *cord* is a 4′ × 4′ × 8′ pile of wood.

328

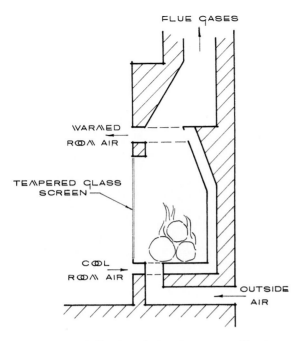

Figure 1 *A fireplace designed to use outside air.*

Industries, 1915 W. Saunders St., Mt. Pleasant, Iowa 52641.

Further efficiency can be achieved by designing the fireplace and chimney so that outside air is used to help support combustion rather than the already-heated house air. When a fireplace is designed to operate on outside air (as shown in Figure 1), a tempered glass door is used to separate the outside air within the fireplace from the house air. The fireplace will then provide heat to the house by means of a fireplace liner such as just described.

The efficiency of existing traditional fireplaces can also be improved by partially enclosing the fireplace opening with glass doors as shown in Figure 2. The doors have air intake dampers below and air outlets above. Cool air is pulled in through the lower damper, heated by the fire, and then directed back to the room rather than up the flue. Also, sufficient air is introduced into the fireplace to support combustion. A leading manufacturer is the American Stovalator Corporation, P.O. Box 1069, East Manchester Rd., Manchester Center, Vermont 05255.

Another method of increasing the heating capacity of a traditional fireplace is by means of a hollow fireplace grate. As shown in Figure 3, cool room air is drawn into hollow pipe grates at the base, warmed by the fire, and discharged back to the room from the top. Efficiency is further increased by grates with electrically driven blower units. These units are manufactured by Thermograte, 301 East Tennessee Street, Florence, Alabama 35631.

WIND ENERGY

For centuries wind was used to move ships, mill grain, and pump water. Today only about fifty thousand working windmills are operating in the

Figure 2 *Tempered glass doors with air ducts increase fireplace efficiency.*

Courtesy of Thermograte.

Courtesy of Thermograte.

Figure 3   *A hollow fireplace grate increases heating capacity.*

Courtesy of Automatic Power Division of Pennwalt Corporation.

Figure 5   *An upwind propeller-type wind machine.*

United States. However, the windmill is experiencing a rebirth in the search for additional energy sources. Two principal manufacturers are Aermotor Division, Braden Industries, Box 1364, Conway, Arizona 72032; and Dempster Industries, P.O. Box 848, Beatrice, Nebraska 68310. Windmills are available with fans in sizes from 6′ to 16′ in diameter. Pumping capacities start at 100 gal./hr. and go up to 3,000 gal./hr.

Figure 6   *A 100-kw depression-type generator.*

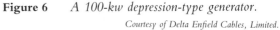

Courtesy of Delta Enfield Cables, Limited.

Figure 4   *Traditional water-pumping windmill.*

There are many forms of wind machines that differ from the traditional water-pumping wind-mill of Figure 4. The *propeller-type* (Figure 5) has propeller blades similar to an aircraft's blades. There are upwind types (with tail vanes) that face the wind and downwind types (without tail vanes) that face away from the wind.

A *depression-type* wind machine (Figure 6) operates in yet another fashion. Its function is not to drive any mechanism by direct gearing but rather to create a partial vacuum within the tubular tower so that air is drawn into the turbine situated in the base of the tower, thus driving an alternator. The propeller blades are hollow and have orifices at their tips through which the air contained in them is expelled by centrifugal force, thus reducing the pressure in the hub and tower interior.

The *Savonius rotor* (Figure 7) is balanced on a vertical shaft and has several curved vanes to catch the wind. A horizontal-shaft windmill must be able to rotate toward the wind, but a vertical-shaft rotor has the advantage that it always faces the wind.

The *Darrieus rotor* (Figure 8) is also balanced on a vertical shaft, but it has thin, curved blades which can rotate at high speed. A 65' unit manufactured by DAF Indal Ltd., 3570 Hawkstone Rd., Mississauga, Ontario, Canada L5C2V8 has a 50kw output.

If the wind is used to provide energy or pump water for a single building, it would be expected that the wind machine would be integrated into the overall design. Occasionally a wind energy collector and a solar energy collector will both be installed on a single building, for the wind often blows when the sun isn't shining. Of course all designs must be able to withstand high winds without damage. Also they must not disturb the occupants by excess noise or vibration.

WATER ENERGY

Hydroelectric turbines. Although flowing river water produces the energy for many large-scale hydroelectric turbines, water is seldom used to provide energy for a single building since the number of suitable sites obviously is limited. Even those persons who are fortunate enough to have a home near a river with sufficient volume, velocity, and head (vertical drop) may not be permitted to interfere with the natural flow.

Hydraulic rams. Many farms have hydraulic rams which use the energy of moving water to pump a portion of the water to storage at a higher level. As shown in Figure 9, when the rush of the

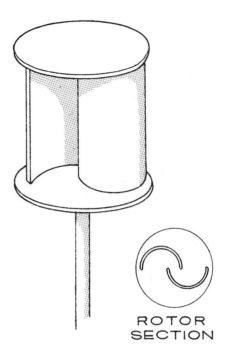

Figure 7 *Savonius rotor.*

Figure 8 *Installing a Darrieus rotor.*

Courtesy of DAF-Indal, Limited.

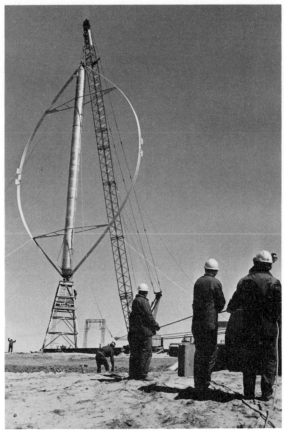

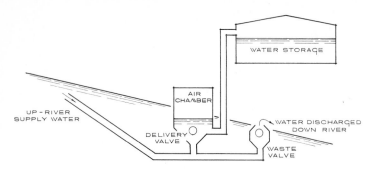

Figure 9 *Hydraulic ram used to raise water.*

supply water closes the waste valve, the momentum of the suddenly checked current opens the delivery valve and forces water into the air chamber, thus compressing the air. The compressed air shuts the delivery valve and forces water up to storage. When the waste valve drops open, the operation starts to repeat. A hydraulic ram having a 50-gal./min. intake with a head of 8′ will pump about 9.6 gal./min. to a height of 25′. More delivery height can be obtained by increasing the intake volume, increasing the head, or decreasing the delivery volume. A principal manufacturer of hydraulic rams is Rife Hydraulic Engine Manufacturing Company, P.O. Box 790, Norristown, Pennsylvania 19401.

STUDY QUESTIONS

1. Describe briefly each of the following terms:
    a. Cord of wood
    b. Head of water
    c. Fossil fuels
    d. Living filter
    e. Hydraulic ram
    f. Turbine
2. What is the difference between:
    a. Solar energy and geothermal energy
    b. Propeller-type and depression-type wind machines
    c. Darrieus rotor and Savonius rotor
3. List four methods of increasing fireplace efficiency.
4. List four types of nontraditional wind machines.
5. What is the advantage of:
    a. A vertical- over a horizontal-shaft wind machine
    b. A vertical- over a horizontal-shaft water turbine.

LABORATORY PROBLEMS

1. For the building assigned by your instructor, draw the mechanical details of its nontraditional energy source.
2. For your original house design, prepare the details for:
    a. A supplemental wood-burning heating system
    b. A wind energy source
    c. A water energy source
3. (For the advanced student) Design a building using a nontraditional:
    a. Heating source
    b. Hot-water heating source
    c. Electrical power source

IX / Presentation Drawing

36 / Perspective

In addition to *working drawings,* an architectural drafter must be able to prepare *presentation drawings.* A presentation drawing is used to help describe, or *present,* the proposed building to the client. For this purpose, a *perspective drawing* is nearly always used since it shows the appearance of the finished building exactly. Even persons trained in other types of drawing are able to visualize a design better in perspective. The architectural drafter, for example, will prepare thumbnail perspectives of each alternate scheme so that the most satisfactory design can be chosen.

A perspective drawing shows exactly how the building will appear to the eye or to a camera. The illustrator in Figure 1, drawing on a window with a wax pencil, will obtain the same perspective as a camera—as long as the relative positions of the observer, object, and picture plane are identical.

THREE TYPES OF PERSPECTIVE

If the picture plane is placed parallel to a face of the object, the resulting perspective is called a *one-point perspective.* If it is placed parallel to one set of lines (usually vertical lines), the resulting perspective is called a *two-point perspective.* When the picture plane is oblique to all of the object's lines and faces, a *three-point perspective* results (see Figure 3).

The two-point perspective is more commonly used than either the one-point or three-point perspective. A one-point perspective of the exterior of a building is unsatisfactory for most purposes since it looks very much like a standard elevation drawing. Room interiors, however, may well be drawn in one-point perspective, as shown in Figure 2. A three-point perspective of a building

exterior is not often used since it means that the observer must be looking *up* at the building (*worm's-eye view*) or *down* on the building (*bird's-eye view,* Figure 4). Obviously, neither of these is considered a normal line of sight.

There are many methods of obtaining a two-point perspective, but the most often used are the *common method* (Figures 5-13), the *direct projection method* (Figure 14), and the *perspective grid method* (Figure 15). Let us look at each.

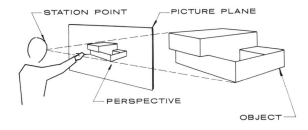

Figure 1   *Perspective sketch.*

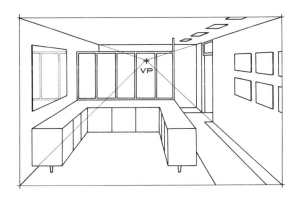

Figure 2   *One-point interior perspective.*

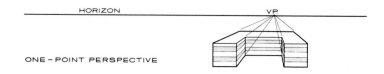

ONE – POINT PERSPECTIVE

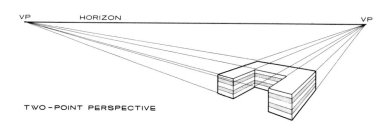

TWO – POINT PERSPECTIVE

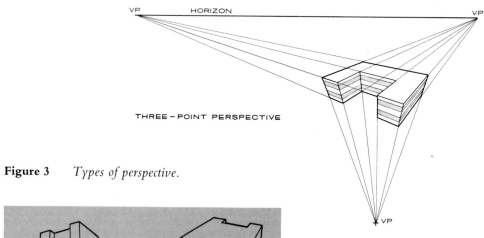

THREE – POINT PERSPECTIVE

Figure 3 *Types of perspective.*

WORM'S-EYE VIEW   BIRD'S-EYE VIEW

Figure 4 *Three-point perspective.*

TWO-POINT PERSPECTIVE BY THE COMMON METHOD

Step 1: Locate the plan view behind the picture plane so that the front face is inclined 30° and the desired end face is inclined 60° to the picture plane. Actually, any set of complementary angles may be used, but the 30°–60° combination is most often used.

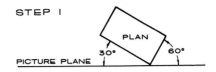

Step 2: Select any elevation view and position it on the ground line. Locate the horizon 6′ (to scale) above the ground line. This means the eye of the observer is 6′ above the ground. Other eye heights may be used if desired.

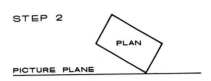

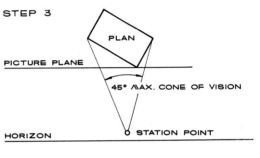

Step 3: Locate the station point (representing the location of the eye of the observer) directly in front of the plan view with a 45° maximum cone of vision. Occasionally a greater cone of vision angle is used to produce more dramatic results. The station point, however, should not be moved sideways because it will give a distorted perspective that does not represent the true proportions of the building.

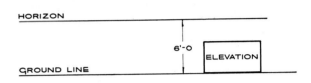

Step 4: Find both vanishing points. In two-point perspective, a vanishing point is the perspective of the far end of an infinitely long horizontal line. The vanishing point for all horizontal lines extending 60° to the right (VPR) is found by drawing a parallel sight line 60° to the right until it intersects the picture plane. This is the plan view of the VPR. The perspective view of the VPR is found by projecting from the plan view down to the horizon. The VPL (vanishing point left) is located in a similar manner.

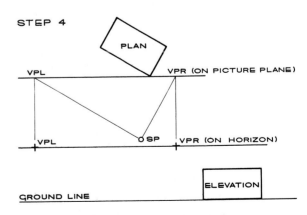

Figure 5   *Two-point perspective by the common method.*

STEP 5

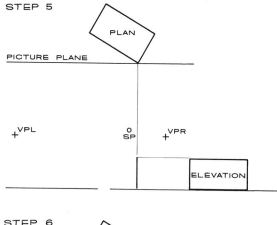

Step 5: Only lines located on the picture plane are shown true length in a perspective drawing. If a line is behind the picture plane, it will appear shorter; if it is in front, it will appear longer. Project the front corner that is located on the picture plane to the perspective view and lay off its true height by projecting from the elevation view.

STEP 6

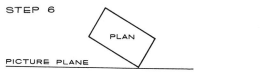

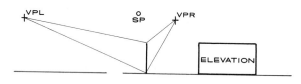

Step 6: Find the perspective of horizontal lines by projecting from the vertical true-length line to the vanishing points.

STEP 7

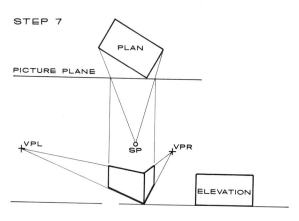

Step 7: Draw sight lines from the station point to the corners of the plan view. The intersections of these sight lines with the picture plane are projected to the perspective view to find the extreme corners.

STEP 8

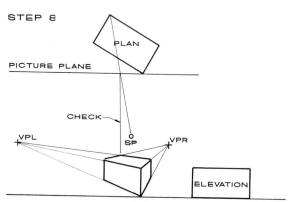

Step 8: Complete the perspective by projecting from the extreme corners to the vanishing points. The far corner may be checked by projecting from the picture plane. Notice that invisible lines are omitted in a perspective drawing.

Figure 5 *continued*

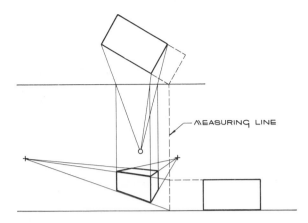

Figure 6   *Use of the measuring line.*

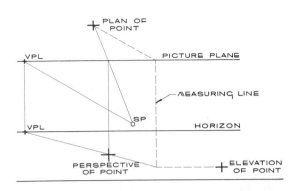

Figure 7   *Perspective of a point.*

Measuring line.   In the preceding step-by-step illustration of the common method of drawing two-point perspective, the plan view was located so that the front corner touched the picture plane. This corner, then, was used to show the true height of the object in the perspective drawing. Occasionally *no* line in the plan view is located on the picture plane. When this occurs, as in Figure 6, a *measuring line* must be used. Simply imagine the plan view to be extended until a corner touches the picture plane. This corner is then projected to the perspective drawing for the true-height measurement.

Perspective of a point.   Figure 7 shows the method of finding the perspective of any point. This is a very useful exercise because the perspective of the most complicated object can be constructed merely by finding the perspectives of a sufficient number of points on the object. The perspective of an inclined line, for example, can be constructed by finding the perspective of both ends of the line. The perspective of a curved line can be constructed by finding the perspective of a number of points along the line.

Vanishing points of inclined lines.   Figure 8 shows that vanishing points of *inclined* lines (such as the inclined rafters of the shed roof) will lie directly above or below the vanishing point of horizontal lines that are in the same plane. Figure 8 also shows that vanishing points of all *horizontal* lines (such as the top and bottom rails of the open shed door) will always lie on the horizon.

Enlarging a perspective drawing.   Often a perspective layout requires so much additional drawing space for the plan, elevation, and vanishing points that the resulting perspective drawing is smaller than desired. A number of "tricks" may be used to correct this.

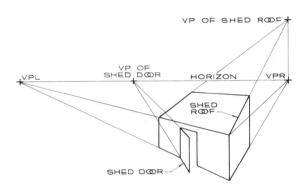

Figure 8   *Finding vanishing points.*

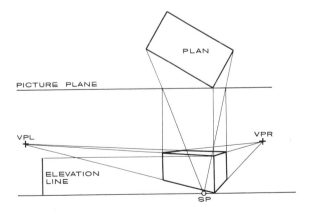

Figure 9   *Overlapping views.*

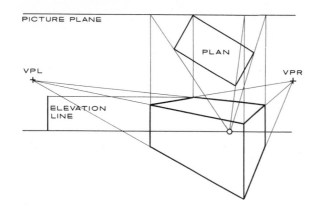

Figure 10   *Plan in front of picture plane.*

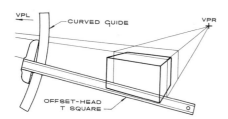

Figure 11   *Use of curved guide.*

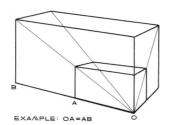

Figure 12   *Use of radiating lines.*

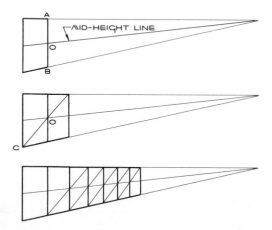

Figure 13   *Spacing of lines.*

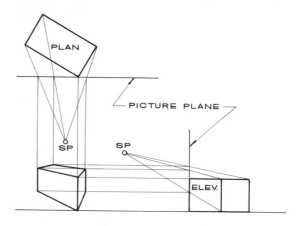

Figure 14   *Direct projection method.*

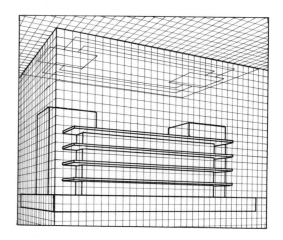

Figure 15   *Perspective grid method.*

1. Overlap the plan, elevation, and perspective drawings. Also, only an elevation *line* is needed — not an entire elevation view (Figure 9).
2. Place the plan view *in front* of the picture plane to obtain larger perspectives (Figure 10).
3. Allow the vanishing points to fall beyond the limits of the paper (Figure 11). The vanishing points may fall off the drawing table entirely. In this case, a curved cardboard strip is prepared so that the T square will project non-parallel lines.
4. A perspective can be enlarged by the use of radiating lines. Each radiating line shown in Figure 12 has been doubled in size. There are many other enlarging devices (such as pantographs) that may be used.

Spacing of lines. In perspective drawing, it is often desirable to show features that are evenly spaced without going through the trouble of projecting from the plan and elevation views. For

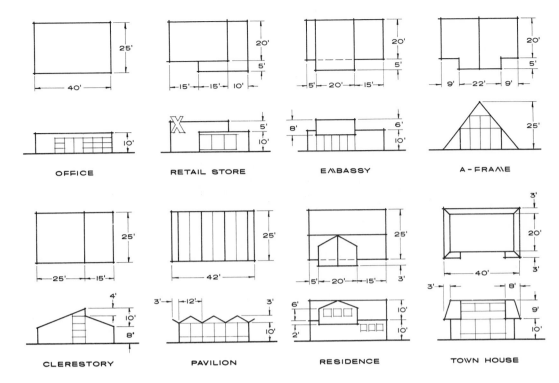

Figure 16

example, a row of adjacent windows will appear smaller as they recede into the distance. If the first window is drawn in perspective, adjacent windows may be found as follows (Figure 13):

1. Draw a mid-height ($OA = OB$) line to the vanishing point.
2. Draw a diagonal (CO) and project it to locate the adjacent window.
3. Repeat as often as required to accurately locate each window.

DIRECT PROJECTION

The direct projection method of perspective drawing is similar to the common method with the exception of the addition of the end elevation view of the object, station point, and picture plane (Figure 14). Perspective widths are obtained as previously, by projecting from the plan view, and perspective heights are obtained by projecting from the end elevation view. This system has the advantage of not requiring a measuring line. In fact, even the vanishing points may be omitted if desired. In this case, however, very accurate projection is required.

PERSPECTIVE GRIDS

Perhaps the simplest method of constructing a perspective drawing is by the use of prepared grid sheets obtainable in a number of sizes (Figure 15).

The perspective may be drawn directly on these grids or on tracing overlays.

STUDY QUESTIONS

1. What is the principal difference between one-, two-, and three-point perspective? When is each used?
2. Sketch a two-point perspective layout of a simple object and label the picture plane, horizon, station point, right and left vanishing points, plan view, elevation view, and perspective view.
   a. Use the common method
   b. Use the direct method
3. Sketch a two-point perspective layout illustrating the correct method to obtain the perspective of a horizontal line making an angle of 30° with the picture plane.
   a. Use the common method
   b. Use the direct method
4. Sketch a two-point perspective layout illustrating the correct method to obtain the perspective of a point.
   a. Use the common method
   b. Use the direct method
5. Give the four methods used to enlarge a perspective drawing.

LABORATORY PROBLEMS

1. Prepare two-point perspectives of the buildings shown in Figure 16. Use the method assigned by your instructor.
2. Prepare a two-point perspective of the A residence.
3. Prepare a two-point perspective of the building assigned by your instructor.
4. Prepare a two-point perspective of your original house design.

37 / Shadows

A knowledge of shadows is important to both the architectural designer and the architectural drafter. The designer will consider the effect of shadows upon the proposals. The drafter will show these shadows on the presentation drawings to give them an extra three-dimensional quality.

Historically, shadows have greatly influenced architectural design. For example, Greek architecture evolved in a latitude where the bright sunlight exquisitely modeled the bas-relief carvings and fluted columns. Gothic cathedrals would lose their mystic beauty in the same climate. Today, much emphasis is given to the sun shielding and the patterns created by overhangs. In some instances, the shadows may be a major element in the final solution.

TERMINOLOGY

In a study of shadows, these terms should be understood (Figure 1):

Shade: A surface turned away from light
Umbra: The space from which light is excluded by the shaded surface
Shadow: A surface from which light is excluded by the shaded surface

Of the three, only the umbra is never shown on a drawing. Shaded surfaces are usually shown as a light gray, and shadows are shown as a darker gray or black. It is very easy to determine the surfaces in shade since they are merely the surfaces turned away from the direct rays of light. Shadows, though, are harder to find.

MULTIVIEW SHADOWS

Presentation drawings may include elevation views and a plot plan rendered to give a pictorial quality. Shadows are always included as shown in Figure 2 to increase the three-dimensional appearance.

In architectural renderings it is conventional to employ a distant source of light (the sun) as the basis for establishing the shade and shadow lines. The sun's rays are parallel and are usually assumed to have the direction of the diagonal of a cube extending from the upper left front to the lower right rear as shown in Figure 3. This is a convenient direction since the orthographic views of this diagonal are 45° lines.

To find shadows in multiview projection, two rules are used:

Rule 1 The shadow of a point upon a plane may be easily found in the view showing the plane as an edge.

Rule 2 The shadow of a line may be found by first

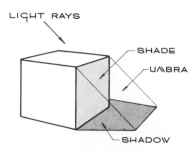

Figure 1   *Terminology.*

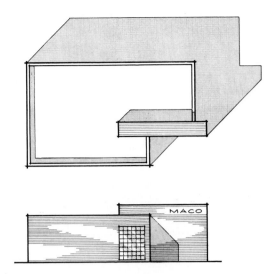

Figure 2   *Multiview shadows.*

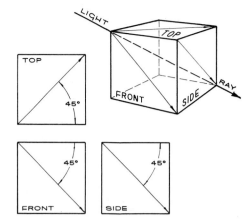

Figure 3   *Conventional light direction in multiview drawing.*

finding the shadows of both ends of the line and then connecting these points.

EXAMPLE

Find the shadow cast upon the ground by a flat-roofed structure (see Figure 4).

Step 1: The points A, B, and C will cast shadows upon the ground. Therefore draw lines through both views of these points parallel to the light direction (45°).

Step 2: Find where these 45° lines intersect the ground plane. This is found in the front view since the ground plane appears as an edge in the front view (rule 1).
Project from the front view to the top view.

Step 3: Connect the shadows of points A, B, and C (rule 2).

A_sB_s represents the shadow of line AB.
B_sC_s represents the shadow of line BC.

Notice that the shadow of a line upon a parallel plane will appear as a parallel line.

AA_s and CC_s represent the shadows of vertical lines (rule 2).

Figures 5–16 show the multiview shadows cast by a variety of architectural shapes. Study each to find how the shadows were determined.

SHADOWS IN PERSPECTIVE—PARALLEL LIGHT RAYS

There are two methods of constructing the shadow of a building in a perspective drawing:

1. The shadow may be first obtained in the multi-view drawings and then projected to the per-

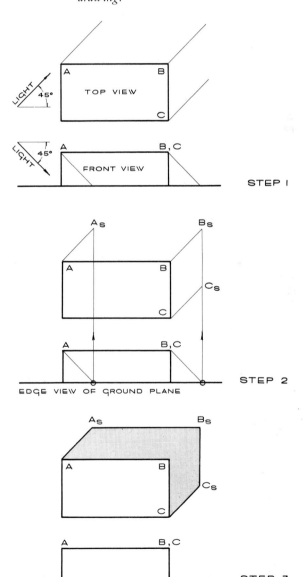

Figure 4   *Finding a shadow in a multiview projection (new steps in dark blue).*

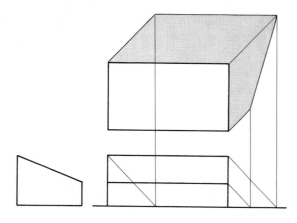

Figure 5   *Shed roof.*

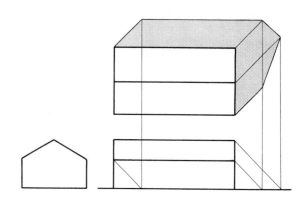

Figure 6   *Gable roof.*

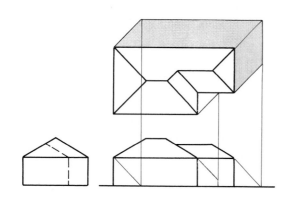

Figure 7   *Hip roof.*

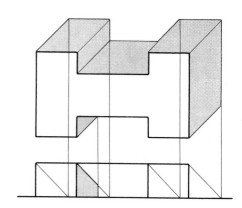

Figure 8   *Irregular plan.*

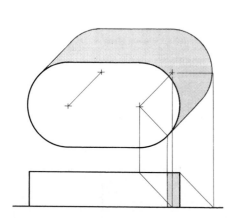

Figure 9   *Rounded plan.*

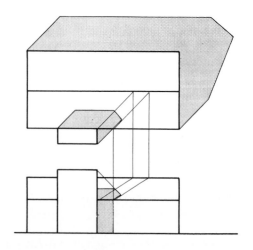

Figure 10   *Chimney.*

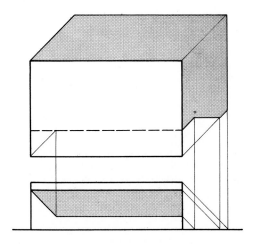

Figure 11   *Flat-roof overhang.*

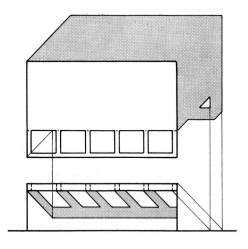

Figure 12   *Open overhang.*

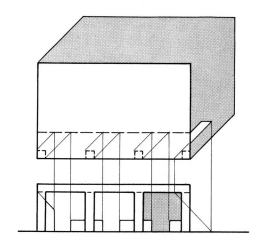

Figure 13   *Colonnade.*

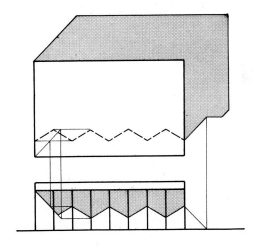

Figure 14   *Accordion wall.*

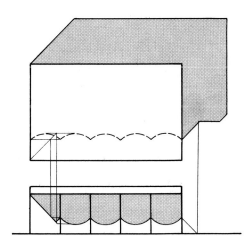

Figure 15   *Fluted wall.*

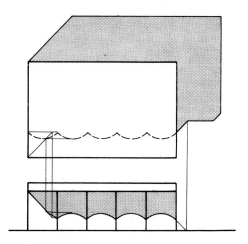

Figure 16   *Beaded wall.*

spective view in the same manner as any other line. This method is easy to understand but requires more work.

2. The shadow may be constructed directly in the perspective view. This method requires a bit of explanation but is often used since it is shorter and more direct. To further simplify this method, the direction of light rays is assumed to be parallel to the picture plane and to make

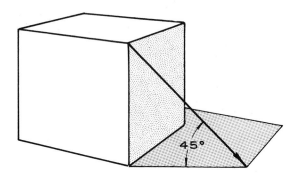

Figure 17 *Conventional light direction in perspective.*

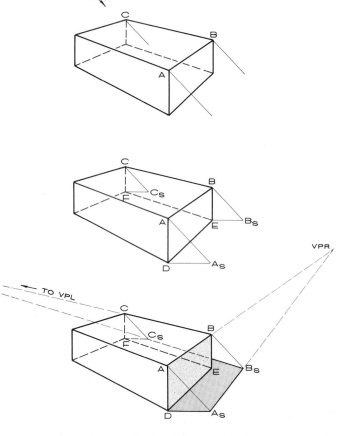

Figure 18 *Shadow in perspective (new steps in dark blue).*

an angle of 45° (or some other convenient angle) with the ground, as shown in Figure 17.

To find shadows in a perspective view, two rules are again used:

Rule 1 The shadow of a vertical line upon the ground (or any horizontal plane) is a horizontal line.

Rule 2 The shadow of a horizontal line upon the ground (or any horizontal plane) is parallel to the line.

EXAMPLE

Find the shadow cast upon the ground by a flat-roofed structure (Figure 18).

Step 1: The points *A*, *B*, and *C* will cast shadows upon the ground. Therefore draw 45° lines through these points parallel to the assumed light direction.

Step 2: Find where the 45° lines intersect the ground plane by drawing horizontal lines from points *D*, *E*, and *F* (rule 1).

DA_s represents the shadow of line *DA*.
EB_s represents the shadow of line *EB*.
FC_s represents the shadow of line *FC*.

Step 3: Connect the shadows of points *A*, *B*, and *C*.

A_sB_s represents the shadow of line *AB* and appears parallel to line *AB* (rule 2).
B_sC_s represents the shadow of line *BC* and appears parallel to line *BC* (rule 2).

Notice that these lines will not be drawn exactly parallel to each other, but will be connected to their vanishing points.

Figures 19–26 show the perspective shadows cast by a variety of architectural shapes. As before, study each to learn how the shadows were determined.

SHADOWS IN PERSPECTIVE— OBLIQUE LIGHT RAYS

In perspective drawing, a shadow found by light rays parallel to the picture plane is not always entirely satisfactory. Although it is a difficult process, finding the shadow may be accomplished by using light rays oblique to the picture plane. The main difference is that the light rays must be drawn from their vanishing point rather than 45° with the ground. Figure 27 illustrates how the vanishing point of the light rays is found.

In actual practice, shadows are seldom determined by accurate construction since this is a time-consuming process. Rather, architectural

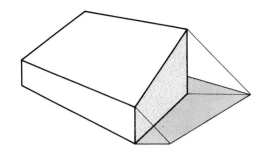

Figure 19   *Shed roof.*

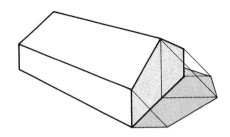

Figure 20   *Gable roof.*

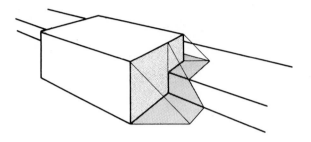

Figure 21   *Offset surface.*

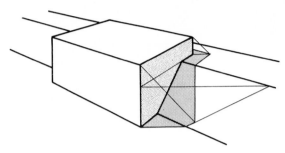

Figure 22   *Sloping surface.*

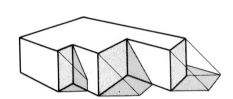

Figure 23   *Irregular plan.*

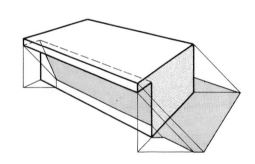

Figure 24   *Flat-roof overhang.*

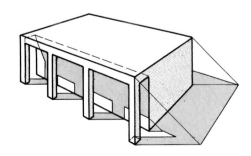

Figure 25   *Colonnade.*

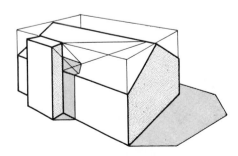

Figure 26   *Chimney.*

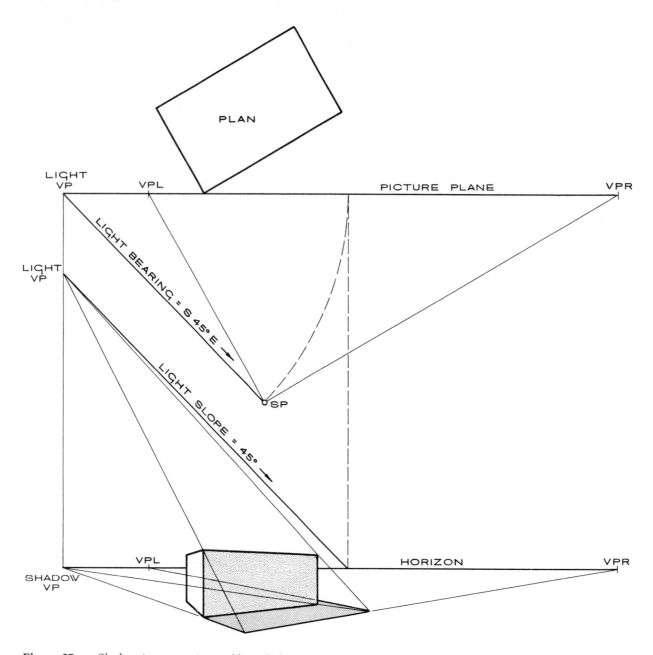

Figure 27 *Shadow in perspective—oblique light rays.*

drafters draw upon their knowledge of the general form of shadows to estimate the position and shape of the shadows. After a little experience, a fairly accurate estimation is possible.

SHADOW INTENSITY

In addition to determining the location of a shadow, the architectural drafter must also make decisions concerning the intensity of the shadow, which may vary from black to a very light tone. This variation is due principally to the amount of light reflected upon the surface. This reflected light causes shadows to assume varying tones rather than one uniform tone. This variation may be useful for several purposes: to sharpen the shadow outline, to show changes in the direction of adjacent surfaces, to express changes in the depth of receding surfaces, and to show changes in surface texture. In general, the drafter must use a great deal of imagination and "artistic license" to obtain the desired result.

STUDY QUESTIONS

1. Define each of the following:
   a. Shade
   b. Umbra
2. What is meant by *conventional light direction?* Why is it used?
3. Give two methods that may be used to find the shadow of a building in a perspective drawing.
4. Give a method that may be used to find the shadow of any line.
5. Give four reasons to vary shadow intensity.

LABORATORY PROBLEMS

1. Add shadows to the two-point perspectives you drew for problem 1 of Chapter 36. Use the method assigned by your instructor.
2. Add shadows to (a) the presentation drawing and (b) the perspective of the A residence.
3. Add shadows to (a) the presentation drawing and (b) the perspective of the building assigned by your instructor.
4. Add shadows to (a) the presentation drawing and (b) the perspective of your original house design.

38 / Architectural Rendering

The ability to prepare a finished rendering is a desirable goal for every architectural drafter. Even a large architectural firm with a separate art department occasionally needs help to meet a deadline. Smaller offices must depend upon the regular staff for renderings or send the work out to companies specializing in presentation drawings. These companies produce excellent results but, of course, time and coordination must be considered.

Since a rendering shows a structure as it actually appears to the eye, it is used for presentation drawings that will be seen by clients who, in all likelihood, cannot read ordinary blueprints. As a matter of fact, the quality of the rendering may well influence the final decision of the client to continue with the proposed building. Most clients feel (and rightly so) that the finished product will look and function no better than the drawings. In addition to finished renderings, the architectural draftsman should be able to make quick sketches of alternate solutions to a problem to show to the architect who makes the final decision.

TYPES OF RENDERING

There are many kinds of renderings. Among the most common are:

Pencil
Pen-and-ink
Marker
Scratch-board
Appliqué
Watercolor
Tempera
Spray

Photographic
Combination of the preceding

In this chapter we will study each of these techniques—putting the emphasis upon those that will be most useful to you. *Pencil rendering* is most often used since it requires no special equipment and is very versatile. Drawings from small, quick sketches all the way up to large, finished presentation displays can be rendered in pencil. *Ink,* however, is preferred for drawings to be reproduced in media such as newspapers, books, and brochures. *Appliqués* offer a quick and effective method of applying a professional-looking shading. *Scratchboard* is occasionally used, as is *watercolor*. *Tempera* applied by brush or spray is the normal medium used by the professional artist for a colored rendering.

PENCIL RENDERING

Pencil rendering is the most popular form of rendering because it is quick, errors are easily corrected, no special equipment is needed, and it is very versatile. Pencil renderings range from rough freehand sketches to accurate drawings using a straightedge for outlines and shading.

Pencils. The softer lead grades are used in pencil rendering. Although the final choice will depend upon the paper texture and personal preference, the following selection is ordinarily satisfactory:

2H for layout
F for medium-tone rendering
2B for dark tones

A sharp conical point is used for the layout work and detailing, but a flat chisel point is used to obtain the broad rendering strokes.

Paper. The paper selected should take pencil lines and erasures nicely. Bristol board, Strathmore paper, and tracing vellum meet these requirements. Fine- or coarse-textured paper may be used depending upon the result desired. During rendering, keep the paper clean by working with a paper shield under your hand. A fixative spray is used to protect the finished rendering from smudges.

Textures. The success of a pencil rendering depends, to a large extent, upon the ability of the drafter to indicate the proper texture of surfaces and materials. Some of the most common materials encountered are:

Glass and mirrored surfaces (Figure 1). Small areas are quite simply rendered by blackening with a 2B pencil. Larger window areas may be toned from a dark corner to an opposite light corner. Very large expanses of glass, however, require more thought. Normally some of the surroundings are shown reflected in the glass. Highlights are made with an eraser and erasing shield. If desired, the glass rendering may be omitted in order to show interior features.

Brick. Brick surfaces are indicated by closely spaced lines made with a flat-pointed F pencil. The length of the lines does not matter since the horizontal brick joints are more important to show than the vertical joints (see Figure 2).

Stone. Stone surfaces are rendered by drawing a few individual stones, leaving large expanses of "white" space. In Figure 3, notice that the shadow line is darkest near its extremity.

Roof. Shingled roofs are shown by long, closely spaced lines—somewhat like brick. The lines may fade into light areas as in Figure 4. Built-up roofs, concrete, and plaster are stippled.

Foliage. A variety of foliage can be shown by varying the stroking and the pencil grade as shown in Figure 5. Usually, however, a single foliage type is selected and repeated in various sizes rather than mixing different types.

Procedure. The usual procedure for rendering in pencil follows. We will use the A residence for illustration (see Figure 6).

Step 1: A rough pencil sketch is made to determine the most suitable perspective angle, light

Figure 1   *Glass renderings.*

Figure 2   *Brick rendering.*

Figure 3   *Stone rendering.*

Figure 4   *Shingled-roof rendering.*

Figure 5   *Pencil grades indicate depth and texture.*

STEP 1

STEP 2

STEP 3

STEP 4

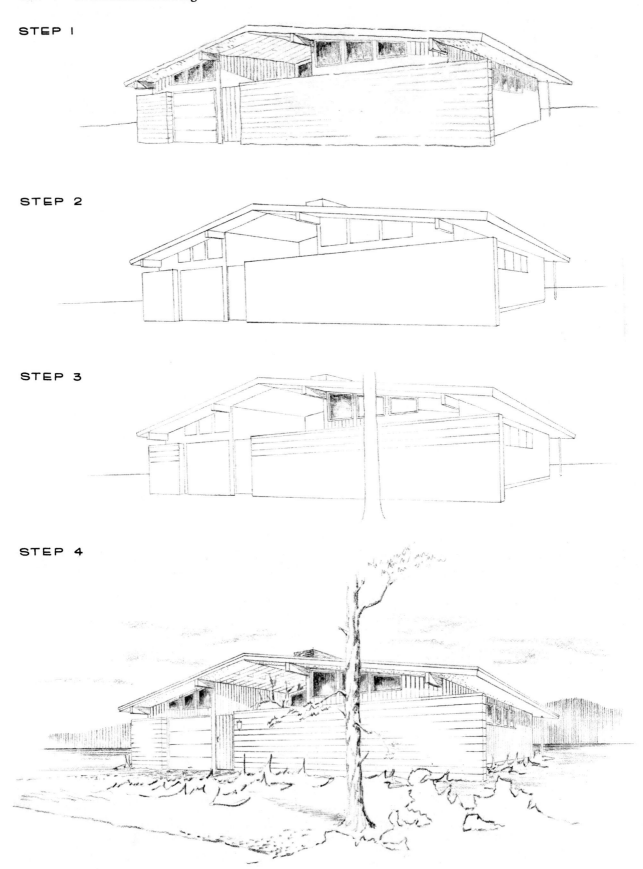

Figure 6 *The procedure for pencil rendering.*

direction, and shadow locations. In general, there should be a balance between white, black, and gray areas.

Step 2: Transfer the mechanically drawn perspective to the finished paper. Outline with a sharp 2H line. Portions of these outlines may be erased later to provide highlights (bright areas).

Step 3: Render the central structure using an F or 2B pencil, depending upon the desired blackness. Windows are done first, followed by walls and roofs.

Step 4: Render the foreground details followed by the background elements. Use an eraser to provide highlights.

Study Figures 7–10 for examples of different techniques in pencil rendering.

Color. Pencil renderings may be colored with light watercolor washes. Select the colors carefully

Figure 7 *Pencil sketch of a summer camp. A successful sketch must blend perspective, shadows, and rendering.*

Courtesy of Scholz Homes, Inc.

Figure 8 *Showing texture and shading in pencil rendering.*

Courtesy of Scholz Homes, Inc.

Figure 9 *Professional pencil renderings. Study these examples and start a collection of additional samples of pencil renderings.*

to prevent disappointing results. Colored pencils are often used on colored mat boards. Monochromatic schemes (various tones and shades of one color) are particularly effective. White pencil or ink is used for highlighting.

INK RENDERING

Black ink rendering is the most suitable medium for drawings to be reproduced by any of the printing processes. Colored drawing inks are occasionally used for display drawings. Ink rendering differs from pencil rendering in that the shades of gray are more difficult to obtain. A wash of ink diluted with water may be used, but usually shading is done by varying the width of stroke or spacing between strokes as shown in Figures 11 and 12. The stippling technique (Figure 13) is also often used. Notice that the completely black shading in Figure 14 requires that the mortar joints be changed from black to white.

Paper. The paper used for ink rendering must take ink without fuzzing, allow ink erasures, and be smooth-surfaced. Some satisfactory materials are:

    Mat boards (available in white and colors)
    Bristol boards, plate surface
    Strathmore paper, plate surface
    Tracing paper (use only better-quality)
    Tracing cloth

Figure 10   *Window rendering.*

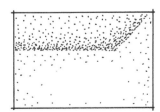

Figure 11   *Vertical siding.*

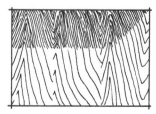

Figure 12   *Plywood.*

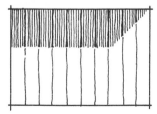

Figure 13   *Concrete.*

Figure 14   *Stone.*

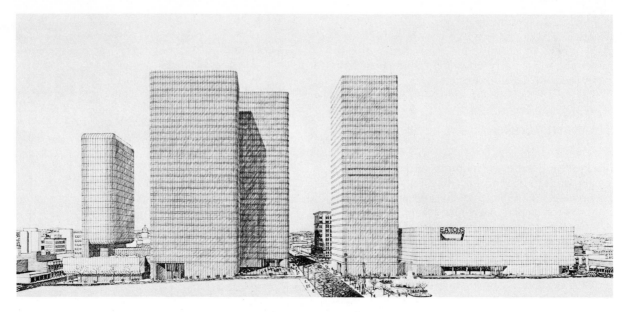

Figure 15   *An ink-and-pencil rendering of Canada's Pacific Centre, Vancouver, British Columbia.*

Figure 16   *Ink rendering.*

Figure 17   *Realistic rendering obtained by rapid ink strokes.*

Pens. The technical fountain pen or ordinary pen nibs and holder may be used. A ruling pen (drafting pen), of course, is not used to draw freehand lines. Technical fountain pen points are sized:

00 Fine
 0 Medium fine
 1 Medium
 2 Medium heavy
 3 Heavy

The most popular pen nibs are:

Crow-quill: Hunt 102 or Gillott 659   Very fine
Hawk-quill: Hunt 107 or Gillott 837   Fine
Round-pointed: Hunt 99 or Gillott 170   Medium
Bowl-pointed: Hunt 512 or Speedball B-6 Heavy

Inks. Satisfactory drawing inks are produced by Higgins, Weber, and Pelikan. The following colored inks are available. Other shades are obtained by mixing.

Yellow	Violet	Brick red
Orange	Blue	Russet
Red orange	Turquoise	Brown
Red	Green	Indigo
Carmine red	Leaf green	White
Red violet	Neutral tint	Black

Ink erasing is done with a pencil eraser to prevent damage to the paper's surface. A sharp razor blade is used to pick off small ink portions.

Procedure. The usual procedure for an ink rendering is the following:

1. Make a charcoal study or rough ink sketch to determine the most suitable light direction and shadow locations. Try to obtain a balance between white, black, and gray areas.
2. Outline lightly in pencil on finished paper.
3. Ink in outlines with fine lines (unless the surfaces are to be defined by shading differences only).
4. Render each feature separately—first windows, then walls, and so on, working from foreground to background.

The student wishing to learn the technique of ink rendering would be well advised to copy a good rendering before attempting an original. Also, he should start a collection of ink renderings by various artists so that he can study the numerous methods of handling the details. In Figure 15, ink was used for outlines, but pencil was used for shading. In Figure 16, notice how the entourage is subordinated to direct your attention to the pavilion structure. Also notice that every shingle and blade of grass need not be drawn. Figures 17-19 show ink renderings drawn with a coarser pen in a freer style. Ruled ink lines were used in Figure 20.

MARKER RENDERING

Markers are usually called *Magic Markers* (a trade name), but *AD Markers, Design Art Markers,* and other companies manufacture markers in over 100 colors, tints, and degrees of transparency. Point widths are available from very fine to broad brush. Markers can be used successfully on a medium of any color or thickness. They have the advantage of drying quickly and, unlike watercolors, they do not wrinkle tracing vellum.

SCRATCH BOARD

A simple method to create a rendering of white lines on a black background is provided by a *scratch board,* which is a board having a white, chalky surface. The surface is coated with black ink, and a rendering is obtained by drawing with a sharp-pointed stylus. The stylus will scratch through the black coating, leaving a white line. A knife-edged tool is used to whiten larger areas. If desired, large portions of the scratch board may be left white (not coated with black ink). In these areas, ink rendering is done in the usual manner.

The pictorial detail at the bottom of Figure 19 was done on scratch board.

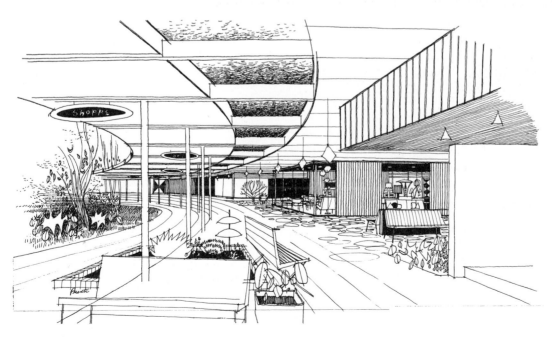

Figure 18   *Ink rendering.*

The labels visible in the detail drawings include: FLASHING, FASCIA, JOIST, HEADER, WIRE LATH, PLATE, PLASTER TRIM, MASONITE SHADOWVENT, METAL CHANNEL, ROYALCOTE WALNUT, BUILDING PAPER, SHEATHING, INSULATION, MASONITE SHADOWVENT, 2" x 4" STUDS, PLATE, MASONITE PRESDWOOD 1/4" STARTER STRIP, ANCHOR BOLT, 2" x 4" PLATE (NAILER FOR RIDGELINE), 2" x 6", 5/16" MASONITE RIDGELINE, BATTENS NAILED INTO 2" x 4" POSTS SPACED 24" O.C.

Figure 19 *Scratch-board rendering.*

Figure 20 *Ink rendering of proposed interior, United Nations Organizations Headquarters.*

Figure 21   *Typical appliqué patterns.*

Figure 22   *Typical appliqué symbols.*

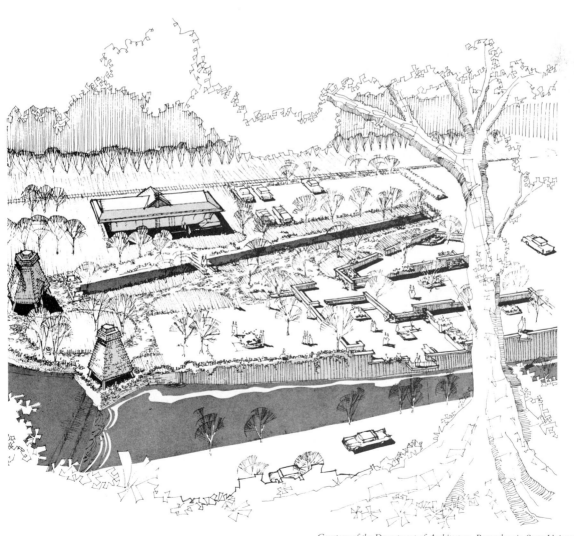

Courtesy of the Department of Architecture, Pennsylvania State University

Figure 23   *Ink-and-appliqué rendering.*

APPLIQUÉ

An appliqué (pressure-sensitive transfer) is a thin transparent plastic sheet with a printed pattern of black dots or lines. The sheet is coated on one side with a special adhesive to make it stick to the drawing. A wide variety of patterns are available; some are illustrated in Figure 21. Various shades of gray can be obtained by choosing the proper transfer or by applying several transfer sheets over each other for darker shades. In addition to patterns, a number of architectural symbols for trees, shrubbery, people, automobiles, and furniture may be obtained. Examples of such appliqué symbols are shown in Figure 22.

Procedure. The order of procedure is:

1. Outline in ink.
2. Select the desired transfer, remove its protective backing, and place it over the area to be rendered, adhesive side down. Rub gently with your fingernail to increase adherence.
3. Lightly score around the outline with a razor blade without cutting the paper underneath.
4. Peel off the excess material and rub again with your fingernail to ensure permanent adherence.

Figure 23 shows a very simple—yet effective—presentation. One sheet of appliqué was the sole rendering medium.

WATERCOLOR AND TEMPERA RENDERING

Watercolor refers to a transparent water-based paint; *tempera* refers to an opaque water-based paint. Both are used (separately or together) to render large presentation drawings, watercolor giving a refined, artistic effect, tempera giving a more vivid and striking effect.

Watercolor may be applied with a brush using a very thin mixture of paint and water called a *wash*, or it may be applied directly from a *palette* used for mixing the colors. The professional obtains his watercolors in tubes and half-tubes rather than in dried cake form.

Tempera (known also as *poster paint, opaque watercolor,* and *showcard color*) is usually applied directly from the palette. Tempera is obtainable in jars and tubes. In addition to color illustration, tempera is very effective when used as a monotone medium. Black, white, and several tones of gray are often used. Figure 24 shows an example of such a rendering.

SPRAY RENDERING

The smooth gradation of tones seen in professional renderings is usually obtained by spraying with an airbrush. This technique is excellent for the indication of smooth, glassy surfaces and background sky.

Courtesy of Scholz Homes, Inc.

Figure 24   *Monotone rendering.*

An airbrush is simply a nozzle that sprays a fine mixture of paint and air. The compressed air is obtained from a compressor or tank of carbonic gas. Since this equipment is expensive and not available to the average student, other methods are often used. Hand spray guns, pressurized spray cans, and even spattered paint (toothbrush rubbed on screening) have been used successfully. Tempera paint is used because it is fast-drying.

Procedure. The procedure for a typical spray rendering is as follows:

1. Block in the desired illustration using a sharp pencil line. The paper must be clean and smudge-free. A spray rendering is transparent and all smudges will show.
2. Select the area to be sprayed. Usually the structure is completed first, then sky, and finally the entourage. Mask out all other areas so that they will not be painted also. Transparent *frisket* paper, which is applied like an appliqué, is used.
3. Make a few test sprays upon scratch paper to determine the proper distance and motion of the spraying device. A light spray is preferred since a too-dark spray cannot be corrected. Carefully lift the frisket paper occasionally to compare relative shades and tones.
4. When the paint is dry, remove the frisket and move on to the next area.
5. Accent details with tempera using a fine brush.

See Figures 25–27 for examples of professional renderings which utilize a combination of media.

PHOTOGRAPHIC RENDERING

When a presentation model of a proposed structure is built, photographs of the model are also prepared for purposes of publication, ease of transportation, and file records. If no presentation model is available, a stage set cardboard model can be built using only those faces that will be seen by the camera. Often both panoramic photographs and close-ups are taken and touched up using standard darkroom methods. See the chapter on Architectural Modeling for several examples of photographic rendering.

See Figures 25–27 for examples of professional renderings that utilize a combination of techniques.

STUDY QUESTIONS

1. Give the principal uses of each of the following types of renderings:
   a. Pencil
   b. Pen-and-ink
   c. Scratch board
   d. Appliqué
   e. Watercolor
   f. Tempera
   g. Spray
2. In pencil rendering, how are each of the following materials treated?
   a. Windows
   b. Brick walls

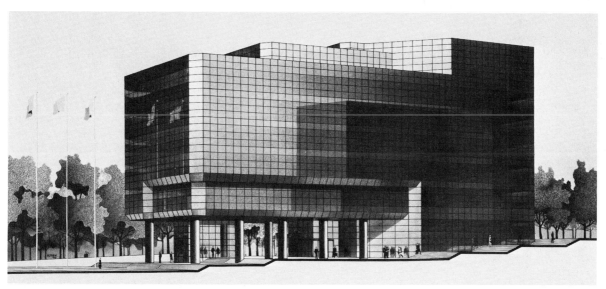

Courtesy of Gruen Associates.

Figure 25   *Ink-and-airbrush rendering.*

Figure 26 *Architectural rendering of the World Trade Center, New York City. Minoru Yamasaki and Associates, architects.*

Figure 27 *Professional rendering of Canada's Pacific Centre using several media. Note reflections of existing buildings in window walls.*

   c. Stone walls
   d. Concrete walls
   e. Shingled roofs
3. In ink rendering, what is meant by the following terms?
   a. Wash
   b. Stipple
   c. Crow-quill
4. How does watercolor differ from tempera?
5. Give four methods of producing a spray rendering.

LABORATORY PROBLEMS

1. Start a collection of renderings by various artists in the medium of your choice.

2. Obtain a good example of a rendering in the medium of your choice and make an accurate copy.
3. Prepare a *style sheet* showing how various materials and textures may be rendered. Use the medium of your choice.
4. Render (a) the presentation drawing and (b) the perspective of the A residence in the medium of your choice.
5. Render (a) the presentation drawing and (b) the perspective of the building assigned by your instructor. Use the medium of your choice.
6. Render (a) the presentation drawing and (b) the perspective of your original building design using the medium of your choice.

39 / Entourage

In architectural design, a structure is planned in relation to its environment. The characteristics of the land, trees, and surrounding buildings are all considered. The quantity and location of traffic—both vehicle and pedestrian—affect the design. To present the design in its proper context, then, an architectural rendering also includes an indication of the character and quantity of these surrounding elements. If this is done well, the client will be able to identify the surroundings and visualize the proposed building in them. If it is done poorly, the client may reject the entire plan. Subconsciously he will feel that a poorly executed drawing means a poorly designed building.

In architectural drawing, the word used to describe the surroundings is *entourage*.* It is used to describe objects—trees, shrubbery, background mountains, human figures, and vehicles—that are included to increase the realistic appearance or decorative effect of the drawing. In addition to its use on perspective renderings, entourage may be used on presentation plans and elevations to increase their pictorial quality.

Contrary to what you might expect, entourage is drawn in a simplified, stylized manner rather than in a detailed, photographic style. There are three good reasons for this:

1. Only a trained artist can draw objects like trees, vehicles, and people to look exactly as they are.
2. There is a constant shortage of time in an architectural drafting room, so shortcut techniques must be used whenever possible.
3. Entourage drawn in great detail would detract from the central structure.

The stylized forms of trees, human figures, and vehicles shown in this chapter may be traced directly or increased in size to fit a particular requirement. The student is advised, however, to develop his own style by improving upon these drawings. In addition to entourage in perspective, the plan and elevation symbols are included, since a presentation drawing often contains the plan and elevations.

Nearly all of the plan-view trees in Figure 1 are based upon a lightly drawn circle. Remember to change the size of the circles for variety, but do not mix many different symbols on the same drawing.

Choose trees that will fit the location. Palm trees, for example, would be appropriate in southern states; cacti in western states (Figure 3). The foreground in Figure 2 may be drawn across the bottom of a rendering, indicating shrubbery near the observer.

Choose a style of background mountains or trees from those shown in Figure 3 that is compatible with your tree style.

The perspective automobiles (Figure 4) are easily traced from advertisements found in magazines. The plan-view autos are drawn by adapting standard templates.

Human figures are most difficult to draw realistically, and therefore the outline forms shown in Figure 5 are used.

---

* Pronounced *n-tur-ahge*. This is a French word with the accent on the last syllable, which is pronounced like the last three letters in the word *garage*.

Figure 1 *Trees in plan view.*

SOFTWOOD TREES

FOREGROUND SHRUBBERY

HARDWOOD TREES

Figure 2 *Trees in elevation.*

BACKGROUND

EXOTIC

Figure 3 *Planting.*

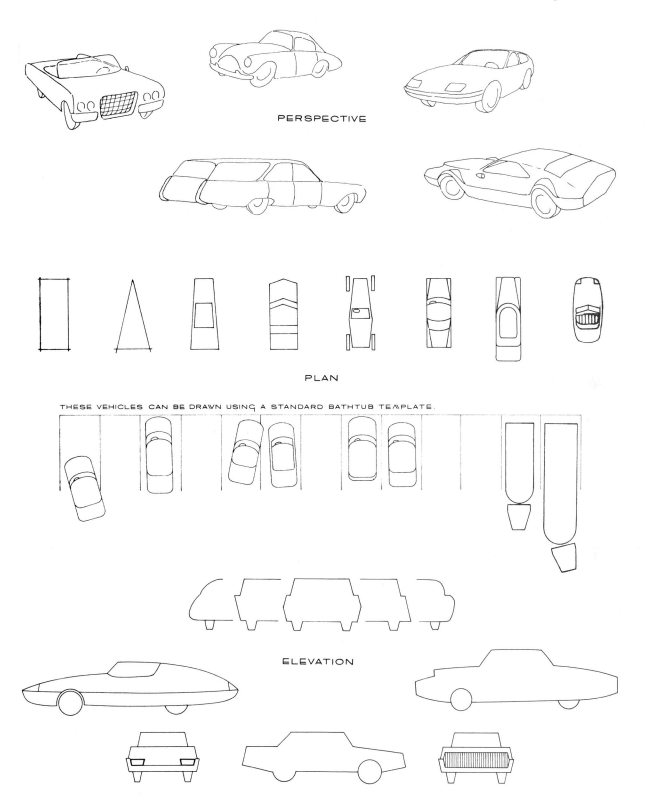

PERSPECTIVE

PLAN

THESE VEHICLES CAN BE DRAWN USING A STANDARD BATHTUB TEMPLATE.

ELEVATION

Figure 4 *Vehicles.*

Figure 5 *Human figures.*

STUDY QUESTIONS

1. What is the meaning of the word *entourage*?
2. Why is it important to include entourage on a presentation drawing?
3. Give three reasons why entourage is drawn in a simplified rather than detailed manner.

LABORATORY PROBLEMS

1. Prepare a *style sheet* of your individual treatment of the following elements:
   a. Evergreen trees in plan
   b. Evergreen trees in elevation
   c. Deciduous trees in plan
   d. Deciduous trees in elevation
   e. Foreground shrubbery
   f. Background scenery
   g. Human figures
   h. Vehicles
2. Include entourage on (a) the presentation drawing and (b) the perspective of the A residence.
3. Include entourage on (a) the presentation drawing and (b) the perspective of the building assigned by your instructor.
4. Include the entourage on (a) the presentation drawing and (b) the perspective of your original house design.

X / Commercial Design and Drafting

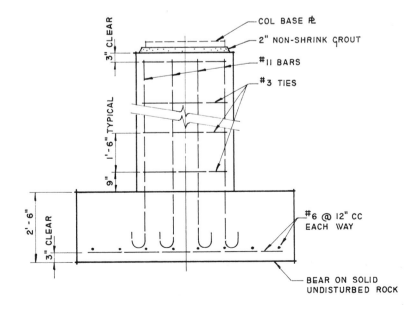

40 / Commercial Drafting

There are important differences between the design, drafting, and construction of a residence and that of a commercial building:

1. *Design.* A single individual can design and draft the plans for a residence, but a number of specialists, including a registered architect and professional engineer, are needed to plan a commercial building. This involves all the consequent problems of coordination, cooperation, and human relations.
2. *Drafting.* More drawings are required for a commercial building due to its sheer size. But in addition, the plans must be more completely detailed to permit all interested builders to bid on a competitive basis.
3. *Construction.* A light wood-frame construction, as described in Chapter 28, is adequate for a residence, but a commercial building is usually framed in steel or reinforced concrete and finished with masonry or prefabricated composition panels.

A small commercial structure, the South Hills Office Building recently designed and built in State College, Pennsylvania, will be used in this chapter to illustrate each of these aspects.

DESIGN

Three businesspeople—the owners of a law office, a real estate firm, and an advertising agency—joined together to solve a common problem—that of finding suitable space for their offices. They formed a partnership, purchased a half-acre site, and asked a local architect to design a building

to satisfy their needs. As is customary with most architects, the design procedure consisted of four major stages:

1. The program
2. Presentation drawings of several schemes
3. Preliminary drawing of the chosen scheme
4. Working drawings

At one of the early meetings, a *program* was prepared which indicated the owners' requirement of 4,000 sq. ft. of office space plus an additional 12,000 sq. ft. of rentable space for other companies. An attractive contemporary exterior appearance was considered to be an important requirement. A preliminary study of the zoning and building code requirements showed that building height would be limited to 55' (not including mechanical features occupying less than one-tenth of the roof area). It was also determined that one off-street parking stall would have to be provided for each office, for a total of twenty-four stalls.

The architect proceeded to develop *sketch plans* and *presentation drawings* of three alternate solutions: a two-, three-, and five-story building. The solution preferred by the owners was a five-story basementless building with the first (plaza) level open to provide adequate parking. This solution included glass window walls and a central elevator shaft.

Preliminary drawings consisting of 4' modular plans and elevations were then prepared for this chosen solution. The framing was visualized as consisting of steel beams supported by ten steel columns. Each pair of columns would form a bent spanning 40', and adjacent bents would be 24' oc. Welded connections would be used where necessary to obtain a rigid frame. To provide uninterrupted glass window walls, the outer wall was cantilevered 4' beyond the columns, resulting in a rectangular floor plan of 48' × 104'. Stairwells were placed at both ends of the floor plan and were connected by a longitudinal corridor. The elevator shaft, rest rooms, and maintenance room were placed in a central location. The remaining area was then available as clear floor space for maximum flexibility. A hydraulic piston elevator was chosen in preference to a hoist elevator to eliminate the unsightly elevator penthouse needed for the hoisting machinery. The piston elevator, however, does require that a piston shaft be drilled into the ground equal to the distance of the total lift. Piston elevators generally are not specified for lifts exceeding 60' in height. Heating and cooling were provided by electric air-conditioning space units installed in wall panels.

The preliminary drawings were approved by the owners with only one major change: the glass window walls were rejected due to the additional air-conditioning capacity required. The architect replaced the window walls with vertically aligned windows and air-conditioning units set in exterior brick walls. Vertical lines were emphasized by mullions framing each stack of windows.

DRAFTING

Working drawings of the final solution were prepared as shown in Drawings No. 1–S5. These drawings are nearly identical* to the set of working drawings used to construct the South Hills Office Building and were redrawn in ink to assure good reproduction in this book. Study these plans until you are confident that you understand how they are used to describe this project. The following remarks may help.

Drawing No. 1: Index. This is the cover sheet for the entire set of working drawings. In addition to the index of drawings, it includes a legend of all abbreviations and symbols used on the drawings. Some architectural offices also include a sketch of the building on the cover sheet.

Drawing No. 2: Plot plan. This plot plan positions the building on the site, shows the existing and proposed land contour, landscaping, parking, walks, gas lines, water lines, and sanitary waste lines. The note "Swale to CB" indicates a downward slope to a catch basin. The designation "BC 100.5″" fixes the bottom of the curb (road level) at an elevation of 100.5', and "TC 101.5″" fixes the top of the curb (ground level) at an elevation of 101.5'.

Notice that two indications for north are given at the lower right corner. The large arrow enclosed in a circle is the direction of north, and "building north" shows the side of the building that is termed the *north elevation*. This is particularly important when a building is positioned such that two sides might both be considered north elevations.

Drawing No. 3: Foundation plan. A 4' modular grid system is used with coordinate identification letters and numbers. This identification system helps to locate details on the plans, in the written specifications, and in the field. Notice that this system was adapted to use arrowheads to indicate both on-grid and off-grid dimensions. The callouts "0" and "6" refer to masonry courses, each 8″ high. Thus the CMU (concrete masonry unit) wall marked "6" can be started 6 courses (48″) above the walls marked "0." Refer to Drawing No. 11 for a better understanding of these masonry-course identification numbers.

A test boring was taken at each column location. Firm rock was only 6'–8' deep at the three "A" locations, but was 16'–18' deep at the seven "B" locations. Therefore two types of footings were designed. Notice on Drawing No. 4 that the contractor was given the option of using the reinforced footing "A" at all ten locations and chose that alternative in preference to driving piles as required for footing "B." To support walls, either 8″- or 12″-thick CMU foundations were used, depending upon the weight of the wall to be supported. This and all similar plans were originally drawn to a scale of $\frac{1}{4}″ = 1'$-0.

Drawing No. 4: Footing details. Four details are included on this sheet to show the reinforced concrete construction of footing "A," steel pile footing "B," the column waterproofing, and the reinforced concrete footing for the CMU walls. The note "HP 10 × 42" refers to a 10″ × 10″ bearing pile weighing 42 lb. per foot of length; "5-#11 bars" means five reinforcing steel bars, each $\frac{11}{8}″$ in diameter. See Drawing No. 1 for the meaning of all abbreviations. These and similar details were originally drawn to a scale of $\frac{1}{2}″ = 1'$-0.

Drawing No. 5: Plaza floor plan. Dashed lines are used to indicate overhead features such as the building line or overhead simulated beams. Each room, stairway, or corridor has an identification number (such as "P2"). Doors also have an identification number which is coded to the proper room (such as "P2/1" and "P2/2"). See the legend on Drawing No. 1 for the meaning of all such identification numbers.

Drawing No. 6: First-floor plan. Six air-conditioning units are located on the south wall, but only

---

* Some details such as stair and elevation sections are omitted.

four units are required for the north wall because the south-wall cooling requirements are greater than the north-wall heating requirements.

Drawings No. 7–9: Elevations. Although 4′ horizontal modules are used on the plans, 8″ vertical modules are used on elevations to indicate courses of masonry 8″ apart (a CMU course of 8″ or three brick courses of $2′-\frac{2}{3}″$). For example, the balloon "39" means that the second floor is 39 courses, or 26′ ($39 \times 8″ = 26′$), above the top of the footing marked with a balloon "0." Control joints are formed by raking and caulking masonry joints. This directs any cracking along these joints rather than allowing it to occur at random. These elevations were originally drawn to a scale of $\frac{1}{4}″ = 1′-0$.

Drawing No. 10: Interior elevations. Interior elevations of all specially equipped rooms would be included in addition to these rest-room elevations. The elevation identification "10/1" indicates Elevation No. 1 on Drawing No. 10.

Drawing No. 11: Longitudinal section. This section is needed to explain the structural system and assure proper clearances and room heights. Only the more useful coordinate identification numbers are included. Note "AC CLG BD" is an abbreviation for acoustical ceiling boards.

Drawing No. 12: Typical sections. Section 12/1 is a vertical section cut through a window (see Drawings No. 6 and 7). Section 12/2 is a vertical section through a simulated plaza roof beam (see Drawing No. 7). Section 12/3 is a horizontal section through a column (see Drawing No. 7). Multiple balloons such as "B" and "L" on Section 12/3 show that this section is typical of columns centered on both grid B and grid L.

Drawing No. 13: Typical details. Plan detail 13/1 is a horizontal section cut through the window mullions (see Drawing No. 6). The two alternate details show the installation of panels and louvers. The callout "362 DS 16 PUN @ 16″ oc" refers to $3\frac{5}{8}″$ prefabricated metal studs as manufactured by the Keene Company: model no. 362, double stud, 16-gauge, punched, 16″ on center.

Drawings No. 14 and 15: Schedules. Room finish information is contained in schedules such as shown on these two sheets. Complete schedules for all floors require many more pages. The written specifications contain even more detailed information.

Drawing No. E1: Electrical plan. The dark rectangles represent the fluorescent ceiling fixtures, and dark circles represent incandescent fixtures. The letter within each fixture symbol identifies the type of fixture (see "Lighting Fixture Schedule" on Drawing No. 14). The alphameric designation at the end of each home run identifies the floor level and circuit number (see "Legend" on Drawing No. 1). An emergency lighting circuit is indicated by "E." See the legend for exit light information.

Drawing No. H1: Heating-cooling plan. The dark rectangles with diagonal lines represent the Remington electric heating-cooling units, and the dark hexagons indicate Electromode electric baseboard heaters. See Drawing No. 14 for more detailed information. The two hash marks on each home run indicate 208-V circuits.

Drawings No. P1 and P2: Water supply and sanitary plan. Drawing No. P1 shows the hot- and cold-water supply piping and the dry fire piping both in plan and pictorial projection. The plan also includes an air circulation system for the rest rooms. Drawing P2 shows the waste and soil disposal systems.

Drawing No. S1: First-floor structural plan. Each heavy line indicates the location of a steel member. The note "W 16 × 36 (−4)" refers to a 16″-wide flange beam weighing 36 lb./ft. with its upper flange 4″ below the concrete slab surface. This and all similar plans were originally drawn to a scale of $\frac{1}{8}″ = 1′-0$.

Drawing No. S2: Roof structural plan. Note "12 H5 EXT END ($-2\frac{1}{2}$)″" refers to a 12″-deep, H5-series, open-web joist with an extended end and located $2\frac{1}{2}″$ below the roof surface. Notation "DO" means ditto. The dashed lines show the location of cross-bridging. The note "ship lone" means that elevator beam 6 B 16 should be shipped without any shop connections because this beam is to be installed by the elevator technicians rather than the structural fabricators.

Table I   *Structured Steel Designations*

Type of Shape	"Old" Designation	"New" Designation
W shape (formerly *wide flange*)	8 W 31	W 8 × 31
W shape. (formerly *light beam*)	8 B 20	W 8 × 20
S shape (formerly *American Standard I beam*)	8 I 18.4	S 8 × 18.4
American Standard channel	8 [11.5	C 8 × 11.5
Angle	∠ 4 × 4 × ¼	L 4 × 4 × ¼
HP shape (formerly *bearing pile*)	8 BP 36	HP 8 × 36

Note: Designations "8 W 31" and "W 8 × 31" refer to a wide-flange beam 8″ high weighing 31 lb. per foot of length.

Structural steel designations were revised by the American Institute of Steel Construction in 1970. Although the "new" designations are used on the plans of the South Hills Office Building and throughout this book, the "old" designations are shown on Drawing No. S2. It would be well to become familiar with these earlier designations since they will still be seen on plans for many years. See Table I.

Drawing No. S3: Column schedule. Refer to Drawing No. S1 for an explanation of the double designations "S3/1" and "S3/2." The column schedule shows a typical bent. Notice that the column sections are spliced between floors where the bending moment is smaller.

Drawing No. S4: Structural details. The location of Sections S4/1 and S4/2 is indicated on Drawings No. S1 and S2. The welding symbols used on this sheet include a closed triangle for a fillet weld, an open triangle for a vee weld, a closed circle for a field weld, and an open circle for an all-around weld.

Drawing No. S5: Concrete slab plan. Notation "#4@9 TOP" refers to $\frac{4}{8}$″-diameter steel reinforcing rods placed 9″ apart and near the top surface of the concrete slab. "Granco" is the trade name for a decking manufacturer.

CONSTRUCTION

Careful design and detailing of the South Hills Office Building permitted the construction to be completed in three months without any major design changes or emergencies.

Although two column foundations were designed, the contractor was given the option of using the reinforced concrete foundation at all ten locations and chose that alternative.

The main steel members (Figure 25) were erected and held in place by temporary bolting until the weldments were made. Secondary members were fastened by high-strength bolts or unfinished bolts as specified. In Figure 26, notice that steel angles were welded to the exterior I beams to form a masonry shelf at each floor level. Also notice that intermediate floor beams are required to support the concrete floor at each level except the roof. At the roof, steel open-web joists are sufficient to support the roof deck. All structural steel was fireproofed as specified by the architect (Figure 28).

Six-inch batt insulation was installed with a special attention to the plaza roof. The plaza roof beams and tapered columns were simulated by light channels wired to shape (Figure 31) and covered with a metal lath base used under the final coating of cement plaster (Figure 32). Two-inch rigid insulation was used for the exterior walls.

A specialty metal company supplied the anodized aluminum components for window mullions which are so important to the exterior design. Figure 34 shows the entire four-floor section being field-fabricated before final erection. After erection, the electric heating-cooling units and window frames were placed in the mullions.

Interior partitions were framed in lightweight metal as shown in Figure 36 using the system marketed by the Keene Company. The partition members were shop-welded into convenient wall sections and then field-welded in the final position. The vertical metal studs are supplied with a nailing groove to facilitate fastening the finished drywall. This groove is formed by two channels fastened together in such a way that a nail can be driven between them. The nail is not only held by friction but is also deformed when driven to provide greater holding power. The stairwells and elevator shaft were built of concrete masonry units. Wood strapping (Figure 37) was nailed to the masonry units to provide a base for the drywall of $\frac{1}{2}$″, vinyl-covered gypsum board. A suspended system of steel channels was used to support the finished ceiling panels (Figure 38), and vinyl-asbestos tile flooring was laid directly over the concrete floor. The electrical and plumbing work was completed in appropriate steps during the various stages of construction. Figures 39–42 show the completed structure.

Study the photographs in this chapter until you are familiar with the main construction steps. Also try to visit construction sites near you at least once a week to become familiar with the latest construction techniques.

STUDY QUESTIONS

1. Name the four major steps in the design and drafting of a commercial structure.
2. List the drawings normally included in a set of commercial working drawings.
3. What is the principal reason for including details of alternate construction methods in the working drawings?
4. On the working drawings of the South Hills Office Building, the vertical modular grid system is different from the horizontal grid system. Why?
5. Are the same number of heating-cooling units used on opposite walls of the South Hills Office Building? Why?
6. Describe briefly each term:
   a. Structural bent
   b. Swale
   c. Control joint
   d. Building north
   e. Roof scuttle

7. Give the meaning of these abbreviations:
   a. FTG, HTG, LTG
   b. HTR, WTR
   c. CMU, DO, GL, VAT
   d. ℄, ℗
   e. WC, ⊮
8. Give the meaning of:
   a. Detail 12/3
   b. Door S2/2
   c. Elevation 10/6
9. Give *two* meanings for each of the following abbreviations:
   a. E
   b. ELEV
   c. W
   d. φ
   e. #

LABORATORY PROBLEMS

1. Complete the working drawings for the South Hills Office Building as assigned:
   a. Second-floor plan
   b. Roof plan
   c. Interior elevations of lobby
   d. Transverse section
   e. Stair section and details
   f. Elevator section and details
   g. Roof cornice detail section
   h. Lobby sill detail section
   i. Second-floor schedules
   j. Plaza electrical plan
   k. Telephone plan
   l. Fire alarm diagram
2. Prepare working drawings of the building assigned by your instructor:
   a. Title page
   b. Plot plan
   c. Foundation plan
   d. Floor plan
   e. Elevations
   f. Sections
   g. Details
   h. Schedules
   i. Electrical plan
   j. Heating-cooling plan
   k. Plumbing plan
   l. Structural plan
3. The presentation drawings of a community church are shown in Figures 43–46. Using 6″ × 24″ laminated roof beams 8″ oc, prepare the working drawings as assigned:
   a. Floor plans
   b. Elevations
   c. Transverse section through auditorium

   d. Typical wall sections
   e. Stair details
   f. Schedules
   g. Electrical plan
   h. Heating and air circulation plan
   i. Plumbing plan
4. Design and prepare preliminary drawings for the project assigned:
   a. An innovative children's playground for a 50′-wide × 150′-deep urban site.
   b. A drive-in movie screen structure. The screen is to be 120′ wide × 50′ high and at an angle of 12° from the vertical. The bottom of the screen is 12′ above the ground level. Use timber or steel construction as assigned.
   c. An 80′ × 160′ unheated storage warehouse for a building-supply distributor. Clear ceiling height should be 12′-0″. Use masonry (10″ CMU) or wood-frame construction (2″ × 6″ studs 24″ oc with corrugated aluminum siding). Provide a small heated office and lavatory, rail receiving dock, and truck shipping dock. Fire protection will include a dry sprinkler system.
   d. A single-story retail candy store for a 24′-wide × 120′-deep commercial site. Use a brick bearing-wall and steel-joist roof construction. Provide an attractive front elevation with display window, rear office of 200 sq. ft., and storage of 300 sq. ft. with delivery door. Show details of interior planning.
   e. A two-story community college academic building containing an auditorium seating 200 students; five classrooms, each seating 40 students; a drafting room for 30 students, eight two-man faculty offices, rest rooms, and maintenance. Use steel and masonry construction.
   f. (For the advanced student) A world's fair pavilion representing your state. Provide for a 4,000-sq. ft. major working attraction, 3,000 sq. ft. small products display and sales area, offices, rest rooms, and maintenance. Use a progressive structural system.
5. (For the advanced student) Design and prepare presentation drawings for:
   a. A community action center
   b. An urban pedestrian mall
   c. A low-cost housing module
   d. A manufacturing plant for the production of low-cost housing modules
   e. A processing plant for the conversion of sewage into potable water
   f. A processing plant to convert scrapped automobiles into structural units
   g. A processing plant to convert residential waste into building blocks
   h. A seagoing processor to neutralize floating oil slick

CONSTRUCTION DRAWINGS
FOR THE
SOUTH HILLS OFFICE BUILDING
STATE COLLEGE, PENNSYLVANIA

ABBREVIATIONS

ACOUSTIC	AC	HOLLOW METAL	HM
ALUMINUM	ALUM	HOT	H
AMPERES	A	BEARING PILE	HP
ANGLE	L		
AT	@	INSULATION	INSUL
		IRON PIPE	IP
BEAM	B		
BEARING PILE	HP	JUNCTION BOX	JB
BITUMINOUS	BIT		
BOARD	BD	LAVATORY	L or LAV
BOTTOM OF CURB	BC	LIGHTING	LTG
BRITISH THERMAL UNIT	BTU		
BUILDING	BLDG	MANUFACTURER	MANUF
		MATERIAL	MAT'L
CABINET	CAB	MAXIMUM	MAX
CATCH BASIN	CB	METAL	MET
CEILING	CLG	MINIMUM	MIN
CEMENT	CEM		
CENTER LINE	₵	NORTH	N
CENTER TO CENTER	CC	NUMBER	NO or #
CERAMIC TILE	CER T		
CHANNEL	C or C	ON CENTER	o c
CLEAN OUT	CO		
CLEAR	CLR	PARTITION	PART
COLD	C	PHASE	Ø
COLUMN	COL	PLASTER	PLAST
CONCRETE	CONC	PLATE	R
CONCRETE MASONRY UNIT	CMU	PORCELAIN	PORC
CONSTRUCTION	CONST	POUNDS PER SQUARE INCH	PSI
CUBIC FEET PER MINUTE	CFM	PUNCHED	PUN
DIAMETER	Ø	RAIN WATER CONDUIT	RWC
DITTO	DO or "	RECEPTACLE	REC
DOUBLE STUDS	DS	RIGHT OF WAY	R/W
DOWN	DN	RISER, RADIUS	R
EACH	EA	SHOCK ABSORBER	SA
EAST, EMERGENCY	E	SLOP SINK	SS
ELEVATION, ELEVATOR	ELEV	SOUTH	S
EQUAL	EQ	SPECIFICATIONS	SPECS
EXHAUST	EXH	STEEL	STL
EXISTING	EXIST	SYSTEM	SYS
EXPANSION JOINT	EXP JT		
EXTENDED	EXT	THRESHOLD	THRESH
		TOP OF CURB	TC
FINISH	FIN		
FLASHING	FLASH	UNPUNCHED	UNP
FLOOR	FL	URINAL	U
FOOTING	FTG		
FRESH AIR	FA	VINYL ASBESTOS TILE	VAT
FURRING	FUR	VOLTS	V
GYPSUM	GYP	WASTE, WATTS, WEST	W
GLASS	GL	WATER CLOSET	WC
		WATER HEATER	WTR HTR
HEATING	HTG	WIDE FLANGE	W
HEXAGONAL	HEX	WITH	w/

INDEX OF DRAWINGS

1	INDEX
2	PLOT PLAN
3	FOUNDATION PLAN
4	FOOTING DETAILS
5	PLAZA FLOOR PLAN
6	FIRST FLOOR PLAN
7	SOUTH ELEVATION
8	NORTH ELEVATION
9	EAST & WEST ELEVATIONS
10	INTERIOR ELEVATIONS
11	LONGITUDINAL SECTION
12	TYPICAL SECTIONS
13	TYPICAL DETAILS
14	ROOM SCHEDULES
15	DOOR & WINDOW SCHEDULES
E1	ELECTRICAL PLAN
H1	HEATING-COOLING PLAN
P1	WATER SUPPLY PLAN
P2	SANITARY PLAN
S1	FIRST FLOOR STRUCTURAL PLAN
S2	ROOF STRUCTURAL PLAN
S3	COLUMN SCHEDULE
S4	STRUCTURAL DETAILS
S5	CONCRETE SLAB PLAN

LEGEND

100 ---	EXIST CONTOUR
100 —	REVISED CONTOUR
	PROPERTY LINE
	BRICK
	CMU
	CRUSHED STONE
	EARTH
	STEEL
	CONCRETE SECTION
	" IN PLAN
	BITUMINOUS
	RIGID INSULATION
	BATT "
	ROUGH WOOD
	GYPSUM BOARD
	PLASTER
	CERAMIC TILE
	SHEET NO / SECTION NO
	SHEET NO / ELEVATION NO
	ROOM NO / DOOR NO
	WINDOW SYMBOL
	ROOM SYMBOL

	SWITCH LEG
	SWITCHED CIRCUIT
	BRANCH CIRCUIT
D-1	HOME RUN w/ CIRCUIT NO
	208V HOME RUN
	INCANDESCENT FIXTURE, CLG
	" " WALL
	FLUORESCENT "
	" "
	CONVENIENCE OUTLET
S	SWITCH
S3	THREE WAY SWITCH
S4	FOUR " "
E	EMERGENCY CIRCUIT
	" " LIGHTING
	EXIT LIGHT, CKTH B1412
	" " B1414
	HEATING-COOLING UNIT
	BASEBOARD HEATING "
	COLD WATER
	HOT WATER
	SANITARY WASTE
	VENT

Drawing No. 1   *Index of the South Hills Office Building.*

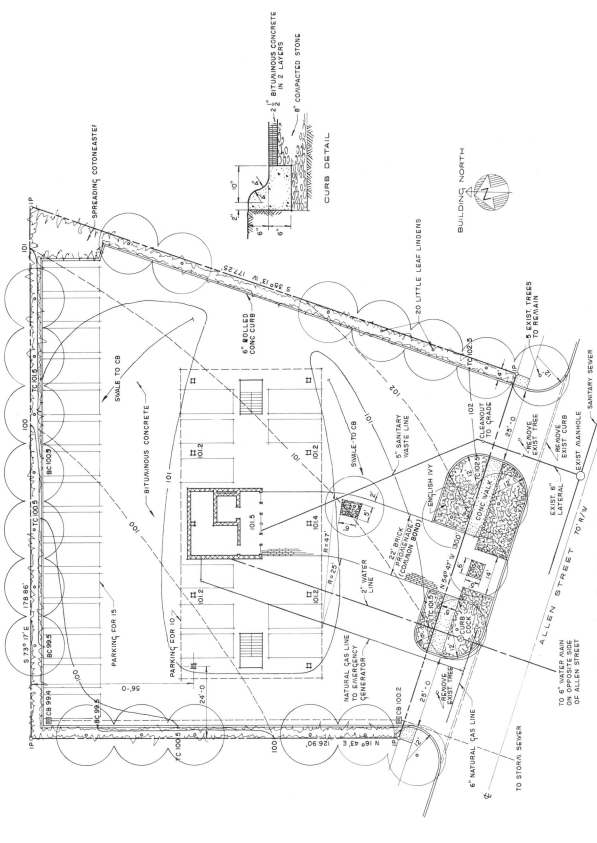

Drawing No. 2 *Plot plan of the South Hills Office Building.*

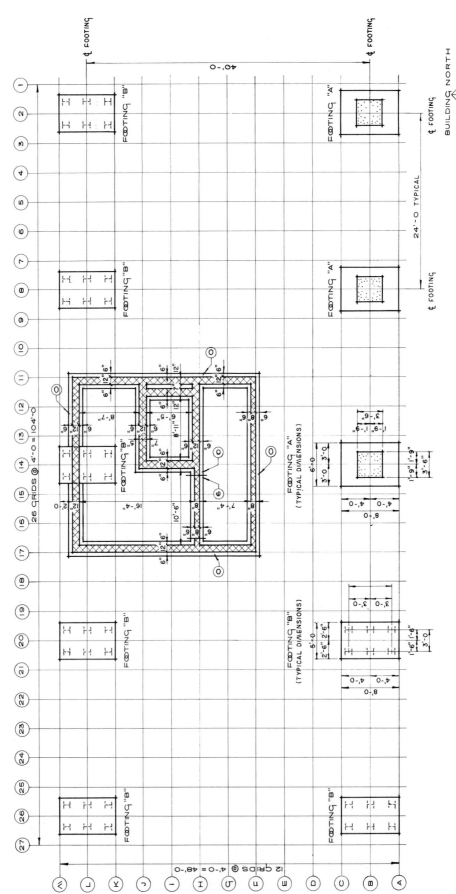

Drawing No. 3   *Foundation plan of the South Hills Office Building.*

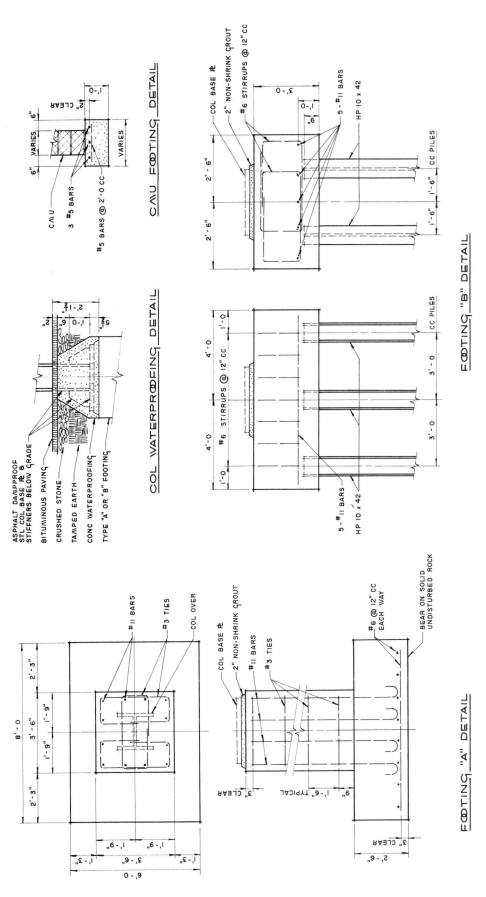

CMU FOOTING DETAIL

CMU
3 #5 BARS
#5 BARS @ 2'-0 CC
VARIES
6"
CLEAR
1"-0
6"
VARIES

COL WATERPROOFING DETAIL

ASPHALT DAMPPROOF
STL COL BASE ℄ &
STIFFNERS BELOW GRADE
BITUMINOUS PAVING
CRUSHED STONE
TAMPED EARTH
CONC WATERPROOFING
TYPE "A" OR "B" FOOTING
2'-1"
1'-0"
6"
1"

FOOTING "B" DETAIL

COL BASE ℄
2" NON-SHRINK GROUT
#6 STIRRUPS @ 12" CC
5 - #11 BARS
HP 10 x 42
3'-0
2'-6"
2'-6"
1'-0"
6"
CC PILES
1'-6"
1'-6"

#6 STIRRUPS @ 12" CC
5 - #11 BARS
HP 10 x 42
4'-0
4'-0
1'-0
3'-0
3'-0
1'-0
CC PILES

FOOTING "A" DETAIL

#11 BARS
#3 TIES
COL OVER
8'-0
2'-3"
3'-6"
1'-9"
1'-9"
2'-3"
9'-0
1'-3"
3'-6"
1'-3"
1'-9"
1'-9"

COL BASE ℄
2" NON-SHRINK GROUT
#11 BARS
#3 TIES
#6 @ 12" CC EACH WAY
BEAR ON SOLID UNDISTURBED ROCK
3" CLEAR
1'-6" TYPICAL
9"
3" CLEAR
2'-6"

GENERAL FOUNDATION NOTES

1. FOOTING "A" MAY BE SUBSTITUTED FOR FOOTING "B" AT CONTRACTOR'S OPTION.

2. ALL CONCRETE SHALL HAVE AN ULTIMATE 28 DAY COMPRESSIVE STRENGTH OF 3000 PSI.

3. ALL REINFORCING STEEL SHALL BE ASTM A15 INTERMEDIATE GRADE.

4. STEEL BEARING PILES FOR FOOTING "B" SHALL BE ASTM A36. PILES SHALL BE DRIVEN TO REFUSAL ON SOLID ROCK. SEE TEST BORING RESULTS FOR APPROXIMATE DEPTH OF ROCK.

Drawing No. 4 *Footing details of the South Hills Office Building.*

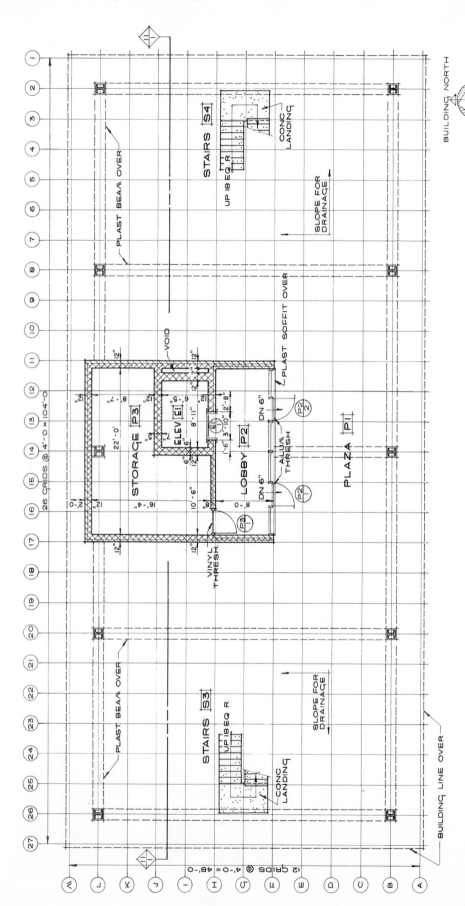

Drawing No. 5 *Plaza floor plan of the South Hills Office Building.*

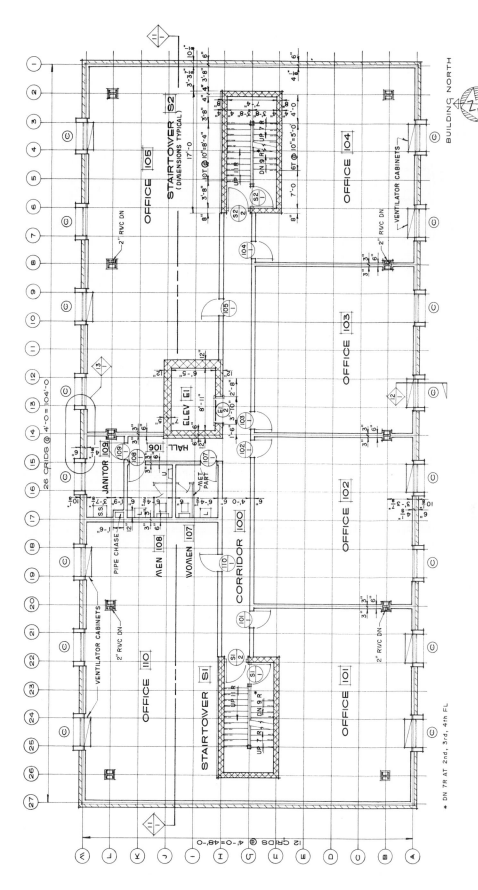

Drawing No. 6 *First-floor plan of the South Hills Office Building. (Second-, third-, and fourth-floor plans similar.)*

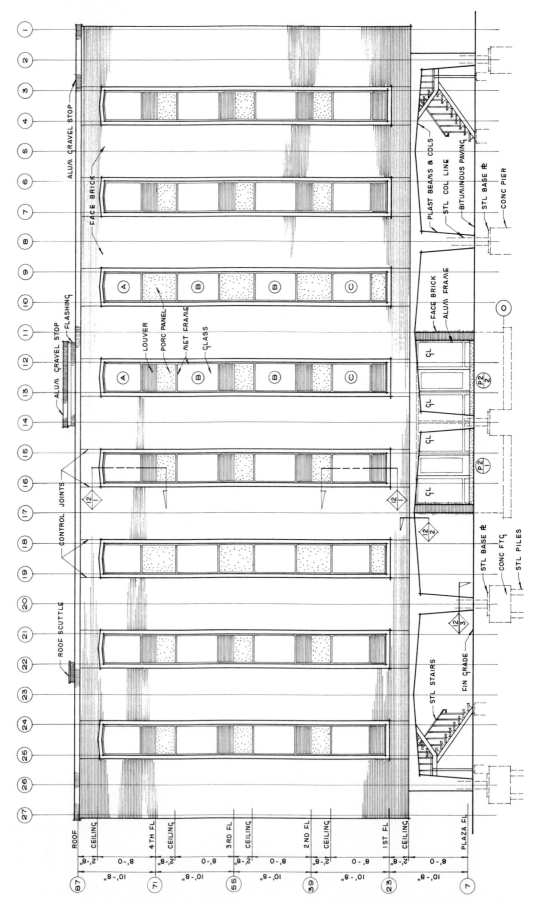

Drawing No. 7 *South elevation of the South Hills Office Building.*

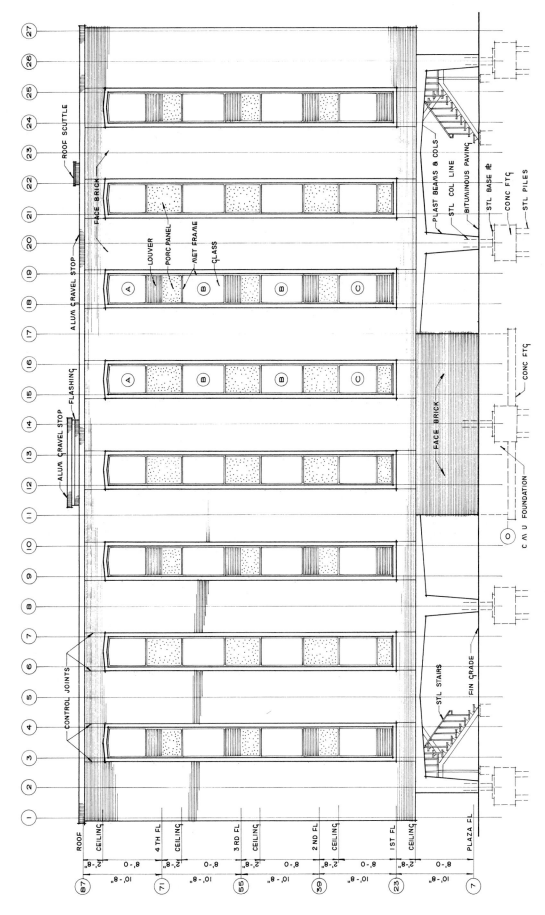

Drawing No. 8 *North elevation of the South Hills Office Building.*

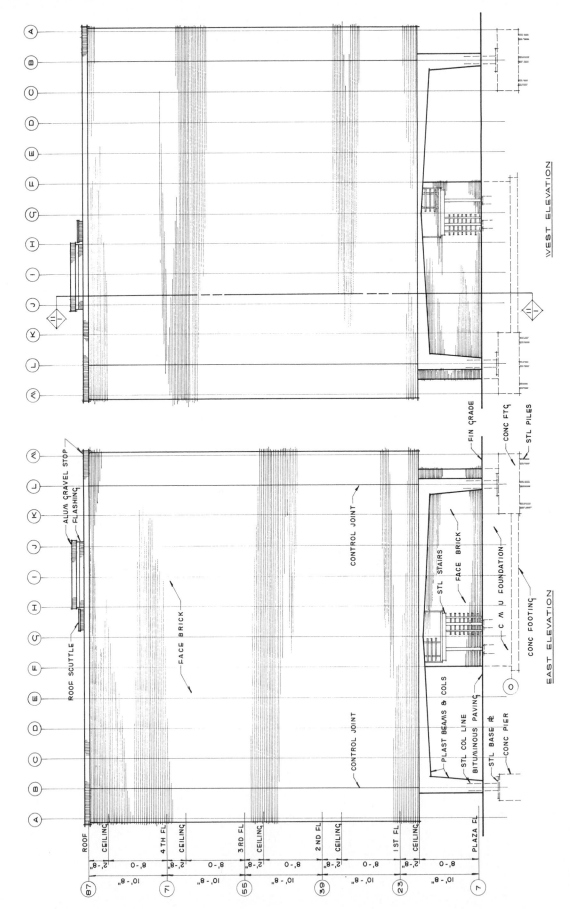

Drawing No. 9   *East and west elevations of the South Hills Office Building.*

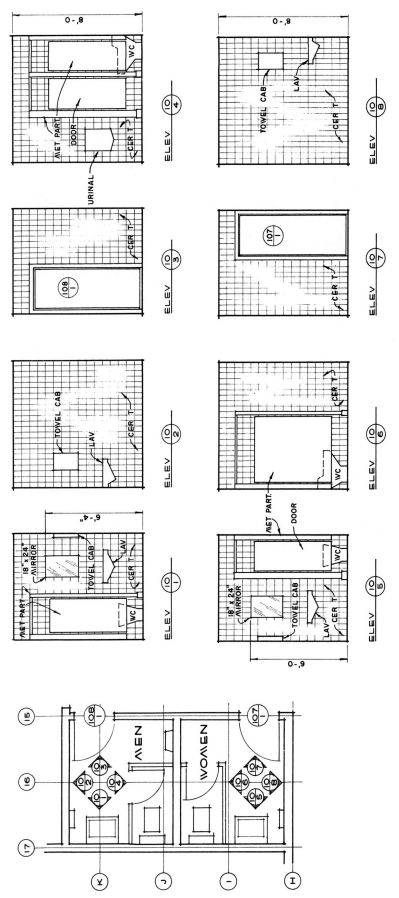

Drawing No. 10   *Interior elevations of the South Hills Office Building.*

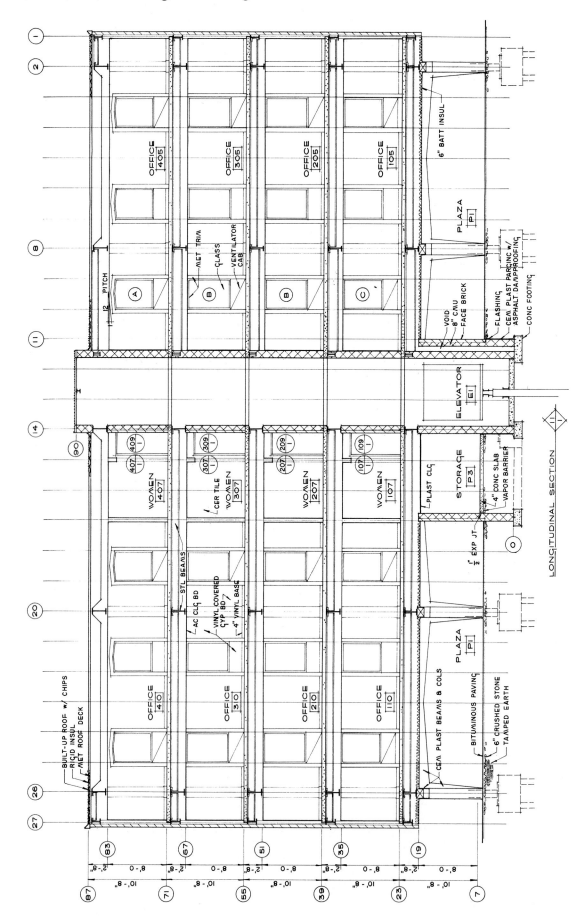

Drawing No. 11 *Longitudinal section of the South Hills Office Building.*

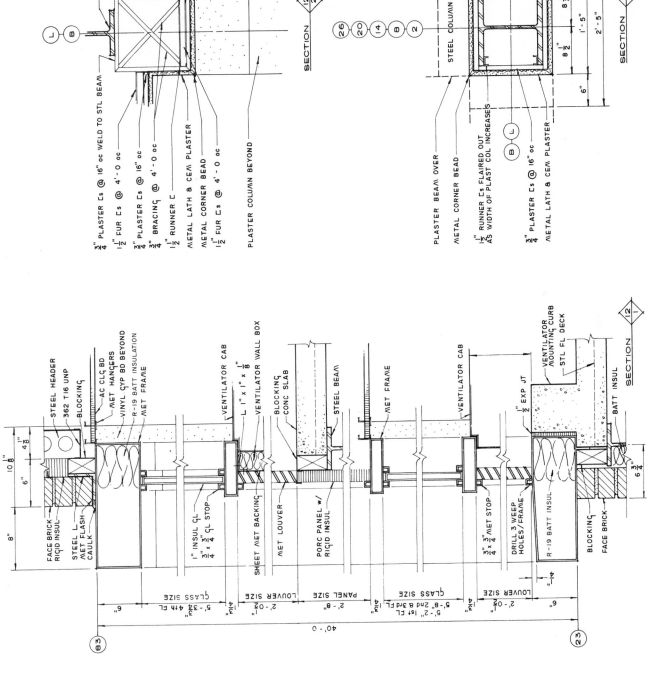

Drawing No. 12 *Typical sections of the South Hills Office Building.*

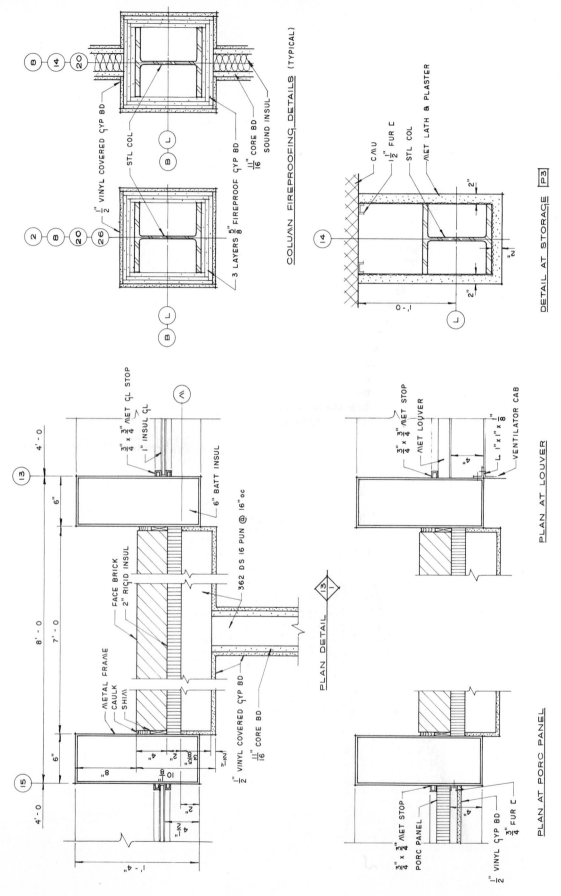

Drawing No. 13 *Typical details of the South Hills Office Building.*

LIGHTING FIXTURE SCHEDULE

NO	MANUFACTURER	CATALOG NO	FINISH	WATTS
A	LIGHTOLIER	7792		300
B	"	7794		100
C	"	7827 & 7821	WHITE	150
D	"	7827 & 7822	ALUM	150 & 25
F	PRESCOLITE	WB-28-2	ALUM	150 & 100
G	LIGHTOLIER	81675	WHITE	4L-40
H	STONCO	QD8501	ALUM	500

MAIN DISTRIBUTION PANEL

400A-3P-SW-W/3-300A-FU- PANEL A
400A-3P-SW-W/3-225A-FU- PANEL B
400A-3P-SW-W/3-225A-FU- PANEL C
400A-3P-SW-W/2-275A-FU- PANEL D
100A-2P-SW-W/2-100A-FU- PANEL E
60A-2P-SW-W/2-50A-FU- PANEL E/W SW
*200A-3P-SW-W/3-200A-FU- ELEVATOR
*TIME DELAY FUSES (FUSETRON)
1200A-BUS 3Ø-4W-120/208V

PANEL D (TYPICAL)

3I-20A-2P-CB-LTG, REC
9-30A-2P-CB-HTG, WTR HTR
3-20A-2P-CB-HTG
2-20A-2P-CB-SPARES
4-20A-IP-SPACE ONLY
400A-M/LO 3Ø-4W-120/208V

PANEL E

9-20A-2P-CB-LTG, FA SYS EXH FAN
4-20A-IP-CB-LTG, REC
4-20A-IP-CB-SPARES
100A-M/LO IØ-3W-120/208V

PANEL E/W

5-20A-IP-FU-LTG, ELEV JB
5-20A-IP-FU-SPARES
100A-M/LO IØ-3W-120/208V

ELECTRICAL PANEL SCHEDULES

ELECTRIC HEATING-COOLING UNITS

NO	MANUFACTURER	HEATING BTU	WATTS	COOLING BTU	WATTS
EK-7S	REMINGTON	8400	2460	6500	1240
EK-10S	"	8400	2460	9000	1520
EK-10M	"	11330	3320	9000	1520
EK-12S	"	8470	2480	11700	1770
EK-12L	"	15300	4480	11700	1770
EK-15L	"	15370	4500	14100	2220

ELECTRIC BASEBOARD HEATING

NO	MANUFACTURER	CATALOG NO	BTU	WATTS
A	ELECTROMODE	8950-D	2560	750
B	"	8950-A	1707	500
C	"	8960-C	4439	1300

ROOM FINISH SCHEDULE

NO	NAME	FLOOR	BASE	WALL	TRIM	WINDOW STOOL	CEILING	HGT	REMARKS
P1	PLAZA	BITUM		BRICK 5	ALUM 9		PLAST 11	VARIES	CEM PLAST BEAMS & COLS
P2	LOBBY	VAT 1		" 5	" HM 10		" 13	8'-0	
P3	STORAGE	CONC 17		CMU 6	HM 10		" 11	8'-0	
100	CORRIDOR	VAT 1	VINYL	VINYL BRICK 3	HM 7/5	10	ACCLG BD 14	8'-0	
101	OFFICE	"	"	VINYL 3	" 7	ALUM 9	" 14	8'-0	NO BASE AT BRICK WALL
102	"	"	"	" 3	" 7	9	" 14	8'-0	
103	"	"	"	" 3	" 7	9	" 14	8'-0	
104	"	"	"	" 3	" 7	9	" 14	8'-0	
105	"	"	"	" 3	" 7/5	9	" 14	8'-0	
106	HALL	"	"	VINYL BRICK 3	" 8	9	" 14	8'-0	
107	WOMEN	CER T	CER T 2	CER T 4	" 8	9	PLAST 12	8'-0	PROVIDE MIRROR, TOWEL CAB, MET PART
108	MEN	"	2	" 4	" 8	10	" 12	8'-0	
109	JANITOR	VAT 1	VINYL	VINYL CMU 3	" 7/6	ALUM 9	ACCLG BD 14	8'-0	
110	OFFICE	"	"	VINYL 3	" 7	9	" 14	8'-0	

STAIRTOWER FINISH SCHEDULE

NO	RISER	TREAD	STRINGER	INTERMEDIATE FLOOR	FLOOR BASE	FLOOR LANDING	BASE	SOFFIT	CEILING	RAILING	WALL RAILING	WALLS
S1	STL 15	STL 15	STL 15	VAT 1	VINYL 3	VAT 1	VINYL 3	PLAST 13	PLAST 13	VINYL 3	VINYL 16	CMU 6
S2	" 15	" 15	" 15	" 1	" 3	" 1	" 3	" 13	" 13	STL 15	" 16	" 6
S3	CONC 17	CONC 17	CONC 17	CONC 17				" 11	" 11	STL 11	" 15	PLAST 11
S4	" 17	" 17	" 17	" 17				" 11	" 11	" 11	" 15	" 11

INTERIOR MATERIAL SCHEDULE

NO	MATERIAL	SIZE	TYPE	FINISH
1	VINYL ASBESTOS TILE	9" x 9" x 1/8"	SEE SPECS	WAX
2	CERAMIC FLOOR TILE	1 1/16" x 1 1/16"	CERAMIC MOSAIC	FACTORY FINISH, UNGLAZED
3	VINYL COVE BASE	4" HIGH	COVE BASE	"
4	CERAMIC BASE TILE	4 1/4" x 6" x 5/16"	"	MATTE GLAZE
5	BRICK	3 COURSES = 8"	SEE SPECS, COMMON BOND	1/4" CONCAVE JOINT 3/8"
6	CONCRETE MASONRY UNIT	1 COURSE = 8"	"	ALUM BATTENS
7	VINYL COVERED GYP BD	4'-0 x 8'-0 x 1/2" SHEETS	"	PAINT
8	CERAMIC WALL TILE	4 1/4" x 6" x 5/16"	WALL TILE	FACTORY FINISH, MATTE GLAZE
9	ALUMINUM		SEE SPECS	PAINT
10	HOLLOW METAL			SPRAYED ON WHITE
11	PLASTER		CEMENT	WHITE COAT
12	"		KEENE CEMENT	PAINT
13	"		SAND FINISH GYPSUM	
14	ACOUSTICAL CEILING BOARD	2'-0 x 2'-0 x 5/8"	SEE SPECS, EXPOSED "T" BARS	FACTORY FINISH
15	STEEL		STEEL STAIR PARTS	PAINT
16	STAIR RAILING	2" x 2" x 3/8" STEEL BASE PLATE	VINYL STAIR RAIL	FACTORY FINISH, PAINT BASE
17	CONCRETE			SEAL w/ LIPIDOLITH

Drawing No. 14 Room schedules of the South Hills Office Building.

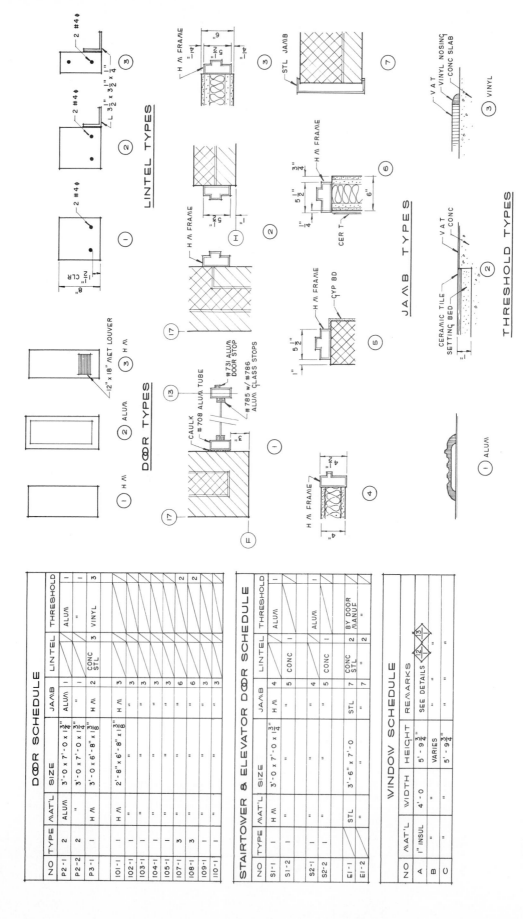

Drawing No. 15   *Door and window schedules of the South Hills Office Building.*

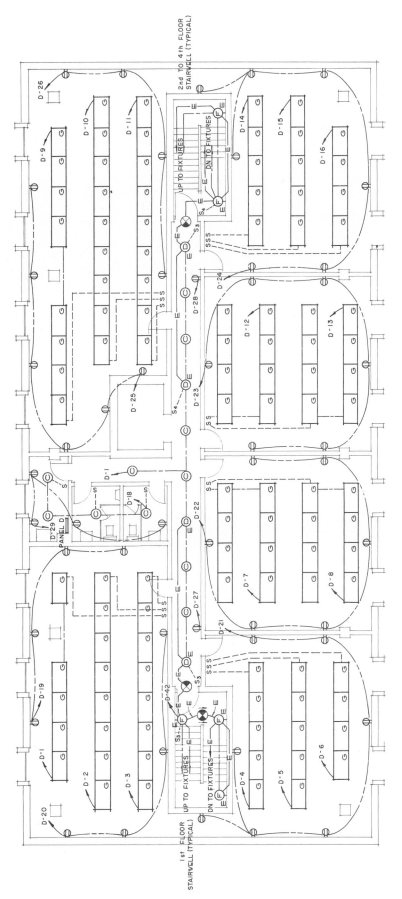

Drawing No. E1   *Electrical plan of the South Hills Office Building.*

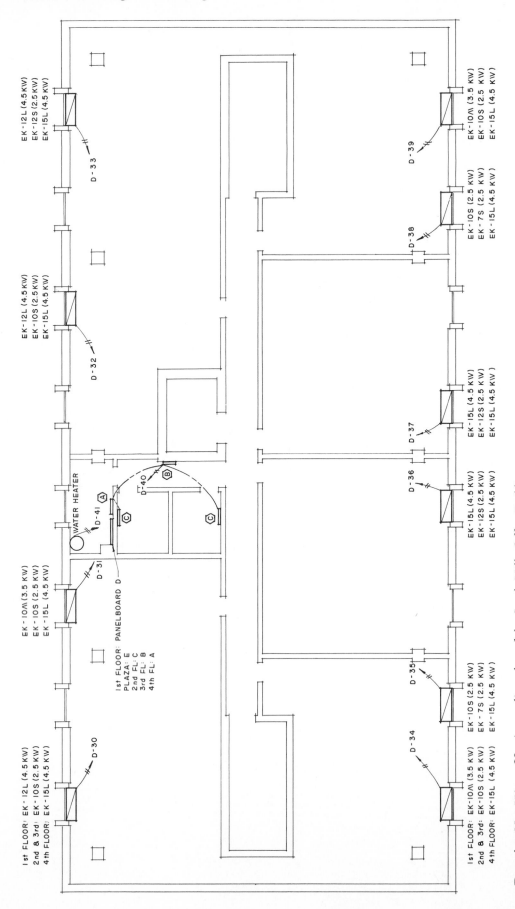

Drawing No. H1 *Heating-cooling plan of the South Hills Office Building.*

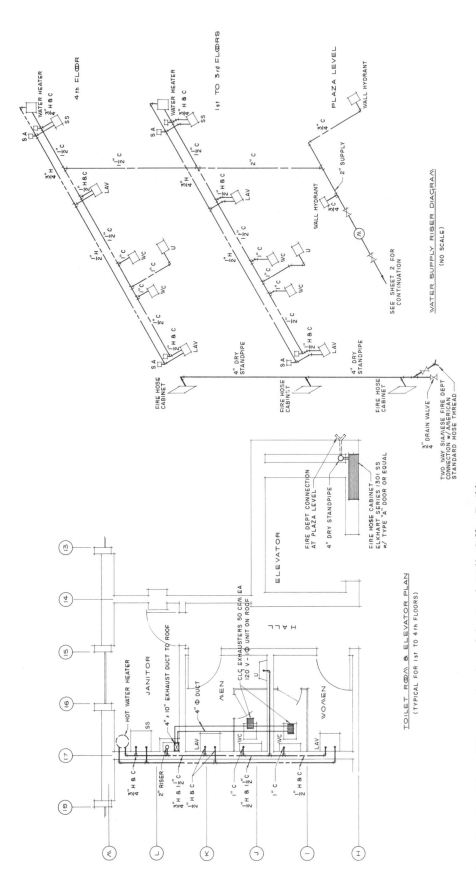

Drawing No. P1   *Water supply plan of the South Hills Office Building.*

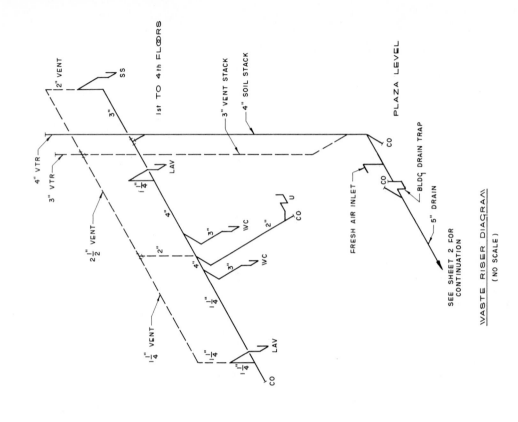

WASTE RISER DIAGRAM
(NO SCALE)

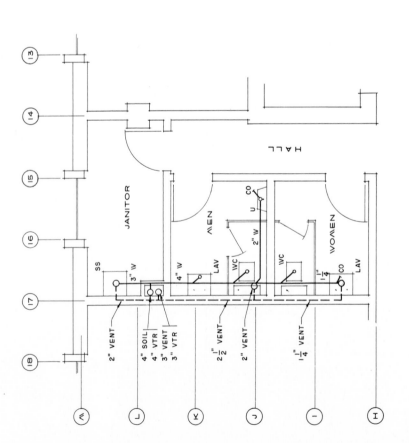

TOILET ROOM PLAN
(TYPICAL FOR 1st TO 4th FLOORS)

Drawing No. P2 *Sanitary plan of the South Hills Office Building.*

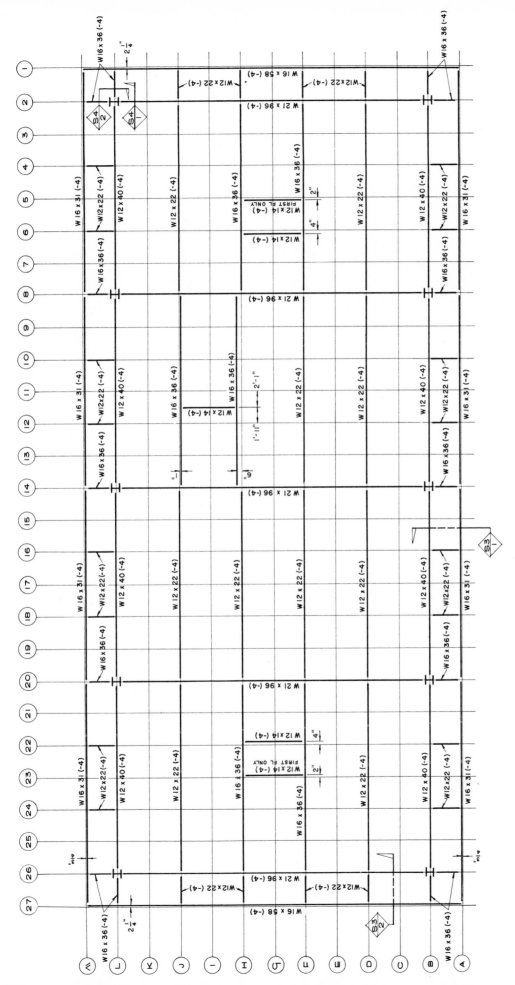

Drawing No. S1   *First-floor structural plan of the South Hills Office Building. (Second-, third-, and fourth-floor structural plans similar.)*

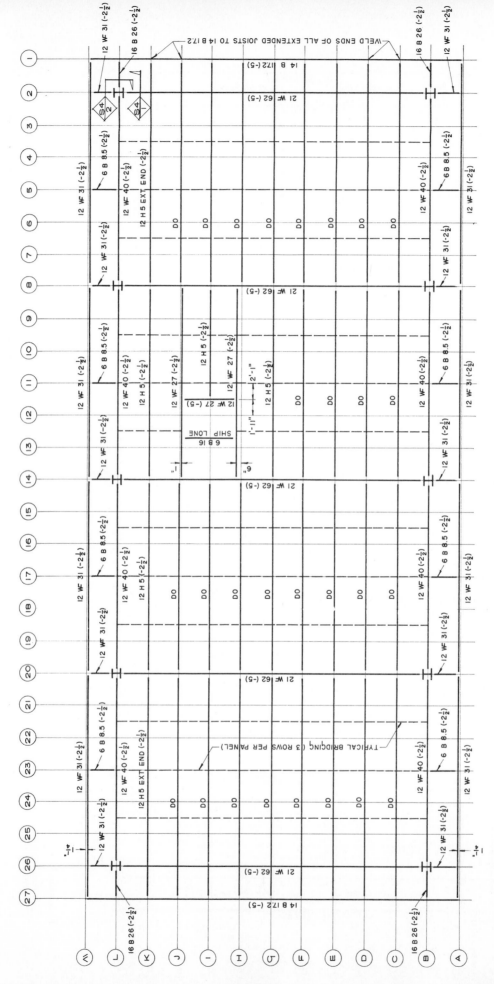

Drawing No. S2   *Roof structural plan of the South Hills Office Building (using "old" steel designations).*

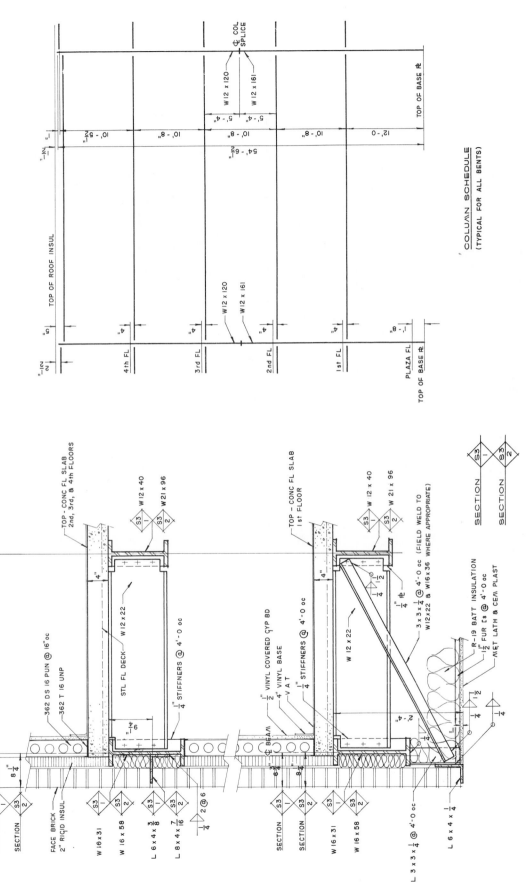

Drawing No. S3 *Structural section and column schedule of the South Hills Office Building.*

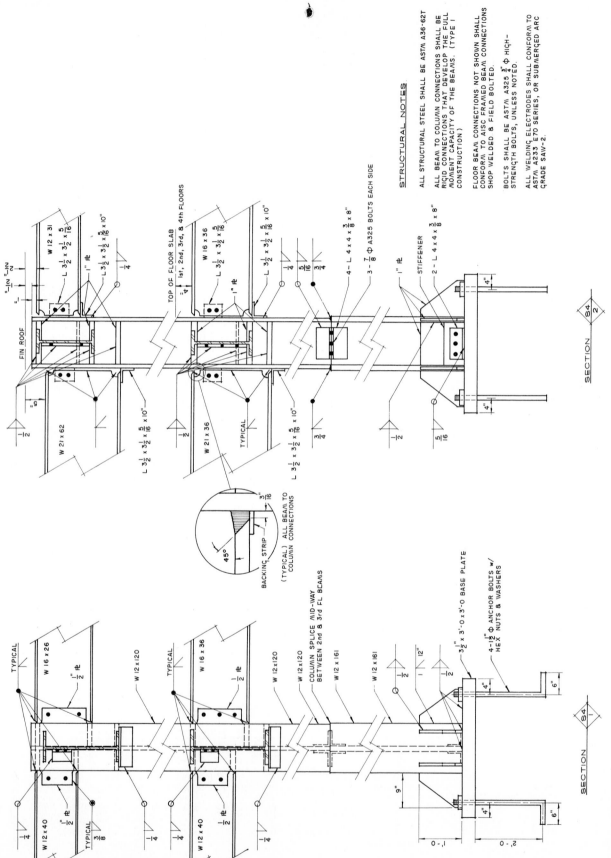

Drawing No. S4   *Structural details of the South Hills Office Building.*

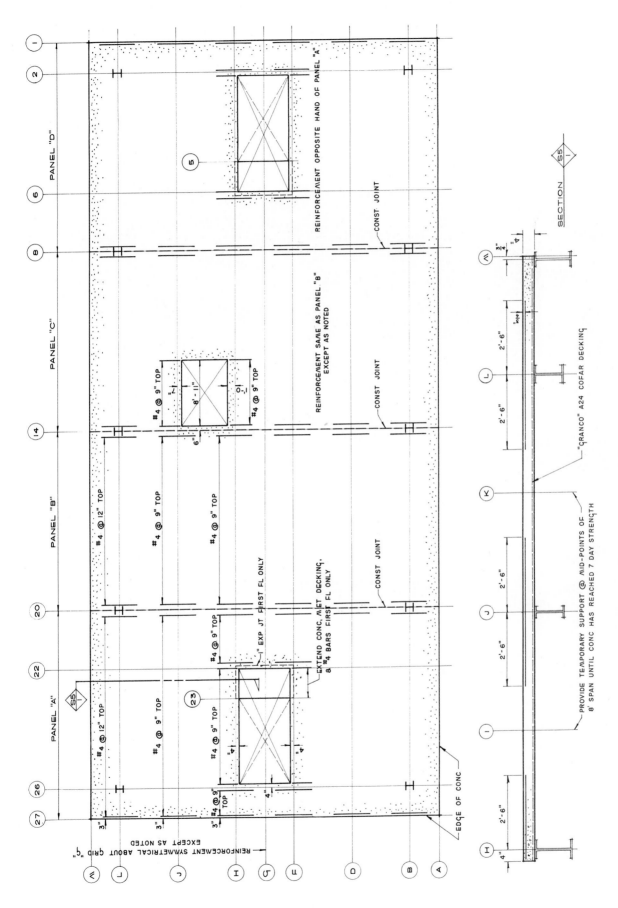

Drawing No. S5 *Concrete slab plan of the South Hills Office Building. (First, second, third, and fourth floors.)*

Figure 25   *Steel framing of the South Hills Office Building.*

Figure 26   *Close-up of framing showing masonry shelves.*

Figure 27   *Detail of welded beam-to-column connection.*

Figure 28   *Detail of fireproofing sprayed on steel beams.*

Figure 29   *Corrugated forms for reinforced concrete floors.*

Figure 30   *Corrugated decking over open-web roof joists.*

Figure 31   *Installing forms for simulated beams over plaza level.*

Figure 32   *Metal lath installed prior to plastering.*

Figure 33 *Outside wall detail before mullion installation.*

Figure 34 *Assembling aluminum window mullions before erection.*

Figure 35 *Outside wall detail after mullion installation.*

Figure 36 *Steel interior partition framing.*

Figure 37 *Wood strapping nailed to masonry stairwell in preparation for drywall installation.*

Figure 38 *Hung metal channels will support ceiling panels.*

Figure 39   *Exterior view of the completed South Hills Office Building.*

Figure 40   *The law office in the South Hills Office Building.*

Figure 41 *The real estate office in the South Hills Office Building.*

Figure 42 *The advertising agency's conference room in the South Hills Office Building.*

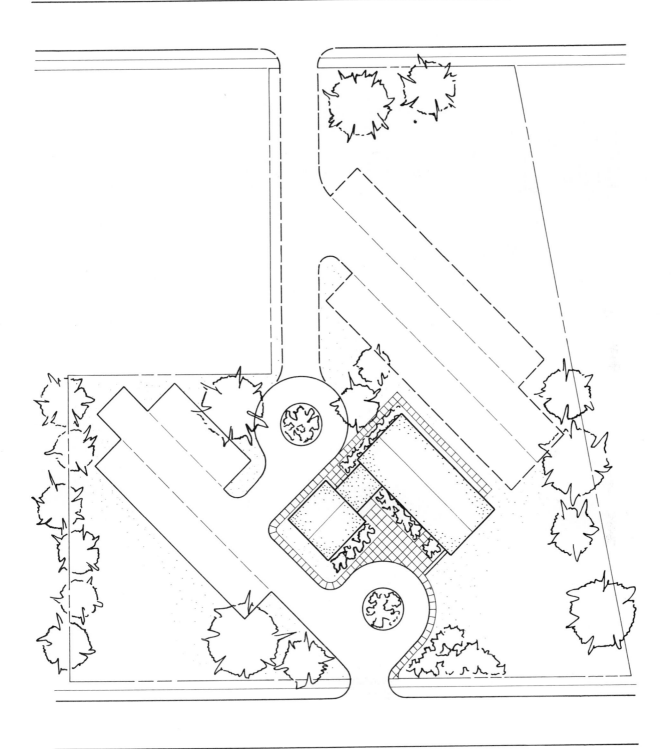

Figure 43 *Plot plan of a community church.*

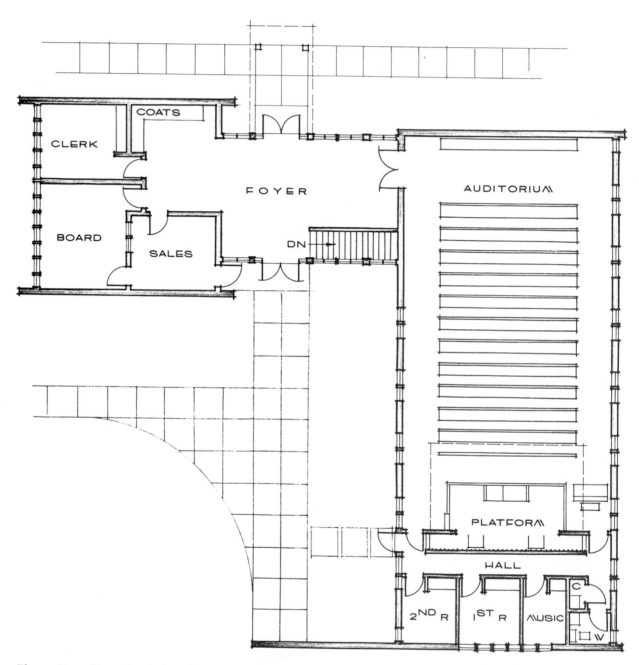

Figure 44 *Upper-level plan of a community church.*

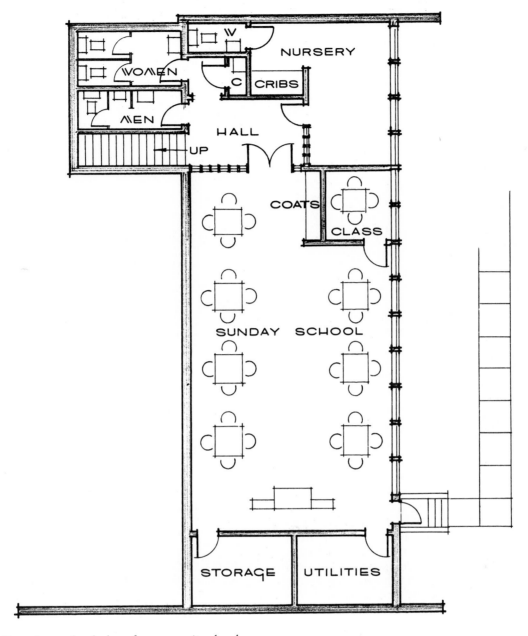

Figure 45 *Lower-level plan of a community church.*

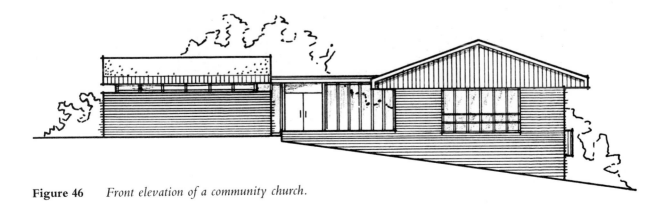

Figure 46 *Front elevation of a community church.*

41 / Design for Accessibility

For a public building to be used as intended, it must be accessible to *all* individuals, including those with walking, sight, and hearing impairments. Although the design and construction of a new building for accessibility is easily accomplished, it often is quite difficult to correct design errors and remove architectural barriers at a later time. In a few instances, accessibility features will help one group but hinder another. This, of course, is often true in architectural design where no one solution is ideal for everyone. However, designers still have a moral, as well as a legal, obligation to include accessibility considerations in their designs.

The cost of accessibility varies greatly. Depending upon what is required, it can range from almost no additional cost to virtually prohibitive costs. Usually in a new building, accessibility can be designed into the job and the building can be constructed without major deviations from the original designs. Thus in new construction provision for accessibility is accomplished at low cost. For most projects, additional costs incurred to provide accessible facilities, elevators, and ramps should not exceed from 0.5 to 5 percent of the total construction costs. In retrofitting existing facilities, the costs will depend on how easily accessibility can be attained.

STANDARDS

The basis for most federal, state, and local legislation on accessible design is standard ANSI A117.1–

* This chapter courtesy of Professor John N. Grode. The Behrend College of The Pennsylvania State University.

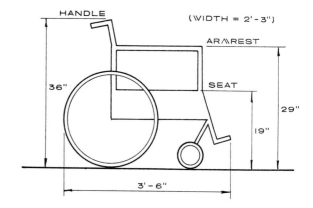

Figure 1   *Dimensions of a typical wheelchair.*

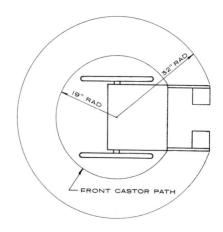

Figure 2   *Turning radius of a typical wheelchair.*

1980 entitled *Specifications for Making Buildings and Facilities Accessible to and Usable by Physically Handicapped People*. This standard establishes minimum design requirements for buildings and facilities so that they are usable by people with such physical disabilities as the inability to walk, difficulty in walking, reliance on walking aids, lack of coordination or stamina, reaching or manipulation difficulty, extremes of physical size, sight or hearing impairment, or difficulty in interpreting and reacting to sensory information. Accessibility and usability allow a disabled person to get to, enter, and use a building or facility. Although this standard refers primarily to public building and facilities, many of the recommendations can be easily adapted to residential buildings and facilities as well.

The recommendations in this chapter are not entirely based on ANSI A117.1–1980 or its predecessor ANSI A117.1–1961 (R 1971), but instead are the most common design considerations found in the many accessibility codes in effect throughout the Americas. These recommendations are not all-inclusive, and obviously a designer must consult the federal, state, and local accessibility regulations that apply to the particular project. Failure to comply with the accessibility sections of the applicable codes may well result in the designer's facing legal action and the project being closed by court order until the violations are corrected.

COMPENSATING FOR IMPAIRED MOBILITY

Persons requiring wheelchairs do not constitute the majority of the disabled population, but since their requirements for mobility demand the most space (based on the size of the wheelchair, Figure 1, and its turning requirements, Figures 2–4), most spatial design criteria have been written with them in mind. Additional limitations such as maximum reach from a wheelchair further affect the criteria. It should be noted that electric wheelchairs may be slightly larger than the standard self-propelled model. With few exceptions, spatial considerations defined for chairbound individuals will benefit other disability groupings.

Parking spaces.

1. Parking space should be set aside and clearly marked for disabled use. The United States Architectural and Transportation Barriers Compliance Board (A&TBCB) has reviewed many of the various state and local building codes and has developed the recommendations indicated in Table I. This table represents an adequate minimum for most types of facilities.
2. Parking should be located as close as possible to an accessible entrance.

Table I *Recommended Number of Parking Spaces*

Total Parking in Lot	Required Minimum Number of Accessible Parking Spaces
1 to 25	1
26 to 50	2
51 to 75	3
76 to 100	4
101 to 150	5
151 to 200	6
201 to 300	7
301 to 400	8
401 to 500	9
501 to 1000	2% of total
Over 1000	20 plus 1 for each 100 over 1000

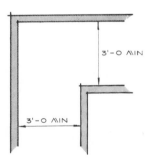

Figure 3 *Minimum dimensions for a 90° corner.*

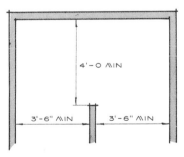

Figure 4 *Minimum dimensions for a 180° turn about a partition.*

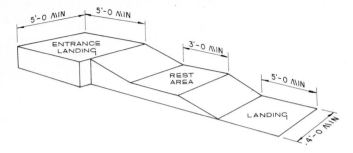

Figure 5 *Ramp dimensions.*

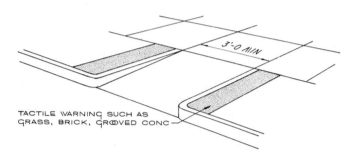

Figure 6 *Radiused curb cut (preferred).*

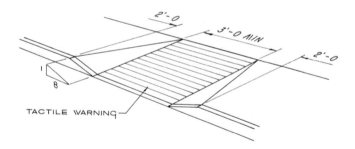

Figure 7 *Flared curb cut.*

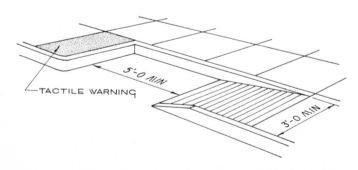

Figure 8 *Parallel curb cut used when depth is small.*

3. The approach from the parking space to any walkway should be ramped if necessary.
4. The width of each parking space should be at least 12'–0 to allow room for transfer from an automobile to a wheelchair. A minimum 13'–0 is more realistic to permit the use of vans equipped with side door lifts. This recommendation includes an 8'–0 wide access aisle adjacent to each van parking space instead of the typical 5'–0.
5. Care should be taken when laying out parking spaces to ensure that chairbound individuals need not travel behind or between other vehicles.
6. Vans fitted with raised roofs are increasingly being used by the disabled, so designers of parking garages must provide sufficient overhead clearance. Where accessible parking is provided in garages, a 9'–6" clear height should be provided for van headroom along the entire route between entry, parking spaces, and exit.
7. Accessible parking stalls should be on as level a surface as possible. In general the surface should not slope in excess of 1:50.
8. Surfaces of parking stalls and adjacent walkways should be stable, firm, and slip resistant. Gravelled surfaces generally are not usable by the disabled.

Walks.

1. Walkways should be a minimum 5'–0 wide with hard, nonskid surfaces. Some codes will permit 3'–0 or 4'–0 wide walkways, but this is an insufficient width for two wheelchairs to pass each other. Furthermore, on the narrower walkways there is the danger of walking persons tripping over crutches, canes, or walkers used by semi-ambulatory persons.
2. Furniture and other obstacles such as benches, mailboxes, and refuse containers should not be within the minimum 5'–0 width of the walkway.
3. Surfaces should be level. Abrupt changes in level surface of over $\frac{1}{2}$" tend to jam the small front wheels of wheelchairs and to cause the unstable walker to trip.
4. Water, ice, and snow should be removed from outside walkways. In some climates this may require covered or heated walkways.
5. A minimum overhead clearance of 6'–8" should be maintained.
6. Below the overhead clearance, no object should overhang the side of the walkway by more than 4".

Ramps.

1. The maximum slope of a ramp should be 8.3 percent (1:12).
2. The minimum width should be 4'–0 and is sub-

ject to the same considerations as walkway widths.

3. Ramps should have a continuous 1½″ diameter handrail 32″ high. The handrail permits some chairbound persons to pull themselves up the ramp. Handrails are not necessary for ramps sloping less than 5 percent (1:20) with no drop-offs.

4. Handrails should extend 12″ to 18″ beyond the top and bottom of the ramp if they do not project into a main pathway.

5. If many children will be using the ramp, include an additional lower handrail at a height of 24″.

6. Ramps with a drop-off should have a 2″ curb.

7. Every 30′ there should be a level area 3′–0 long to be used as a resting area (Figure 5).

8. A level landing should be provided at the top and bottom of the ramp. The landings should be at least 5′–0 long.

9. The ramp should have a nonskid surface and be kept free of water, ice, and snow.

Curb cuts.

1. Curb cuts should be placed where they will not be blocked by parked vehicles.

2. The width of the curb cut should be at least 3′–0 exclusive of flared sides (Figures 6–8), but 4′–0 is recommended.

3. A curb cut is a ramp, and the slope should not exceed 5 percent (1:20). However, when the curb cut is a short ramp, some states permit a slope up to 16.7 percent (1:6), although there is some danger of a wheelchair tipping over backwards at slopes greater than 8.3 percent (1:12).

4. Care must be taken that the curb cut is not a hazard to pedestrians, particularly to persons with impaired sight. Thus the curb cut should be clearly marked with a planting strip, railing, or some form of tactile (capable of being *felt*) warning system. Further, it is advisable to not place the curb cut directly in line with the major pedestrian walkway.

5. A diagonal curb cut (Figure 9) is usable for both directions of travel and the hazardous, up and down, effect of two adjacent ramps is avoided. Further, in parts of the country where snow removal is a concern, the diagonal ramps are more likely to be cleared whereas ramps off to the side may be buried under snow.

  Persons with impaired sight frequently use curb cuts to orient themselves at intersections. Thus diagonal curb cuts may tend to be confusing and care must be exercised when incorporating them.

Entrances, doors, and doorways.

1. Entrances should have a continuous level or ramped surface.

2. The outer surface of an entrance should have a slope no greater than 2 percent (1:50) within 5′–0 of a door. Ideally there should be a level entranceway to permit the chairbound to conveniently manage the wheelchair and the door.

3. If an exterior threshold is absolutely necessary, it should have beveled edges and be a maximum ¾″ high. Interior thresholds should be flush.

4. Doors should have a minimum 2′–8″ clear passageway when the door is open (Figure 10). Double-leaf doors should have at least one door leaf meeting this requirement.

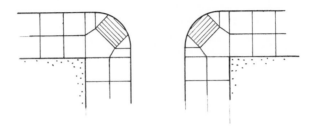

Figure 9   *Diagonal curb cuts.*

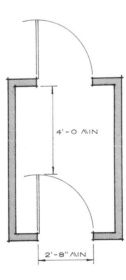

4′–0 MIN

2′–8″ MIN

Figure 10   *Minimum door dimensions for accessibility.*

5. Doors placed in a series should open in the same direction or open away from the area between them. A minimum 4'-0 of clear space should be provided between such doors (Figure 10).

6. Revolving doors cannot be used at all by people in wheelchairs, and are difficult, if not impossible, for those individuals with walkers, crutches, canes, or sight impairments. If a revolving door must be used to maintain an efficient air seal, a suitable accessible auxiliary entrance or exit must be provided nearby.

7. Turnstiles are often used to control pedestrian traffic. They present the same types of problems to the physically handicapped population as revolving doors. There are other one-way gates that perform the same function but that have wider openings and require less opening force. If turnstiles are necessary, some alternate type of entrance must be provided.

8. Door closures may be necessary for energy conservation, security, noise control, or fire control, and must have sufficient force to overcome friction, wind, and indoor and outdoor air pressure. If door closures are installed, they should require no more than 5 lbs. opening force on an exterior door. Automatic doors are recommended if greater opening forces will be required. Sliding automatic doors are preferred to swinging doors.

9. Manual doors should have single-action lever, toggle, or paddle-type handles. Some persons cannot grasp, pinch, or twist knobs.

10. Doors should have a smooth push panel extending at least 12″ up from the bottom to permit pushing the door open with a wheelchair's foot pedal. This greatly minimizes damage to the door and helps by providing a smooth pushing surface.

11. Thick, bristly floor mats and plush carpeting should be avoided since they greatly increase the effort required to push a wheelchair.

12. Grates or grilles used in entrances to trap dirt and gravel are by their very nature, tripping hazards. Great care must be exercised when specifying their design and use. Their openings may be rectangular if their smaller dimension (measured parallel to the traffic flow) is less than $\frac{3}{8}″$ while the other dimension may be up to 4″.

13. The disabled should be able to use the principal entrances of a building and not be restricted to using service entrances.

Stairs and stairways.

1. Tread run should not be less than 11″, and tread rise should not exceed 7″.

2. Tread nosing should not exceed $1\frac{1}{2}″$, and the radius of the tread nose should not exceed $\frac{1}{2}″$. (See Figure 11.)

3. Tread runs and rises should be consistent for the length of the stairway.

4. Continuous handrails should be provided, preferably on both sides of the stairway, and extend 12″–18″ beyond the ends of the stairway.

5. Handrails should be 32″ high and have $1\frac{1}{2}″$ clearance between the railing and wall to prevent hands from getting caught.

6. Open stairways are very decorative. However, they are hazardous to those with leg braces who have difficulty clearing the stair nose. Persons with seriously impaired sight also have difficulty climbing an open staircase since they are unable to feel the front face of the next step with their shoe tips.

Elevators and wheelchair lifts.

1. All elevators and elevator lobbies intended for use by the public and by employees should be accessible.

2. Elevators should be provided for all buildings of two or more levels.

3. The elevator should be large enough for at

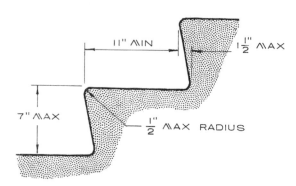

Figure 11 *Stair dimensions for accessibility.*

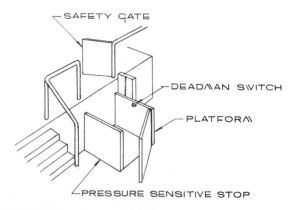

Figure 12 *A vertical platform lift.*

least one wheelchair to enter, turn 180°, and exit.

4. The positioning of the control panel is important. It should be mounted on the front or side wall within diagonal reach from a wheelchair. Also, the uppermost control buttons should not be higher than 4'-6".
5. Controls should have tactile identification to be read by those with impaired sight, as well as tactile markings on both sides of the door jamb to identify the floor.
6. Emergency safety controls and devices should be located no higher than 3'-4".
7. The elevator should have automatic controls, with automatic open and close features as well as automatic reopening if the closing door strikes an obstacle.
8. The elevator should have automatic leveling within $\frac{1}{2}$" of the floor level.
9. Lobby call buttons should be centered no higher than 3'-6".
10. Visual and audible signals to indicate arriving elevator cars should be used, with one ring for an "up" car and two for a "down" car.
11. Ideally, visual and audible signals to identify each floor should be provided.
12. The wheelchair lift (Figure 12) is rather new in the building industry and is primarily used for less than two-floor operations when a ramp is impractical. These lifts have a capacity of 400 to 500 lbs. There are two types of wheelchair lifts, one that operates vertically like an elevator and the other that runs on an incline following the flight of stairs.

   At present, there is a movement underway to create an ANSI standard for wheelchair lifts that are not regulated by A17.1 elevator standards. Further, some local codes do not permit their use.

Building controls.

1. Building controls such as light switches, thermostats, air-conditioner controls, window and drapery hardware, call buttons, electrical outlets, and fire alarms, intended for use by visitors and employees, should be within reach of the chairbound.
2. These controls should be located no higher than 4'-0, but 3'-4" is recommended.
3. Electrical outlets should be located at least 18" high.

Restrooms.

1. If public restrooms are provided, at least one restroom per sex should meet accessibility requirements.
2. When the toilet is enclosed in a stall, the stall should meet the following requirements:

a. Minimum width 3'-0.
b. Stall door 2'-8" wide that swings out or slides.
c. Minimum depth 5'-0 if a wall-hung toilet is used; otherwise, minimum depth 6'-0.
d. Handrails 2'-8" high on both sides, minimum 4'-0 long, 1½" diameter, with 1½" clearance from wall, capable of supporting 250 lbs. (See Figure 13.)

This minimum toilet stall arrangement requires transfer from the front or rear of the wheelchair to the toilet. Transfers of this type are difficult for many chairbound, and thus a layout such as shown in Figure 14 is recom-

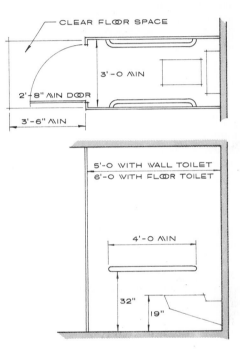

Figure 13   *Stall dimensions for front/rear transfer.*

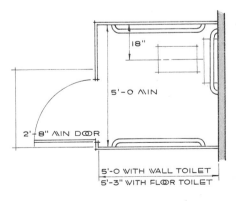

Figure 14   *Stall dimensions for side transfer.*

mended. This permits side transfers as well as the more awkward front/rear transfers.

3. The flushing control should be no higher than 3'–0 and easily reached.
4. The toilet tissue dispenser should be conveniently positioned.
5. The top of the lavatory should be no higher than 2'–8", and the lower edge should be no lower than 2'–3" (2'–5" is recommended). This will permit a wheelchair to wheel under the unit.
6. Single-lever faucet handles should be used.
7. All plumbing should be mounted close to the wall to provide for knee and toe clearance. Pipes carrying hot water should be insulated to protect those chairbound who have no sensation in their legs.
8. Accessories such as towel racks, towel dispensers, electric hand dryers, sanitary napkin dispensers, soap dispensers, refuse disposal units, vending machines, and shelves should have operating parts no higher than 3'–4".
9. The bottom of at least one mirror should be mounted no higher than 3'–2". Full-length mirrors are acceptable.
10. Baffle walls or partitions used to block public view of toilet facilities should not impede access.

Drinking fountains and watercoolers.

1. The waterspout of a watercooler should be 2'–8" high. Sufficient clearance must be provided for the wheelchair to be wheeled under the cooler with appropriate knee and toe clearance, especially if the cooler is hung in an alcove.
2. The watercooler should have a front-position waterspout and water trajectory approximately parallel to the front of the cooler.
3. The watercooler should have controls that do not require manual dexterity to grasp, pinch, or twist. If a foot pedal is used, auxiliary single-action hand controls should be provided.

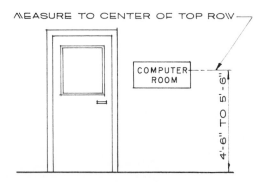

Figure 15 *Height of tactile signs.*

4. If cups are required, they should be in a convenient position.

Public telephones.

1. At least one telephone on each floor should be accessible to those with impaired mobility.
2. The height of the telephone's uppermost operating mechanism (usually the coin slots) should not exceed 4'–0.
3. Push-button telephones should be used whenever available.
4. The telephone receiver cord should be at least 2'–6" long.
5. The receiver should have a volume-control adjustment for use by individuals with impaired hearing.
6. The telephone book should be within easy reach.
7. The telephone should be mounted so that a wheelchair can make a parallel approach to the face of the phone.
8. The size of a telephone booth should be approximately 4'–0 × 5'–0 with at least a 2'–8" opening and a 3'–6" clear depth. A fixed seat would only be in the way of a wheelchair, so a hinged seat is preferred. The telephone should be mounted on a side wall of the booth enclosure or diagonally in a corner.
9. The telephone may be mounted in an alcove if sufficient knee and toe clearance is provided.

COMPENSATING FOR IMPAIRED SIGHT

Today most persons with seriously impaired sight use a long cane or a seeing-eye dog, enabling them to be more active than they were in the past. Typically, individuals who use a long cane will have sighted persons guide them through a building while they become familiar with room shapes and the positions of obstacles such as furniture and columns. Persons using seeing-eye dogs move about more easily, relying on dogs to direct them around obstacles.

The following are accessibility considerations for the sight-impaired:

1. Avoid low-hanging obstacles. A minimum overhead clearance of 6'–8" should be adhered to at all times.
2. Tactile senses are often used to compensate for impaired sight. Thus a change in floor surface, such as from carpet to tile, can be used to identify key areas such as restrooms or lobbies and danger areas such as stairs or ramps.

3. Persons with impaired sight can identify abrupt changes in surface such as a curb, but they are not always able to identify gradual changes such as a ramp. Thus some type of tactile surface change should occur 2'–4" before a potentially dangerous obstacle.

4. Handles and knobs on doors leading to danger areas such as boiler rooms, equipment rooms, fire escapes, stage doors, loading platforms, and the like should have knurled surfaces. This tactile identification serves as an immediate warning.

5. The sense of sound also is used to aid in moving about. An overly *live* acoustical environment can thus lead to confusion.

6. Ideally, all written directions and information should be accompanied by verbal instructions. Where this is impractical, signs should be constructed of raised capital Arabic letters and numerals at least ⅝" high with color contrast between the letter and its background. This will permit the individual to use the sense of touch to read the sign. Furthermore, many persons have residual sight and can read signs when there is high contrast between the message and its background. To avoid confusion, keep signs brief.

7. Some persons read only Braille. For such persons, Braille identification and instructions should be available if possible.

8. All signs should be placed consistently between 4'–6" and 5'–6" high. (Figure 15)

COMPENSATING FOR IMPAIRED HEARING

Most people with hearing impairment are able to hear some sounds, given a reasonable environment for sound transmission. Others are able to hear only certain frequencies of sound. Designers can accommodate both groups without extensive modifications. Some recommendations follow.

1. Fire alarms, telephones, doorbells, and other devices using sound signals should use sound frequencies that can attract the attention of individuals with partial hearing. For individuals with severe hearing impairment, visual signals such as blinking lights are the solution.

2. As noted earlier, at least one telephone in a bank of public telephones should be equipped with an adjustable sound amplifier. This aid is available from nearly all telephone companies. Also, private telephones for persons unable to hear the audible ring of a telephone should be equipped with a blinking light to indicate incoming calls.

3. Signs and directions should be composed with

Figure 16   *International symbol of access.*

Table II   *Dimensions for International Symbol of Access*

Size	Location	Viewing Distance
2½ in.	Interior	Up to 30 ft.
4 in.	Interior	Greater than 30 ft.
4 in.	Exterior	Up to 60 ft.
8 in.	Exterior	Greater than 60 ft.

care to ensure clarity of understanding so that the hearing-impaired individual need not ask questions.

4. Public address systems should not have excessively loud volume. The increased volume results in sound distortion for individuals with reduced hearing as well as for those with normal hearing.

INTERNATIONAL SYMBOL OF ACCESS

The International Symbol of Access (Figure 16) is used to identify special facilities for the disabled. It should always be used in the design and proportions shown and in contrasting colors of black or dark blue and white. The A&TBCB has recommended the dimensions shown in Table II.

STUDY QUESTIONS

1. List three design considerations of aid to chairbound persons:
   a. Parking an automobile
   b. Leaving an automobile
   c. Moving over a curb
   d. Moving down a level walk
   e. Moving up a ramp

f. Moving through a doorway
2. List six design considerations of aid to persons with impaired sight.
3. List three design considerations of aid to persons with impaired hearing.
4. For accessibility, indicate the maximum recommended height for:
   a. Building controls
   b. Ramp handrails
   c. Elevator door controls
   d. Elevator emergency controls
   e. Top of lavatory
5. Indicate the minimum recommended height for overhead clearance.
6. For accessibility, indicate the minimum width of:
   a. Walkways
   b. Ramps
   c. Doorways

LABORATORY PROBLEMS

1. Check your original building design for compliance with local and statewide accessibility codes.
2. Prepare details for an original design to improve accessibility:
   a. Between floors for chairbound persons
   b. Between rooms for persons with impaired sight
   c. For communications between rooms for persons with impaired hearing

42 / Design for Acoustics

Proper environment benefits all human activities. It has long been recognized that proper lighting, decorating, and air conditioning will reduce stress, but sound conditioning has only recently* been accepted as equally important. Sounds, as well as other factors affecting senses, can make us happy or annoyed, contented or distracted, efficient or careless. A building is a controlled environment and should be designed for sound control just as it is planned for durability and weather protection. Obviously theaters and auditoriums should be sound-conditioned, but attention should also be given to single- and multifamily buildings, offices, factories, and schools.

The acoustical design of an important building would be entrusted to a consulting firm specializing in architectural acoustics. Although architectural drafters would not be expected to be acoustical experts, they can prevent many noise problems by using common sense in their design and materials specifications. In planning a building for sound conditioning, designers have four factors under their control:

1. Layout
2. Sound transmission
3. Sound reflection
4. Sound absorption

Each of these elements will be studied in the same order in which they should be considered during design.

* Minimum specifications for sound transmission were established by the Federal Housing Administration in 1963 in its *Minimum Property Standards for Multifamily Housing*.

LAYOUT

Intelligent site selection and room layout can prevent many acoustical problems from developing. For example, a school should not be located adjacent to a superhighway or a hospital located near a jet air terminal. Also, quiet and noisy areas in the same building should be removed from each other or separated by buffer zones such as storage walls or corridors. For example, the placement of an office adjacent to a noisy manufacturing area (Figure 1) can be improved by using the storage room and lavatories as a sound buffer. Figure 2 shows how office windows and doors can be separated to reduce sound transmission.

SOUND TRANSMISSION

Whenever it is not possible to separate quiet and noisy rooms, their common wall should be de-

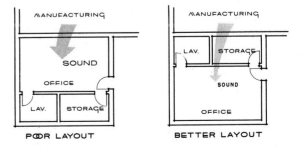

Figure 1   *Buffer zones reduce noise transmission.*

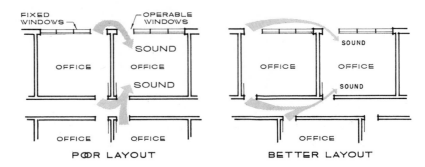

Figure 2 *Increased transmission paths reduce noise.*

STAGGERED STUDS   SLOTTED STUDS   RESILIENT BRACKETS

Figure 3 *Construction of acoustical double walls.*

signed to reduce sound transmission to an acceptable level. It is not necessary to prevent *all* sound transmission, but rather just to reduce it to a level below the normal sound level in the quieter room.

Table I *Sound Transmission Classification (STC) of Walls*

Type of Wall	STC
2″ × 4″ wood studs with dry-wall finish, both sides	32
2″ × 4″ staggered wood studs with dry-wall finish, both sides	41
2″ × 4″ wood studs with plastered finish, both sides	35
2″ × 4″ staggered wood studs with plastered finish, both sides	44
8″ hollow CMU	48
8″ hollow CMU with furred dry-wall finish, both sides	58
12″ hollow CMU	
12″ doubled CMU	53
(4″ CMU + 4″ air space + 4″ CMU)	63
4″ solid brick	41
8″ solid brick	49
12″ solid brick	54
6″ reinforced concrete	46
8″ reinforced concrete	51
12″ reinforced concrete	56

Sound travels through most building materials by causing vibrations in the material. The vibrations can be caused by *structure-borne* sound or *airborne* sound. Most sound transmitted through *floors* (such as footsteps and furniture scraping) is structure-borne. Structure-borne sound can be reduced most economically by carpeting or resilient cork tiling. Most sound transmitted through *walls* (such as voice and typewriter clatter) is airborne. In general, heavy walls do not vibrate as readily as lighter walls and are therefore better barriers to airborne sound. Thus a solid brick wall would be more effective than a wood stud wall. Another method of reducing sound transmission is through the use of a *double wall,* that is, splitting a wall into two unconnected layers. In this manner, the sound vibrations are not directly transmitted from one room to another through the solid building material in a common wall. Figure 3 shows some methods of constructing double walls.

Table I can be used to compare the acoustical effectiveness of various types of walls. The ratings are given in *sound transmission classifications* (STCs), which can be considered simply as dimensionless numbers that rank the relative acoustical effectiveness of various wall types. For example, a plastered stud wall (STC = 35) is only slightly better than a dry-wall finished stud wall (STC = 32), but an 8″ CMU wall (STC = 48) or 8″ brick wall (STC = 49) is considerably better. Recommended minimum STC ratings for various conditions are given in Table II.

In addition to traveling through the walls and floors, sound will travel through any openings in the building materials and will also travel around them. An opening of only 1 sq. in. in area will transmit as much sound as 100 sq. ft. of wall area. Some possible openings are ventilating ducts, oversized pipe openings, and door cracks. Back-to-back electric outlets or medicine cabinets will also transmit sound and therefore should be avoided.

Often a partition will extend only as high as a suspended ceiling, with the area above the ceiling serving as a plenum for wiring and piping (Figure 4). Sound will then travel right *over* the partition into the next room. Often such transmission by *flanking* is greater than transmission by wall vibration. This can be avoided by extending the partitions through the plenum to the floor above. Special closure panels are available for this purpose. Another solution is the use of acoustical insulation blankets laid over the top of the suspended ceiling and extending 3′ beyond the partitions. See Figure 5. Flanking paths *around* walls are also created by some contemporary construction methods that use continuous glass walls with interior partitions that do not completely connect to the window mullions. Even a crack between wall and floor offers a flanking path.

Special sound problems caused by vibrating machinery bolted to the structure can be solved by specifying resilient machinery mountings. Any piping or duct work connected to such machinery should be attached with flexible bellows or isolated from the structure with resilient gaskets. Figure 6 illustrates these solutions.

SOUND REFLECTION

Special attention to acoustics is needed in the design of large assembly rooms where a principal function is listening to speech or music. Examples are auditoriums, theaters, churches, classrooms,

gymnasiums, and courtrooms. When these rooms are properly designed, the audience is able to hear without difficulty: the sound will be loud enough, it will be evenly distributed throughout the room, and there will be no distracting echoes.

Loudness. The sound heard by members of an audience reaches them by at least two paths: (1) *directly* from the source and (2) by *reflection* from

Table II   *Recommended Sound Transmission Classifications*

Type of Building	STC
Private residence or apartment (same occupancy)	
Bathroom/living area	40
Living area/child's bedroom	40
Kitchen/living area	38
Kitchen/bedroom	38
Bedroom/bedroom	38
Other	32
Motel, hospital, or apartment (separate occupancy)	
Bathroom/living area	50
Bathroom/bedroom	50
Bathroom/bathroom	50
Living area/living area	50
Living area/bedroom	50
Bedroom/bedroom	50
Rooms/corridor	42
Other	45
Offices	
Washroom/private office	47
Washroom/general office	40
Private office/private office	45
Private office/general office	45
Other	38
Schools	
Music room/classroom	50
Shop/classroom	47
Mechanical equipment/classroom	45
Washroom/classroom	42
Classroom/classroom	40

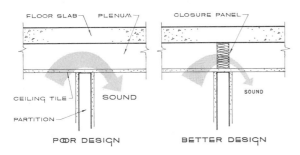

Figure 4   *Reduction of sound through plenum by closure panel.*

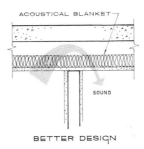

Figure 5   *Reduction of sound through plenum by ceiling blanket.*

one or more surfaces as shown in Figure 7. Some surfaces, such as acoustical tile, absorb sound and reflect very little. But hard surfaces, such as wood, concrete, plaster, and glass, absorb very little and reflect nearly all sound, just as light reflects from a

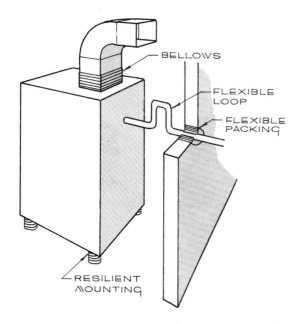

Figure 6 *Reduction of sound from vibrating machinery.*

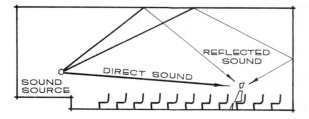

Figure 7 *Direct and reflected sound.*

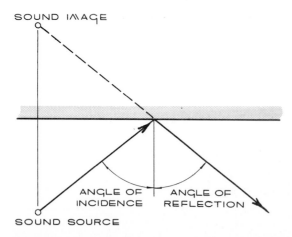

Figure 8 *Sound reflected from a plane surface.*

polished surface. The angle of sound reflection is determined by the same physical law governing light reflection: the angle of incidence equals the angle of reflection. See Figure 8. To the listener, the reflected sound appears to come not from the actual source but rather from the sound *image*. When a room is being designed, the sound image is often plotted behind the reflecting surface to serve as a graphical shortcut to determine the path of the reflection.

The loudness of a direct sound depends upon the power output of the source and the distance from the source. The loudness of a reflected sound is always less than that of the direct sound because the path is longer and some of the sound is absorbed by the reflecting surface. But the total sound reaching the listener by direct and reflected paths may be substantially louder than the direct sound alone.

Distribution. An auditorium can be designed so that sound is evenly distributed throughout the audience, allowing those seated at the rear to hear as readily as those seated at the front. This is done by shaping the floor, ceiling, and walls to accomplish specific acoustical tasks.

A good rule of thumb in acoustics is that a poor sight line from stage to audience will also produce a poor hearing line. For example, direct sound to the audience seated at the rear of the level auditorium shown in Figure 9 will diminish as it is absorbed by the people and upholstered seats in the front rows. This sound loss can be as much as 2 decibels* per row. Refer to Table III for an approximate indication of common sound levels in decibels. A sound level change of 5 decibels is quite noticeable, and a change of 10 decibels appears to the listener to double (or halve) the sound. Figure 10 illustrates common solutions to this problem: the stage is raised or the auditorium floor is sloped (preferably both).

Another method of reinforcing the sound delivered to the rear seats is through the installation of hard, sound-reflecting ceilings. As shown in

* A decibel is a unit of measuring the relative loudness of sound and is equal to the smallest change in sound level detectable by the human ear.

Table III *Common Sound Levels (in decibels)*

120 decibels	Threshold of pain (ear damage)
100 decibels	Rock band
80 decibels	Factory
60 decibels	Office
40 decibels	Home
20 decibels	Whisper
0 decibels	Threshold of hearing

Figure 11, the sound reflects from the ceiling and reinforces the direct sound. The ceiling is the most important reflective surface in an auditorium, and it is a good rule of thumb not to use sound-absorbing materials (such as acoustical tile) unless echoes must be prevented. Ceilings and other surfaces can be shaped to evenly distribute reflected sound. Figure 12 illustrates a ceiling designed to increase the reflection toward the rear of an auditorium. If a balcony is included, it is important that those persons seated under the balcony are able to "see" the ceiling (Figure 13) in order to receive sound reflected from it.

In addition to flat surfaces, convex and concave surfaces (Figure 14) may be desired. Deep convex surfaces of 6″ or more (not fine ridges as in striated plywood) will diffuse sound, but concave surfaces will cause the reflected sound waves to focus on one spot—with a consequent loss of sound at other locations. Also, the reflected sound may be louder than the direct sound, which gives the impression that the sound is coming from the wrong direction. Curved rear walls often cause such a problem, but this can be corrected by segmenting the wall into separate panels positioned in different directions, or the wall can be treated with sound-absorbing material.

Side walls also can reflect sound, resulting in undesirable effects. Figure 15 shows an auditorium with wide parallel side walls which cause the reflected sound to travel a great distance before reaching the listener and may result in echoes. Figure 16 illustrates the focusing effect of a fan-shaped side wall combined with a concave rear wall. Although there is no shape that is best for all conditions, Figure 17 shows the plan and elevation of an auditorium designed for even distribution of direct and reflected sound.

Echoes. When the first reflection of a sound reaches the listener within $\frac{1}{20}$ second of the direct sound, it tends to blend with and reinforce the direct sound. But when a reflected sound reaches the listener after $\frac{1}{20}$ second, it is heard as a distinct repetition of the direct sound—called an *echo*. Reinforced sound is desirable, but echoes are undesirable. Sound travels through the air at a velocity of 1,125 ft./sec. Consequently a reflected path that is about 50′ longer than the direct path will produce echoes.

EXAMPLE

A person seated 15′ from the front of a 45′-deep auditorium (Figure 18) will receive an echo from the rear wall since the reflected path is 75′, the direct path is only 15′, and the difference is 75′ − 15′ = 60′.

Surfaces that will produce echoes can be corrected

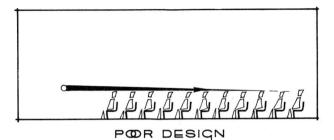

POOR DESIGN

Figure 9   *Sound distribution in a level auditorium.*

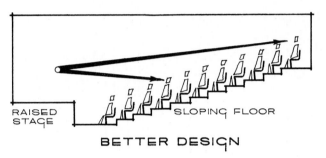

RAISED STAGE   SLOPING FLOOR

BETTER DESIGN

Figure 10   *Sound distribution in a sloping auditorium.*

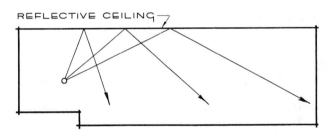

REFLECTIVE CEILING

Figure 11   *Sound reinforcement from a reflective ceiling.*

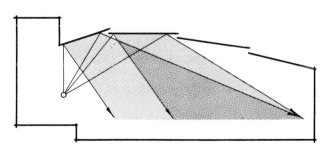

Figure 12   *Ceiling designed to increase reflected sound delivered to the rear of the audience.*

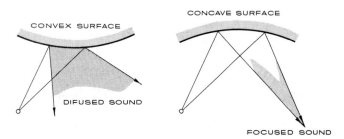

Figure 13 *Balcony designed to permit reflected sound to the audience below.*

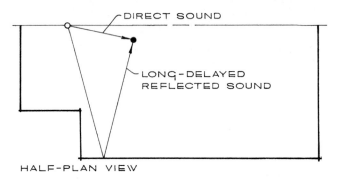

Figure 14 *Effect of convex and concave surfaces.*

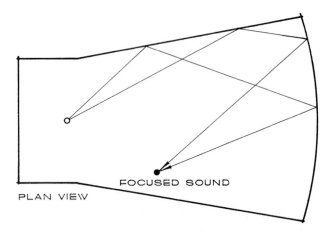

Figure 15 *Echo caused by wide side walls.*

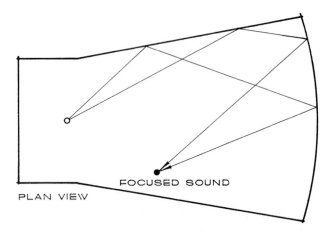

Figure 16 *Focusing effect of fan-shaped side wall combined with a concave rear wall.*

by covering with sound-absorbing material. Also, the auditorium can be designed to reduce the length of the reflected sound paths by lowering the ceiling height near the stage and narrowing the auditorium width near the stage (Figure 17). Such a design is effective for medium-sized auditoriums (seating 500–2,000). For smaller auditoriums, the first reflections usually reach the audience quickly enough to prevent echoing. In larger auditoriums, it is nearly impossible to shape them to obtain even distribution of sound without echoing. Natural hearing in the front center section is nearly always more difficult than in the farthest sections. Electronic sound amplification is the best solution.

SOUND ABSORPTION

Sound-absorbing materials are used in rooms to reduce noise or prevent echoes caused by reflected sound. They cannot reduce the level of direct sound, nor prevent sound transmission from another room (such as footsteps from the floor above). In practice, the addition of sound-absorbent material can reduce the reflected sound level in a room about 5–7 decibels, but it can never reduce the total sound below the level of the direct sound itself.

The most efficient sound-absorbing materials are fiber blankets, porous ceiling tile, carpeting, drapes, and upholstered furniture. They work by converting sound into heat due to friction on the walls of the capillaries within the material. If the surface fissures of the sound-absorbent are blocked (by excessive painting, for example), the material will no longer be effective. Fiber products are usually applied by spray gun to a 3″ depth or installed in 1″- or 2″- thick blankets. A *transparent*

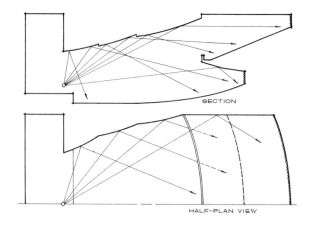

Figure 17 *Auditorium designed for sound distribution.*

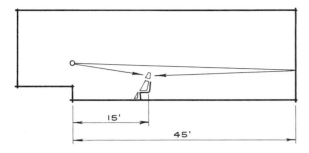

Figure 18   *Echo caused by reflected sound.*

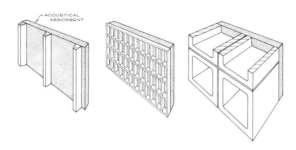

Figure 19   *Architectural facings over acoustical absorbents.*

Figure 20   *Acoustical ceiling tile used in the Air Force Museum, Dayton, Ohio.*

Figure 21   *Acoustical wall panels used in the board room of the U.S. Steel Pittsburgh headquarters.*

(acoustically speaking) facing may be installed over the fibers to achieve specific architectural effects. Some possibilities are shown in Figure 19.

Sound-absorbing materials are often specified in office buildings, schools, and auditoriums. Figures 20–21.

Office buildings. Cover ceilings with absorbents. In large office areas, wall treatment is also recommended. In large conference rooms, provide a hard, sound-reflective panel in the center of the ceiling equal to 50 percent of the ceiling area. This panel aids conversation between opposite ends of the room. The remaining ceiling and walls should be treated.

Schools. In elementary school classrooms, cover ceilings with absorbents. In higher-level classrooms of more than 700 sq. ft. of area, provide a reflective ceiling panel equal to 50 percent of the ceiling area. A 2′-wide strip of absorbent above chalkboards is recommended on two adjacent walls.

Auditoriums. Place absorbents on surfaces that will cause echoes, but not on surfaces that will provide useful sound reinforcement. Usually ceilings over 25′ high must be treated. In theaters, it may be desirable to adjust the sound-absorbent quality depending upon the performance (high reverberation for music but low for lecture). This can be done by designing flexible components such as retractable drapes as shown in Figure 22.

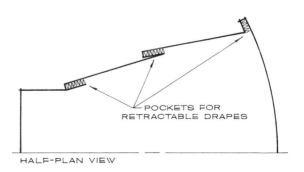

Figure 22   *Adjustable sound absorbency.*

For auditoriums, expert advice should always be obtained.

AMPLIFICATION

In large rooms (over 100,000 cu. ft. volume), electronic sound amplification will generally be required. Amplification will also be useful in rooms like lecture halls down to a size of 20,000 cu. ft. Amplification is seldom required in smaller rooms.

Electronic amplification systems may be *central* or *distributed*. The central system is usually preferred because the loudspeaker (or group of loudspeakers) is located above the sound source, giving maximum realism of sound direction. The distributed system is used when a line of sight between the central loudspeaker and audience is not feasible. The distributed system consists of a number of loudspeakers distributed over the entire audience. This is often used in airport terminals and large convention halls.

The controls of amplified sound systems should be located at the rear of the audience rather than in a glassed-in booth. The sound system operator should be able to hear the sound just as it is heard by the audience.

SOUND MASKING

In addition to reduction of noise, it is sometimes possible to mask undesirable sound by the addition of pleasant sound. This has been called *acoustic perfume*. Some examples are background music in commercial and industrial buildings, the sound of a water fountain in a busy lobby, and even the sound of air-conditioning units in motels located on noisy highways. It has been found that such a bland, continuous sound is more agreeable than intermittent noise.

STUDY QUESTIONS

1. List the four major factors to be considered during the design of a building for sound conditioning.
2. List methods of reducing sound transmission:
   a. From room to room
   b. From vibrating machinery
3. List methods of increasing the sound delivered to the rear of an auditorium.
4. List methods of increasing sound absorption in:
   a. Homes
   b. Office buildings
   c. Schools
   d. Auditoriums
5. Distinguish between:
   a. Structure-borne and airborne sound
   b. Direct and reflected sound
   c. Central and distributed amplification systems
6. Describe briefly each term:
   a. Sound transmission classification
   b. Flanking
   c. Sound image
   d. Acoustic perfume
   e. Decibel
7. Why does a reflected path 50' longer than the direct path produce an echo?

LABORATORY PROBLEMS

1. Draw the sound conditioning details for:
   a. 12' × 28' conference room
   b. 30' × 40' high school classroom
   c. 600 seat high school auditorium
2. Complete the sound conditioning plan and details for:
   a. The building assigned by your instructor
   b. Your original building design

43 / Fire Protection

BUILDING CODES

The earliest record of an attempt to improve building safety is the Code of Hammurabi, a Babylonian king and lawmaker in 2100 B.C.

> In the case of collapse of a defective building the architect is to be put to death if the owner is killed, and the architect's son if the owner's son is killed.

Laws governing building construction and land use were first introduced by the ancient Romans. During the reign of Julius Caesar, Rome grew rapidly, and tall, speculative apartments were built which often collapsed. Roman laws first limited heights to 70', and later reduced them to only 60'. In the fourteenth century the City of London adopted a law that prohibited the building of wooden chimneys. Building codes governing building construction methods and zoning ordinances governing land use were adopted in English, French, and Prussian cities by the ninteenth century, and were accepted by all U.S. cities and most towns in the early twentieth century.

The basic concept of a building code or a zoning ordinance is that individual actions should be regulated in favor of the welfare of the general public. It has been shown many times over that such protection is necessary, and courts have supported the inherent power of the government to protect citizens from unsafe building practices. Building codes specify acceptable building materials and construction methods, allowable loads and stresses, mechanical and electrical requirements, and other specifications for health and safety. Architects have both a moral and a legal obligation to study and follow the building code requirements*

of the city in which they build. Architectural drafters, also, are more effective when they understand some of these requirements.

Among the most important portions of any building code are the sections on fire protection. One need not experience the terror of fire to realize how necessary it is to design buildings that will not be a hazard to their occupants. In the United States over ten thousand persons are killed each year in fires. Many of these deaths occur in buildings that are in violation of fire protection codes.

BUILDING CLASSIFICATIONS

Building code requirements vary depending upon such factors as type of occupancy, building contents, type of construction, location, and fire-extinguishing systems. The codes permit "trade-offs" between these classifications with the goal of obtaining that degree of public safety as can be reasonably expected. For example, greater fire protection is required for a building that will be high-rise, densely occupied, constructed of flammable materials, or have hazardous contents. Building codes try to avoid requirements that involve unnecessary inconvenience or interference with the normal use of a building. However, the codes do set minimum standards for public safety which must be followed even though a financial hardship may be imposed upon individuals or groups.

Classification by occupancy. The Life Safety Code* developed by the National Fire Protection

---

* Building codes are minimum requirements and may be outdated. When this occurs, architects, as professionals, are expected to design at the current state-of-the-art.

* The Life Safety Code is only one portion of the ten-volume *National Fire Codes*. These codes are purely advisory but are widely used as a basis for establishing local or state building codes.

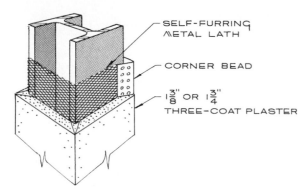

Figure 1 *Plaster-on-metal-lath fire protection of columns. (See Table IV.)*

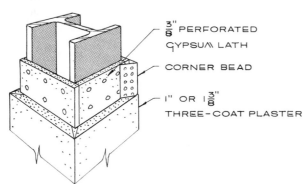

Figure 2 *Plaster-on-gypsum-lath fire protection of columns. (See Table IV.)*

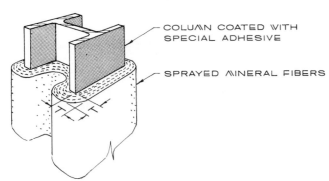

Figure 3 *Sprayed fibrous fire protection of columns. (See Table IV.)*

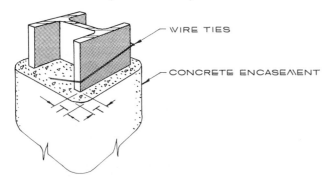

Figure 4 *Concrete fire protection of columns. (See Table IV.)*

Association classifies buildings by eight types of occupancy:

1. Assembly (theatres, restaurants, churches, and museums)
2. Educational
3. Institutional (hospitals and prisons)
4. Residential (hotels, apartments, and dwellings)
5. Mercantile
6. Offices
7. Industrial
8. Storage

The code deals with the design of various types of buildings to reduce the danger from fire, panic, fumes, and smoke. It specifies the number, size, and arrangement of exits to allow prompt escape from buildings of each occupancy type. The code recognizes that safety is more than a matter of exits and therefore recommends a number of additional requirements. Following are some abstracts from the Residential and Assembly sections of this code to give you an idea of the variety of regulations that have been included. This is only a partial list of requirements, and local building codes should always be consulted for complete, updated requirements.

ONE- AND TWO-FAMILY DWELLINGS

The requirements for residences are far short of complete requirements for fire safety, but are those which can reasonably be enforced by law. Some of these requirements are:

1. In all residences, every occupied room (except storage rooms) must have at least two means of exit (such as a doorway or window). At least one exit must be a doorway. Below-grade sleeping areas must have direct access to the outside.
2. Exit doors must be at least 24″ wide (30″ preferred).
3. Occupied rooms must not be accessible only by folding stairs, trapdoor or ladder.
4. All door-locking devices must be such that they can be easily disengaged from the inside by quick-release catches. All closet door latches must be such that they can be easily opened by children from inside the closet. All bathroom door locks must be such that they can be opened from the outside without the use of a special key.
5. The path of travel from any room to an exit must not be through a room controlled by another family, nor through a bathroom or other space subject to locking.
6. Passages from sleeping rooms to exits must be at least 3′-0 wide.
7. Stairs must be at least 3′-0 wide with risers no greater than 8″ and treads not under 9″.
8. Every sleeping room, unless it has a direct exterior

exit or two interior exits, must have a window which can be easily opened from the inside without use of tools. This window must provide a clear opening of at least 5 sq. ft. with not less than 22″ in the least dimension. The bottom of the opening must not be more than 4′-0 above the floor. Awning and hopper windows must be designed to permit full opening.

9. Storm windows, screens, and burglar guards must have quick-opening devices.

10. Combustion heaters and stoves must not be so located as to block escape in case of a malfunction.

11. Smoke detectors should be installed in the immediate vicinity outside of each separate sleeping area and on each additional story of a living unit including the basement.

See the *National Fire Codes* or local codes for more detailed requirements.

ASSEMBLY BUILDINGS

1. An assembly area must be at least fifteen square feet per person. Seating area must be at least seven square feet per person. Standing area (such as waiting rooms) must be at least three square feet per person.

2. A satisfactory grade-level door must be provided for each 100 persons. A door to a stair or fire escape must be provided for each 75 persons.

3. Assembly buildings with a capacity of over 1,000 persons must have at least 4 exits widely separated from each other. Assembly buildings with a capacity of over 600 persons must have at least 3 widely separated exits. Smaller assembly buildings must have at least 2 widely separated exits.

4. Exits must be arranged so that the total length of travel from any point to the nearest exit does not exceed 150′ for unsprinklered areas, and 200′ in areas protected by automatic sprinklers.

5. Exit doors must be at least 2′-4″ wide. The floor on both sides of a door must be level and at the same elevation for a distance at least equal to the width of the door; except exterior doors which may be one step (7½″) higher inside.

6. Exit doors must swing in the direction of travel. Screen or storm doors must also swing in the direction of travel. Sliding, rolling, or folding doors must not be used.

7. Exit doors must be readily opened from the inside of the building. Latches must be simple and easily operable, even in darkness. Conventional hardware such as panic bars or doorknobs are satisfactory, but an unfamiliar method of operation (such as a blow to break glass) is prohibited. Exit doors of assembly buildings with a capacity over 100 persons must have panic bars.

8. Locks must not require a key to operate.

9. Doors to stair enclosures and smoke stop doors must be provided with reliable self-closing mechanisms and never secured open unless provided with a reliable release device.

10. No mirrors shall be placed on exit doors. Doors must not harmonize in appearance with the rest of the wall.

11. Revolving doors must never be installed at the foot or top of stairs. They must not be considered as a portion of the required exits. No turnstiles which restrict exit are permitted.

12. Approved exit signs, lighting, and emergency lighting must be provided at all exits and approaches. Doors which lead to dead-end areas must be identified by signs indicating their character (such as "linen closet").

13. No open flames (such as candles) are permitted unless adequate precautions are made to assure that no other material is ignited.

14. Assembly buildings must be designed so the principal floor is not below grade unless protected by automatic sprinklers. Non-fire-resistive assembly buildings must have the principal floor not more than 28′ above grade.

15. All interior stairways must be enclosed to prevent spread of fire.

16. All interior decorations must be of fire-resistive or nonflammable materials.

17. A row of seats between aisles must not exceed 14 seats. A row of seats opening to an aisle at one end only must not exceed 7 seats.

18. Seats must be at least 18″ wide, spaced at least 33″ between rows, with at least 12″ leg room (measured between plumb lines).

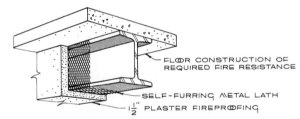

Figure 5   *Plaster fire protection of beams. (See Table V.)*

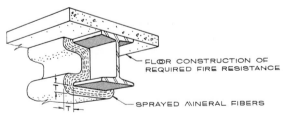

Figure 6   *Sprayed fibrous fire protection of beams. (See Table V.)*

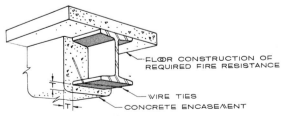

Figure 7   *Concrete fire protection of beams. (See Table V.)*

19. Aisles must be at least 3'-0 wide. Steps must not be used in aisles unless the slope exceeds 1' rise in 8' run. Ramps must not exceed 1' rise in 8' run.
20. Balcony rails must be substantial and at least 26" high, at least 30" high at the foot of an aisle, and at least 36" high at the foot of a stepped aisle.
21. Rooms containing pressure boilers, refrigerating machinery, transformers, or other service equipment subject to possible explosion must not be located adjacent to or under the exits.
22. Special regulations govern air conditioning, ventilating, and heating equipment. For example, automatic devices must be provided to prevent circulation of smoke through ductwork.
23. Areas used for painting or repair must be effectively cut off from assembly areas or protected by automatic sprinklers.
24. Fire alarm systems must be visual and coded to alert employees rather than audible to alert the entire audience. Audible devices such as gongs or sirens may create panic in conditions where fire drills are not feasible. Employees must be drilled and present when the building is occupied by the public.
25. Automatic sprinklers are required for any stage rigged for movable scenery, as well as for under-stage areas, dressing rooms, and storerooms. An approved fire-resisting curtain with an emergency closing device must be provided. The stage roof must contain an approved, operable ventilator having a free-opening area at least 5 percent of the stage floor area.
26. Motion picture projection apparatus must be enclosed by a fixed, fire-resistive booth.

See the *National Fire Codes* or local codes for more detailed requirements.

Classification by contents. The Life Safety Code also classifies buildings according to their contents by three ratings: ordinary-hazard contents, extra-hazard contents, and light-hazard contents.

1. *Ordinary-hazard contents* represents the conditions found in most buildings having contents that are moderately combustible but that are not explosive and will not release poisonous fumes.
2. *Extra-hazard contents* are liable to burn rapidly, explode (such as gasoline), or release poisonous fumes. All extra-hazard-contents buildings must have sufficient exits to allow occupants to escape with a travel distance not over 75'. It is assumed that this distance can be traveled in 10 sec., which is the time normal individuals can hold their breath.
3. *Light-hazard contents* have low combustibility and, consequently, the primary danger will be from panic.

Classification by construction type. The *National Fire Codes* of the National Fire Protection Association classify buildings into five principal construction types as follows:

Type I: Fire-resistive construction. Members are of noncombustible materials with fire ratings not less than:

4 hours for bearing walls
4 hours for columns and beams supporting more than 1 floor
3 hours for columns and beams supporting only 1 floor
2 hours for interior partitions

Type II: Heavy timber construction. Bearing walls are of noncombustible materials (usually masonry) with a minimum two-hour fire rating, and laminated or solid wood members are not less than:

8" × 8" for columns
6" × 10" for beams
4" × 6" for trusses or arches supporting roof loads
4" for flooring
2" for roof deck

Type III: Noncombustible construction. Structural members, walls, and partitions are of noncombustible construction such as unprotected steel.

When bearing walls are protected to a two-hour fire rating, and columns, floors, and roofs are protected to a one-hour fire rating, this is designated *Protected Noncombustible Construction.*

Type IV: Ordinary construction. Exterior bearing walls are of noncombustible materials (usually masonry) with a minimum two-hour fire rating, and interior framing, roofs, and floors are combustible (usually wood).

When roofs, floors, and their supports have a one-hour fire rating, this is designated *Protected Ordinary Construction.*

Type V: Wood-frame construction. All elements are of wood or other combustible material, but it does not qualify as heavy timber construction or ordinary construction.

Table I *Construction Classifications*

Type I.	Fire-resistive construction: noncombustible materials with four-hour bearing members
Type II.	Heavy timber construction: timber interior with two-hour masonry walls
Type III.	Noncombustible construction: unprotected steel
Type IV.	Ordinary construction: wood interior with two-hour masonry walls
Type V.	Wood-frame construction: wood interior and walls

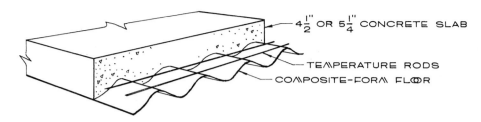

Figure 8   *Unprotected floors and roofs. (See Table VI.)*

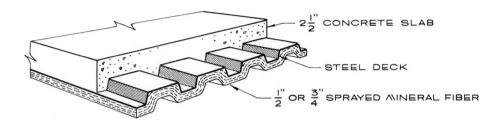

Figure 9   *Sprayed fibrous fire protection of floors and roofs. (See Table VI.)*

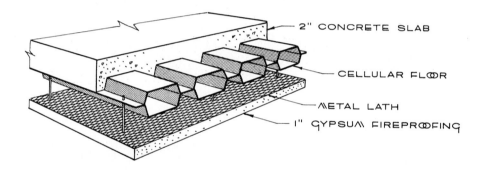

Figure 10   *Membrane fire protection of floors and roofs. (See Table VI.)*

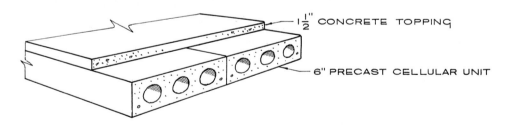

Figure 11   *Unprotected cellular floors and roofs. (See Table VI.)*

When roofs, floors, and their supports have a one-hour fire rating, this is designated *Protected Wood-frame Construction*.

Table I simplifies these definitions.

Fire ratings. The fire protection sections of building codes are based upon studies made by fire protection engineers who have tested various building methods to determine the fire resistance of each. The *standard fire test* (E119-58) of the American Society for Testing Materials is the accepted standard for such tests. The degree of fire resistance of each building method is measured in terms of its ability to withstand fire from one to four hours. For example, a two-hour fire rating would indicate that a structural member could withstand the heat of fire (or the cooling of a fire hose) for two hours before serious weakening; or that a wall, floor, or roof would not allow passage of flame and hot gasses for two hours.

The fire resistance ratings for typical walls, columns, beams, floors, and roofs are given in Tables II–VI. Notice that the fire ratings of masonry and concrete walls can be improved simply by increasing their thickness. Steel members, however, must be screened by additional fire protection. Usually gypsum, perlite, vermiculite, or mineral fiber is used.

Classification by location. Buildings constructed in closely packed communities are a greater threat to the general public than buildings located in an open area. Therefore building codes establish *fire limits,* or *fire zones.* Within the limits of a fire zone, all buildings must be designed so that a fire will remain contained and not sweep on to adjacent building after building.

Originally, fire codes required masonry exterior walls to act as fire barriers, but present codes

Table II   *Fire Resistance Ratings for Masonry Walls*

	Minimum Thickness for Ratings of:			
Type of Masonry Wall	4 hr.	3 hr.	2 hr.	1 hr.
Heavyweight concrete masonry units* (coarse aggregate, siliceous gravel)	6.7″	6.7″	4.5″	3″
Lightweight concrete masonry units* (coarse aggregate, expanded slag)	5.9″	5″	4″	2.7″
Lightweight concrete masonry units* (coarse aggregate, expanded slag)	4.7″	4″	3.2″	2.1″
Solid brick masonry**	8″	8″	8″	4″ (nonbearing)
Clay tile masonry**	16″	12″	12″	8″
Solid stone masonry*	12″	12″	12″	8″

* Abstracted from National Building Code.
** Abstracted from Uniform Building Code.

Table III   *Fire Resistance Ratings for Concrete Walls*

	Minimum Thickness for Ratings of:			
Type of Concrete Wall	4 hr.	3 hr.	2 hr.	1 hr.
Plain concrete	$7\frac{1}{2}$″	$6\frac{1}{2}$″	$5\frac{1}{2}$″	4″ (nonbearing)
Reinforced concrete (unplastered)	$7\frac{1}{2}$″	$6\frac{1}{2}$″	$5\frac{1}{2}$″	4″ (nonbearing)
Reinforced concrete ($\frac{3}{4}$″ portland cement or gypsum plaster, each side)	6″	5″	4″	3″

Abstracted from National Building Code.

Table IV   *Fire Resistance Ratings for Steel Columns*

	Minimum Thickness for Ratings of:			
Type of Column Protection	4 hr.	3 hr.	2 hr.	1 hr.
Vermiculite or perlite-gypsum plaster on self-furring metal lath (see Figure 1)	$1\frac{3}{4}$″	$1\frac{3}{8}$″		
Perlite-gypsum plaster on $\frac{3}{8}$″ perforated gypsum lath (see Figure 2)		$1\frac{3}{8}$″	1″	
Sprayed mineral fiber (see Figure 3)	$2\frac{1}{2}$″	2″	$1\frac{1}{2}$″	
Concrete encasement (see Figure 4)	3″	$2\frac{1}{2}$″	2″	$1\frac{1}{2}$″

Abstracted from *Fire-resistant Construction in Modern Steel-framed Buildings,* AISC.

allow other construction methods having satisfactory wall fire ratings. Such walls must also be able to remain standing under fire conditions.

Extinguishing systems. Building codes often require automatic water-sprinkler systems, for they give excellent fire protection in all types of buildings. Records show that when fires occurred in sprinkler-protected buildings, 80 percent of those fires were extinguished by the sprinklers, and another 18 percent held in check.

A sprinkler system consists of a network of piping placed under the ceiling and provided with a number of nozzles called *sprinklers* (Figure 12). When activated, the sprinklers spray water downward in a hemispherical pattern. The sprinkler systems are *fixed-temperature* and *rate-of-rise*.

Fixed-temperature sprinkler heads. These heads are usually designed so temperatures of 135°F–170°F will cause them to open automatically. Fixed-temperature sprinkler heads are color-coded to show their temperature ratings. Fixed-temperature sprinkler systems are *wet-pipe* when water is stored in the piping and *dry-pipe* with no water is in the piping.

The *wet-pipe system* is commonly used for most indoor conditions where temperatures will not fall below freezing. The water in the piping is kept under pressure behind each sprinkler. Sprinklers contain fusible links which are melted by heat and automatically open the sprinkler. Only sprinklers exposed to heat will open, thus preventing unnecessary water damage. A fire alarm sounds when the first sprinkler is opened. An anti-

Table V   *Fire Resistance Ratings for Steel Beams, Girders, and Trusses*

	Minimum Thickness for Ratings of:			
Type of Beam Protection	*4 hr.*	*3 hr.*	*2 hr.*	*1 hr.*
Vermiculite or perlite-gypsum plaster on self-furring metal lath (see Figure 5)	$1\frac{1}{2}''$			
Sprayed mineral fiber (see Figure 6)	$1\frac{7}{8}''$	$1\frac{7}{16}''$	$1\frac{1}{8}''$	
Concrete encasement (see Figure 7)	$3''$	$2\frac{1}{2}''$	$2''$	$1\frac{1}{2}''$

Abstracted from *Fire-resistant Construction in Modern Steel-framed Buildings*, AISC.

Table VI   *Fire Resistance Ratings for Floor and Roof Systems*

	Minimum Thickness for Ratings of:			
Type of Floor and Roof Protection	*4 hr.*	*3 hr.*	*2 hr.*	*1 hr.*
Light-gauge steel, not fireproofed (see Figure 8) Sand-limestone concrete slab of thickness equal to:			$5\frac{1}{4}''$	$4\frac{1}{2}''$
Light-gauge steel, contact fireproofing (see Figure 9) $2\frac{1}{2}''$ sand-gravel slab with sprayed mineral fiber of thickness equal to:		$\frac{3}{4}''$	$\frac{1}{2}''$	
Light-gauge steel, membrane fireproofing (see Figure 10) $2''$ sand-gravel slab and $1''$ vermiculite-gypsum fireproofing on metal lath installed at a distance of:	$2''$	$15''$		
Precast cellular system, not fireproofed (see Figure 11) $1\frac{1}{2}''$ sand-gravel concrete topping over a limestone concrete precast unit of thickness equal to:		$6''$		

Abstracted from *Fire-resistant Construction in Modern Steel-framed Buildings*, AISC.

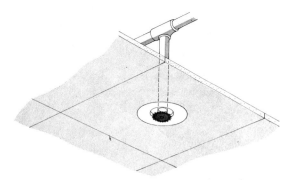

Figure 12   *A flush-type ceiling sprinkler.*

freeze solution may be used in the piping for limited protection from freezing.

Buildings likely to have temperatures below freezing (such as unheated warehouses) can be protected by the *dry-pipe system*. The piping contains air under pressure rather than water. When heat from a fire opens one of the sprinklers, the air is released and water flows into the piping network and through any opened sprinklers. A fire alarm also sounds.

Rate-of-rise sprinkler systems. Detectors open valves to the sprinkler piping rather than to the sprinkler heads. Rate-of-rise detectors open valves upon any abnormal increase of temperature. They are very sensitive and consequently give quicker warning of a fire hazard. Rate-of-rise sprinkler systems are *deluge* and *preaction*.

The *deluge system* is used for extra-hazard conditions. All sprinkler heads are open, but the piping is dry. When a rate-of-rise detector opens the water supply valve, water rushes into the piping and out through all heads simultaneously, giving better protection for difficult conditions such as flammable liquid fires. An alarm also sounds.

The *preaction system* is used when it is important to reduce the possibility of accidental water damage. The principal difference between a preaction and a standard dry-pipe system is that in a preaction system, the water supply valve operates independently of the sprinkler heads; that is, a rate-of-rise detector first opens the valve and sounds an alarm. The fixed-temperature sprinkler heads do not open until their temperature ratings are reached. This gives time for small fires to be extinguished manually before the heads open.

Sprinkler layout. The layout of a sprinkler system is performed by a professional engineer using established standards as a guide. Sprinkler layout depends upon the building classifications. For example, the *National Fire Codes* specifies the following under a smooth ceiling construction:

1. *Light hazard:* The protection area per sprinkler must not exceed 200 sq. ft. The maximum distance between lines and between sprinklers on lines is 15 ft. Sprinklers need not be staggered. See Figure 13.
2. *Ordinary hazard:* The protection area per sprinkler must not exceed 130 sq. ft. The maximum distance between lines or between sprinklers on lines is 15 ft. Sprinklers on alternate lines must be staggered if the distance between sprinklers on lines exceeds 12 ft.
3. *Extra hazard:* The protection area per sprinkler must not exceed 90 sq. ft. The maximum distance between lines and between sprinklers on lines is 12 ft. The sprinklers on alternate lines must be staggered.

See the *National Fire Codes* or local codes for more detailed requirements.

Standpipes. Standpipes are vertical water pipes with fire-hose outlets at each floor. They can be designed for small-hose ($1\frac{1}{2}''$) to be used by the building occupants in the event of fire or large-hose ($2\frac{1}{2}''$) to be used by fire departments—or both. Standpipes are usually wet-pipe rather than dry-pipe. At ground level, branches extend outside the building and are finished with *Siamese connections*. Should there be insufficient pressure in the public water system, the fire department can pump water into the standpipe through these connections to increase the pressure. Check valves relieve the pumps from back-pressure.

Standpipes are located so that any fire can be reached by a stream from not more than 75' of small-hose or 100' of large-hose.

See the *National Fire Codes* or local codes for more detailed requirements.

Some other extinguishing systems are foam, carbon dioxide, halons, and dry chemical. Foam is an aggregate of tiny gas-filled or air-filled bubbles used to smother fire by excluding air. Because foam contains water, it also has cooling properties. The principal use for foam is in fighting fires involving flammable liquids. Carbon dioxide, the halons, and dry chemical are nonconductive and therefore can be used on electrical fires as well as on flammable-liquid fires.

High-rise buildings. Research is constantly being conducted to find better ways to prevent or control fires in buildings. Special attention is being given to the problem of fire safety in high-rise buildings, for their construction is increasing—some to heights of 1,000 ft. and more. These buildings may contain more than twenty-five thousand persons—equivalent to the population

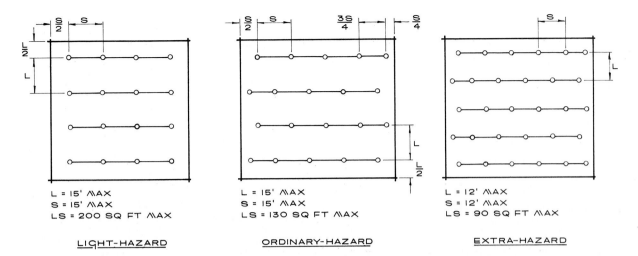

L = 15' MAX
S = 15' MAX
LS = 200 SQ FT MAX

LIGHT-HAZARD

L = 15' MAX
S = 15' MAX
LS = 130 SQ FT MAX

ORDINARY-HAZARD

L = 12' MAX
S = 12' MAX
LS = 90 SQ FT MAX

EXTRA-HAZARD

Figure 13 *Sprinkler layouts for smooth ceiling.*

of a small city. Special precaution for fire protection must be taken in such buildings, for prompt evacuation is usually not possible. In addition, the building height may contribute to a stack effect, and many floors may be beyond the reach of fire department aerial equipment. Therefore, fire must be controlled and fought internally. A combination of three methods is usually used:

1. All building materials and furnishings selected to provide no potential fuel for a fire, including no potential for emitting smoke or toxic gasses
2. Compartmented structures capable of resisting and containing a fire within a relatively small portion of the building
3. Automatic fire-extinguishing systems capable of prompt and effective operation

An innovative fire protection system was used in the U.S. Steel Building of Pittsburgh, Pennsylvania (Figure 14). Conventional sprayed cementitious fire protection was used for interior columns, beams, and floors. However, exterior columns were protected by using hollow box-columns of weathering steel filled with water plus antifreeze and corrosion-inhibiting additives. In the event of fire, the water will absorb heat and keep the temperature of the columns below a critical point. Any steam generated escapes through vents. To prevent excessive hydrostatic pressure, the columns are divided into four separate sections, each sixteen stories high.

STUDY QUESTIONS

1. List the eight building classifications by occupancy as established by the National Fire Protection Association.

Figure 14 *U.S. Steel Building in Pittsburgh contains water-filled columns for fire protection.*

2. List the three building classifications by hazard as established by the National Fire Protection Association.
3. List the five building classifications by construction type as established by the National Fire Protection Association.
4. What is the difference between:
   a. Fire-resistive and noncombustible construction
   b. Heavy timber, ordinary, and wood frame construction
   c. Wet- and dry-pipe sprinkler systems

5. Give the meaning of *three-hour fire rating*.
6. Give the minimum thickness required to achieve a three-hour fire rating for:
   a. Lightweight CMU walls (with unexpanded slag)
   b. Solid brick masonry walls
   c. Reinforced concrete walls, unplastered
   d. Sprayed mineral fiber on steel columns
   e. Sprayed mineral fiber on steel beams
   f. Sprayed mineral fiber on $2\frac{1}{2}''$ concrete slab poured on light-gauge steel decking

LABORATORY PROBLEMS

1. Check your original building design for compliance with your local exits code or the National Building Exits Code.
2. Using local codes or the National Fire Protection Association codes, draw the fireproofing details for the building assigned by your instructor;
   a. Columns
   b. Beams or girders
   c. Trusses
   d. Floors
   e. Roof
3. Using local codes or the National Fire Protection Association codes, draw the fireproofing details for your original building design:
   a. Columns
   b. Beams or girders
   c. Trusses
   d. Floors
   e. Roof
4. Using the National Fire Protection Association codes, lay out the sprinkler system for the building assigned by your instructor.
5. Using the National Fire Protection Association codes, lay out the sprinkler system for your original building design.

44 / The Construction Documents

In addition to the working drawings, any large project also requires a number of written documents that are needed to advertise for and obtain bids, award a contract, and assure the satisfactory completion of the project. The index of a typical set of construction documents will give an idea of the many different documents required.

I INDEX

Document	Title	
I	Index	
II	Invitation to Bid	Bidding Require-ments
III	Instructions to Bidders	
IV	Bid Form	
V	Agreement	
VI	Performance Bond	
VII	Labor and Material Bond	Contract Forms
VIII	Estimate of Payment Due	
IX	General Conditions	
X	Supplementary Conditions	
XI	Specifications	
XII	Working Drawings	

Some of the sections listed are comparatively short, simple documents; others (like the specifications) may consist of many hundreds of pages. The specifications are prepared by a *specs* writer who is specially trained to do this work. To give a better idea of the makeup of the various sections of the construction documents, let us look at each in more detail.

II INVITATION TO BID

In public work, bid invitations are mailed to all contractors who might be interested in the proposed project. Also newspaper advertisements for bids are placed. (Occasionally in private work only selected contractors are invited to bid.) The advertisements are placed three times in three weeks, and they include a brief description of the work and location, together with the requirements (time and place) of bid delivery. A sample Invitation to Bid is shown in Figure 1. A sample Advertisement for Bids is shown in Figure 2.

III INSTRUCTIONS TO BIDDERS

This section gives more detailed information that a bidder needs to intelligently prepare and submit a bid. The information includes the following:

1. Availability of construction documents
2. Examination of construction documents and site
3. Resolution of questions
4. Approval for substitution of materials
5. Basis of bids
6. Preparation of bids
7. Bid security information
8. Requirements for the Performance Bond and the Labor and Material Bond
9. Requirements for listing any subcontractors
10. Identification and submission of bid

```
Jones and Brown, Architects              INVITATION TO BID
5555 Main Street            STATE UNIVERSITY SCIENCE BUILDING
Smithville, Ohio                             Project 3813
Phone:  888 777-6666                        October__,19__
```

You are invited to bid on a General Contract, including mechanical and electrical work, for a two-story, thin-shell concrete, circular Science Building, approximately four hundred feet in diameter. All Bids must be on a lump sum basis; segregated Bids will not be accepted.

The State University Board of Governors will receive Bids until 3:00 p.m. Central Standard Time on Tuesday, November 8, 19__, at 233 Uptown Street, Room 313, Smithville, Ohio. Bids received after this time will not be accepted. All interested parties are invited to attend; Bids will be opened publicly and read aloud.

Drawings and Specifications may be examined at the Architect's office and at:

```
    The Plan Center              Associated Plan Bureau
    382 West Third Street        1177 South Barnes
    Smithville, Ohio             Smithville, Ohio
```

Copies of the above documents may be obtained at the office of the Architect in accord with the Instructions to Bidders upon depositing the sum of $100.00 for each set of documents.

Any bona-fide bidder, upon returning the documents in good condition immediately following the public opening of said bids, shall be returned his deposit in full. Any non-bidder returning the documents in good condition will be returned the sum of $75.00.

Bid Security in the amount of _____ percent of the Bid must accompany each Bid in accord with the Instructions to Bidders.

The Board of Governors reserves the right to waive irregularities and to reject Bids.

```
                             By order of the Board of Governors

                             State University
                             Smithville, Ohio

                             Hirmats J. Downe, Secretary
```

Figure 1 *Sample Invitation to Bid.*

11. Modification or withdrawal of bid
12. Disqualification of bidders
13. Governing laws and regulations
14. Opening of bids
15. Award of contract
16. Execution of contract

A sample Instructions to Bidders is shown in Figure 3.

IV BID FORM

The Bid Form is a sample bidding letter from the bidder to the prospective owner. It contains blank spaces to be filled in by the bidder and a place for his signature (and for the seal of corporations) to indicate agreement with all provisions. The Bid Form includes the following:

1. Acknowledgment that all construction documents were received by bidder.
2. Agreement statements that bidder will hold bid open until a stated time and that bidder will abide by the Instructions to Bidders.
3. Price of project including price of any alternatives. Alternate bids should be included in addition to the base bid as a means of keeping the project cost within the budget and as a "keep-honest" feature; that is, the bid may be higher if there are no allowable substitutes for materials for competitive bidding. Some alternate bids for a large project might be the following:
    a. Asphalt tile as an alternative to rubber tile in corridors
    b. Quarry tile as an alternative to terrazzo on interior floor slabs
    c. Asphalt and slag roof as an alternative to a pitch-and-slag roof.
    d. Cold-mixed bituminous surfacing as an alternative to hot-mixed asphaltic concrete surfacing course on driveways and service areas
4. Attachment statement that required information (such as a subcontractor listing or evidence of bidder's qualifications) is enclosed.

A sample Bid Form is shown in Figure 4.

V AGREEMENT

The Agreement is one of several forms that are preprinted to simplify contract preparation. The contract forms supplied by the American Institute of Architects are commonly used, but many gov-

Figure 2 *Sample Advertisement for Bids.*

Jones and Brown, Architects
5555 Main Street
Smithville, Ohio
Phone: 888 777-6666

INSTRUCTIONS TO BIDDERS
STATE UNIVERSITY SCIENCE BUILDING

To be considered, Bids must be made in accord with these instructions
to Bidders.

DOCUMENTS. Bonafide prime bidders may obtain _____ sets of
Drawings and Specifications from the Architect upon deposit of $_____
per set. Those who submit prime bids may obtain refund of deposits by
returning sets in good condition no more than _____ days after Bids
have been opened. Those who do not submit prime bids will forfeit
deposits unless sets are returned in good condition at least _____
days before Bids are opened. No partial sets will be issued; no sets
will be issued to sub-bidders by the Architect. Prime bidders may
obtain additional copies upon deposit of $_____ per set.

EXAMINATION. Bidders shall carefully examine the documents and the
construction site to obtain first-hand knowledge of existing
conditions. Contractors will not be given extra payments for
conditions which can be determined by examining the site and
documents.

QUESTIONS. Submit all questions about the Drawings and
Specifications to the Architect, in writing. Replies will be issued
to all prime bidders of record as Addenda to the Drawings and
Specifications and will become part of the Contract. The Architect
and Owner will not be responsible for oral clarification. Questions
received less than _____ hours before the bid opening cannot be
answered.

SUBSTITUTIONS. To obtain approval to use unspecified products,
bidders shall submit written requests at least ten days before the
bid date and hour. Requests received after this time will not be
considered. Requests shall clearly describe the product for which
approval is asked, including all data necessary to demonstrate
acceptability. If the product is acceptable, the Architect will
approve it in an Addendum issued to all prime bidders on record.

BASIS OF BID. The bidder must include all unit cost items and all
alternatives shown on the Bid Forms; failure to comply may be cause
for rejection. No segregated Bids or assignments will be considered.

PREPARATION OF BIDS. Bids shall be made on unaltered Bid Forms
furnished by the Architect. Fill in all blank spaces and submit two
copies. Bids shall be signed with name typed below signature. Where
bidder is a corporation, Bids must be signed with the legal name of
the corporation followed by the name of the State of incorporation
and legal signatures of an officer authorized to bind the corporation
to a contract.

BID SECURITY. Bid Security shall be made payable to the Board of
Governors, State University, in the amount of _____ percent of the
Bid sum. Security shall be either certified check or bid bond issued
by surety licensed to conduct business in the State of Ohio. The
successful bidder's security will be retained until he has signed the
Contract and furnished the required payment and performance bonds.
The Owner reserves the right to retain the security of the next _____
bidders until the lowest bidder enters into contract or until _____
days after bid opening, whichever is the shorter. All other bid
security will be returned as soon as practicable. If any bidder
refuses to enter into a Contract, the Owner will retain his Bid
Security as liquidated damages, but not as a penalty. The Bid
Security is to be submitted _____ day(s) prior to the Submission of
Bids.

Figure 3   *Sample Instructions to Bidders.*

PERFORMANCE BOND AND LABOR AND MATERIAL PAYMENT BOND. Furnish and pay for bonds covering faithful performance of the Contract and payment of all obligations arising thereunder. Furnish bonds in such form as the Owner may prescribe and with a surety company acceptable to the Owner. The bidder shall deliver said bonds to the Owner not later than the date of execution of the Contract. Failure or neglecting to deliver said bonds, as specified, shall be considered as having abandoned the Contract and the Bid Security will be retained as liquidated damages.

SUBCONTRACTORS. Names of principal subcontractors must be listed and attached to the Bid. There shall be only one subcontractor named for each classification listed.

SUBMITTAL. Submit Bid and Subcontractor Listing in an opaque, sealed envelope. Identify the envelope with: (1) project name, (2) name of bidder. Submit Bids in accord with the Invitation to Bid.

MODIFICATION AND WITHDRAWAL. Bids may not be modified after submittal. Bidders may withdraw Bids at any time before bid opening, but may not resubmit them. No Bid may be withdrawn or modified after the bid opening except where the award of Contract has been delayed for _____ days.

DISQUALIFICATION. The Owner reserves the right to disqualify Bids, before or after opening, upon evidence of collusion with intent to defraud or other illegal practices upon the part of the bidder.

GOVERNING LAWS AND REGULATIONS
NON DISCRIMINATORY PRACTICES. Contracts for work under the bid will obligate the contractor and subcontractors not to discriminate in employment practices. Bidders must submit a compliance report in conformity with the President's Executive Order No. 11246.

U.S. GOVERNMENT REQUIREMENTS. This contract is Federally assisted. The Contractor must comply with the Davis-Bacon Act, the Anti-Kickback Act, and the Contract Work Hours Standards.

OHIO EXCISE TAX. Bidders should be aware of the Ohio Law (_____) as it relates to tax assessments on construction equipment.

OPENING. Bids will be opened as announced in the Invitation to Bid.

AWARD. The Contract will be awarded on the basis of low bid, including full consideration of unit prices and alternatives.

EXECUTION OF CONTRACT. The Owner reserves the right to accept any Bid, and to reject any and all Bids, or to negotiate Contract Terms with the various Bidders, when such is deemed by the Owner to be in his best interest.

Each Bidder shall be prepared, if so requested by the Owner, to present evidence of his experience, qualifications, and financial ability to carry out the terms of the Contract.

Notwithstanding any delay in the preparation and execution of the formal Contract Agreement, each Bidder shall be prepared, upon written notice of bid acceptance, to commence work within _____ days following receipt of official written order of the Owner to proceed, or on date stipulated in such order.

The accepted bidder shall assist and cooperate with the Owner in preparing the formal Contract Agreement, and within _____ days following its presentation shall execute same and return it to the Owner.

Figure 3 *continued.*

TO: STATE UNIVERSITY SCIENCE BUILDING
The Board of Governors   Project 3813
State University
233 Uptown Street, Room 313
Smithville, Ohio

I have received the documents titled "Specifications for State University Science Building" and Drawings A-1 through A-27, S-1 through S-10, and M-1 through M-15. I have also received Addenda Nos. _____, and have included their provisions in my Bid. I have examined both the documents and the site and submit the following Bid:

In submitting this Bid, I agree:

  1. To hold my bid open until December 8, 19 _.

  2. To accept the provisions of the Instructions to Bidders regarding disposition of Bid Security.

  3. To enter into and execute a Contract, if awarded on the basis of this bid, and to furnish Guarantee Bonds in accord with Article 30 of the General Conditions of this Contract.

  4. To accomplish the work in accord with the Contract Documents.

  5. To complete the work by the time stipulated in the Supplementary Conditions.

I will construct this project for the lump-sum price of _____ _____ dollars ($_____).

I will include the following alternatives as specified substitutes for the additional costs listed:

  1. Elevators Nos. 5 and 6   +$_____

  2. Steam pipe system   +$_____

If the following items, which are based on unit prices, vary more than 10 percent from the estimates furnished by the Architect, I will adjust the Contract Sum in accord with the following rates:

Concrete piling   +$_____   -$_____

Interior gypsum partitions, including plaster and paint, per square foot   +$_____   -$_____

I have attached the required Bid Security and Subcontractor Listing to this Bid.

         Date:_____   Signed:_____

Figure 4   *Sample Bid Form.*

ernment agencies have developed standard contract forms for their own uses.

The Owner-Architect Agreement includes a statement of the architectural services ordinarily considered necessary and the owner's usual obligations. Many different forms of Agreement are used, but they differ mainly in the method by which the architect's compensation is determined. The fee can be as follows:

1. A percentage of the construction cost (usually from 5 to 15 percent)
2. A professional fee plus expenses
3. A multiple of personnel expenses

VI PERFORMANCE BOND

The Performance Bond is a guarantee to the client that the contractor will perform all the terms and conditions of the contract, and if defaulted will protect the client up to the bond penalty. The Performance Bond should be distinguished from the Labor and Material Bond, which protects the laborers and material men.

VII LABOR AND MATERIAL BOND

The Labor and Material Bond guarantees that the bills of the materials suppliers and subcontractors will be paid.

VIII ESTIMATE OF PAYMENT DUE

A first payment of 10 percent of the architect's fee is paid upon the execution of the Agreement. Additional payments of the fee are made monthly in proportion to the services performed. The total payments are increased to the following percentages at the completion of each phase:

1. Schematic design   15 percent
2. Design development   35 percent
3. Construction documents   75 percent
4. Receipt of bids   80 percent
5. Construction   100 percent

IX GENERAL CONDITIONS

This section is among the most important in the construction documents. The General Conditions contain additional contractual-legal requirements not covered by other contract forms. Whereas some architects use A.I.A. Document A-201 without change, others write the General Conditions to satisfy their own requirements. It is also possible to note only those modifications of the A.I.A. Document that apply to each job. Typical subsections are the following:

1. Definitions
2. Architect's supervision
3. Architect's decision
4. Notice
5. Separate contracts
6. Intent of plans and specifications
7. Errors and discrepancies
8. Drawings and specifications furnished to contractors
9. Approved drawings
10. Patents
11. Permits, licenses, and certificates
12. Supervision and labor
13. Public safety and guards
14. Order of completion
15. Substitution of materials for those called for by specifications
16. Materials, equipment, and labor
17. Inspection
18. Defective work and materials
19. Failure to comply with orders of architect
20. Use of completed parts
21. Rights of various interests
22. Suspension of work due to unfavorable conditions
23. Suspension of work due to fault of contractor
24. Suspension of work due to unforeseen causes
25. Request for extension
26. Stoppage of work by architect
27. Default on part of contractor
28. Removal of equipment
29. Monthly estimates and payments
30. Acceptance and final payment
31. Deviations from contract requirements
32. Estoppel and waiver of legal rights.
33. Approval of subcontractors and sources of material
34. Approval of material samples requiring laboratory tests
35. Arbitration
36. Bonds
37. Additional or substitute bonds
38. Public liability and property damage insurance
39. Workmen's Compensation Act

40. Fire insurance and damage due to other hazards
41. Explosives and blasting
42. Damages to property
43. Mutual responsibility of contractors
44. Contractor's liability
45. Familiarity with contract documents
46. Shop drawings
47. Guarantee of work
48. Cleanup
49. Competent workmen (state law)
50. Prevailing wage act (state law)
51. Residence of employees
52. Nondiscrimination in hiring employees (state law)
53. Preference to employment of war veterans (state law)
54. Hiring and conditions of employment (state law)

X SUPPLEMENTARY CONDITIONS

The Supplementary Conditions contain special modifications to the basic articles of the General Conditions, together with any additional articles of a contractual legal nature that might be needed for a particular project.

XI SPECIFICATIONS

The Specifications give detailed instructions on the required materials, finishes, and workmanship—all grouped by building trades. Each trade is included in the order of actual construction. Nearly all offices use the standardized specification system as recommended by the Construction Specifications Institute. This system is called the *CSI Format* and consists of sixteen *Divisions* (grouped by building trades) and a number of related *Broadscope Sections* (grouped by units of work). The *Divisions* are shown in Table I, and the *Broadscope Sections* of the first ten Divisions are shown in Figure 5. The Broadscope Sections (printed in capital letters) are further refined into *Narrowscope Sections*. The *Narrowscope Sections* (printed in lowercase letters) of Division 8 are shown in Figure 6. A specifications writer will select only those sections that apply to a particular job. Notice that a five-digit numbering system is used for the designation of all Broadscope and Narrowscope Sections. This helps offices that use automated printing and data retrieval systems.

The Construction Specifications Institute also recommends a uniform three-part approach for writing each section:

Part 1—General
  Description
  Quality Assurance
  Submittals
  Product Delivery, Storage, and Handling
  Job Conditions
  Alternatives
  Guarantee

Part 2—Products
  Materials
  Mixes
  Fabrication and Manufacture

Part 3—Execution
  Inspection
  Preparation
  Installation/Application/Performance
  Field Quality Control
  Adjust and Clean
  Schedules

Although architects still refer to "writing" specifications, actually the majority of sections are assembled from a data book of carefully worded and approved paragraphs.

Three basic sentence structures are commonly used in specifications to convey the architect's intent clearly and concisely: the indicative mood, the imperative mood, and streamlining.

The indicative mood, requiring the use of *shall* in nearly every sentence, is the traditional language of specs writing: "Two coats of paint shall be applied to each exposed surface."

The imperative mood is more concise. A verb begins the sentence and immediately defines the required action: "Apply two coats of paint to each exposed surface."

Table I   *The Divisions of the CSI Format*

DIVISION 1—GENERAL REQUIREMENTS
DIVISION 2—SITEWORK
DIVISION 3—CONCRETE
DIVISION 4—MASONRY
DIVISION 5—METALS
DIVISION 6—WOOD AND PLASTICS
DIVISION 7—THERMAL AND MOISTURE PROTECTION
DIVISION 8—DOORS AND WINDOWS
DIVISION 9—FINISHES
DIVISION 10—SPECIALTIES
DIVISION 11—EQUIPMENT
DIVISION 12—FURNISHINGS
DIVISION 13—SPECIAL CONSTRUCTION
DIVISION 14—CONVEYING SYSTEMS
DIVISION 15—MECHANICAL
DIVISION 16—ELECTRICAL

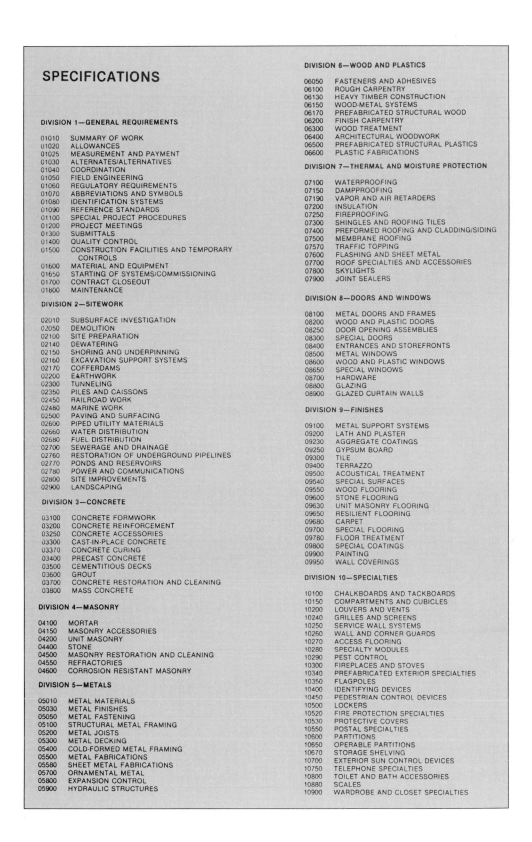

SPECIFICATIONS

DIVISION 1—GENERAL REQUIREMENTS

01010	SUMMARY OF WORK
01020	ALLOWANCES
01025	MEASUREMENT AND PAYMENT
01030	ALTERNATES/ALTERNATIVES
01040	COORDINATION
01050	FIELD ENGINEERING
01060	REGULATORY REQUIREMENTS
01070	ABBREVIATIONS AND SYMBOLS
01080	IDENTIFICATION SYSTEMS
01090	REFERENCE STANDARDS
01100	SPECIAL PROJECT PROCEDURES
01200	PROJECT MEETINGS
01300	SUBMITTALS
01400	QUALITY CONTROL
01500	CONSTRUCTION FACILITIES AND TEMPORARY CONTROLS
01600	MATERIAL AND EQUIPMENT
01650	STARTING OF SYSTEMS/COMMISSIONING
01700	CONTRACT CLOSEOUT
01800	MAINTENANCE

DIVISION 2—SITEWORK

02010	SUBSURFACE INVESTIGATION
02050	DEMOLITION
02100	SITE PREPARATION
02140	DEWATERING
02150	SHORING AND UNDERPINNING
02160	EXCAVATION SUPPORT SYSTEMS
02170	COFFERDAMS
02200	EARTHWORK
02300	TUNNELING
02350	PILES AND CAISSONS
02450	RAILROAD WORK
02480	MARINE WORK
02500	PAVING AND SURFACING
02600	PIPED UTILITY MATERIALS
02660	WATER DISTRIBUTION
02680	FUEL DISTRIBUTION
02700	SEWERAGE AND DRAINAGE
02760	RESTORATION OF UNDERGROUND PIPELINES
02770	PONDS AND RESERVOIRS
02780	POWER AND COMMUNICATIONS
02800	SITE IMPROVEMENTS
02900	LANDSCAPING

DIVISION 3—CONCRETE

03100	CONCRETE FORMWORK
03200	CONCRETE REINFORCEMENT
03250	CONCRETE ACCESSORIES
03300	CAST-IN-PLACE CONCRETE
03370	CONCRETE CURING
03400	PRECAST CONCRETE
03500	CEMENTITIOUS DECKS
03600	GROUT
03700	CONCRETE RESTORATION AND CLEANING
03800	MASS CONCRETE

DIVISION 4—MASONRY

04100	MORTAR
04150	MASONRY ACCESSORIES
04200	UNIT MASONRY
04400	STONE
04500	MASONRY RESTORATION AND CLEANING
04550	REFRACTORIES
04600	CORROSION RESISTANT MASONRY

DIVISION 5—METALS

05010	METAL MATERIALS
05030	METAL FINISHES
05050	METAL FASTENING
05100	STRUCTURAL METAL FRAMING
05200	METAL JOISTS
05300	METAL DECKING
05400	COLD-FORMED METAL FRAMING
05500	METAL FABRICATIONS
05580	SHEET METAL FABRICATIONS
05700	ORNAMENTAL METAL
05800	EXPANSION CONTROL
05900	HYDRAULIC STRUCTURES

DIVISION 6—WOOD AND PLASTICS

06050	FASTENERS AND ADHESIVES
06100	ROUGH CARPENTRY
06130	HEAVY TIMBER CONSTRUCTION
06150	WOOD-METAL SYSTEMS
06170	PREFABRICATED STRUCTURAL WOOD
06200	FINISH CARPENTRY
06300	WOOD TREATMENT
06400	ARCHITECTURAL WOODWORK
06500	PREFABRICATED STRUCTURAL PLASTICS
06600	PLASTIC FABRICATIONS

DIVISION 7—THERMAL AND MOISTURE PROTECTION

07100	WATERPROOFING
07150	DAMPPROOFING
07190	VAPOR AND AIR RETARDERS
07200	INSULATION
07250	FIREPROOFING
07300	SHINGLES AND ROOFING TILES
07400	PREFORMED ROOFING AND CLADDING/SIDING
07500	MEMBRANE ROOFING
07570	TRAFFIC TOPPING
07600	FLASHING AND SHEET METAL
07700	ROOF SPECIALTIES AND ACCESSORIES
07800	SKYLIGHTS
07900	JOINT SEALERS

DIVISION 8—DOORS AND WINDOWS

08100	METAL DOORS AND FRAMES
08200	WOOD AND PLASTIC DOORS
08250	DOOR OPENING ASSEMBLIES
08300	SPECIAL DOORS
08400	ENTRANCES AND STOREFRONTS
08500	METAL WINDOWS
08600	WOOD AND PLASTIC WINDOWS
08650	SPECIAL WINDOWS
08700	HARDWARE
08800	GLAZING
08900	GLAZED CURTAIN WALLS

DIVISION 9—FINISHES

09100	METAL SUPPORT SYSTEMS
09200	LATH AND PLASTER
09230	AGGREGATE COATINGS
09250	GYPSUM BOARD
09300	TILE
09400	TERRAZZO
09500	ACOUSTICAL TREATMENT
09540	SPECIAL SURFACES
09550	WOOD FLOORING
09600	STONE FLOORING
09630	UNIT MASONRY FLOORING
09650	RESILIENT FLOORING
09680	CARPET
09700	SPECIAL FLOORING
09780	FLOOR TREATMENT
09800	SPECIAL COATINGS
09900	PAINTING
09950	WALL COVERINGS

DIVISION 10—SPECIALTIES

10100	CHALKBOARDS AND TACKBOARDS
10150	COMPARTMENTS AND CUBICLES
10200	LOUVERS AND VENTS
10240	GRILLES AND SCREENS
10250	SERVICE WALL SYSTEMS
10260	WALL AND CORNER GUARDS
10270	ACCESS FLOORING
10280	SPECIALTY MODULES
10290	PEST CONTROL
10300	FIREPLACES AND STOVES
10340	PREFABRICATED EXTERIOR SPECIALTIES
10350	FLAGPOLES
10400	IDENTIFYING DEVICES
10450	PEDESTRIAN CONTROL DEVICES
10500	LOCKERS
10520	FIRE PROTECTION SPECIALTIES
10530	PROTECTIVE COVERS
10550	POSTAL SPECIALTIES
10600	PARTITIONS
10650	OPERABLE PARTITIONS
10670	STORAGE SHELVING
10700	EXTERIOR SUN CONTROL DEVICES
10750	TELEPHONE SPECIALTIES
10800	TOILET AND BATH ACCESSORIES
10880	SCALES
10900	WARDROBE AND CLOSET SPECIALTIES

Figure 5   *Some Broadscope Sections of the CSI Format.*

Streamlining is used to itemize products, materials, and reference standards: "Materials shall meet the following requirements:

Portland cement: ASTM C 150, Type I.
Aggregate: ASTM C 33."

Some additional rules of thumb for specifications writing are the following:

1. Use short sentences and simple declarative statements.
2. Avoid complicated sentences whose meanings are so dependent on punctuation that inadvertent omission or insertion of punctuation changes the meaning or creates ambiguity.
3. Choose words and terms that are plain and well understood to convey the information. Avoid pompous or highly embellished language. For example, use "shall" rather than "it is incumbent upon" or "it is the duty." Use "the contractor may" rather than "if the contractor so elects, he may" or "the contractor is hereby authorized to." Use "means" rather than "shall be interpreted to mean." Use "by" rather than "by means of." Use "to" rather than "in order to." Never use "herein," "hereinbefore," "hereinafter," or "wherein." Avoid using "and/or," "etc.," and as per."
4. Use "shall" for the work of the contractor. Use "will" for acts of the owner or architect. Do not use "must."
5. Use numerals (figures) instead of words for numbers over twelve. For example: one, six, twelve, 13, 18, 100. But use numerals for all sums of money, e.g., $1.00. Give numbers preceding a numeral as words, e.g., fifteen 8-hour days.

To get a better idea of the specifications, let us look at one of the sections in more detail. We have chosen Division 8 (Doors and Windows), Broadscope Section 08800 (Glazing) for this study.

Section 08800 Glazing*

08801 STIPULATION

Applicable requirements of the "General Conditions" apply to this entire Specification, and shall have the same force and effect as if printed here in full.

---

* Section 08800 courtesy of Jack W Risheberger & Associates, Registered Architects and Engineers.

08802 SCOPE OF WORK

The work covered by this Section consists of furnishing all labor, materials, equipment, and services necessary to complete all glass and glazing required for the project, in strict accordance with this Section of the Specifications and the Drawings; including, but not limited to, the following:

a. Glazing of exterior doors, sidelights, transoms, and fixed metal window frames;
b. Glazing of interior doors, sidelights, and frames;
c. Mirrors

08803 WORK EXCLUDED

The following items are included in other sections of the General Contract Specifications:

a. All bank equipment shall be factory glazed.

08810 GLASS

All glass shall comply with Federal Specification DD-G-45a for glass, flat, for glazing purposes.

08813 TEMPERED GLASS **(Exterior doors and sidelights at doors)**

Tempered glass for the above locations shall be "Solarbronze Twindow" with $\frac{1}{4}$" polished plate Solarbronze exterior sheet and $\frac{1}{4}$" clear tempered plate interior sheet. Glass in doors shall be $\frac{13}{16}$" thick and $\frac{1}{4}$" air space. Other glass shall be $1\frac{1}{16}$" thick with $\frac{1}{2}$" air space. Set in metal glazing beads.

08823 INSULATING GLASS **(Fixed exterior windows and transoms in aluminum frames)**

Insulating glass shall be $1\frac{1}{16}$" thick "Solarbronze Twindow" set in metal glazing beads. Glass shall have a $\frac{1}{4}$" polished plate Solarbronze exterior sheet, $\frac{1}{2}$" air space, and $\frac{1}{4}$" clear polished plate interior sheet.

08830 MIRRORS

Over lavatories in toilet rooms, provide and install mirrors. Each mirror shall be of size indicated on the Drawings, equal to No. 53020, as manufactured by the Charles Parker Company, 50 Hanover Street, Meriden, Connecticut, complete with $\frac{1}{4}$" polished plate glass, moisture proof backing, removable back, narrow channel type plated brass or stainless steel frame, with concealed vandalproof mirror hangers. Mirrors shall be centered over lavatories, and set at height shown on Drawings or as directed by the Architect.

08840 GLAZING COMPOUND

Glazing compound for bedding glazing, Federal Specification TT-P-791a, Type I, elastic glazing compound.

DIVISION 8—DOORS AND WINDOWS

Section Number	Title
08100	METAL DOORS AND FRAMES
-110	Steel Doors and Frames
	Standard Steel Doors and Frames
	Standard Steel Doors
	Standard Steel Frames
	Custom Steel Doors and Frames
	Custom Steel Doors
	Custom Steel Frames
-115	Packaged Steel Doors and Frames
120	Aluminum Doors and Frames
-130	Stainless Steel Doors and Frames
140	Bronze Doors and Frames
08200	WOOD AND PLASTIC DOORS
-210	Wood Doors
	Flush Wood Doors
	Plastic Faced Flush Wood Doors
	Metal Faced Wood Doors
	Panel Wood Doors
-220	Plastic Doors
08250	DOOR OPENING ASSEMBLIES
08300	SPECIAL DOORS
-305	Access Doors
-310	Sliding Doors
	Sliding Glass Doors
	Sliding Metal Fire Doors
	Sliding Grilles
-315	Blast-Resistant Doors
-318	Security Doors
320	Metal-Clad Doors
325	Cold Storage Doors
330	Coiling Doors
	Coiling Counter Doors
	Overhead Coiling Doors
	Side Coiling Doors
340	Coiling Grilles
	Overhead Coiling Grilles
	Side Coiling Grilles
350	Folding Doors and Grilles
	Accordian Folding Doors
	Panel Folding Doors
	Accordian Folding Grilles
355	Flexible Doors
360	Sectional Overhead Doors
365	Multi-leaf Vertical Lift Overhead Doors
	Vertical Lift Telescoping Doors
370	Hangar Doors
380	Sound Retardant Doors
385	Safety Glass Doors
390	Screen and Storm Doors
395	Flood Barrier Doors
398	Chain Closures
08400	ENTRANCES AND STOREFRONTS
-410	Aluminum Entrances and Storefronts
-420	Steel Entrances and Storefronts
-430	Stainless Steel Entrances and Storefronts
-440	Bronze Entrances and Storefronts
-450	All-Glass Entrances
-460	Automatic Entrance Doors
-470	Revolving Entrance Doors

Section Number	Title
08500	METAL WINDOWS
-510	Steel Windows
-520	Aluminum Windows
-530	Stainless Steel Windows
-540	Bronze Windows
-550	Metal Jalousie Windows
-560	Metal Storm Windows
08600	WOOD AND PLASTIC WINDOWS
-610	Wood Windows
	Metal Clad Wood Windows
	Plastic Clad Wood Windows
	Wood Storm Windows
-630	Plastic Windows
	Reinforced Plastic Windows
	Plastic Storm Windows
08650	SPECIAL WINDOWS
-655	Roof Windows
660	Security Windows
-665	Pass Windows
08700	HARDWARE
-710	Finish Hardware
-720	Operators
	Automatic Door Operators
	Window Operators
-730	Weatherstripping and Seals
	Thresholds
740	Electrical Locking Systems
-750	Door and Window Accessories
	Flood Barriers
08800	GLAZING
-810	Glass
	Mirror Glass
840	Plastic Glazing
-850	Glazing Accessories
08900	GLAZED CURTAIN WALLS
-910	Glazed Steel Curtain Walls
-920	Glazed Aluminum Curtain Walls
-930	Glazed Stainless Steel Curtain Walls
-940	Glazed Bronze Curtain Walls
950	Translucent Wall and Skylight Systems
960	Sloped Glazing Systems
-970	Structural Glass Curtain Walls

```
JONES AND SMITH,  Architects: John Doe Bldg.
                    Washington, D. C.
First National Bank of Brownsville: Project No. 11863


ADDENDUM NO. 2: August 15, 19 —

To: All prime contract bidders of record.

This addendum forms a part of the Contract Documents and modifies the
original specifications and drawings, dated July 1, 19  , and
Addendum 1, dated August 1, 19—, as noted below. Acknowledge receipt
of this Addendum in the space provided on the Bid Form. Failure to do
so may subject bidder to disqualification.

This Addendum consists of _____. (Indicate the
number of pages and any attachments or drawings forming a part of the
addendum.)

ADDENDUM NO. 1

1. Drawings, page AD 1-1. In line 3, number of the referenced Drawing
is changed from "G-1" to "G-7."

INSTRUCTIONS TO BIDDERS
2. Proposals. The first sentence is changed to read: "Proposed
substitutions must be submitted in writing at least 15 days before
the date for opening of bids."

GENERAL CONDITIONS
3. Article 13, Access to Work. The following sentence is added: "Upon
completion of work, the Contractor shall deliver to the Architect all
required Certificates of Inspection."

SUPPLEMENTARY CONDITIONS
4. Article 19, Correction of Work Before Substantial Completion. This
Article is deleted and the following is inserted in its place: "If
proceeds of sale do not cover expenses that the Contractor should
have borne, the Contractor shall pay the difference to the Owner."

SPECIFICATIONS
5. Division 7
Waterproofing: Page 4, following Paragraph 7C-02 Materials, add the
following: "(d) Option. Factory mixed waterproofing containing
metallic waterproofing, sand and cement, all meeting the above
requirements, may be used in lieu of job-mixed waterproofing."

6. Division 15
Refrigeration: Page 10, Paragraph 4--Chillers item "e" Line 4: Change
total square feet of surface from 298 to 316.

Liquid Heat Transfer: Page 17, Paragraph 10--Convectors item "b" Line
3: Delete "as selected--or owner."
Page 23, Paragraph 13--Wall Fin: Omit entirely.

DRAWINGS
7. S-9, Beam Schedule. For B-15 the following is added: "Size, 12 x
26; Straight, 3 - #6; Bent, 2 - #8, Top Over Columns: 3 - #7."

8. M-1: At room 602 change 12 x 6 exhaust duct to 12 x 18; at room
602 add a roof ventilator. See print H-1R attached and page 16,
paragraph 13 Roof Ventilators addenda above.
```

Figure 7 *Sample Addendum.*

```
JONES AND SMITH, Architects/Engineers John Doe Bldg.,
                  Washington, D.C.
CHANGE ORDER NO. 5: September 9, 19 —
JOB NO. 11863: First National Bank of Brownsville
OWNER: ABC Corp., Brownsville, Virginia
CONTRACTOR: Bildum Construction Co., Washington, D.C.
CONTRACT DATE: July 4, 19 —



TO THE CONTRACTOR: You are hereby authorized, subject to Contract
provisions, to make the following changes:
Bulletin No. 1                                          ADD $ 73.24
Bulletin No. 2                                          ADD   138.07
Bulletin No. 3 No Charge,/No Credit
Bulletin No. 4                      DEDUCT $ 75.32
Bulletin No. 5                      DEDUCT   36.99

TOTAL                               DEDUCT $112.31      ADD $211.31
NET ADD $99.00



ORIGINAL CONTRACT AMOUNT:           $1,234,567.89
PRIOR CHANGE ORDERS (+, —):             +2,000.00
THIS CHANGE ORDER (+, —):                  +99.00

REVISED CONTRACT AMOUNT:            $1,236,666.89



TIME EXTENSION/REDUCTION: None



OTHER CONTRACTS AFFECTED: None



SUBMITTED BY:_____DATE:_____
             (arch/engr's signature)



APPROVED BY:_____DATE:_____
            (owner's signature)



ACCEPTED BY:_____DATE:_____
            (contractor's signature)



DISTRIBUTION: Owner, Contractor, Architect/Engineer,
              Field Representative, Other _____.
```

Figure 8   *Sample Change Order.*

Glazing compound shall be specially prepared for the purpose, tinted to match frames, and shall remain plastic under a strong surface film similar to the product manufactured by "Tremco," "Pecora," or "Kuhls." *No putty will be accepted* (glass in doors and windows shall be set in glazing compound secured by glazing beads).

08841 SAMPLES

Samples of each type of glass and glazing compound shall be submitted for approval of the Architect.

08842 SETTING

All glass shall be properly bedded in glazing compound previously specified. Glazing compound shall not be applied in temperatures below 40°F, or during damp or rainy weather. Surfaces shall be dry and free of dust, dirt, or rust.

Glazing compound shall be used as it comes from the container without adulteration and only after thorough mixing. If thinning is required, use only such type of thinner as recommended by the manufacturer.

08843 REPLACEMENT AND CLEANING

Upon completion of the glazing, all glass shall be throughly cleaned, any paint spots and labels and other defacements removed, and all cracked, broken, and imperfect glass, or glass which cannot be properly cleaned, shall be replaced by perfect glass.

At the time of acceptance of the building, all glass shall be clean, whole, and in perfect condition, including glazing compound. Glazing compound applied after completion of painting shall be painted not less than two (2) coats.

08844 LABELS

Each light shall bear the manufacturer's label indicating the name of the manufacturer and the strength and quality of the glass. Labels shall remain in place until after final acceptance of the building, at which time the labels shall be removed and glass shall be given its final cleaning.

XII WORKING DRAWINGS

The Working Drawings together with the Specifications are the most important parts of the documents constituting the contract. Information on the design, location, and dimensions of the elements of a building is found on Working Drawings, and information on the quality of materials and workmanship is found in the Specifications. A good Working Drawing gives the contractor the exact information he needs, is clear and simple, arranged in an orderly manner, and accurately drawn so that scaled measurements will agree with dimensions. (See Chapter 21 for more information.)

ADDENDA AND CHANGE ORDERS

Addenda and Change Orders are used to correct or change the original construction documents. The main difference between an Addendum and a Change Order is the timing. An Addendum revises the original construction documents *before* the contract is awarded, and a Change Order is a revision *after* award of the contract. A sample Addendum is shown in Figure 7, and a sample Change Order is shown in Figure 8.

STUDY QUESTIONS

1. Why is it important to prepare specifications for every architectural project?
2. List the twelve documents included in a typical set of construction documents.
3. List the sixteen divisions of a typical set of specifications.
4. Give the reasons for including the following documents in a set of construction documents:
   a. Specifications
   b. Working drawings
   c. Agreement
   d. Bid form
   e. Performance bond
   f. Labor and material bond

LABORATORY PROBLEMS

1. Prepare an outline of the specifications for the building assigned by your instructor.
   a. Include the broadscope section headings only.
   b. Include the broadscope and narrowscope section headings.
   c. Write a detailed specification for the section assigned by your instructor.
2. Obtain a set of specifications from a local architect for classroom study.

XI / Building Materials

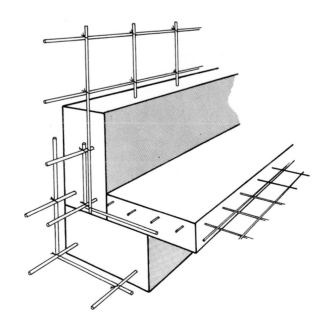

45 / Wood Products

Wood is one of the oldest and most widely used of building materials. Today, in spite of diminishing forest stands, it is still extremely popular for a number of structural and decorative applications. In addition, new methods of processing and combining wood with other materials have been developed. Approximately 75 percent of processed wood is used for building purposes.

TREE GROWTH

The growth of a tree is one of the wonders of nature. The process is not completely understood, but it is often compared to a continuously operating chemical factory that manufactures a product called *cellulose,* for wood cells are made almost entirely of cellulose cemented together with *lignin.* Cellulose is a carbohydrate composed of carbon, hydrogen, and oxygen. The tree absorbs these elements from the earth and air. With energy from the sun, the leaves of hardwood trees and the needles of softwood trees change these elements into carbohydrates and then into new cellulose cells. The process can be traced from the roots to the leaves to new growth as follows.

Roots not only anchor the tree in place but also gather nourishment from the soil through tiny white root hairs called *feeding roots.* Feeding roots grow wherever there is moisture. They push between soil particles and wrap around any wet particles to absorb the moisture. The moisture is mixed with mineral salts and becomes the tree sap. Every spring the sap flow increases as it is pulled up through the *sapwood* by capillary action, osmosis, and evaporation through the leaves. In the leaves, the mineral salts react with chlorophyll in the presence of sunlight to produce carbohydrates which the tree uses as plant food. This process is called *photosynthesis.* The plant food flows back down the *inner bark* to feed every living cell of the tree.

Separating the inner bark and sapwood is a microscopically thin layer of tissue called the *cambium* which is the wood-manufacturing part of the tree. Each year when the sap starts to flow, the cambium forms new wood and bark cells by cell division. New wood cells form on the inside of the cambium and new bark cells on the outside. No growth ever takes place in either diameter or length of *existing* wood; rather growth occurs by the addition of *new* cells. This growth forms the *annual rings,* which are used to date a tree. Figure 1 shows some of these features from outer bark to the inner heartwood.

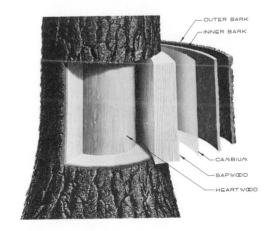

Figure 1   *Parts of a tree.*

Outer bark, formed of dry, dead tissue, is the tree's protective coating. It insulates the tree from cold, heat, excessive evaporation, and insects.

Inner bark returns food from the leaves to the rest of the tree. It lives for a short time and then dies and turns to cork to become outer bark.

Cambium cell layer produces new sapwood and new inner bark.

Sapwood carries sap from the roots to the leaves. As new rings of sapwood are formed on the outside, the inner rings die and turn into heartwood.

Heartwood is formed from former sapwood. Although dead, it does not decay and is the principal structural support for the tree.

Reading a tree. The wood formed early in the growing season is called *springwood,* and the wood formed later is called *summerwood.* The cells of springwood have thin walls and large cavities, but the walls thicken as the growing season progresses. There is enough difference between springwood and summerwood for the annual growth rings to be clearly visible on the cross section of a tree trunk or branch. In Figure 2 the wide, light-colored rings are springwood; the narrow, dark-colored rings are summerwood.

The cross section of a tree stump can be "read" like a natural history book since it gives much information on the tree's life. The number of rings indicates the tree's age. Broad, evenly spaced rings indicate rapid growth under abundant rainfall and sunshine. Narrow rings indicate slow growth because of crowding, a prolonged dry spell, or infestation by a leaf-eating insect. Egg-shaped rings show that something pushed against the tree, causing it to lean. In this case, the rings are wider on the lower side since the tree builds reaction wood to support itself. Dark scars on an annual ring give the date of a forest fire.

LUMBER MANUFACTURE

The terms *wood, lumber,* and *timber* are often used interchangeably. To be completely accurate, however, *wood* refers to the unprocessed fibrous material of the tree. *Lumber* is wood that has been sawed and planed to size. *Timber* refers to lumber in the larger sizes. Specifically, timber must be a nominal 5″ or larger in the least dimension.

Lumber manufacture begins with *fellers,* who cut down (*fell*) trees that have been selected and marked by *foresters.* A gas-powered hand chain saw is the usual tool. *Toppers* are persons who remove the tops of large trees such as redwoods and Douglas firs to prevent possible splintering when the tree is felled. *Buckers* follow the fellers to lop off limbs and cut the tree trunks into lengths of 40′

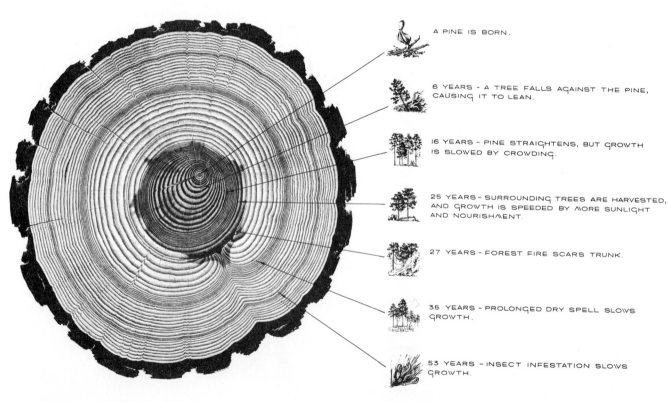

A PINE IS BORN.

6 YEARS - A TREE FALLS AGAINST THE PINE, CAUSING IT TO LEAN.

16 YEARS - PINE STRAIGHTENS, BUT GROWTH IS SLOWED BY CROWDING.

25 YEARS - SURROUNDING TREES ARE HARVESTED, AND GROWTH IS SPEEDED BY MORE SUNLIGHT AND NOURISHMENT.

27 YEARS - FOREST FIRE SCARS TRUNK.

35 YEARS - PROLONGED DRY SPELL SLOWS GROWTH.

53 YEARS - INSECT INFESTATION SLOWS GROWTH.

Figure 2   *Reading a tree.*

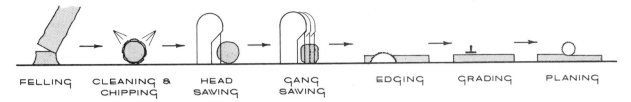

Figure 3   *Lumber manufacture.*

or less. The logs are hauled to a central storage landing until they can be moved to a sawmill. Sawmills range in size. A smallmill may have truck-mounted machinery which can be moved into the woods to be closer to the cutting operation. Larger mills are built near a *log pond* which is used to store the logs until needed. The water protects the logs from decay and fire. Also, the *boom man,* who walks on the floating logs, can sort them by size and type of wood. A selected log is carried to the sawmill by a moving conveyor chain. High-pressure water jets clean off all dirt which might dull the saw blades. See Figure 3. Before sawing, most mills remove the bark by means of a steel *chipper.* The log is then rolled onto a carriage which carries the log to the *head saw.* This heavy band saw squares the log in several passes and then is used to slice the wood into timber or smaller lumber. Figure 4 shows a log cut into typical sections of lumber. *Gang saws* may be used to reduce the number of passes. Circular *edger saws* and *trimmer saws* are used to square the edges of the wood to the desired width and trim the ends square to the desired length. The *rough lumber* is then inspected by a *grader* who marks the proper grade on each piece. Lumber of better appearance is selected for *planing* into *finished lumber.*

Defects. When grading lumber, the inspector looks for natural and manufacturing defects that affect strength and appearance. Some of the most common defects are:

1. *Knot:* A limb embedded in the lumber.
2. *Shake:* A natural separation of the annual rings. See Figure 5.
3. *Check:* A radial separation occurring during seasoning. See Figure 5.
4. *Warp:* A twist. See Figure 5.
5. *Cup:* A curve across the grain. See Figure 5.
6. *Wane:* Bark left on the lumber (or lack of wood). See Figure 5.
7. *Mold* and *stain:* Discoloration caused by fungi.

WOOD CLASSIFICATION

Wood is classified as softwood and hardwood. These terms are confusing because all softwoods are not softer than all hardwoods. Softwoods are obtained from conifers* (evergreen trees) and are commonly used in construction. Hardwoods are obtained from deciduous** trees (which usually shed their leaves each season) and are used for flooring, treads, rails, and veneers, and extensively for better grades of furniture. Some common softwoods and hardwoods used in building are listed in Table I.

PRODUCT STANDARDS

Nearly all products—from paper bags to prefabricated homes—are manufactured according to specifications found in *Product Standards.* Product Standards are published by the National Bureau of

* Conifer means "cone bearing."
** Deciduous means "fall off."

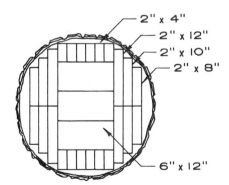

Figure 4   *A typical sawed log.*

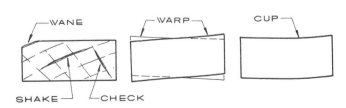

Figure 5   *Common lumber defects.*

Standards of the U.S. Department of Commerce. The adoption and use of a Product Standard is voluntary, but when a standard is made part of a legal document such as a purchase order, sales contract, or building code, compliance with the standard is enforceable. Also, Product Standards are not published unless there is general agreement by nearly all segments of an industry.

The Product Standard for softwood lumber is *PS 20-70 American Softwood Lumber Standard,* published in 1970. Lumber graded by these standards is called *American Standard Lumber.* The following paragraphs on lumber classification, grading, sizes, and measurement are condensed from the American Softwood Lumber Standard.

Lumber classification. American Standard softwood lumber is classified by nominal size, extent of manufacture, and use:

Size classification.

1. Boards (lumber less than 2″ thick)
2. Dimension lumber (lumber 2″ up to 5″ thick)
3. Timber (lumber 5″ or more thick)

Table I   *Some Common Softwoods and Hardwoods Used in Building*

Softwood	Hardwood
Cedars	Beech
Cypress	Birch
Douglas Fir	Cherry
Firs	Chestnut
Hemlocks	Hickory
Junipers	Mahogany
Larch	Maple
Pines	Oak
Redwood	Teak
Spruces	Walnut

Table II   *Comparison of Nominal and Finished Sizes*

Nominal Size	Finished Size
1″	$\frac{3}{4}$″
2″	$1\frac{1}{2}$″
4″	$3\frac{1}{2}$″
6″	$5\frac{1}{2}$″
8″	$7\frac{1}{4}$″
10″	$9\frac{1}{4}$″
12″	$11\frac{1}{4}$″

Manufacturing classification.

1. Rough lumber (lumber sawed, edged, and trimmed, but not planed)
2. Dressed lumber (lumber surfaced* by a planer)
3. Worked lumber (lumber shaped, such as tongue-and-grooved)

Use classification.

1. Yard lumber (general-purpose lumber such as studs, joists, boards, siding, and finishing material)
2. Structural lumber (lumber 2″ or more thick and graded by working stresses)
3. Factory and shop lumber (lumber graded by appearance to be further manufactured into doors, sash, trim, and the like)

Lumber grading. Lumber is further classified by *grade* according to the number of natural, seasoning, and manufacturing defects that affect strength or appearance:

1. Yard lumber
   a. Select (for good appearance and finishing qualities)

      Grade A (for natural finishes, clear)
      Grade B (for natural finishes, generally clear)
      Grade C (for high-quality paint finishes)
      Grade D (for standard paint finishes)

   b. Common (for general construction)

      No. 1 Common (for high-quality construction)
      No. 2 Common (for standard construction)
      No. 3 Common (for economy or temporary construction)
      No. 4 Common (low quality)
      No. 5 Common (just strong enough to hold together, dunnage)

2. Structural lumber

   Stress graded (by species of timber according to load-bearing properties as specified by the National Lumber Manufacturers Association)

3. Factory and shop lumber

   Grade A (for natural finishes, clear)
   Grade B (for natural finishes, generally clear)
   Grade C (for high-quality paint finishes)
   Grade D (for standard paint finishes)

* Such as surface one side (S1S), two sides (S2S), all sides (S4S), one edge (S1E), two edges (S2E), or some combination (S1S1E, S2S1E, S1S2E).

Size standards. The *nominal size* is the size of rough lumber. After planing, the actual *finished size* is about $\frac{1}{2}''$ smaller than nominal. The difference between nominal and finished size will vary depending upon the size of the lumber, ranging from $\frac{3}{4}''$ for lumber over 6″ to only $\frac{1}{4}''$ for 1″ lumber. Table II shows the variations between nominal and finished size of American Standard Lumber.

Seasoning. The moisture content* of *green lumber* (freshly cut lumber) is approximately 40 percent by weight. Before use, the lumber must be *seasoned* or *kiln dried* to reduce the moisture content to about 12 percent. Seasoning refers to the natural drying of lumber. This is usually accomplished by stacking covered lumber for several months. During these months, the lumber is separated by 1″ strips so air can circulate freely. Kiln drying refers to accelerated drying in a kiln where both temperature and humidity are carefully controlled. Lumber after seasoning or kiln drying is less likely to shrink, warp, or check. However, lumber will continue to slightly shrink or swell depending upon any variations in the moisture content of the surrounding atmosphere. Warping is caused by the wood fibers absorbing unequal amounts of moisture on the two sides of a board. Such warping can occur when only one side of a board is painted or one side is exposed to excessive moisture.

Lumber measurement. Structural calculations for the strength of lumber are made using the actual dimensions, but lumber is specified and sold by the *board foot*—based upon nominal dimensions. A board foot is the amount of wood contained in a piece of rough green lumber 1 inch thick × 12 inches wide × 1 foot long. The abbreviation for board feet is *BM* (meaning literally "board measure"). The abbreviation for one thousand is M, and a thousand board feet is abbreviated MBM.

The board feet in any piece of lumber can be calculated as follows: BM = thickness (inches) × width (feet) × length (feet).

EXAMPLE

1. The board feet in a 2″ × 4″ stud 8′ long is: $2 \times \frac{4}{12} \times 8 = 5.3$ BM.
2. The board feet in sixty pieces of 2″ × 10″ joists 14′ long is: $2 \times \frac{10}{12} \times 14 \times 60 = 1,400$ BM = 1.4 MBM.

Although most lumber is sold by the board foot, some wood products are specified and sold

---

* The *Voluntary Product Standards* define green lumber as having a moisture content over 19 percent and seasoned lumber as 19 percent or less.

by the square foot (plywood), running foot (molding), or number of pieces (rails).

FIRE RESISTANCE

Heavy lumber, such as used in timber construction, has high ratings for fire protection. But light lumber, such as used in standard frame construction, is quite combustible. Limited fire protection can be obtained by pressure impregnation of the lumber with mineral salts. The surfaces of treated lumber must be sealed, however, to prevent the salts from being leached out of the lumber by atmospheric humidity. This treatment is useless when lumber is exposed to rain. This method provides fire protection by causing heated lumber to release noncombustible gases and water vapor at temperatures just below its ignition point. Also, a hard layer of carbon char forms on the surface of the lumber. In addition to fire protection, this treatment provides termite and decay protection.

Fire-retardant paint also gives some fire protection. The paint forms blisters when heated which serve to insulate the lumber.

WOOD PRESERVATIVES

Lumber can be protected from attack by decay and insects by treating with preservatives. Pressure is used to drive the preservative deep into the lumber. The lumber is loaded on cars and pushed into steel chambers capable of pressures up to 200 psi.

Creosote is the oldest wood preservative against decay and wood-destroying insects. Creosoted lumber is not paintable. It also has increased flammability and consequently is seldom used above ground. Pentachlorophenol, an oil-borne treatment, has the same effects and limitations of creosote.

A gas-borne treatment for decay and termite protection uses liquid petroleum gas solvents to force the preservative into the wood. With this treatment, pentachlorophenol is still the preservative, but the lumber is paintable.

Several water-borne salt treatments are available for decay and termite protection. Painting over water-borne salt treatment is possible.

PROCESSED WOOD

Wood may undergo further processing into a variety of products such as plywood, fiberboard, and hardboard.

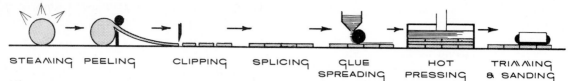

Figure 6 *Plywood manufacture.*

Figure 7 *Direction of plywood plies.*

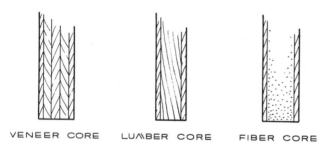

Figure 8 *Plywood core types.*

Plywood. The art of veneering was practiced in Egypt as early as 1500 B.C. Thin layers of rare wood were inlaid and overlaid on furniture using animal glue and sandbag weights. Ancient Greeks and Romans also used veneer and plywood to achieve intricate designs. In 1830 plywood was used extensively in the manufacture of pianos, and in 1890 plywood-paneled doors were first manufactured. Stock plywood sheets were first sold in 1910. These early sheets were 3' × 6'; the standard size today is 4' by 8'. Synthetic resin adhesives were developed around 1925. Urea-formaldehyde glue was introduced in 1937 and is still used today in nearly all interior plywood. Resorcinol glues are highly resistant to water and are used extensively in the manufacture of exterior plywood.

Plywood is a popular and strong wood product. Its strength is nearly equal in length and width, it is easily fabricated, and it resists shrinking and warping. Plywood is manufactured by glueing together thin wood veneers that have been sliced from steamed logs mounted in lathes. See Figure 6. The veneers, or *plies,* are bonded together with the grain of adjacent plies perpendicular to each other as shown in Figure 7. Depending upon the type of glue used, plywood is designated *dry-bond, water-resistant-bond,* and *waterproof-bond.* Dry-bond plywood is used in interiors where there is no exposure to dampness, water-resistant plywood will resist occasional exposure to moisture, and waterproof plywood can be used for exteriors.

Plywood is manufactured with a number of different kinds of cores. See Figure 8. The *veneer*

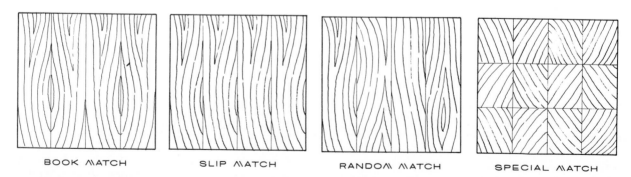

Figure 9 *Matching face veneer.*

core, consisting of an odd number of plies, is most common. The *lumber core,* of solid wood more than $\frac{3}{8}''$ thick, permits better edge staining. A *particle-board core* of chips of wood and adhesive formed under pressure into an homogeneous panel is extremely stable and has good acoustical properties. Other cores for special purposes include mineral cores for fire resistance and aluminum or kraft-paper honeycomb for lightweight panels.

The usual sizes of stock plywood panels are $\frac{1}{16}''$–$1\frac{1}{4}''$ thick, 4' wide, and 8', 10', or 12' long. Softwood plywood of Douglas fir is commonly used for construction. Hardwood plywood has a face ply of hardwood such as birch, cherry, hickory, mahogany, maple, oak, pine (knotty), teak, or walnut. When only the face ply of a panel is finished hardwood, the back face ply must be of the same or equivalent wood to prevent warping. An example of hardwood plywood with a face ply of wormy chestnut is shown in Figure 10. Face veneers for decorative wall panels are selected for their pattern and are termed flat slice, burl, crotch, or butt depending upon where they are *flitched* from the log. When the edges of hardwood plywood are exposed, they can be finished by glueing veneer or a lumber edgeband of the matching species to the edges.

Matching veneers. The term *matching* refers to the joining of adjacent veneers to form special patterns. Adjacent strips of veneer *within* a panel can be matched, and the panels themselves can be matched. Some of the combinations (Figure 9) are:

1. *Book match.* Alternate sheets of veneer are turned over as are the leaves of a book, providing continuity of grain from panel to panel.
2. *Slip match.* Sheets are joined side by side without turning, providing a repetitive pattern.
3. *Random match.* Sheets are joined at random to produce a casual effect.
4. *Special matchings.* Matchings such as diamond, herringbone, and vee matches can be specified to provide the desired design. This is achieved by placing the grain of each panel at an angle.

Plastic veneers. In addition to hardwood veneers over plywood or particle-board cores, a variety of plastic veneers are manufactured over these cores. Plastic veneers are also available separately in $\frac{1}{32}''$ to $\frac{1}{4}''$-thick sheets. All are resistant to weather, acids, alkalies, and alcohol. One of the most popular trade names is *Formica*. Formica is a thin, flexible sheet from $\frac{1}{32}''$ to $\frac{1}{16}''$ thick consisting of layers of resin-impregnated kraft paper that has been molded under high temperature and pressure. Available in a large selection of colors and patterns, Formica is widely used for wall surfaces and

Figure 10   *Wormy chestnut plywood paneling.*

countertops. Contact cement is used to fasten the Formica veneer to its backing core.

Fiberboard. *Fiberboard* is used as sheathing and insulation. It is composed of loosely compressed fibers of wood, cane, mineral, or glass. Common panel sizes are $\frac{1}{4}''$–$1''$ thick × 4' wide × 8' long. Sections 16" wide × 12' long called *planks* are also stocked.

Wood fiberboard, also called *particle board,* is composed of small wood particles or chips. It is an ideal core for hardwood and plastic veneers.

Cane fiberboard is manufactured from sugarcane fiber. When impregnated with asphalt to increase its water resistance, it is used for roof insulation.

Mineral fiberboard, made of rock wool, has the advantage of being incombustible.

Glass fiberboard is composed of fiber glass between layers of kraft paper. It has excellent insulating properties and is not damaged by moisture.

Hardboard. *Hardboard* is used for exterior siding, interior finishing, and concrete forms. It is commonly called by the trade name *Masonite*. Hardboard is manufactured from wood fibers molded under heat and high pressure into dense, hard panels that are much harder than the initial wood. *Tempered hardboard* is manufactured by chemically treating standard hardboard under additional heat

457

Figure 11   *Patterned interior hardboard with wood-grain finish used for interior partitions and doors.*

Figure 12   *Tempered exterior hardboard with simulated planked siding.*

to increase its resistance to water. Standard hardboard is used for interiors and tempered hardboard for exteriors.

Hardboard is available with smooth surfaces or with a smooth front face and a screen-indented rear surface. Also available are patterned front faces such as tile, brick masonry, wood grain, burlap, and striated. Punched hardboard is used for filigree. The natural color of hardboard is dark brown, but prefinished hardboard in colors is popular. Some interior patterns are shown in Figure 11 and exterior uses in Figure 12. Common sizes are $\frac{1}{8}''$ to $\frac{5}{16}''$ thick $\times$ 4' wide $\times$ 8' long.

STUDY QUESTIONS

1. How old is the tree shown in Figure 2?
2. What is the difference between:
   a. Outer bark and inner bark
   b. Sapwood and heartwood
   c. Springwood and summerwood
   d. Wood, lumber, and timber
   e. Nominal size and finished size
   f. Seasoned lumber and kiln-dried lumber
   g. Deciduous and conifer trees
3. Describe the process of:
   a. Tree growth
   b. Lumber manufacture
   c. Plywood manufacture
4. Describe briefly each term:
   a. Check
   b. Cup
   c. Knot
   d. Shake
   e. Wane
   f. Warp
5. List the American Standard lumber classifications by size, extent of manufacture, and use.
6. List the American Standard lumber classifications by grade.
7. List five examples of:
   a. Softwood
   b. Hardwood
8. How many board feet are contained in one hundred pieces of 2″ × 6″ lumber 16′ long?
9. Name the methods of increasing the fire resistance of a wood-framed structure.
10. Name four types of wood preservatives. Indicate those types that permit the wood to be painted.
11. What is the difference between dry-bond, water-resistant, and waterproof plywood?
12. Sketch hardwood plywood installed in a pattern of each of the following. What is the advantage of each?
    a. Book match
    b. Slip match
    c. Random match
13. Name four types of fiberboard and give the advantages of each.
14. What is the principal advantage of tempered hardboard?

LABORATORY PROBLEMS

1. Calculate the quantity and cost of lumber required for your original building design.
2. Detail customized plywood cabinets for:
   a. The building assigned by your instructor
   b. Your original building design
3. Draw detailed sections of a typical asbestos cement spandrel panel installation.
4. Prepare a class list of material cost for your area after obtaining information from your local building suppliers.
5. (For the advanced student) Construct a model showing:
   a. How lumber is manufactured
   b. The parts of a tree from outer bark to heartwood

46 / Timber Construction

Timber construction was one of the earliest methods of building used by settlers in the New World. It has continued in popularity through the years, but not for the same reasons. Originally timber was used because of the difficulty in hand sawing logs into smaller lumber. Later, when lumber was readily available in all sizes, a type of timber construction called *mill construction* was often used for factories and warehouses where the loads were heavy and the fire danger high. In mill construction, a few heavy posts and beams support a solid wood floor 3″–6″ thick—since a few large members will resist fire longer than many small members. In recent years mill construction for industrial buildings has been replaced by steel and concrete construction methods. Timber construction still continues in popularity for structures such as residences, churches, schools, gymnasiums, and commercial buildings where the timber is left exposed to present a permanent, yet warm, effect. Some of the most outstanding examples of contemporary architecture have used this method of framing (Figure 1).

HEAVY TIMBER

Heavy timber construction is similar to plank-and-beam framing in principle, but heavier members are used. Heavy timber construction, as defined by many building codes, consists of solid or glue-laminated wood columns at least 6″ × 8″ for supporting roof and ceiling loads and at least 8″ × 8″ for supporting floor loads. Beams are at least 6″ wide × 10″ deep. Floors and roofs have no concealed spaces but are built of solid or glue-lam-

inated, continuous-span planking, splined or tongue-and-grooved, at least 2″ thick for roof support and at least 3″ thick for floor support. Major advantages are:

1. A few large structural members replace many small members.
2. Fire hazard is reduced.
3. Timbers and planks are often left exposed, eliminating the need for additional interior finish.

Figure 1   *Visitor Information Center of timber construction, Jamestown, Virginia.*

459

Some disadvantages of this type of construction are:

1. Special furring must be used to conceal pipes and electrical conduits installed on the ceiling.
2. Additional roof insulation must be used due to the elimination of dead air spaces between the roof and ceiling.
3. It is more difficult to control condensation. Exhaust fans are used to reduce moisture in the building to a minimum.

It should be mentioned that combinations of heavy timber and conventional construction are possible using the advantageous features of each type.

Construction details. Figures 2–7 illustrate recommended construction details that have been found through experience to be satisfactory. The location of fasteners in these figures is indicated by center lines. Bolts are usually used with shear plates which distribute the load over a greater area. Shear plates are shown in Figure 8. They are completely embedded flush with the timber surface in precut daps (circular grooves). Shear plates are used for both timber-to-timber and timber-to-steel connections. Shear plates are $2\frac{1}{2}''$–$4''$ in diameter. The number and size of timbers and hardware connectors are determined through analysis of the loads to be supported.

Theory of continuous spans. Compare the deflection of single-span planks and continuous-span

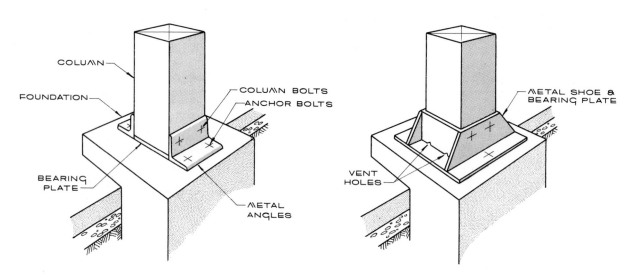

Figure 2 *Column anchorages.*

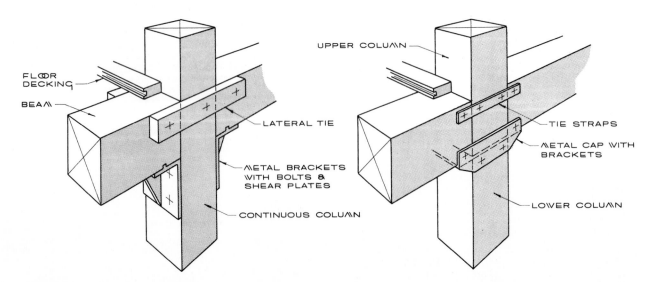

Figure 3 *Floor-beam and column framing.*

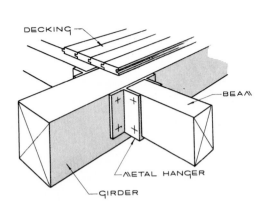

Figure 4 *Beam-and-girder framing.*

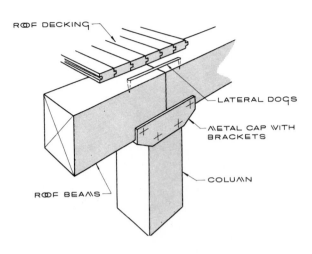

Figure 5 *Roof-beam framing.*

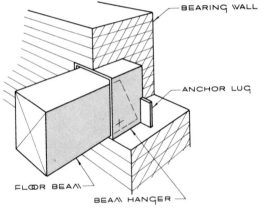

Figure 6 *Beam framing at wall.*

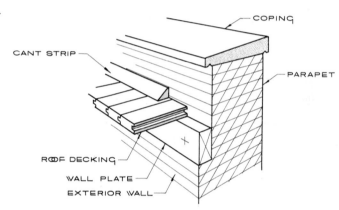

Figure 7 *Plank framing at wall.*

planks as shown in Figure 9 and notice that the continuous span will deflect less. In fact, the continuous span will have about twice the stiffness of the single span. Of course, it is important that the floor be constructed so that it acts as one homogeneous unit. This is done by using tongue-and-groove or splined planking with staggered end joints.

Continuous-spliced joists. The added stiffness of a continuous beam is also used to advantage in conventional platform framing. Although joists are not normally available in lengths sufficient for a double span, a system of staggered splices is almost as effective. As shown in Figure 10, a joist is cantilevered over the girder and spliced to a shorter supported joist. It is important, of course, that splices be staggered, and their location is critical. Details can be obtained from the American Plywood Association.

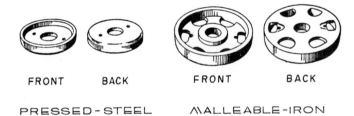

Figure 8 *Shear plates.*

LAMINATED TIMBER

Laminated timber is fabricated in sizes and shapes that are difficult to obtain in solid timber. Also, seasoning and inspection of laminations can be better controlled, and select lumber can be used

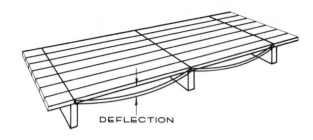
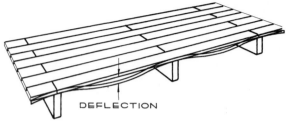

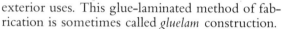

SINGLE SPAN   CONTINUOUS SPAN

Figure 9   *Continuous-span theory.*

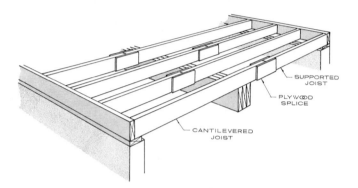

SUPPORTED JOIST

PLYWOOD SPLICE

CANTILEVERED JOIST

Figure 10   *Continuous-spliced joists.*

where good appearance and strength are desired, with less costly lumber used elsewhere.

Laminations are usually 2″ thick and glued together under pressure. This is best accomplished at a factory since nails or other fasteners are not used to hold the laminations in contact while the glue sets. Water-resistive casein glue is used for interior uses, and waterproof resin glue is employed for exterior uses. This glue-laminated method of fabrication is sometimes called *gluelam* construction.

Laminated timber is usually fabricated of Douglas Fir, Southern Yellow Pine, or Ponderosa Pine. The laminations can be vertical as in Figure 11 or horizontal as in Figure 12. Vertically laminated timbers are often used for straight beams of moderate size (Figure 13); horizontally laminated timbers are used for curved or special shapes in large spans such as arches (Figure 14), rigid frames, or tapered girders. Laminations 2″ thick can be bent to a radius of 24′. When the laminations must be spliced, scarfed end joints, beveled 1 in 8, are used. Laminated timber is typically spaced 6′–20′ oc.

Laminated timber is often finished at a factory. To protect the timber from moisture and the finish from scratches, it is wrapped in a waterproof membrane at the factory. See Figure 15. The membrane is kept in place until the beam is in place and protected from moisture and construction damage.

Typical connection details are similar to those shown in Figures 16–18. Notice that metal connectors can be exposed or concealed when desired.

Figure 11   *Vertically laminated beam with tongue-and-grooved planking.*

Figure 12   *Horizontally laminated arch—buttress connection detail.*

Figure 13   *Laminated timber used for exposed residential beams.*

Figure 14   *Laminated timber used for arch construction.*

Laminated decking. Laminated decking (Figure 19) is available in thicknesses from 2″ to 5″ and widths from 6″ to 12″. Typically the core and back laminations will be Douglas Fir or West Coast Hemlock with the face lamination of Red Cedar. Routing for concealed wiring can be cut in the top of the decking parallel to the span. When perpendicular to the span, routing must be done only over support members. It is also possible to cover wiring with rigid insulation without routing. See Table XII in Chapter 29 to determine allowable loads for laminated decking.

BOX BEAMS

Box beams are lightweight, economical, and easily fabricated into a variety of tapered, arched, or curved shapes (Figure 20). They may be used as an

Figure 15   *Casein-glued interior arches delivered with waterproof membrane.*

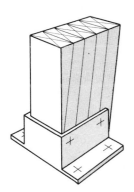 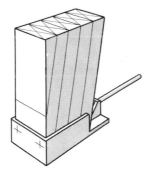 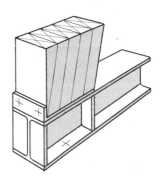

HORIZONTAL THRUST TO FLOOR SLAB   HORIZONTAL THRUST TO TIE ROD   HORIZONTAL THRUST TO STEEL BEAM

Figure 16   *Arch anchorages.*

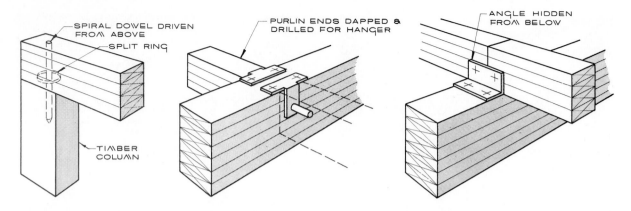

Figure 17   *Concealed beam connections.*

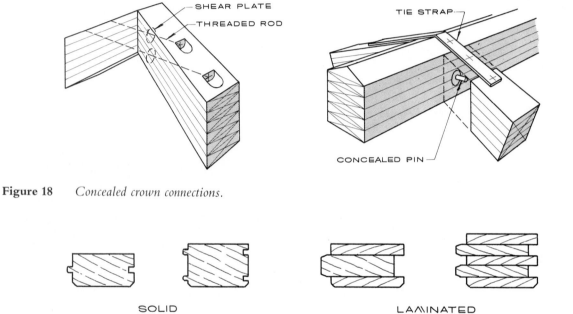

Figure 18   *Concealed crown connections.*

SOLID   LAMINATED

Figure 19   *Types of tongue-and-grooved planking.*

alternate to built-up girders and lintels in light-frame construction and as an alternate to solid or laminated beams in post-and-beam construction. They are used for spans from 8′ to 120′.

Box beams are hollow structural units composed of vertical plywood webs fastened to seasoned lumber flanges. Vertical spacers are also included to prevent web buckling and to provide a backup at the joints of the plywood. See Figure 21.

Four types of beam cross section are common, each suited for different loadings and space requirements. These sections are called Type A, Type B, Type C, and Type I, and are illustrated in Figure 22.

Type A box beams consist of lumber flanges and plywood webs glued or nailed together. The

size of sections depends upon the span and loading, with flanges ranging from a 2″ × 4″ wood member for an 8′ span to six 2″ × 10″ wood members for an 80′ span. Webs range from $\frac{1}{2}$″ plywood for an 8′ span to $1\frac{1}{8}$″ plywood for an 80′ span. The cross section is uniform throughout the length.

Type B box beams are different from Type A box beams only in that the webs are doubled where shear reinforcement is needed. This is at the outer portions of uniformly loaded single-span beams, but special conditions may require reinforcing at any position. Where the webs do not need to be doubled, shims are provided which are of the same thickness as the plywood.

Type C box beams also have extra webs where necessary for shear, but these webs are sandwiched between flanges. Type C1 beams have a single interior web; Type C2 beams have two interior webs.

Type I beams (named after their shape) are also occasionally used for short spans and light loads.

Several typical box-beam designs are detailed in Figures 23 and 24. The 16′ garage-door header is for a 24′-deep building with 25 lb./sq. ft. live roof load. The 22′ ridge beam is for a 32′-deep building with 30 lb./sq. ft. live roof load. Notice how the plywood web joints were staggered in both instances. Figure 25 illustrates the use of box beams in a rigid-frame type of construction.

STRESSED-SKIN PANELS

Stressed-skin panels are used for floors, roofs, and walls in all types of prefabricated building construction. Flat stressed-skin panels are made by glueing and nailing plywood sheets to lumber joists as shown in Figure 26. Usually 4′-wide sheets are glued to four joists and two headers, thus replacing conventional joist and subflooring construction.

In conventional floor and roof framing, joists act as the sole structural support for dead and live loads, including the dead load of the subflooring. In stressed-skin panel construction, plywood sheets are bonded to the joists to provide an integral structural unit. The upper sheet of plywood aids in resisting compressive stresses, and the lower sheet aids in resisting tensile stresses in much the same manner that the upper and lower flanges of a steel beam resist compressive and tensile stresses. Figure 27 shows workmen installing

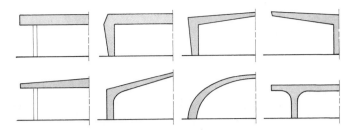

Figure 20   *Some box-beam shapes.*

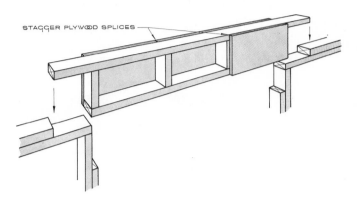

Figure 21   *Installing a 12′ box-beam lintel.*

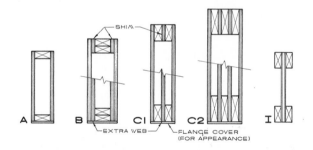

Figure 22   *Box-beam types.*

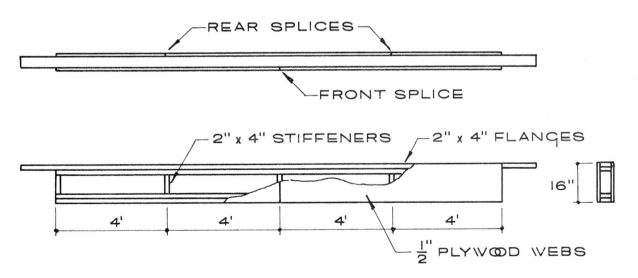

Figure 23   *Detail of a 16′ garage-door-header box beam.*

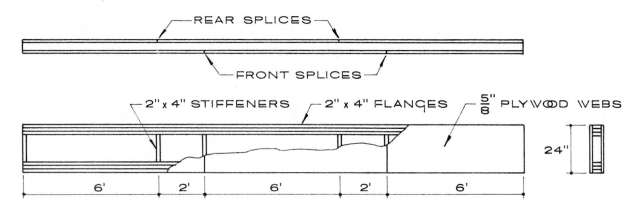

Figure 24   *Detail of a 22' ridge box beam.*

Figure 25   *Box beams used for rigid-frame construction.*

stressed-skin panels. Figure 28 illustrates the use of box beams and stressed-skin panels in combination.

Folded-plate roofs are often constructed of stressed-skin panels. The inclined panels lean against one another and are stabilized by tie rods. The end of each valley is supported by columns (Figure 29). Folded-plate sections may be assembled at the factory and delivered to the job site (Figure 30).

Curved stressed-skin panels (Figure 31) are used for the construction of unique roof shapes. Construction of curved panels is similar to the construction of flat panels, but curved, laminated ribs are used to replace straight joists. Figure 32 shows workers installing curved stressed-skin panels. Some completed units are shown in Figures 33 and 34.

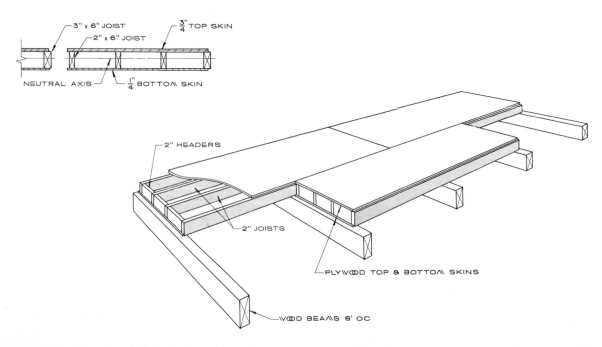

Figure 26   *Flat stressed-skin panel.*

Figure 27   *Installing stressed-skin panels.*

Figure 28   *A structure of box beams and stressed-skin panels.*

Figure 29   *A folded-plate roof of stressed-skin panels.*

Figure 30   *Delivering folded-plate sections to the job site.*

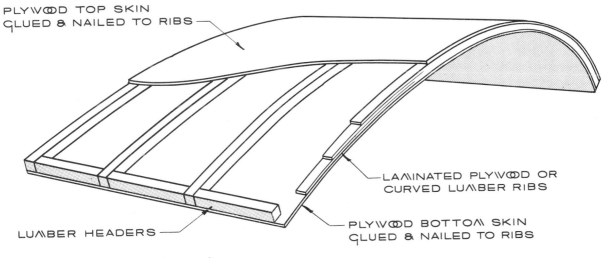

PLYWOOD TOP SKIN
GLUED & NAILED TO RIBS

LAMINATED PLYWOOD OR
CURVED LUMBER RIBS

LUMBER HEADERS

PLYWOOD BOTTOM SKIN
GLUED & NAILED TO RIBS

Figure 31   *Curved stressed-skin panel.*

Figure 32 *Installing curved stressed-skin panels.*

Figure 33 *A roof of curved stressed-skin panels.*

Figure 34 *A contemporary church roof of curved stressed-skin panels.*

STUDY QUESTIONS

1. Define *heavy timber construction* as specified by most building codes.
2. Give three advantages and three disadvantages of heavy timber construction.
3. Why are shear plates used?
4. What is the advantage of:
   a. A continuous-span joist over a single-span joist
   b. A continuous-spliced joist over a continuous-span joist
5. Indicate the primary application of:
   a. Vertically laminated timbers
   b. Horizontally laminated timbers
6. Sketch a typical Type A, Type B, Type C, and Type I box beam.
7. How do box beams differ from stressed-skin panels?

LABORATORY PROBLEMS

1. Prepare the following detailed drawings for a two-story timber building with masonry walls:
   a. 8″-square column at its footing
   b. 8″ × 12″ horizontal beam supported by an 8″-square column at the first-floor level
   c. 8″ × 12″ horizontal beam supported by an 8″-square column at the roof level
   d. 8″ × 12″ horizontal beam framed into 12″-thick exterior masonry wall
2. For the building assigned by your instructor, complete:
   a. Heavy timber details
   b. Laminated timber details
   c. Box-beam details
   d. Stressed-skin panels
3. For your original building design, complete:
   a. Heavy timber details
   b. Laminated timber details
   c. Box-beam details
   d. Stressed-skin panels
4. (For the advanced student) Design and detail a series of concealed connectors for typical timber-to-timber construction joints.

47 / Concrete Masonry

MASONRY CONSTRUCTION

Masonry construction refers to buildings made of stone, brick, concrete block, and structural clay tile—all materials used by masons. Stone and brick have been important building materials for thousands of years, stone being the oldest natural building material and brick the oldest manufactured material. Later, new materials such as concrete block and structural clay tile were developed.

CONCRETE MASONRY

Manufacture. Concrete masonry units, usually called *concrete block,* * are commonly used as a construction material. Their use exceeds the combined use of all other types of masonry units. Concrete block are manufactured by molding under

*The words *block,* *brick,* and *tile* are used to describe both singular and plural units.

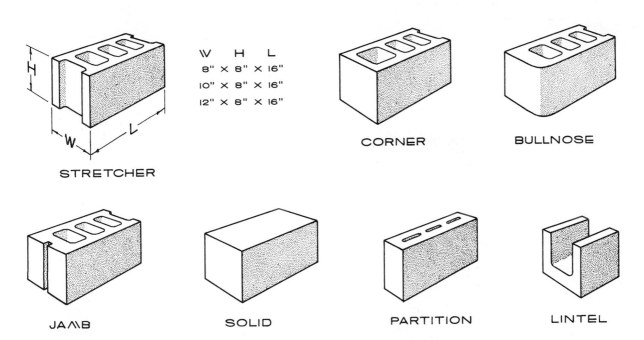

W   H   L
8" × 8" × 16"
10" × 8" × 16"
12" × 8" × 16"

STRETCHER

CORNER

BULLNOSE

JAMB

SOLID

PARTITION

LINTEL

Figure 1   *Typical concrete block units.*

pressure a stiff mixture of portland cement, aggregates, and water in steel molds. The *green* block holds its shape even though immediately removed from the mold. Curing (drying) is accomplished within a day by treatment with steam in a drying kiln. Both heavyweight units (concrete block) and lightweight units (cinder block) are available. The stronger heavyweight unit is composed of crushed stone or gravel aggregate. The aggregate of the lightweight unit is crushed coal cinders and is superior for insulation, nailability, and resistance to fire.

Sizes. Concrete block, like all masonry units, are manufactured in modular sizes based upon the 4″ module. The 8″ × 8″ × 16″ *stretcher* (Figure 1) is

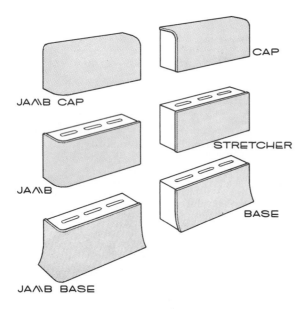

the unit most often used. The actual size of such a unit is $7\frac{5}{8}″ \times 7\frac{5}{8}″ \times 15\frac{5}{8}″$ to allow for $\frac{3}{8}″$ mortar joints. Block in 10″ and 12″ nominal widths are manufactured for use in thicker walls. The *corner block* is used for squared corners, and the *bullnose block* for rounded corners. *Jamb block* are laid around window and door openings. *Solid* (uncored) *block* are available in widths of 2″, 3″, 4″, 6″, 8″, 10″, and 12″. They are used as bearing block. When used in the construction of fallout shelters, they give increased protection from radioactivity. *Partition block* are available in 3″, 4″, and 6″ widths and are used to form interior partitions, exterior cavity walls, and composite walls. *Lintel block* are used as forms for reinforced concrete when constructing lintels over openings or bond beams around the entire structure. They have the added advantage of continuing the pattern formed by the stretcher block. Half-length units 8″ long are available for most of the block shown in Figure 1.

Color and texture. Concrete block are often painted to improve their appearance. Paint applied with a brush tends to close the surface pores and reduce the sound insulation value by about half, but spray painting does not have as great an effect. The paints used for exterior masonry walls will reduce rain penetration but will still allow water vapor to escape from the building. If this "breathing" is retarded, trapped moisture may freeze within the masonry units and cause them to disintegrate.

Block *glazed* on the exposed surfaces are available in all colors. Some types of units are shown in Figure 2. The glazed facing is $\frac{1}{8}″$ thick and quite resistant to abrasion, impact, and chemicals. Units glazed on opposite sides are used for interior partitions. Also available are units in a vari-

Figure 2 *Glazed partition block.*

Figure 3 *Slump block.*

Figure 4 *Split block.*

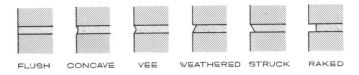

Figure 5 *Types of mortar joints.*

ety of patterned surfaces. Pierced grille block are used for solar screens and special effects.

Slump block (Figure 3) are manufactured by molding a concrete mixture of a consistency that sags or slumps when removed from the mold. The result is a block varying in size and texture that resembles stone.

Split block offer another variation in wall finish. They are manufactured by splitting solid block and are laid with these fractured faces exposed as shown in Figure 4.

Mortar and joints. Mortar may be applied to the webs as well as to the edges of concrete block (called *full mortar bedding*) or to the edges only (called *face-shell bedding*). Full mortar bedding is used in laying the starting course of block on a footing or to support heavy loads. Face-shell bedding is used for all ordinary work.

Although wood-bonding materials are stronger than wood itself, masonry-bonding materials are not as effective as the masonry units and must be carefully specified. Selection of a mortar type depends upon the required type of wall. For load-bearing walls, mortar with a high *compressive* strength is needed; for walls to resist strong winds, high *tensile* bond strength is needed. No one mortar type listed in Table I is best for all requirements. A mortar is excellent for one requirement at the expense of other requirements. The letter designations in Table I are not in alphabetical order. The ASTM* committee that chose these designations deliberately avoided an alphabetical order to indicate that no single mortar is "best."

Type M mortar has the highest compressive strength and durability. It is recommended for unreinforced masonry below grade in contact with the earth such as foundations and walks.

Type S mortar has the highest tensile bond strength. It is recommended for reinforced masonry and wherever strong mortar adhesion is needed such as ceramic veneer fastened to a masonry backing.

Type N mortar is an all-purpose mortar for exterior use above grade. It is recommended for

* American Society for Testing and Materials.

walls subject to severe exposure, parapets, and chimneys.

Type O mortar is recommended for non-load-bearing interior walls. It can be used in exterior walls if no freezing will be encountered.

Mortar should not be applied in freezing temperatures, and it should be protected against freezing for several days after being used in masonry construction. Calcium chloride may be added to the mortar in an amount not greater than 2 percent by weight of the portland cement content. This will not lower the freezing point of the mortar to any great extent, but it will accelerate the setting and hardening of the mortar. Salts such as sodium chloride (table salt) should not be added, since they may weaken the mortar.

The simplest masonry joint is the *flush joint* (Figure 5) which is made by trimming excess mortar with the trowel. A hairline crack may appear between mortar and block, and so this is not always a watertight joint. When the mortar has begun to stiffen, it is good practice to compact it with a jointing tool (Figure 7). The *concave joint* is produced by a circular tool, and the *vee joint* by a square tool. These are very weather resistant joints and are recommended in areas of heavy rain and wind or freezing. The *weathered joint* and the *struck joint* are cut with a trowel. The weathered joint is somewhat compacted and sheds water. The struck joint is commonly used because it is easy to make when the mason is working from the inside of a wall. There is some compaction, but the small ledge tends to holds moisture longer. The *raked joint* is made with a square edge tool. It is not a dependable weather-resistant joint, but is often specified by architects to emphasize the mortar joints. A popular treatment is raked horizontal joints with flush vertical joints to create strong horizontal lines.

Surface bonding. Surface bonding is a relatively new masonry process in which the concrete blocks are stacked without mortar in a stretcher bond. Then both sides of the wall are dampened and plastered with a surface bonding cement to a thickness of at least $\frac{1}{8}''$. The cement is spread over both the joints and the block and can be finished to a variety of stucco-like finishes. Surface bonding cement is composed of portland cement, graded sand, and glass fiber. Surface bonding should not be used for

Table I *Mortar Types*

Mortar Type	Parts by Volume			Compressive Strength
	Cement	Lime	Sand	
M	1	$\frac{1}{4}$	3 times	2,500 psi
S	1	$\frac{1}{2}$	the sum	1,800 psi
N	1	$1\frac{1}{4}$	of cement	750 psi
O	1	$2\frac{1}{2}$	and lime	350 psi

Figure 6 *Laying a single-wythe block wall.*

Figure 7 *Tooling mortar joints.*

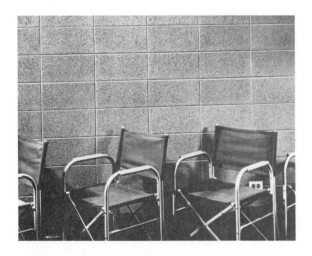

Figure 8 *Stretcher units stacked horizontally.*

Figure 9 *Stretcher units stacked vertically.*

Figure 10 *Square units stacked.*

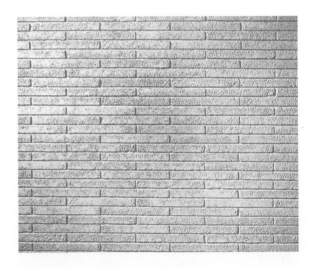

Figure 11 *Roman concrete brick.*

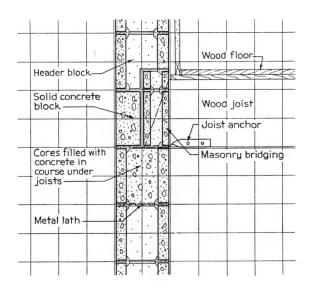

Figure 12 *Wood joist floor framing into a single-wythe wall.*

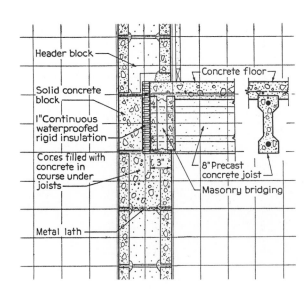

Figure 13 *Precast concrete joist floor framing into a single-wythe wall.*

chimneys or other construction where high temperatures or high humidity is present.

CONCRETE MASONRY CONSTRUCTION

Concrete block are used for bearing and curtin (non-load-bearing) walls and partitions. A stacked bond such as shown in Figures 8–10 is often used for best appearance. Concrete block can also serve as a backing for brick, stone, and other facings, and as fireproofing for steel structural members. Properly reinforced, they are used as columns and lintels. Concrete *brick* units are also available. A Roman concrete brick wall laid in a stretcher bond is shown in Figure 11.

Single-wythe walls. The starting course of block is laid to a chalk line snapped on the footing. A full bed of mortar is spread on the footing, and a corner block is laid to the line, level and plumb. Adjacent block are laid and constantly checked for accurate positioning. When the starting course has been completed, the usual practice is to lay the corner block first, and then stretch lines between them to serve as guides in laying the stretcher block (Figure 6). Concrete block should not be wetted before laying, since this will cause shrinkage and cracks in the finished walls.

When beams or floor slabs frame into a block wall, the supporting course should be of solid masonry. This serves to distribute the load on the

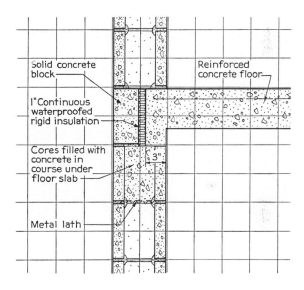

Figure 14 *Concrete slab floor framing into a single-wythe wall.*

wall and also provides a termite deterrent. Either a course of solid block can be used, or the cores of hollow block can be filled with mortar as shown in Figures 12–14. The mason places strips of metal lath in the joint below to support the mortar filling the cores.

It is common practice to strengthen concrete block walls by the use of a *bond beam* at each story height. Bond beams are constructed by placing two reinforcing bars in a continuous course of lintel block and filling the trough with concrete. Vertical reinforcing is also possible by pouring concrete around reinforcing rods set in the cores of

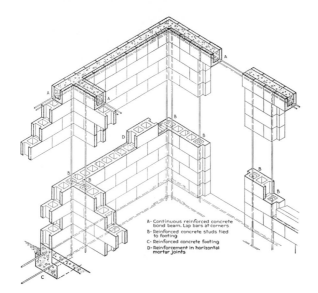

Figure 15   *Reinforcing block walls.*

Figure 17   *Joining nonbearing walls with hardware cloth.*

Figure 16   *Joining bearing walls with tie bar.*

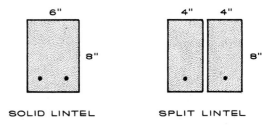

Figure 18   *Reinforced concrete lintels.*

block at corners, wall openings, and regular intervals between wall openings. The vertical reinforcing should be tied in with the horizontal bond beams as shown in Figure 15.

Intersecting concrete block walls are not tied together by a masonry bond (except at corners). Rather, metal tie bars are used to tie bearing walls together (Figure 16), and metal lath to tie nonbearing walls to bearing walls (Figure 17). The metal tie bars are spaced 4′ oc vertically, the lath 16″ oc vertically.

Jamb block are used to form the sides of window and door openings. Precast concrete sills are available for use with both metal and wood sash. Reinforced concrete beams, used as window and

door lintels, are commonly available in 4″ and 6″ nominal widths and an 8″ nominal height (Figure 18). Lengths vary from 40″ to 144″ in 8″ increments. The minimum bearing permitted at each end is 8″. Therefore a 40″ lintel would be used to span a 24″ opening. Two lintels placed side by side (called *split lintels*) are used in walls thicker than 6″. Thus two 4″ lintels are placed in an 8″ wall, two 6″ lintels in a 12″ wall, and one 4″ with one 6″ lintel in a 10″ wall. Split lintels are easier to handle than one heavy, solid lintel, but care must be taken to assure that superimposed loads are proportionately supported by both split lintel blocks. If a floor load has to be supported by the lintel in addition to the normal wall load, a special beam designed by an architectural engineer is required.

When a block wall is to be covered by a wood-framed roof, wood top plates are fastened to the top of the wall by $\frac{1}{2}$″, $\frac{5}{8}$″, or $\frac{3}{4}$″ anchor bolts spaced 4′ apart as shown in Figure 19. The bolts are set 15″ deep in mortar poured in the cores of the top two courses of block.

Masonry walls may also be finished by *parapets*. A parapet acts as a safety wall for anyone

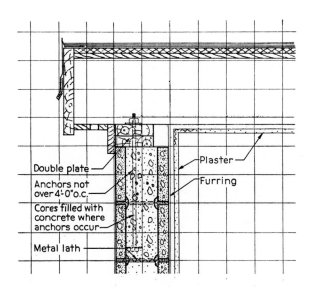

Figure 19 *Roof construction on a single-wythe wall.*

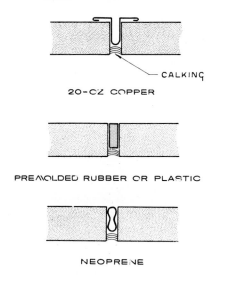

20-OZ COPPER

PREMOLDED RUBBER OR PLASTIC

NEOPRENE

Figure 21 *Expansion joints.*

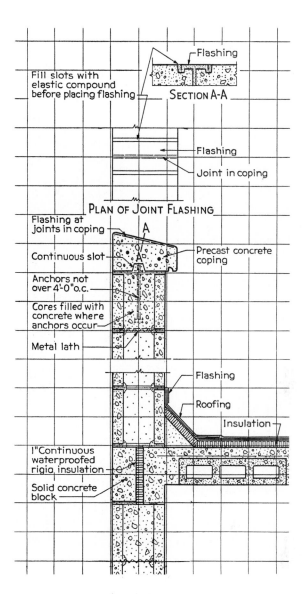

SECTION A-A

PLAN OF JOINT FLASHING

Figure 20 *Coping and parapet construction on a single-wythe wall.*

walking on the roof. It also screens unsightly roof projections such as ventilators and stacks. Parapets are completely exposed to the weather, so special care in weatherproofing is necessary to prevent cracking at the junction of the parapet and roof. To prevent moisture from entering the cores of the block, the parapet is topped with a *coping* as shown in Figure 20. To reduce cracking from expansion and contraction, a parapet can be reinforced by two #2 bars 16″ oc horizontally and #3 bars 24″ oc vertically. The height of a parapet wall should not exceed three times the thickness.

Expansion joints. Building materials are in a state of relative motion at many times. This mo-

tion is quite small, but sufficient enough to seriously damage a building not designed for this factor. There are three major causes for movement: temperature changes, moisture changes, and settlement. A 100′-long masonry wall, for example, expands nearly ½″ due to a 100°F temperature increase from winter to summer. Unless *expansion joints* (separations filled with a flexible material) were provided in such a wall, cracks would appear. Vertical expansion joints are specified at about 20′ intervals in exterior walls, at offsets, pilasters, and at the intersections of bearing walls and nonbearing partitions. Figure 21 illustrates some forms of expansion joints. The 20-oz. copper water stop is constructed of short lengths of

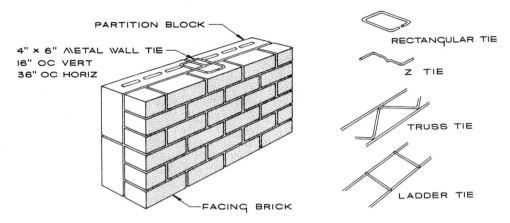

Figure 22 *Eight-inch composite wall—wall tie bonded.*

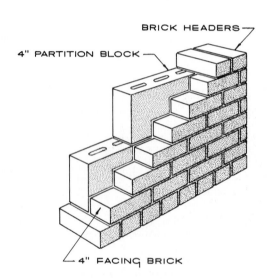

Figure 23 *Eight-inch composite wall—masonry bonded.*

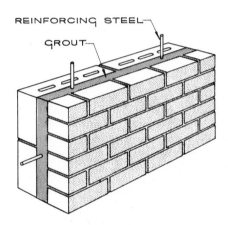

Figure 24 *Reinforced masonry.*

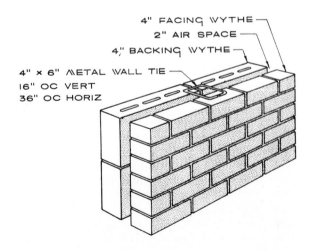

Figure 25 *Ten-inch cavity wall.*

sheet metal overlapped at their joints. Premolded rubber and plastic fillers are popular because they are compressible and will return to the original shape after compression. The weather side of the joint is sealed with calking compound or the newer polymer sealing compound. A form of expansion joint called a *control joint* may be provided by raking the mortar from a continuous vertical joint to a depth of $\frac{3}{4}''$. The recess is then filled with calking compound. Obviously a control joint is not compressible, but it does reduce unsightly random cracks. Expansion joints are costly to install and maintain, so overdesign should be avoided.

Composite walls. Concrete block can be used as a backing for a more costly facing such as brick (Figure 22). In this manner, the required wall thickness is efficiently obtained, as well as the desired architectural effect. Commonly used are 8″ and 12″ composite walls (also called *faced* walls). Bonding between the wythes of facing and backing may be accomplished in several ways.

1. The wythes may be bonded using brick headers every seventh course as shown in Figure 23. An

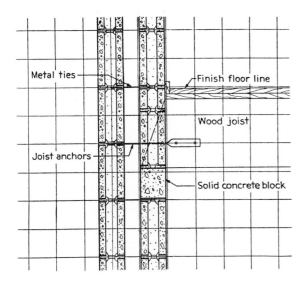

Figure 26 *Wood joist floor framing into a cavity wall.*

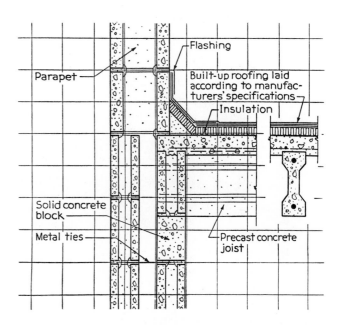

Figure 27 *Parapet construction on a cavity wall.*

Figure 28 *Installation of plumbing and electrical conduits in block wall.*

8″ composite wall is comprised of 4″ partition block faced by 4″ of brick or other material. A 12″ wall is composed of 8″ stretcher block with the 4″ facing. When joists frame into such walls, the block immediately under the joists should be either solid block or hollow block with the cores filled with concrete.

2. A more popular method of bonding is through the use of $\frac{3}{16}$″-diameter steel wall ties (Figure 22) having a maximum vertical spacing of 16″ and horizontal spacing of 36″. The ties are staggered in alternate courses. Additional ties 36″ apart are set around the perimeter of all wall openings. This method has the advantage of reducing moisture penetration paths as offered by the header brick. Construction is somewhat easier. Also, a slight movement between the wythes is possible which reduces stresses and cracking.

3. Bonding may also be achieved by pouring grout* into the cavity between wythes. A $2\frac{1}{2}$″-minimum cavity is required, and the masonry must cure three days to gain strength before grout is poured in 4′ lifts. When reinforcing rods have been placed between the wythes as shown in Figure 24, they are surrounded and also bonded by the grout. This produces a reinforced masonry wall and is often specified in areas subject to earthquakes. The design of reinforced masonry walls is similar to the design of reinforced concrete walls.

A composite wall is shown in Figure 28. Notice that the cores of the hollow block wythe provide a passage for the installation of plumbing and electrical conduits.

* *Grout* is mortar thinned to a pouring consistency.

Cavity walls. A cavity wall consists of two wythes of masonry separated by a 2″ air space (Figure 25). Often the 4″ exterior wythe is built of brick, and the interior wythe of 4″ or 6″ concrete block. The air space provides greater protection against rain penetration than does a composite wall. The air space also provides insulation. The two wythes are tied together with #6-gauge metal ties embedded in alternate courses and 32″ oc horizontally. Some cavity wall details are shown in Figures 26 and 27.

Every design and construction precaution should be taken to ensure weathertight masonry walls. Many designers assume that the outside barrier to water will leak, and they provide a second line of defense. This is done by cavity wall construction, staggered joints in a composite wall, parging, stucco, portland cement base paint, flash-

Figure 29 *Nailing wood furring to masonry using hardened nails.*

ing, calking, and furring. The weakest spots are usually at joints and intersections of different materials.

Flashing is important in cavity wall construction to prevent moisture from entering the cavity. Flashing is also installed at the bottom of the cavity to direct any moisture in the cavity outside through weep holes. Weep holes are located just over the base flashing and 2′ apart. They may be formed by omitting mortar from the vertical joints or by placing wicks such as sash cord in the joints to draw moisture out of the cavity.

Concrete masonry walls may be finished by nailing wood strips called *furring* to the masonry using hardened nails as shown in Figure 29. The interior or exterior finish material is then nailed to the furring. In Figure 30 the concrete masonry wall was left exposed as the finished surface.

Figure 30 *The Playhouse in the Park, Cincinnati, Ohio.*

STUDY QUESTIONS

1. Describe briefly the manufacture of concrete masonry units.
2. Distinguish between:
   a. Composite wall and cavity wall
   b. Expansion joint and control joint
   c. Slump block and split block
   d. Full mortar bedding and face-shell bedding
3. Describe briefly each term:
   a. Jamb block
   b. Bond beam
   c. Split lintel
   d. Parapet
   e. Wall tie
4. Sketch the following masonry joints:
   a. Flush
   b. Concave
   c. Vee
   d. Weathered
   e. Raked
5. Give the principal advantage of each mortar:
   a. Type M
   b. Type S
   c. Type N
   d. Type O
6. List some methods of obtaining weathertight masonry walls.
7. Why is it important to provide vertical expansion joints?
8. Why is it unnecessary to provide horizontal expansion joints?

LABORATORY PROBLEMS

1. Draw a detail plan section for the following:
   a. 10″, single-wythe CMU wall at an exterior corner
   b. 10″ composite wall at an exterior corner (4″ brick and 6″ CMU)
   c. 12″ cavity wall at an exterior corner (4″ brick, 2″ air space, 6″ CMU)
   d. Intersection of two 8″, single-wythe CMU interior partitions
2. Draw a vertical section for the following:
   a. 8″, single-wythe CMU wall from 8″ × 16″ concrete footing, to 2″ × 10″ horizontal roof joists.
   b. 10″ composite wall from 10″, single-wythe CMU foundation to 2″ × 10″ rafter (sloping 3 in 12)
   c. 12″ cavity wall from 12″, single-wythe CMU foundation to 2″ × 12″ horizontal roof joists. Include an 8″ × 12″ bond beam.
   d. 12″ reinforced masonry wall
3. Draw the sections showing window jamb, sill, and head details for the following:
   a. 8″, single-wythe CMU wall
   b. 10″ composite wall
   c. 12″ cavity wall
4. For the building assigned by your instructor, complete:
   a. CMU detail plan sections
   b. CMU vertical sections
5. For your original building design, complete:
   a. CMU detail plan sections
   b. CMU vertical sections
6. (For the advanced student) Design and detail an innovative pattern for an exterior CMU wall.

48 / Clay Masonry

Brick, structural clay tile, and architectural terra-cotta are all classified as *clay* masonry as distinguished from *concrete* masonry. Of the various forms of clay masonry, brick is the most popular by far.

BRICK MASONRY

Manufacture. Brick and tile are produced from clay, the most plentiful raw material used to manufacture any building product. Clay is obtained in three forms: *surface clays,* found near the surface of the earth; *shales,* also found near the surface but pressure-hardened almost to slate; and *fire clays,* found at greater depths. The surface clays and shales are mined in open pits by power equipment, but the fire clays must be removed from underground mines. These processes are called *winning* (which means "obtaining"). The clay is crushed, ground, screened, and mixed with water in a *pug mill* to a plastic consistency. See Figure 1. The clay can be molded by several different processes: stiff-mud, soft-mud, and dry-press.

Stiff-mud process. The plastic clay is extruded through a rectangular die like toothpaste squeezed from a tube, and sections are cut off by taut wires, each section forming a brick.

Soft-mud process. The plastic clay is mixed to a softer consistency and pressed into gang molds. To prevent sticking, the molds are lubricated with either sand (producing *sand-struck* brick) or water (producing *water-struck* brick).

Dry-press process. A very stiff mix of clay containing only the natural water content is pressed into gang molds by plungers exerting pressures as high as 1,500 psi.

After being molded into shape, the wet clay units are dried in ovens and then *burned* (fired) in kilns. If the brick is to be glazed, the glazes are sprayed on before burning. Face, common, glazed, and fire brick are all produced by these processes. *Face brick* is manufactured with special color and texture for exposed surfaces. Attachments are used to scratch, brush, or roughen the face as the clay leaves the die of the stiff-mud process. Face brick may be backed with *common brick* which is used for

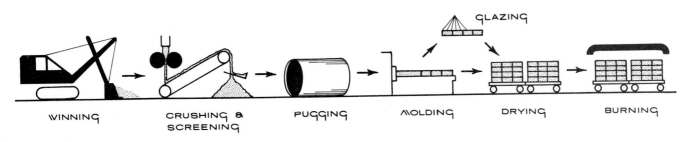

Figure 1 *Brick manufacture.*

479

Table I *Brick Sizes*

	Actual Dimensions			Modular Dimensions			
	Width	*Height*	*Length*	*Width*	*Height*	*Length*	*Coursing*
Standard	$3\frac{3}{4}''$	$2\frac{1}{4}''$	$8''$				
Modular	$3\frac{1}{2}''$	$2\frac{1}{6}''$	$7\frac{1}{2}''$	$4''$	$2\frac{2}{3}''$	$8''$	$3C = 8''$
Roman	$3\frac{1}{2}''$	$1\frac{1}{2}''$	$11\frac{1}{2}''$	$4''$	$2''$	$12''$	$2C = 4''$
Norman	$3\frac{1}{2}''$	$2\frac{1}{6}''$	$11\frac{1}{2}''$	$4''$	$2\frac{2}{3}''$	$12''$	$3C = 8''$
SCR	$5\frac{1}{2}''$	$2\frac{1}{6}''$	$11\frac{1}{2}''$	$6''$	$2\frac{2}{3}''$	$12''$	$3C = 8''$

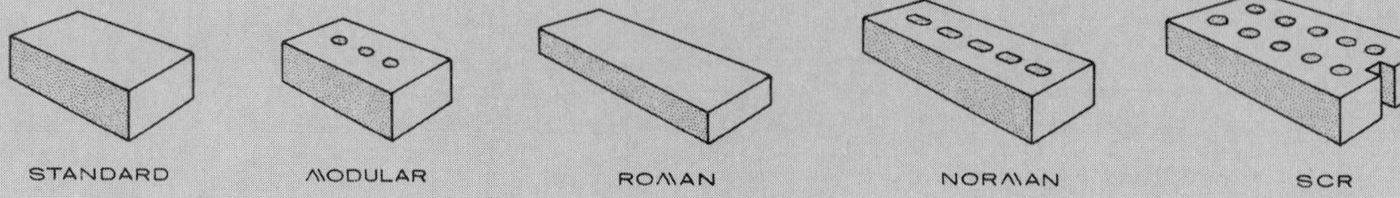

general construction. Common brick is graded SW (severe weather) for use in wet locations subject to freezing, MW (moderate weather) for use in dry locations subject to freezing, and NW (no weather) for use where no freezing occurs, such as interior partitions. *Fire brick* is made from deep-mined fire clays. Their resistance to heat permits them to be used in furnaces and chimneys. *Glazed brick* are also made from fire clay and are finished with ceramic, clay-coated, or salt glaze. The ceramic glaze produces a surface with a high-gloss or a matte finish in many colors. The clay-coated glaze produces a dull surface in softer tones. The salt glaze is transparent, allowing the brick color to show through the finish.

Sizes. The size of a standard brick is often $3\frac{3}{4}'' \times 2\frac{1}{4}'' \times 8''$, but brick sizes vary widely with the locality and manufacturer. Four common types of modular brick are listed in Table I. Their modular dimensions will not vary, but their actual dimensions will vary depending upon the intended thickness of the mortar joint. The actual dimensions shown in this table are based upon $\frac{1}{2}''$ mortar joints. Notice that the joint thickness can be added to the actual dimensions to obtain the modular dimensions. In general, $\frac{1}{2}''$ joints are used for general construction, $\frac{3}{8}''$ joints for facing brick, and $\frac{1}{4}''$ joints with glazed brick. Figure 2 shows how various brick types fit in a 4″ modular system. The Roman and Norman brick are shown in a one-third *bond*. This means that each brick is covered by one-third of a brick in the course above, thus reducing the amount of cutting.

Brick may be manufactured with cores to reduce their weight. As long as the cored area does not exceed 25 percent of the gross area, these masonry units would be considered to be *solid*. A *hol-*

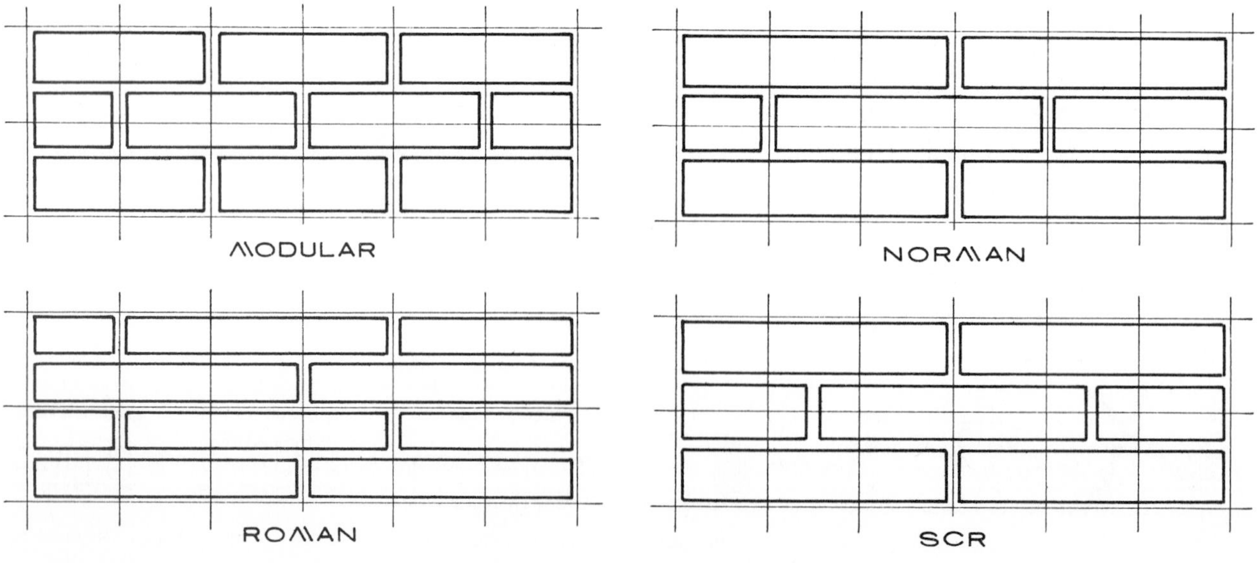

Figure 2 *Modular coordination of brick types.*

Smooth

Stippled

Rugs

Barks

Sand-struck

Water-struck

Salvaged

Figure 3   *Brick textures.*

low masonry unit (such as structural clay tile) is defined as a unit having cores that exceed 25 percent of the area.

The SCR* brick is formed with a $\frac{3}{4}'' \times \frac{3}{4}''$ jamb slot at one end. The SCR brick is intended for use in 6″ solid, load–bearing masonry walls for all types of single-story structures. The walls of these structures should not exceed 9′ to the eaves or 15′ to the gable peak. Ordinarily 2″ × 2″ furring is applied to the interior face to provide a moisture barrier and to permit installation of blanket insulation, electrical fixtures, pipe, and ducts. Building codes do not permit pipe or duct chases to be built into walls less than 8″ thick.

Brick is also available in a variety of special shapes for use as sills, caps, lintels, and corners.

* SCR brick was developed and named by the Structural Clay Products Research Foundation.

Occasionally, custom-designed brick will be ordered to meet unique needs. For example, one nationwide motel chain always uses a made-to-order brick in keeping with the company image. As another example, the decorative sculpture of molded brick shown in Figure 4 was designed for the University Baptist Student Union Center in Austin, Texas. The original design was modeled in clay. Then the sculptor made a four-piece plaster casting into which was pressed the same clay of which the other bricks were made. Wooden spacers were used to obtain the proper mortar joint widths. The molded pieces were then burned in a kiln, as with regular brick, and finally laid in the wall along with the other brick.

Color and texture. The colors of nearly all face brick could be classified as red, buff, or cream. The red colors range from pink through brick red to deep maroon. The buffs and creams range from dark brown to off-white. Glazed brick, however, are manufactured in all colors.

Figure 4 *A molded brick sculpture.*

Brick is specified for exterior finish due to its color and texture as well as its inherent durability, so there is little reason to paint it. Trim adjacent to masonry should be painted with nonchalking paints. Self-cleaning (chalking) paints work on the theory that rain will wash away chalked paint, exposing clean surfaces, but the chalky water may soak into a brick wall and stain it.

A few of the many brick textures are shown in Figure 3. Since there is such a wide variety of both colors and textures, it is normal practice to select from samples and then require that the shipment match the approved sample.

Walls of salvaged brick are often desired due to the interesting variation in color and texture. However, salvaged brick should not be permitted to be used in bearing walls because of the chance of rapid disintegration. Rather, blends of new brick are available which provide a similar appearance.

Brick wall patterns are most interesting when headers or bull headers (Figure 5) are used in structural bonding. Some of the more traditional bonds are shown on page 249, and some contemporary bonds formed by projected and recessed units are shown in Figure 6. Building codes require that headers make up at least 4 percent of the wall surface in structural bonding, with headers not more than 24″ apart vertically or horizontally. Of course all the pattern bonds shown can be formed using half-brick headers called *snap headers* in a veneer wall. In Figure 7 notice that brick can be used to form a screen wall.

The color and texture of the mortar joint can also be specified to contrast or blend with the brick. Colored mortars can be obtained by using colored aggregate or special pigments. Either the entire mix is colored or the uncolored mortar joint is raked out 1″ deep and tuck-pointed with colored mortar.

Efflorescence. Efflorescence is an undesirable white crystallization which may form on masonry walls. This is caused by water-soluble salts originally present in the brick and brought to the surface by moisture movement and evaporation. Efflorescence can be removed by scrubbing with water or with a solution of water and muriatic (hydrochloric) acid in 9 to 1 proportions.

A green stain resulting from water-soluble vanadium or molybdenum compounds in the clay is called *green efflorescence.* This is removed with a solution of water and caustic soda.

Water containing iron rust or dirt will also cause stains if it is constantly running over the brick. This can be prevented by proper design of flashing and downspouts. Any iron fastened to the wall should be separated from the brick with a noncorrosive gasket shaped to form a drip to di-

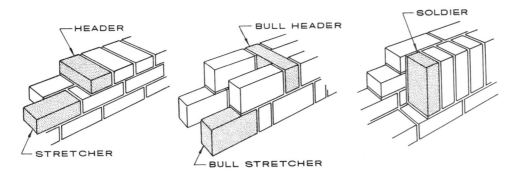

Figure 5 *Brick terminology.*

rect the water away from the fixture or the wall. Sills are shaped to direct water from the corners to the center of the sill and then away from the wall. A vee slot on the underside of the sill projection prevents water from running under the sill and down the wall.

Mortar and joints. Brick mortar joints should be completely filled to ensure a strong, watertight wall. The mason spreads a thick, uniform mortar bed over a few brick of the course previously completed. He also throws mortar on the end of each brick before it is laid. The brick is then shoved into place and tapped to its final position, squeezing out excess mortar, which is cut off. The same mortar joints are used for brick as are used for concrete block (Figure 5, Chapter 47).

Bond strength. The ability of mortar to adhere to the masonry unit is called *tensile bond strength* and is an important factor in a structurally sound wall. For best tensile bond strength:

1. Use type S mortar (Table I, Chapter 47).
2. Use maximum water consistent with good workmanship.
3. Use fresh mortar, or replace water that has evaporated (called *retempering*).
4. Use brick with rough rather than smooth surfaces, but:
5. When brick has very high suction, soak the brick and allow to surface-dry before laying. This is necessary to prevent such brick from sucking water from the mortar.
6. Do not use air-entrained cement. Air entraining agents do decrease mortar deterioration from frost action and salt applications (such as used on walks to melt snow), but tensile bond strength is also decreased.
7. Do not wet-cure mortar. Although wet curing strengthens concrete, it has the opposite effect upon mortar, and both the bond strength and the compressive strength are decreased.

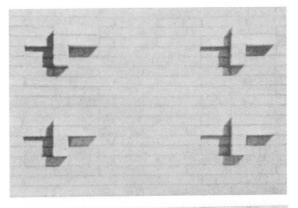

Figure 6 *Contemporary pattern bonds.*

Figure 7 *Brick screen wall.*

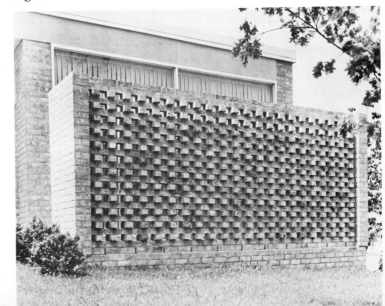

BRICK CONSTRUCTION

Although many brick walls look similar, there are a number of different ways in which brick can be used in those walls. The brick can be merely a facing—a 4″ non-load-bearing veneer covering a wood, steel, or concrete skeleton. Or the brick may be used to construct a load-bearing wall—a solid brick wall of 6″ single-wythe or 8″ (or more) multiple wythes, a reinforced brick masonry wall, or a cavity wall. Often the face brick you see is only on the outside of a building and is backed up by less costly units such as concrete block or structural clay tile.

The design of a masonry wall as well as the design of all structural elements of a building is the responsibility of registered architectural engineers specializing in structures. For tall buildings, they perform a structural analysis to achieve a reliable and economical solution. For small buildings, however, they may depend a good deal upon the local building codes in specifying wall thickness and height. Many building codes are modeled after the ANSI (American National Standards Institute) code for masonry. Some portions of this code have been included in the following discussion.

Solid brick walls. Solid brick load-bearing walls may be 6″ thick if not over 9′ high. The gable peak may not exceed 15′. Figure 8 shows these limitations. A single wythe of 6″ SCR brick is often used for this purpose.

In residence buildings not over three stories and 35′ high, an 8″, double-wythe solid wall may be used. For other kinds of buildings not over 35′ high, the top-story bearing wall may be 8″ for the upper 12′, but 12″ walls are required for the first two stories.

In taller buildings, 12″ walls are required for the upper 35′, and the wall must be increased 4″ for each 35′ or portion thereof. If the solid masonry bearing walls are stiffened every 12′ by masonry cross walls or reinforced concrete floors, the

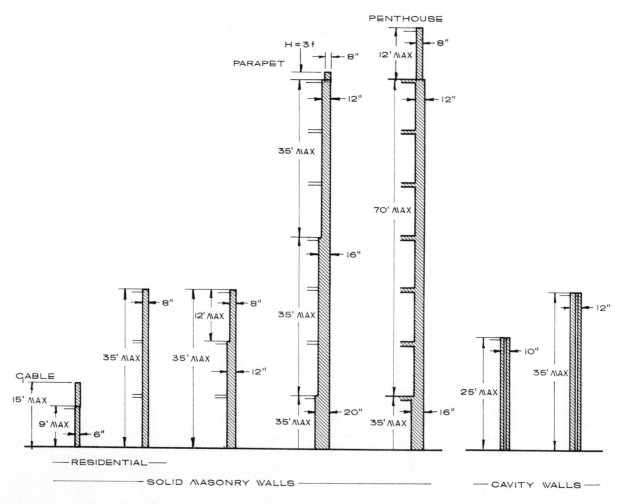

Figure 8   *Allowable wall heights. (Note: The horizontal scale is double the vertical scale.)*

12″ requirement may be applied to the upper 70′. In all these instances, the roof must be designed to give no horizontal thrust to the walls. Masonry *penthouses* (housings for elevator machinery) and stair enclosures no more than 12′ above the roof line may be 8″ thick. A parapet may be 8″ thick but no higher than three times its thickness.

Structural bonding. When a multiple-wythe wall is constructed, it is important to tie together each wythe so that the wall acts as a single structural unit. Structural bonding may be accomplished by:

1. The use of headers as shown in Figure 23, Chapter 47
2. The use of metal ties embedded in the mortar joints as shown in Figure 25, Chapter 47
3. Grout poured between wythes of masonry

Cavity walls. The American Standard Building Code permits 12″ cavity walls to be no higher than 35′, and 10″ cavity walls to be no higher than 25′. The facing and backing wythes must be at least 4″, and the cavity between 2″ minimum and 3″ maximum.

The insulation value of a cavity wall can be increased by pouring loose-fill (fibrous glass, vermiculite, or perlite) in the cavity. Rigid insulation (glass fiberboard, foamed glass, or foamed plastic) should be at least 1″ less in thickness than the cavity, and it should be placed against the interior wythe to allow moisture drainage in the cavity.

Lateral support. Both solid and cavity brick walls must also be supported laterally. Lateral support may be obtained by cross walls or piers (measured horizontally) or by floors or roofs (measured vertically). The ratio of the unsupported length or height of a solid bearing wall to its thickness cannot exceed 20. The ratio of a cavity bearing wall (or a solid wall of hollow masonry units) should not exceed 18. The sum of the thicknesses of both wythes is used in cavity wall calculations. In non-load-bearing partitions, the ratio should not exceed 36.

EXAMPLES

Although many brick bearing walls are designed using the wall thicknesses and heights permitted by building codes, a structural analysis is usually performed for buildings over several stories high to achieve the optimum design. Among such buildings built recently are the seventeen-story Park Mayfair East apartment building in Denver, Colorado (Figure 9), with 11″ reinforced brick bearing walls, and the ten-story Housing for the Elderly building in Rock Island, Illinois (Figure 10), with 8″ transverse brick bearing walls spaced 12′ apart.

Masonry arches. The arch shape appealed to many ancient civilizations and is still used in contemporary structures. One of the principal advan-

Figure 9   *Park Mayfair East, Denver, Colorado.*

Figure 10   *Housing for the Elderly, Rock Island, Illinois.*

Figure 11 *High school in Columbus, Indiana.*

Figure 12 *St. Anastasia Church, Waukegan, Illinois.*

Figure 13 *Bucks County Courthouse, Doylestown, Pennsylvania.*

tages of the arch is its ability to bridge a space using materials that have a greater resistance to compression than to tension, such as brick. Arches may be used as minor design elements such as window and door lintels as shown in Figure 11 or as major design elements as shown in Figure 12.

Arches are built over temporary forms which carry the dead load of the masonry until the mortar has hardened. These forms can be removed seven days after the masonry work is finished. Usually mortar joints are tapered to provide the required curvature of the arch, but specially tapered brick may also be obtained. As shown in Figure 14, both soldier and header bonds are commonly used in brick arch work. The *flat* arch is often supported by a steel lintel. When this occurs, it is not considered a true arch. A *segmental* arch is in the form of a circular arc but is less than a *semicircular* arch. *Multicentered* arches have several tangent circular arcs. A *three-centered* arch and the four-centered *Tudor* arch are illustrated. The *parabolic* arch is the most structurally efficient for uniformly distributed loads since each brick is in pure compression. Whenever designing an arch, remember that the outward thrust must be counteracted. Notice how this was done in Figure 13.

STRUCTURAL CLAY TILE

Structural clay tile is made from the same raw material and by the same process as brick, but the units are hollow and therefore are lighter and can be made larger. Consequently, tile walls can be erected more quickly than brick walls.

In contrast to the long history of the use of brick, structural clay tile was first manufactured about 1875 for fireproofing steel skeleton buildings. Solid brick was used for most masonry walls of that period, but eventually the structural clay tile was used as a backup material for an exterior wythe of brick to provide a wall of lighter weight. In addition to its fire resistance and light weight, structural clay tile offers good insulation from heat, sound, and moisture, together with excellent stability. In fact, it is probably the most dimensionally stable building material available. Recently, the construction grades of structural clay tile have been almost entirely replaced by concrete masonry units, but structural clay *facing* tile is still popular.

STRUCTURAL CLAY FACING TILE

Sizes. Facing tile is available in nominal thicknesses of 2″, 4″, 6″, and 8″, nominal face dimen-

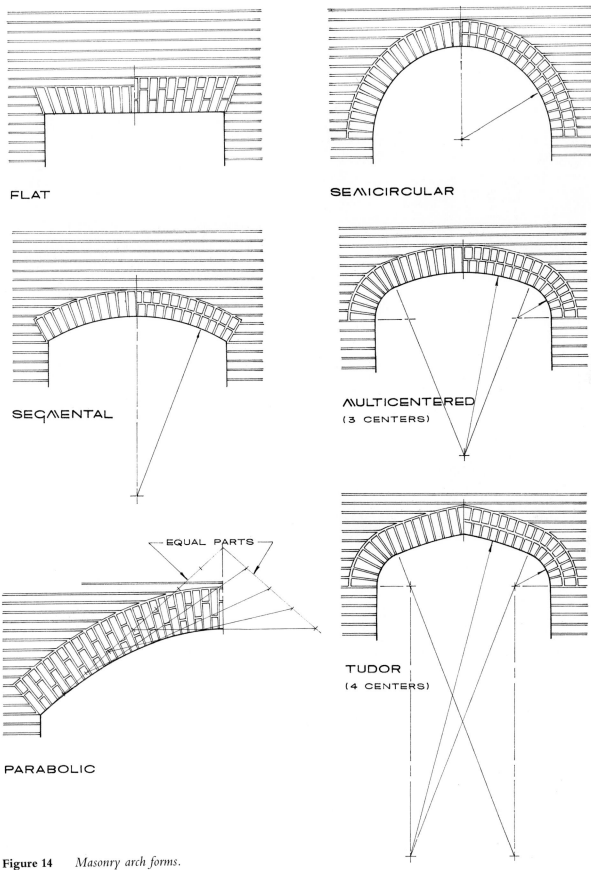

FLAT

SEMICIRCULAR

SEGMENTAL

MULTICENTERED
(3 CENTERS)

EQUAL PARTS

PARABOLIC

TUDOR
(4 CENTERS)

Figure 14 *Masonry arch forms.*

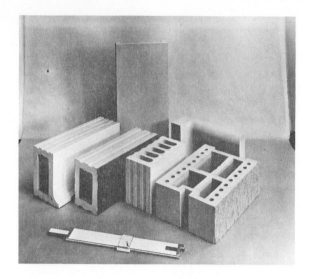

Figure 15   *Structural clay facing tile.*

Figure 16   *Structural clay facing tile laid in stack bond, YMCA Natatorium, Ontario, Canada.*

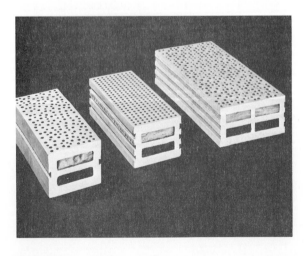

Figure 18   *SCR acoustile.*

sions of $2\frac{2}{3}''$, $4''$, $5\frac{1}{3}''$, $8''$, $12''$, and $16''$. Notice that all units are based upon a $4''$ module or a multiple of $4''$. Actual sizes are only $\frac{1}{4}''$ less than nominal to allow for $\frac{1}{4}''$ mortar joints. Some available shapes are shown in Figure 15.

Construction. Although most masonry walls are laid in a stretcher bond, facing tile is often laid in stack bond as shown in Figure 16. Since the stack bond does not have the interlocking quality of stretcher bond, it is good practice to specify one $\frac{3}{16}''$ steel reinforcing rod or its equivalent in horizontal joints $16''$ oc for each $6''$ or less of wall thickness.

Facing tile is made in a number of series based on the face dimensions of the stretcher unit. The standard depth of most series is a modular $4''$.

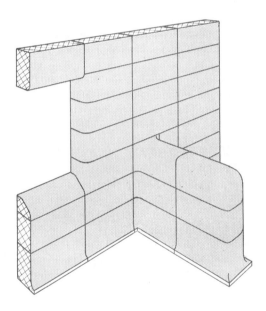

Figure 17   *Structural clay facing tile forms.*

Figure 19   *SCR acoustile installed in John J. Pershing Junior High School, Houston, Texas.*

Table II *Structural Clay Facing Tile Series*

Series	Modular Sizes
4D	4″ × 5⅓″ × 8″
6T	4″ × 5⅓″ × 12″
8W	4″ × 8″ × 16″

Many shapes used for stretcher and soldier stack bond are available in all series. Some are shown in Figure 17. The three most common series are shown in Table II.

Color and texture. Facing tile may be glazed or unglazed. The glazed tile is available in single shades or multicolor mottles of white, gray, cream, tan, light yellow, light green, and light blue. Accent colors include red, orange, yellow, green, blue, brown, and black. Unglazed tile is available in colors and textures similar to those of facing brick.

Although color affects different people in different ways, there are some rules of thumb that generally apply and help in selection of finish materials:

1. All areas should be kept uniform in brightness within a 10:1 ratio. For example, a white wall reflecting 80 percent light used with a black floor reflecting only 2 percent light would give an undesirable 40:1 ratio.
2. Ceilings should nearly always be white for best light distribution.
3. Light reflection from walls should range between 30 and 40 percent in areas where work will demand extreme concentration (such as an operating room) and 40 and 60 percent in ordinary working areas. In nonworking areas, over 60 percent reflection may be acceptable.

4. Warm tints (yellow, coral) may be preferred for cool, barren areas; cool tints (green, aquamarine) may be preferred for areas exposed to excess heat.
5. Warm, bright colors may be best for areas used for physical tasks; cool, subdued colors for areas used for visual tasks.

SCR acoustile. Load-bearing facing tile are also available with perforations through the face and fibrous glass pads behind the faces. See Figures 18 and 19. This produces a tile with high sound *absorption* and low sound *transmission,* which are both desirable acoustical properties—important to the room in which the sound originates and to adjacent rooms as well.

REINFORCED MASONRY LINTELS

Special tile shapes are produced to be used for reinforced lintels. Standard tile and brick units may also be adapted for the same purpose. Reinforced tile lintels have several advantages over structural steel lintels. Since the reinforcing steel is completely surrounded by concrete, it is more resistant to weathering and to fire. Reinforced brick lintels have the aesthetic advantage of using the same material for both the wall surface and the lintel surface.

Reinforced tile and brick lintels are usually built in place using temporary shoring. The lintel thickness is equal to the wall thickness. After the soffit tile or brick are laid, reinforcing steel is placed and surrounded by grout. Tile lintels can also be precast and installed as complete units.

Some examples of reinforced tile and brick lintels are shown in Figure 20.

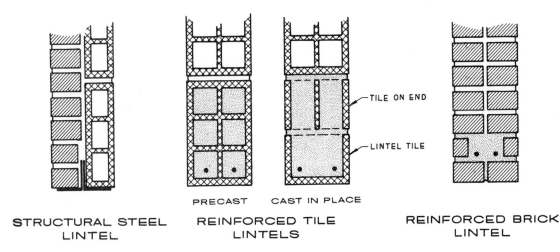

PRECAST   CAST IN PLACE

STRUCTURAL STEEL LINTEL   REINFORCED TILE LINTELS   REINFORCED BRICK LINTEL

TILE ON END

LINTEL TILE

Figure 20 *Tile and brick lintels.*

Figure 21 *Architectural terra-cotta, Memorial Evangelical United Brethern Church, Silver Spring, Maryland.*

Figure 22 *Ceramic veneer, Hebrew Educational Alliance, Denver, Colorado.*

ARCHITECTURAL TERRA-COTTA

Architectural terra-cotta* is a masonry veneer used on both interior and exterior walls. Terra-cotta is either molded by hand or extruded by machine. Both are custom products and are available in a wide range of glazes, colors, and sizes. The hand-molded terra-cotta can be shaped to any decorative form as shown in Figure 21. The machine-extruded units, often called *ceramic veneer,* are large slabs with face dimensions usually greater than brick or facing tile. See Figure 22. Ceramic veneer slabs are fastened to the backing units by either adhesion or anchoring.

Adhesion. The ceramic veneer slabs (usually $1\frac{1}{8}'' \times 18'' \times 30''$) are set in a $\frac{3}{4}''$ mortar bed with $\frac{1}{4}''$ joints as shown in Figure 23. The mortar bed can be applied directly to brick and concrete, or it can be applied to metal lath fastened on wood or metal studs.

Anchoring. Anchoring is used for larger slabs ranging from $2''$ to $2\frac{1}{2}''$ thick. Wire loops set in masonry or concrete backing are used to fasten $\frac{1}{2}''$-diameter *pencil rods* at least $1''$ out from the backing wall. Nonferrous wire anchors are hooked around the pencil rods and into holes in the edges of the veneer. The space between the veneer and backing wall is then filled with grout. Grooves on the veneer and concrete backing wall provide keys as shown in Figure 24.

STUDY QUESTIONS

1. Describe briefly the manufacture of brick.
2. What mortar joint thickness is usually specified for:
   a. General construction
   b. Facing brick
   c. Glazed brick

* *Terra-cotta* means literally "baked earth."

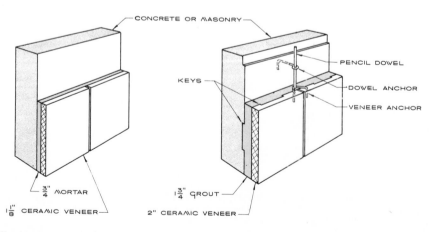

Figure 23 *Adhesion-type ceramic veneer.*

Figure 24 *Anchored-type ceramic veneer.*

3. Sketch:
   a. Roman brick laid in a ⅓ bond
   b. An 8″ × 12″ ventilator installed in an SCR brick wall
4. How does a cored brick differ from a structural clay tile?
5. What is the difference between:
   a. Stiff-mud process and soft-mud process
   b. Face brick and fire brick
   c. Efflorescence and green efflorescence
   d. Semicircular arch and multicentered arch
6. Briefly describe the following terms:
   a. Winning
   b. Glazed brick
   c. Retempering
   d. Penthouse
7. Is wet curing recommended for both mortar and concrete?
8. When SCR brick is laid in a stretcher bond wall, does it look like Roman brick?
9. Briefly describe the manufacture of structural clay facing tile.
10. Distinguish between:
    a. Clay masonry and concrete masonry
    b. Architectural terra-cotta and ceramic veneer
11. Describe the construction of a reinforced tile lintel built in place.
12. List several rules of thumb for the color selection of facing tile.
13. Briefly describe the installation of ceramic veneer by the method of:
    a. Adhesion
    b. Anchoring

LABORATORY PROBLEMS

1. Draw a detail plan section for the following:
   a. SCR brick wall at an exterior corner
   b. 8″ composite brick wall at an exterior corner
   c. 12″ composite brick wall at an exterior corner
   d. 10″ cavity brick wall at an exterior corner
   e. 12″ cavity brick wall at an exterior corner
   f. Intersection of two 8″ brick interior partitions
2. Draw a vertical section for the following:
   a. SCR brick wall from footing to 2″ × 8″ horizontal roof joists
   b. 8″ composite brick wall from footing to 2″ × 10″ horizontal roof joists
   c. 10″ cavity brick wall from 10″, single-wythe CMU foundation to 2″ × 10″ rafters (sloping 2 in 12)
3. For the building assigned by your instructor, complete:
   a. Brick detail plan sections
   b. Brick vertical sections
4. For your original building design, complete:
   a. Brick detail plan sections
   b. Brick vertical sections
5. Complete the clay masonry details for:
   a. The building assigned by your instructor
   b. Your original building design
6. (For the advanced student) Design and detail an original pattern for an interior partition of brick.
7. (For the advanced student) Design and detail a bas-relief sculpture of architectural terra-cotta.

49 / Stone Masonry

Stone has been the favorite building material for large structures for thousands of years. Although it is now seldom used for structural purposes, stone is still a popular finish material, as a result of a combination of desirable characteristics. Stone represents strength, permanence, and quality. It also looks more natural than the manufactured appearance of most other building materials.

Rocks are classified according to their method of formation as *igneous, sedimentary,* or *metamorphic.* Stones* from each classification have unique characteristics which determine their use as a building material. The major building stones— granite, sandstone, limestone, marble, and slate —are listed in Figure 1.

Igneous rocks are formed from molten material which erupted from the interior of the earth and

---

* Stone refers to quarried pieces of *rock,* but these terms are also used synonymously.

Figure 1   *Common building stone.*

solidified near the surface. In the United States igneous rocks are found in the older mountain ranges: Appalachians, Rocky Mountains, Sierra Nevada, Cascades, and Coast Ranges. Igneous rocks are usually formed without planes of stratification. Granite (Figure 2) is an important igneous rock because of its durability and hardness, which permit it to be exposed to weather. Granite is often used for steps and thresholds. The color is generally gray, although some quarries produce

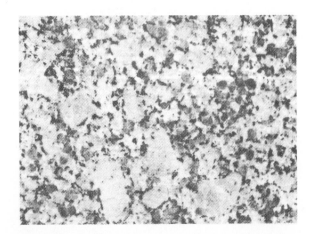

Figure 2   *Granite.*

Figure 3   *Sandstone.*

Figure 4 *Limestone.*

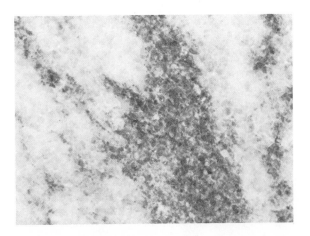

Figure 5 *Marble*

granite in various shades of brownish red when in combination with feldspar, hornblende, or mica.

Sedimentary rocks are formed from the sediment deposited by seas in beds, or strata. The sediment can be composed of igneous or other sedimentary rocks that have disintegrated into sand to form *sandstone* (Figure 3), or the sediment can be composed of disintegrated shells and coral which form into *limestone* (Figure 4). Sedimentary rocks are most abundant in the central part of the country, which was a sea bottom in past ages. Sedimentary rocks are usually stratified, and the cleavage faces aid in the quarrying and the final placing of the stone. Sandstones are easy to work, but some sandstones, such as *brownstone,* are not very resistant to weather. The lighter-colored gray *Ohio sandstone* is quite durable. The bluish-gray *bluestone* is a sandstone that is easily split into flagstones or building stones. *Indiana limestone* is the most popular limestone for building purposes. Although soft and workable when quarried, it hardens to a weather-resistant surface upon exposure to air. This phenomenon occurs with the evaporation of the *quarry sap,* or water, in the rock. Indiana limestone is gray or buff in color.

Metamorphic rocks are either igneous or sedimentary rocks that have been changed physically and chemically due to great heat and pressure. Like igneous rocks, metamorphic rocks are found in the older mountain regions. *Marble* (Figures 5 and 6) and *slate* (Figure 7) are the most popular building stones of metamorphic rock. Marble is derived from limestone, and the dividing line between marble and limestone is difficult to determine. In fact, some polished limestones are called marble. Pure marble is white, but it is streaked with color at some quarries depending upon the mineral composition. Some marbles cannot be safely exposed to weather and are satisfactory only for interior use. Marble presents the most dignified appearance of any building stone. Slate is eas-

Figure 6 *Wall and floor marble.*

Figure 7 *Slate wall panels in the Residence Hall at University of Chicago, Eero Saarinen & Associates, architects.*

Figure 8 *Cut stone used on the Manufacturers & Traders Trust Company Building, Buffalo, New York, Minoru Yamasaki & Associates, architects.*

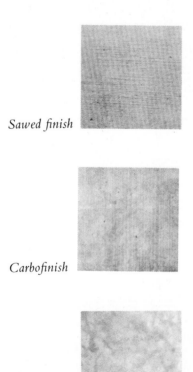

Sawed finish

Carbofinish

Honed finish

Figure 9 *Stone finishes.*

ily split along cleavage lines into thin roofing slate or thicker slabs for flagstone, shower partitions, countertops, and blackboards.

QUARRYING

Quarry rock is exposed by removing the overburden by machine. Explosives may also be used. The exposed rock may be stratified in horizontal *beds* such as sandstone, or have a massive structure such as granite. In both instances, the rock may be separated by *seams* which can run in any direction. When the rock is already broken up by beds and seams, it is removed by wedges and crowbars. But when it is unbroken, vertical cuts are made by channeling machines or by drilling a line of closely spaced holes. A channeling machine can make cuts 15' deep. The holes are used to receive steel wedges which are hammered in until the rock splits. Horizontal separations are made by wedges between the bedding planes or by an additional line of horizontal, drilled holes. Channeling is commonly used to quarry the softer stones such as sandstone, limestone, and marble. Drilled holes and wedges are used to quarry granite and the harder varieties of sandstone. Flame drills are used to cut hard rock by heating to a high temperature followed by water quenching to disintegrate the rock.

MILLING

Stone may be used as it comes from the quarry without additional dressing. The faces of such stone are called *seam-faced* when caused by a natural seam, *split-faced* when split along beds, and *quarry-faced* when caused by the quarrying operations. Additional forming and finishing may be done at a stone mill where power gang saws are used to cut stone into 4″ building stone for facing, 2″ flagstones, or 1″ veneers. When cut to specification for a particular project, each stone is numbered in accordance with the shop drawings to facilitate identification and installation. Such stone is called *cut stone* (Figure 8).

Various sawed stone finishes are possible and are specified as *shot-sawed finish, chat-sawed finish,* or *sand-sawed finish* depending upon the abrasive used under the saw blade. A *planer finish* refers to a smooth finish produced by a planer, and a *carbofinish* is a very smooth finish produced by a carborundum machine instead of a planer (Figure 9). Additional grinding machine processes will produce a *honed finish,* which is almost free from scratches, or a *polished finish,* which is completely

Random rubble

Coursed rubble

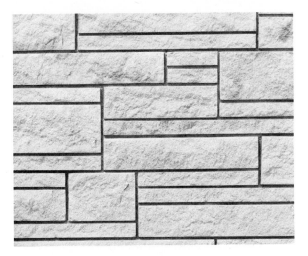

Random ashlar

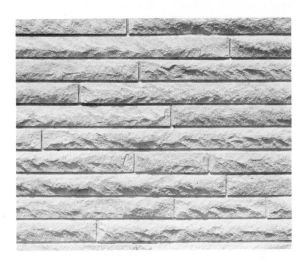

Coursed ashlar

Figure 10 *Types of stone masonry.*

free from scratches. Only granite and marble will hold a polished finish. Limestone and sandstone are usually finished only by sawing. Stone columns are turned on lathes.

Lettering (such as on a granite cornerstone) is cut by *sandblasting*. This is accomplished by painting the stone with a material called *dope* which hardens to a tough surface. The lettering or design is cut into this covering and peeled away. Compressed air is then used to blow sand against the stone for cuts to the desired depth.

STONE CONSTRUCTION

Three general classifications of stone masonry are *rubble, ashlar,* and *cut stone.* Rubble masonry con-

sists of stones that have not been cut to any special shape. When the stones are stratified, the bed faces are laid horizontally, resulting in *coursed rubble.* Uncoursed rubble is called *random rubble.* Ashlar consists of stones whose edge surfaces have been cut into plane surfaces. The stones are laid with horizontal bed joints and either vertical or inclined head joints. When the bed joints are continuous, the masonry is termed *coursed ashlar;* when not continuous, it is called *random ashlar.* Figure 10 shows these classifications. The term *cut stone* designates stone that has been individually cut to the architect's specifications—usually in an ashlar pattern.

Stone work is set in full mortar joints $\frac{1}{4}''$–$\frac{1}{2}''$ thick. Ashlar stone facing can be backed with rubble stone, concrete, concrete block, brick, or structural clay tile. The facing and backing wythes are bonded together by metal anchors, bond stones, or bond courses. When both wythes act as a single structural unit, the wall is called a *faced* wall. When the facing wythe is merely attached to its backing which carries the load, the wall is called a *veneered* wall. The veneer can also be hung from a steel-frame backing using noncorrosive metal anchors.

Openings in a stone wall may be spanned by stone arches or lintels. Stone lintels no longer than 6′ are usually supported by a steel angle. An I beam or channel section is used for longer lintels.

Stone window- and doorsills are called *slip sills* when they are the same length as the opening and *lug sills* when they are longer to enable them to be built into the wall on either side. Slip sills are less likely to crack upon settlement of the wall, but the mortar may wash out of their end joints.

Stone-faced precast concrete. Stone can be used as a facing for precast concrete spandrel panel and window units. Figure 11 illustrates the steps in casting the marble-faced window units for the Life of Georgia Tower in Atlanta. Step 1 shows the cut marble needed for one complete unit. The marble is placed in the form (step 2) and stainless steel anchors are set in holes predrilled in the marble (step 3). After reinforcing steel is positioned in the form (step 4), concrete is placed and vibrated (step 5). The completed window unit is shown in step 6.

Cast stone. Cast stone is an imitation stone of cast concrete. Most stone shapes and textures can be obtained, in addition to original finishes which do not imitate any natural stone. Installation is similar to the laying of stone or brick facing.

STUDY QUESTIONS

1. Briefly describe the production of building stone.
2. Briefly describe how lettering is cut into building stone.
3. Distinguish between:
   a. Stone and rock
   b. Igneous, sedimentary, and metamorphic
   c. Sandstone and limestone
   d. Marble and limestone
4. Describe briefly each term:
   a. Quarry sap
   b. Shot-sawed
   c. Carbo finish
   d. Ashlar
   e. Slip sill
5. Distinguish between:
   a. Seam facing, split facing, and quarry facing
   b. Rubble and ashlar
   c. Coarsed ashlar and random ashlar
   d. Faced wall and veneer wall
   e. Stone-faced precast concrete and cast stone

Figure 11

LABORATORY PROBLEMS

1. Prepare a display chart showing:
   a. Classifications of rocks
   b. Classifications of stone masonry
2. Draw sectional details for:
   a. 12″ faced wall of 4″ stone facing and 8″ concrete block backing
   b. 12″ veneered wall of 4″ stone facing and 8″ concrete block backing
3. Complete the stone masonry details for:
   a. The building assigned by your instructor
   b. Your original building design

Step 1: Cut marble for one unit.

Step 2: Marble placed in form.

Step 3: Setting anchors.

Step 4: Placing reinforcing steel.

Step 5: Placing concrete.

Step 6: Completed window unit.

Figure 12 *Precasting window units for Life of Georgia Tower, Atlanta, Georgia.*

50 / Glass Masonry

Building units of glass, commonly called *glass block*, are often specified for their decorative effect, but in addition they provide controlled light transmission, insulation, condensation protection, and sound reduction. Glass block are available in transparent, translucent,* and opaque units.

MANUFACTURE

Glass block are formed of two cast glass shells that are hermetically fused together to form a hollow unit containing a partial vacuum (Figure 1). This

* Translucent means that light will be transmitted, without a clear image.

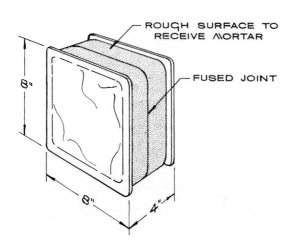

ROUGH SURFACE TO RECEIVE MORTAR

FUSED JOINT

8"

8"

4"

Figure 1 *Glass block.*

partial vacuum decreases heat transmission and surface condensation. Some units also have fibrous glass inserted in the interior which further reduces heat transmission and glare. The faces of the block can be smooth to provide vision through the block, textured to provide only light transmission, or fired with a ceramic finish to provide an opaque surface. The textured patterns are often cast on the interior surfaces, allowing the exposed surfaces to be smooth. This aids in cleaning. Some of these units are shown in Figure 2. Light-directing units are also illustrated in Figure 2. These units direct light up to the ceiling, from which it reflects down on work surfaces some distance from the wall. Such units should not be placed lower than 6' to prevent light being directed up into the eyes.

Some units have deep sculptured patterns on the exposed surfaces. Figure 3 shows how these can be combined to form various decorative patterns. Units are available which are formed of translucent glass framed by an opaque ceramic finish. Such a unit, having small openings which create gemlike effects, is shown in Figure 4. Framed units can be combined with completely opaque ceramic units of matching color and texture to form varied patterns as shown in Figure 5.

SIZES

The common modular size of glass block is 8" square by 4" thick. Also available are 6" square, 12" square, and 4" × 8" and 4" × 12" rectangular units —all 4" thick. Actual sizes are $\frac{1}{4}$" smaller to allow for $\frac{1}{4}$" mortar joints.

Transparent

Translucent ‖ flutes

Translucent ⊥ flutes

Sculptured interior

Sculptured exterior

Light-directing

Figure 2   *Forms of glass block.*

A BASIC UNIT   PATTERNS FORMED BY VARYING BASIC UNITS

Figure 3   *Combining sculptured block.*

CONSTRUCTION

Glass block are used to construct both interior and exterior panels, but they are not structural building units and can support only their own weight. Each panel is limited to a maximum area of 144 sq. ft. with a maximum height of 20′ and width of 25′. When larger areas are desired, vertical mullions or horizontal shelf angles are introduced to support smaller areas.

Glass block are laid using a stack bond. A glass block panel is illustrated in Figure 6. Notice that chases were provided in the masonry jamb and head to hold expansion strips. These strips are $\frac{3}{8}''$ thick and allow the glass block panel to expand

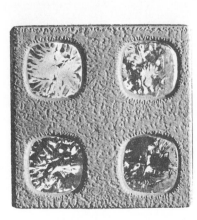

A BASIC UNIT

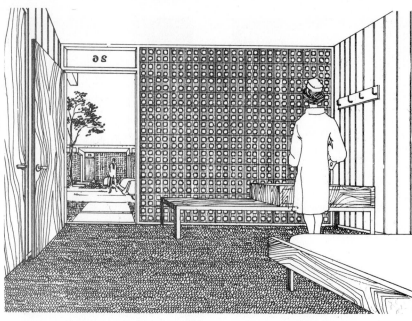

SCREEN WALL FORMED BY MULTIPLE USE OF BASIC UNIT

Figure 4   *Screen wall formed of framed block.*

FRAMED UNIT   OPAQUE UNIT   PATTERN FORMED BY COMBINING
                                          FRAMED AND OPAQUE UNITS

Figure 5   *Combining framed and opaque block.*

without cracking. Mortar is applied only at the sill and between units. Glass block are manufactured with coarse edges to aid in bonding with the mortar. Oakum is tightly packed at the jamb and head. Sill, jamb, and head are then all caulked.

GLASS BRICK

A solid glass brick is shown in Figure 7. Available in two sizes (8″ square × 3″ thick and 5″ square × $2\frac{5}{8}$″ thick), these units are recommended for fallout shelters to provide light during daylight hours and some limited vision, thus eliminating the "closed-in" feeling inherent in shelters. When installed back to back in the same thickness as the shelter wall, these units provide radiation protection equivalent to concrete.

STUDY QUESTIONS

1. List the advantages of glass masonry.
2. Distinguish between:
   a. Glass block and glass brick
   b. Transparent and translucent
3. Are textured patterns cast on the interior or exterior surfaces of glass block? Why?
4. Why is fibrous glass cast inside some glass block?
5. Give the height and width limits for a single glass masonry panel.

LABORATORY PROBLEMS

1. Complete the sectional details for an 8′-high × 3′-wide × 4″-thick glass masonry panel.
2. Complete the glass masonry details for:
   a. The building assigned by your instructor
   b. Your original building design
3. (For the advanced student) Design and detail an innovative architectural use for a commercially available glass block.

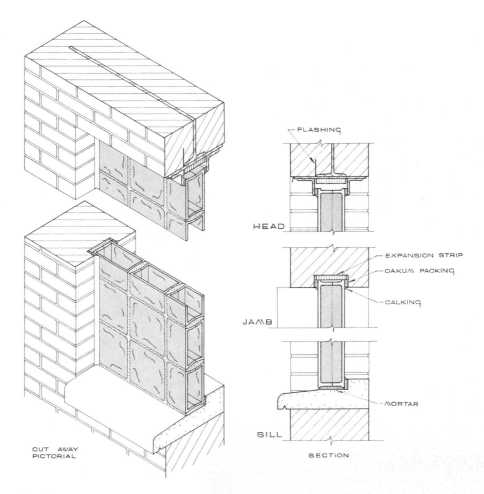

Figure labels: FLASHING, HEAD, EXPANSION STRIP, OAKUM PACKING, CALKING, JAMB, MORTAR, SILL, SECTION, CUT AWAY PICTORIAL

Figure 6 *A glass block panel in a masonry wall.*

Figure 7 *Eight-inch solid glass brick.*

HAIR STYLISTS

Figure 8 *A glass masonry wall.*

51 / Reinforced Concrete

Concrete is one of the most widely used and important building materials today. Concrete made of natural cement was initially developed by the ancient Romans and, to their credit, some of their concrete structures still exist—two thousand years later. Amazingly, the art of making concrete was nearly lost after the decline of the Roman empire until the invention of *portland cement* by Joseph Aspdin, a British bricklayer, in 1824. He named it *portland cement* because its gray color resembled the gray limestone mined in Portland, England. Rather than a mix of volcanic ash and slaked lime* as used by the Romans, portland cement is a mix of finely crushed burned limestone and clay. Jack Monier, a French gardener, is credited with inventing *reinforced concrete* as early as 1850 by reinforcing garden pots with embedded wire. The first plant to produce portland cement in quantity was built near Allentown, Pennsylvania, in 1871. Each successive manufacturer used a different formula until 1917, when the U.S. Bureau of Standards and the American Society for Testing Materials (ASTM) approved standards for portland cement. The United States now manufactures and uses more than twice as much portland cement as any other country. *Prestressed concrete* was developed in 1927 by Eugene Freyssinet, a French engineer.

* *Slaked lime* is lime with water added.

PORTLAND CEMENT MANUFACTURE

Cement manufacturing plants are located near limestone quarries and clay deposits. These raw materials, together with iron ore, are hauled to the plants by conveyor belts or trucks to be processed by crushing, burning, and fine grinding.

Portland cement requires about 60 percent lime and 25 percent silica together with smaller proportions of alumina, iron oxide, and gypsum. The lime is obtained from limestone, silica and alumina from clay, and iron oxide from iron ore. The gypsum is added after burning to regulate the *set*, or hardening time of the cement.

Cement manufacture begins by crushing man-sized pieces of quarried limestone into smaller fist-sized pieces using *hammer mills* (Figure 1). After other raw materials are added, further grinding is accomplished in rotating *ball mills*, which contain steel balls. Two types of grinding are possible: *wet-process* and *dry-process*. In the wet process, water is added to produce a *slurry*. No water is added in the dry process.

The finely ground mixture is fed into the higher end of a huge, 15° sloping, rotating kiln. These kilns are among the largest moving machinery used in any industry. They may be 15' in

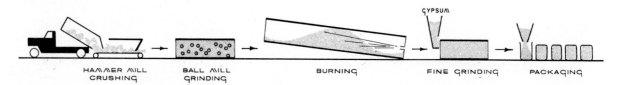

Figure 1   *Cement manufacture.*

502

diameter and over 500' long. The kiln rotates once a minute and is heated to 2,700°F. The raw materials emerge from the lower end four hours later as a new, marble-sized substance called *clinker*. After this substance has been cooled, gypsum is added and the mixture is again ground into cement powder, and then packaged in sacks of 1 cu. ft. (weighing 94 lb. each) or shipped in bulk by rail, truck, or barge.

CEMENT

The standards of ASTM include eight types of portland cement.

Type I: General-purpose-use. Type I is the cement stocked by all suppliers and will be delivered unless another type of cement is specified.

Type II: Moderate-heat. All concrete gives off considerable heat during the curing process. Type II is used where less heat is desired, such as in large abutments, since too much heat speeds the curing and weakens the concrete. Type II is also moderately sulfate-resistant.

Type III: High-early-strength. Freezing temperatures also weaken the concrete. Type III cures rapidly and is used in cold weather or when freezing weather is expected.

Type IV: Low-heat. Type IV is used in very large masses, such as dams, to reduce the amount of heat generated.

Type V: Sulfate-resistant. Type V is used where exposure to sulfate action is expected, such as in western states having water and soil of high alkali content.

Types IA, IIA, IIIA: Air-entrained. These types are similar to types I, II, and III, but include air entrainment (minute air bubbles) to reduce damage from salt and frost. Air-entrained concrete is often used for highway pavements.

CONCRETE

Concrete is produced by mixing a batter of cement and water with a *fine aggregate* such as sand. Usually a *coarse aggregate* such as crushed stone or gravel is also included. When mixed in proper

Figure 2 *Mixing trucks deliver concrete to the footing forms for the U.S. Steel Building, Pittsburgh.*

Figure 3 *Conveyor belt used for concrete placement on the U.S. Steel Building.*

proportions, the cement unites chemically with the water and can be poured into *forms*. After several hours, the concrete *sets* and binds the aggregates into a dense mass similar to stone. Freshly placed concrete is protected from rapid evaporation of water for seven days. During this *curing* period, the concrete continues to gain strength. The ultimate strength is reached after twenty-eight days.

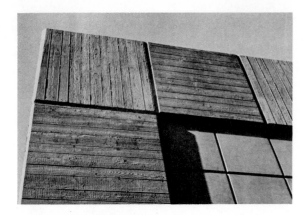

Figure 4   *Textured concrete created by forms of wood planks.*

Proportioning. The proportioning of the ingredients in concrete greatly affects the strength and durability. For ordinary work, concrete is specified by its dry proportions of cement, fine aggregate, and coarse aggregate, all by volume. For example, a *1 : 2 : 4 mix* consists of 1 part by volume of cement, 2 parts sand, and 4 parts crushed stone. This will produce concrete with a compressive strength of at least 2,000 psi. For more critical work, the *water-cement* ratio is used, because the proportion of water to cement is the most important ratio in controlling the strength of concrete. This ratio is expressed in terms of gallons of water per sack (1 cu. ft.) of cement. For example, a water-cement ratio of 6 indicates 6 gal. of water per cubic foot of cement. With a 1 : 2 : 3 dry mix, this would produce a compressive strength of 3,000 psi. In general, concrete is weakened by adding more water than is necessary for workability. Another adverse effect of excess water is that a watery layer forms puddles on the upper surface of the curing concrete. This is called *laitance** and is very weak and undesirable.

Mixing. Concrete is mixed by machine either on the site or at a central plant. After water is added, an *agitator* can keep the concrete in a workable condition for about an hour before placing. Often the concrete is dry-mixed centrally, and then water is added automatically by *transit mixers* on the way to the job site (Figure 2).

Placing. If connected chutes from the truck cannot reach the form, wheelbarrows, powered buggies, or conveyor belts are used (Figure 3). Also, it is possible to pump concrete from the

---

* Pronounced *le-tarns*. This is a French word with the accent on the last syllable, which is pronounced like *barns*.

truck to its final position using hoses or pipes. Pumped concrete is called *pumpcrete*.

Concrete can be sprayed in place through a pneumatic spray gun at high velocity to cover shell surfaces such as domes and pools. This is called *shotcrete* when wet mix is shot and *gunite* when dry mix and water is pumped to the gun through separate hoses and then shot into place by force of the compressed air.

Curing. For concrete to obtain its maximum strength, the chemical reaction between cement and water must continue for about twenty-eight days. During this period the concrete is sprinkled and covered to retard the loss of moisture.

Protection from freezing or excess heat is also important for the first seven days of curing. During freezing weather the water or aggregates may be heated before mixing and kept above 50°F for the seven days after placing. Often this is done by building a temporary framework covered by tarpaulins over the concrete and heating with *salamanders* (oil-burning stoves). *High-early-strength* cement (type III) can be used when freezing weather is expected since it cures rapidly and gains "seven-day strength" in only three days. The heat produced during this rapid curing also helps protect the concrete from low temperatures.

Excess heat is a problem when large masses of concrete are placed since the heat causes rapid curing, which lowers the strength of the concrete and causes cracking due to early surface contraction. Type II or Type IV cement is used, or the heat is removed by cooling water pipes embedded in the concrete.

Forms. Forms are nearly always required to mold fresh concrete into the desired shape. Forms must be accurate and sturdy, yet economical since they often cost more than both the concrete and reinforcing steel.

It is easy to underrate the strength needed to support wet concrete, and construction accidents caused by collapsed formwork are all too common. Concrete is more than twice as heavy as water. Also, the pressure of fresh concrete increases in proportion to its depth, just as the pressure water exerts on a dam increases. Thus the lower portion of a form for a concrete column must be able to resist tremendous bursting forces. As with water, the horizontal area does not affect this pressure.

Wood forms are framed of well-braced beams covered with waterproof plywood. Wood planks are used in place of plywood to achieve special textured effects as shown in Figure 4. Before concrete is placed, wood forms are moistened or covered with form oil or plastic liners so that moisture will not be absorbed from the concrete. All forms

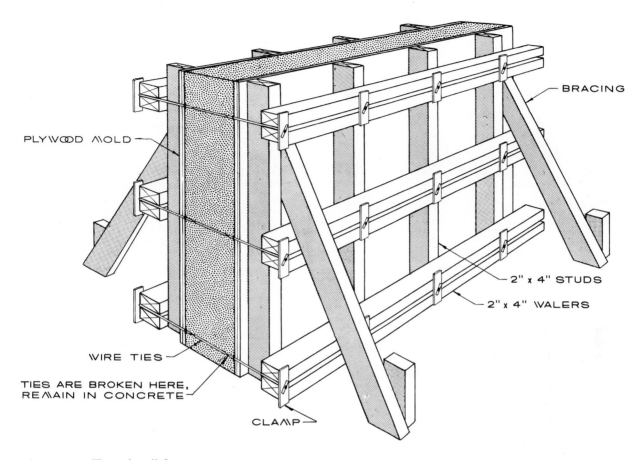

PLYWOOD MOLD

BRACING

2" x 4" STUDS

2" x 4" WALERS

WIRE TIES

TIES ARE BROKEN HERE,
REMAIN IN CONCRETE

CLAMP

Figure 5   *Typical wall form.*

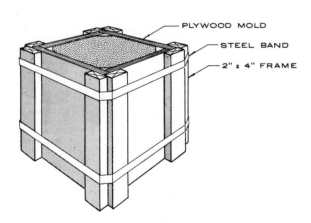

PLYWOOD MOLD

STEEL BAND

2" x 4" FRAME

Figure 6   *Typical column form.*

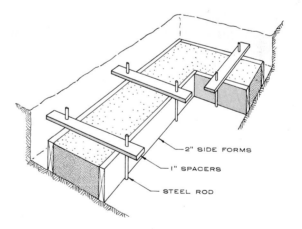

2" SIDE FORMS

1" SPACERS

STEEL ROD

Figure 7   *Typical footing form.*

are designed to facilitate later *stripping* (removal of the forms). Plywood forms are factory- or field-coated with commercial compounds to prevent adhesion to the concrete. Some common methods of building wood forms are illustrated in Figures 5–7.

Reusable steel forms are also used. Sometimes they are rented from companies specializing in formwork. Steel forms are commonly used to shape ribbed or waffled floors. Steel floor forms

are supported by wood *centering,* which is in turn supported by *shoring.* See Figures 8–11.

Plastic-surfaced cardboard tubes are used for cylindrical posts. Sizes range from 6"-diameter to 18"-diameter in 2" increments and to 36" in 6" increments. Stripping is accomplished by making a vertical cut with a circular saw whose blade is set to the thickness of the tube.

As discussed in the chapter on concrete masonry, *expansion joints* must be provided to control

Figure 8   *Installing steel forms on open centering for a ribbed concrete floor.*

Figure 9   *Installing steel forms on plywood centering for a waffled concrete floor.*

Figure 10   *Forms omitted to permit additional reinforcing about column.*

cracking in large areas due to temperature changes, moisture changes, and settlement.

Reinforcing. Concrete can be mixed to develop a *compressive* strength of 7,000 psi after twenty-eight days curing, but the *tensile* strength of concrete is only about one-tenth the compressive strength. Actually it is standard design practice to assume that concrete has no ability at all to withstand tension. Rather, steel rods called *reinforcing bars** are embedded in the concrete to resist any tensile forces. This is called *reinforced concrete.* Concrete without reinforcing is called *plain concrete.*

Reinforcing bars are available in sizes from #2 ($\frac{1}{4}$"-diameter) to #18 ($2\frac{1}{4}$"-diameter) and with minimum yield strengths from 40,000 psi to 70,000 psi. As shown in Table I, the bar designations indicate the diameter in eighths of an inch. For example, a #4 bar is $\frac{4}{8}$" ($=\frac{1}{2}$") in diameter. The ASTM Standard A-615 (approved in 1968) designates three grades of billet steel for reinforcing bars: grade 40 with a minimum yield level of 40,000 psi, grade 60 with 60,000 psi, and grade 75 with 75,000 psi.

For maximum bond strength, the reinforcing bars must be completely surrounded by concrete. The wet concrete is rodded or vibrated mechanically, as it is placed, to remove any possible voids. To ensure a strong bond between the reinforcing steel and concrete, reinforcing bars are rolled with ridged surfaces. These bars are called *deformed bars.*

* *Reinforcing bar* is abbreviated *rebar.*

Figure 11   *Forms are stripped using air guns applied to nozzle at center of each form.*

See Figure 12. The only bars that are not available with these deformations are #2 bars. The ends of reinforcing bars are often bent into hooks to obtain greater holding strength.

Bars are identified by a set of marks rolled on the surface of the bar to show, in order:

1. Point of origin: A symbol identifying the producer.
2. Size: The bar number.
3. Type of steel: The letter N indicating the bar was produced from new-billet steel, I from rail steel, or A from axle steel.
4. Minimum yield: The numeral 60 or a single line indicating 60,000 psi, or the numeral 75 or double lines indicating 75,000 psi. The minimum yield is 40,000 psi if no mark is shown.

EXAMPLE

A rebar marked B6N60 indicates a Bethlehem Steel #6 bar ($\frac{3}{4}''$ diameter) of new-billet steel having a 60,000 psi minimum yield point.

Bar placement. A structural engineer calculates the number, size, shape, and placement of reinforcing steel necessary to meet all design requirements. The reinforcing steel is ordered to these specifications, placed in the form, and wired in position.

Steel *saddles* and *chairs* are used to help hold the reinforcing bars in place.

A typical reinforced concrete beam would contain several horizontal reinforcing bars located near the *bottom* of the beam to resist tension at the middle of the span. But when the beam passes over a support, the *top* of the beam is in tension, and consequently the bars are bent to be located near the top of the beam over supports. Also the beam must resist *shear* near its supports. This is accomplished by the use of reinforcing steel *stirrups*. These are usually U-shaped bars placed vertically.

A typical reinforced concrete slab would also contain reinforcing bars located near the bottom of the slab. In a one-way slab, all these bars would be parallel to one another. To prevent cracking between these bars due to moisture and temperature

Figure 12 *Deformed reinforcing bars.*

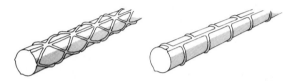

Figure 13 *A rebar clamp.*

Table I *Reinforcing Bars*

Bar Designation	Approximate Diameter
#2	$\frac{1}{4}''$
#3	$\frac{3}{8}''$
#4	$\frac{1}{2}''$
#5	$\frac{5}{8}''$
#6	$\frac{3}{4}''$
#7	$\frac{7}{8}''$
#8	$1''$
#9	$1\frac{1}{8}''$
#10	$1\frac{1}{4}''$
#11	$1\frac{3}{8}''$
#14	$1\frac{3}{4}''$
#18	$2\frac{1}{4}''$

Table II *Recommended Clear Concrete Cover for Reinforcing Steel*

	Protected from Weather and Ground	Exposed to Weather or Ground
Beams and girders	$1\frac{1}{2}''$ min.	$2''$ min.
Floor slabs and walls	$\frac{3}{4}''$ min.	$3''$ min.

Figure 14 *Welded wire mesh used for wall reinforcing at U.S. Air Force Museum, Dayton, Ohio.*

Table III   *Bends Permitted for Reinforcing Bars*

Bar Designation	Minimum Inside Radius of Bend		
	Grade 40	Grade 60	Grade 75
#3, #4, #5	3 DIA	4 DIA	*
#6, #7, #8	4 DIA	5 DIA	*
#9, #10	5 DIA	6 DIA	*
#11	5 DIA	6 DIA	8 DIA

* Grade-75 bars are available only in sizes #11, #14, and #18.

Table IV   *Common Welded Wire Mesh Sizes*

Square	Rectangular
6 × 6 - 10/10	6 × 12 - 4/4
6 × 6 - 8/8	6 × 12 - 2/2
6 × 6 - 6/6	6 × 12 - 1/1
6 × 6 - 4/4	
	4 × 12 - 8/12
4 × 4 - 10/10	4 × 12 - 6/10
4 × 4 - 8/8	
4 × 4 - 6/6	4 × 16 - 8/12
4 × 4 - 4/4	4 × 16 - 6/10

Table V   *Steel Wire Gauge Sizes*

	Gauge	Diameter
◦	10	0.1350″
◦	8	0.1620″
○	6	0.1920″
○	4	0.2253″
○	2	0.2625″
○	1	0.2830″

changes,* additional horizontal reinforcing bars called *temperature steel* are placed at right angles to the tension bars.

To be protected from corrosion, the bars must be completely encased in concrete. Most codes specify minimum distances depending upon the type of weather exposure, the significance of the member, and the required fire rating. Table II gives some rule-of-thumb guidelines.

To ensure an adequate bond and permit the proper placing of concrete, there also must be adequate clearance between parallel bars. A distance of 1″ is considered to be the minimum. The maximum spacing for effectiveness in floor slabs and

* A 100′ concrete slab will change approximately $\frac{1}{2}$″ in length due to moisture changes and an additional $\frac{1}{2}$″ during a 100° change in temperature.

walls is 18″ or three times the thickness of the slab or wall. For example, the distance between parallel bars in a 5″-thick floor slab should not exceed 3 × 5″ = 15″.

Reinforcing bars are often bent into special shapes, but if the bend is too sharp, excessive stresses will be created. Consequently, ASTM has established the minimum permissible inside radius expressed in terms of the nominal diameter, as shown in Table III. Example: A #4 grade-60 bar can be bent to an inside radius of $\frac{1}{2}$″ × 4 = 2″.

Bars must often be spliced by clamping, lapping, or welding. One form of mechanical clamp is illustrated in Figure 13. A rule of thumb for lapped splices is that the bars should be overlapped and wired together for a distance of at least thirty bar diameters. For example, spliced #4 bars should overlap 30 × $\frac{1}{2}$″ = 15″. Splices should not be made in critical areas, of course.

Wire mesh. For slabs, *welded wire mesh* is often used to prevent cracking (Figure 14). Wire mesh (also called *welded wire fabric*) is produced from cold-drawn steel wire welded together in a square or rectangular pattern. A popular wire mesh is 6 × 6 - 10/10, which indicates a 6″-square pattern of 10-gauge wire in each direction. A heavier wire mesh with a tighter pattern is 4 × 4 - 8/8. A 4 × 16 - 8/12 wire mesh indicates 8-gauge wire spaced 4″ apart with 12-gauge wire spaced 16″ apart. Table IV shows some common sizes. Table V shows the size of some steel wire gauges.

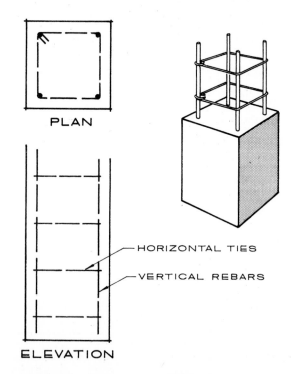

PLAN

ELEVATION

HORIZONTAL TIES

VERTICAL REBARS

Figure 15   *Typical reinforced concrete column.*

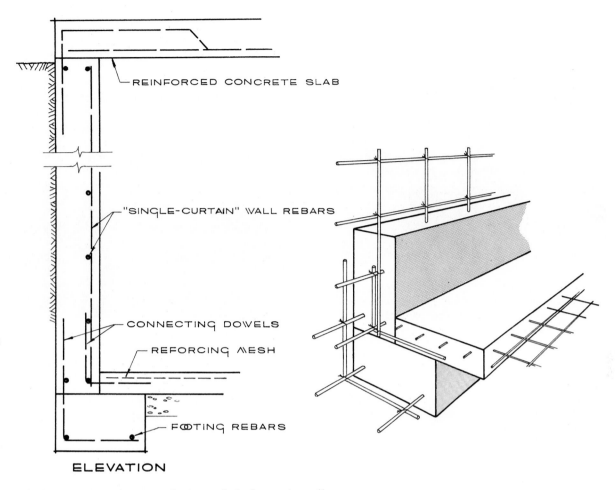

Figure 16   *Typical concrete footing and single-curtain wall.*

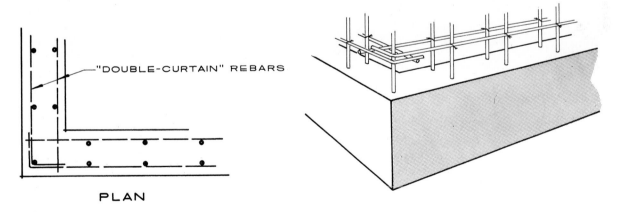

Figure 17   *Typical double-curtain concrete wall.*

EXAMPLES

Examples of typical footing, slab, wall, and beam reinforcing are shown in Figures 15–17. Notice that the end
view of a reinforcing bar is shown as a small, solid circle;
the side view is shown as a dashed line. Figures 18–21
show the use of reinforced concrete in the construction
of a folded-plate roof.

REINFORCED CONCRETE STRUCTURES

A typical reinforced concrete structure consists of
round or square reinforced columns supporting
one-way or two-way floor slabs. The term *one-
way* refers to tension rebars all placed parallel to

Figure 18 *Installing forms over open centering for a folded-plate roof on the Treasure Island Shopping Center near Milwaukee, Wisconsin.*

Figure 19 *Folded-plate-roof reinforcing steel in place.*

Figure 20 *Forms for folded-plate roof removed.*

each other, or *one way*. For example, the structure shown in Figure 22 has a slab containing parallel rebars that stretch from beam to beam. Of course the concrete beams also contain rebars, as do their supporting girders and columns.

The intermediate beams of Figure 22 can be replaced by two sets of rebars installed in each direction as shown in Figure 23. This is called a *two-way slab*. Two-way slabs are commonly used for square or nearly square floor panels.

When the column-to-column girders are also omitted under a two-way slab, a *flat-slab* floor system results, as shown in Figure 24. The upper portion of the columns in flat slab floors are strengthened by flaired capitals and drop panels.

Ribbed (Figure 25) and *waffle* (Figure 26) floor systems are efficient refinements of the one-way and two-way systems. These floors are cast with the aid of reusable steel forms (previously shown in Figures 8–11).

Needless to say, the design and construction of reinforced concrete buildings should be attempted only by competent engineers and contractors since once the steel is placed and the concrete has been poured, an important commitment has been made by the engineer, builder, and owner.

PRECASTING

Precasting refers to the casting of a reinforced concrete member in a mold that is not located at its final position in the structure. The principle of precasting is not new, but precasting in quantity began only about 1955 with the establishment of specialized manufacturing plants. Precast concrete is manufactured by placing reinforcing steel and concrete in forms which may be made of wood, plastic, concrete, or steel. Waterproof plywood forms are most common. Fiberglass-reinforced plastic molds are used for fabrication into intricate shapes. These molds are usually stripped within twenty-four hours after casting and can be reused about seventy-five times.

Members such as face panels can be precast with exposed aggregate facings. A thin layer of

Figure 21 *Completed folded-plate roof for Treasure Island Shopping Center.*

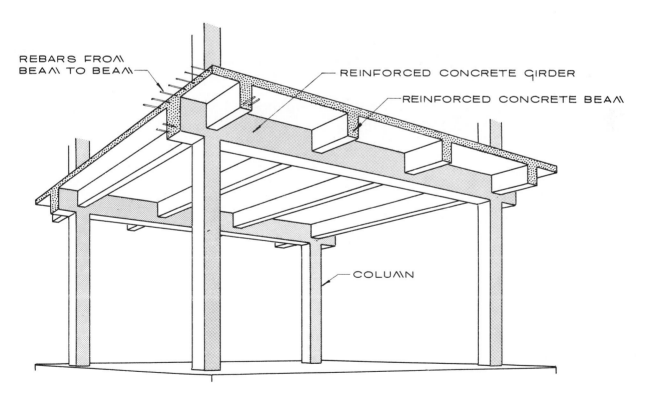

Figure 22 *A one-way slab-and-beam floor.*

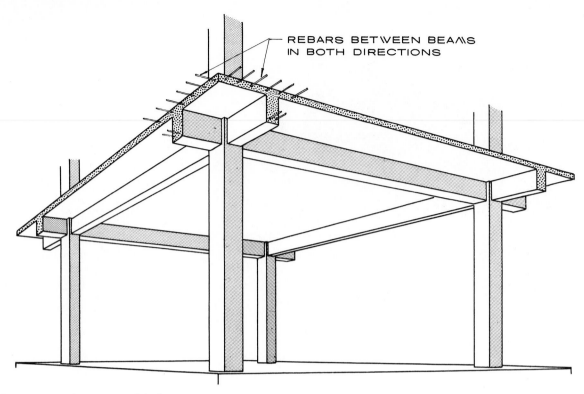

Figure 23 *A two-way slab floor.*

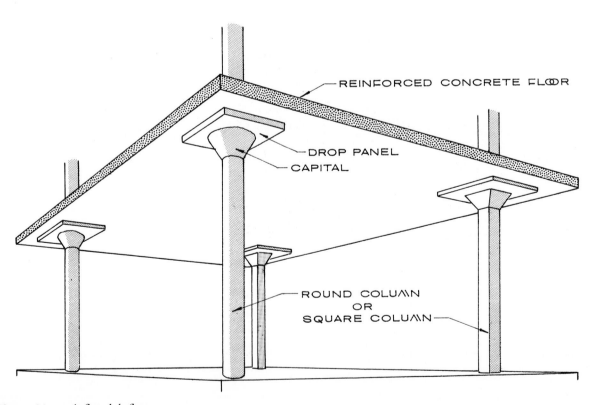

Figure 24 *A flat slab floor.*

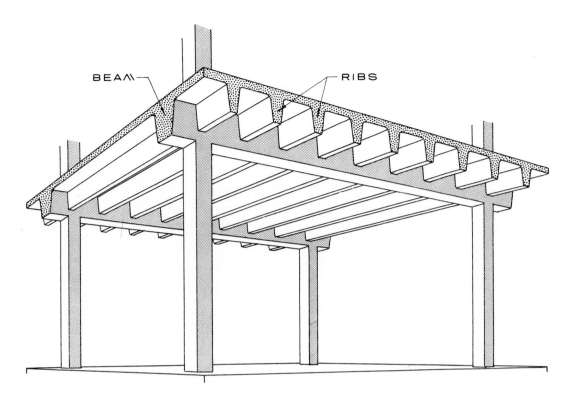

Figure 25   *A ribbed concrete floor.*

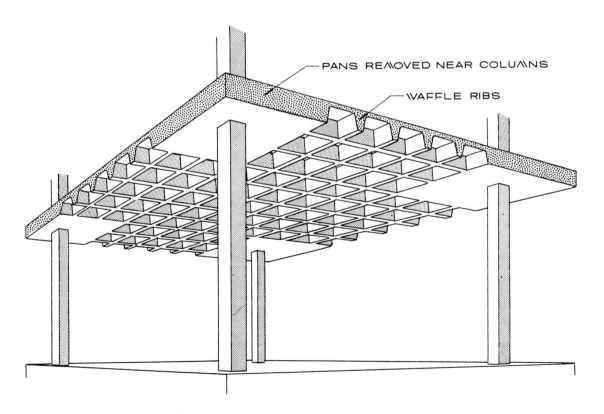

Figure 26   *A waffled concrete floor.*

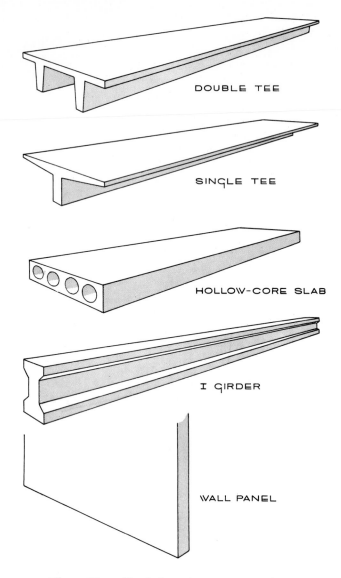

Figure 27 *Typical precast concrete members.*

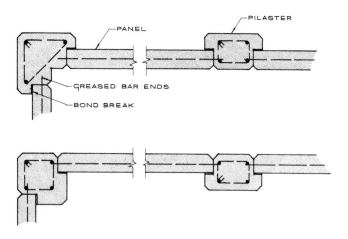

Figure 28 *Joint details for tilt-up construction.*

facing concrete containing the aggregate to be exposed is cast first and backed up with reinforced concrete. After initial curing, the facing concrete is partially removed by brushing, sandblasting, or chemical treatment to expose the desired amount of aggregate.

Precast members are trucked to the construction site and hoisted into position by attaching to hooks cast into the beams or panels. These hooks may serve double duty to anchor the member to the structure. Field connections between the precast member and structure may be in the form of welding, bolting, or cast concrete connections. Joints are sealed by caulking over a flexible joint filler. Some typical precast members are illustrated in Figure 27. These members are also often *prestressed.*

A *double tee* is a basic shape used for floor and roof construction as a combined deck and joists. Spans to 60' are common. Double-tee shapes may be cantilevered or used vertically as a wall.

Single tees are used for floor and roof decks with larger spans to 125'.

Hollow-core slabs are commonly used for decks up to 40' span where flat ceilings are required. The cores are used as raceways for electrical and mechanical systems.

I *girders* are used for long spans and heavy loads. They often serve as the principal girder in a beam-and-deck system.

Wall panels are used for bearing and curtin walls, often with special textured finishes. They are sometimes called *cast stone,* as discussed in Chapter 49. These panels may be combined with insulating material such as a 6"-thick panel that is composed of 2" outer shells of concrete surrounding a 2" inner layer of rigid insulation.

TILT-UP CONSTRUCTION

Precast concrete generally refers to members precast at a factory. Tilt-up construction refers to walls and other members that have been custom-precast on the site and then lifted by crane (*tilted up*) into their final vertical position. Tilt-up construction has the advantages of reducing formwork, simplifying the placing of reinforcement and concrete, and permitting ground-level installation of components such as window frames. Some typical joint details for tilt-up construction are shown in Figure 28. Columns may be placed either before or after the tilt-up panels are in position. Usually the columns and panels are not bonded, so slight movement is permitted for temperature and moisture expansion.

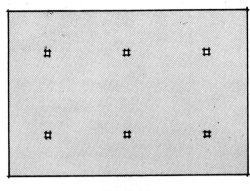

PLAN

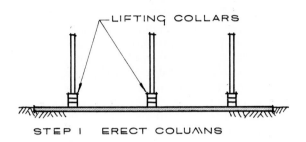

STEP 1   ERECT COLUMNS

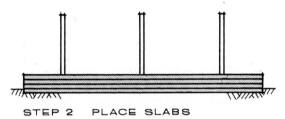

STEP 2   PLACE SLABS

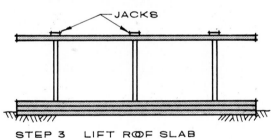

STEP 3   LIFT ROOF SLAB

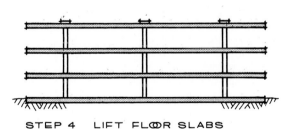

STEP 4   LIFT FLOOR SLABS

ELEVATIONS

Figure 29   *Sequence of operations for lift-slab construction.*

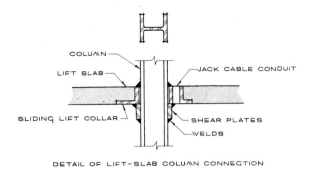

DETAIL OF LIFT-SLAB COLUMN CONNECTION

Figure 30   *Detail of lift-slab column connection.*

LIFT-SLAB CONSTRUCTION

Another method of site precasting is called lift-slab construction. The sequence of operations is shown in Figure 29. After columns are erected, each floor slab is cast on the ground, one on top of the other, using a membrane to prevent adhesion. The slabs are cast directly below their final position surrounding the columns with sliding steel collars (Figure 30) cast in each slab about each column. Special hydraulic jacks are located at the top of each column and connected first to the cured roof slab. The roof slab is hoisted slowly (about 1″/minute) to its final position and fastened to each column by welding or by some other method. The procedure is repeated for each additional floor slab.

PRESTRESSING

A concrete beam or slab will deflect downward under live and dead loading as shown in Figure 31 (A). The upper side will be compressed, but the lower side will be stretched (in tension) and may weaken and crack. Prestressing refers to a method of compressing concrete members so that they do not deflect when in position, and both upper and lower sides remain in compression. Steel rods or strands inserted through the member near the lower side are tensioned to produce a slight upward arch or camber as shown in Figure 31 (B). When in position and loaded, the member flattens but remains in compression throughout.

Most precast concrete construction is also prestressed. Prestressing can be accomplished by *pretensioning* or *posttensioning*. In pretensioning, steel tendons are placed in empty concrete forms and stretched (tensioned) using hydraulic jacks. The tendons are usually high-strength, spiraled wire strands $\frac{1}{4}″-\frac{1}{2}″$ in diameter and are often *draped*

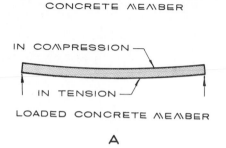

CONCRETE MEMBER

IN COMPRESSION

IN TENSION

LOADED CONCRETE MEMBER

A

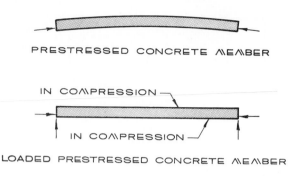

PRESTRESSED CONCRETE MEMBER

IN COMPRESSION

IN COMPRESSION

LOADED PRESTRESSED CONCRETE MEMBER

B

Figure 31 *The principle of prestressed concrete.*

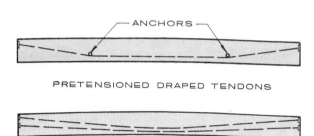

ANCHORS

PRETENSIONED DRAPED TENDONS

POST-TENSIONED DRAPED TENDONS

Figure 32 *Draped tendons for prestressing concrete.*

Figure 33 *The towers were slip-formed on an around-the-clock basis and posttensioned. Knights of Columbus building, New Haven, Connecticut.*

as shown in Figure 32. Draping increases the effectiveness of the pretensioning. Concrete is placed about the tendons and cured. Tendons are *bonded* to the concrete, and when the jacks are removed, part of the tension in the tendons is transferred to the concrete as compression. Some of the tension of course is lost due to concrete shrinkage upon curing, shortening under compression, and *creep* (further shortening under continued pressure over a long time).

In posttensioning, unbonded tendons are stressed *after* the concrete has cured. The tendons are either surrounded with tubing or are greased to prevent adhesion to the concrete. The tension is applied by hydraulic jacks, and anchors at the end of each tendon are installed. To protect tendons from corrosion, they may be bonded *after* posttensioning by forcing cement grout around them. Posttensioning is not as commonly used as pretensioning but may have advantages when used for members too large or heavy to permit moving from factory to site.

Several reinforced concrete buildings are shown in Figures 33 and 34.

STUDY QUESTIONS

1. Briefly describe the manufacture of portland cement.
2. Give the advantage of each of the eight types of portland cement.
3. Why is concrete curing necessary?
4. Describe the special steps needed to place concrete during freezing weather.
5. Describe briefly the following concrete mixes:
   a. 1:2:4 mix
   b. Water-cement ratio of 6
6. Describe the probable form used for each shape:
   a. 8″ foundation wall
   b. Cylindrical post
   c. Waffle floor slab

7. Concrete floors of apartment buildings are commonly precast, but the concrete floors of a spiral parking garage are commonly cast in place. Why?
8. Distinguish between:
   a. Cement and concrete
   b. Fine aggregate and coarse aggregate
   c. Pumpcrete and gunite
   d. Stripping and shoring
   e. Pretensioning and posttensioning
9. Describe briefly the following terms:
   a. Laitance
   b. Salamander
   c. Centering
   d. Rebar
   e. Stirrup
   f. Cast stone
   g. Creep
10. List the precautions for the proper installation of reinforcing bars.
11. Describe the following concrete construction methods:
    a. Precasting
    b. Prestressing
    c. Tilt-up construction
    d. Lift-slab construction
12. Sketch the cross section of a typical precast:
    a. Single tee
    b. Double tee
    c. Hollow-core slab

Figure 34   *Cadet dormitory at the U.S. Air Force Academy, constructed of reinforced concrete.*

LABORATORY PROBLEMS

1. Draw the sectional details for:
   a. 8″, single-wythe reinforced concrete wall
   b. 5″-thick reinforced concrete floor slab
   c. 8″-square reinforced concrete column
   d. 3″-thick tilt-up wall at column and pilaster
2. Complete the reinforced concrete details for:
   a. The building assigned by your instructor
   b. Your original building design

52 / Structural Steel

The nature of architecture is greatly affected by the kind of building materials available. At first, humans depended only upon natural materials such as wood and stone for the construction of shelter. The baking of clay into brick was an early attempt to alter and improve a natural material. But only recently with the production of steel in large quantities has an artificial material been available with such desirable properties of strength and workability. Although we have had hand-crafted tools and weapons of iron for nearly five thousand years, we have been able to build structures of mass-produced steel for only two hundred years.

As early as 3000 B.C. Egyptians formed iron tools by hammering meteorites into saws and sickles. Later, iron was made by heating iron ore until soft enough to be forged or worked. This was called *wrought iron* (*wrought* means "worked"). To make hotter fires, bellows were used to blow air into the fire. The first *blast furnace* to force a steady blast of air into the furnace to melt the ore was built in the fourteenth century, but iron was not produced in large quantity until the eighteenth century.

Refined iron, called *steel,* also has a history of several thousand years, but steel was first produced in quantity only late in the nineteenth century.

MANUFACTURE OF IRON

Iron is made from iron ore, which is found in nearly every country in the world. Iron ore is simply rock containing some proportion of iron. The proportion is about 70 percent in ore mined in the United States. Most iron ore is mined in open pits by stripping away the surface to uncover the ore, which is loaded by power shovel directly to railroad hopper cars. The ore is combined with coke*

---

* *Coke* is manufactured by heating coal without the presence of air in coking ovens. As a fuel, coke produces intense heat.

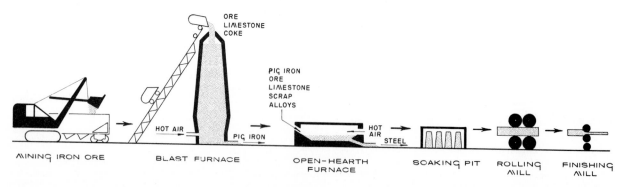

Figure 1   *Steel manufacture.*

for fuel, limestone for flux, and heated air in a blast furnace to produce pig iron.** See Figure 1. To produce 1 ton of pig iron, about $1\frac{3}{4}$ tons of ore, $\frac{3}{4}$ of a ton of coke, $\frac{1}{4}$ of a ton of limestone, and 4 tons of air are needed. The blast furnace is a steel cylinder about 150' high lined with fire brick. Once lighted, it is kept running day and night for several years until the fire brick burns out and has to be replaced. The iron ore, coke, and limestone are dumped in continuously at the top of the furnace. Heated air is blasted in through openings near the bottom. The melted iron is separated from its impurities, and the lighter impurities, called *slag,* float on top of the molten iron. Every few hours the pig iron and the slag are separately drawn off or *tapped,* in batches of several hundred tons at a time.

MANUFACTURE OF STEEL

Pig iron is not used as a finished product but rather as the major ingredient in the manufacture of cast iron, wrought iron, steel, and alloy steels. Cast iron is manufactured by melting a mixture of pig iron and iron scrap in a coke-burning furnace called a *cupola.* The molten iron is then cast in molds to its final shape. Cast iron has high compressive strength but low tensile strength. Also it is quite brittle. Cast-iron products are seldom used in buildings.

Wrought iron is manufactured by pouring refined pig iron in a molten state over silicate slag (melted sand) to form puddle balls which are then squeezed and rolled to shape. Wrought iron is low in compressive and tensile strengths, but it is easily worked and welded and is resistant to corrosion. Wrought iron is used for pipe and ornamental iron work.

Most steel is manufactured in basic oxygen furnaces or electric furnaces. Steel is made in a *basic oxygen furnace* by pouring molten pig iron over scrap iron and then blowing pure oxygen at high pressure onto the surface of the charge to increase the temperature and oxidize impurities. In an *electric arc furnace* scrap iron is heated by an electric arc between two electrodes within the charge. Basic oxygen furnaces supply about 75 percent of steel and electric furnaces about 25 percent. Alloys are carefully added when making steel to obtain desired characteristics. For example, when chromium is added, corrosion resistance is greatly increased. This is called *stainless steel.*

Most *structural steel* is made by reheating the steel ingots produced by the basic oxygen fur-

** This was called *pig iron* because formerly it was cast into bars called *pigs.* Today the molten pig iron runs directly to the steelmaking furnaces.

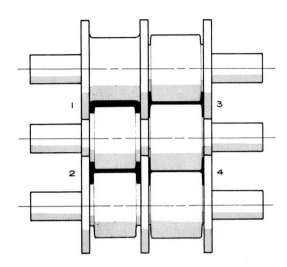

Figure 2   *Rolling a structural steel shape.*

naces in *soaking pits* until white-hot.* The soft ingots are then squeezed between the rollers of *rolling mills.* As the ingots are passed back and forth between rollers, they are flattened and stretched. The rolling improves strength and workability. Finished shapes are rolled in *finishing mills,* where rollers gradually change the ingots to their desired shape. As shown in Figure 2, a rectangular ingot is shaped into an I section by passing through each roller in the numbered order. In addition to structural steel shapes, the finishing mill rolls bars, plates, sheets, and strips.

STRUCTURAL STEEL SHAPES

Structural steel members are extruded in the finishing mill to various cross-sectional shapes (Figure 4). The shape most commonly used for beams and columns is in the form of an I or H. As a beam, this shape is economical because a large proportion of the material is located at the extremity of the shape, where the bending stresses are greatest. It is also more useful as a column than a channel or angle due to its symmetry in both directions. There are two standard shapes in this form. They are called the *S shape* (formerly *American Standard I beam*) and the *W shape* (formerly *wide-flange shape*).

S shapes are available in several weights for each nominal size. The heavier members are made by spreading the rollers, causing the web thickness

* The steel ingots cannot be sent directly to the rolling mill from the furnace due to the difference in temperature between the interior and exterior of the ingots. Either the interior is too soft or the exterior is too cold and hard for working.

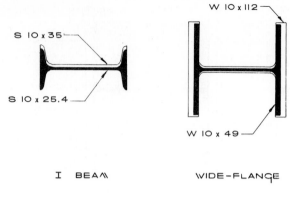

I BEAM   WIDE-FLANGE

Figure 3 *Comparison of sections rolled in different weights.*

and flange width to increase while the depth remains constant, as shown in Figure 3. The inner faces of the flanges have a taper of 2 in 12 as shown in Figure 4. S shapes are available in sizes from 3″ deep to 24″ deep. S shapes are not as popular as W shapes, but they do have the advantages of constant depth, which permits several beam weights to be specified with the same height; thicker webs, which are more resistant to shear and buckling; and narrower flanges, which may be desirable for some designs.

W shapes have wider flanges and thinner webs than the S shapes. Thus they have even more material located at the extremity and are more efficient in resisting bending. W shapes vary from a square proportion to a rectangular proportion.

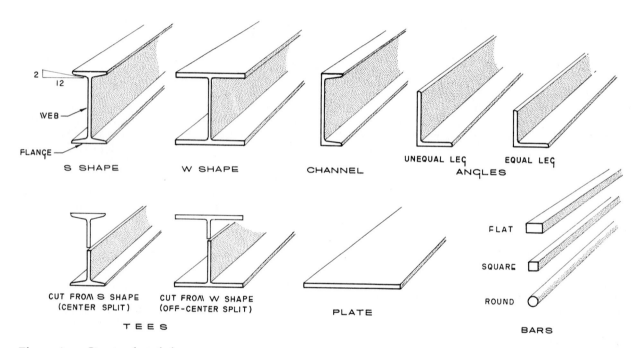

Figure 4 *Structural steel shapes.*

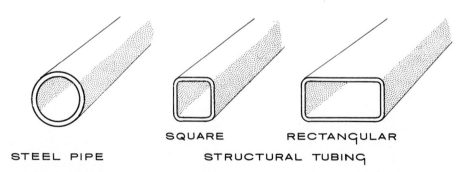

Figure 5 *Steel pipe and structural tubing.*

The shapes with square proportions are often used as columns; the shapes with rectangular proportions are often used as beams. Unlike S shapes, the various weights of W shapes are manufactured by spreading the rollers both horizontally and vertically, thus increasing all dimensions of the flanges and web, as shown in Figure 3. The inner faces of the flanges remain parallel to the outer faces. W shapes are available in sizes from 4″ deep to 36″ deep.

Channel shapes are rolled in shapes from 3″ to 15″ deep. The inner faces of channel flanges are sloped 2 to 12 like S shape flanges. The heavier weights for each depth are made by spreading the rollers in a manner similar to S shapes, giving the same advantage of constant depth.

Channels are used in pairs for the top and bottom chords of heavy steel trusses. Because of the flat face on one side, channels are often used to frame floor openings such as stairwells and elevator shafts. They are also used for stairway supports, roof purlins, and lintels.

Lighter-weight sections are available in both beam and channel shapes. The beams are called *M shapes* and the channels are called *miscellaneous channels*. They are used in the same manner as regular shapes but for lighter loads or shorter spans. See Figures 6 and 7. The differences in flange size and weight between the W shapes, S shapes, and M shapes of 8″ beams are shown in Table I.

Figure 6 *Columns fabricated from four 12″ M shape beams.*

Table I *Comparison of W-, S-, and M-shape 8″ Sections*

Beam Size (depth × width)	Weight	
8″ × 8″	67 lb./ft.	
	58	
	48	
	40	
	35	
	31	
8″ × 6½″	28	W shape
	24	
8″ × 5¼″	20	
	17	
8″ × 4″	15	(formerly
	13	called
	10	*lightweight*)
8″ × 4″	23 lb./ft.	S shape
	18.4	
8″ × 8″	37.7 lb./ft.	
	34.3	M shape
	32.6	(formerly
8″ × 5¼″	22.5	called
	18.5	*junior*)
8″ × 2¼″	6.5	

Figure 7 *Prefabricated stairways of miscellaneous channels.*

Angles are rolled with legs of equal and unequal length. Equal-leg angles range in size from $1'' \times 1'' \times \frac{1}{8}''$ to $8'' \times 8'' \times 1\frac{1}{8}''$. Unequal-leg angles range from $1\frac{3}{4}'' \times 1\frac{1}{4}'' \times \frac{1}{8}''$ to $9'' \times 4'' \times 1''$.

Angles are often used for built-up trusses, beams, and columns, for connectors, and for lintels of short span to support masonry.

Structural tees are manufactured by shearing or flamecutting the webs of either I beams or wide-flange shapes. Orders may be placed for center or off-center splitting. Tees can also be rolled by special order.

Tees are used for the top and bottom chords of welded steel trusses. Inverted tees are used to support roof slabs of gypsum or concrete.

Plates and *bars* are usually specified by size rather than weight. In general, bars are 8'' or less in width; plates are over 8'' wide. Rectangular bars (called *flat bars*) are rolled in increments of $\frac{1}{8}''$ thickness and $\frac{1}{4}''$ width. *Square* and *round bars* are rolled in $\frac{1}{16}''$ increments. Plates are rolled at most mills in width increments of even inches to 60''. Thickness increments of plates are:

$\frac{1}{32}''$ increments up to $\frac{1}{2}''$ thick
$\frac{1}{16}''$ increments $\frac{1}{2}''$–2'' thick
$\frac{1}{8}''$ increments 2''–6'' thick
$\frac{1}{4}''$ increments over 6'' thick

Plates are used for the webs of built-up columns and girders, and for reinforcement of the web or flange of steel shapes. Plates are called *bearing plates* when used to provide bearing areas under columns and beams resting upon concrete. Bars are used for bracing, hangers, and special structural applications.

Availability. S shapes, W shapes, channels, and angles are manufactured by the major steel producers listed in Table II. They are available from local or regional distributors who handle the product of the steel mills. All larger sizes are produced by the two principal steel companies: Bethlehem Steel Corporation and United States Steel Corporation. Some M shapes are produced only by Jones & Laughlin Steel Corporation. Lengths are

available to a maximum of 60' to 90' depending upon the mill. There is a steady demand for the regular shapes shown in Figure 4, and therefore they are easily obtained. Special shapes can be rolled upon special order, but it is more economical to specify regular shapes whenever possible.

STEEL PIPE AND STRUCTURAL TUBING

Steel pipe (round) and *structural tubing* (square and rectangular) (Figure 5) are available in several sizes and wall thicknesses. Nominal pipe diameters range from $\frac{1}{2}''$ to 12'' in three weights: *Standard, Extra-strong,* and *Double Extra-strong.* Square tubing ranges from $2'' \times 2''$ to $10'' \times 10''$ outside dimensions. Rectangular tubing ranges from $3'' \times 2''$ to $12'' \times 8''$ outside dimensions. As columns, these sections have aesthetic and structural advantages over W shapes, but at the sacrifice of fastening convenience.

DESIGNATION OF SHAPES

Rolled steel shapes are specified by the shape symbol, the nominal depth in inches, and the weight in pounds per foot of length. No reference is made to producers; inch marks and pound symbols are omitted. Some examples are shown in Table III.

The quantity of rolled steel shapes of a given length is indicated as shown in Table IV.

AISC Manual. The most useful reference used by structural designers is the *Manual of Steel Construction,* Eighth Edition, published by the American Institute of Steel Construction. This book is usually called the *Steel Construction Manual.* It contains tables that give the dimensions and properties of all available steel shapes. A typical *Dimensions* page is shown in Figure 8, and a typical *Properties* page is shown in Figure 9.

Table II *Major Steel Producers*

Producer	General Office Address
Armco Steel Corporation	Box 600, Middletown, Ohio 45043
Bethlehem Steel Corporation	Martin Tower, Bethlehem, Pennsylvania 18016
Inland Steel Company	30T West Monroe Street, Chicago, Illinois 60603
Jones & Laughlin Steel Corporation	3A Gateway Center, Pittsburgh, Pennsylvania 15263
Northwestern Steel & Wire Company	121T Wallace Street, Sterling, Illinois 61081
United States Steel Corporation	71 Broadway, New York City, New York 10006

Table III *Designation of Rolled Steel Shapes*

New Designation	Interpretation	Old Designation
S 8 × 18.4	S shape, 8″ depth, 18.4 lb./ft.	8 I 18.4
W 8 × 31	W shape, 8″ nominal depth, 31 lb./ft.	8 W 31
C 8 × 11.5	American Standard channel, 8″ depth, 11.5 lb./ft.	8 [11.5
M 8 × 6.5	M shape (formerly junior beam)	8 JR 6.5
MC 10 × 6.5	Miscellaneous channel (formerly junior channel)	10 JR [6.5
∠ 4 × 4 × ¼	Equal-leg angle, 4″ leg × 4″ leg × ¼″ thickness	∠ 4 × 4 × ¼
∠ 6 × 4 × ¼	Unequal-leg angle, 6″ leg × 4″ leg × ¼″ thickness	∠ 6 × 4 × ¼
ST 4 × 9.2	Structural tee cut from an S 8 × 18.4	ST 4 I 9.2
WT 4 × 15.5	Structural tee cut from a W 8 × 31	ST 4 W 15.5
PL ½ × 12	Plate, ½″ thick × 12″ wide	PL 12 × ½
Bar 1¾ × 1	1¾″ × 1″ flat bar	Bar 1¾ × 1
Bar 1 ▱	1″-square bar	Bar 1 ▱
Bar 1 ⌀	1″-diameter round bar	Bar 1 ⌀

Table IV *Designation of Multiple Steel Units*

Designation	Interpretation
10-W 8 × 31 × 12′-8″	10 units of W 8 × 31, each unit 12′-8″ long

TYPES OF STRUCTURAL STEEL

Structural steel shapes, plates, and bars are available in carbon steel, high-strength steel, and weathering steel. Plates are also available in heat-treated steel. The designer specifies the type of steel that gives the desired combination of strength, economy, weldability, and corrosion resistance. Standards for steel are specified by ASTM (American Society for Testing Materials), and the commonly used types are summarized in Table V.

Carbon steel contains carbon and manganese as the main alloys and is the basic structural steel. Carbon steel is the most economical steel on a cost-per-pound basis but has the lowest yield point.

High-strength steel (also called *high-strength, low-alloy steel*) contains alloy elements in addition to carbon and manganese. It is stronger than carbon steel and offers a weight reduction which may result in a cost savings of foundation or erection. Resistance to corrosion is improved.

Weathering steel is high-strength steel with a

Table V *Types of Structural Steel*

ASTM Designation	Yield Point	Use in Construction
		Carbon Steel
A36	36,000 psi	All-purpose steel for building construction
A283	24–33,000 psi	Less expensive than A36
		High-strength Steel
A440	42–50,000 psi	An economical high-strength steel for bolted or riveted structures, but not recommended for welding. Has twice corrosion resistance of A36.
A441	42–50,000 psi	Characteristics similar to A440, but may be welded
A572	42–65,000 psi	Very high strength steel for bolted, riveted, or welded structures
		Weathering Steel
A242	42–50,000 psi	High-strength steel with four times the corrosion resistance of A36
		Heat-treated Steel
A514	90–100,000 psi	Only available in plate

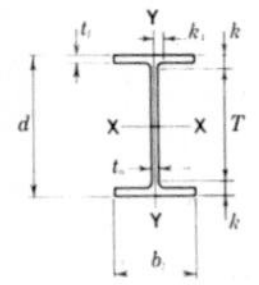

W SHAPES
Dimensions

Designation	Area A	Depth d		Web Thickness t_w		$\frac{t_w}{2}$	Flange Width b_f		Flange Thickness t_f		Distance T	Distance k	Distance k_1
	In.²	In.		In.		In.	In.		In.		In.	In.	In.
W 12×336	98.8	16.82	16 7/8	1.775	1 3/4	7/8	13.385	13 3/8	2.955	2 15/16	9 1/2	3 11/16	1 1/2
×305	89.6	16.32	16 3/8	1.625	1 5/8	13/16	13.235	13 1/4	2.705	2 11/16	9 1/2	3 7/16	1 7/16
×279	81.9	15.85	15 7/8	1.530	1 1/2	3/4	13.140	13 1/8	2.470	2 1/2	9 1/2	3 3/16	1 3/8
×252	74.1	15.41	15 3/8	1.395	1 3/8	11/16	13.005	13	2.250	2 1/4	9 1/2	2 15/16	1 5/16
×230	67.7	15.05	15	1.285	1 5/16	11/16	12.895	12 7/8	2.070	2 1/16	9 1/2	2 3/4	1 1/4
×210	61.8	14.71	14 3/4	1.180	1 3/16	5/8	12.790	12 3/4	1.900	1 7/8	9 1/2	2 5/8	1 1/4
×190	55.8	14.38	14 3/8	1.060	1 1/16	9/16	12.670	12 5/8	1.735	1 3/4	9 1/2	2 7/16	1 3/16
×170	50.0	14.03	14	0.960	15/16	1/2	12.570	12 5/8	1.560	1 9/16	9 1/2	2 1/4	1 1/8
×152	44.7	13.71	13 3/4	0.870	7/8	7/16	12.480	12 1/2	1.400	1 3/8	9 1/2	2 1/8	1 1/16
×136	39.9	13.41	13 3/8	0.790	13/16	7/16	12.400	12 3/8	1.250	1 1/4	9 1/2	1 15/16	1
×120	35.3	13.12	13 1/8	0.710	11/16	3/8	12.320	12 3/8	1.105	1 1/8	9 1/2	1 13/16	1
×106	31.2	12.89	12 7/8	0.610	5/8	5/16	12.220	12 1/4	0.990	1	9 1/2	1 11/16	15/16
× 96	28.2	12.71	12 3/4	0.550	9/16	5/16	12.160	12 1/8	0.900	7/8	9 1/2	1 5/8	7/8
× 87	25.6	12.53	12 1/2	0.515	1/2	1/4	12.125	12 1/8	0.810	13/16	9 1/2	1 1/2	7/8
× 79	23.2	12.38	12 3/8	0.470	1/2	1/4	12.080	12 1/8	0.735	3/4	9 1/2	1 7/16	7/8
× 72	21.1	12.25	12 1/4	0.430	7/16	1/4	12.040	12	0.670	11/16	9 1/2	1 3/8	7/8
× 65	19.1	12.12	12 1/8	0.390	3/8	3/16	12.000	12	0.605	5/8	9 1/2	1 5/16	13/16
W 12× 58	17.0	12.19	12 1/4	0.360	3/8	3/16	10.010	10	0.640	5/8	9 1/2	1 3/8	13/16
× 53	15.6	12.06	12	0.345	3/8	3/16	9.995	10	0.575	9/16	9 1/2	1 1/4	13/16
W 12× 50	14.7	12.19	12 1/4	0.370	3/8	3/16	8.080	8 1/8	0.640	5/8	9 1/2	1 3/8	13/16
× 45	13.2	12.06	12	0.335	5/16	3/16	8.045	8	0.575	9/16	9 1/2	1 1/4	13/16
× 40	11.8	11.94	12	0.295	5/16	3/16	8.005	8	0.515	1/2	9 1/2	1 1/4	3/4
W 12× 35	10.3	12.50	12 1/2	0.300	5/16	3/16	6.560	6 1/2	0.520	1/2	10 1/2	1	9/16
× 30	8.79	12.34	12 3/8	0.260	1/4	1/8	6.520	6 1/2	0.440	7/16	10 1/2	15/16	1/2
× 26	7.65	12.22	12 1/4	0.230	1/4	1/8	6.490	6 1/2	0.380	3/8	10 1/2	7/8	1/2
W 12× 22	6.48	12.31	12 1/4	0.260	1/4	1/8	4.030	4	0.425	7/16	10 1/2	7/8	1/2
× 19	5.57	12.16	12 1/8	0.235	1/4	1/8	4.005	4	0.350	3/8	10 1/2	13/16	1/2
× 16	4.71	11.99	12	0.220	1/4	1/8	3.990	4	0.265	1/4	10 1/2	3/4	1/2
× 14	4.16	11.91	11 7/8	0.200	3/16	1/8	3.970	4	0.225	1/4	10 1/2	11/16	1/2

Figure 8 *A typical* Dimensions *page from the* AISC Manual.

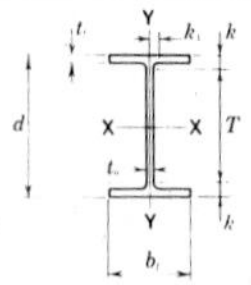

W SHAPES
Properties

Nominal Wt. per Ft.	Compact Section Criteria $\frac{b_f}{2t_f}$	F_y'	$\frac{d}{t_w}$	F_y'''	r_T	$\frac{d}{A_f}$	Elastic Properties Axis X-X I	S	r	Axis Y-Y I	S	r	Torsional constant J	Plastic Modulus Z_x	Z_y
Lb.		Ksi		Ksi	In.		In.⁴	In.³	In.	In.⁴	In.³	In.	In.⁴	In.³	In.³
336	2.3	—	9.5	—	3.71	0.43	4060	483	6.41	1190	177	3.47	243	603	274
305	2.4	—	10.0	—	3.67	0.46	3550	435	6.29	1050	159	3.42	185	537	244
279	2.7	—	10.4	—	3.64	0.49	3110	393	6.16	937	143	3.38	143	481	220
252	2.9	—	11.0	—	3.59	0.53	2720	353	6.06	828	127	3.34	108	428	196
230	3.1	—	11.7	—	3.56	0.56	2420	321	5.97	742	115	3.31	83.8	386	177
210	3.4	—	12.5	—	3.53	0.61	2140	292	5.89	664	104	3.28	64.7	348	159
190	3.7	—	13.6	—	3.50	0.65	1890	263	5.82	589	93.0	3.25	48.8	311	143
170	4.0	—	14.6	—	3.47	0.72	1650	235	5.74	517	82.3	3.22	35.6	275	126
152	4.5	—	15.8	—	3.44	0.79	1430	209	5.66	454	72.8	3.19	25.8	243	111
136	5.0	—	17.0	—	3.41	0.87	1240	186	5.58	398	64.2	3.16	18.5	214	98.0
120	5.6	—	18.5	—	3.38	0.96	1070	163	5.51	345	56.0	3.13	12.9	186	85.4
106	6.2	—	21.1	—	3.36	1.07	933	145	5.47	301	49.3	3.11	9.13	164	75.1
96	6.8	—	23.1	—	3.34	1.16	833	131	5.44	270	44.4	3.09	6.86	147	67.5
87	7.5	—	24.3	—	3.32	1.28	740	118	5.38	241	39.7	3.07	5.10	132	60.4
79	8.2	62.6	26.3	—	3.31	1.39	662	107	5.34	216	35.8	3.05	3.84	119	54.3
72	9.0	52.3	28.5	—	3.29	1.52	597	97.4	5.31	195	32.4	3.04	2.93	108	49.2
65	9.9	43.0	31.1	—	3.28	1.67	533	87.9	5.28	174	29.1	3.02	2.18	96.8	44.1
58	7.8	—	33.9	57.6	2.72	1.90	475	78.0	5.28	107	21.4	2.51	2.10	86.4	32.5
53	8.7	55.9	35.0	54.1	2.71	2.10	425	70.6	5.23	95.8	19.2	2.48	1.58	77.9	29.1
50	6.3	—	32.9	60.9	2.17	2.36	394	64.7	5.18	56.3	13.9	1.96	1.78	72.4	21.4
45	7.0	—	36.0	51.0	2.15	2.61	350	58.1	5.15	50.0	12.4	1.94	1.31	64.7	19.0
40	7.8	—	40.5	40.3	2.14	2.90	310	51.9	5.13	44.1	11.0	1.93	0.95	57.5	16.8
35	6.3	—	41.7	38.0	1.74	3.66	285	45.6	5.25	24.5	7.47	1.54	0.74	51.2	11.5
30	7.4	—	47.5	29.3	1.73	4.30	238	38.6	5.21	20.3	6.24	1.52	0.46	43.1	9.56
26	8.5	57.9	53.1	23.4	1.72	4.95	204	33.4	5.17	17.3	5.34	1.51	0.30	37.2	8.17
22	4.7	—	47.3	29.5	1.02	7.19	156	25.4	4.91	4.66	2.31	0.847	0.29	29.3	3.66
19	5.7	—	51.7	24.7	1.00	8.67	130	21.3	4.82	3.76	1.88	0.822	0.18	24.7	2.98
16	7.5	—	54.5	22.2	0.96	11.3	103	17.1	4.67	2.82	1.41	0.773	0.10	20.1	2.26
14	8.8	54.3	59.6	18.6	0.95	13.3	88.6	14.9	4.62	2.36	1.19	0.753	0.07	17.4	1.90

Figure 9 *A typical* Properties *page from the* AISC Manual.

unique means of corrosion protection as described in Chapter 30. Shapes, bars, plates, sheets, structural rivets, common machine bolts, and heat-treated, high-strength bolts including nuts and washers are available in weathering steel.

Heat-treated steel differs from high-strength steel in that the strength is developed by quenching and tempering. Available only in plate, heat-treated steel is used in high-rise buildings, television towers, and missile transporting and erecting equipment.

STUDY QUESTIONS

1. Describe the manufacture of:
   a. Iron
   b. Steel
2. Distinguish between:
   a. Iron and steel
   b. S shapes, W shapes, and M shapes
   c. High-strength steel and heat-treated steel
3. Describe briefly each term:
   a. Wrought iron
   b. Blast furnace
   c. Slag
   d. Coke
   e. Pig iron
   f. Rolling mill
   g. Weathering steel
4. Give some common applications for the use of:
   a. W shapes
   b. S shapes
   c. Channels
   d. Angles
   e. Tees
   f. Plates
   g. Bars
5. How does a standard steel pipe differ from an extra-strong steel pipe?
6. Give the meaning of the following designations:
   a. W 12 × 120
   b. S 18 × 70
   c. M 10 × 9
   d. C 5 × 9
   e. MC 13 × 50
   f. L 4 × 3 × $\frac{1}{4}$
7. List the advantages and disadvantages of weathering steel.

LABORATORY PROBLEMS

1. Prepare a display chart showing the cross sections of commonly used structural steel shapes.
2. Draw the structural steel details for:
   a. The building assigned by your instructor
   b. Your original building design

XII / Building Fabrication

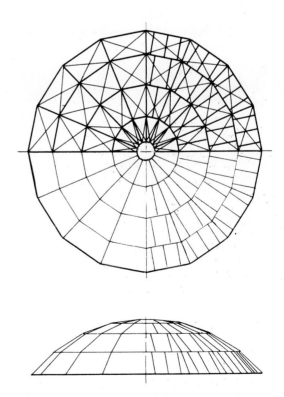

53 / Steel Fabrication

Figure 1 *Steel erection by* crawler cranes (*which operate from ground level*) *and* creeper cranes (*which move up every third floor as construction progresses*).

Structural steel shapes are cut to size and fastened together to form structural units of convenient size at the *fabricating plant*. These structural units are then shipped to the building site and are eventually placed in position, or *erected* (Figures 1 and 2). Connections made at the fabricating plant are called *shop connections* and are usually welded. Connections made at the building site are called *field connections* and are usually bolted. For example, in the steel framework of Figure 3, the angle seats would be shop-welded to the columns, and the angle connections would be shop-welded to the girders. Erection is then completed by simply resting the girder on its seat and bolting the connection through predrilled holes. When alterations are made to existing buildings, new structural steel is often connected to the existing steel by welding.

BOLTING

Bolts are classified as *unfinished* bolts and *high-strength* bolts as listed in Table I. ASTM A307 unfinished bolts are made of low-carbon steel and are quite inexpensive. ASTM A325 high-strength bolts are made of heat-treated medium-carbon steel and are about twice as strong as A307 bolts. ASTM A490 high-strength bolts are made of heat-treated alloy steel and are about 50 percent stronger than A325 bolts. A325 and A490 bolts are identified by the mark "A325" or "A490" on the top of the bolt head as shown in Figure 4. All sizes of A325 bolts are available in weathering steel.

The American Institute of Steel Construction recommends high-strength bolts, welds, or rivets for the following connections:

526

Figure 2 *Ironworkers await delivery of shop-fabricated structural steel for the U.S. Steel Building, Pittsburgh.*

1. Beams and girders connected to columns (and any connections for column bracing) in structures over 125′ high
2. Column splices in:
   a. Structures under 100′ high if a horizontal dimension is less than 25 percent of the height
   b. Structures 100′–200′ high if a horizontal dimension is less than 40 percent of the height
   c. Structures 200′ or more in height
3. Connections, splices, supports, and braces in all structures carrying live loads (such as large cranes or running machinery) that produce impact or reversal of stress. This is to prevent loosening of joints by continued vibration.

Unfinished bolts may be used for all other connections. Unfinished bolts are also used temporarily in all structures to hold members in alignment during high-strength bolting or welding operations.

Installation. Holes for bolts are drilled $\frac{1}{16}''$ larger than the nominal bolt diameter.

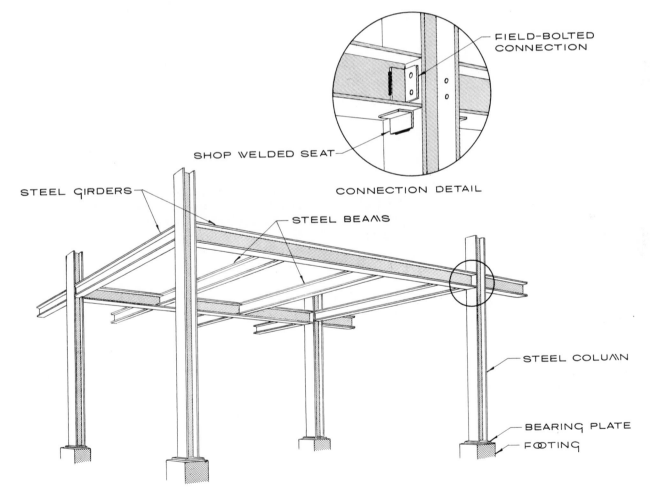

Figure 3 *Typical building framework fabricated of steel.*

Figure 4 *High-strength bolts.*

Table I *Types of Structural Steel Bolts*

ASTM Designation	Bolt Type
A307	Unfinished bolt
A325*	High-strength bolt*
A490	High-strength bolt

* Also available in weathering steel or as interference-body bolts.

The quantity and spacing of bolts are determined by an engineering analysis, but there are some rules of thumb. The center-to-center distance between adjacent bolts (called the *pitch*) should not be less than three nor more than six times the bolt diameter. The distance from the center of a bolt to the edge of the structural member should not be less than one and one-half nor more than six times the bolt diameter. The distance from the bolts to the webs of beams and channels is shown in handbooks and allows clearance for wrenches.

High-strength bolts (Figure 4) are tightened to their required tension by the *turn-of-nut* method using hand or powered impact wrenches (Figure 8). The nut is drawn up to a snug position and then tightened an additional $\frac{1}{2}$ turn. Washers are not needed with A325 bolts, but the harder A490 bolts and nuts do require hardened washers to prevent galling of the softer steel members. When the steel members are sloped, bevel washers are used to compensate for the slope, as shown in Figure 6. Clipped washers are used where clearances are too small for regular washers, as shown in Figure 7.

A325 *interference-body bolts* (Figure 5) combine the best features of high-strength bolts and rivets. They have raised ribs on the shank and are driven into smaller-diameter holes with a maul. This interference fit provides a firm bearing between the bolt and the sides of the hole.

Figure 5 *Interference-body bolt.*

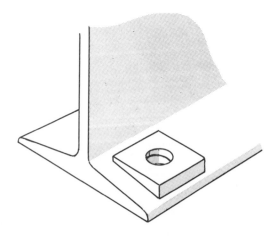

Figure 6 *Bevel washer.*

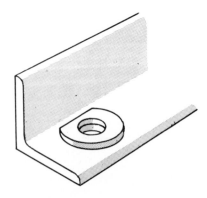

Figure 7 *Clipped washer.*

WELDING

Welding is a popular method of connecting structural steel members and has some advantages over bolting:

1. Fabrication is simplified by reducing the number of individual parts to be cut, punched with holes, handled, and installed.
2. Welded joints may be considered to be rigid, but bolted joints are not considered rigid. This is an important consideration when designing because a uniformly loaded beam with the ends rigidly fixed will deflect only one-fifth the amount of a simply supported beam, as shown in Figure 9.
3. A welded joint is stronger than the joined members; the weld metal itself is 50 percent stronger than the members.

There are a number of different methods of welding, but the *electric arc process* (Figure 10) is almost exclusively used for structural welding. In this process, a generator is used to supply high voltage to the structural metal and to a coated welding rod which serves as an electrode. When the rod is close to the metal, an electric arc is formed which creates enough heat to melt and fuse both members being welded. In addition, the tip of the core of the welding rod melts and is transferred through the arc to the weld seam. The coating of the welding rod also melts to provide gaseous and slag *shields* which protect the weld from oxidation. This slag is easily removed when cool. Self-shielded electrodes are used when working in the open at high, windy elevations. Supplying its own shielding from the ingredients in the flux-cored electrode, this process is impenetrable to wind and eliminates the need for windbreaks. Gravity has little effect on the welding process, so welds can be made in vertical and overhead positions.

Stud welding. Stud welding is a form of electric arc welding used to fasten threaded studs to structural steel. This is accomplished by the use of a

Figure 8 *Madison Square Garden's compression ring sections being bolted with A490 high-strength bolts.*

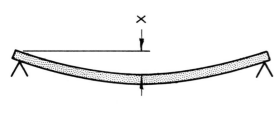

SIMPLY SUPPORTED

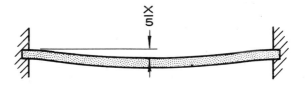

ENDS RIGIDLY FIXED

Figure 9 *Deflection of uniformly loaded beam.*

special gun that holds the stud. When the trigger of the gun is squeezed, the current is turned on, and the stud is positioned to draw an arc which melts its tip. The gun then pushes the stud into the molten pool to complete the weld. Figures 11–13 show studs welded to steel plates set in the concrete fireproofing of the Chicago First National Bank Building. These threaded studs are then used to attach the granite cladding.

Semiautomatic welding. Semiautomatic welding (Figures 14 and 15) is provided by feeding the electrode and flux automatically to the welding head. This increases the rate of weld metal deposit by a factor of three: from the hand rate of 10 lb. of weld metal per hour to 30 lb. per hour. Also, the welder's helper is no longer needed.

Figure 16 shows a beam-to-column connection made by semiautomatic welding. The beam is first bolted to an erection angle. This angle also serves as a backing bar for the web-to-column

weld. The angle and bolts are left in place after welding. Notice that $\frac{3}{8}'' \times 1''$ backing bars are also needed under the flanges and extending 1″ beyond them. These are called run-on and run-off tabs. They assure a complete weld by allowing it to be started before the beginning of the flange and running past the end of the flange. They also prevent runoff of molten puddles of weld metal. These tabs and the excess weld metal are later cut off.

Figure 12   *Completed weld studs.*

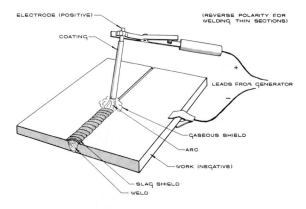

Figure 10   *Electric arc welding.*

Figure 11   *Studs being end-welded to embedded stainless steel plates.*

Figure 13   *Granite cladding attached with stainless steel weld studs, First National Bank Building, Chicago.*

Figure 17 shows a partially completed column splice. Notice that small triangular gates were tacked on to eliminate the need for run-off tabs.

Power is supplied to the electrode feeders through gas or electric dc generators. The electric generators receive their current from utility power lines through portable switching substations such as shown in Figure 18. The substations are moved up the building as the erection progresses. To receive power, a cable is plugged into one of the substation's quick disconnects, and its switch is closed. To provide oxygen and fuel gas for cutting torches and heating torches, portable fuel stations are also provided as shown in Figure 19. Workers can connect their torches to one of the manifold systems of the fuel station to get the fuel needed for each job.

Automatic welding. Automatic welding is seldom used in the field but is often used for shop fabrication. There are many types of automatic welding equipment. The most advanced processes can deposit 200 lb. of weld metal per hour. Figure 20 shows a self-propelled *tractor* fastened to a semi-automatic welding gun. The tractor controls the speed of travel and is equipped with a magnetic wheel to guide it along the curved joint.

Figure 21 shows fully automatic tandem heads mounted on a self-propelled tractor. This unit is making a two-pass, $\frac{3}{8}''$ fillet welded in one pass at a speed of 30 in./min.

The welding heads can also be mounted on a carriage suspended from a rail. The carriage carries the power sources, electrode feeders, and flux tanks. Figure 22 shows such a setup equipped with sensing devices to keep the head automatically centered over the joint.

EXAMPLES

A small welded structure is shown in Figures 23 and 24. This fire station is literally a steel-framed, transparent glass box, designed to put fire equipment on display. Welded steel members were specified to provide clean, narrow sight lines and a sculptural quality to the structure. The South Hills Office Building illustrated in Chapter 40 is another example of welded steel design.

The Tulsa Exposition Center is a welded structure with the largest suspended steel roof ever built. Masts and girders were fabricated by shop welding and then transported to the site. The 80′ masts and 52′ elbow girders were raised by crane (Figure 25), pinned together, and welded to the base plates. The two remaining girder sections—one 95′ long and the other 58′ long—are spliced together by welding on the ground and then lifted into place (Figure 26), hooked on to the suspension cables, and welded to the elbow section. Girders are connected by lightweight beams (Figure 27). Steel decking, insulation, asphalt-impregnated felt, and marble chips complete the roof.

Figure 14   *Welding a beam web-to-column connection with the semiautomatic open-arc process.*

Figure 15   *Welders working in pairs to make column splices.*

Figure 16   *A completed beam-to-column welded connection.*

Figure 17   *A partially completed column weld.*

Figure 18   *A portable power substation for supplying current to electric dc generators.*

Figure 19   *A portable fuel supply station for supplying oxygen and fuel gas.*

Figure 20   *A self-propelled tractor, equipped with a semiautomatic welding gun, guides itself along curved joints by means of a magnetic wheel.*

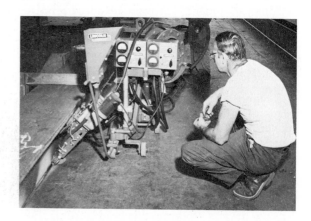

Figure 21   *Fully automatic tandem welding heads mounted on a self-propelled tractor.*

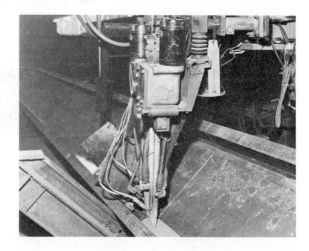

Figure 22   *Tandem welding heads mounted on a boom.*

Figure 23   *Welded steel fire station for Kansas City, Missouri.*

Figure 24   *Detail of welded steel connections on Kansas City fire station.*

Figure 25   *Crane positioning mast for Tulsa Exposition Center.*

Types of welded joints. The most commonly used weld for structural steel is the *fillet weld*. As shown in Figure 28, the size of a fillet weld refers to the length of a leg of its triangular cross section.

Butt welds can be made in several ways. The ends of the members to be joined can be squared, mitered, or grooved. The butt weld is called a *bevel weld* when only one member is mitered, and it is called a *vee weld* when both members are mitered. These miters must be cut before assembling the member. When a fabricator is equipped to gouge rather than miter, *J-groove* and *U-groove welds* have some advantages. Gouging can be done either before or after the assembly. In addition, J-groove and U-groove welds usually require less weld metal than bevel and vee welds do. The members to be joined can be either adjacent or slightly separated by a distance that is called the *root opening*. Members can be welded on one or both sides.

Figure 26 *A girder section being erected by iron-workers.*

Figure 27 *Construction of the Tulsa Exposition Center with suspended roof.*

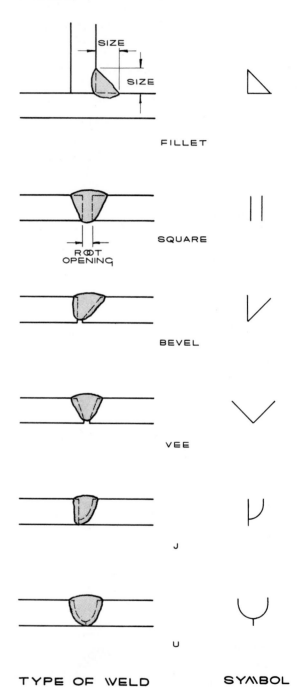

Figure 28 *Basic welds and their symbols.*

Welding symbols. Welds are specified by a standardized *bent arrow* as shown in Figure 29. The arrow points to the joint to be welded, and the appropriate weld symbol from Figure 28 is attached to the horizontal shank. This weld symbol is placed *below* the shank when only the near side (arrow side) of the joint is to be welded, *above* the shank when the opposite side of the joint is to be welded, and on *both* sides of the shank when both sides of the joint are to be welded. See Figure 30. The vertical (perpendicular) leg of the weld symbol is always drawn on the left side, and the other specifications are always arranged from left to right regardless of the direction of the arrow. Although a number of specifications are shown in Figure 29, some may not apply on occasion and are omitted. The weld symbol and weld size are always shown, and the field-weld symbol and all-around symbol are often shown. Study Drawings S3 and S4 in Chapter 40 to understand how welding symbols are used in actual drafting-room practice.

STUDY QUESTIONS

1. Compare the advantages of bolting and welding as methods of building fabrication.
2. Compare the advantages of unfinished bolts and high-strength bolts.
3. Compare the strength of A307, A325, and A490 bolts.
4. What size drilled hole is required for a $\frac{3}{4}''$ bolt?
5. How are high-strength bolts tensioned?
6. What is the advantage of:
   a. Bevel washers
   b. Clipped washers
   c. Interference-body bolts
7. Describe briefly:
   a. Electric arc welding
   b. Stud welding
   c. Semiautomatic welding
   d. Automatic welding
8. By means of sketches, show the cross section of a:
   a. Fillet weld
   b. Square weld
   c. Bevel weld
   d. Vee weld
   e. J-groove weld
   f. U-groove weld
9. Sketch a *bent-arrow* welding symbol for:
   a. $\frac{1}{4}''$ fillet weld, near side
   b. $\frac{1}{2}''$ bevel weld, opposite side
   c. $\frac{5}{16}''$ square weld, both sides 12" long
   d. $\frac{3}{4}''$ vee weld, all around

LABORATORY PROBLEMS

1. Draw the structural details for:
   a. W 12 × 120 column to 2" base plate, welded connection
   b. W 12 × 120 column to W 12 × 31 floor beams, A307 bolts
   c. W 12 × 120 columns to W 16 × 31 floor beams, A490 bolts
   d. W 12 × 31 beam to W 16 × 31 beams, A325 bolts
2. Complete the structural steel plans for the building assigned by your instructor.
3. Complete the structural steel plans for your original building design.
4. Design and detail an original:
   a. High-strength bolted steel protector for a loading dock
   b. Welded steel stair railing for a commercial building
   c. Weathering steel fascia for a shopping plaza

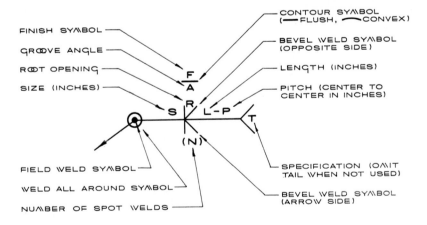

Figure 29 *The welding symbol.*

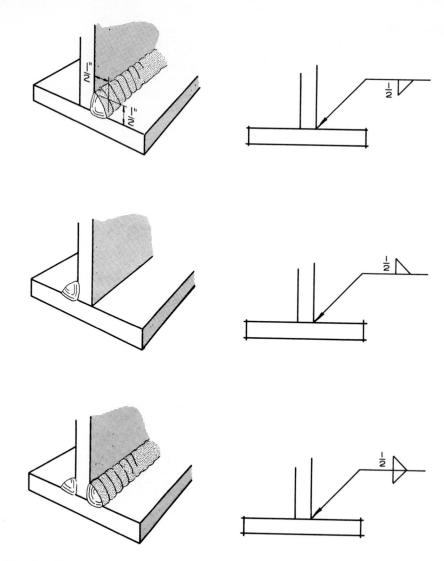

Figure 30 *Use of welding symbols.*

54 / Rigid Frames

UNIFORMLY DISTRIBUTED HORIZONTAL LOAD

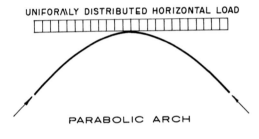

PARABOLIC ARCH

UNIFORMLY DISTRIBUTED SECTION LOAD

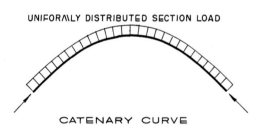

CATENARY CURVE

CONCENTRATED LOADS

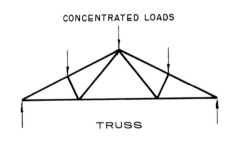

TRUSS

Figure 1   *Structural forms having no bending stress.*

For each type of roof loading, there is a theoretically "best" structural form—a form having only tensile and compressive stresses without any bending stresses. Some examples are in Figure 1. As indicated, the parabolic arch is the ideal form for the usual uniformly distributed loading. The catenary* was discovered by Galileo as the shape of a heavy chain suspended between two points, and is inversely, therefore, the ideal form for a load distributed uniformly along the curve itself. The truss can be an ideal solution for concentrated loads.

Although these forms would require the least amount of material for each given condition, they might not be the most desirable solution for architectural or other reasons. For example, if there are strong reasons to provide a structure with a flat roof, the arch shown in Figure 2 would not be an acceptable solution, even though it would appear to be most economical from a theoretical stress standpoint.

A rigid frame of laminated timber or welded steel is a satisfactory answer to the problem of

---

* *Catenary* is from the Latin word for "chain."

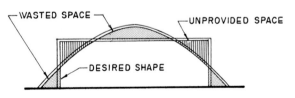

Figure 2   *The ideal structural form may not be the best solution.*

537

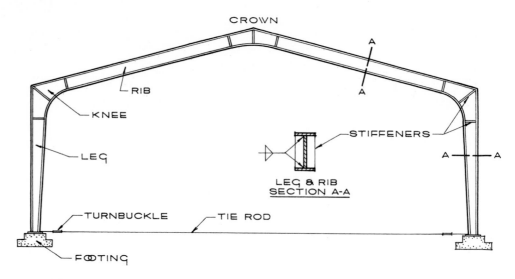

Figure 3 *Rigid-frame nomenclature.*

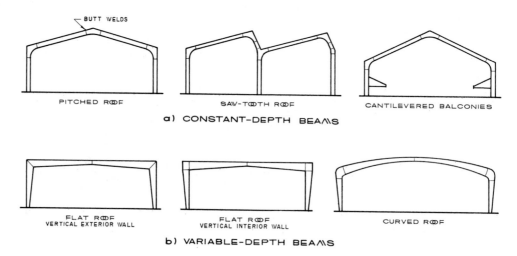

Figure 4 *Some rigid-frame shapes.*

spanning distances from 30′ to 80′ (timber) and 60′ to 120′ (steel) since it can offer a good compromise between the ideal structural shape and the desired enclosed space. In addition, an exposed rigid frame can be a handsome feature in any building. When well designed, it appears both functional and graceful. A rigid frame can take on almost human form: a combination of masculine muscle at the knees and crown with feminine slender at the legs and ribs (Figure 3).

Rigid frames can be built in a variety of shapes (Figure 4). The legs and ribs can be made of rolled steel beams which will give constant depths as shown in Figure 4(a), or they can be fabricated from flat steel plate into I-shaped beams of varying depths as shown in Figure 4(b). Also, they can be constructed of laminated timber into curved

beams of any shape. In wood, constant-depth beams are impractical because of the difficulty in designing knee connections capable of resisting the increased stresses there. In steel, the constant-depth rolled beams are less costly and therefore more commonly used even though more total material is required. Fabricated steel beams are used only when the frame is too large to use available rolled beams.

Some means must be provided to strengthen the knee. In wood and in steel construction, this is usually done by increasing the section depth at the knee. In steel, stiffeners are added to prevent buckling. Stiffeners are often added at the crown and may also be used to strengthen the legs and ribs. Bracing struts at the knees are used between adjacent bents as shown in Figure 5.

Although a rigid frame is not an arch, it has some characteristics similar to an arch. For example, the legs transmit outward thrust to the ground. This thrust can be resisted by ground footings or by tie rods connecting the pairs of legs as shown in Figure 3. Turnbuckles are included for final adjustment. Then the tie rods are embedded in concrete to resist corrosion.

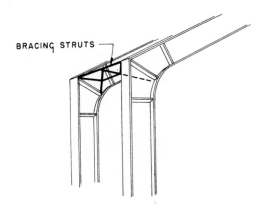

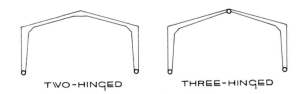

Figure 5 *Use of bracing struts between knees.*

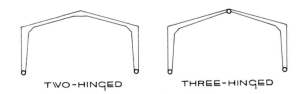

TWO-HINGED   THREE-HINGED

Figure 6 *Basic forms of the rigid frame.*

For design purposes, most rigid frames of steel are considered to be two-hinged frames (Figure 6). Pins are not used at the base of the legs as illustrated, but rather the legs are welded to base plates that are anchored to concrete footings. But since it would increase the cost of the footings considerably to design them to resist rotation completely, pin or hinged connections are assumed. The three-hinged frame is not as rigid as the two-hinged frame and therefore is seldom used in steel construction. However, rigid frames in timber are usually three-hinged since the transportation of fabricated laminated timber causes the frame to be made in two parts.

Details of a rigid-framed auditorium of laminated timber are given in Figure 7. The cross section shows that the ribs have been extended to provide wide eaves. Notice that the gluelam ribs are protected from weather by the 3″ tongue-and-grooved decking turned down to form a fascia. The legs are protected from weather by the exterior wall.

EXAMPLES

The manufacturing plant shown in Figure 8 was designed for the production of high-output hand tools. A rigid steel structure was specified to support an intricate conveyor system in addition to normal wind and snow loads.

The church shown in Figure 9 has five rigid frames of laminated timber. The frames are 5¼″ × 36′ spaced 17′ apart.

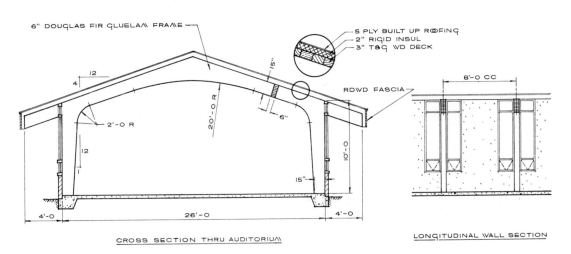

CROSS SECTION THRU AUDITORIUM   LONGITUDINAL WALL SECTION

Figure 7 *A rigid-framed auditorium.*

The factory-built modular apartment building shown in Figure 10 used a rigid steel frame to provide minimum weight with maximum strength. Erection of the modular units is shown in Figure 11.

STUDY QUESTIONS

1. Give the theoretically ideal structural form for:
   a. Load uniformly distributed horizontally
   b. Load uniformly distributed along the form itself
   c. Concentrated loads
2. What is the principal disadvantage of constant depth rigid timber frames?

3. What is the principal disadvantage of varying depth rigid steel frames?
4. In a rigid frame, what is the reason for including:
   a. Tie rods
   b. Concrete around tie rods
   c. Turn buckles
   d. Stiffeners

LABORATORY PROBLEMS

1. Complete the details for the rigid frame structure as assigned by your instructor.
2. Complete the rigid frame details for your original building design.

Figure 8 *Skil Tools manufacturing plant, Wheeling, Illinois.*

Figure 9 *A three-hinged, rigid-frame structure, Emmaus Lutheran Church, St. Paul, Minnesota.*

Figure 10 *Factory-built modular apartments in Westlake, Ohio.*

Figure 11 *Erection of modular apartments, Westlake, Ohio.*

55 / Trusses

Wooden trusses were developed in the Middle Ages as a natural outgrowth of the gable roof. Builders used horizontal joists to tie together opposite walls in order to resist the outward thrust of sloping rafters. The resulting triangular structure was rigid, and it was discovered that a combination of triangular forms would also be rigid. Thus large spaces could be spanned by a number of pinned beams, each lighter and shorter than required for a single lintel. Truss members can be smaller than lintels because truss members are subjected only to tension or compression, but lintels are subjected to bending stress. Most materials resist tension and compression better than bending. For example, it is difficult to break a pencil in two by pulling the ends apart (tension) or pushing them together (compression), but it is easy to break a pencil by bending it. Trusses may be of wood, steel, or a combination of wood and steel. Steel rods are efficient tension members of a truss; timber or steel angle is better for the compression members.

TERMINOLOGY

Trusses consist of principal members called *top chords* and *bottom chords* which are joined together by vertical or diagonal members called *webs*. The webs divide the truss into a number of segments called *panels*, usually of equal width. The top chords may be horizontal (or nearly horizontal) for flat roofs, or inclined for pitched roofs. The depth of flat trusses is usually one-eighth to one-tenth of the span. For normal slopes, the depth of pitched trusses is one-fourth to one-fifth of the span. Depending upon the number of panels and strength of members, most trusses are economical from 20' to 80' spans.

Adjacent trusses are usually spaced about 15' or 16' apart (but also 8'–20') and are joined by horizontal *purlins* on the top chords. When adjacent trusses are spaced close enough that purlins or similar framing are unnecessary, the trusses are called *trussed rafters*.

TYPES

Some of the more common types of trusses are shown in Figure 1. The heavy lines indicate members that usually are in compression for vertical loading, and the light lines indicate members that usually are in tension. The number of panels will depend upon the material and span.

King-post truss. The king-post truss is often used for relatively short spans (20'–30'). The top and bottom chords are often of wood, and the vertical web of steel rod.

Inverted king-post truss. This is also called a *trussed beam*. The tension rods greatly increase the load-bearing capacity of the horizontal beam.

Pratt truss and Howe truss. Pratt and Howe trusses are somewhat similar. They both contain vertical webs that can be extended up through the roof for framing *monitors*. A monitor is a clerestory that permits light or ventilation at the middle of the trussed roof. The Pratt truss contains diagonal webs in tension; the Howe truss contains vertical webs in tension.

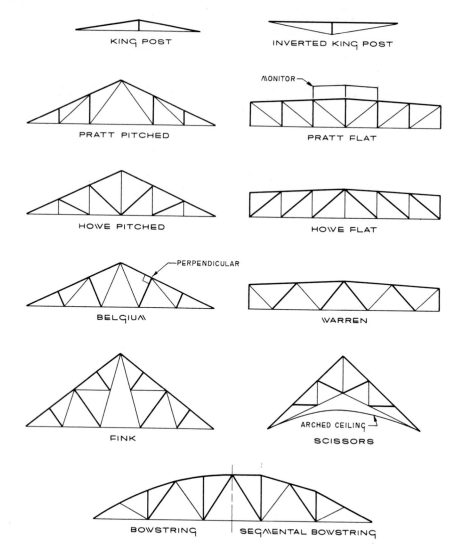

Figure 1 *Common truss types.*

The Pratt flat truss is preferred when it is built integral with columns since the direction of the diagonal webs permits columns to extend to the crown, giving better wind bracing. The Howe truss, however, is usually more economical for similar loading conditions. When several bays of trusses frame to each side of a common column, a Pratt may be used on one side and a Howe on the other since both webs do not then frame to the same place.

Belgium truss. The compression web members of the Belgium truss are perpendicular to the top chords, permitting easy framing of the purlins at these panel points.

Warren truss. Warren trusses are not often used for built-up roof trusses, but the Warren principle is the basis for all open-web joists.

Fink truss. Fink trusses are used with steep roofs to reduce the length of the compression members. In Belgium trusses, for example, the compression members may be too long for reasonably sized members.

Scissors truss. Scissors trusses are used in buildings such as churches where an arched ceiling is to be hung from the bottom chords.

Bowstring truss. For spans from 80′ to 250′, the Bowstring truss is particularly economical in comparison to other types of trusses. Wood bowstring trusses have been made with laminated curved top chords. Segmental bowstring trusses have straight top chords.

Steel trusses. Fabricated two-dimensional trusses of steel are commonly used in bridge design, and

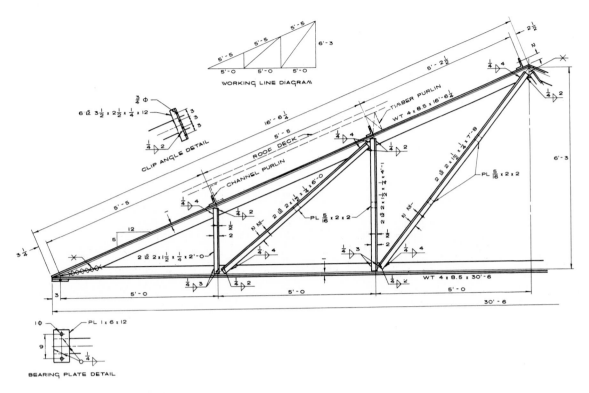

Figure 2 *A welded steel Pratt truss.*

three-dimensional trusses (called *space frames*) are commonly used in contemporary building design. One of the earliest large steel-trussed structures, the 986'-high Eiffel Tower, was built for the 1889 World's Fair in Paris. The steel cantilever truss of the Quebec Bridge, built in 1917, contains one span of 1,800'. The tallest man-made structure is a steel-trussed television transmission tower 2,063' high built in 1963 at Fargo, North Dakota.

For buildings with spans less than 144', open-web joists are usually preferred for light loading. For heavy loading or large spans, fabricated steel trusses may be specified. The Pratt and Warren trusses are commonly used for flat roofs, and the Fink for steeply sloping roofs. The bowstring truss is often specified for buildings that have very long spans, such as field houses. Welding and high-strength bolting are the usual methods of fabrication.

The construction drawing of a welded steel Pratt truss is illustrated in Figure 2. The top and bottom chords of this truss are 4" structural tees cut from W shapes. The web members are doubled 2" × 1½" unequal-leg angles. The 2"-square plates tend to keep each pair of angles in alignment. The chord members are joined by vee welds, and the web members are fastened to the chords by ¼" fillet welds.

In designing a truss, the first step is the preparation of the working line diagram which establishes the theoretical principal dimensions. Then the designer attempts to lay out the truss members so that the center-of-gravity axes of each member coincide with the working lines. In this instance, the flange faces of the structural tees are 1" from the working lines, and the angle faces are ½" from the working lines.

Wood trusses. Wooden-trussed rafters (page 245) are commonly used for small spans of 20'–50', and wooden trusses are often used for spans to 80'. Wooden bowstring trusses are the most economical form of wooden truss for large spans over 100' and have been used for spans of 250'.

Wood trusses can be factory- or shop-fabricated. Connections are made by machine bolts with washers and split rings (Figure 4) or shear plates (Figure 5). Split rings transmit forces from one wooden member to another, the only function of the bolt being to hold the members together. Shear plates transmit the forces to the bolt, which then resists the entire shearing stress. Split rings are used for wood-to-wood connections. Shear plates are used for wood-to-wood or wood-to-steel connections. Both split rings and shear plates are embedded in precut daps routed in the wooden

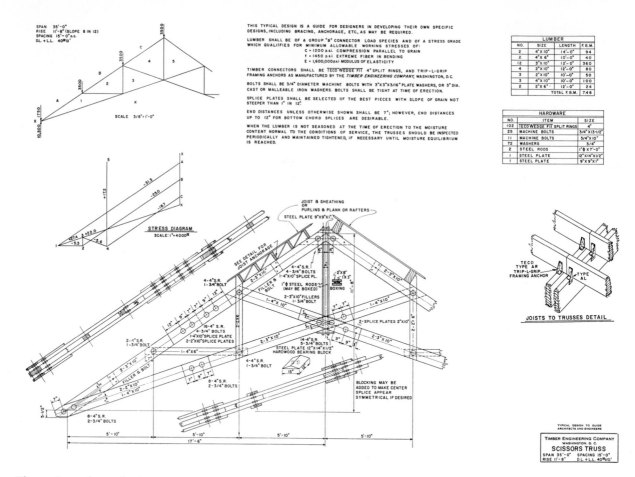

Figure 3   *A wood scissors truss.*

members. They serve the function of distributing the forces over a greater area of each member. Thus larger forces can be transmitted than possible with a bolt alone.

A wood scissors truss of 35′ span is shown in Figure 3. Notice the central steel tension rod. The stress diagram was used to calculate the stress in each member before determining its size. The positive signs indicate tension; the negative signs indicate compression.

OPEN-WEB JOISTS

Small prefabricated steel Warren trusses, called *open-web joists,* are commonly used to support floors and roofs (Figures 6 and 7). Available in sizes to span distances from 8′ to 144′, open-web joists are economical, strong, lightweight, and easily erected. The open webs permit installation of electric conduits, heating pipes, and air ducts. When used with an incombustible top slab and metal-lath plaster ceiling, open-web joists can carry fire protection ratings of four hours. As

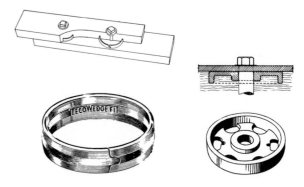

Figure 4   *Split ring.*   **Figure 5**   *Shear plate.*

shown in Figure 8, open-web joists can be obtained with underslung or square ends. Ceilings can be better hung from joists with square ends. Open-web joists can also be obtained either with the top chord parallel to the bottom chord (for floors) or pitched in one or both directions (for roofs). The standard pitch is $\frac{1}{8}$″/ft., which permits roof drainage. An upward camber of $\frac{3}{8}$″–$8\frac{5}{8}$″ (depending upon the span) is also provided.

Figure 6 *Open-web steel joists for floor and roof support.*

Figure 7 *Open-web steel joists for roof support of the Air Force Museum.*

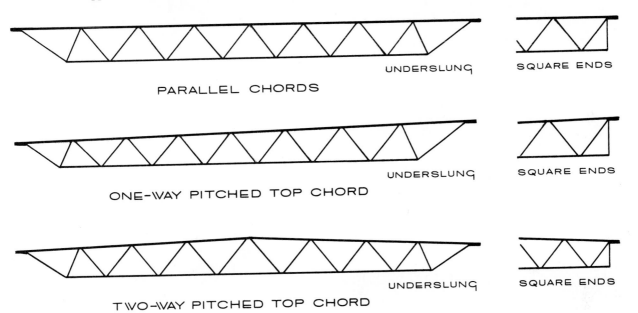

PARALLEL CHORDS — UNDERSLUNG — SQUARE ENDS

ONE-WAY PITCHED TOP CHORD — UNDERSLUNG — SQUARE ENDS

TWO-WAY PITCHED TOP CHORD — UNDERSLUNG — SQUARE ENDS

Figure 8 *Types of open-web joists.*

Steel joists are manufactured in three series as shown in Table I: open-web steel joists, long-span steel joists, and deep long-span steel joists.

Table I *Open-web-joist Designations*

	Based upon Available Stress of:	
	22,000 psi	*30,000 psi*
Open-web steel joists	J	H
Long-span steel joists	LJ	LH
Deep long-span steel joists	DLJ	DLH

Open-web steel joists. Open-web steel joists, called the *J Series,* are available in lengths from 8′ to 48′ and depths* from 8″ to 24″. They are manufactured with cold-formed chords (Figure 9) or hot-rolled chords (Figure 10). The J Series is based upon a tensile working stress of 22,000 psi. A heavier H Series, based upon a tensile working stress of 30,000 psi, will support heavier loads.

Long-span steel joists. Long-span steel joists, called the *LJ Series,* are available in lengths from 25′ to 96′ and depths from 18″ to 48″. Hot-rolled

---

* The joist depth refers to the nominal depth at the middle of the span.

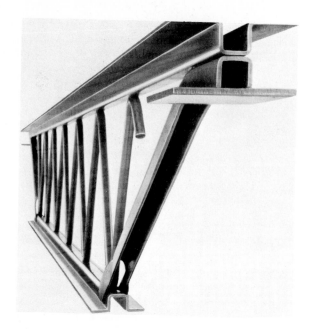

Figure 9   *Open-web joist with cold-formed chords.*

Figure 10   *Open-web joist with hot-rolled chords.*

Figure 11   *Long-span joists with tee-section chords.*

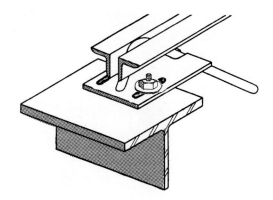

Figure 12   *Bolted connection.*

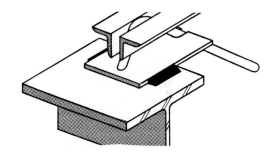

Figure 13   *Welded connection.*

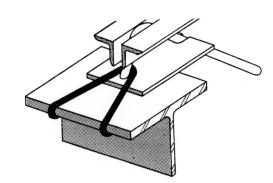

Figure 14   *Hairpin anchor.*

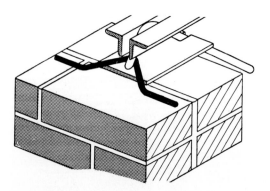

Figure 15   *Masonry rod anchor.*

tee sections are used for the top and bottom chords (Figure 11). The LJ Series is also based upon a tensile working stress of 22,000 psi. A heavier LH Series, based upon a tensile working stress of 30,000 psi, will support heavier loads.

Deep long-span steel joists. Deep long-span steel joists, called the DLJ Series, are available in lengths from 89' to 144' and depths from 52" to 72". These lengths and depths are shown in Table II. The DLJ Series is based upon a tensile working stress of 22,000 psi, and the heavier DLH Series is based upon 30,000 psi.

Table II *Comparison of Open-web-joist Series*

Joist Series	Joist Depth	Span
J and H	8"–24"	8'–48'
LJ and LH	18"–48"	25'–96'
DLJ and DLH	52"–72"	89'–144'

Erection details. Open-web joists can be lifted into place by two men or a simple rig; only bolting or field welding is required to anchor them permanently. Details of anchoring to walls and columns are shown in Figures 12–16. For bolted connections (Figure 12), $\frac{3}{4}$" slotted holes are used for field adjustments. A 1"-long weld on each side of the bearing plate (Figure 13) is the accepted method of welding steel joists to supporting structural steel. If not bolted or welded, the joists are anchored by means of $\frac{1}{4}$"-round hair-pin anchors bent around the flange of the supporting member (Figure 14). Where masonry or concrete walls support joists (Figure 15), $\frac{3}{8}$" rod anchors are built into the wall to secure the joist. Minimum bearing on steel supports is $2\frac{1}{2}$"; minimum bearing on masonry or concrete is 4". Column connections are made by bolting the top bearing plate to the bearing beam or to an angle (Figure 16) and field-welding the extended lower chord to a shelf angle.

For framing small floor openings for shafts and ducts (up to 4' wide), header angles are used (Figure 17). The header angle is welded to the trimmer joists; the tail joist is then welded to the header angle. Large openings over 4' wide should be framed in structural steel.

After the joists are in place, bridging of round rods (Figure 18) or steel angles is installed and welded to the joists. This holds the joists in alignment and provides lateral bracing. The ends of the lines of bridging are welded to a steel framework, and bridging anchors (Figure 19) are used to secure the ends of bridging lines to masonry walls. When joists are used as purlins on a sloping roof, $\frac{1}{2}$"-round sag rods should be used (Figure 20). The

Figure 16 *Column connection.*

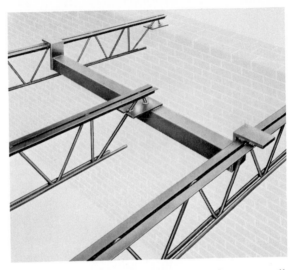

Figure 17 *Use of a header angle to frame a small opening.*

Figure 18 *Bridging.*

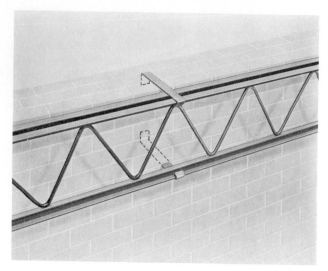

Figure 19 *Bridging anchors.*

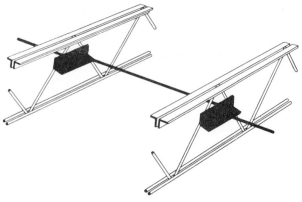

Figure 20 *Sag rods.*

Figure 21 *Joist extensions.*

Figure 22 *Joist outriggers.*

Figure 23 *Wood nailer.*

Table III *Spacing of Bridging or Sag Rods*

Span	Number of Lines of Bridging or Sag Rods
Up to 14′	1 row
14′–21′	2 rows
21′–32′	3 rows
32′–40′	4 rows
40′–48′	5 rows

number of lines of sag rods needed are the same as for bridging (Table III).

To support overhanging roofs, joists may be obtained with top chords extended up to 4′ (Figure 21). For greater extension, outriggers are shop-welded to the joists (Figure 22). When a nailing surface is needed, wood nailers are attached to the joists by lag screws or carriage bolts between the chord angles as shown in Figure 23.

Joist substitutes. For short spans (such as corridors no wider than 12′), cold-formed joist substitutes may be economically used to frame floors and ceilings. See Figures 24 and 25. Joist substitutes are available in lengths from 4′ to 12′ and depths from $2\frac{1}{2}''$ to 10″. No bridging is required.

Roof decking. Floor and roof decks are installed on the top chords of open-web joists, and ceilings may be hung from the bottom chords. The floor and roof decks may be precast concrete planks, concrete, poured-on formed steel decking, wood-fiber panels, or wood planking. The ceiling is often of metal lath and plaster to serve as fire protection for the joists.

Figure 24 *Joist substitute.*

Poured floor and roof slabs are constructed by attaching formwork of ribbed, corrugated, or cellular steel sheets, ribbed metal lath, or paper-backed welded wire fabric to the top chords of the joists. This formwork is called *centering* (Figure 26). Steel centering sheets are available in lengths to 24′ and widths to 32″. They are laid with nesting side laps and 2″ minimum end laps. The centering sheets are securely fastened to the top chords by welding or by metal clips. These attachments also serve to stay the top chords laterally.

Concrete is poured on the centering to a minimum thickness of 2″. The centering acts as positive reinforcement* in addition to being a form. Often reinforcing steel near the top of the slab is included for negative reinforcement. Utilities may also be embedded in the poured slab. Lightweight poured concrete, although not as structural, gives fire protection for the joists. When lightweight concrete is used, vent clips are installed along the side laps between supports to permit escape of moisture.

---

* Positive reinforcement resists U-shaped bending; negative reinforcement resists inverted U-shaped bending.

STUDY QUESTIONS

1. Distinguish between:
   a. Tension, compression, and bending
   b. Truss, trussed rafter, and trussed beam
   c. Open-web, long-span, and deep long-span steel joists
   d. Split ring and shear plate
2. What is the principal advantage of a truss compared to a lintel?
3. With the aid of a sketch, define each term:
   a. Top chord
   b. Bottom chord
   c. Web
   d. Panel
   e. Purlin
4. Define briefly each term:
   a. Space frame
   b. Centering
   c. Monitor
   d. Working line diagram
   e. Stress diagram

Figure 25 *Installing joist substitutes.*

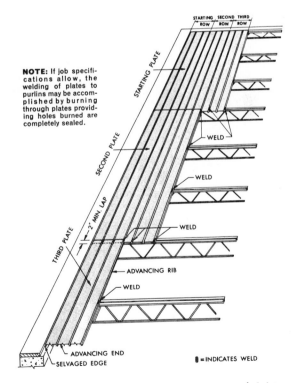

NOTE: If job specifications allow, the welding of plates to purlins may be accomplished by burning through plates providing holes burned are completely sealed.

STARTING ROW   SECOND ROW   THIRD ROW

STARTING PLATE

SECOND PLATE

THIRD PLATE

2′ MIN. LAP

WELD
WELD
WELD
WELD

ADVANCING RIB

ADVANCING END
SELVAGED EDGE

▮ = INDICATES WELD

Figure 26 *Installing centering on open-web joists.*

5. Sketch each truss and give its advantages:
   a. King-post
   b. Inverted king-post
   c. Pratt
   d. Warren
   e. Fink
   f. Scissors
   g. Bowstring
6. Indicate the common methods of connecting the members of a:
   a. Steel truss
   b. Wood truss
7. Describe the erection details for a roof framed of open-web joists if the exterior wall is 12″, single-wythe masonry.

LABORATORY PROBLEMS

1. Draw the plan and structural details for:
   a. 26′ wood-trussed rafter for a roof slope of 4 to 12
   b. 32′ wood Pratt truss for a roof slope of 6 to 12
   c. 36′ welded steel Fink truss for a roof slope of 9 to 12
2. Draw the plan and structural details for a flat roof with dimensions of:
   a. 34′ × 60′ with 2′ roof overhang and hung ceiling
   b. 60′ × 60′ with a 4′ × 4′ centered opening
3. Draw the truss details for:
   a. The building assigned by your instructor
   b. Your original building design

56 / Space Frames

Although all forms in nature are three-dimensional, humans often think and design in a two-dimensional manner. Even some spatial systems are really only superimposed planar systems. The spatial truss system shown in Figure 1, for example, is composed of two planar truss systems perpendicular to each other. The folded-plate trussed roof in Figure 2 is merely a system of inclined planar trusses. A truly integrated spatial truss system is called a *space frame*.

True space frames may take many forms but are often based upon a spatial tetrahedron (a pyramid with a triangular base) rather than a planar triangle. Just as the triangle is a rigid structure, so is the tetrahedron a rigid structure. Figure 3 shows a popular form of space frame based upon the tetrahedron.

Any regular polyhedron can be made rigid by making all its faces rigid. This is often accomplished by triangulation. The upper horizontal planes in Figures 3–5, though, are not triangulated

since it is assumed that an attached floor or roof system will be used to achieve rigidity in these planes. The examples in Figures 4 and 5 show space frames based upon rectangular forms and triangular forms. As shown in Figure 6, the space-frame concept can be expanded for use as columns or towers. A complete roof and column design is illustrated in Figure 7.

Space frames are usually constructed of steel or aluminum tubing. For modular purposes, all tubular members have the same outside diameter, but thicker walls are specified when increased strength is needed.

The major feature in any space-frame system is the manner of connecting the truss members. Welding is probably the most common method, but some alternate methods are shown in Figure 8. The Mannesmann System of clamping was first developed for scaffolding. The clamps can be used to fasten tubing at any desired angle. The Unistrut System uses specially formed plates to which

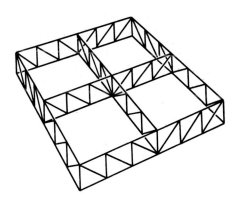

Figure 1   *A spatial truss system.*

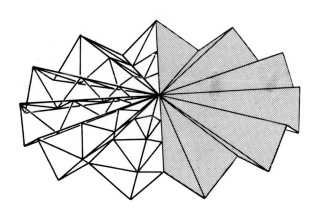

Figure 2   *A folded-plate trussed roof.*

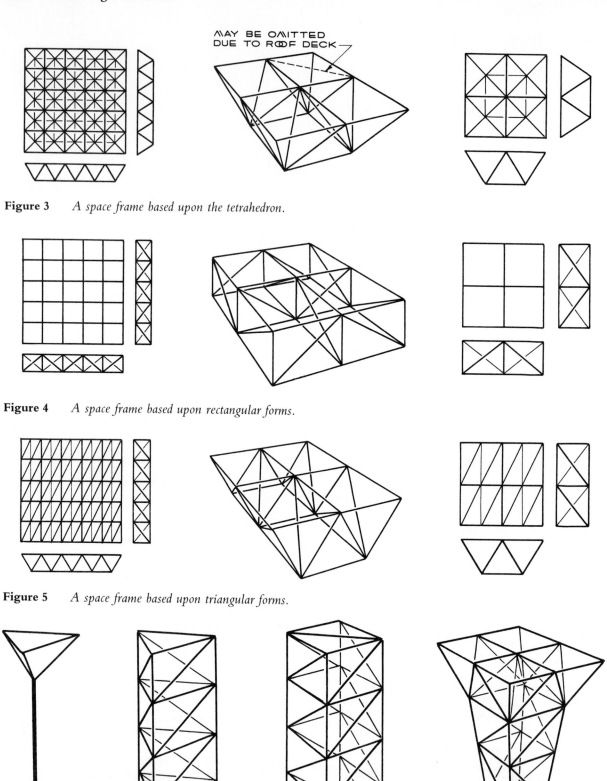

MAY BE OMITTED
DUE TO ROOF DECK

Figure 3   *A space frame based upon the tetrahedron.*

Figure 4   *A space frame based upon rectangular forms.*

Figure 5   *A space frame based upon triangular forms.*

Figure 6   *Space-frame columns.*

channel members are bolted. This system produces square panels 49″ center to center, permitting the use of 48″ panel materials with 1-in. joints. The Mero System consists of spherical connectors having threaded holes. Up to 18 members can be fastened to each connector.

EXAMPLES

Frank C. Bishop Library, The York School, Monterey, California (Figures 9 and 10). This library's entire structure is a space frame that permits a column-free interior. The truss members are $2\frac{1}{2}$″ steel angles and tees that were shop-welded to a large extent. Roofing is wood shakes.

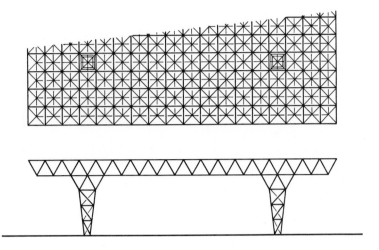

Figure 7   *A space-framed structure.*

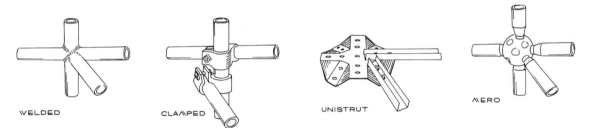

Figure 8   *Fastening space frames.*

Figure 9   *Interior of the Bishop Library, Monterey, California.*

Figure 10   *Exterior of the Bishop Library.*

U.S. Air Force Academy Field House, Colorado (Figure 11). The roof of this field house is a welded structural steel space frame. The lighting fixtures and air-conditioning ducts shown in the illustration will be concealed, together with the frame, by an acoustical ceiling.

U.S. Air Force Academy Dining Hall, Colorado (Figures 12–15). Built as a complete unit on the ground (Figure 12), the steel framework of this 4,400-capacity dining hall was lifted into place as a complete unit and bolted to the supporting steel columns. It was engineered to compensate for the structural sag that occurred when it was placed on the columns.

Figure 11   *Space-framed roof of the U.S. Air Force Academy Field House.*

Figure 12   *U.S. Air Force Academy Dining Hall roof being assembled on the ground.*

Figure 13   *Dining Hall roof in place.*

Figure 14   *Roof facade and ceiling of Dining Hall near completion.*

Figure 15   *Dining Hall interior.*

Figure 16 *U.S. Air Force Chapel under construction.*

U.S. Air Force Chapel, Colorado (Figures 16–18). The roof of this famous building is a space frame. Prefabricated sections were swung into position by a ground crane (Figure 16) and bolted in place.

STUDY QUESTIONS

1. Distinguish between a truss and a space frame.
2. Why are space frames usually based upon connected tetrahedrons?
3. Sketch several common methods of connecting space-frame members.
4. Why is it usually not necessary to triangulate the upper horizontal plane of a space frame?

LABORATORY PROBLEMS

1. Build a study model of a space-frame roof based upon:
    a. Rectangular forms
    b. Triangular forms
    c. Tetrahedrons
2. Complete the space-frame plans for:
    a. The building assigned by your instructor
    b. Your original building design
3. (For the advanced student) Design an original space-frame connection system.

Figure 17 *Space framework of the Air Force Chapel.*

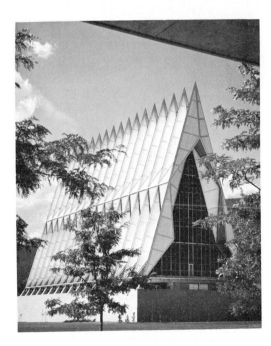

Figure 18 *Completed Air Force Chapel.*

57 / Vaults and Domes

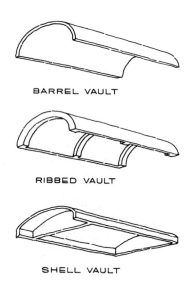

Figure 1   *Common vault types.*

BARREL VAULT

RIBBED VAULT

SHELL VAULT

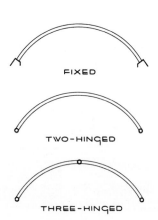

FIXED

TWO-HINGED

THREE-HINGED

Figure 2   *Vault classifications.*

Vaulted and domed structures have been designed and built for many centuries. The Roman, Byzantine, and Gothic civilizations all used arches, vaults, and domes extensively for their public buildings. Similar methods are still used today.

VAULTS

A *vault* is a curved surface supporting an entire roof. An *arch* is a curved structure usually supporting the weight over the opening in a wall. Masonry arches are often made of wedge-shaped members with their joints perpendicular to the curve of the arch. Some popular forms are shown in Chapter 48.

Vaults may be monolithic structures of concrete or framed structures of timber or steel. For maximum rigidity with economy of materials, vaults may be *ribbed* as shown in Figure 1. The ribs may be girders with solid cross sections, or they may be trussed. Very thin ribbed vaults are called *shells*. Shells have been constructed of reinforced concrete and plywood. The edge and end ribs are an integral part of shell construction since they are needed for added strength.

Vaults may be fixed or contain two or three hinges as shown in Figure 2. The ends of a fixed vault are rigidly anchored to buttresses. The ends of a two-hinged vault may be pinned or constructed in some other manner that permits bending. Three-hinged vaults with long spans present a special design problem. Temperature changes cause a vertical movement of the central hinge which may break the roof seal at the crown.

A vault exerts not only a *downward* thrust, but an *outward* thrust as well. The outward thrust can be counteracted by either buttresses or tie rods. Tie rods may be underground or overhead as shown in Figure 3. Underground tie rods are embedded in concrete to resist corrosion; overhead tie rods may require sag rods to keep the ties from sagging. Turnbuckles are included for final adjustment.

Vaults are constructed of timber, steel, or concrete. Timber barrel vaults of laminated wood are used to span distances of 40'–120'. Ribbed vaults of trussed timber are used to span distances to 200'. Welded steel ribbed vaults of solid-plate section are usually three-hinged and may span up to 300'. They are often used for aircraft hangars which require great column-free spans. Concrete vaults are also built with spans up to 300'. They usually are two-hinged and of ribbed construction. They may be cast in place or precast in sections and lifted into position.

Two types of steel vaults are illustrated in Figures 4 and 5. The three-hinged girder vault of Figure 4 is modeled after the University of Vermont field house, which spans 150'. The girder ribs were fabricated of steel plate cold-bent to the curve of the roof. Each rib was shop-welded in

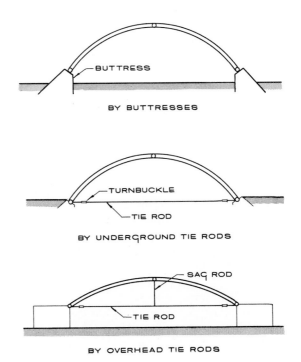

Figure 3 *Containment of horizontal thrust.*

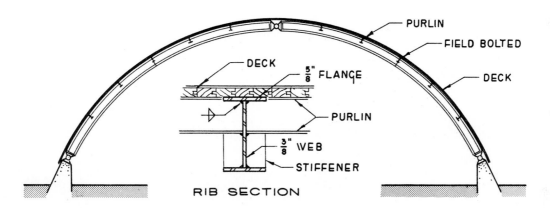

Figure 4 *A three-hinged girder vault.*

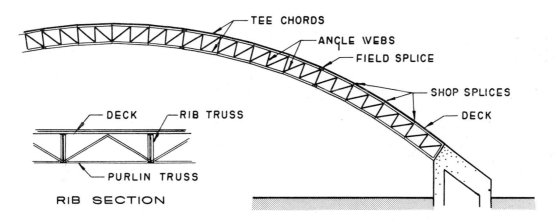

Figure 5 *A fixed truss vault.*

four sections, assembled on the ground with high-strength bolts into two halves, and pinned to the buttresses. Then the rib halves were raised to position by cranes and pinned at the crown. A 4″-thick tongue-and-groove roof deck was installed and covered with built-up roofing.

The fixed truss of Figure 5 illustrates the construction of the Navy Hangar at Patuxent, Maryland, which spans 300′. Top and bottom chords are straight members for two panels. Sets of these panels were butt-welded into five sections of equal length. Each section was then erected and field-welded. Lateral support against buckling is provided by welded purlin trusses that are the same depth as the ribs.

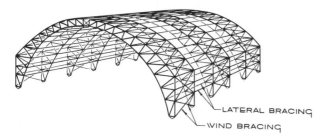

Figure 6 *Lateral and wind bracing.*

BRACING

In addition to resisting vertical live and dead loads, buildings must be rigid enough to resist a variety of horizontal and inclined forces. Bracing to resist such forces is called *wind bracing.* The structure of a typical steel-trussed vault might consist of ribs joined by purlins as shown in Figure 6. Lateral wind bracing of steel rods is installed in the plane of the top chords. It is often sufficient to place wind bracing only in the outside and alternate inside bays.

To prevent sideways buckling of the bottom chords, lateral bracing is also installed. Lateral bracing often consists of trussed purlins whose depth is the same as that of the trussed ribs.

EXAMPLES

Blossom Music Center, Akron, Ohio (Figures 7 and 8). The Cleveland Orchestra's summer house is supported by a 572′ steel arch tilted 16° from the horizontal. The arch is a welded box girder of trapezoidal cross section 7′ wide at the bottom and 4′ wide at the top. It is fabricated of $1\frac{1}{2}$″ weathering steel plate internally stiffened by structural tees. The fan-shaped convex roof is supported by a network of steel-pipe trusses. The facility seats 4,600 under the roof and an additional 10,000 on the sloping hillside.

Figure 7 *The Blossom Music Center at Akron, Ohio.*

Figure 8 *Steel arch of the Blossom Music Center.*

U.S. Air Force Museum, Dayton, Ohio (Figures 9–12). This museum at Wright Patterson Air Force Base consists of two-hinged, steel-trussed vaults 80' high at the crown and spanning 240'. The sixteen trussed ribs spring from 10' × 10' reinforced concrete buttresses. The section halves of the trusses were pinned to the buttresses and then hoisted to final position for final welding at the crown.

DOMES

Domes are usually hemispherical in shape and consequently exert outward thrusts continuously around the perimeter. These thrusts are often counteracted by a steel *tension ring* as shown in Figure 13. A *compression ring* is also included at the crown. Domes may be constructed of a reinforced concrete shell or framed in wood or steel. Several framing patterns are illustrated in Figure 15. No-

tice that the tension ring may be constructed of straight rather than curved members.

Framing patterns. The common patterns for framing a dome are radial, lamella, and geodesic.

A *radial dome* contains curved ribs radiating from the crown to the tension ring. Ribs usually number from twelve for small domes to forty-eight for domes to 400' in diameter. The ribs form curved sections called *gores*. Gores can be identical in size and shape and therefore are ideal for prefabrication. Opposite gores are erected, forming an arched structure that serves as the base for attaching additional gores. Roofing panels can be fastened to horizontal purlins that span adjacent ribs or can be fastened to inclined rafters that span adjacent purlins.

The *Schwedler dome* is a radial dome with diagonals to divide all surfaces into rigid triangles. The diagonals and other members can be straight or curved.

Figure 9   *Pinning a rib to its buttress.*

Figure 10   *Hoisting a rib to position.*

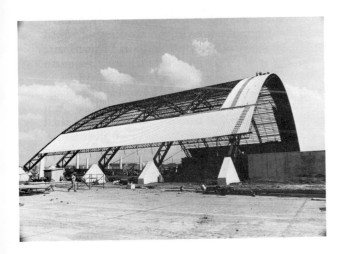

Figure 11   *Installing the roof deck.*

Figure 12   *The U.S. Air Force Museum at Dayton, Ohio.*

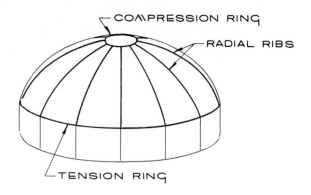

Figure 13   *Elements of a dome.*

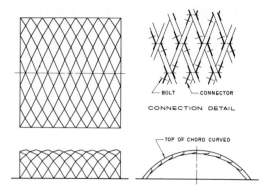

Figure 14   *A lamella vault.*

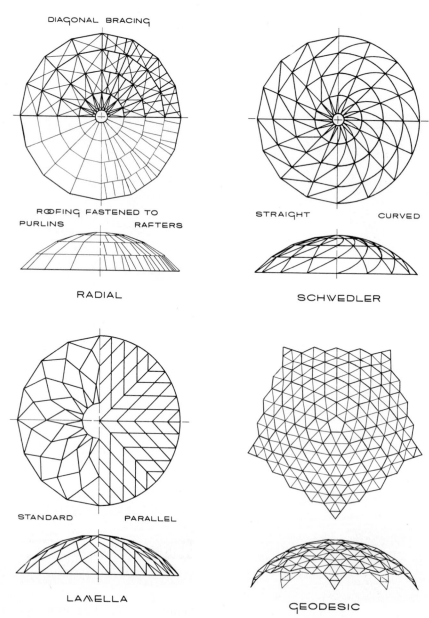

Figure 15   *Types of domes.*

A *lamella roof* is formed of short members assembled in diamond-shaped patterns. In vault construction (Figure 14), the diamond-shaped panels are all the same shape and size. In dome construction, the panels must become smaller as they approach the crown. The parallel lamella dome solves this problem by having fewer panels near the crown. However this system tends to visually emphasize those few ribs that reach the crown, which causes the dome to appear divided into large segments. The world's largest steel dome, the Louisiana Superdome in New Orleans, is a 680' diameter lammella dome 273' high. The world's largest dome, the National Center of Industries and Technology in Paris, is a 720' diameter concrete dome.

A *geodesic dome* is framed of members nearly equal in length that are joined to form triangular patterns. The triangles are then joined to form pyramids (tetrahedrons), giving a double-faced structure of great strength. See Figure 16. The framing members are usually straight rather than curved, which causes the geodesic dome to look like a polyhedron rather than a hemisphere. All the bottom members of a geodesic dome are not al-

ways at the same elevation. Consequently the supporting buttresses may have to be of different heights.

The inventor of the geodesic dome is R. Buckminster Fuller, who has received over one hundred patents since 1954 on a number of designs, some based upon shapes other than the tetrahedron. One popular system is based upon the octahedron as shown in Figure 17.

Construction of a geodesic dome proceeds by erecting a complete ring of the lower sections and then adding on higher sections. Each ring of sections is stable by itself, and consequently formwork is not required. These domes have also been built starting with the uppermost sections fastened around a telescoping mast. The mast is then extended as additional lower sections are added.

EXAMPLES

Trade Fair Dome, Kabul, Afghanistan (Figure 18). This 100'-diameter pavilion for an Afghanistan trade fair was assembled in forty-eight hours. Afghans regard the geodesic dome as a modern Mongolian *yurt* (tent) and therefore representative of native Afghan architecture.

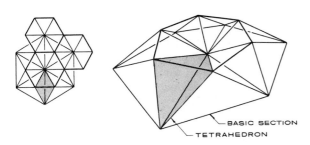

Figure 16   *Detail of a tetrahedral-based geodesic dome.*

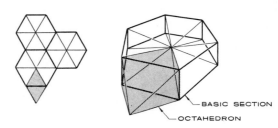

Figure 17   *Detail of an octahedral-based geodesic dome.*

Figure 18   *Trade Fair Dome, Kabul, Afghanistan.*

Figure 19   *U.S. Exhibition at Expo 67, Montreal, Canada.*

U.S. Exhibition at Expo 67, Montreal, Canada (Figure 19). This spherical structure is 250' in diameter and 197' high. It is based upon a tetrahedral system. The covering is plexiglass.

American Society for Metals Headquarters, Cleveland, Ohio (Figure 20). Designed as the national headquarters for the American Society for Metals, this structure is the same diameter as the pavilion in Figure 19 but is based upon an octahedral system.

Figure 20 *American Society for Metals Headquarters, Cleveland, Ohio.*

STUDY QUESTIONS

1. Distinguish between:
   a. Arch, vault, and dome
   b. Barrel, ribbed, and shell vault
2. Indicate three methods of resisting the horizontal thrust of a vault.
3. Indicate the usual method for resisting the horizontal thrust of a dome.
4. Briefly describe each term:
   a. Wind bracing
   b. Gore
   c. Tension ring
   d. Compression ring
   e. Lamella vault
   f. Geodesic dome
5. With the aid of a sketch, describe a:
   a. Tetrahedral-based geodesic dome
   b. Octahedral-based geodesic dome

LABORATORY PROBLEMS

1. Design and detail the plans for a 20'-diameter, plastic-covered domed structure to be used as a temporary exhibition building at a school fair.
2. For the building assigned by your instructor, draw the plan and details for a:
   a. Vaulted roof
   b. Domed roof
3. For your original building design, draw the plan and details for its vaulted or domed roof.

58 / Cable Roof Structures

Builders of suspension bridges have long known that a cable is the most efficient method to span wide distances. Recently the steel cable has also been used to support roofs of large public buildings. Cable-suspended roofs are light in weight and therefore require lighter supporting members and foundations. They are also ideal for structures such as arenas that must have a column-free floor area.

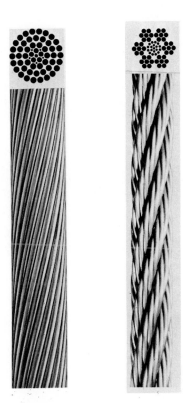

Figure 1   *Steel cable.*

HISTORY

Among the oldest suspension structures were foot bridges in Burma and Java made of hemp and bridges in China made of iron chains. In the Americas, a suspension bridge of 148' span was built by the Incas in 1350. Known as the Bridge of San Luis Rey, it lasted for 540 years with annual replacement of the rope plaited from leaves of the century plant. In the United States toward the end of the eighteenth century, suspension bridges were built of flat iron links. The first wire-cable suspension bridge was built in 1816. John Roebling's Brooklyn Bridge, finished in 1883, had a secondary cable system which solved the problem of vibration and sway (called *flutter*).

The oldest building with a cable-supported roof was probably the Roman Colosseum (A.D. 80). As indicated in Chapter 12, rope cables were stretched across the 600' × 500' elliptical wall to support silk awnings over the galleries. But other than temporary buildings such as tents, few permanent cable-suspended buildings were built before 1950. The State Fair Arena at Raleigh, North Carolina (Figures 2–5) was finished in 1953 and is considered to be the first major cable-suspended building in the United States.

MANUFACTURE OF COMPONENTS

Cable. Steel cables may be either strands or wire rope. A *strand* is an arrangement of galvanized steel wires twisted together. A *rope* is an arrangement of strands twisted together. The wire used in steel

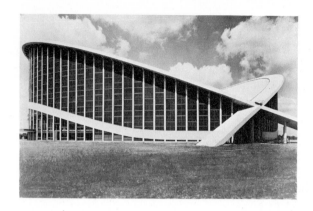

Figure 2   *A warped cable roof for the North Carolina State Fair Arena, Raleigh, North Carolina.*

Figure 3   *Clamping intersecting strands together at the Raleigh Arena.*

Figure 4   *Installing the corrugated metal roof deck of the Raleigh Arena.*

cable is manufactured by drawing hot-rolled steel rod through a series of dies to finish size. The wire is wound on bobbins which are placed in a stranding machine (Figure 6), which twists the wires into a strand. A closing machine (Figure 7) twists the strands into rope. Both strands and rope are used as cables (Figure 1). Strands provide maximum strength, and rope provides maximum flexibility. The breaking strength of a 1″ strand is 115 kips, compared to 91 kips for a 1″ rope. Rope is used when the cable runs over saddles of small radii. Strands are manufactured in diameters from $\frac{1}{2}$″ containing 7 wires to $5\frac{1}{2}$″ containing over 300 wires. Rope is manufactured in diameters from $\frac{3}{8}$″ with 6 strands of 7 wires each (specified as 6 × 7) to 4″ with 6 strands of 37 wires each (specified as 6 × 37). Before installation, steel cables are *prestretched* (Figure 8) to squeeze the wires closer together and assure that all cables will stretch uniformly when loaded. This is important because the positions of intersecting members can then be accurately marked on the cable before it is positioned.

Fittings. Various types of fittings are used with steel cable. Some common fittings are shown in Figure 9. The cable is fastened to the end fittings by either socketing (Figure 11) or swaging (Figure 12). In socketing, the socket is slipped over the end of the cable, the wire ends are separated, or *broomed*, and molten zinc is then poured into the socket. In swaging, the cable end is inserted into the fitting, and they are squeezed together in a 1,000-ton hydraulic press. Both of these types of connections are as strong as the cable itself.

Some details of cable fittings and their applications are shown in Figure 14. A detail of the Raleigh State Fair Arena is shown in Figure 10.

Figure 5   *Interior of the Raleigh Arena.*

Figure 6 *Laying a strand in a stranding machine.*

Figure 7 *Laying a wire in a closing machine.*

Figure 8 *Prestretching track for steel cable.*

CLOSED SOCKET   OPEN SOCKET   BRIDGE SOCKET

SWAGED EYE   SWAGED CLEVIS

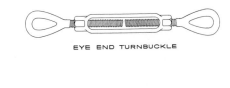

EYE END TURNBUCKLE

JAW END TURNBUCKLE

SHACKLE   CLIP   THIMBLE

Figure 9 *Typical cable fittings.*

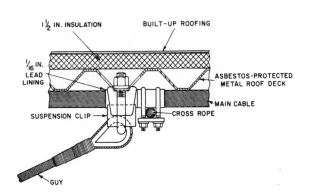

1½ IN. INSULATION   BUILT-UP ROOFING

1/16 IN. LEAD LINING   ASBESTOS-PROTECTED METAL ROOF DECK

SUSPENSION CLIP   CROSS ROPE   MAIN CABLE

GUY

Figure 10 *Roof detail of the State Fair Arena, Raleigh, North Carolina. (See page 568.)*

DESIGN

A cable can be considered to be an inverted arch. A uniformly loaded cable assumes a parabolic shape. This explains why the parabolic arch is the most structurally efficient arch for uniformly distributed loads since each portion of the arch is in pure compression. But unlike arches, cable roofs are economical only for spans greater than 150′. The cable connections and anchors represent a large proportion of the cost of a cable roof, and a 50′ span might require the same number of connections as a 500′ span. Cable economy is also dependent upon the amount of sag. The stress in a cable increases dramatically as the sag is reduced, as shown in Figure 13.

Figure 11   *Socketing.*

Figure 12   *Swaging.*

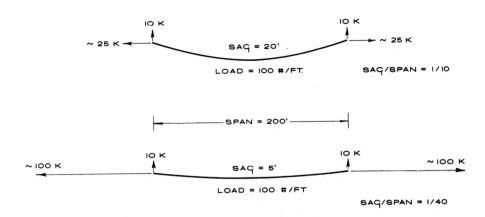

Figure 13 *Cable tension related to sag.*

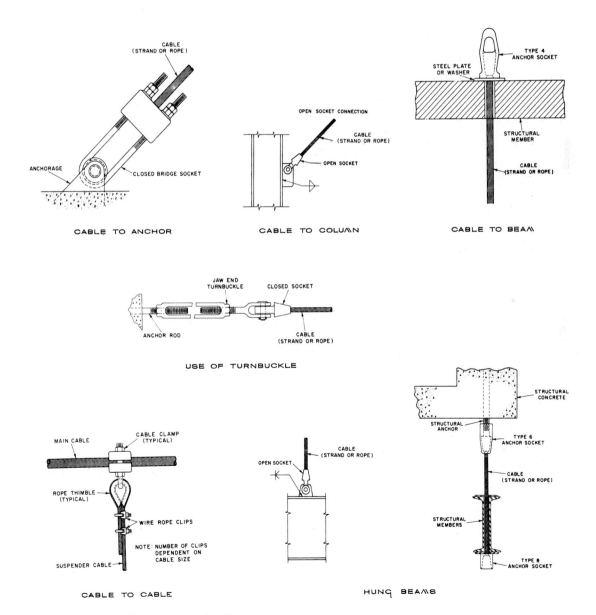

Figure 14 *Typical cable connection details.*

In addition to the usual static considerations of strength and stability, a cable-supported structure must also be designed for dynamic considerations. Just as a violin string will vibrate when plucked, a steel cable will oscillate under forces such as wind, moving loads, or earth movements. Such oscillations are called *flutter* and must be controlled by *damping*. Damping can be accomplished by a heavy, rigid roof; by connection to a secondary set of cables using *struts*; or by direct connection to a secondary set of cables in a grid pattern. Notice how flutter is solved in each of the following examples. Also notice the various methods of anchoring the cables: by ground anchors, by a continuous structural member, or by the geometry of the structure itself.

Single curved roof (Figure 15). This roof of parallel cables is typically designed with a ratio of vertical sag to horizontal span of 1:8–1:9 for spans of 100′–200′. To decrease flutter that would occur when the wind frequency matches one of the natural frequencies of the cables, a heavyweight roof deck must be specified. The cables, spaced 4′–12′ oc, assume a parabolic shape when loaded uniformly as in the alternate design. The roof deck could also be suspended below the cables rather than resting directly upon them.

Single curved roof with secondary cables (Figure 16). The secondary cables are tensioned to provide damping of the primary cables. Thus flutter is eliminated and a lightweight roof deck can

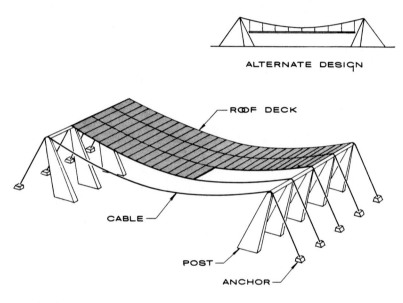

ALTERNATE DESIGN

ROOF DECK

CABLE

POST

ANCHOR

Figure 15   *Single curved cable roof.*

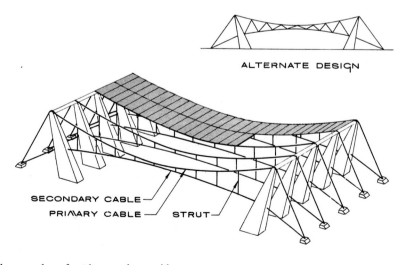

ALTERNATE DESIGN

SECONDARY CABLE

PRIMARY CABLE   STRUT

Figure 16   *Single curved roof with secondary cables.*

be used. Cables are spaced 4′–8′ oc. The sag-to-span ratio is 1:10–1:11 for spans of 150′–300′.

Compression ring with single set of cables (Figure 17). The radial cables connect the interior tension ring to the surrounding compression ring. The roof deck rests directly on the cables. To reduce flutter, the cables are prestressed against a

concrete deck. The sag-to-span ratio is 1:9–1:10 for spans of 150′–300′.

Compression ring with double set of cables (Figure 18). The roof deck rests on the primary cables, with rigid struts separating the primary and secondary cables. The secondary cables have a tension different from the primary cables to pre-

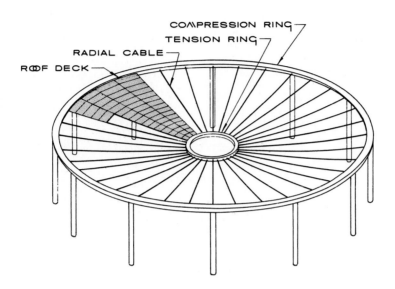

Figure 17   *Compression ring with single set of cables.*

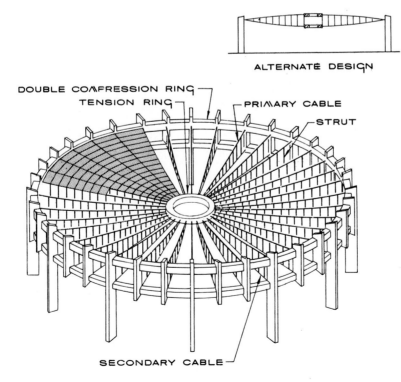

Figure 18   *Compression ring with double set of cables.*

vent flutter. The typical sag-to-span ratio is only 1:12–1:15. Large spans of 200′–400′ are common.

Compression ring with cable grid (Figure 19). The concave primary cables and convex secondary cables are in the same surface and tensioned to press against each other. This can efficiently damp the cables to prevent flutter so that a lightweight roof deck can be used. The sag-to-span ratio is 1:12–1:15 for primary cables and 1:25–1:75 for secondary cables at 150′–300′ spans.

Warped roof formed by cables (Figure 20). An infinite variety of warped roofs can be formed by a grid of primary and secondary cables. The warped surface illustrated is a hyperbolic paraboloid. Both primary and secondary cables connecting *adjacent* framing members are parabolic in shape.

Warped roof formed by beams (Figure 21). The hyperbolic paraboloid roof formed by parabolic cables in Figure 20 can also be formed by straight roof beams connecting *opposite* framing members.

* This warped surface is termed a *hyperbolic paraboloid* because a plane perpendicular to the ground can cut a *parabolic* intersection with the roof, and a plane parallel to the ground can cut a *hyperbolic* intersection with the roof.

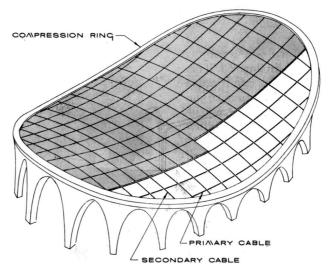

Figure 19   *Compression ring with cable grid.*

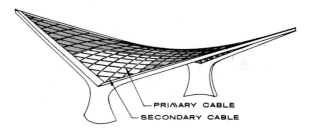

Figure 20   *Warped roof formed by cables.*

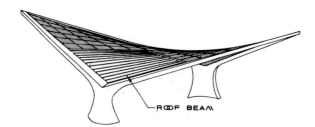

Figure 21   *Warped roof formed by beams.*

Boundary cable (Figure 22). Strong boundary cables can replace the tension element in grid systems. Typical sag-to-span ratios are 1:10–1:12 for primary cables and 1:8–1:12 for secondary cables at 150'–300' spans.

Cable-supported roof (Figure 23). Rigid, cantilevered roofs hung from cables are termed *supported* roofs rather than *suspended* roofs. The cable tension keeps the cables almost free of sag. Spans are typically 50'–150'.

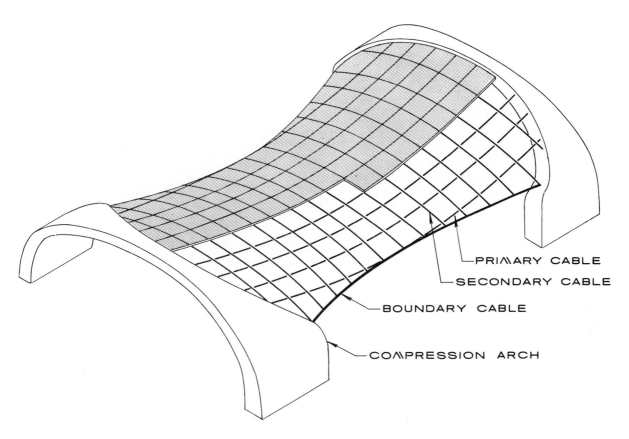

Figure 22   *Boundary cable roof.*

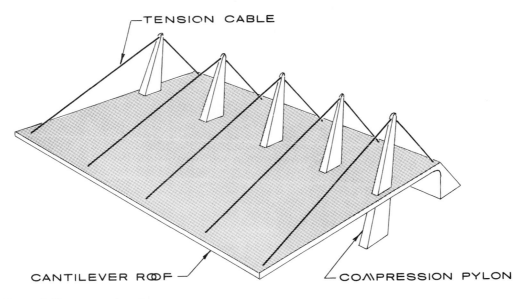

Figure 23   *Cable-supported roof.*

CONSTRUCTION

The construction of a cable roof is a rapid operation once the materials have been assembled. The steps in the erection of a typical double compression ring roof (similar to Figure 18) are as follows:

1. Exterior walls are constructed, including the concrete or steel compression rings.
2. A temporary scaffold is erected at the center of the building to support the steel tension ring.
3. Cables are delivered to the site, cut to proper length with the end fittings attached.
4. With the aid of a truck crane or movable scaffold, the cables are anchored to the tension and compression rings.
5. The primary and secondary cables are jacked apart, and the vertical struts inserted and clamped in place.
6. The cables are further tensioned to predetermined stresses* by use of turnbuckles. The primary cable stress must be different from the secondary cable stress to obtain different natural frequencies to damp vibration. It is important that all cables remain in tension under *all* loading conditions.
7. Diagonal cross-bracing is installed by clamping rods to cables and struts.
8. Light-gauge steel roof deck is bolted directly over the primary cables, using intermediate cross-purlins when the span is too great for the deck itself. Roof topping is then applied to the roof deck.

* Cable stress is determined by measuring elongation by mechanical or electronic devices.

EXAMPLES

Pan-American Terminal (Figure 24). This 528' × 422' elliptical roof is cable-supported, permitting a deep overhang to shelter passengers while boarding. The cantilever extends 114' beyond the walls. Cables are mounted in groups of six strands of $1\frac{1}{2}''$-diameter each. Double-thickness zinc coating on the exposed steel strands was specified to protect against corrosion.

Cables pass over saddle on post

Cantilevered roof on concrete columns

Night view of completed terminal

Aerial view of completed terminal

Figure 24   *Pan-American Terminal, John F. Kennedy International Airport, New York.*

Villita Assembly Hall (Figure 25). Two hundred galvanized strands of $\frac{11}{15}$"-diameter connect the steel tension and compression rings. The circular roof is 132' in diameter.

Academic-Athletic Building (Figure 26). The 300'-diameter domed roof is supported by steel trusses. These exert an outward thrust on the walls which is balanced by the inward pull of seventy-two strands of $1\frac{1}{8}$"-diameter.

Nicholson Pavilion (Figure 27). This field house at Central Washington State College measures 150' × 390'. Galvanized strands of $\frac{15}{16}$"-diameter support laminated timber girders.

Swaged clevis fastened to tension ring

Aerial view of construction

View of Villita Hall during construction

Completed exterior of hall

Completed interior of hall

Figure 25   *Villita Assembly Hall, San Antonio, Texas.*

Great Flight Cage (Figure 28). This aviary at the Smithsonian's National Zoological Park is constructed of six parabolic steel arches inclined 30° from vertical, surrounding a 90′ steel mast. Seventy-two steel cables stabilize the arches by connecting them to the mast. The cables also extend from the arches to the concrete foundation wall. Wall and roof covering is vinyl-covered steel wire mesh.

Other examples of cable roof structures appearing in this book are Dulles International Airport Terminal and Yale University Hockey Rink (both on page 101).

STUDY QUESTIONS

1. Distinguish between:
   a. Steel strand and steel rope
   b. Socketing and swaging
   c. Parabola and catenary
2. Why are cable roof structures economical for large spans but not economical for short spans?
3. Describe briefly each term:
   a. Prestretching
   b. Flutter
   c. Brooming
4. With the aid of a sketch, describe each cable roof:
   a. Single curved
   b. Compression ring with single set of cables
   c. Compression ring with a grid of cables
   d. Warped roof
   e. Boundary cable roof
   f. Cable-supported roof

LABORATORY PROBLEMS

1. Draw the cable roof details for the following connections:
   a. ½″ cable to anchor
   b. ½″ cable to W 10 × 60 steel column
   c. ½″ vertical suspender cable hanging from 1″ main cable
   d. ½″ vertical suspender cable supporting a horizontal S 8 × 23 steel beam
2. Draw the cable roof details for:
   a. The building assigned by your instructor
   b. Your original building design

Figure 26 *Academic-Athletic Building, Bowling Green, Kentucky.*

Figure 27 *Nicholson Pavilion, Ellensburg, Washington.*

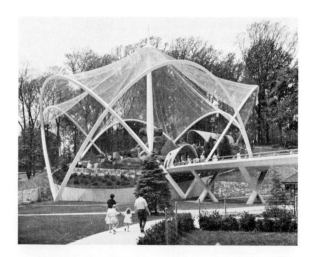

Figure 28 *Great Flight Cage, Washington, D.C.*

Appendices

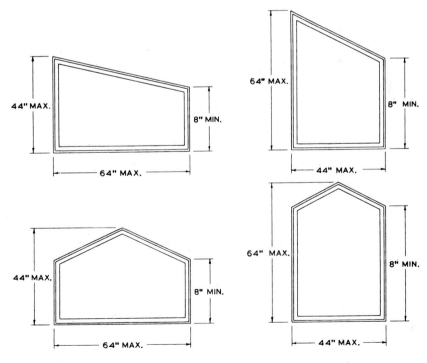

PELLA TRAPEZOIDAL WINDOW – TABLE OF SIZES

A / Plans of a Two-Story Residence and a Solar A-Frame

A single story contemporary home* designed for Mr. and Mrs. A has been used as an example throughout the preceding chapters. In addition, the plans of a split-level home**—also of contemporary design—for Mr. and Mrs. M were used to illustrate dimensioning in metric units in Chapter 11.

To provide a wider base of comparison, plans of two quite different homes follow. The Z residence is a two-story traditional house in an English garrison styling. The S residence is an A-framed solar house*** with direct passive, indirect passive, and active solar features.

* Courtesy of Mr. and Mrs. Donald W. Hamer, State College, Pennsylvania

** Courtesy of Professor Emeritus M. Eisenberg, The Pennsylvania State University

*** Courtesy of Professors Richard E. and Mary J. Kummer, The Pennsylvania State University

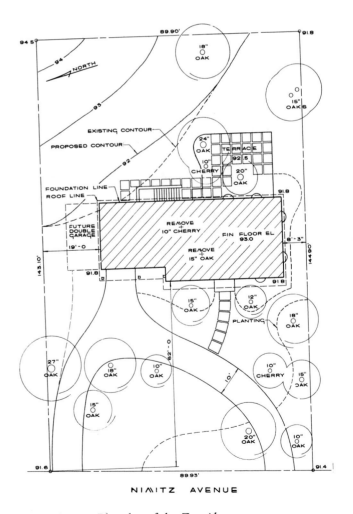

Figure 1   *Plot plan of the Z residence.*

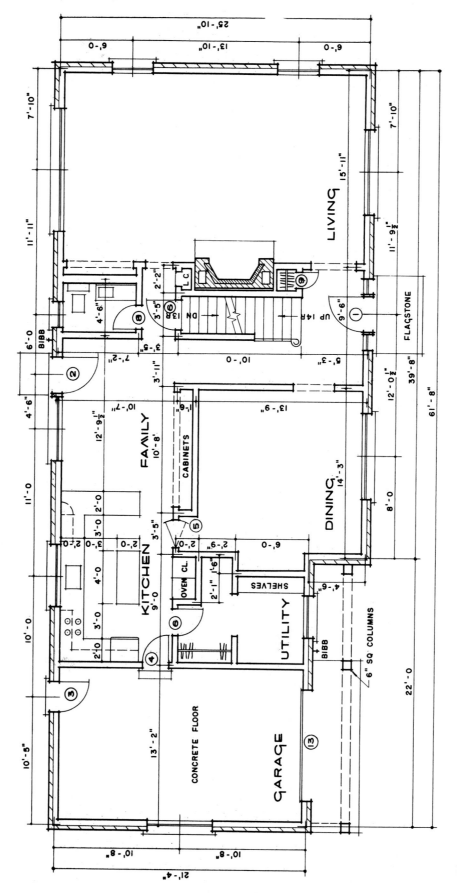

Figure 2 *First-floor plan of the Z residence.*

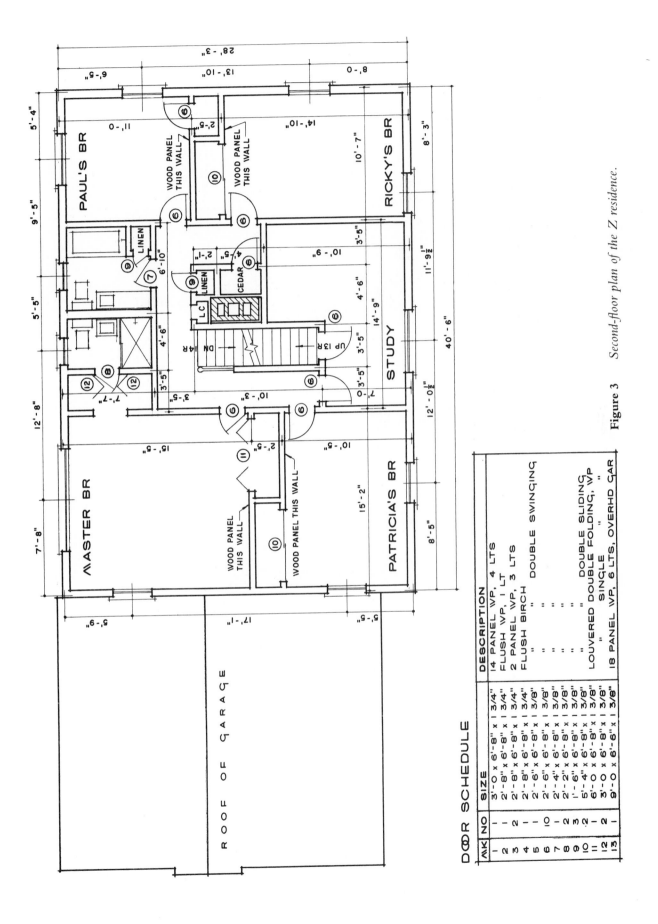

Figure 3 *Second-floor plan of the Z residence.*

DOOR SCHEDULE

MK NO	NO	SIZE	DESCRIPTION
1	1	3'-0 × 6'-8" × 1 3/4"	14 PANEL WP, 4 LTS
2	1	2'-8" × 6'-8" × 1 3/4"	FLUSH WP, 1 LT
3	1	2'-8" × 6'-8" × 1 3/4"	2 PANEL WP, 3 LTS
4	1	2'-8" × 6'-8" × 1 3/8"	FLUSH BIRCH
5	10	2'-6" × 6'-8" × 1 3/8"	" " DOUBLE SWINGING
6	1	2'-4" × 6'-8" × 1 3/8"	" "
7	2	2'-2" × 6'-8" × 1 3/8"	" "
8	3	1'-6" × 6'-8" × 1 3/8"	" " DOUBLE SLIDING
9	2	6'-0 × 6'-8" × 1 3/8"	LOUVERED DOUBLE FOLDING, WP
10	1	6'-0 × 6'-8" × 1 3/8"	" SINGLE " "
11	2	3'-0 × 6'-8" × 1 3/8"	" "
12	2	3'-0 × 6'-8" × 1 3/8"	" "
13	1	9'-0 × 6'-6" × 1 3/8"	18 PANEL WP, 6 LTS, OVERHD GAR

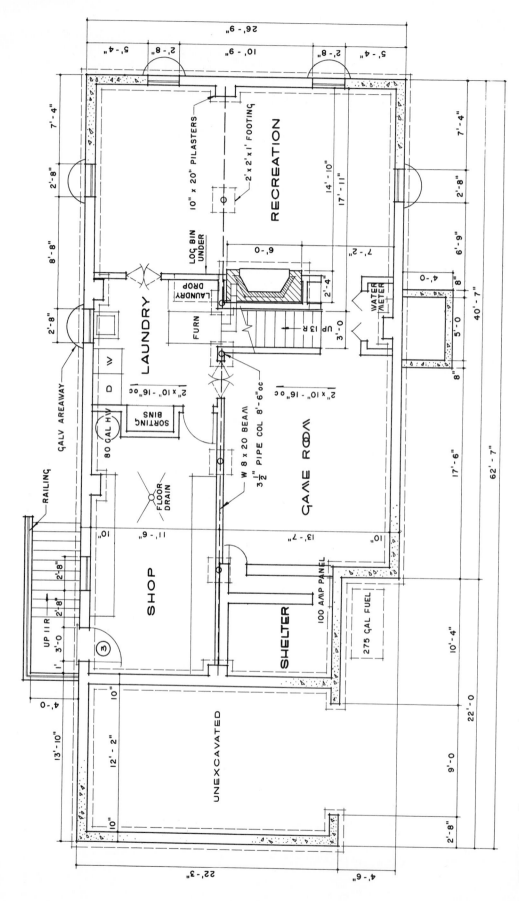

Figure 4 *Basement plan of Z residence.*

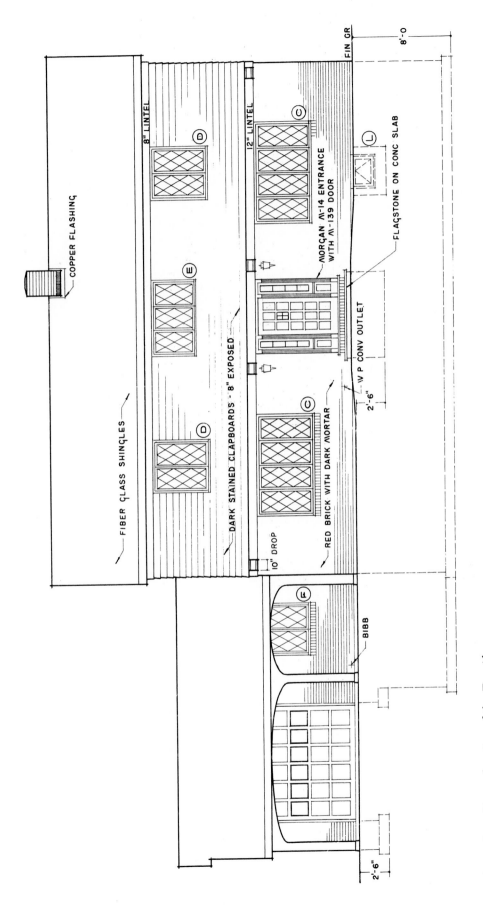

Figure 5 *Front elevation of the Z residence.*

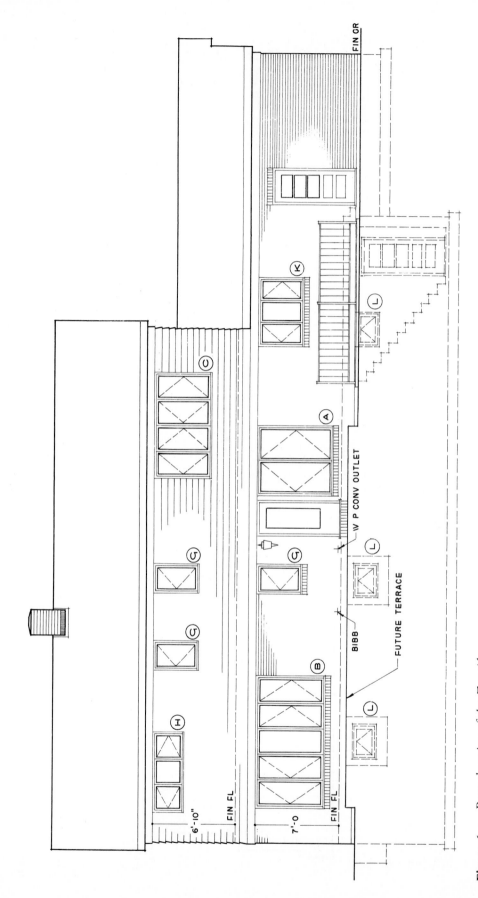

Figure 6 *Rear elevation of the Z residence.*

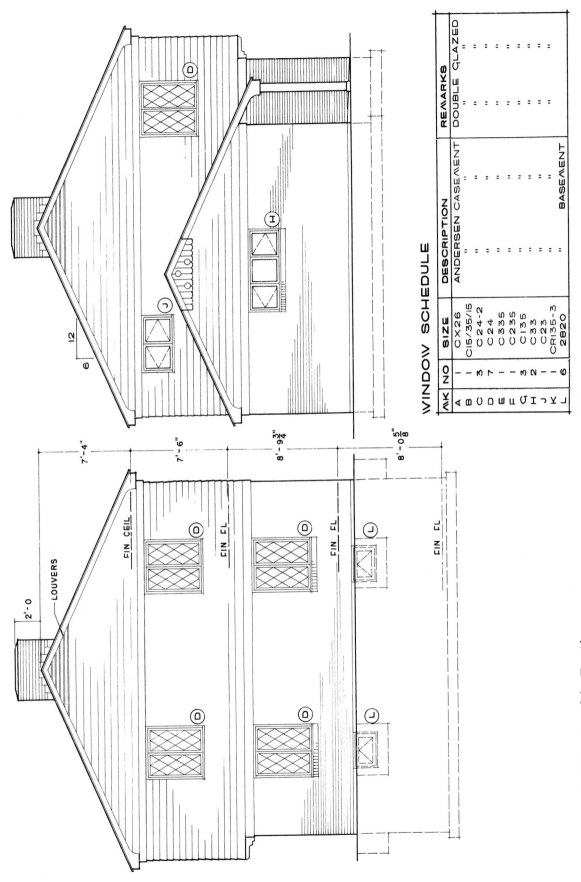

WINDOW SCHEDULE

MK	NO	SIZE	DESCRIPTION	REMARKS
A	1	CX26	ANDERSEN CASEMENT	DOUBLE GLAZED
B		C15/35/15	"	"
C	3	C24-2	"	"
D	7	C24	"	"
E	1	C335	"	"
F	1	C235	"	"
G	3	C135	"	"
H	2	C33	"	"
I	1	C23	"	"
J	1	CRI35-3	"	"
L	6	2820	BASEMENT	"

Figure 7 *End elevations of the Z residence.*

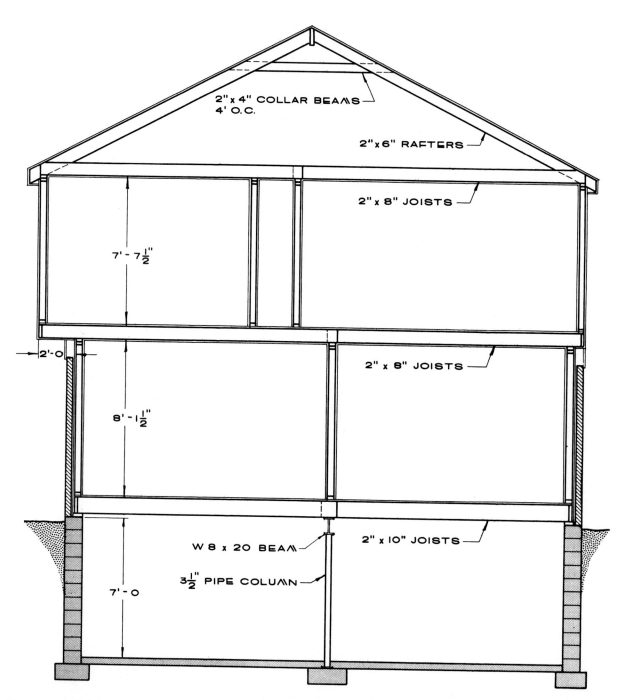

Figure 8 *Structural section of the Z residence.*

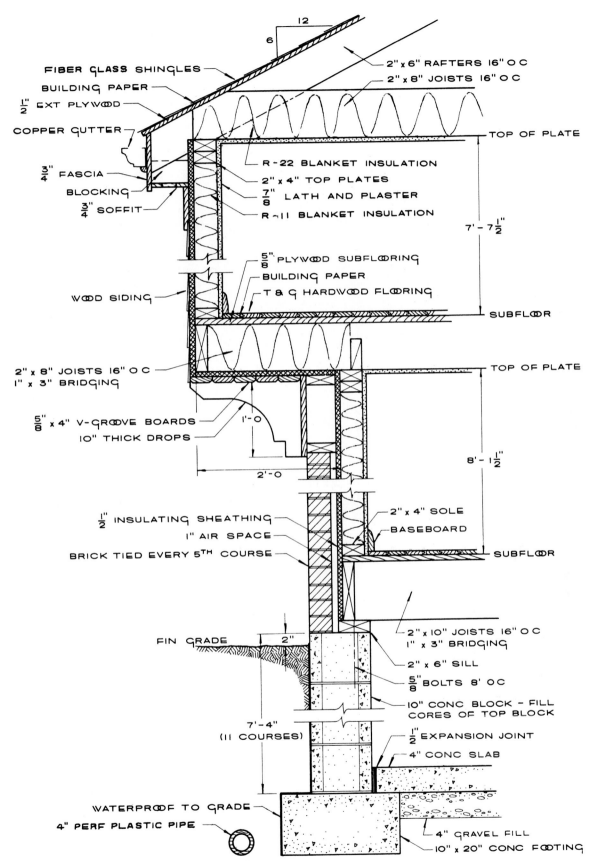

Figure 9 *Typical wall section of the Z residence.*

FIBER GLASS SHINGLES
BUILDING PAPER
$\frac{1}{2}$" EXT PLYWOOD
COPPER GUTTER

12
6

2" x 6" RAFTERS 16" O C
2" x 8" JOISTS 16" O C

TOP OF PLATE

R-22 BLANKET INSULATION
2" x 4" TOP PLATES
$\frac{7}{8}$" LATH AND PLASTER
R-11 BLANKET INSULATION

$\frac{3}{4}$" FASCIA
BLOCKING
$\frac{3}{4}$" SOFFIT

7' - 7$\frac{1}{2}$"

$\frac{5}{8}$" PLYWOOD SUBFLOORING
BUILDING PAPER
T & G HARDWOOD FLOORING

WOOD SIDING

SUBFLOOR

2" x 8" JOISTS 16" O C
1" x 3" BRIDGING

TOP OF PLATE

$\frac{5}{8}$" x 4" V-GROOVE BOARDS
10" THICK DROPS

1'-0

8' - 1$\frac{1}{2}$"

2'-0

$\frac{1}{2}$" INSULATING SHEATHING
1" AIR SPACE
BRICK TIED EVERY 5TH COURSE

2" x 4" SOLE
BASEBOARD

SUBFLOOR

2" x 10" JOISTS 16" O C
1" x 3" BRIDGING

FIN GRADE   2"

2" x 6" SILL
$\frac{5}{8}$" BOLTS 8' O C
10" CONC BLOCK - FILL
CORES OF TOP BLOCK

7'-4"
(11 COURSES)

$\frac{1}{2}$" EXPANSION JOINT
4" CONC SLAB

WATERPROOF TO GRADE
4" PERF PLASTIC PIPE

4" GRAVEL FILL
10" x 20" CONC FOOTING

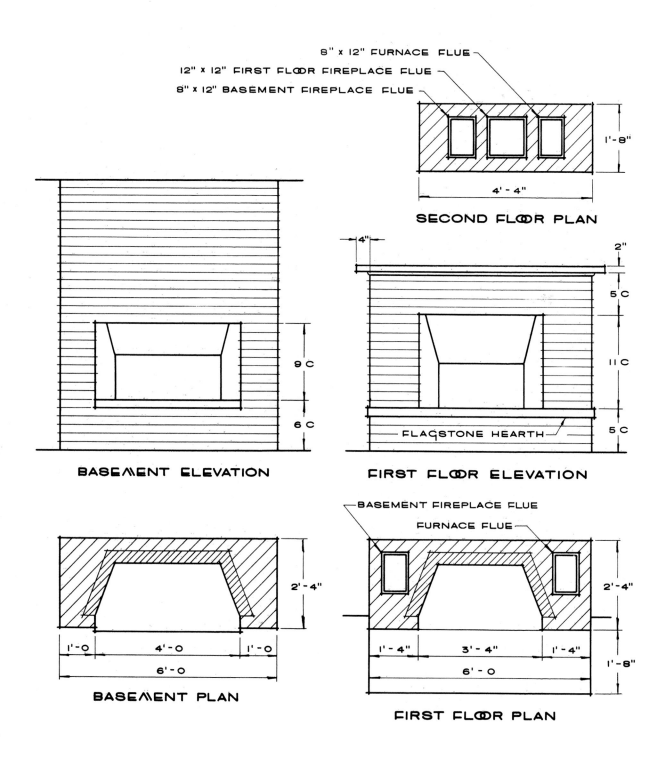

Figure 10 *Fireplace details of the Z residence.*

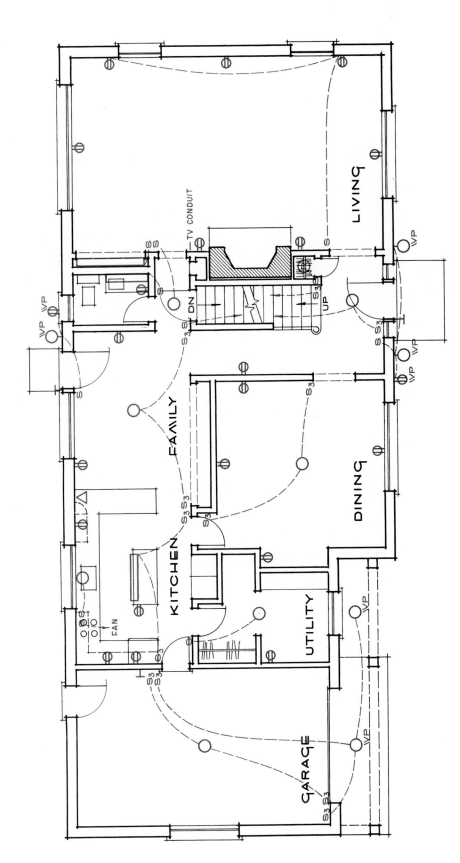

Figure 11 *Electrical plan of the Z residence.*

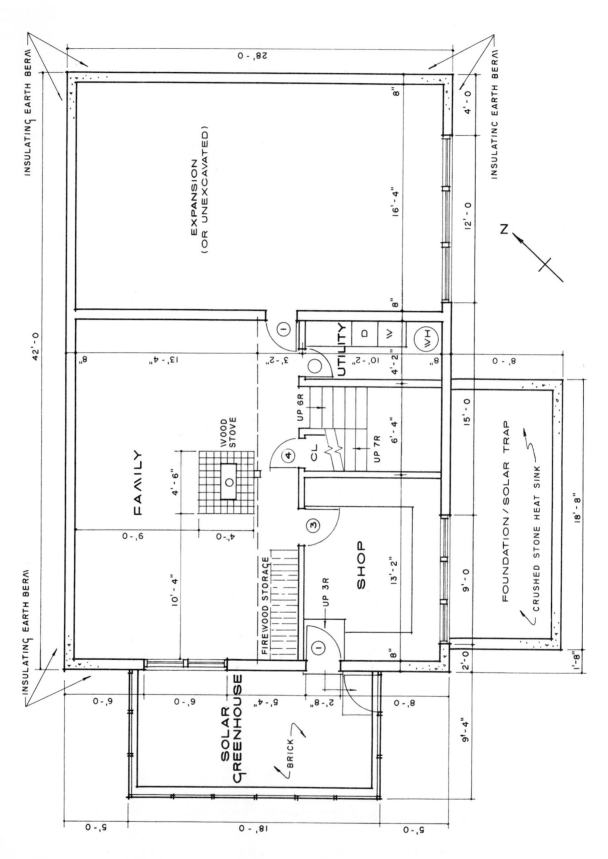

Figure 12 *Basement level of the solar S residence.*

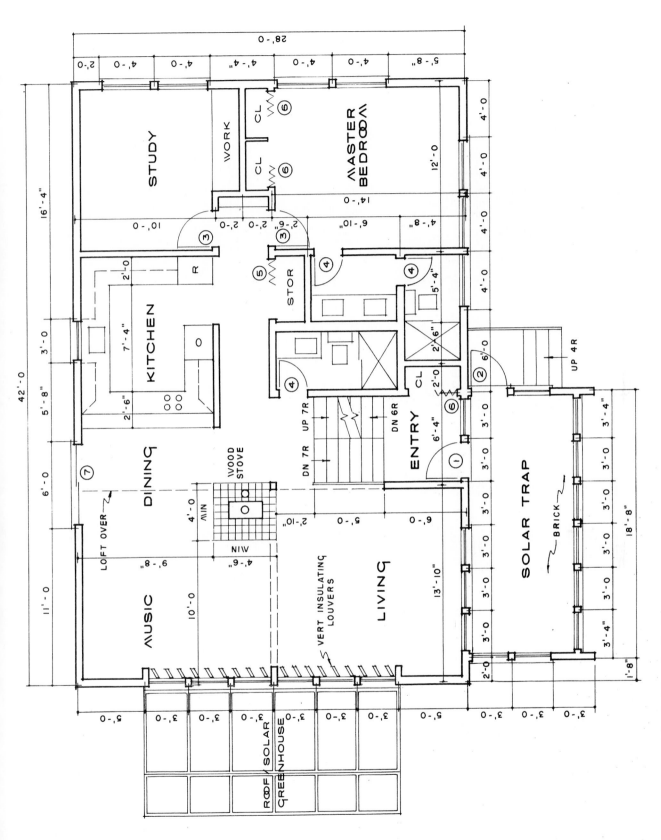

Figure 13 *Living level of the solar S residence.*

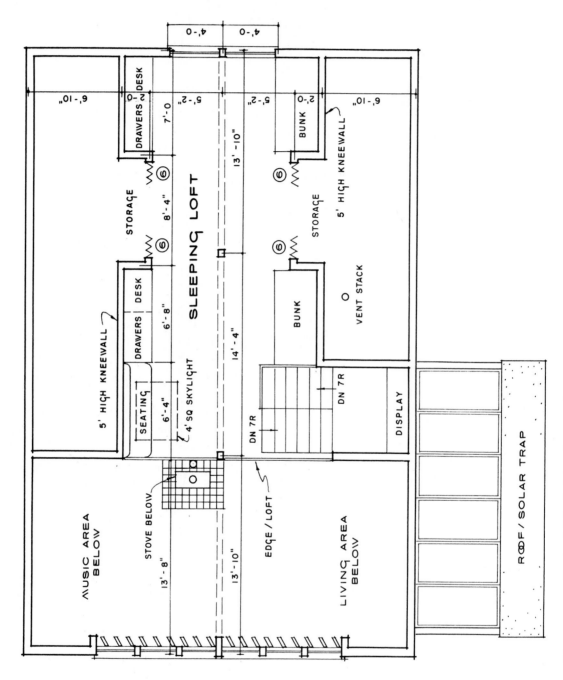

Figure 14 *Sleeping loft level of the solar S residence.*

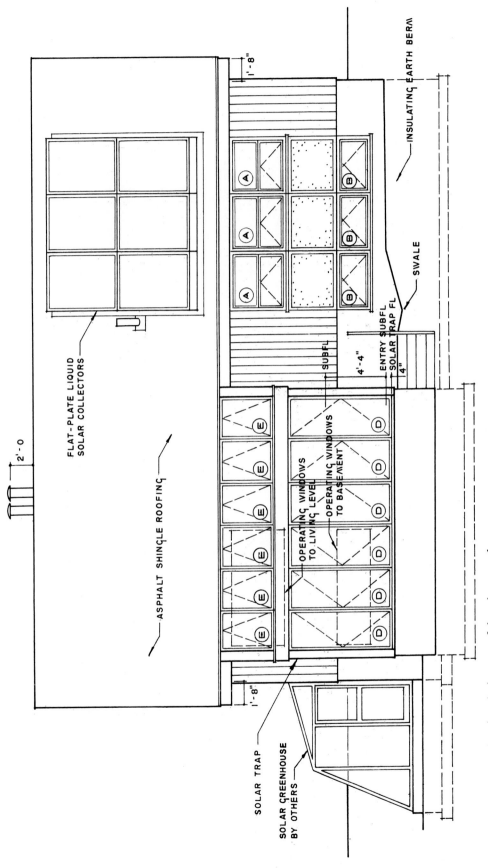

Figure 15 *Front (southeast) elevation of the solar S residence.*

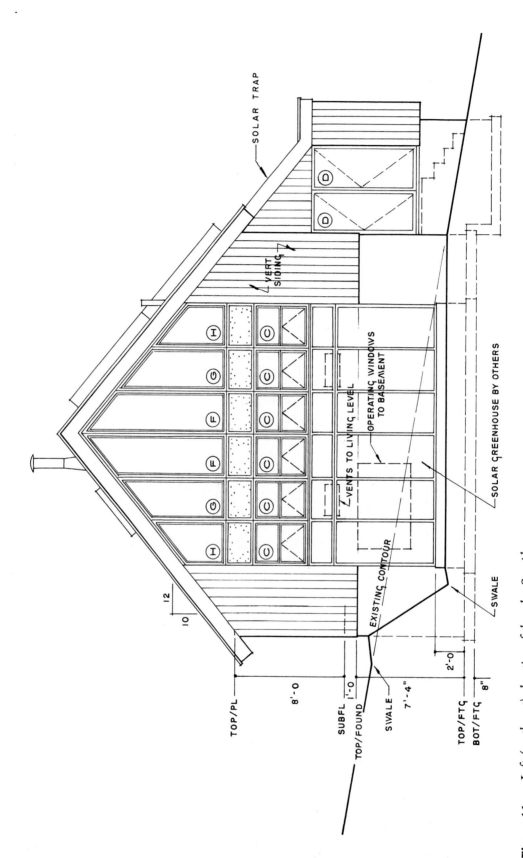

Figure 16 *Left (southwest) elevation of the solar S residence.*

B / Windows

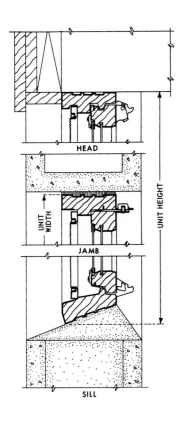

BASEMENT WINDOW IN
CONCRETE BLOCK WALL

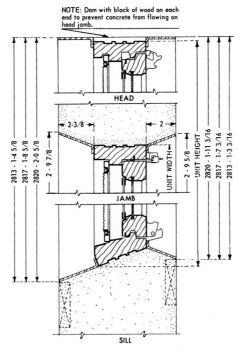

NOTE: Dam with block of wood on each end to prevent concrete from flowing on head jamb.

HEAD

JAMB

SILL

2813 - 1-4 5/8
2817 - 1-8 5/8
2820 - 2-0 5/8

2 - 9 7/8

UNIT HEIGHT

2820 - 1-11 3/16
2817 - 1-7 3/16
2813 - 1-3 3/16

2-3/8   2

2 - 9 5/8

UNIT WIDTH

NOTE: Split Steel Bucks are shown in these details for the purpose of positioning window in wall form. Sash and screen must be removed from frame when using split bucks in order to bolt assembly together and to drive nails into wall form. Temporary cleats shown in sill sections are for resting assembled buck in position while securing to wall form. Only one cleat needed depending on whether inner or outer wall form is erected first. Cleat must be removed after split buck assembly is nailed to form.

BASEMENT WINDOW IN
POURED CONCRETE WALL

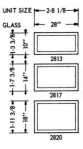

UNIT SIZE ← 2-8 1/8
GLASS ← 28"

1-3 3/8   10"
2813

1-7 3/8   14"
2817

1-11 3/8   18"
2820

MODULAR SIZES: Fit typical 8 x 16 inch block walls for masonry openings 2 blocks wide by 2, 2-1/2, or 3 blocks high. All three sizes glazed one light only.

ANDERSEN BASEMENT
WINDOW - TABLE OF SIZES

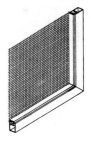

Corner section of aluminum framed screen.

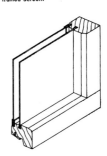

Corner section of sash with Removable Double Glazing panel applied.

Figure 1   *Andersen basement window.*

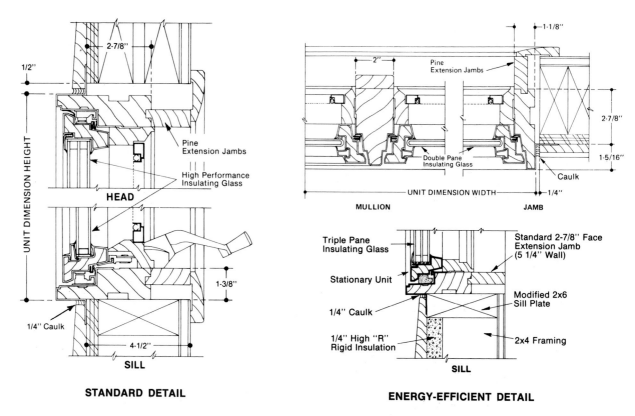

Figure 2 *Andersen casement windows—tracing details.*

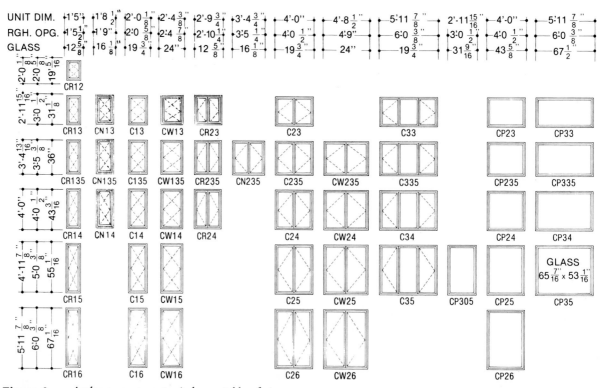

Figure 3 *Andersen casement windows—table of sizes.*

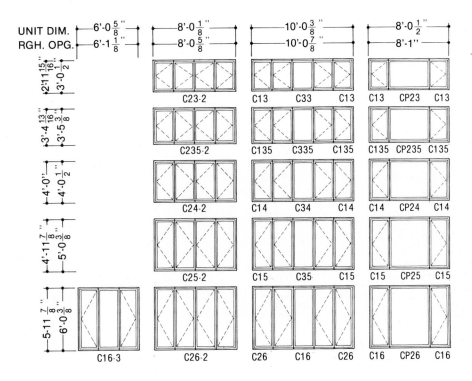

Figure 4   *Andersen casement window combinations–tables of sizes, C series.*

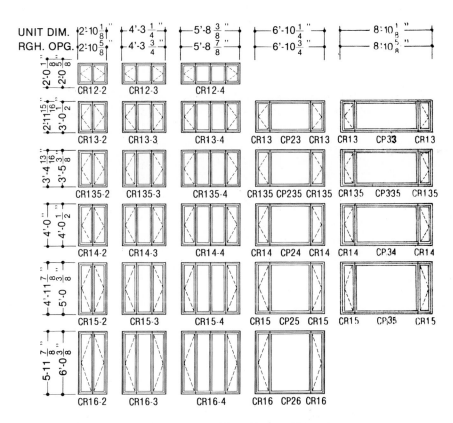

Figure 5   *Andersen casement window combinations–tables of sizes, CR series.*

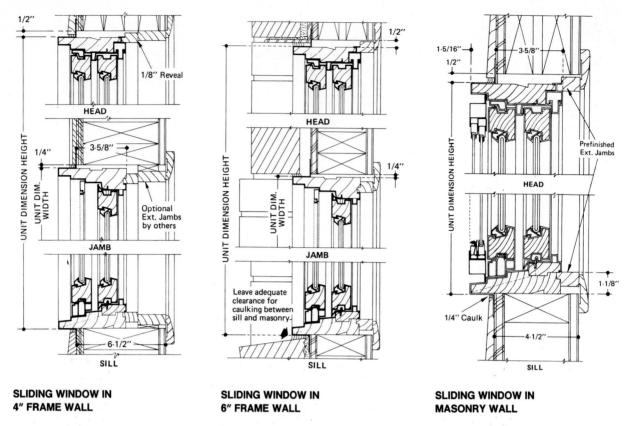

Figure 6   *Andersen sliding windows—tracing details.*

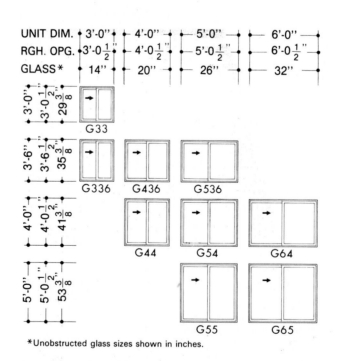

*Unobstructed glass sizes shown in inches.

Figure 7   *Andersen sliding windows—table of sizes.*

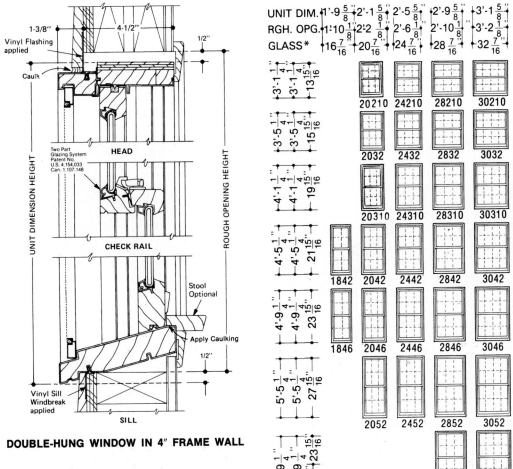

*Unobstructed glass sizes shown in inches.
Glass height for one sash only.

Figure 9   *Andersen double-hung window—table of sizes.*

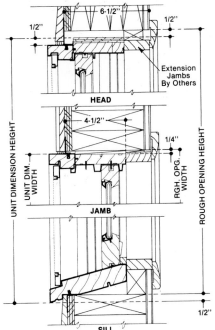

DOUBLE-HUNG WINDOW IN 4″ FRAME WALL

DOUBLE-HUNG WINDOW IN 6″ FRAME WALL

Figure 8   *Andersen double-hung window—tracing detail.*

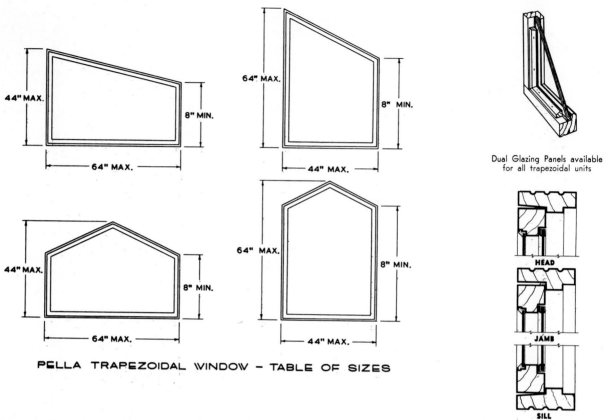

Dual Glazing Panels available
for all trapezoidal units

PELLA TRAPEZOIDAL WINDOW - TABLE OF SIZES

Figure 10 *Trapezoidal fixed windows.*

PELLA TRACING DETAIL

C / Doors

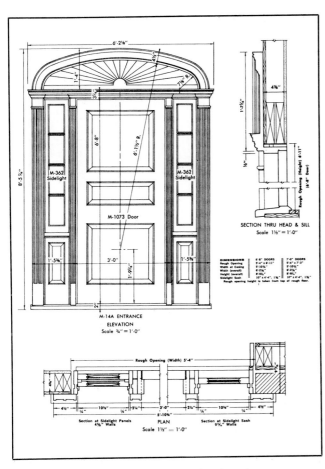

Figure 1 *A Morgan entrance—details and sizes.*

Units Made in Sizes as Shown:

Thickness	Width	Height
1¾″	× 2′-6″ ×	6′-8″
1¾″	× 2′-8″ ×	6′-8″
1¾″	× 3′-0 ×	6′-8″
1¾″	× 3′-0 ×	7′-0

Some doors available in additional sizes.

M—Designates Pine Doors
F—Designates Fir Doors

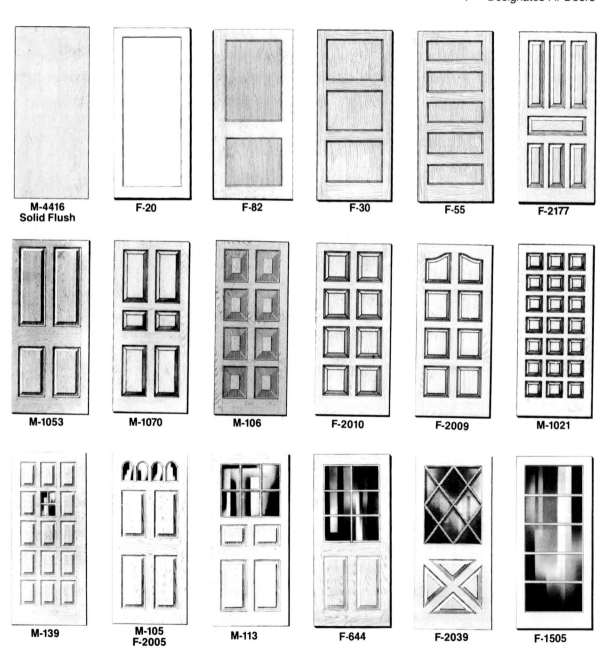

Figure 2 *Some Morgan exterior door styles.*

Units Made in 6'-6", 6'-8", and 8'-0 Heights and in Widths as Shown:

2-door Units (M-2FD)		4-door Units (M-4FD)	
Width of Doors	Jamb Opening Width	Width of Doors	Jamb Opening Width
11$\frac{11}{16}$"	2'-0	8$\frac{11}{16}$"	3'-0
1'-1$\frac{11}{16}$"	2'-4"	11$\frac{11}{16}$"	4'-0
1'-2$\frac{11}{16}$"	2'-6"	1'-2$\frac{11}{16}$"	5'-0
1'-3$\frac{11}{16}$"	2'-8"	1'-5$\frac{11}{16}$"	6'-0
1'-5$\frac{11}{16}$"	3'-0		

M—Designates Pine Doors
F—Designates Fir Doors

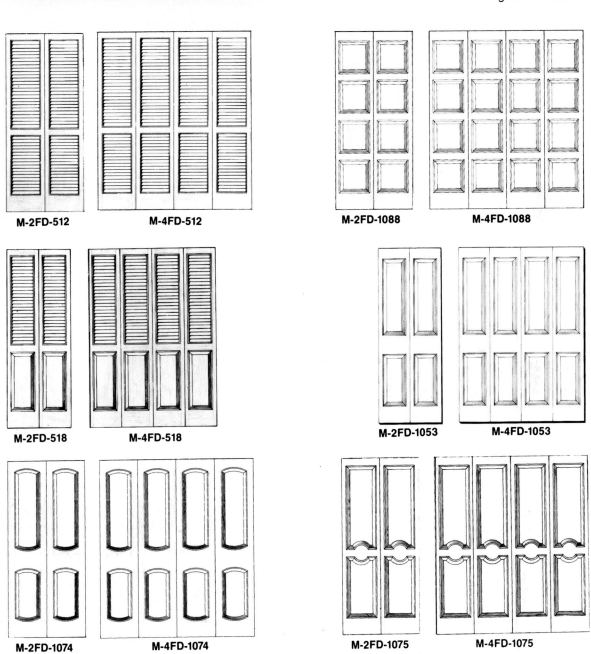

M-2FD-512   M-4FD-512   M-2FD-1088   M-4FD-1088

M-2FD-518   M-4FD-518   M-2FD-1053   M-4FD-1053

M-2FD-1074   M-4FD-1074   M-2FD-1075   M-4FD-1075

Figure 3 *Some Morgan folding interior door styles.*

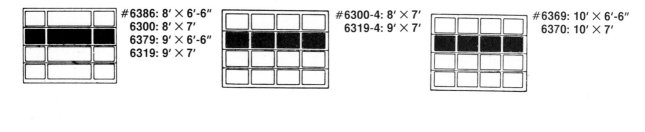

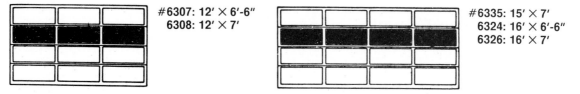

1⅜″ SECTIONAL DOORS WITH EXTENSION SPRING HARDWARE

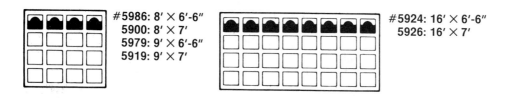

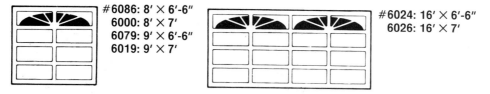

1⅜″ DECORATOR SECTIONAL DOORS

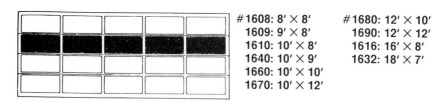

1⅜″ LIGHT COMMERCIAL SECTIONAL DOORS WITH TORSION SPRING HARDWARE

Figure 4 *Some Frantz sectional garage doors—styles and sizes.*

D / Abbreviations

Abbreviations must often be used by architectural drafters to fit notes into the available space. However, a list of the abbreviations used should be included on each set of drawings so that the meanings of the abbreviations are perfectly clear to all reading the drawings. The abbreviations shown in this section have been approved by architectural and engineering societies. They are based upon the following rules:

1. Capitals are used almost universally
2. Periods are used only when necessary to avoid a misunderstanding (like the use of *IN.* in place of *IN*)
3. Spaces between letters are used only when necessary to clarify the abbreviation (such as *CU FT* in place of *CUFT*)
4. The same abbreviation may be used for the singular and plural

Abbreviation	ABBREV
Acoustic	ACST
Acoustical plaster	ACST PLAS
Actual	ACT.
Addition	ADD.
Adhesive	ADH
Aggregate	AGGR
Air conditioning	AIR COND
Alternating current	AC
Aluminum	AL or ALUM
American Institute of Architects	AIA
American Institute of Steel Construction	AISC
American National Standards Institute	ANSI
American Society for Testing Materials	ASTM

American Society of Heating, Refrigerating, and Air Conditioning Engineers	ASHRAE
American Standards Association	ASA
American wire gauge	AWG
Amount	AMT
Ampere	A or AMP
Anchor bolt	AB
Angle	⌐
Apartment	APT
Approved	APP
Approximate	APPROX
Architect, architectural	ARCH
Architectural terra-cotta	ATC
Area	A
Asphalt	ASPH
Assemble	ASSEM
Assembly	ASSY
Associate, association	ASSOC
At	@
Atmospheric pressure	ATM PRESS
Automatic	AUTO
Avenue	AVE
Average	AVG
Balcony	BALC
Barrel, barrels	BBL
Basement	BASMT
Bathroom	B
Beaded one side	B 1S
Beam	BM
Bedroom	BR
Bench mark	BM
Better	BTR
Between	BET.
Beveled	BEV
Blocking	BLKG
Blower	BLO
Board	BD
Board feet	BD FT or FBM

Board measure	BM	Countersink	CSK
Book shelves	BK SH	Courses	C
Bottom	BOT	Cover	COV
Boulevard	BLVD	Cross section	X-SECT
Bracket	BRKT	Cubic	CU
Brass	BR	Cubic feet per minute	CFM
British thermal unit	BTU	Cubic foot, feet	CU FT
Bronze	BRZ	Cubic inch, inches	CU IN
Broom closet	BC	Cubic yard, yards	CU YD
Brown & Sharpe gauge	B&S GA	Cylinder	CYL
Building	BLDG		
Built-in	BLT-IN		
Bulletin board	BB	Damper	DMPR
Button	BUT.	Decibel	DB
Buzzer	BUZ	Deep, depth	DP
By	× (as 2′ × 4′)	Degree	° or DEG
		Detail	DET
		Diagram	DIAG
Cabinet	CAB.	Diameter	φ or DIA
Calking	CLKG	Dimension	DIM
Candela	cd	Dining room	DR
Candlepower	CP	Direct current	DC
Carpenter	CARP.	Dishwasher	DW
Casing	CSG	Distance	DIST
Cast iron	CI	Ditto	" or DO
Catch basin	CB	Division	DIV
Ceiling	CLG	Door	DR
Cement	CEM	Dozen	DOZ
Cement floor	CEM FL	Double-hung	DH
Celsius	C	Dowel	DWL
Center	CTR	Down	DN
Center line	CL or ₵	Downspout	DS
Center matched	CM	Drain	D or DR
Center to center	OC	Drawing	DWG
Centimeter, centimeters	cm	Drawn	DR
Ceramic	CER	Dressed and matched	D&M
Cesspool	CP	Drinking fountain	DF
Chamfer	CHAM	Dryer	D
Change	CHG	Dry well	DW
Channel	C or [(old designation)	Duplicate	DUP
Check	CHK		
Cinder block	CIN BL		
Circle	CIR		
Circuit	CKT	Each	EA
Circuit breaker	CIR BKR	East	E
Class	CL	Edge grain	EG
Clean-out	CO	Elbow	ELL
Clear	CLR	Electric	ELEC
Closet	C or CL or CLO	Elevation	EL, ELEV
Coefficient	COEF	Elevator	ELEV
Cold water	CW	Emergency	EMER
Column	COL	Enclosure	ENCL
Combination	COMB.	Engineer	ENGR
Common	COM	Entrance	ENT
Company	CO	Equipment	EQUIP
Concrete	CONC	Equivalent direct radiation	EDR
Concrete block	CONC B	Estimate	EST
Concrete floor	CONC FL	Excavate	EXC
Concrete masonry unit	CMU	Extension	EXT
Construction	CONST	Exterior	EXT
Construction Specifications Institute	CSI	Extra heavy	XH or XHVY
Contractor	CONTR		
Copper	COP or CU	Fabricate	FAB
Counter	CTR	Face to face	F to F

Family room	FAM R	Inch, inches	" or IN.
Fahrenheit	F	Information	INFO
Feet	' or FT	Inside diameter	ID
Feet board measure	FBM	Insulation	INSUL
Feet per minute	FPM	Interior	INT
Feet per second	FPS	Iron pin	IP
Figure	FIG.		
Finish	FIN.		
Finish all over	FAO	Joint	JT
Finished floor	FIN FL	Junior beam	M or JR (old designation)
Fire brick	FBRK		
Fire extinguisher	F EXT		
Fire hose	FH	Kalamein	KAL
Fireproof	FP	Kelvin	K
Fireproof self-closing	FPSC	Kilogram	kg
Fitting	FTG	Kilowatt	kw
Fixture	FIX.	Kitchen	K
Flange	FLG	Kitchen cabinet	KC
Flashing	FL	Kitchen sink	KS
Floor	FL		
Floor drain	FD		
Flooring	FLG	Laboratory	LAB
Fluorescent	FLUOR	Ladder	LAD.
Foot	' or FT	Landing	LDG
Footing	FTG	Latitude	LAT
Foundation	FDN	Laundry	LAU
Free-on-board	FOB	Laundry chute	LC
Front	FR	Lavatory	LAV
Fuel oil	FO	Leader	LDR
Full size	FS	Leader drain	LD
Furnace	FURN	Left	L
		Left hand	LH
		Length	LGTH
		Level	LEV
Gallon, gallons	GAL	Library	LIB
Galvanized	GALV	Light	LT
Galvanized iron	GI	Limestone	LS
Gauge	GA	Linear feet	LIN FT
Glass	GL	Linen closet	L CL
Glass block	GL BL	Lining	LNG
Glue-laminated	GLUELAM	Linoleum	LINO
Government	GOVT	Living room	LR
Grade	GR	Long	LG
Grating	GRTG	Lumber	LBR
Gypsum	GYP		
		M-shape steel beam	M or JR (old designation)
Hall	H	Machine	MACH
Hardware	HDW	Manufacture, manufacturer	MFR
Hardwood	HDWD	Manufactured	MFD
Head	HD	Manufacturing	MFG
Heater	HTR	Mark	MK
Height	HT or HGT	Masonry opening	MO
Hexagonal	HEX	Material	MATL
Hollow metal	HM	Maximum	MAX
Horizon, horizontal	HOR or HORIZ	Mechanical	MECH
Horsepower	HP or HP	Medicine cabinet	MC
Hose bibb	HB	Medium	MED
Hot water	HW	Metal	MET
Hour	HR	Meter, meters	m
House	HSE	Millimeter, millimeters	mm
Hundred	C	Minimum	MIN
		Miscellaneous	MISC
I beam	S or I (old designation)		

Model	MOD	Quantity	QTY
Moderate-weather (a common brick grade)	MW	Quart, quarts	QT
Molding	MLDG	Radiator	RAD
Mole	mol	Radiator enclosure	RAD ENCL
		Radius	R
National	NATL	Random length and width	RL&W
National Electrical Code	NEC	Range	R
National Lumber Manufacturers Association	NLMA	Receptacle	RECP
		Rectangle	RECT
No-weather (a common brick grade)	NW	Redwood	RDWD
Nominal	NOM	Reference	REF
North	N	Refrigerator	REF
Not applicable	NA	Register	REG
Not in contract	NIC	Reinforce, reinforcing	REINF
Number	# or NO.	Reinforcing bar	REBAR
		Required	REQD
		Return	RET
Oak	O	Revision	REV
Octagon	OCT	Revolutions per minute	RPM
Office	OFF	Right	R
On center	OC	Right hand	RH
Opening	OPG	Riser	R
Opposite	OPP	Road	RD
Ornament	ORN	Roof	RF
Ounce, ounces	OZ	Roof drain	RD
Outside diameter	OD	Roofing	RFG
Overhead	OVHD	Room	RM
		Rough	RGH
		Rough opening	RO
Page	P	Round	ϕ or RD
Painted	PTD		
Pair	PR	S-shape steel beam	S or I (old designation)
Panel	PNL	Schedule	SCH
Paragraph	PAR	Screw	SCR
Parallel	‖ or PAR	Second, seconds	s
Partition	PTN	Section	SECT
Passage	PASS.	Self-closing	SC
Pedestal	PED	Service	SERV
Penny (nail)	d	Severe-weather (a common brick grade)	SW
Per	/	Sewer	SEW.
Percent	%	Sheathing	SHTHG
Perforate	PERF	Sheet	SHT
Perpendicular	⊥ or PERP	Shower	SH
Pi (ratio of circumference to diameter of circle)	π	Siding	SDG
Piece	PC	Sill cock	SC
Plaster	PLAS	Sink	S or SK
Plate	℞ or PL	Slop sink	SS
Plate glass	PL GL	Socket	SOC
Platform	PLAT	Soil pipe	SP
Plumbing	PLMB	South	S
Plywood	PLYWD	Specifications	SPEC
Point	PT	Square	□ or SQ
Polish	POL	Square foot, square feet	SQ FT
Position	POS	Stairs	ST
Pound, pounds	lb or #	Standard	STD
Pounds per square inch	PSI	Standpipe	ST P
Poured concrete	P/C	Station	STA
Prefabricated	PREFAB	Station point	SP
Property	PROP.	Steel	STL
Push button	PB	Stirrup	STIR.
		Stock	STK
		Storage	STOR
		Street	ST

Structural	STR
Structural clay research	SCR
Substitute	SUB
Supersede	SUPSD
Supplement	SUPP
Supply	SUP
Surface	SUR
Surface 1 side	S1S
Surface 2 sides	S2S
Surface 4 sides	S4S
Surface all sides	S4S
Surface 1 edge	S1E
Surface 2 edges	S2E
Surface 1 side 1 edge	S1S1E
Surfaced and matched	S&M
Suspended ceiling	SUSP CLG
Switch	S or SW
Symbol	SYM
System	SYS
Tar and gravel	T&G
Technical	TECH
Tee	T
Telephone	TEL
Television	TV
Temperature	TEMP
Terra-cotta	TC
Thermostat	THERMO
Thick, thickness	T or THK
Thousand	M
Thousand board feet	MBM
Thread	THD
Tongue-and-groove	T&G
Tread	TR
Typical	TYP
Ultimate	ULT
Unfinished	UNFIN
U.S.A. Standards Institute	USASI
U.S. standard gauge	USG

Vanishing point	V
Vent or ventilator	V
Ventilate, ventilation	VENT.
Vertical	VERT
Vestibule	VEST.
Volt, volts	V
Volume	VOL
W-shape steel beam	W, WF or WF (old designations)
Wall cabinet	W CAB
Wall vent	WV
Water	W
Water closet	WC
Waterproof	WP or WP
Watt, watts	W
Weatherproof	WP or WP
Weight	WT
Weep hole	WH
West	W
White Pine	WP
Wide flange	W, WF or WF (old designations)
Width	WTH
Window	WDW
Wire glass	W GL
With	W/
Without	W/O
Wood	WD
Wrought iron	WI
Yard, yards	YD
Year	YR
Yellow Pine	YP
Zinc	Z or ZN

E / Architectural Spelling

These words are commonly used in architectural drafting and are often misspelled. Anyone seriously interested in drafting should know the proper spelling of the words of the trade.

Acoustical
Acre
Aisle (*isle* is an island)
Alcove
Aluminum
Appliance
Asphalt

Barbecue
Bathroom (one word)
Batten
Batter board (two words)
Bedroom (one word)
Bevel, beveled
Bracing
Brickwork
Bridging
Built-up roof

Cabinet
Calk, calking (preferred spelling)
Canopy, canopies
Cant strip
Cantilever
Carport (one word)
Casement
Center (*centre* is British spelling)
Centimeter (*centimetre* is British spelling)
Channel
Chromium

Cleanout door
Clerestory
Colonnade
Coping
Cornice
Corridor
Corrugated
Creosote
Cupola

Dampproof (one word)
Dining room (two words)
Dishwasher (one word)
Disposal unit
Double-hung
Dovetail
Downspout
Downstairs (one word)
Draft, drafting, drafter (*draught* is obsolete)
Dry wall (two words)

Eave (*eve* is evening)
Enclose, enclosure (*inclose* is used by land surveyors)

Fascia, facia
Fiberboard
Fiber glass (*Fiberglas* is trade name)
Fieldstone (one word)
Fire brick (two words)
Fireplace (one word)
Flagstone (one word)
Flue (*flu* is a disease)
Fluorescent
Formica
Freezer
Furring

Gable
Galvanized
Game room (two words)
Grill (a grid for broiling)
Grille or grill (a grating for protection)
Gypsum

Handrail (one word)
Hangar (for airplanes)
Hanger (for hanging)
Horizontal

Jalousie (*jealousy* is resentment)

Kiln

Lanai (a Hawaiian porch)
Lath (*lathe* is a machine tool)
Lavatory (a sink; *laboratory* for experiments)
Level, leveled, leveling
Linoleum
Lintel
Living room (two words)
Loggia (a roofed, open porch)
Louver (*Louvre* is an art museum in Paris)

Mantel (*mantle* is a cloak)
Masonry
Meter (*metre* is British spelling)
Millimeter (*millimetre* is British spelling)
Miter, mitered
Molding or moulding
Mortar
Mortgage
Movable
Mullion
Muntin

Nosing

Ordinance (*ordnance* are artillery)
Oriel (*oriole* is a bird)

Paneled, paneling
Parallel
Perpendicular
Playroom (one word)
Projector

Rabbet (*rabbit* is an animal)
Receptacle
Remove, removable

Sheathing
Sheetrock (one word)
Siding
Solder (*soldier* is a military man)
Stile (of a door)
Story, storey
Style (of architecture)
Subfloor (one word)

Template
Terrazzo

Upstairs (one word)

Veneer
Vertical
Vinyl

Wainscot, wainscoting
Wallboard (one word)
Waterproof (one word)
Weatherstripping
Weep hole (two words)
Woodwork (one word)
Wrought iron (means "worked iron")

Zinc

F / Glossary of Architectural Terms

Active solar system: A solar heating system in which the heat flow is forced by some mechanical means.

A-frame: Any frame in the shape of an inverted V.

Aggregate: Material such as broken stone, gravel, cinders or slag used as one of the constituents of concrete, the other constituents being sand, cement, and water.

Alcove: A recessed space connected with or at the side of a larger room.

Anchor: A metal piece used to attach building members to masonry.

Anchor bolt: A threaded rod used to fasten the sill plate to the foundation.

Angle iron: A metal bar, L-shaped in section.

Apron: The finish board immediately below a window-sill.

Arcade: A series of arches supported by a row of columns.

Arch: A curved structure that carries the weight over an opening.

Architect: A person who plans buildings and oversees their construction.

Architectural terra-cotta: Terra-cotta building blocks having a ceramic finish.

Areawall: The wall of an areaway.

Areaway: A subsurface enclosure to admit light and air to a basement.

Ashlar masonry: Masonry composed of squared units laid with horizontal bed joints.

Asphalt: An insoluble material used in waterproofing.

Backfill: Earth replaced around a foundation.

Balcony: A platform projecting from the wall of a building, above the ground.

Balloon frame: A type of building frame in which the studs extend from sill to eaves without interruption.

Balusters: The small vertical members of a railing between the bottom and top rail.

Banister: A handrail.

Baseboard: The finishing board covering a wall where it meets the floor.

Basement: The lowest story of a building, partially or entirely below ground.

Batten: A strip of board for use in fastening other boards together.

Batter: Sloping a masonry or concrete wall.

Batter board: A horizontal board nailed to posts and used to lay out the excavation and foundation.

Bay: Any division or compartment of an arcade, roof, building, space between floor joists, or other area.

Beam: A horizontal structural member that carries a load.

Bearing partition: A partition supporting any vertical load other than its own weight.

Bearing plate: A support member used to distribute weight over a larger area.

Bench mark: A reference point used by surveyors to establish lines and grades.

Bent: A rigid, transverse framework.

Bevel weld: A butt weld with one mitered member.

Bibb: A threaded faucet.

Blocking: Small wood framing members.

Bluestone: A hard, blue sandstone.

Board foot: The amount of wood contained in a piece of rough green lumber 1″ thick × 12″ wide × 1′ long.

Bond: Mortar bond between mortar and masonry units; structural bond between wythes; pattern bond for decorative effect.

Bond beam: A reinforced concrete beam used to strengthen masonry walls.

Book match: A veneer pattern of alternate sheets turned over as are the leaves of a book.

Box beam: A hollow, built-up structural unit.

Brick veneer: A brick facing laid in front of frame construction.

Bridging: Cross-bracing between floor joists to add stiffness to the floors.

Brownstone: A brown sandstone.

Btu: A unit used to measure heat (British thermal unit).

Building board (also **Wallboard**): Boards made from repulped paper, shredded wood, or similar material.

Building line: An imaginary line on a plot beyond which the building may not extend.

Building paper: A heavy, waterproof paper used over sheathing and subfloors to prevent passage of air and water.

Built-up beam: A beam constructed of smaller members fastened together with the grains parallel.

Build-up roof: A roofing composed of several layers of felt and asphalt, pitch, or coal tar.

Butt: See Door butt.

Butt weld: A weld of members butting against each other.

Calking: A waterproof material used to seal cracks.

Canopy: A sheltering roof.

Cant strip: A form of triangular molding.

Cantilever: A beam or girder fixed at one extremity and free at the other. To *cantilever* is to employ the principle of the lever to carry a load.

Carbon steel: A basic structural steel containing carbon and manganese as main alloys.

Carport: A garage not fully enclosed.

Casement: A window whose frame is hinged at the side.

Casing: The framing around a door or window.

Catch basin: An underground structure for surface drainage in which sediment may settle.

Catenary: The shape of a chain hanging freely between two supports.

Cavity wall: A masonry wall having an air space of about 2″.

Cement: A masonry material purchased in the form of a highly pulverized powder usually medium gray in color. The approximate proportions for portland cement are as follows:

Lime (CaO)	60%–67%
Silica (SiO$_2$)	20%–25%
Iron oxide and alumina	7%–12%

Centering: Form work for poured concrete floor and roof slabs; temporary form work for the support of masonry arches or lintels during construction.

Center to center: Measurement from the center of one member to the center of another (noted "oc").

Ceramic veneer: Architectural terra-cotta having large face dimensions and thin sections.

Channel: A standard form of structural rolled steel, consisting of three sides at right angles in channel form.

Check: A lumber defect caused by radial separation during seasoning. Also see Door check.

Chord: A principal member of a truss.

Circuit: The path for an electric current.

Clapboard: A narrow board, thicker at one edge, for weather-boarding frame buildings; siding.

Clerestory: A window between roof planes.

Client: A person who employs an architect.

Collar beam: A horizontal member tying two opposite rafters together at more or less a center point on the rafters.

Column: A vertical supporting member.

Common brick: $3\frac{3}{4}″ \times 2\frac{1}{2}″ \times 8″$ brick used for general construction.

Composite wall: A masonry wall of at least two adjacent wythes of different materials.

Concrete: A masonry mixture of portland cement, sand and aggregate, and water in proper proportions.

Condensation: Water formed by warm, moist air contacting a cold surface.

Conductor: A vertical drainpipe or material permitting passage of electric current.

Conduit: A pipe or trough that carries water, electrical wiring, cables, and so forth.

Conifer: See Softwood.

Contractor: A builder.

Control joint: An expansion joint in a masonry wall formed by raking mortar from a continuous vertical joint.

Convector: A heat transfer surface that uses convection currents to transmit heat.

Coping: A masonry cap on top of a wall to protect it from water penetration.

Corbel: A bracket formed in a wall by building out successive courses of masonry.

Corner bead: A metal molding, built into the plaster corners to prevent the accidental breaking off of the plaster.

Cornice: That part of a roof which extends or projects beyond the wall; the architectural treatment thereof, as a *box cornice.*

Counterflashing: A flashing used under the regular flashing.

Course: A horizontal row of bricks, tile, stone, building blocks, or similar material.

Court: An open space surrounded partly or entirely by a building.

Crawl space: The space between the floor joists and the surface below when there is no basement. This is used in making repairs on plumbing and other utilities.

Cricket: A roof device used at intersections to divert water.

Cupola: A small structure built on top of a roof.

Curtain wall: An exterior wall which provides no structural support.

Cut stone: Stone cut to given sizes or shapes.

Damper: A movable plate to regulate the draft in a chimney.

Dap: A circular groove (used for split rings and shear plates).

Decay: Disintegration of wood through the action of fungi.

Decibel: A unit of measuring the relative loudness of sound.

Deciduous: See Hardwood.

Door buck: A door frame (usually metal).

Door butt: A hinge.

Door check: A device to slow a door when closing.

Doorstop: A device to prevent a door from hitting the wall when opening.

Dormer: A structure projecting from, or cut into, a sloping roof, usually to accommodate a window or windows.

Double-faced fireplace: A fireplace having two fireplace openings.

Double-hung window: A window having top and bottom sashes each capable of movement up and down in its own grooves.

Downspout: A vertical drainpipe for carrying rainwater from the gutters.

Drain: A pipe for carrying waste water.

Dressed size: See Finished size.

Drip: A molding designed to prevent rainwater from running down the face of a wall, or to protect the bottom of a door or window from leakage.

Drafter: A man or woman who prepares plans using drafting instruments or computer equipment.

Dry rot: A dry, crumbly wood rot.

Dry wall: A wall finished with wallboard in place of plaster; stone wall built without mortar.

Dry well: A shallow well used for the disposal of rainwater.

Duct: A sheet-metal conductor for air distribution.

Eave: The lower portion of a roof which extends beyond the wall.

Efflorescence: An undesirable white crystallization that may form on masonry walls.

Elbow: An L-shaped pipe fitting.

Electric arc process: A welding process that uses an electric arc to fuse both members.

Elevation: An orthographic projection of the vertical side of a building.

Escalator: A moving stairway.

Excavation: A hole formed by removing earth.

Expansion joint: A separation in a masonry or concrete wall to permit wall expansion due to temperature and moisture changes.

Facade: The front or face of a building.

Face brick: A special brick used for facing a wall. Face bricks are more uniform in size than common bricks and are made in a variety of colors and textures.

Faced wall: See Composite wall.

Facing: Any material, forming a part of a wall, used as a finished surface.

Fascia (Facia, Fascia board): A flat banded projection on the face of the cornice; the flat vertical member of the cornice; the flat surface running above a shop window on which the name of the shop may be displayed.

Fenestration: The arrangement of windows in a wall.

Fiber glass: A material composed of thin glass threads used for insulation or with resin for a finished surface.

Fiberboard: Sheet material of refined wood fibers.

Fieldstone: Building stone found loose on the ground (field) regardless of its exact variety. Don't confuse with Flagstone.

Filigree: Fine, decorative openwork.

Fillet weld: A butt weld with the weld metal filling an inside corner.

Finish lumber: Dressed wood used for building trim.

Finished size: The *nominal size* is the size of rough lumber. After planning, the actual *finished size* is about ½″ smaller than nominal. The difference between nominal and finished size will vary depending upon the size of the lumber, ranging from ¾″ for lumber over 6″ to only ¼″ for 1″ lumber. The variations between nominal and finished size of American Standard Lumber are:

Nominal Size	Finished Size
1″	¾″
2″	1½″
4″	3½″
6″	5½″
8″	7¼″
10″	9¼″
12″	11¼″

Fire brick: A brick made of a refractory material (fire clay) that withstands great heat; used to line furnaces, fireplaces, and so on.

Fire cut: An angular cut at the end of a joist framing into a masonry wall.

Fireproofing: Any material protecting structural members to increase their fire resistance.

Fire stopping: Obstructions across air passages in buildings to prevent the spread of hot gasses and flames; horizontal blocking between wall studs.

Fire wall: A wall extending from foundation through the roof to subdivide a building in order to restrict the spread of fire.

Fixture: A piece of electric or plumbing equipment.

Flagstone: Flat stone used for floors, steps, and walks.

Flashing: The sheet-metal work used to prevent leakage over windows and doors, around chimneys, and at the intersections of different wall surfaces and roof planes.

Floor plan: An orthographic projection of the floor of a building.

Flue: A passage in the chimney to convey smoke to the outer air.

Flue lining: Terra-cotta pipe used for the inner lining of chimneys.

Footing: The bases upon which the foundation and posts rest.

Formica: A plastic veneer trade name.

Foundation: The supporting wall of a building below the first-floor level.

Framing: Lumber used for the structural framing of a building.

Frost line: The depth of frost penetration in soil.

Furring: Wood strips fastened to a wall or ceiling for the purpose of attaching wallboards or ceiling tile.

Gable: The triangular portion of an end wall formed by a sloping roof.

Gambrel: A gable roof, each slope of which is broken into two planes.

Geodesic dome: A double-faced dome formed of members of nearly equal length.

Girder: A large horizontal structural member, usually heavier than a beam, used to support the ends of joists and beams or to carry walls over openings.

Glazed brick: Brick finished with ceramic, clay-coated, or salt glaze.

Grade or grade line: The level of the ground around a building.

Granite: A durable and hard igneous rock.

Green efflorescence: An undesirable green stain that may form on masonry walls.
Ground cover: Usually roll roofing laid on the ground in crawl spaces to reduce moisture.
Grounds: Wood strips attached to the walls before plastering, serving as a plaster stop and nailing base for trim.
Grout: Mortar of pouring consistency.
Gunite: Sprayed concrete using a dry mix and water.
Gutter: A trough or depression for carrying off water.
Gypsum board (also Plaster board): Board made of plaster with a covering of paper.

Half-timbering: A frame construction where the spaces are filled in with masonry.
Hanger: An iron strap used to support a joist or beam.
Hardboard: Sheet material of compressed wood fibers.
Hardwood: Wood from trees having broad leaves in contrast to needles. The term does not necessarily refer to the hardness of the wood.
Header: A beam perpendicular to joists, into which they are framed; a masonry unit laid horizontally with the end exposed.
Headroom: The vertical clearance in a room or on a stairway.
Hearth: The masonry portion of a floor in front of a fireplace.
Heartwood: The dead, inner layer of a tree formed from former sapwood.
Heat-treated steel: A high-strength steel that has been quenched and tempered.
High-strength bolt: A medium-carbon or heat-treated alloy steel bolt.
High-strength steel: A high-strength, low-alloy steel.
Hip roof: A roof with four sloping sides.
House drain: Horizontal sewer piping within a building which receives waste from the soil stacks.
House sewer: Horizontal sewer piping 5′ outside the foundation wall to the public sewer.
Humidifier: A device to increase relative humidity in a building.

I beam: A steel beam with an I-shaped cross section.
Insulation: Material for obstructing the passage of sound, heat, or cold from one surface to another.
Interference-body bolt: A high-strength bolt with raised ribs on the shank.

Jack rafter: A short rafter placed between the ridge and the hip rafter or valley rafter.
Jacuzzi: Trademark for whirlpools manufactured by Jacuzzi, Inc.
Jalousie: A type of window consisting of a number of long, thin, hinged panels.
Jamb: The inside vertical face of a door or window frame.
J-groove weld: A butt weld with one gouged member.
Joist: A member directly supporting floor and ceiling loads and in turn supported by bearing walls, beams, or girders.

Kalamein door: A fireproofed door covered with metal.
Keystone: The last wedge-shaped stone placed in the crown of an arch.
Kiln: A heating chamber for drying lumber (pronounced "kill").
Kip: 1,000 pounds.
Knot: A lumber defect caused by an embedded limb.
Kraft paper: A strong, brown paper made from sulphate pulp.

Laitance: An undesirable watery layer found in the upper surface of curing concrete.
Lally column: A steel column.
Lamella roof: A roof formed of short members assembled in diamond-shaped patterns.
Laminate: To bond together several layers of material.
Lanai: A roofed living area or passage with open sides.
Landing: A stair platform.
Lath (metal): Sheet-metal screening used as a base for plastering.
Lath (wood) (also Furring): Thin wood used to level a surface in preparation for plastering or composition tiles.
Lattice: Openwork made by crossed or interlaced strips of material.
Lavatory: A washbasin or room equipped with a washbasin.
Ledger: A wood strip nailed to the lower side of a girder to provide a bearing surface for joists.
Lift-slab: A precast concrete construction method of casting all slabs on the ground and lifting them into final position.
Limestone: A sedimentary rock of calcium carbonate.
Lintel: The horizontal member supporting the wall over an opening.
Lobby: An entrance hall or reception room; vestibule.
Lookout: A short timber for supporting a projecting cornice.
Lot line: The limit of a lot.
Louver: A ventilating window covered by sloping slats to exclude rain.
Low-E glass: Low-emissivity glass manufactured with a microthin transparent coating that reflects heat.
Lumber: Wood that has been sawed, resawed, planed, crosscut, or matched.
    Boards: Lumber less than 2″ thick and more than 1″ wide.
    Dimension: Lumber from 2″ to 5″ thick and more than 2″ wide.
    Dressed size: See Finished size.
    Finished size: The size of lumber after shrinking and planing; about ½″ less than the nominal or rough size. Nominal size: The "name" size by which lumber is identified and sold.
    Rough lumber: Lumber that has been sawed but not planed.
    Structural lumber: Lumber over 2″ thick and 4″ wide, used for structural support.
    Timber: Lumber over 5″ in least dimension.
    Yard lumber: Lumber of all sizes intended for general building purposes.

Manhole: A sewer opening to allow access for a man.

Mansard: A hip roof, each slope of which is broken into two planes.

Mantel: The shelf over a fireplace.

Marble: A metamorphic rock used for building.

Masonite: A hardboard trade name.

Masonry: Material such as stone, brick, and block used by a mason.

Mastic: A waterproof material used to seal cracks.

Meeting rail: The horizontal rails of double-hung sash that fit together when the window is closed.

Member: A part of a building unit.

Millwork: Woodwork that has been finished (*milled*) in a milling plant.

Miter: A beveled cut.

Modular brick: $4'' \times 2\frac{2}{3}'' \times 8''$ brick.

Module: A standardized unit of measurement.

Molding: Strips used for ornamentation.

Mortar: A mixture of cement, sand, and water used as a bonding agent by the mason.

Motif: The basic idea or theme of a design.

M shape: A lightweight structural steel I-beam.

Mullion: The large vertical or horizontal division of a window opening.

Muntin: The small members that divide the glass in a window frame.

Newel or newel post: The post where the handrail of a stair starts or changes direction.

Niche: A small recess in a wall.

Nominal size: See Lumber.

Norman brick: $4'' \times 2\frac{2}{3}'' \times 12''$ brick.

Nosing: The rounded edge of a stair tread.

On center: Measurement from the center of one member to the center of another (noted "oc").

Outlet: An electric socket.

Overhang: The horizontal distance that a roof projects beyond a wall.

Panel: A flat surface framed by thicker material.

Panelboard: The center for controlling electrical circuits.

Parapet: The portion of a wall that extends above the roof.

Parging (Pargeting): Cement mortar applied to a masonry wall.

Parquetry: An inlaid floor in a geometrical pattern.

Particle board: Wood fiberboard.

Partition: An interior wall. (Wall: An exterior wall.)

Passive solar system: A solar heating system in which heat flows naturally rather than being forced by some mechanical means.

Penny: A term for the length of a nail, abbreviated *d*. Originally, it meant the price per hundred nails (i.e., 8 penny = 8 cents per hundred nails).

Penthouse: A housing above the roof for elevator machinery.

Pier: A rectangular masonry support either freestanding or built into a wall.

Pilaster: Specifically, an attached pier used to strengthen a wall.

Pitch: A term applied to the amount of roof slope. It is found by dividing the height by the span. Also a

liquid material used in roofing. Also the center-to-center distance between bolts.

Plank: Lumber $2''$ and over in thickness.

Plate: A horizontal member in a wall framework on which rafters, joists, studs, and so forth rest, or to which they are secured, as in *sole plate, sill plate, top plate*.

Plumb: Vertical.

Ply: The number of layers of roofing felt, plywood veneer, or other materials.

Plywood: Wood made up of three or more layers of veneer bonded with glue.

Poché: To darken in a wall section with freehand shading.

Pointing: Filling of joints in a masonry wall.

Post-and-beam: A type of building frame in which cross-beams rest directly upon vertical posts.

Precasting: A casting in a mold that is not located at its final position in the structure.

Prestressing: A method of compressing concrete members so that they will not deflect when in position.

Priming: The first coat of paint, mixed and applied so as to fill the pores of the surface preparatory to receiving the subsequent coats.

Pumpcrete: Pumped concrete.

Purlin: A horizontal roof framing member, laid perpendicular to main trusses and supporting the roof.

Radiant heating: Heating by radiating rays without air movement.

Radon: A harmful, radioactive gas that may leak into buildings.

Rafter: A member in a roof framework running from the eave to the ridge. There are hip rafters, jack rafters, and valley rafters.

Random match: A veneer pattern of sheets randomly placed.

Rebar: Reinforcing bar.

Reflective insulation: Sheet material with a surface of low heat emissivity used to reduce heat loss.

Reinforced concrete: Concrete containing more than 0.2 percent of reinforcing steel.

Resistance number: See R value.

Relative humidity: Ratio of the amount of water vapor in air to the maximum possible amount at the same temperature.

Retaining wall: A wall designed to resist lateral pressure of earth.

Retemper: To replace water evaporated from wet mortar.

Return: A molding turned back to the wall on which it is located.

Reveal: The depth of masonry between its outer face and a window or door set in an opening.

Ribbon: A wood strip let into the studding to provide a bearing surface for joists.

Ridge: The top edge of the roof where two slopes meet.

Ridge cap: A wood or metal cap used over roofing at the ridge.

Ridgepole: The highest horizontal member in a roof. It supports the heads of the jack rafters.

Riprap: Stone placed on a slope to prevent erosion.

Riser: The vertical board of a step. It forms the front of the stair step.

Rocklath: A flat sheet of gypsum used as a plaster base.

Roll roofing: Roofing material of fiber and asphalt.

Roman brick: $4'' \times 2'' \times 12''$ brick.

Roof boards (Roofers): The rough boarding over the roof framework on which is laid the roof covering.

Rubble: Irregularly shaped building stone, partly trimmed.

R value: A classification number that indicates the effectiveness of insulation.

Saddle: A small, double-sloping roof to carry the water away from the back of chimneys. Sometimes called Cricket.

Salvaged brick: Used brick.

Sandstone: A sedimentary rock of cemented quartz.

Sandwich wall: A wall of at least two adjacent and connected panels, usually reinforced concrete panels protecting an insulating panel.

Sapwood: The living layer of a tree surrounding the heartwood.

Sash: A framing for windowpanes. A sash window is generally understood to be a double-hung, vertically sliding window.

Scab: A small member used to join other members, fastened on the outside face.

Scarf joint: A joint made by tapering the ends of each piece.

Schedule: A list of parts (as a *window schedule*).

SCR brick: $6'' \times 2\frac{1}{2}'' \times 12''$ brick developed by Structural Steel Products Research for use in $6''$ solid, load-bearing walls.

Scratch coat: The first coat of plaster. It is scratched to provide a good bond for the next coat.

Seasoning: Removing moisture from green wood.

Section: An orthographic projection that has been cut apart to show interior features.

Septic tank: A sewage-settling tank.

Setback: The distance between a building and its front or side property lines.

Shake: A hand-split shingle; a lumber defect caused by a natural separation of the annual rings.

Shear plate: A metal connector for timber-to-timber and timber-to-steel construction which distributes the load over a greater area.

Sheathing: The rough boarding on the outside of a wall or roof over which is laid the finished siding or the shingles.

Shim: A piece of material used to true up or fill in the space between two surfaces.

Shingles: Roof covering made of wood cut to stock lengths and thicknesses and to random widths. Also fiber glass shingles, asphalt shingles, slate shingles, and tile shingles.

Shotcrete: Sprayed concrete using a wet mix.

Sidelight: A narrow window adjacent to a door.

Siding: The outside layer of boards on a frame wall.

Sill: The stone or wood member across the bottom of a door or window opening. Also the bottom member on which a building frame rests (sill plate).

Slate: A metamorphic rock used for roofing and flagstone.

Sleeper: A wood member placed over a concrete slab to provide a nailing base for a wood floor.

Slip match: A veneer pattern of sheets joined side by side.

Slump block: A concrete block resembling stone.

Smoke chamber: The portion of a chimney flue located directly over the fireplace.

Snap header: A half-brick header.

Soffit: The undersurface of a cornice, molding, or beam.

Softwood: Wood from trees having needles rather than broad leaves. The term does not necessarily refer to the softness of the wood.

Soil stack: A vertical pipe in a plumbing system that carries the discharge from a toilet.

Soldier: A masonry unit laid vertically with the narrow side exposed.

Sole: The horizontal framing member directly under the studs.

Sovent: A single-stack, self-venting sewage disposal system.

Space frame: A three-dimensional truss system.

Spackle: To cover wallboard joints with plaster.

Span: The distance between structural supports (i.e., the length of a joist, rafter, or other member).

Spandrel: The area between the top of a window and sill of the above window.

Spandrel wall: An exterior wall which provides no structural support.

Specifications: The written description accompanying the working drawings.

Split block: A fractured solid concrete block laid with the split face exposed.

Split lintels: Two lintels placed side by side in a wall.

Square: 100 sq. ft. of roofing.

S shape: A structural steel I beam.

Stack: A vertical pipe.

Stile: A vertical member of a door, window, or panel.

Stirrup: A metal U-shaped strap used to support framing members.

Stool (Water closet): The wood shelf across the bottom and inside of a window.

Stop: See Doorstop.

Story (Storey): The space between two floors, or between a floor and the ceiling above.

Stressed-skin panel: A hollow, built-up panel used for floors, roofs, and walls.

Stretcher: A masonry unit laid horizontally with the long face exposed.

Stringer: The sides of a flight of stairs; the supporting member cut to receive the treads and risers.

Stucco: A face plaster or cement applied to walls or partitions.

Stud: The vertical member that forms the framework of a partition or wall.

Stud welding: An electric arc welding process used to weld threaded studs to structural steel.

Subfloor: The rough flooring under the finish floor.

Tail beam: Framing members supported by headers or trimmers.

Tee: A structural steel member in a shape of a T.

Tempered hardboard: Water-resistant hardboard.

Tensile bond strength: Ability of mortar to adhere to masonry unit.

Termite shield: Sheet metal used to block the passage of termites.

Terra-cotta: Hard-baked clay and sand often used for chimney flues.

Terrace: A raised flat space.

Terrazzo: Floor covering of marble chips and cement ground to a smooth finish. Metal strips are used to separate different colors and create designs.

Thermostat: An instrument that automatically controls the heating plant.

Threshold: The stone, wood, or metal piece directly under a door.

Tie bar: A tie rod.

Tie beam: A framing member between rafters.

Tie rod: A steel rod used to keep a member from spreading.

Tilt-up construction: A method of precasting members horizontally on the site and lifting into their final vertical position.

Toenail: To drive nails at an angle.

Tongue: A projection on the edge of a board that fits into a groove on an adjacent board.

Track: A horizontal member in metal framing, as in *top track, bottom track.*

Translucent: Having the ability to transmit light without a clear image.

Transom: A small window over a door.

Transparent: Having the ability to clearly transmit images.

Trap: A device providing a liquid seal to prevent passage of air and odor.

Tread: The horizontal part of a step.

Treillage: An ornamental screen.

Trim: The finish frame around an opening.

Trimmer: A joist or rafter around an opening in a floor or roof.

Truss: A braced framework capable of spanning greater distances than the individual components.

Trussed rafter: A truss spaced close enough to adjacent trusses that purlins are unnecessary.

U-groove weld: A weld with one gouged member.

Unfinished bolt: A low-carbon steel bolt.

Valley: The trough formed by the intersection of two roof slopes.

Valve: A device that regulates the flow in a pipe.

Vapor barrier: A thin sheet used to prevent the passage of water vapor.

Vault: A curved surface supporting a roof.

Vee weld: A butt weld with both members mitered.

Veneer: A facing material not load-bearing.

Vent pipe: A small ventilating pipe extending from each fixture of a plumbing system to the vent stack.

Vent stack: A vertical pipe in a plumbing system for ventilation and pressure relief.

Vestibule: A small lobby or entrance room.

Wainscot: An ornamental covering of walls often consisting of wood panels, usually running only part way up the wall.

Wall: An exterior wall. (Partition: An interior wall.)

Wallboard: A large, flat sheet of gypsum or wood pulp used for interior walls.

Wall tie: A metal piece connecting wythes of masonry to each other or to other materials.

W shape: A structural-steel, wide-flanged beam.

Warp: A lumber defect of a twist.

Waste stack: A vertical pipe in a plumbing system that carries the discharge from any fixture.

Waterproof: Material or construction that prevents the passage of water.

Weathering steel: A high-strength steel that is protected from further corrosion by its own corrosion.

Weatherstrip: A strip of metal or fabric fastened along the edges of windows and doors to reduce drafts and heat loss.

Weep hole: An opening at the bottom of a wall to allow the drainage of moisture.

Well opening: A floor opening for a stairway.

Whirlpool: A jetted tub.

Wind bracing: Bracing designed to resist horizontal and inclined forces.

Winder: A tapering step in a stairway.

Working drawing: A drawing containing information for the workers.

Wythe (Withe): A masonry partition, such as separating flues.

G / Microcomputer References and Programs

These microcomputer references are some of the most helpful introductions to interactive graphic programs:

Byte. Monthly magazine containing articles and advertisements on microcomputers. (Subscription) P.O. Box 6807, Piscataway, NJ 08855–9940.

Computer Buying Guide. Reviews and ratings of computers, peripherals, and programs. (320-page paperback, purchase) Publications International, Ltd., 3841 W. Oakton St., Skokie, IL 60076.

Computer Tutor 1. Components and functions of Apple II/IIe. (40 minute, color, $\frac{1}{2}''$ Beta and VHS videocassette, purchase) Penn State University Audio-Visual Services, Special Services Building, University Park, PA 16802.

Computer Tutor 2. Programming in BASIC for AppleII/IIe. (60 minute, color, $\frac{1}{2}''$ Beta and VHS videocassette, purchase) Penn State University Audio-Visual Services, Special Services Building, University Park, PA 16802.

Computers, the Friendly Invasion. Microcomputers as a creative tool for designers. (19 minute, 16 mm color film, rental) Penn State University Audio-Visual Services, Special Services Building, University Park, PA 16802.

Compututor: Using Your Machine. Self-paced instruction for IBM and compatible computers. (90 minute, color, $\frac{1}{2}''$ VHS videocassette, rental) Penn State University Audio-Visual Services, Special Services Building, University Park, PA 16802.

Compututor: Using Database Systems. Self-paced instruction for IBM and compatible computers. (115 minute, color, $\frac{1}{2}''$ VHS videocassette, rental) Penn State University Audio-Visual Services, Special Services Building, University Park, PA 16802.

Creative Computing Buyer's Guide. Personal computer programs. (Annual subscription) P.O. Box 13010, Philadelphia, PA 19101.

Devon, R., *The First Few Bytes.* Provides programming literacy in Applesoft BASIC and DOS file management for the Apple II+ and IIe. (82-page booklet, purchase) Kendall/Hunt Publishing Company, 2460 Kerper Blvd., Dubuque, IA 52001.

Directory of Computer Graphics Suppliers, 5th Ed. Computer graphics hardware, software, systems, and services. (225-page paperback, purchase) The S. Klein Newsletter on Computer Graphics, Directory Dept., P.O. Box 915, Sudbury, MA 01776.

Hearn, D. and Baker, P., *Computer Graphics.* Programming your personal microcomputer. (352-page hardcover and paperback, purchase) Prentice-Hall, 301 Sylvan Ave., Englewood Cliffs, NJ 07632.

Meyers, R., *Microcomputer Graphics.* Programming for microcomputer graphics with BASIC programs for Apple II. (282-page paperback, purchase) Addison-Wesley Publishing Co., Inc., 1 Jacob Way, Reading, MA 01867.

Park, C., *Interactive Microcomputer Graphics.* Programming for microcomputer graphics with BASIC programs for the IBM personal computer. (458-page text, purchase) Addison-Wesley Publishing Co., Inc., 1 Jacob Way, Reading, MA 01867.

Poole, L., McNiff, M., and Cook, S., *Apple II® User's Guide.* Complements the Apple II+ and Apple IIe owner's manual. (388-page paperback, purchase) Osborne/McGraw-Hill, 630 Bancroft Way, Berkeley, CA 94710.

Software Reference Guide. List of 600 software programs for Tandy/Radio Shack computers. (75-page directory, no charge) Available at local Radio Shack computer centers.

These microcomputer programs are typical of some of the architectural design programs available for use with popular microcomputers:

AE/CADD. Provides a library of architectural symbols for walls, stairs, furniture, structural, electrical, and plumbing fixtures. (Software supported by Autodesk for Tandy 1000/1200/2000/3000, purchase) Local Radio Shack computer centers.

Architectural Specification. Prepares CSI specifications, (software for Apple II/III, purchase) Microcomputing Research, 29 Estancial Drive, Marana, AZ 85238.

Architectural Specifications. Prepares CSI specifications. (software on disk for TRS-80 Models I through IV, purchase) Disco Tech, 600 B Street, P.O. Box 1659, Santa Rosa, CA 95402.

Autocad Standard. A computer-aided drafting and design system allowing the user to interactively create and edit plans of any size and scale. (Software supported by Autodesk for Tandy 1000/1200/2000/3000, purchase) Local Radio Shack computer centers.

Building Performance Profile. Calculates heat loss, heat gain, and energy consumption. (Software on cassette for TRS-80 Model I, purchase) Compass Systems, Village Square Center, Box 388, East Hampstead, NH 03826.

Cadapple—Entry Level. An introductory computer-aided drafting system. (Software for Apple II/IIe/IIc, purchase) Career Aids, 20417 Nordhoff St., Chatsworth, CA 91311.

Caddraw. A computer-aided drafting system with a library of 800 symbols for architectural drawings up to 12″ × 16″. (Software for Apple II/IIe/IIc, purchase) Career Aids, 20417 Nordhoff St., Chatsworth, CA 91311.

Caddraw Symbol Maker. A program allowing the user to create symbols for Caddraw. (Software for Apple II/IIe/IIc, purchase) Career Aids, 20417 Nordhoff St., Chatsworth, CA 91311.

Computer Data Base for Structural Shapes. Dimensions and properties of steel shapes, channels, tees, angles, and tubing. (Disks for IBM-PC, HP-150, Wang PC, and DEC Rainbow PC, purchase) American Institute of Steel Construction, P.O. Box 4588, Chicago, IL 60680–4588.

Conbeam. Calculates reactions, shears, and moments of continuous beams. (Software on disk or cassette for Apple II/III, purchase) Technical Software, P.O. Box 73043, Metairie, LA 70033.

Concrete Beam Design. Designs reinforced concrete beams by ultimate strength or working stress methods. (Software on disk for TRS-80 Model II or Model 16, purchase) Ecom Associates, 8634 West Brown Deer Road, Milwaukee, WI 53224.

Concrete Column Design. Designs reinforced concrete columns by moment magnification method. (Software on disk for TRS-80 Model II or Model 16, purchase) Ecom Associates, 8634 West Brown Deer Road, Milwaukee, WI 53224.

Energy Audit Analysis, Residential. Computes energy savings. (Software on disk for TRS-80 Model I or II, purchase) Eloret Corporation, 1178 Maraschino Drive, Sunnyvale, CA 94087.

The Framing Calculator. Calculates labor and material cost for wood-framed construction. (Software on disk for TRS-80 Model I or III, purchase) Mendocino Software, P.O. Box 1564, Willits, CA 95490.

Hydraulic Calculations Sprinkler Systems. Calculates water flow and pressure requirements for sprinkler systems. (Software on cassette for TRS-80 Model I, purchase) W. O. Lintz, 2522 Edge-O-Lake Drive, Nashville, TN 37217.

Isolated Footing Design. Designs continuous or isolated concrete footings. (Software for Apple II/III with CP/M or TRS-80 Models I thru IV, purchase) Disco Tech, 600 B Street, P.O. Box 1659, Santa Rosa, CA 95402.

MGI/CADD. A computer-aided drafting system allowing the user to create architectural symbols, drawings, and schematics. (Software supported by Microcomputer Graphics for Tandy 1000/1200/2000/3000, purchase) Local Radio Shack computer centers.

Pier and Grade Beam Design. Designs concrete pier and grade beam foundations. (Software for Apple II/III with CP/M or TRS-80 Models I thru IV, purchase) Disco Tech, 600 B Street, P.O. Box 1659, Santa Rosa, CA 95402.

Retaining Wall Design. Designs concrete or masonry retaining walls. (Software for Apple II/III with CP/M or TRS-80 Models I thru IV, purchase) Disco Tech, 600 B Street, P.O. Box 1659, Santa Rosa, CA 95402.

Solar Energy for the Home. Calculates heat loss and gain through south-facing windows. (Software for Apple II/III, purchase) Instant Software, Elm Street, Peterborough, NH 03458.

Steel Beam Design. Checks W, S, and C beams for lightest steel section. (Software on disk for TRS-80 Model I or Model 16, purchase) Ecom Associates, 8634 West Brown Deer Road, Milwaukee, WI 53224.

T.CAD Professional. A computer-aided drafting system for architectural drawings up to 24″ × 36″. (Software supported by Microdex for Model III/4, purchase) Local Radio Shack computer centers.

Versacad—Entry Level. An introductory computer-aided drafting system. (Software for IBM PC/XT, purchase) Career Aids, 20417 Nordhoff St., Chatsworth, CA 91311.

Index

Aalto, Alvar, 101
Abbreviations, A27–A31
Absorption of sound, 423–25
Accessibility, design for, 408–16
Accordion doors, 131
Acoustics, 417–24
Active solar heating systems, 310
Adjustable rate mortgage, 115
A-frame roof, 189
Agreement, Owner-Architect, 437, 441
Airbrush, 360–61
Air conditioning, 302–19
    cooling, 317
    filtering, 318
    heating, 302–16
    humidity control, 317
    solar, 319
    ventilation, 317
Air entrained concrete, 503
AISC Manual, 524
Alpha-numeric keyboard, 8
Aluminum wiring, 287
Amplification of sound, 424
Angles, steel, 522
Appliqué
    lettering, 58
    rendering, 360
Arch, 84
Arches, masonry, 485–87
Arch order, 90
Architectural terra cotta, 490
ARK-2 computer system, 8
Arrowheads, 60
Artificial intelligence, 169
Ashlar masonry, 495
Assyrian architecture, 86–87
Attic
    advantages and disadvantages, 110
    expansion, 110–11
Automatic drafting table, 7
Automatic welding, 531
Auxiliary views, 47–48
Awning windows, 122
Axonometric projection, 39, 50

Balcony railing, 216
Balloon framing, 258
Bar joists, 251, 544–48
Barrel vault, 557
Basement
    advantages and disadvantages, 109–10
    plans, 176–78
    windows, 124, A17
Basic Building Code, 111
Basilica, 90
Bathroom design, 154–55
Beams, 245–47
    calculations, 267–68

Bearing, compass, 179
Bearing angles, 63
Bedroom design, 152–54
Belgium truss, 542
Bid form, 437
Bid invitation, 435
Bolting, 526–28
Bond beams, 473–74
Bonding, surface, 469–70
Bonds, brick, 255, 483
Bowspring truss, 542
Box beams, 463–65
Braced framing, 258
Brick masonry, 479–91
    arches, 485–87
    bonds, 255, 483
    cavity walls, 477–78, 485
    colors, 478
    efflorescence, 482
    joints, 483
    load-bearing walls, 484–85
    manufacture, 479
    sizes, 480–82
    textures, 478
Bridging, 248
Broken-out sections, 45
Building code, 111, 179, 182, 425
Building paper, 250
Built-up roofing, 191
Butterfly roof, 188
Byzantine architecture, 91

Cabinet drawing, 52
Cable, steel, 563–64
Cable roof structures, 563–74
    construction, 572
    design, 566–68
    fittings, 564
    manufacture of components, 563–64
Cairns, 84
Cantilever framing, 250
Cape Cod house, 97
Capitol building, national, 94
Carbon steel, 523
Carpenter ant control, 276
Caryatid Porch, 89
Casement windows, 122, A18–A19
Casing, window, 126
Cast stone, 496
Catenary, 24, 537
Cathode-ray tube, 7–11, 168–70
Cavalier drawing, 52
Cavity masonry walls, 475–76, 483
Cellulose insulation, 323
Cement, 503
Center lines, 43
Change order, 448
Channel shapes, 521

Checking, 164, 176
Chimney
    construction, 222–25
    details, 226
    flue, 224
    location, 220–21
Circuit-breaker, 290
Circuits, electrical, 286–87
Circulation, design for, 160
Circus Maximus, 90
Clad windows, 122
Classic Revival, 94
Clay masonry, 479–91
Clean drawings, 28–29
Cleanouts, 298
Clerestory, 86, 188
Closet sizes, 154
Clustered design, 108
Cohesive construction, 84, 90, 243, 504–19
Cold water supply system, 295
Colonial architecture, 97–99
    Cape Cod, 97
    Dutch Colonial, 98
    French Colonial, 99
    Garrison, 97
    New England Colonial, 97
    Southern Colonial, 98
    Spanish, 99
Colosseum, 90
Columns, 246
    calculations, 265–67
Commercial
    construction, 374
    design, 371–72
    drafting, 372–74
Common perspective method, 337–40
Compass bearing, 179
Composite masonry walls, 478–79
Composite order, 89
Computer-aided design, 7–11, 166–70
Computer-aided drafting station, 7
Computer center, home, 157, 286
Computer database, 168
Computer programs, A43–A44
Computers, 7–11, 166–70
Computervision system, 166–67
Concrete, 243, 502–17
    curing, 504
    forms, 504–5
    manufacture of cement, 502–3
    mixing and placing, 504
    precast, 510, 514
    prestressed, 515–16
    reinforcing, 506–10
Concrete masonry, 243, 255, 469–78
    bond beams, 473–74
    cavity walls, 477–78
    composite walls, 476–77
    expansion joints, 475–76

Concrete masonry (cont.)
  glazed partition block, 470
  joints, 471
  lintels, 474
  manufacture, 469–70
  parapets, 474–75
  single wythe, 473–74
  sizes, 470
  slump block, 471
  split block, 471
Condensation, 273–75
Conic sections, 22–24
Conservation of
  air conditioning, 325
  electricity, 325–26
  energy, 321–27
  heat, 321–25
  hot water, 325
  water, 326
Construction
  balloon frame, 258
  braced frame, 258
  building, 239–58
  cantilever, 250
  chimney, 222–25
  cohesive, 84, 90, 243, 502–17
  fireplace, 222–25
  footing, 241
  foundation, 109–10, 243–45
  model, 230–35
  plank and beam, 258–59, 459–63
  platform frame, 239–58
  roof, 194, 250–54
  stair, 213
Construction dimensions, 63
Construction document, 435–48
Construction lines, 43
Construction loan, 113
Contemporary architecture, 99–103
Continuous-spliced joists, 461
Contour lines, 179, 183
  dimensioning, 63
Corbel, 84
Cording of the temple, 86
Corinthian order, 89
Cornices, 251–54
Corrosion prevention, 277
Cost
  estimation, 115
  of home, 112
  reducing, 116
Critical Path Method, 168
CRT computer display, 7–11, 168–70
Cut-away models, 235
Cutting plane lines, 43
Cybernetics, 169

Darrieus rotor wind machine, 331
Database, computer, 168
Data plotter, 7, 166, 168
Decay prevention, 276–77
Deep longspan steel joists, 547
Deflection of continuous spans, 460–61
Depression-type wind machine, 331
Detectors, smoke, 290

Digitizer, 8, 166, 168
Dimensioning, 60–73
  arrowheads, 60
  dimension lines, 43, 60
  dual, 73
  elevations, 62–63, 202–3
    construction, 63
    finish, 63
  extension lines, 43, 60
  gird dimensions, 65
  metric, 67–73
  modular, 64–66
  plans, 60–62, 176
  sectional, 63
  topographical, 63
Dining area design, 152
Direct perspective method, 341
Dividing a line, 20
Domes, 90–91, 190, 561–63
  geodesic, 190, 563
Doors, 130–37, A23–A26
  accordion, 131
  conventional representation, 201
  Dutch, 131
  folding, 131, A25
  French, 131
  garage, 135, A26
  hardware for, 134
  hinged, 130
  installation of, 131
  kalamein, 131
  louvered, 131
  materials, 131
  paneled, 130, A23–A25
  sectional details, 131–32, A23
  sliding, 131
  specifying, 133–34, 138, A23–A26
  terminology, 131–32
  types, 130
Doric order, 88–89
Dormer roofs, 187–88
Double glazing, 126, 323, A17, A22
Double hung windows, 123, 125, A21
Drafting, 17–18
  catenary, 24
  circles and arcs, 18
  conic sections, 22–24
  helices, 24–25
  lines, 17–18
  machines, 6
  parallel lines, 19
  pencils, thin lead, 4
  perpendicular lines, 19
  polygons, 21–22
  table, automatic, 7
  tangent arcs, 20
  tangent lines, 19
  tools, 3–11
Drain pipe, 241–43
Drawing board, 3
Drawing sets, 4
Drip cap, 126
Dry wall construction, 257–58
Dual dimensioning, 73
Dutch Colonial house, 98
Dutch doors, 131

DVST computer storage, 7

Earthquake, design for, 278, 477
Earth-sheltered house, 101
Echoes, 421–22
Eclecticism, 94
Efficiency, designing for, 160, 166
Efflorescence, 482
Egyptian architecture, 84–86
Electrical circuits, 286–87
Electrical conventions
  examples, 288–89
  fixtures, 283
  outlets, 285
  switches, 284–85
Electrical lighting, 283
Electrical requirements, minimum (table), 287
Electrical service, 284
Electrical systems
  electroluminescence, 292
  low voltage, 287, 290
Electric heating, 305–6
Electroluminescence, 292
Electronic pen, 8
Elevations
  dimensioning, 62–63, 202–3
  drafting, 195–203
  finished sketches, 201–3
  interior, 195
  labeling views, 202
  material representation, 201–2
  preliminary sketches, 196–98
  thumbnail sketches, 195–96
Elevator, accessibility, 412–13
Elevator, piston, 372
Ellipse
  concentric circle method, 23
  four-center method, 51–52
  trammel method, 22
Energy
  conservation, 321–27
  sources, 328–32
  system, 106
English style house, 95–96
Entourage, 363–68
  human figures, 368
  trees, 364–66
  vehicles, 367
Entrances, 134, A23
Equilateral triangle, 21
Erasers, 5
Erechtheion, 89
Evacuated tube solar collector, 310
Excavation, 240–41
Expandable mobile home, 261
Expansion, design for, 110–11
Expansion joints, 475–76
Extension line, 43, 60
Exterior walls, 254–55
Extinguishing systems, 431–32

Fenestration, 200

FHA mortgage interest rate, 114
Fiberboard, 457
Filtering, 318
Financing, home, 113–15
Finish dimensions, 63
Finished lumber sizes, 455
Finished sketches
    elevations, 201–3
    plans, 164
Fink truss, 542
Fire
    extinguishing systems, 431–32
    protection, 425–33
    ratings, 429–31
Fireplaces
    construction, 222–25
    details, 226
    flue, 224
    fuel, 220
    liner, 224–25
    location, 220–21
    metal, 225–26
    sizes, 221–22
    styling, 220
First angle projection, 42
Fittings, plumbing, 294–95
Fixed windows, 124, A22
Fixtures, electrical, 283
Flashing, 192, 223
Flat-plate solar collectors, 308
Flat roof, 188, 251
    advantages and disadvantages, 110
    construction of, 188, 251
Floor plans
    dimensioning, 176
    drafting, 172–178
    finished sketches, 164
    preliminary sketches, 163
    shape of, 109
    thumbnail sketches, 163
Floors, number of, 107–9
Flue, prefabricated, 224
Flue tile, 224
Fluorescent lighting, 283
Foamed plastics, 191–92
Focusing solar collectors, 310
Folded roof, 189, 551
Folding doors, 131, A25
Footings, 202, 241
    calculations, 265
    for columns and chimneys, 241
    reinforced, 243, 506–10
Formica, 457
Foundation
    construction, 109–10, 243–45
    plan, 176–78
Frame window, 126
Framing
    balloon, 258
    braced, 258
    cantilever, 250
    metal, 260–61
    plank and beam, 259, 459–63
    platform, 239–58
    roof, 194, 250–54
Free-form roof, 189

Freehand sketching, 12–15
French Colonial house, 99
French doors, 131
Fresh air inlet, 298
Full sections, 45
Functionalism, 94, 101
Future trends
    building design, 166–70
    construction methods and materials,
      261
    drafting tools, 7–11
    interiors, 157–58

Gable roof, 187
Galvanic corrosion, 278
Gambrel roof, 187
Garage
    design, 157
    doors, 135, A26
Garrison house, 97
Geodesic domes, 190, 561
Georgian style house, 96
Ghizeh, pyramids at, 84
Girders, 245–47
    calculations, 267
Glass, low-E, 126, 323
Glass brick, 500
Glass masonry, 498–501
    construction, 499–500
    glass brick, 500
    manufacture, 498
    sizes, 498
Glazed partition block, 470
Gliding windows, 123, A20
Glossary of architectural terms, A35–A41
Gluelam construction, 461–62
Gothic architecture, 92
Grading lumber, 454
Graduated payment mortgage, 115
Granite, 492
Greek architecture, 87–89
Gropius, Walter, 95, 101
Ground fault interrupter, 290
Ground loadings, safe, 265
Ground water, 325
Gruen, Victor, 101
Guide lines, 5, 43, 55
Gunite, 504
Guttering, 193
Gypsum board, 258

Hagia Sophia, 91
Half-sections, 45
Halicarnassus, Mausoleum at, 89
Handicapped design for, 408–16
Handrails, 215–19
Hardboard, 457–58
Hard conversion to metric, 67
Hardwood, 453
Headers, 245
    calculations, 270
Heat conservation, 321–25

Heat gain calculations, 318–19
Heating, 302–16
    electric, 305–6
    history of, 93
    hot water, 295, 303–5
    solar, 307–12
    system design, 315–16
    warm air, 302–3
Heat loss calculations, 312–16
Heat pump, 306
Heat-treated steel, 524
Helix
    conical, 24–25
    cylindrical, 24
    spherical, 25
Hexagon, 21
High-rise fire protection, 432–33
High-strength bolts, 530
High-strength steel, 524
Hip roof, 187
Home computer center, 157, 286
Hopper window, 122
Hot-water heating, 295, 303–5
Hot-water supply system, 295
House drain, 298
House plans for Mr. and Mrs. A
    electrical plan, 291
    elevations, 204–6
    fireplace details, 228
    floor plans, 173, 177
    interior (kitchen), 197
    plot plan, 181
    pool detail, 209
    rendering, 352
    sections, 207–8
    stair details, 217
House plans for Mr. and Mrs. Z, A1–A12
    electrical plans, A11
    elevations, A5–A7
    fireplace details, A10
    floor plans, A2–A4
    plot plans, A1
    rendering, A12
    sections, A8–A9
House sewer, 298
House traps, 298
Howe truss, 543–44
Humidity control, 273–75, 317
Hydraulic ram, 331–32
Hydro-electric turbine, 331
Hydronic heating, 293, 301–3
Hyperbola, 24

Infiltration, air, 313–15, 318
Inks, for rendering, 356
Insulation, 321–25
Interactive computer systems, 10–11
Interference-body bolts, 528
Interior walls, 255–58
International style, 94–95
Interrupter, ground fault, 290
Inverted king-post truss, 541
Invisible lines, 43
Ionic order, 89

Iron manufacture, 518–19
Isometric drawing, 51–52
Isometric projection, 50

Jalousie windows, 124
Johnson, Philip, 101
Joists, 247–48
    calculations, 268
Joist substitutes, 548

Kahn, Louis, 101
Kalamein doors, 131
Karnak, Great Hypostyle Hall, 86
King-post truss, 541
Kitchen
    design, 143–50
    equipment, 145

Labor and Material Bond, 441
Lamella roofs, 561
Laminated decking, 270, 463
Laminated timber, 461–62
Landscaping, 182
Lateral bracing, 558
Laundry design, 155–57
Le Corbusier, 95, 101
Left-handed drafting, 17
Left-handed sketching, 12
Lettering
    architectural, 54–59
    Commercial Gothic, 55
    condensed, 56
    density, 56
    devices for, 5, 6
    extended, 56
    floor plans, 176
    form, 56
    Gothic, 54
    guide lines, 5, 43, 55
    ink, 58
    instrumental, 59
    Old English, 54
    proportion, 56
    Roman, 54
    spacing, 56
    stability, 56
    stencils, 6, 58
    technique, 57–58
    title box, 59
Lift-slab construction, 515
Light pen, 8
Lighting
    electrical, 283
    history of, 93
Lightning protection, 278
Limestone, 493
Lines
    character, 28–29
    drafting, 17–18
    sketching, 12–14
    technique, 29

Lintels, 84, 474, 489
    calculations, 270
Living area design, 150–52
Load calculations, 264–65
Longspan steel joists, 545, 547
Loudness, 419–20
Louvre, The, 93
Low-E glass, 126, 323
Low-voltage system, 287, 290
Lumber
    classification, 454
    defects, 453
    fire resistance, 455
    grading, 454
    manufacture, 452–53
    measurement, 455
    preservatives, 455
    seasoning, 455
    size standards, 455
Lysicrates, Monument of, 89

Magic marker, 357
Mansard roof, 187
Manual of Steel, 524
Marble, 493
Marker, magic, 357
Masking of sound, 424
Masonry, 255
    brick, 479–86
    clay, 479–91
    concrete, 243, 469–78
    glass, 498–501
    sizes (tables), 223, 225
    stone, 492–97
Mastabas, 85
Mausoleum at Halicarnassus, 89
Measuring line, perspective, 339
Mechanical systems, 93
Membrane roofing, 191
Metal framing, 260–61
Metric
    angles, 69
    conversions, 67, 73
    design, 72
    dimensioning, 67–73
    lumber, 69
    masonry, 71
    modules, 69
    plans, 75–79
    plot plans, 68, 74
    plywood panels, 70
    prefixes, 67
    rebars, 71
    scales, 72
    sizes, 69–71
    steel beams, 72
    units, 67
Metric, house plans for Mr. and Mrs. M, 74–79
    basement plan, 75
    elevations, 77–78
    floor plan, 76
    heating plan, 316
    piping plan, 299
    plot plan, 74

plumbing plan, 300
    section, 79
Microcomputer programs, A43–A44
Microwave oven, 146
Mies van der Rohe, Ludwig, 101
Mineral wood insulation, 323
Minimum room sizes, 143
Miscellaneous Channels, 521
Mobile homes, 261
Models, architectural, 229–36
    construction, 230–35
    cut-away, 235
    mass, 229
    materials, 230–31
    presentation, 230
    scale conversions (table), 235
    study, 229–30
Modern architecture, 100–1
Modular brick, 480
Modular coordination, 63–66
Modular dimensioning, 64–66
Modular housing units, 261
Module, size of, 64
Moisture control, 273–75, 317
Mortar, 471
Mortgage, home
    adjustable rate, 115
    calculations, 113
    down payment, 113
    graduated payment, 115
    interest rate, 114
    length of, 114
    nonconventional, 115
    points, 113
    renegotiated rate, 115
    satisfaction piece, 114
Mullions, 126
Multiview projection, 39–45
Muntins, 126

National Building Code, 111
Nervi, Pier Luigi, 101
Neutra, Richard, 102
New England Colonial house, 97
Niemeyer, Oscar, 102
NLMA (National Lumber Manufacturers Association), 63, 65
Nominal dimensions, 63
Nominal lumber sizes, 455
Nonconventional mortgages, 115
Norman brick, 480
Notre Dame Cathedral, 92

Oblique projection, 52–53
Octagon, 21
Offset sections, 45
One-point perspective, 335
Open-web joists, 251, 544–48
Orders, architectural
    Greek, 88–89
    Roman, 89
Orientation, 159–60
    solar, 159

topographical, 159
    view, 159
    wind, 159
Orthographic projection, 37
Oscilloscope, 7–11, 168–70
Outlets, electrical, 285
Outlines, 43
Owner-Architect agreement, 437, 441

Pagoda roof, 190
Pantheon (Paris), 92–93
Pantheon (Rome), 90
Paper
    for ink rendering, 355
    for pencil rendering, 351
Parabola, 23–24
Parabolic arch, 537
Parallel lines, 19
Parallel projection, 37
Parallel rule drawing board, 6
Parapets, 474–75
Parasol roof, 189
Parthenon, 88–89
Partial sections, 45
Partition block, 470
Passive solar heating systems, 307–9
Pei, Ioh Ming, 102
Pen and ink rendering, 355–57
Pencil points for
    compasses, 18
    drafting, 17
    sketching, 12
Pencil rendering, 350–54
Pencils
    drafting, 4
    grades, 5, 28
    for rendering, 350–54
    sharpening of, 5, 28
    thin-lead, 4
Pens, for rendering, 355–57
Pentagon, 21
Performance bond, 441
Perimeter heating, 303
Perpendicular lines, 19
Persian architecture, 87
Perspective drawing, 335–49
    common method, 337–40
    by computer, 8–10
    direct projection method, 341
    enlarging, 339–40
    grid method, 341
    of an inclined line, 339
    of a point, 339
    types of, 335
Perspective projection, 37
Photographic rendering, 361
Photovoltaic cell solar collector, 310
Physically handicapped, design for,
    408–16
Pictorial projection, 50–53
Picture windows, 124
Pilaster, 243
Piping, 294
    plans, 298–99
    sizes, 294

Pitch of a roof, 192
Pitch of a stair, 212
Pivoted windows, 124
Plank-and-beam framing, 259
    459–63
Plans
    electrical, 291
    heating, 316
    piping, 298–99
    plumbing, 298–99
Plaster walls, 257
Plastic roofs, 191–92
Plastic veneers, 457
Platform framing, 239–58
Plot, 105, 169
    cost, 116
    dimensioning, 63
    plan, 179–84
Plumbing, 294–301
    plans, 298–99
    sewage disposal, 298–99
        branches, 297
        cleanouts, 298
        stacks, 297–98
        traps, 297
    water distribution, 294–96
        fittings, 294–95
        piping, 294
Plywood, 456–57
Points, mortgage, 113
Polygons, 21–22
Porch design, 157
Portland cement, 503
Postmodern architecture, 102
Posts, 246, 265–66
Pratt truss, 541–42
Precast concrete, 496, 510, 514
Preliminary layout, 159–70
    interior planning method, 163–64
    over-all planning method, 164
    prototype method, 162
    template method, 162–63
Preliminary sketches
    elevations, 196–98
    plans, 163
Prestressed concrete, 515–16
Primary auxiliary views, 47
Product standards, 453–54
Program, architectural planning, 117
Projected windows, 122
Projections
    auxiliary, 47–48
    axonometric, 39, 50
    first angle, 42
    isometric, 50
    multiview, 39–45
    oblique, 52–53
    orthographic, 37
    parallel, 37
    perspective, 37
    pictorial, 50–53
    third angle, 42
    types of, 37–39
Propeller-type wind machine, 331
Property lines, 179
Proportion, principles of, 14, 198
Proportional dividers, 6

Pumpcrete, 504
Pyramids, 84–85

Radial dome, 559
Radiant panel heating, 305
Radon control, 278
Rafters, 250
    calculations, 268
    trussed, 251
Railings, 215–19
Ranch house, 99–100
Reading a drawing, 43
Real-time computer systems, 11
Reflection of sound, 419–22
Refresh CRT, 7
Regency style house, 96–97
Regular polygons, 22
Reinforced concrete, 243, 502–17
    lift-slab construction, 515
    precast, 510, 514
    prestressed, 515–16
    tilt-up construction, 514
Reinforcing steel, 243, 245, 506–10
Removed sections, 45
Renaissance architecture, 92
Rendering, 350–62
    appliqué, 360
    magic marker, 357
    pen and ink, 355–57
    pencil, 350–54
    photographic, 361
    scratch board, 357
    spray, 360–61
    tempera, 360
    water color, 360
Renegotiated rate mortgage, 115
Resistance values, 321
Revolved sections, 45
Ribbed vault, 557
Rigid frames, 522–24
Rigid insulation, 323
Rock wool insulation, 323
Roman architecture, 89–91
Roman brick, 480
Romanesque architecture, 92
Roof decking, 548
Roof thrust, design for, 250–51
Roofing
    built-up, 191
    membrane, 191
    shingles, 191
Roofs, 187–94
    A-frame, 189
    butterfly, 188
    cable, 565–76
    clerestory, 86, 188
    domed, 90–91, 190, 561–63
    flashing, 192, 223
    flat, 188, 251
        advantages and disadvantages of,
        110
        construction of, 188, 251
    folded, 189, 551
    framing plan, 194
    free-form, 189
    gable, 187

Roofs (cont.)
gambrel, 187
hip, 187
lamella, 561
Mansard, 187
materials, 191
pagoda, 190
parasol, 189
pitched, 187
advantages and disadvantages of, 110
pitch of, 192
plastic, 191–92
shed, 188
terminology, 193
urethane foam, 191
vaulted, 190
warped, 189, 574
windmill, 190
Room design, 143–58
bathroom, 154–55
bedroom, 152–54
dining area, 152
kitchen, 143–50
laundry, 155–57
living area, 150–52
porch, 157
storage, 157
Rooms, number of, 106–7
Rope, steel, 564
Rubble masonry, 495
R-values, 321

Saarinen, Eero, 102
Sandstone, 493
Sanitation, history of, 93
Sash, window, 126
Savonius rotor wind machine, 331
Scale, drawing, 62
Scales
architect's, 4
bevel, 4
engineer's, 63, 179
triangular, 4
Schedules, 138–40, 389–90
Schwedler dome, 559
Scissors truss, 542
SCR acoustile, 489
SCR brick, 481
Scratch board rendering, 357
Seasoning of lumber, 455
Secondary auxiliary views, 47
Section lines, 43
Sections, 45
detail, 209
dimensioning, 63
structural, 209
wall, 209
Semiautomatic welding, 532–33
Sensitivity, 105
Septic tank, 298
Service, electrical, 284
Sewage disposal. See Plumbing
Shade, 342

Shadows, 200, 342–49
intensity of, 348
in multiview drawing, 342–43
in perspective drawing, 343–46
oblique light rays, 346, 348
parallel light rays, 343, 346
terminology, 342
Shape of plan, 109
Sheathing, 250
Shed roof, 188
Shell vault, 558
Shingle roofing, 191
Shotcrete, 504
SI metric system, 67–79
Sill, 245
Site, 105, 169
Size of house, 106–7
Sketches
finished, 164, 201–3
preliminary, 163, 196–98
Sketching, 12–15
circle and arcs, 14
ellipses, 15
lines, 12–14
proportion, 14
Skylights, 193–94
Slab construction, 243
advantages and disadvantages, 109–10
Slate, 495
Sliding doors, 131
Sliding windows, 123, A20
Slump block, 471
Smoke detectors, 290
Socketing, 568
Soft conversion to metric, 67
Softwood, 453
Soil stack, 298
Solar
active systems, 310
air conditioning, 316
farming, 301
heat distribution, 312
heat storage, 310–12
heating, 307–12
house, 101
orientation, 159
passive systems, 307–9
radiation, 318
stills, 300–1
water heating, 299–300
Solar house plans for Mr. and Mrs. S, A12–A16
basement plan, A12
elevations, A15–A16
floor plans, A13–A14
Sound
absorption, 422–24
amplification, 424
distribution, 420–21
echoes, 421–22
loudness, 419–20
masking, 424
reflection, 419–22
transmission, 417–19
Southern Colonial house, 98
Southern Standard Building Code, 111

Sovent plumbing, 299
Space frames, 551–55
Spanish house, 99
Specifications, technical, 169, 442–48
Speech, synthetic, 170
Spelling list, A33–A34
Spiral stairs, 211
Split block, 471
Split level house, 100
Sprayed concrete, 506
Spray rendering, 360–61
Sprinkler systems, 431–33
Square, 21
S shapes, 519–20
Stairs
construction, 213
design, 212
details, 214–16
terminology, 211–12
types of, 211
Steel designation, 373, 522–23
Steel manufacture, 519
Steel pipe, 522
Steel tubing, 522
Stencils, lettering, 6, 58
Stepped footings, 241
Stone, Edward Durell, 102
Stone masonry, 492–97
ashlar, 495
milling, 494
quarrying, 494
rubble, 495
Storage design, 157
Strand, steel, 563–64
Stressed-skin panels, 465–66
Structural calculations, 264–71
beams, 267–68
columns, 265–67
footings, 265
girders, 267
headers, 270
joists, 268
lintels, 270
loads, 264–65
rafters, 268
tributary areas, 265
Structural clay tile, 487
Structural steel, 518–24
availability, 522
designation of, 373, 522–23
manufacture, 519
shapes, 519–22
tubing, 522
types, 523–24
Structural systems, 83
Stud welding, 529–30
Studs, wall, 249
Styling, house, 95–102, 106
Subflooring, 248
Sullivan, Louis, 102
Superinsulation, 322–23
Surface bonding, 471–72
Survey map, 239
Swaging, 566
Switches, electrical, 284–85
Symbols, architectural, 30–33

Synthetic speech processing, 170

Table, automatic drafting, 6
Tangent arcs, 20
Tangent lines, 19
Technical fountain pen, 5, 7
Technique, architectural drafting, 28–33
Tees, structural, 522
Telephones, 284
Tempera rendering, 360
Templates
    commercial, 6
    furniture, 6, 162
    use of for entourage, 363
Temples
    Egyptian, 85–86
    Greek, 87–89
    Roman, 89
Termite control, 275–76
Thermae, 91
Thermal insulation, 321–25
Thin-lead drafting pencils, 4
Third angle projection, 42
Three-point perspective, 335
Thumbnail sketches
    elevations, 195–96
    plans, 163
Tilt-up construction, 514
Timber construction, 459–68
Time sharing, 169
Title box, 59
Topographical dimensioning, 63
Traditional architectural styles, 95–99
Transmission, heat, 313, 318
Transmission, sound, 417–19
Trapezoidal windows, 124, A22
Traps, plumbing, 297
Trees, 182, 451–52
Treillage, 216
Triangles
    drafting, 4
    lettering, 5
Tributary area calculations, 265
Trickle solar collector, 310
Triple glazing, 323
Trombe solar system, 308
Trussed rafters, 251
Trusses, 84, 251, 541–50

    open web, 544–48
    spatial, 551
    steel, 542–43
    wood, 543–44
T-square, 3
Tuscan order, 89
Two-point perspective. See Perspective

Umbra, 342
Underground house, 101
Unicom system, 65
Uniform Building Code, 111
Urethane foam, 191, 323
Utilities, design for, 183

Vapor barriers, 274
Vapor pressure, 273
Variance, zoning, 111
Vaults, 556–59
    contemporary, 190
    inclined, 86
    Roman, 89
Veneers, 457
Vent stacks, 297
Ventilation, 274–75, 317–18
Vesuvius, houses at, 91
Voice, synthetic, 170

Walls
    exterior, 254–55
    interior, 255–58
Warm air heating, 302–3
Warped roofs, 189, 570
Warren truss, 542
Waste stack, 298
Water color rendering, 360
Water distribution system, 294–96
Water energy, 331–32
Water table, 325
Water vapor, 273–75, 317
Weathering steel, 523–24
Welded wire mesh, 508
Welding, 529–36
    automatic, 531
    electric arc process, 529
    semiautomatic, 530–31

    stud welding, 529–30
    symbols, 535
Westminster Abbey, 92
Whirlpool bath, 155
White House, 94
Wills, Royal Barry, 98
Wind bracing, 558
Wind energy, 329–31
Windmill roof, 190
Windows, 121–29, A17–A22
    awning, 122
    basement, 124, A17
    casement, 122, A18–A19
    clad, 122
    conventional representation, 201
    double glazing, 126, 323, A17, A22
    double hung, 123, 125, A21
    fenestration, 200
    fixed, 124, A22
    hopper, 122
    installation of, 124
    jalousie, 124
    low-E glass, 126, 323
    pivoted, 124
    projected, 122
    sectional details, 125–27, A17–A22
    sliding, 123, A20
    specifying, 126–27, 138, A17–A22
    terminology, 125
    trapezoidal, 124, A22
    triple glazing, 323
    types, 121
Wire-frame computer drawing, 9–10
Wire mesh, 508
Wiring, aluminum, 287
Wood energy, 328–29
Wood products, 451–58
Working drawings, 172, 448
Wright, Frank Lloyd, 102
W shapes, 520

Xerxes, Great Hall of, 87

Yamasaki, Minoru, 102

Zoning
    design for, 179, 182
    limitations, 111–12